MALRAUX

MALRAUX

❧ *A Life* ❧

OLIVIER TODD

Translated by Joseph West

ALFRED A. KNOPF   NEW YORK 2005

THIS IS A BORZOI BOOK
PUBLISHED BY ALFRED A. KNOPF

Originally published in France as *André Malraux: Une Vie* by
Éditions Gallimard, Paris, in 2001.
Copyright © 2001 by Éditions Gallimard and Olivier Todd.

Library of Congress Cataloging-in-Publication Data

Todd, Olivier.
[André Malraux. English]
Malraux : a life / Olivier Todd ; translated by Joseph West.
—1st American ed.
p. cm.
Includes bibliographical references and index.
ISBN 0-375-40702-2
1. Malraux, André, 1901–1976.   2. Novelists, French—20th
century—Biography.   3. Art historians—France—Biography.
4. Statesmen—France—Biography.   I. Title.
PQ2625.A716Z946513   2004
843'.912—dc22   2004044216

Manufactured in the United States of America
First American Edition

For Anne-Orange Poilpré,
Helmut Sorge,
and John Weightman

CONTENTS

L'Eau du Coeur

Declaration of interest: Malraux mattered a lot to me. I was eight. Near the orchard in the Jardin du Luxembourg, my mother—a Communist at the time—introduced me to an American friend: Tom, a towering, jovial redhead. "Tom," she explained, "is joining the International Brigades in Spain." They sat on the beige metal seats and chatted. I overheard "Madrid . . . Comrades . . . Barcelona . . ." Tom left. Mother told me about a writer fighting in Spain, a man named Malraux, who commanded a squadron. I looked at his photograph in *L'Humanité*. A few weeks later, my mother announced that Tom was dead.

I met the essential André Malraux, the writer, in 1943 under German occupation, once again at the Luxembourg. I had read *L'Espoir*. I did not know the book had been banned. Luftwaffe soldiers in rough blue-gray uniforms were standing guard at the entrance to the gardens.

I was fourteen. The first paragraphs of the novel rang in my head: "The uproar of trucks loaded with rifles covered a tense Madrid in the summer night." Dialogues crackled between the stations occupied by the government and those in the hands of Franco's men.

"Hello, Sepulveda? This is Madrid North, workers' committee."

"Your train has gone past, blockheads. You're a load of dickless assholes, and we're coming this week to cut your balls off."

"Physiologically impossible. *Salud!*"

In 1943, for me, in the Jardin du Luxembourg, the Francoists in Sepulveda became allies of the German soldiers. The motto "*Gott mit uns*" on the silvery buckle of their belts corresponded to the motto of Franco's troops: "*Viva Cristo Rey.*" The war in Spain has dragged on in our memories with Manichean simplicity. At the time, I overlooked certain questions. Francoism was abominable, but even at its worst it did not turn into

Nazism. Let us dare ask, even if our first sympathies lie with the Spanish Republic: What if the Communists had taken power in Spain? What would have been the result of a Republican victory? A "people's democracy" and a gulag?

Several generations of Frenchmen have slipped into one war or another by proxy. Readers have made sense of their own experiences through the prism of Malraux's works and life. For a long time, I thought that no better life and death could be imagined than with the members of an International Brigade. In the contagious naïveté of the years before the Second World War, some equations seemed obvious: Francoists = Fascists = Nazis = Evil. We cultivated these simplified formulae. The ideological path in the other direction was Communists = Antifascists = Democrats = Good. How can we investigate André Malraux today with lucidity without renouncing some of the generous notions carried along by his works? Another tough question for whoever sets out looking for Malraux: Does lying matter? The hesitant biographer looks for factual truths about the life of a subject, even if that subject glosses over an episode in the name of the rights or duties of the imagination. "For the most part," Malraux claimed, "man is what he hides." No: he is also what he shows and what he does.

André Malraux was resuscitated for a few weeks—protean Lazarus that he was—on November 23, 1996, when Jacques Chirac, fifth president of the Fifth French Republic, had his remains transferred to the Panthéon in Paris. Why?

Chirac welcomes me one Saturday to a deserted Élysée Palace.

"Who are your favorite modern authors, Monsieur le Président?"

Chirac's answer flows out: "Saint-John Perse, Aragon . . ."

He does not take a position either for or against Malraux as a novelist: "For me, Malraux is not a great writer but a great man."

In this the president agrees with André Gide, an attentive and perplexed friend of Malraux. Why, then, did Chirac agree to the "transfer of the ashes"?

"In 1996, we needed to celebrate the twentieth anniversary of his death. He was the General's companion, he invented the Ministry of Culture. . . . He had panache . . ."

The president has recently reread *L'Espoir:* "His best novel, perhaps . . ."

Chirac, it seems, would give him six and a half out of ten. He nevertheless sees "a rare intensity" in this book, "a tremendous scale, a metaphysical quest." Malraux, for him, embodies a "French nostalgia for the will and brotherhood."

Chirac's contact with Malraux was limited. In the 1960s, sitting at the end of the table in Cabinet meetings, Chirac brimmed with ambition and looked on glory; Malraux the *ministre d'état*, sitting next to President Charles de Gaulle, gazed on majesty.

"Malraux dozed with a certain distinction," says Chirac. "He would screw up his face and push his chin into a restless hand. . . . He had a great capacity for making others listen."

When Malraux started to speak, Chirac would see a "certain tenderness" in the eyes of General de Gaulle. Sometimes the junior minister went over to the Ministry of Cultural Affairs: "In his office, Malraux fascinated and irritated me. . . . For art, there was no hierarchy. He saw Michelangelos everywhere."

I take notes. Chirac feigns (I think) a worried look: "You're not going to put that, are you?"

"Why not?"

The president smiles. Chirac doesn't think much of Malraux's books on art: "They lack scientific rigor. But nobody spoke better than he about fetishes."

Chirac is more excited when evoking Malraux the Gaullist high priest. With a veteran's verve, he recalls an electoral meeting in Seine-Saint-Denis (a "red" suburb): "I was sitting behind Malraux. Chairs were flying. Communists were booing Malraux, who was sitting on the platform. When there was a silence, he jumped in—extraordinary actor—and started to address the militants and the Party sympathizers: 'I was on the Guadalquivir. I waited for you. I did not see you coming.' "

We return to the General. Chirac suggests, "In every civilization, leaders have a fool. It relaxes them. . . ."

Malraux remained at Charles de Gaulle's side until the very last: the theatrical, moving, and pointless abdication in 1969.

"Malraux's personality," says the president, "gives rise to emotion, not necessarily admiration. The water of the heart [*l'eau du coeur*] rises to the eyes."

ONE NEEDS to have heard his voice.* At twenty as much as at fifty, Malraux wielded a weapon: a dark beauty and a magnetism that could make an impression of familiarity or shamanic intensity. Imagine Malraux prophetic, cocky at times, sneezing, juddering with nervous tics, expelling his repetitive interjections: *It's complex . . . seriously . . . a huge*

---

*His voice can be heard on a recent radio program, *Culture Vive*, at the Radio France Internationale Web site (www.rfi.fr/fichiers/evenements/articles_evenements/malraux/malraux0111.asp). [Tr.]

issue . . . major point . . . A finger on his chin whether pacing a room, a ministry office, or a battlefield. He kept the leading role for himself, except when faced with Charles de Gaulle. Malraux punctuated his remarks with a stamp of irrefutability, addressing servants or dictators, a museum curator or a museum attendant, in reverberating tones: *Never mind about that . . . secondly . . . At Borobudur, which you know better than I . . . Stalin is all statistics . . .*

In his speech at the Panthéon, Chirac dehydrated Malraux's misadventures in Cambodia. The president declared that Malraux had "the intention of taking samples of bas-reliefs" from a temple. Why the euphemism?

Malraux's biography is neglected by current doctoral dissertations in France. The focus is on the *I, esthetics*, the *transformation of civilizations*, the writer's *oriental inspirations*. Especially under the academic monopoly of Malraux gurus, the often fashionable structuralist and postmodernist approach imposes its restrictions: texts, of course, refer to other texts, never to life. Malraux comes out as pure intellect, stripped of his lively characteristics. By turning him into a statue, we forget his stature. Malraux played with his biography, supplied it, and massaged it: "Biographies that go from the age of five to the age of fifty," he suggested, "are false confidences. *Experiences* set a man in place."

Taking on the biography of a writer does not mean taking it out on his life or works. A reliable Malraux specialist, Robert S. Thornberry, rightly remarks, "There is a lamentable tendency to let one's sympathy or aversion for the man and his legend obscure the critical faculties." In every biographer lurks a detective in love struggling to get out; sometimes jealous, sometimes fulfilled or filled with wonder or shocked—carried away, let down, and caught again by his or her own uncertainty. Every question must be raised, not with cynicism but with skepticism. Malraux's childhood, which he said he hated: Was it unhappy? Was Malraux a revolutionary? Did he really converse with the world's high and mighty? In what way? Was he friendly in private, or indifferent? Was he a member of the Resistance? Was his devotion to Gaullism motivated by real passion or calculated self-interest? Was he afflicted by illness, a syndrome, or was he a drug addict? In 1978, I asked Raymond Aron what he thought of the most sibylline remarks of his friend Malraux. Smiling, Aron answered, "One third genius, one third false, one third incomprehensible."

Contemporaries of Malraux who are still alive are pushing a hundred. I called on witnesses and documents, letters, fragments from newspapers and manuscripts, untapped public and private archives in Russia, Britain, France, and the United States; I consulted the French Foreign Office, the Prime Minister's Office, and the President's Office. I followed Malraux's course from Bondy on the outskirts of Paris to Banteay Srei in Cambodia, via Barcelona, Moscow, Delhi, and Haiti. Archives drag legends back into history. I also relied on the work of my predecessors—Robert Payne, Jean Lacouture, Curtis Cate, and others, including one unpublished work—often without agreeing with them as to the facts or their interpretation.

A painter mixes pigments with a binding medium to obtain colors. In his fiction, in all his writing, Malraux mixed the realities of his life and his imagination. The biographer must separate pigments and binding, respecting the relationship between them. Sartre claimed that the life of a dead man is unguarded, one can walk straight in. Far from it.

MALRAUX

CHAPTER ONE

Heroes and Confectioners

THE *JEANNE-CAROLINE* WAS a squat, heavy dogger of ninety-three tons, fitted out in Dunkirk; a decked vessel with three masts, heavy but fragile in bad weather. In careful, slanted handwriting, the muster roll of the *Jeanne-Caroline* gives an account of the shipwreck in which Jean-Louis Malraux, sailor and ancestor of André Malraux, met his end: "Today, the 25th day of April in the year 1836, at three o'clock in the night, being at 63° latitude 11° longitude west fishing for cod in Iceland . . . ," an ordinary seaman was "summoned for the duration of the storm and in the call of duty to replace the fishing captain, who had fallen overboard, lost and presumed dead." The testimonies of a novice cooper and a ship's boy agree: seven men were lost, including Malraux, Jean-Louis, thirty-two. Jean-Louis's father also died at sea.

Four years before the death of ordinary seaman Jean-Louis, his wife, Françoise, a greengrocer, had given birth to a son, Émile-Alphonse, André Malraux's paternal grandfather.

Among Jean-Louis's forebears figure a plumber, a shoemaker, a vintner, a cooper, a dock laborer, a ship's carpenter, and an unmarried mother; Françoise's ancestors include an employee of the city toll office, a concierge in a Paris hotel, and an infantry major glowing with campaigns in America and Spain.

Malraux fathers died young—killed by seas or oceans off every coast and by firedamp in the mines to the east of Dunkirk, toward Lille and Valenciennes. Untimely bereavement force-fed orphans and wives a compost of suffering and uncertainty.

Émile-Alphonse, Jean-Louis's son, was born on July 14, 1832. Breaking with tradition, he kept mainly to dry land. On a rare sea excursion, he was thrown overboard in broad daylight. He was a little deaf and talked in a loud, high voice. He could read, write, and count very well. He dropped "Émile" and kept "Alphonse" as a first name. He was ambitious: he turned cask maker, wine taster, seller of spirits, and master cooper before becoming a ship owner. He was somebody: the town records him as being a maritime expert. Alphonse had his own headed paper and houses in the nicer parts of Dunkirk: Rue du Jeu-de-Paume, Rue Jean-Bart. He lived in the town center, four hundred yards from the port.

He managed his ten-ship fleet with authority. He embarked from time to time to supervise captains and curse crews, or just to please himself. Despite his average height, he cut an imposing figure at home and at work. With his employees, he spoke French and Flemish. At thirty-five, starting to bald but still with a superb mustache, he married Isabelle Mathilde Antoine, without passion, and gave her eight children in fifteen years.[1] The fifth, Mathias-Numa, was not provided with a Christian first name—his father's way of teasing the priest.[2]

Two maids looked after Alphonse's bourgeois residences with their costly furniture, tasseled curtains, padded armchairs, plants in pots, curios, and seascapes. "Bon Papa" Alphonse collected model boats. They amused the children and grandchildren. As his miniature collection increased, the full-scale one dwindled: his shaky fleet suffered from British and Norwegian competition. His fortunes ebbed, and in 1898, Alphonse financed only two ships.

Alphonse was rough with his employees and tough with his children—he once sent two of his sons to the cellars for two days, one down with the wine, the other among the cheeses. Sporting a little goatee and a top hat, he might often have been taken for a dandy. And he was sometimes an eccentric: when the town hall refused to find a public meeting place for the Jews, Alphonse invited them in. The town council wouldn't give a piece of wasteland to some traveling performers; the incorrigibly rebellious Alphonse put up the circus. He was a bad-tempered character—with character. The Malraux clan had its whimsical eccentricities: one was known for drinking wine out of a chalice; others led a "wild life"; others still neglected their children.

Widowed in 1890, Alphonse slept with his dog, a Saint Bernard that looked like a big bear cub. Alphonse scolded his daughter Marie when she cried. Jacquot, their parrot, picked up the phrase *"Pleure Mimi, pleure Mimi."*

Alphonse's sons longed to leave Dunkirk. Not Alphonse: he loved his town, the North Sea, its melancholy dunes, the houses whitewashed with lime, their walls of pink and brown brick, the tiled roofs, the landscapes floating between softness and sadness under the gray and mauve clouds in winter. Alphonse held his rank, expanded in selfishness, saw to his business, raised his children, contemplated with circumspect benevolence the sailors, dockers, and tradesmen around the Freycinet dock.

The third son, Alphonse's fourth child, had the same Christian name as the first son, who died at four. This Fernand-Jean *bis*, a "replacement child" as psychiatrists say, simultaneously expunged and recalled the death of the firstborn.[3] He was known simply as "Fernand," dropping half of the first name: a familial custom began. Fernand lost his mother at fifteen. He quit his studies. At eighteen years old, with blue-gray eyes, average forehead, five feet seven, he enlisted in the army for four years to get away from Dunkirk and his father. The military authorities note that Fernand "has nothing beyond" scraps of secondary education, despite "a basic knowledge of Spanish." This enlisted man "can ride," notes the recruitment service, so he is drafted into the 21st Dragoons Regiment. He makes corporal, then sergeant.

After being discharged as a noncommissioned officer, Fernand takes various jobs in small Parisian banks. His father, Alphonse, made a fortune; why not Fernand, too? The stock exchange beckons him. Panama, Suez, Longwy Steel—it's all there for the taking! Fernand calls himself a broker. In fact, he is a half-commission man, an intermediary between the exchange broker and the clients. He goes after his commissions with a jaunty step, looking good, feeling good, baiting his line with shares, adorning his patter with accounts of booming capitalism and triumphant colonialism. Steering his way among bonds and Treasury bills, Cuba 5%s, Chargeurs Réunis, Fernand was at ease in a world that drew all sorts. The French, at this time, were keen dabblers in the stock market.

Fernand thought up ideas to patent: unbreakable lightbulbs, self-acting pumps, puncture-proof tires. He attempted to master perpetual motion. He worked away on extravagant projects with unshakable optimism but never filed any patents. The broker or banker or engineer—depending on who asks and when—is even better with women than he is with his clients, thanks to his supple gait, good looks, curly, oiled mustache, and fantastical mind. His father, impatient to marry him off, finds him a reasonable heiress with a good dowry. But at Malo-les-Bains, Fernand falls in love with Berthe-Félicie Lamy, the daughter of a baker from the Jura region. Her father died when she was fourteen. Berthe's mother, Adrienne, née Romania, is a seamstress of Italian extraction. Her family includes artisans, businessmen, a sculptor, a soldier.

On March 24, 1900, as Sarah Bernhardt is having a triumphant success in *L'Aiglon*, Berthe Lamy, nineteen, and Fernand Malraux, twenty-four, are married at the town hall of Paris's Eighteenth Arrondissement, despite a grumbling Alphonse. They move into 53, Rue Damrémont, in the west of the Eighteenth. Fernand rents a five-room apartment in a recently finished building by the architect Émile Blais, whose bourgeois houses are popping up all around the Montmartre cemetery. At the turn of the century, it is said that in this neighborhood one meets *plus de rupins et moins de rapins*—more swells, fewer daubers. The newlyweds visit the World's Fair and the first Métro line, from Maillot to Vincennes, opened that year.

At four in the afternoon on Sunday, November 3, 1901, Georges-André Malraux is born. His birthday—a propitious presage, perhaps, or a heinous heritage—falls on his mother's. The name "Georges" is in fashion. The Malrauxs quickly drop it: it will be André. Fernand himself does not register his son at the town hall. The widow Lamy, the infant's maternal grandmother, takes care of that formality with the uncle Maurice Malraux, a traveling salesman. The authorities, in accordance with Mme. Lamy's claims, record the father as "business employee." From one document to another Fernand's profession metamorphoses.

On Christmas Day 1902, Berthe brings Raymond-Fernand into the world. The child lives for three months. Berthe is not getting on with her husband. He seeks reassurance or amusement in increasing numbers of indiscreet affairs. For lack of achievements, he wreaths himself in conquests. At four, André Malraux threatens to call the *garde champêtre* if his parents go on bickering. Berthe screams that she has "had enough of giving birth to dead babies," alluding to a miscarriage. Fernand Malraux goes away, comes back, then leaves for good.

His departure is the third blow in a row for André's mother, after the death of her father and that of a son. Berthe does not show it, but she is hurt. From now on she must depend on God and her mother, the head of the clan. Adrienne has sold the bakery and bought a greengrocery in Bondy, outside Paris. She converts it into a confectionery and moves in with her daughter Marie, André's beloved spinster aunt. Berthe and her son go to live with the two women at Bondy. His parents' separation leaves its mark on André but is also his salvation.

Bondy was a small, suburban town of five thousand inhabitants to the northeast of Paris. Despite its sawmills, ironworks, and boiler works on the banks of the Ourcq Canal, the industrial boom had passed Bondy by; it was neither popular, like Livry Gargan, farther out to the east, nor fashionable, like Saint-Germain-en-Laye to the west. Civil servants, petits bourgeois, farmers, and manual workers rubbed shoulders on its noisy streets. Flat barges, loaded to the brim with coal, lime, fodder, and boards, were towed along the canal by horses or mules. The surrounding flat, open country with its farms, woods, and forest led away to Alsace-Lorraine and beyond, toward Germany, the traditional enemy. During the fall, in this part of the Aulnois region, the countryside is either veiled in mist or covered with fog. In the summer, sometimes the heat becomes stifling.

Adrienne's house is at 16 Rue de la Gare, in the heart of the trading district. On the ground floor is the confectionery with its shelves, bags, and jars and its rich aroma of coffee and chocolate, ginger and tea, spices and brown sugar. Preserves and alcohol are stored in the cellar. The bedrooms are upstairs: André has his own room. He is the only boy in this reconstituted family, and he never helps with the household chores. The women ask nothing of him, not even, when he is old enough, to serve customers in the store. They accept or invent the idea that he is not very practical. At the side of the house, an archway leads through to an inner courtyard. In the same street, old man Gouisard sells prime vegetables. There are a locksmith, an ice cream maker, Dumet's haberdashery, the bar Les Vins de France, the grocery-cum-café Au Rendez-Vous des Archers. Opposite Adrienne's shop stands a large, prosperous café, Au Rendez-Vous du Marché, Maison Girerd. At the end of the week the cover of the trees and Girerd's musicians draw crowds. Near the town hall a stable smells of straw and dung. There is a hairdresser's, then Cartier's hardware store, then Madame Chandel's little café. Farther on are a printer and binder, warehouses and sheds.

André twitches, starts, makes faces, sniffs, sneezes, grunts, and blinks. He has Tourette's syndrome, at the time a little-known ailment, and one that affects only a small number of people, most often male.[4] Doctors say that his tics will disappear with adolescence. André's Tourette's shows in bursts of muscular and vocal activity. Behind the hyperactivity there is a lively yet mellow look, both serious and mocking; this little boy exerts an influence over his friends despite everything. Some earn the right to become his friends. André attends small, private lessons, some at the Institution Dugand, which has twenty pupils. There, in 1907, André meets a greengrocer's son named Louis Chevasson, a calm kid one year older than himself. He becomes André's confidant. He is amazed by the assurance of this Malraux boy, his ease, and his memory. Louis is one of the few local children to be accepted by the Lamy ladies. Henry Robert, another friend, goes to the local school. He observes that André Malraux, the "petit monsieur" with his private lessons, is not allowed to play in the street or on the little squares of Bondy. André does not "hang about" outside.

In theory, Fernand Malraux sees his son once a week; he takes him to a restaurant and boasts about his triumphs on the stock exchange. For the Easter and summer holidays, he packs André off to his grandfather in Dunkirk. The town, the sea, the countryside, and, above all, Alphonse's personality charm the child. At his grandfather's, André lives in the world of a solid, powerful man. Alphonse is more affectionate with his grandchildren than with his sons or daughters. When aunts, uncles, and cousins are rounded up at family reunions, Alphonse plays the patriarch. The role suits him, for a few hours.

These breaks spent in Dunkirk are glorious moments for the boy. A few days after his eighth birthday, on November 20, 1909, his beloved and respected grandfather dies at Dunkirk's town hospital. The local newspaper, *Le Nord-Maritime*, carries the headline "Tragic death of an old man." "Last night, Alphonse Malraux, 76 years old, of independent means . . . fell in the attic while carrying tools. He wounded himself seriously in the head, and the doctor had him taken to hospital. The unfortunate man suffered a stroke at three in the morning." At the cemetery, a menhir gravestone marks where Alphonse Malraux lies.[5] Some mutter that Bon Papa had had too much to drink.

André paints, on cardboard, canvas, and china plates. A year after his grandfather's death, he sketches and colors three black sailboats on a leaden background.[6] Behind these boats, one can make out the trace of a woman's head—perhaps André's mother. This accomplished little work, melancholy in its colors, evinces a precocious talent, as does the profile of a dog's head painted by André at the same period[7]—perhaps the Saint Bernard belonging to Bon Papa.

Fernand was now the only man in André's universe: a disturbing, imposing, but absent father. The Bondy triad surrounded the child without stifling him. But André had, as R. D. Laing would put it, a knot: his mother, enfeebled by her woes, shaped and misshapen by her rudimentary Christian faith, had little physical closeness with her son. A sensual component was missing. Apparently she found him ugly.

André was well educated and stood up straight; a model child in black-and-white or sepia photos. Jabot collar at three years old, gray school apron with a merit badge and skeptical pout at seven, a sailor suit or musketeer's outfit at eight, stiff collar and black jacket at ten, and, a little later, dressed for his First Communion, with an armband. There are few photographs where the little boy, so admired and carefully dolled up, is laughing or smiling. He sniffs, shakes himself, sometimes chases away women and friends with abrupt gestures: the twitching child seems to want to push away those who surround him.

André seems to have been a good student, except in math. He passed his *certificat d'études* at the end of primary school in May 1913. With Louis Chevasson, he became interested in comic books. *L'Épatant, L'Intrépide, La Semaine de Suzette*: all had fat circulations. André joins the École Jules-Ferry scout group, led by the teacher Mr. Suzanne. Scouting, started in 1909, is full of Baden-Powell's military zeal. A scout is true to his word, he is "loyal and chivalrous"; he combines Christian virtues and manual skill, which is alien to André. The group goes on outings to Enghien-les-Bains, plays tracking games in the Marly woods on Thursdays, pitches tents around a campfire during the holidays. André wears a uniform and scarf and carries a flask. Shouting the scout's motto, "*Toujours prêt!*," he sticks the blue-and-white pennant of his group onto the orange bicycle given him by his father. André never becomes a patrol leader. He gets bored with scouting.

He has friends over. He sings *Manon*, *Werther*, and popular songs. His grandmother, keener on reading than her daughters, sends him off to the local library. The librarian notices his appetite for books.

The Great War arrives, long foreseen and badly prepared for. The French Army was supposed to occupy Berlin in a matter of days. The inhabitants of Bondy hear the rumbling of the "Boche" guns before the Battle of the Marne. At night, some see taxis full of soldiers in red trousers going off to the front. Then, more unexpectedly, dazed refugees start arriving on foot or in carts from Reims and Meaux.

André's father is called up; to the boy, he is the embodiment of *la gloire*, glory. There is a shortage of senior NCOs: Fernand Malraux makes warrant officer in November 1914. Seven months later, headquarters finds itself short of officers. Fernand is promoted to second lieutenant and joins the 13th Artillery Regiment. Fernand cuts a fine figure under a kepi or a beret, in boots or leggings, stick in hand, strapped into a shoulder belt. He develops a military swagger and frequently calls himself a captain, and even—why not?—a major. These grand words titillate the ladies, who cannot read the ranks: one stripe or three, what's the difference? Fernand impresses his son. He could be straight out of the patriotic stories in the illustrated *La Croix d'Honneur*. He ranks with the heroes of the flag-waving *Les Trois Couleurs*, which sings the bravery of those in occupied territory and reveals the "savagery" of the enemy. Promoted to lieutenant in 1917, Fernand is posted in May 1918 to the headquarters of the 12th Light Tank Regiment. André imagines his father in a tank, a throbbing mass of metal, stinking of oil and powder. While the lieutenant is in Paris, father and son pose for photographs. They seem happy with each other. André looks the more serious of the two; Fernand is the smiling, edifying warrior.

Lieutenant Fernand Malraux boasts a lot. His superiors recognize his willingness but remark on his "lack of know-how."[8] In 1915, he is "quite satisfactory"; in 1916, "very conscientious." In 1917, he "commands his section with authority" but has "more theoretical than practical knowledge." As group technical officer in 1918, "he has not found great success in this post . . . a middling reserve officer." Forsang, his commanding officer, comments that Lieutenant Malraux "has spent almost the whole campaign with noncombat units."

After so many dead, so many broken heads, so many Legion of Honor medals and Military Crosses awarded in action or posthumously,

Lieutenant Malraux's military record looks meager: "Injuries: none. Dec-orations: none." Only two entries stand out in the file: four days under arrest for "unjustified complaint" and "demobilized . . . no promotion prospects . . . no aptitude for command."

In civilian life, Fernand remains the same, swaying and sassy. Since before the war, he has been living with Marie-Louise Godard, Lilette to her friends, a gap between her front teeth, cheerful; the opposite of Berthe. In 1912, a son is born to this unofficial couple, Roland-Fernand Georges, André's first half brother. The law at the time dictates that Fer-nand cannot recognize the child, since he is still married to Berthe. He appears on the birth certificate as a witness and with a new profession: "industrialist." In 1915, bravely refusing to accept the idea that his son should not carry his name, he declares himself single and recognizes Roland illegally.

The same year, André, fourteen, goes to Paris. Thanks to private lessons with Mlle. Paulette Thouvenin, he is accepted at the *école primaire supérieure* in Rue Turbigo, near Les Halles. He takes the train with Louis Chevasson, who goes to business classes in another establishment. At the end of the afternoon, the boys meet near the station at a well-known café, La Chope de l'Est. They board a third-class carriage. After the inspectors have passed, they jump from step to step, working their way up the outside of the train to sprawl in first class.

Outside school time, Paris is all theirs. They begin their cultural exploration. After raiding the library, André meets Louis at the theater: they go to see *Andromaque, Le Cid, Le Médecin malgré lui*. Chevasson notices Malraux's concentration as he huddles in his seat, then stretches to catch the words rattling out onstage. They see vintage Chaplin but also discover another image of the war, through the jingoistic nationalism of films. Throughout France, there are outdoor mobile screenings of *L'Angélus de la victoire* (1915), *Des canons, des munitions* (1916), *L'Alsace attendait* (1917), *L'Angélus du front* (1918). André Malraux is a little over sixteen in 1918, and Louis Chevasson, seventeen. Books and movies mean more to them than reality. For their generation, the cinema becomes a source of concentrated information and durable emotions, a new tech-nique with which to perceive and record the world. The pictures of war in newspapers and the cinema shake these young people as much as a visit to the battlefields of the Marne. The friends also go to the Louvre and the Guimet Museum. But these sometimes shut early because of lack of coal, as do the concert halls, where they go with a new pal, Georges Van Parys.

André confides to Chevasson: he wants to write. He shows Louis a short story, which he later apparently tears up.[9] Neither top of his class nor a dunce, André has an average school career.[10] But he shapes a culture for himself, on his own. Without the benefit of a classical education, he chooses *his* classics, outside school reading lists. He reads, passionately. Chevasson notices the ease with which André comes and goes from the medieval Froissart to the nineteenth-century Leconte de Lisle, from Balzac and Flaubert to Malherbe and Montaigne. As a young reader, André Malraux stands astride the centuries.

At eighteen, he elects his own lyric, epic, and romantic trilogy of authors: Hugo, Dumas, and Michelet. Hugo most of all, for his works and the man himself, myth and symbol, royalist, republican, peer of the realm, exile. He triumphed with novels and poetic works, branched out into essays, pamphlets, reporting, plays. So many lives in one, so many talents in one man.

Malraux's three favorite authors are anchored in history. They whet his appetite for heroes. In Michelet's *Jeanne d'Arc*, the young Malraux meets an unusual heroine, peasant turned warrior, with her feet on the ground and her head in the heavens: "good sense in exaltation."[11] Plunging into Dumas, he settles on Georges, whose mixed-race hero fights a colonial English governor. Hugo is his fulcrum. Reading *Quatre-vingt-Treize*, he meets the bloodthirsty Saint-Just, pale, sad, and strange. More than Robespierre or Danton, Saint-Just hypnotizes Malraux, and he finds him again in Michelet. Hugo, Michelet, and Malraux commune in the Revolution. An image of transfigured France stays with the adolescent André.

Hugo justifies this special link with history: "History and legend, each has its own truth. The truth of legend is invention which results in reality. For the rest, both history and legend have the same goal: to portray, beneath short-lived man, eternal man." Like Michelet, who gives synthetic interpretations of historic facts, Hugo paints a mystical picture of the Revolution: "What the Revolution is doing at the moment is mysterious. Behind the visible work is the invisible work." The frontiers between history and legend become blurred; André Malraux develops this esthetic tendency almost as an ethical code.

In everyday life, the Lamy-Malraux family feels some of the war's hardships without undergoing its atrocities. Inflation is eating away at savings, prices are rising, sugar is in short supply, and the confectionery business suffers. Adrienne knows people in the country who can get her white flour and chickens instead of the gray bread from the bakeries and refrigerated, tasteless meat from the butchers in town.

There is a cardboard and paper shortage. André Malraux, going through the booksellers' stalls on the banks of the Seine, notices sought-after and expensive works. He starts to think about the price of books.

Just before the end of the war, in 1918, Malraux is turned down by the

Lycée Condorcet. Perhaps he wasn't judged to be up to its standards. André decides not to continue his schooling. He coughs, clears his throat, appears to get worked up easily. His Tourette's is not well adapted to a restricted school environment. To keep his head still and control his tics, he often rests his chin on his hands. His friends forget about these recurrent symptoms. His hoarse, nervous voice makes an impression, even when it runs away with itself. An unusual case, Malraux: rather than Tourette's holding him back it pushes him forward. Only hyperactivity and extreme concentration—or a fever—lessen or temporarily banish the symptoms. André works out his own therapy.

The women around him worry. His father accepts that he wants to leave school. Fernand never got his high school diploma—nor did Grandpa Alphonse—and he found his way to a "good position." Fernand and Adrienne will help André. This break with the lycée, and therefore with university, has some advantages: the curious, inventive André Malraux must educate himself outside traditional institutions, acquiring a precious independence of mind. One disadvantage: he is not exposed to discipline or logic.

André soon leaves behind him a childhood that was neither rosy nor gloomy.[12] He slips away from the three women in Bondy, who are surprised to find him a stubborn, unpredictable teenager. The harsh reality for Berthe is that her life as a woman is "behind her." Fernand the storyteller is a failure. How is the adolescent André to react to his father's lies? He does not know or does not want to know. Malraux clings to the warm and majestic image of Alphonse, the totemic grandfather.

CHAPTER TWO

Adolescence of a Leader

MALRAUX, BETWEEN SIXTEEN and twenty, a precocious but immature young man, wanders Paris in search of his path. His energy, his curiosity, his good manners, and a rare visual memory ease his movement within the world of literature and the visual arts. People find him irritating but charming. He doesn't bother with national or international political news, nor with religion, which he has not thought of since receiving presents at his First Communion. He thinks he lost God around the age of twelve or fourteen, as one might mislay an empty wallet. Since the age of sixteen, he has wanted to become a writer; not quite the same thing as wanting to write books. He admitted this to Louis but not to his parents. Fernand said that Grandpa Alphonse used to grumble about not having had a writer for a son. Perhaps André Malraux might satisfy the ambitions of the kindly ghost of his grandfather, who himself read very little. As a writer, one can revolt, one can remake the world, and in France the aura of the profession brings you fame.

Malraux liked to think of himself as an accursed poet of genius.[1] He could see himself not only in Hugo but in Baudelaire, Verlaine, and Rimbaud. Poetry is an exquisite and painful wonder: it won't earn you a living, but, more than the novel, it pushes you to play with words. And it sanctions narcissism. Malraux wrote:

> O my sensitive and sick soul, O my soul,
> See the still more empty day return, see
> By the darkened lamp and the flameless grate
> The day return as pale and sad as you
> And lines reminiscent of Paul Valéry:
> Alas, friend, alas! You betray yourself!

As sand in the wind your courage runs away,
Fashion your heavy disdain into pointless poems;
You will live by force, O my soul, today![2]

The metered lines run from his pen. The subject, the author's soul, is hackneyed. In other poems, Baudelaire's cat makes an appearance.[3] It is the work of a beginner, feeling for his identity. He also works on a convoluted prose text. The first scene opens on a "laughing moon whose shrill notes fall like teeth"; Pierrots emerge from flower balloons, a lake spirit hangs himself. Pride has a speech that could be applied to the whole text: "I fear, alas, that these institutions are not sufficiently precise." The muddled little work, entitled *Lunes en papier* (Paper Moons), dissolves into allegories. The influences of Rimbaud, Laforgue, Max Jacob, and Lautréamont are all amalgamated. Malraux works on the text for at least three years, churning through adolescent themes: angst at the incoherence of existence, the temptation of suicide, the struggle against death. Even the admiring Louis Chevasson has reservations.

How can one have enough money and still keep one's freedom? Malraux has discovered the intoxicating pleasure of being master of his own time—and master of Paris. He balks at office or shop hours as trivial requirements. From Montmartre to Montparnasse, from Passy to the Bastille, around the Louvre and the Institut de France, Malraux spots works from the seventeenth to the twentieth centuries and researches the price of binding and paper. He goes hunting with Louis, sniffing out secondhand books to read or resell. André learns about the fluctuations of supply and demand. He learns how to judge the quality of a book's paper, the beauty of an ex libris, of signed works by Anna de Noailles, Stendhal, or Voltaire. Is this one a fake? But isn't it beautiful! An object's value, like its beauty, is in the eye of the beholder. Secondhand booksellers, shivering through the winter in front of their green boxes on the banks of the Seine, are less good at judging the value of a book than the established booksellers. André has all the parameters in his head. He mesmerizes the booksellers, talking of laid paper, bastard titles, typography, engravings, lithographs.

First he makes pocket money with ordinary books. Then he starts earning a living from rare books. He gets Louis involved and starts doing business with René-Louis Doyon, a publisher and bookseller, minor writer, and book collector with a reading room at 9a, Galerie de la Madeleine. Malraux the young broker follows the standard routes. In the mornings, he goes up the Rue des Saints-Pères, browses the lanes, takes Rue Bonaparte, then turns back down the Boulevard Saint-Michel. Leaving the Left Bank before noon, he crosses the Seine armed with lists of first editions he has tracked down. Doyon makes an order. They understand and complement each other. Malraux surpasses his role as wily book tinker and Doyon his own as secondhand buyer. André is not yet eighteen, and Doyon is asking him for advice. From all of his five feet, ten and a half inches, the novice suggests titles to the elder, including a French translation of the romantic poet Clemens Brentano's *The Dolorous Passion of Our Lord Jesus Christ* and Görres's *Christian Mysticism*.[4]

Malraux wants to edit and present: not bothering with academic precision, he throws together an edition, mixing literary fragments by Jules Laforgue. Accuracy? Does that really matter? Malraux wants to move fast. Specialists pan his edition. Malraux doesn't like experts. This young autodidact might pass for presumptuous if he weren't so knowledgeable.

Malraux sees himself as a literary critic. Doyon launches a two-franc monthly magazine, *La Connaissance, Revue de Lettres et d'Idées*. In January 1920, five pages are given over to an article by André Malraux (aged eighteen years, two months), "On the Origins of Cubist Poetry." In a sensational summary, the beginner encompasses Guillaume Apollinaire, Max Jacob, Pierre Reverdy, and Blaise Cendrars. Attack is the best form of defense: "While symbolism, that now senile literary movement, was dabbling in the lapping waters of its imminent dissolution," writes Malraux, "those young people who had no particular desire to publish flabby (but nonetheless praiseworthy) poems and bedeck them with stunning commentaries set off on foot to find an artist capable of producing work from which a new esthetic could be extricated without plagiarism." Apollinaire, according to Malraux, imitated Heine. Max Jacob deserves to be commended for his "trim" irony and his carnivalesque images, as do Pierre Reverdy for his "surgical scrutiny" and Blaise Cendrars for his lucid rendition of "the paroxysmal expression of modern life." A first article generally passes unnoticed. Not this one. In the weekly *Comœdia*, a certain Valmy-Baysse takes the upstart to task. Is Malraux really suggesting that symbolism is "senile"? Malraux retaliates with a letter that *Comœdia* publishes: he has been misunderstood; he didn't mean to attack symbolism, he admires it.

His second and last article in *Connaissance*, attracting less attention, deals with three books by Laurent Tailhade. Whether mocking the middle classes or admiring the anarchist Vaillant,[5] Tailhade amuses Malraux; the young critic is trying to find a voice of his own. His article has the feel of a long-drawn-out chore: "Since the day that Stéphane Mallarmé replaced the ordinary grime of women's reviews with a pale soot of his own, nobody has been able to show, as Laurent Tailhade can, how much beauty style alone can contain."

Malraux grew close to *Action*, an artistic and literary review led by Florent Fels. Fels was interested in workers' conditions, the repression of rebellion, George Bernard Shaw, the social and political dimensions of creation, and individual anarchism. He dreamed of a world with no governmental control; he wanted to devote himself to "experience," the final goal of existence. He set great store by experience. He often used the word "comrade," which pleased Malraux, as did "experience." Fels was an avant-gardist when it came to literature but was attracted by a certain form of order where the monuments of the past have their place. At the first dadaist demonstration, in front of the sympathizers Max Jacob and Blaise Cendrars and partisans such as André Breton and Francis Picabia, Fels shows his opposition. Tzara reads the text of a speech given by Léon Daudet in the Chamber of Deputies. In the wings, Breton and Aragon are ringing bells. Florent Fels, yelling from the audience, launches into Tzara: "Go back to Zurich! String him up!"

Fels opens a counterdemonstration with a talk on the new Mind Classics: "If Art cannot be without a certain seriousness, it must die of boredom." He reveals the "Messieurs du Dada" as plagiarists of Italian futurism. He rejects dadaist irrationality and decadent negativism. Malraux agrees with Fels's ideas, although not always with the texts he publishes. But he doesn't follow the surrealists either: they are too fond of psychoanalysis. Malraux enters the flow, but against the current. Sixty years after the publication of *Les Chants de Maldoror*, Isidore Ducasse, the Count of Lautréamont, is being revered by militant dadaists and future surrealists. André Breton, Paul Éluard, Louis Aragon, and Philippe Soupault place Lautréamont alongside Rimbaud. Malraux doesn't: he denounces his methods. Ducasse, notes the young critic, simply substitutes the name "Satan" for the name "God." Malraux loves to display his erudition, even when it is shaky, and takes an unfashionable approach to a fashionable author. For him, the Lautréamont hoax is revealed when one compares his *Songs* of 1868 and of 1874. Indeed, admits Malraux, this count is still a visionary madman. But you have to ask yourself: "Even when it produces such curious results, what is the literary value of a given process?" *Action* publishes more studies by Malraux, on André Salmon and André Gide; the latter earns him a letter from the Great Writer, who asks about this young man with interest. Malraux hesitates, then also gives *Action* some prose poems.[6] They have no narrative thread and no original metaphors and pass unnoticed. The author later uses them in *Lunes en papier*.

Malraux lived through these years on fluctuating finances. Without cutting all bonds with Bondy, he rented a furnished two-room apartment in Avenue Rachel in Montmartre, where he put up good old Louis Chevasson. When one of the friends invited a young lady, the other would go to stay with his mother. Then, before taking a bachelor apartment near

L'Étoile, Malraux moved into an upper-floor room at the Lutétia, Boulevard Raspail. He liked the area and appreciated the service that hotel life offered, with meals and laundry on demand. Trained by the Bondy ladies, Malraux took an interest in his clothes. He tried the English tailors around the Opéra. He would wear cotton or silk poplin shirts and treated himself to accessories: scarves, cravats, sticks, kid gloves, pearl pins (often false) for his ties. He loved to wear a thick coat thrown around his shoulders, like a Napoleonic officer's cape. His feet, he said, were delicate; he went to good shoemakers. He became a dandy, like Fernand and Alphonse Malraux before him but in Parisian style.

His love of books brought him out of adolescent negativity. André now wanted to live a happy and exciting life. In a text published a few years later, he cast himself as both booklover and cat, his totem animal.[7] Malraux the cat says, "If you open *Les Fleurs du mal* more often than *La Légende des siècles*, it is not only because of your partiality for Baudelaire. The book that should be sought out, before any other, by any lucid bibliophile who can fathom the nature of his pleasure, is one in which each page can defend itself. Let us reform the appreciation of books." Malraux the booklover explains what drives him: "Searching for first editions and organizing a Balzac or Marcel Proust evening both illustrate the same feeling, I think; but if what used to signify modernity now signifies archaism, what does that matter? This is also true of the work itself. What I am defending is the quality of my pleasure. I know that a second edition of Racine, even of Balzac, is loaded with as much evocative power, with as much time, one might say, as a first. But all passion merely creates a need which only the illusion of perfection can satisfy." Malraux the cat agrees: "These are excellent reasons to become a forger. What is the difference between a good fake and a bad original? Hoax is eminently creative."

In the publishing world Malraux starts to look for people more original or enterprising than Doyon. He meets gallery owners, small-scale editors with imagination, scouts and crooks. A recently made friend, Pascal Pia, aka Pierre Durand, advises him. Younger than him by two years, a voracious reader, thirsty for literary perfection, and a poet when the fancy takes him, Pia was orphaned by the death of his father and has left his mother. Self-taught like Malraux but with a more marked taste for accuracy, he has been a barman and an employee of a shipping and insurance company. He is a great connoisseur of Hell at the Bibliothèque Nationale[8] and has worked with Frédéric Lachèvre, onetime stockbroker and specialist in libertine authors. Pia puts Malraux onto *Théophile de Viau, Cyrano de Bergerac, Lettres à la Présidente,* and *Lesbia, maîtresse d'école.* For Durand-Pia, a prodigious author of pastiches, fakery becomes a game, a way to trap pedants. Malraux sees it the same way.

When money comes in, the Malraux-Pia-Chevasson trio dine at

Larue's, steering clear of the set menus. They visit the Moulin-Rouge and the Lapin Agile, go to homosexual bars and heterosexual clubs. After a full day, they buy one another drinks at the Chat Noir or in the brothels.

Malraux refines his epistolary tactics. In 1920, he sends a letter from Bondy to Paul Éluard, his elder by six years, whose *Poèmes pour la paix* were received with interest in 1918: "I wish to make your acquaintance because you are for me one of the most interesting dada poets." Malraux doesn't say he likes dada. "The last thing I want to do is to put you to any trouble," he continues, but he points out that he would prefer to visit in either the morning or the afternoon.[9] Again from Bondy, to André Breton: "My sincerest congratulations for your *Exemples*, even more successful when printed than read or handwritten . . . Literature such that the silence of the newspapers is most agreeable, for one doesn't like to see animals walking on the things one loves."[10] Again in 1920, Malraux writes to Jean de Gourmont, looking for further details about George Sand's sex life. In Baudelaire's *Intimate Journals*, explains Malraux, there is a sentence on the writer's capacity for love. The letter lapses into nonsense: "You must find this epistle disgusting and its author a hispid scribbler, you who write so admirably! But since this paper has bad things in store for me. . . . I sink my fingers into the fur of your 'powerful' cat, though not soft (rather clawy) to ward off fate."

In his letters and the margins of his manuscripts, Malraux often draws cats, sometimes seahorses or "devyls"—with captions such as "Music lover," "Monogram," or "Disagree." In *Royaume farfelu* (Nutty Kingdom), his current work, he declares, "Take care, curly devils, pale images are forming noiselessly on the surface of the sea." Do Malraux's drawings, with their ironical smiles, indicate his regret at not being as gifted an artist as William Blake or Victor Hugo?[11]

Unlike his father and grandfather, the young Malraux possesses a sixth sense for literature and a seventh for Art. He explores museums, particularly the new exhibitions at the Louvre and the galleries around the Place Beauvau and the Madeleine. He is knowledgeable about the works of some painters: Braque, Matisse, Picasso, Derain, Vlaminck, Juan Gris. Malraux makes his way through the artistic world, moving from one mutual appreciation society to another. At sculptors' and painters' studios he listens and trains his eye. He learns, questions, analyzes techniques and ideas.

To promote his friend the etcher Demetrios Galanis, he compares him to the primitive Italian artists of the first Renaissance. He is not afraid of exaggerating: "One could compare Galanis to many masters, . . . but he is nobody's student." Malraux thus chances a first step into art criticism, without straying much from generalities: "One can understand only through comparison," he writes; "whoever has read *Andromaque* or *Phèdre* will better grasp what constitutes French genius by reading *A Midsummer Night's Dream* than by studying the rest of Racine. The Greek genius will be understood better through the opposition of a Greek statue and an Egyptian or Asian one than by knowing a hundred Greek statues." Comparison, genius, opposition, knowledge: keywords for the young, imperious André Malraux.

For two years, he keeps company with the poet Georges Gabory, a connoisseur of good restaurants and bad haunts, an expert in champagne and cancan dancers. Gabory's poems are rather thin:

> Toward the azure of another port
> Far from the sick land
> From desire and tediousness
> And our heart fled
> The pomegranate rose
> Opened out for him at last.[12]

Malraux prefers Gabory the man to his work and thinks more of his prose than his poetry. Gabory writes a provocative piece in praise of Landru[13] worthy of a surrealist. They hang out in Montmartre and Montparnasse with friends. René Latouche, an office clerk with a limp, also harbors literary ambitions. Latouche realizes that he does not love his mistress, since he has been sleeping with someone else. Don't worry about it, his friends tell him. Latouche then commits suicide. Malraux had some affection for him.

Gabory introduces André to Raymond Radiguet and Max Jacob, whose importance is quickly apparent to Malraux. The poet is a quarter of a century older; he has known poverty, astrology, and the cabala. He receives the young people he deigns to befriend at 7 Rue Gabrielle, Montmartre. Max Jacob has been visited by God. He recognized Him: God "had a robe of yellow silk with blue facing . . . his face was peaceful and beaming." The young crowd surrounding the poet, often agnostics or atheists, accept his Catholic faith, his outbursts and recantations, his homosexuality and the laughing fits that bring him to the brink of tears. Max Jacob sees André as a handsome, pretentious, and sometimes pedantic Baudelaire figure. They share a *boeuf miroton* and a *navarin aux pommes*. Max breaks off their serious conversations with imitations of pompous academics or foreigners lost in Paris. Malraux, normally touchy, takes in Max's ironic remarks. He would not tolerate them from anyone else.

Malraux makes the acquaintance of Marcel Arland and his traditional approach to literature. The two friends share a passion for Art, classical and modern. Arland is twenty-eight months older than Malraux, which makes a difference when you are twenty. Arland grew up in the country. His heart and his mind often look back to his native Haute-Marne. He is something of an ascetic; he was raised on Stendhal and Baudelaire. He draws Malraux's attention to Barrès's style. Arland went to university, but the barren rhetoric of the lecturers put him off academics, "jugglers of ideas and words." This seduces Malraux, and Malraux captivates Arland. They discuss Pascal, Dostoevsky, and Claudel and argue about the issues they see as essential: What to do with one's life? Which values to defend after the war and the breakup of Europe? Especially after the death of God announced by Nietzsche (the greatest "event" of the last few years, Malraux believes), they want to get to the bottom of the problems presented by Life, Creation, and Art. The word "essential" recurs in their conversations. Arland seems to be the first rigorous mind Malraux associates with.

Malraux cannot live the bohemian life for long. He goes to the Hôtel Drouot often and there meets a proper publisher: Lucien Kra, initiated into manuscripts by Simon, his father. Simon advises Lucien to try luxury editions. Lucien Kra and Malraux become partners.

On April 23, 1920, the *Journal de la Librairie* prints an ad: "Sagittarius Publishing, bookseller and printer, 6 Rue Blanche . . . We will shortly be publishing a series of limited editions (1,000 copies, luxury included)." Sagittarius aims at quality: "Each volume in a charming format, square duodecimo . . . luxuriously printed on Van Gelder Zonen Holland paper or Japanese Imperial paper will be illustrated by one of the best contemporary artists." Sagittarius emphasizes that all the works in the collection will be original editions. The first volume will be *Le Livret de l'imagier* by Remy de Gourmont, the second, Charles Baudelaire's *Causeries*. Malraux chooses fourteen drawings, eleven previously unseen, by Constantin Guys for this volume. These editions will never be reprinted, but they are not meant for the sole enjoyment of the very rich book collectors for whom a book printed in two hundred copies would not count as a rare work. Kra and Malraux launch their semiluxe series with "unpublished" writings by Baudelaire—that have in fact already been published.[14]

They have a sense of prestige and profit: a publishing venture, if it is to last, must reconcile literary requirements with financial benefit. Less than a year after its foundation, Sagittarius prepares a collection of still unpublished works by the masters of new literature and young writers, illustrated by "the most famous artists." André Salmon and Max Jacob will be among them, as well as André Malraux, less well known to book collectors. Sagittarius states that these works "will soon become extremely rare." Malraux's ambitions are not beyond his competence. The perspicacity inherited from his grandfather gets the better of the loquacity he owes to his father. Friendship and business merge. Max Jacob has, for a long time, known Daniel-Henri Kahnweiler, a German who spent the war in Switzerland, came back to Paris in 1920, and took up again as a dealer. He employs Braque and Derain to illustrate Max Jacob, Raymond Radiguet, and Pierre Reverdy. They all meet at Kahnweiler's for tea, intellectual speculation, and gossip—which Malraux and the others love. The third volume of a collection by Kahnweiler, illustrated by Fernand Léger, will be the first real book to come from Malraux the art editor.

Malraux detects financial possibilities in eroticism and pornography. He oversees the making of *Les Amis du crime*, hacked out of *La Nouvelle Justine* by the Marquis de Sade: twelve woodcuts, a limited run of five hundred copies, on Chesterfield laid and white vellum. The original, Malraux asserts, appeared in Paris in 1790. He follows on with *Le Bordel de Venise*, assembled from the story of Juliette, again by Sade, the first edition printed in two hundred copies, decorated with "scandalous watercolors by Couperin," actually by the Belgian artist Géo A. Drains. Malraux mixes licentious text ("We dined all three: they insisted on sucking my mouth and my cunt. They each took quick turns . . .") with illustrations showing erect members, whips, and threesomes.

Malraux and Kra separate in strange circumstances. Max Jacob looks on, as perfidious as he is pious, and comments on their disagreements in a letter to Radiguet: "We must make the most of the fact that these fellows are not yet disillusioned by the publications of the young. A day will come when our friend Malraux will no longer be there and these fellows will think more about Anatole France than about us." A good observation: when Malraux has left, the Kras announce four volumes of Anatole France, not the avant-garde.

Malraux withdraws from publishing, still thinking of becoming a writer. He must straighten out his position with the authorities. In order to obtain a deferment, Malraux alludes to his nervous tics and adds some imaginary ailments, insomnia, and stomach pains. In matters of importance, as in everyday life, he develops a theory of truth: what is true is whatever amuses, suits, or benefits me. Too many young men lost their lives between 1914 and 1918. So why bother with military service?

Le Roi des
Royaumes Imaginaires

CHAPTER THREE

The Strange Foreigner

THE REVIEW *ACTION* publishes studies and translations of foreign literature: Gorky, Aleksandr Blok, Victor Serge. Florent Fels employs polyglots such as the poet Yvan Goll and a young woman of German origin, Clara Goldschmidt. Effervescent, cosmopolitan, five foot nothing; gray eyes, dark brown hair, a rather long nose, and a determined chin. She is three years older than André. An electric presence, she speaks German, English, and a smattering of Italian. Stimulated by poetry and novels, she also manifests an appetite for philosophy. One of her grandfathers still lives in Germany but feels European: during the war, some of his descendants fought with the French, others on the German side. His two sons were prosperous tannery merchants. Otto, Clara's father, died in 1912. With branches in America and Asia, the family remains well off. An Austrian governess and an Irish tutoress look after the children. Clara's widowed mother keeps a housemaid and a cook; she lives in Auteuil with her daughter and two sons.

In this Jewish family, girls enjoy the same rights as boys, except where sexual freedom is concerned. Clara notes that her older brother André spends nights out. Why can't she? André advises his sister to get married and "muck about under another name." Both daughter and son have been urged to cultivate themselves. Clara has heard her mother talk of Hegel and declares herself "magnetized" by "unbearable tensions." She quotes Spengler, Hölderlin, Dickens, and Tolstoy.

At twenty-three, she meets Malraux during a dinner organized by Fels in a restaurant at the Palais-Royal.[1] After conversation with Goll and his wife, Clara and André go to a nightclub, the Caveau Révolutionnaire. They start to tango. Malraux is not a good dancer.

The following Sunday he drops by the Golls'. They live in two rooms furnished by Biedermeier, near the Goldschmidts' villa. Under a Robert Delaunay canvas, around an Aleksandr Archipenko bust, there is chatting in French, in German, in English. Marc and Bella Chagall are frequent visitors.

Malraux comes up to Clara. She notices his wonderful hands, his touching paleness, his Parisian drawl, his glibness. She talks almost as much as he does, and with the same self-assurance. He acts the sibylline peacock; she, the cultured coquette. She quotes Novalis, he El Greco, both of them Nietzsche. She has recently returned from Italy, where she broke off her engagement to a doctor.

"What are you doing this summer?" asks Malraux.

"Going back to Italy."

"Right. I'll come with you."

Si non è vero, è ben trovato . . . Clara finds his bravado romantic. The young are prone to theatrical emotions. She comments to her mother, "It is so nice to be intelligent. It makes you attractive to intelligent men."

André phones her the next day. She has a beautiful voice, he declares in a romantic gambit. He comes to pick her up. There are a visit to the Gustave-Moreau Museum, boat trips on the lake in the Bois de Boulogne; André rows as badly as he dances. He's an artist, Clara decides, and he's brilliant. She senses ambition in this young man. She guesses that he would like to write. He denies it, unconvincingly.

"You know the Chinese theory," he says. "He who appreciates the garden is superior to he who makes the garden."

He adds, sententiously, "The man who can enjoy a work of art is superior to its creator."

Clara perceives in André a need for recognition and a certain pain. Malraux says his father is a banker. Before long, Clara finds out that this is not true. Is André suffering from his origins? Too humble? Bondy is not as chic as Auteuil, but so what? Clara is not a snob. She is as chatty as André but appears more mature. André has had brief liaisons, including a "little dance hall chick," according to Georges Gabory. For the first time, André appears to be in love. He does not spare the compliments: "I know only one person as intelligent as you, and that's Max Jacob."

André and Clara go to exhibitions and to the theater. Clara introduces him to the work of German, Russian, and English writers. He introduces her to cabaret. What, has Clara never been to a public dance? They escape from a literary rout in Palaiseau, go to the Noël Peters cabaret, then on to a dance in Rue Broca, near the Gobelins area. They drink. Someone asks Clara to dance, and Malraux pushes her to accept. As they are coming out of the ball, some men jostle them. André pulls a revolver from his pocket.[2] A shot is fired. André fires back. He is slightly wounded on the hand, and they go to the Goldschmidts' for disinfectant. Madame appears.

"What's your friend doing here in the middle of the night?"

"He's getting a book."

Malraux is allowed to come back to the villa. On July 14, Clara walks André home, and they give way to their feelings. Clara has a lover. Malraux tells Clara he'll meet her at the Ritz but doesn't turn up.

He is not yet of age and will have to persuade his father, retired in Orléans, to give his permission to marry Clara. Fernand finds the idea extravagant: "A German girl? And Jewish!"

Fernand, now remarried, has another two legitimate sons. André meets his younger half brother, Claude. Fernand admires his eldest's ability to earn money and "get by." But the boy is too young to get married. Why had André lied about the meeting at the Ritz? Clara senses his need to conceal his simplest actions.

The departure for Florence is farcical. On the platform at the Gare de Lyon, Clara kisses her mother good-bye. Clara and André board the train separately. They spend the night together. A friend of the Goldschmidt family, traveling on the same train, consults the passenger list. How could a young lady from such a good family come to be sharing a compartment with this stranger? If the friend says anything, Uncle Goldschmidt, who handles the family fortune, will cut his niece off, and Madame will make a scene. André bursts into the friend's compartment, intending to challenge him to a duel. Malraux likes to cultivate a heroic image of himself. The friend won't talk.

According to Clara, André asks, "Would getting married help things?"

"Of course."

Fernand Malraux will lift his veto, promises André. Clara proposes that they divorce after six months. Love and marriage must be free.

Florence—palaces, gardens, museums—impresses Malraux, as does his guide, Clara. She is struck by his pictorial knowledge. He remembers the slightest color details and composition of a picture seen at the Uffizi. For the architecture, she shows him a thing or two. She offers him SS. Annunziata and St. Mark's. He discourses on Giotto and Paolo Uccello. He compares the three fragments of the Battle of San Romano: one at the Louvre, one in Florence, and one in the National Gallery in London (which he has never seen). He invents and lets his imagination inflame his interpretation.

"Just look at this picture as if it didn't contain any anecdotes," he commands.

They are drunk on words. Malraux: "How happy we are."

Or even: "If you were to die, Clara, I would kill myself. How about you?"

"Now, yes. Later, I don't know."

Quite his father's son, André exclaims, "You have to spend the money you don't have faster than the money you do." They make a detour to Sienna and return to Florence. Someone has squealed; Clara gets an imperious telegram from her mother: "Come home immediately without your companion." The word "companion" verges on contempt. They reply by telegram, announcing their engagement.

Then for Venice, settling in at the Hotel Danieli. They are happy but don't always agree. She redefines their contract: they won't be restricted to each other. Deep down, Malraux doesn't accept this rule. Money runs out. After a few hours on the beach at the Lido, they board the Orient Express. At the Gare de Lyon, Clara's aunt, Jeanne Goldschmidt, asks her if this marriage is really necessary. Her mother asks if Clara is happy. André Goldschmidt, the brusque elder son, declares that his sister is bringing dishonor on the family. He calms down, meets Malraux at Fouquet's, and informs his future brother-in-law that Clara is strong and intelligent but mad.

Fernand Malraux grants his permission. Max Jacob, piously established in the presbytery of Saint-Benoît-sur-Loire, is not surprised at the wedding plans. Jacob foresees for André a chair at the prestigious Collège de France and even a fauteuil at the Académie Française: "I congratulate you on your resolution and your choice. . . . You will have for a partner an excellent mind, both positive and artistic."[3] He adds, "I hope that the sweetness of engagement does not harm your work and that we will soon see its succulent fruits." He is impatient to see books come out of "this active, bitter, and tender brain."

On October 21, 1921, six months after their first meeting, Clara and André are married at the town hall of the elegant Sixteenth Arrondissement. She has ordered a black velvet and vair-fur suit by Poiret. Not wanting to meet André's father, the three women from Bondy do not attend the ceremony. Fernand has to turn up to authorize the marriage, and he makes a good impression. Aunt Jeanne suggests to Clara that she should have chosen the father—"much smarter than the son." With 300 francs Clara bribes a registry official into mumbling the dates of birth: the difference in age must not come out.

André, a husband at twenty, does not intend to live in a maid's room. The couple stay on the second floor of the Goldschmidts' villa. Clara comes into 300,000 francs ors and some shares, about $800,000 worth today. Malraux handles the portfolio. With Fernand's know-how the future is assured, especially if they invest in Mexican mining shares. André has warned Clara, "I'm damned if I'm going to work."

Certainly not at a desk job; Malraux doesn't see himself in some government office. The Goldschmidts are merchants, and they work a lot.

Malraux makes a big splash, gives everyone the impression that he is somebody. But who? He is a writer before he has published. He gets through sheets of paper and has trouble finding a subject, a genre, a style. He hovers between prose and poetry.

He is afraid of being poor, more so than Clara. He has a taste for the best restaurants. Against her family's advice, the generous and impulsive Clara does not insist on a marriage contract. It would have been straightforward: everything came from her, André owned nothing. For a while, Malraux thinks of becoming a museum curator. He gives up the idea quickly: after all, at this time the profession requires independent means, and indeed a few days' presence every week.

Like Clara, André wants to travel. Travel remains a conquest, a superb alibi for gathering literary materials or for escaping the discipline of writing a book. The world is at their feet, waiting to be discovered. They go to Prague by plane. Why deny themselves this luxury? Here German is also spoken, which is good from Clara's point of view. André needs people to talk to in French. Vienna, the capital of an empire that no longer exists, is caught in a financial crisis. Sad lines form in front of the soup kitchens. The schilling and the mark are crumbling against the franc. The Malrauxs live in luxury. There are places in the world, says Clara, where the people are having a revolution to take money from the rich. Does a revolution improve the lot of the poor? André, less political, remarks, "You're one of those who wants everybody killed for the good of the few."

Back in France, they visit Chartres and Tournus, leave for Belgium, come back to Paris, off again to Alsace, Brittany . . . They wander rather than travel. Malraux has travelitis, the exquisite illness of emotion collectors and sensation seekers. In Paris, he invests in the stock exchange—badly—while Clara summarizes Spengler or Freud for him. The couple meet up with André's old friends, among them good old Chevasson—whom Clara, somewhat jealous, finds decidedly dull and not artistic enough. Gabory sees Clara as invasive: "A married friend is only half a friend." Then Gabory gets married. In turn, Malraux falls out of touch.

In December 1921, the couple visit Clara's grandfather and uncles in Magdeburg. Malraux is courteous; his charm is all the more effective since the company cannot understand him. They roam from Swabia to Bavaria. Under Clara's influence, André explores the baroque. Berlin interests him, with its museums and fancy-dress cabarets. Prodigious Berlin, where the couple discover expressionist filmmakers, painters, and poets, Carl Einstein's work on the "Negro Arts," and the psychiatrist Hanz Prinzhorn's on the art of the mad. Perhaps Paris is not the only cultural capital in Europe.

The Malrauxs do not notice the political and social cracks in the Weimar Republic. The German grandfather warns of a bad economic outlook, and Malraux listens: he will not invest Clara's dowry in Germany. But the cinematograph—now, there's a promising little industry. Malraux imagines himself selling films to the French, Wiene's *The Cabinet of Dr. Caligari* or Murnau's *Nosferatu*.[4] During meetings with producers, Clara translates and André signs preliminary contracts. In France, the authorities refuse the import permits.

In Brussels, accompanied by Clara, Arland, and his wife, Malraux decides to pay his respects to James Ensor. He is welcomed to Ostende, where he admires the painter's masks fighting over a hanged man, challenging death. André is an honorary Fleming via his grandfather: perhaps these masks bring back memories of the carnival of Dunkirk. Around *Dr. Caligari*, *The Blue Angel*, and Ensor's canvases, André and Clara elaborate on fate and destiny.

For the spring of 1922, looking for sun and sea, they plan excursions to Tunisia and Italy. But weren't they supposed to divorce six months after getting married? The money would be better spent in Jerba and Catania. At hotels, at home, Malraux continues to play at writing, usually in the morning. He produces fragments and would like to turn them into a book. These words are the fruit of painful labor. After "The Tamed Hedgehogs" and "Diary of a Slaughter Game Fireman," published the year before, there follow "Written for a Teddy Bear," "Pneumatic Rabbits in a French Garden," and other artificial texts to be brought together in his *Written for an Idol with a Trunk*.[5] In theory, he distances himself from the surrealists but cannot manage to escape their influence. He creates an atmosphere where the bric-a-brac of a confused irrationality—not equal to that of André Breton or Tristan Tzara—mixes with a fairy-tale world of forced ingenuity. In England, Ronald Firbank manages the cocktail much more successfully.

In his writing, Malraux is short on wit and humor. His heavy style puts editors off. Despite the friendly insistence of Arland, who has contacts at the *Nouvelle Revue Française*, its director, Jacques Rivière, refuses to show interest in these texts, thinking them trifling. Malraux has to make do with *Action*, which still welcomes him, or even with *Signaux de France et de Belgique*. His "Diary of a Fireman," the least obscure of his efforts, shows a Malraux inspired by Maeterlinck, Hoffmann, and Pierre Mac Orlan—without their ability to take literary flight.[6] Malraux continues to shut himself into a fantastical universe, which he describes as "quirky." Trees turn into threatening hands, replaced by a spinning top transformed into a mouth. The painter Victor Brauner also seems to influence the writer. Here and there a pretty sentence: "The sun fell into the sea, which immediately became a lake of scales. A white spinning top comes out of it, so large that it cannot be seen in its entirety."

In contrast to *Lunes en papier*, these texts initiate the description of a character, Malraux himself, with his own sensitivity and temptations. The writer uses brutal transitions, clean filmlike cuts. His "Diary of a Fireman" tells of events in Bhouzylle, freely adapted from his Bondy childhood. A stranger appears, the "charlatan," with his friend, the Petit-Salé. There are catastrophes, episodes where the style borders on the comic book: "All the golden buttons on my jacket fell on the floor and became cats' eyes." A voice asks, "Why is everything going away?" The Fireman, alias the narrator Malraux, answers, "In truth, Sir, I know not. I will tell you all about it . . . everything is going away because there are no more morals." The conservative weekly *Le Figaro* talks of the decline in moral values.

Malraux has a social position but no status. Fels sees a skeptical philosopher in him. He salutes Malraux the traveler, the poet, the man of culture who has yet to prove himself. Malraux pays a respectful visit to François Mauriac, who discerns in him a promisingly fierce nature. Malraux doesn't know where he is going but knows he is on his way. Others feel it too, not least Clara. In his article on Gide, "the greatest living French writer," Malraux writes, "To strive towards a rough goal, aware of one's value and looking for ways to increase it from one's current position: that is the manifestation of all intelligence and all real faith."[7] Barrès lies in wait.

Malraux enlarges his circle of acquaintances. Florent Fels recommends him to Charles Maurras. Malraux has the same tendency as Maurras to flit between order and anarchy. He pays more attention to sensitivity than to reason; a human being "trades a feeling for another feeling, and not for an idea." He appreciates Maurras's liking for a nation in opposition to anarchy. Malraux is twenty-one, Maurras, fifty-six. The young writer appears nationalistic, not jingoistic.

To become known (if not well known), it is essential to be published in the *NRF,* the review that can establish its contributors. Malraux keeps trying, suggests reviews to Paulhan, sends texts to Jacques Rivière, who finds him too aggressive and turns down his offerings, advising him again to get beyond the whimsical, the weird, and the wonderful. Nevertheless, Malraux manages to make his mark as a regular critic for the *NRF.* In 1922, he signs a first, restrained study on *L'Abbaye de Typhaines*, an insipid novel by Gobineau. The following month, he writes a laudatory article on *L'Art poétique* by Max Jacob. He follows on with a gentle critique of *Malice* by Pierre Mac Orlan. He doesn't make a living from these notes but earns a reputation in literary circles, while still not having published a significant book.

The Malrauxs continue to travel. They leave for Greece. Under the influence of his wife, André's curiosity about architecture and sculpture continues to grow. In a few months, Clara has introduced him to foreign civilizations, to whole areas of culture from the Russian novel to architecture, from sculpture to German philosophy. He has rid himself of his Parisian parochialism and owes this to Clara more than anyone else.

Also thanks to her, the couple felt closer to Fernand Malraux and Lilette. Lilette becomes Clara's true mother-in-law. Fernand amuses his daughter-in-law. Despite being an old, flag-waving soldier, Fernand forgets about Clara's German origins: "For a Jew, Clara dresses pretty well."

Clara, like André, forgets the Bondy women until she gets to know Aunt Marie, whose kindness touches them both. There is no more question of divorce between Clara and André.

The Mexican shares aren't rising anymore. That's worrying. They're going down. Tiresome. What's that? They're not worth a penny? André and Clara Malraux are ruined.

Un complexe

CHAPTER FOUR

False Thieves?

F ULL OF AMBITION and an enormous eclectic knowledge, Malraux
proposes to write a history of art. But at twenty-three, he's a bit
young. No publisher will go ahead with him as editor. The intrepid
Malraux insists on an abundant use of illustration, which is lacking in the
works currently available, such as Élie Faure's *History of Art.*[1] Malraux is
not satisfied with black-and-white reproductions.

He tries to find erudite (and preferably adventurous) contacts. He
meets one of the first specialists in comparative visual arts, Alfred Salmony, the deputy curator of the Cologne Museum, a specialist in Siamese
sculpture but interested in all of Asia. The scholar warms to the young
man and introduces him to Thai art. Salmony prods him with questions:
Why should a French Romanesque statue of the twelfth century resemble
a Chinese bodhisattva of the sixth? What links can we find between the
African masks collected by Tzara and Breton and the Japanese or Chinese porcelain in the British Museum? Salmony shows Malraux sepia and
black-and-white photographs. They note similarities and differences.
Malraux steeps himself in the art of every continent: he questions himself
about the Art behind the art, the first sign of his metaphysical inclinations. Having dipped into philosophical works, he becomes a Hegelian
almost without knowing it. For Malraux, Hegel would say, art becomes
"the supreme interest of the mind." But the young writer is not as condescending about non-European art as the German philosopher.

He spends time with the archaeologist Joseph Hackin, another Asia
specialist. He constantly thinks of leaving France. The colonization of
Indochina is turning the French in Cambodia, Tongking, Annam, and
Laos into crack treasure seekers. Navy officers have discovered countless
monuments. In 1902, a "Descriptive Inventory of Cambodia's Monu-

ments" located 290. Two years later, the official count came to 910 monuments, temples, ornamental lakes, and bridges.

In the *Bulletin de l'École Française d'Extrême-Orient* (the French School of the Far East, or EFEO), Malraux reads a hundred-page article by Henri Parmentier, an expert in Khmer art. The article, entitled "The Art of Indravarman," is illustrated with photographs and sketches by the author. It points out the creative originality of the reign of Indravarman, differentiating the preclassical period of the seventh century from that of Angkor in the ninth century. The tiny temple of Banteay Srei, northeast of Angkor, still offers a superb example of Khmer art. This temple, set away from the main monuments of the immense and prodigious Angkor group, was discovered by Lieutenant Marek from the Geographical Service. It has been inspected by other archaeologists and by the architect Demasure. In 1916, Parmentier remarked on its poor condition. On the route from Flanders to Santiago de Compostela, there are sanctuaries, Malraux explains to Clara, with chapels and churches. In Cambodia, on Angkor's ancient Royal Road leading to Siam, there are bound to be isolated temples. Clara and André could go there with Chevasson.

Paul Cassirer gives rough ideas of prices: in London and New York, a ten-inch statuette sells for 30,000 francs; a sculpture of a dancing goddess, an *apsara*, for 200,000 francs (more than $12,000 at the time). Malraux consults Daniel-Henri Kahnweiler, the art dealer and supplier to John Quinn and other American collectors. It's well known in Paris that Malraux trades in paintings and takes a cut in major deals, as when Kahnweiler bought a Le Nain: as an intermediary in the transaction, Malraux demanded his 18,000 francs ($1,000) in cash.[2] An expedition of a few weeks in Asia would provide André and Clara with something to live on for several months. The formula appears magical: art + adventure = living expenses. The vital thing is to find a source and an outlet. Clara is enchanted at the idea of this journey, even if Chevasson, whom she dubs "the colorless one," is to come along.

To prepare the ground, Malraux goes to the Ministry of Colonies with a reference from a curator of the respectable Guimet Museum. He also cites Claude Maître, former head of the École Française d'Extrême-Orient, as a reference and mentions the courses he is following—so he says—at the École des Langues Orientales (School of Oriental Languages). André intended to follow these courses.

On December 25, 1923, a seven-member committee sits at the Ministry of Colonies under the chairmanship of a senior member of the Council of State, the head of political affairs. The conclave includes several active or honorary colonial governors and a chief inspector from the Department of Health. The Malraux dossier is first on the agenda. The

young man requests permission for "a free mission in Indochina, to pur-
sue studies in Khmer archaeology in Cambodia in collaboration with the
EFEO." In return, he offers the EFEO "a large sum, varying according to
the material difficulty of the excavations, but which he already estimates at
100,000 to 200,000 francs" ($6,000 to $12,000). Malraux confidently sells
ahead of time statuettes he does not yet own. In his mind, possibilities are
automatically probabilities and already seem certain. He undertakes to
leave the management of the excavations to the EFEO and not to make
any personal claim to ownership of objects found. He will take casts of
monuments other than those of Angkor and bring them back to the
Guimet Museum.

After a short discussion, the mission is approved unanimously, "under
reserve of the governor of Indochina's assent." The commission covers
itself and leaves it "to the competent departments to obtain more precise
information on the character of Mr. Malraux." That day, two other candidates are not so lucky: Mme. Bellot's mission is "reserved," as is that of Mr.
Péan. The meeting dispatches three cases in forty-five minutes.[3]

Thanks to the Third Republic authorities' lightweight approach,
Malraux can get started. Two weeks later,[4] having borrowed 10,000 francs
($600) from Fernand Malraux and liquidated the few remaining shares in
Clara's portfolio, the couple board the *Angkor* at Marseille. In first class,
Malraux maintains a certain rank at the captain's table. Throughout the
three-week voyage, he scrawls on.

At the stopover in Djibouti, the Malrauxs visit souks and brothels.
The couple arrive in Saigon on November 4, 1923. The headquarters of
the EFEO and of the governor-general's departments are in Hanoi, more
than a thousand miles from Saigon. Malraux goes to see the acting head of
the EFEO, Léonard Aurousseau, a China specialist who does not take to
this amateur. He points out that the zone to the north of Angkor is
"unsubdued" and therefore dangerous. The "natives" have killed two representatives of the EFEO out there. Any objects discovered in the course
of excavations, insists Aurousseau, must remain where they are, in situ. A
decree of 1901 from the governor-general is specific: "Listed objects,
being part of the national estate, are inalienable and immutable." Article
20, Section IV: "No historic monument may be exported, in part or in
whole, from the territories of Indochina, without authorization of the
governor-general." In reality, senior colonial government officials possess
many items of "native" art and take them with them when returning to
France.

Having admired the small lake and the delightful Temple of Literature at Hanoi, André and Clara return to Saigon, where Chevasson has
been waiting for them since November 15. They meet Henri Parmentier,

who waxes lyrical on Khmer art and the beauty of the apsaras. Parmentier jokes about Pierre Loti, who claimed to have observed vultures clustered on banana trees. He is charmed by Clara and falls under the spell of Malraux, this rich, fiery, selfless young man who is putting his fortune to such good use.

Going up the swollen Mekong with another scholar, Victor Goloubow, the group arrives at Phnom Penh on December 3. André and Clara meet up with Chevasson at the Grand Hotel and feign surprise: My dear friend, what are you doing here! The Simon Gallery sends a wire to Malraux: "Cannot find funds without details and photographs. Explanatory letter follows." Malraux had talked of a complete collection. Without any firm buyers, perhaps he should limit himself to a few pieces. A "New York correspondent" is less than encouraging: the U.S. market seems worse than expected. But an American, Miss Gertrude Whitling, would like to examine the "Khmer collection Mr. Malraux has talked about" in Bangkok in February. She asks for news of his "expedition."[5]

The Malrauxs are not exactly given full backing by the French authorities. Before their arrival in Phnom Penh, the governor-general of Indochina alerted the resident superior in Cambodia: "Certain information gathered on Monsieur Malraux's previous history leaves some doubt as to his real intentions. . . . He should limit his activities to the strictly scientific."[6] Nevertheless, the resident in Cambodia gives instructions to help the Malrauxs: rooms are booked for them near Angkor in Siem Reap, the small town near the temples. Telegrams, some encoded, fly between Hanoi, Phnom Penh, Battambang, and Siem Reap. The Malrauxs are under surveillance. Their rooms in the Siem Reap bungalow are next to an annex of the police station. The bungalow manager spies on them for the police. Malraux takes on an Annamese odd-job man, Nguyen Van Xa, known as Sau, an ex-convict known to Mr. Cremazy, *délégué administratif* in Siem Reap. Recruiting in Cambodia a Vietnamese hand who is also being watched by the police is a double blunder that does not go unnoticed.

Siem Reap's European microcosm includes about a hundred government officials, tradesmen, and planters. Malraux and Chevasson begin to arouse suspicions by proclaiming too insistently that they came across each other by chance. Then Chevasson goes to the market and buys chisels, rope, picks, and shovels: rather heavy equipment for an archaeological survey. All that's missing is dynamite. Sray Ouk, a businessman who hires out sampans, horses, and carts to carry pieces from the temple to the bungalow, does his accounts: Chevasson has spent 23.40 piastres; Malraux, 90. Only Malraux's mission is free.

They camp for two days next to the Banteay Srei temple, a small

Mandarin marvel with three sanctuary towers and decorations chiseled into hard pink sandstone. Centuries, rains, and people have hardly damaged the foliations, checkered patterns, and pediments. Malraux forbids his drivers and porters to come near the temple while he is working with Louis. From the resting rooms, overgrown with vegetation, the two friends remove seven pieces. In their clumsiness, they make a gash here, split a block of stone there. The Khmer builders used no cement, fitting their stones flush together with dry joints. Malraux and Chevasson do more ripping out than detaching. The removed pieces range from one to two feet across: bas-reliefs or fragments, a Brahman ascetic sitting in a Javanese pose, a figure with a demonic mask, and apsaras, the celestial dancers. Sometimes damaged, the works are nonetheless well chosen: they belong to the art of the end of the tenth century. All of it, brought back to the bungalow, is transferred on December 22 at 10:30 p.m. to a steamboat. The trunks are addressed to "Berthé & Charrière Chemicals, Saigon." The Malrauxs and Chevasson rely on police attention slackening off over the days leading up to Christmas. But as early as the twenty-third, Cremazy finds out about the transport of the trunks: clearly these explorers have no intention of going back to Phnom Penh. They are fleeing Cambodia by boat to Siam. The acting resident in Cambodia, L. Helgoualc'h, and the police give the order to pick up the "adventurers," Chevasson and the "Malraux couple," in cabin 13.

At first Chevasson passes for a medical student or a tourist in the eyes of the investigators. They request further information from Paris: "Mr. Chevasson seems, according to his statements, never to have had a profession as such. He appears, while in France, to have lived by his wits, writing articles published in avant-garde literary reviews, earning money as a sales representative, or from gambling, principally horse racing. Mr. Chevasson's activity in the latter sphere should be particularly well documented." Evidently, the résumés of André, Louis, and others merge in the investigations, reports, and overimaginative police profiles. The head of the Cambodian Criminal Investigation Department, Mr. Poillot, seizes the trunks and baggage and deposits the works of art at the Albert-Sarraut Museum in Phnom Penh.

When interviewed, Malraux does not falter. He and Chevasson have concocted a plan: Louis will take the blame for everything, leaving Malraux free to organize his defense. Proclaiming his honesty, Malraux thus accuses Chevasson of having abused their friendship to pillage the temple. Louis bears the guilt. Nevertheless, the authorities are convinced that Malraux is the brains behind the operation and Chevasson the "instrument." Witnesses confirm it: from the eighteenth to the twenty-second, the two friends were never apart. Malraux had gone away with empty crates and brought them back full.

In Phnom Penh, on January 1, 1924, detailed charges are brought. In court, the two friends are accused of stealing and defacing public monuments. What's more, they left unpaid bills. They escape being charged with fraud. The police easily extract witness statements from the Cambodians on the expedition. This is colonial justice, and the three white defendants are not imprisoned, as natives would have been for just stealing bananas.

Requested to remain at the judge's disposal, the Malrauxs and Chevasson stay in the Grand Hotel on the banks of the river. The examining magistrate, Bartet, conducts his case with respect for procedure while policemen fill long-winded reports with accusations. Malraux speaks with detached superiority. The police are sure that this was not his first time. Backed up with photographs, the report of the archaeologist Georges Groslier concludes that the stones were ripped out with the clumsiness of a novice. Chevasson is less provocative than his friend and comes out in official reports as "hardworking," a "tertium quid," "a stooge in Malraux's shrewd and audacious scheme." Paris reports moreover on a correspondence between Malraux and Mme. Simon, an antiques dealer, of Rue de Provence in the Eighth Arrondissement. The police want to expose the network, establishing Malraux as the seller, with others he has approached, especially in the United States, as buyers.

Fernand Malraux wires money to settle with the hotel owner, Mr. Manolis. What does the father of the accused do? the police are asking. "Works at the sand quarries company at Gennevilliers . . . Earns 12,000 francs [$720] per year . . . appears to live off his sister-in-law's generosity." Fernand, indeed, is having an affair with Gaby, the sister of his second wife, Lilette. But where is the connection with the Banteay Srei case? As the investigation develops, André Malraux's image darkens, as Louis Chevasson's emerges in a better light. Louis comes across as a minor employee of the Lévy silk works, "hardworking, sober, thrifty," to whom Malraux appears to have given 10,000 francs in travel expenses. Malraux appears more dubious: "Married a Jewess of Austrian origin. Associates with a certain Kahnweiler, a 'German expatriate.'" He sponges off his mother-in-law and sees himself as a man of letters, within the sphere of dada-bolshevik-anarchist reviews. There is "every reason to believe" that he traffics with dealers of stolen works. Malraux's dreadfulness sets off Chevasson's niceness to advantage; his "modesty" and good conduct are highlighted in the magistrate's summing-up.

Those at the top, in Hanoi, want an example to be made. Judge Bartet is too soft and is replaced. Complications begin to emerge in a legal tangle, which is promising for the defense. The archaeologist Groslier goes back on his first report. He made a mistake. There are two temples called Banteay Srei on the site of Angkor, which, he states, are probably of different status.[7] Do they belong to the king of Cambodia, the governor-general, or the École Française d'Extrême-Orient?

From January 5, the Indochinese newspapers pounce on the case. The daily L'Impartial in Saigon attacks Malraux, who is unruffled despite being trapped by his own defense. Neither Malraux nor Chevasson has a criminal record. Is "removing" a few statuettes really that serious? The Grand Hotel, too, exhibits Cambodian statues whose origins are not known to the owner. Surveillance is lax. On the quiet, one of the guides employed by Malraux offers several statuettes to Clara in her room, including a Hindu divinity, a Harihara (half Shiva, half Vishnu), and two apsaras.

Justice is slow. Chevasson and the Malrauxs wait, recite poems, take walks, discover the lifestyles and architecture of Phnom Penh. Getting away from the stone and brick villas of the rich and influential, they notice the misery of the Cambodian working class in the poor areas, the stench of the alleyways. Without exoticism, André Malraux soaks up the social reality of colonialism. The bourgeoisie of Phnom Pehn have no doubt that these "natives" are happy living with malaria, TB, and French rule.

The Malrauxs feel abandoned but find solidarity in their shared solitude. André Malraux writes letters and analyzes his moods: I act, therefore I am. I act no longer: I write, therefore I am. To dear Marcel Arland: "One can describe only the unimportant things to one's friends. By writing down and summarizing the things that are worth saying, one is bound to disfigure them; by taking enough care to convey them accurately, one can end up living all wrong. Still, life is sad, as you well know." Under house arrest, Malraux lets loose: "You have to love the Chinese quarters. Have I told you that the famous Chinese violins, the ones in the shape of a pipe, can now be found only at fairs? China now has no musical instrument but the gramophone." He finds his old quirky tone: "The gramophone hides in the belly of the dragons and, when they get hot, comes out through the monsters' mouths or eyes, to take the air; and this gives the aforesaid monsters an air of deaf men with hearing aids." In Hanoi, he writes, he met old mistresses of rich Europeans. One European lady he met, he swears, "had a little garden in a native street; trees grew there in the shape of a phoenix. In the pools swam turtles with no scales, their shells having been dissolved in complex acids." Malraux's fairy-tale phantasmagoria returns: a dog with three legs, a dwarf with four knees, blind lizards. Armed with his deep knowledge of Asia gathered over a few months, Malraux is bursting with advice: "Don't ever come to the colonies as a university lecturer. I write this solemnly: never. Towns in the colonies are not those of Africa, nor of Asia, but of the most squalid provinciality." He finishes cryptically, "I have written you none of what I should have liked to write, but I will say it to you." He knows the police go through his correspondence. Solitude is hard for Malraux: it deprives him of an audience. Louis listens. Clara seems less receptive to her husband's tirades than in Europe. She finds it hard not to be angry, because she has shared the risks of the expedition, yet the magistrate—what an insult!—fails to charge her along with Malraux and Chevasson. A good wife, Clara was "only following her husband," according to French law.

On February 6, 1924, the resident receives a telegram:

"February two number one hundred thirteen . . . Malraux case being likely to take on bigger proportions and unforeseen developments, I request: firstly: ask magistrate urgently send telegram . . . senior Paris magistrate allows free rein to search and question witnesses . . . thirdly: inspect letters and telegrams Mme. Malraux and accused . . . fifthly: take exceptional measures to guard archaeological treasures sought after at very high price by international gangs . . . Minister.

In Paris, Clara's family rebels. Mme. Goldschmidt sees divorce as the only option for her daughter. Fernand Malraux is indulgent and wires a few more francs. The case is not going anywhere. To be allowed to return to France, Clara simulates suicide. Many medicines are freely available in Phnom Penh. A tube and a half of veronal (barbital) will do it, declares Dr. André. Clara takes more than the prescribed dose. She has to have her stomach pumped at the hospital. The blackmail doesn't work on the magistrate. Mme. Malraux, now weighing less than 90 pounds, must remain at the court's disposal as a witness.

Lukewarm colonial weeks trail by. On May 13, 1924, Malraux sends a letter to the resident: "The case had been going on for two months already when my wife, in worse health and having learned that my mother had fallen ill, decided to return to France. My lawyer, Maître de Parcevaux, having informed His Honor of her departure as a matter of courtesy, was told that he would not allow it. Indeed, two days later, my wife was charged." Malraux cannot help showing his indignation: "The shock caused by this indictment . . . the impossibility of returning home, upon a constitution that was already weakened and bears the weight of a heavy heredity, was such that it triggered a nervous breakdown of the greatest violence with some characteristics of madness. She was taken in time to hospital, where she refused food for quite some time. Since then (more than two months ago) she has remained in a state of extreme depression and has not yet recovered consciousness." Clara has an effervescent, slightly hysterical nature, but she is not mad. Malraux continues, "She was promised indulgence and the dismissal of her case upon confirmation that she has no criminal record." In a document enclosed in Malraux's letter, Émile Vallet, head doctor of the hospital in Phnom Penh, certifies that "the precarious state of this person's physical and mental health requires a prompt return to France." Malraux fears that his wife's recovery may "become altogether impossible." One month later, the public prosecutor mentions that the case will be called in June. A "degree of favorable consideration will given to Mme. Malraux due in particular to her very precarious state of health."

Clara is free. During her return voyage, she flirts with Charles G.,[8] sleeps with him, and meets Paul Monin, a progressive lawyer.

Malraux and Chevasson's trial opens at 7:30 a.m. on July 16, in Phnom Penh. The heat is already sticky. The two friends are accused of "trespass of monuments" and "misappropriation of stolen bas-reliefs." Malraux's strategy collapses: he was supposed to play the simpleton and Chevasson the brains. Malraux can play many roles, but not that of an imbecile. According to a journalist from the *Écho du Cambodge*, André gives a lecture on archaeology. He paints a picture of Fernand Malraux, director of a large oil company, "a legendary personality on the stock exchange" (which Fernand—like André?—would certainly have liked to be). When he holds forth, Malraux addresses a wider public than just the judges. He has found an audience. With disarming cheek, he informs the press that this whole affair is "a misunderstanding." He may, on his way past an isolated temple in the jungle, have inadvertently removed some bas-reliefs that were "already cut." Malraux *saved* these bas-reliefs. The witnesses' statements weigh against him. The archaeologist Henri Parmentier generously expresses admiration for Malraux and speaks highly of his intelligence. But the young man has nonetheless taken advantage of his burgeoning friendship. And Clara, during the raid on the temple ruins, distracted him with a show of simpering: "I won't be accompanying my husband," she told him. "Show me some photographs. You explain so well."

In bit parts as well as major roles, Clara is easily André's equal. Parmentier doesn't hold this playacting against her.[9] The two defense lawyers get bogged down. Not so Jordiani the prosecutor, who stands on morality and legality. After three hearings and four days of consideration,[10] Georges-André Malraux is sent down for three years' imprisonment without remission and receives a five-year ban on re-entering the country. Louis Chevasson gets eighteen months. The grounds given by the trial court are severe, citing fraud, deliberate damage, an act "not of pointless and profitable vandalism but of actual burglary." The verdict also adds, "The theft of these wonderful and voluminous sculptures might have caused particularly serious harm to the artistic and archaeological heritage." Harm, certainly. But particularly serious? Thousands of borrowers went before Malraux, tens of thousands of pieces had already been stolen.[11] He is thought to be in continued contact with "traders of German nationality, dealers in archaeological pieces." To flesh out the image of Malraux as a corrupting influence, they accuse him of having "promised gifts worthy of a Roland Bonaparte."[12] They appeal, which will at least delay their imprisonment. They get to Saigon, where the court of appeal sits, and move into the Hôtel Continental, for decades the only place to stay for visitors of standing. Malraux can now observe Saigon's colonial classes.

Back in Paris, Clara and Marcel Arland mobilize intellectual society. The Goldschmidt family, standing firm on its principles, provides neither help nor protection, but Fernand Malraux puts himself at his daughter-in-law's disposal. Clara also discovers the compassion and tenderness of André's mother. The maternal grandmother has sold the grocer's shop in Bondy and lives with her daughters in a small flat on the Boulevard Edgar-Quinet in the Fourteenth Arrondissement. The Malraux-Lamy clan closes ranks around the accused.

A letter from René-Louis Doyon in an issue of *L'Éclair* of August 9 touches Clara, often hurt by the harsh, ironical reports in the Parisian press, such as *Le Journal* and *Le Matin*. Doyon was abandoned by Malraux three years earlier for another publisher but bears no grudge. He evokes the image of a young writer who has "Rimbaud as a model" and "an uncontrollable taste for the aesthetic." Clara rushes to thank Doyon.

In Indochina, Malraux is growing restless. How can he resist the temptation of an interview in *L'Impartial*?[13] Articles favoring André have appeared in France, Clara's telegrams tell him.

"I am here to tell you," Malraux declares to the interviewer, "that a countercampaign is being led by two other major newspapers, *L'Éclair* and *L'Intransigeant*. Many French intellectuals feel moved by my plight, and a petition has been presented, bearing forty-eight signatures, demanding the complete remission of my sentence. You will find Anatole France's name on it and that of Claude Farrère, as well as others known to the people of Indochina."

At the Décades de Pontigny, where writers hold an annual symposium, Marcel Arland has indeed gathered some signatures, but not those of Anatole France or Claude Farrère. André Gide, André Maurois, François Mauriac, and Jean Paulhan, among others, support the amateur archaeologist. In the *Nouvelles Littéraires* of September 6, Breton praises Malraux's heroic character. What of the apsaras from Banteay Srei? "Who in their homeland really cares about the preservation of these works of art?" writes Breton. A good crop of names—Jacques Rivière, Maurice Martin du Gard, Gaston and Raymond Gallimard—also sign a letter of protest written by Clara, with Breton and Monin's help. The text has a curious logic: "The undersigned, moved by the condemnation of André Malraux, have confidence in the consideration that justice is wont to show to all those who help increase the intellectual wealth of our country." So fine minds deserve preferential treatment? The undersigned also "hold themselves guarantors of the intelligence and real literary value of this person, whose youth and completed works encourage great hopes for the future." One book and a dozen articles—his works? The signatories ask that no sanction be enforced that would prevent André Malraux from accomplishing what everybody "has a right to expect of him." A more aggressive press campaign is developing in Cochin China. If the *Courrier Saigonnais* appears moderate, *L'Impartial* wants to nail Malraux. Documents and leaks move among police offices, the corridors of justice, and newsrooms. Ludicrous instances of "evidence" are reported. The French Embassy in Siam had a catalog of Chinese sculptures of the fifth to fourteenth centuries that was sent to Malraux. The embassy forwards it to the judicial authorities, along with (according to the diplomatic sender) a damning conclusion: "This missive thus helps situate Mr. Malraux among the specialists enjoying a certain notoriety in the relevant European circles." Some officials want to apply deductive reasoning to the case, however absurd: Malraux stole seven pieces from a temple. We see in him an expert in Asiatic art. Therefore, he is a plunderer on a large scale. Malraux hurries to the offices of *L'Impartial* to seek compensation and challenge the editor in chief, Henri de Lachevrotière, to a duel.

On October 8, Malraux and Chevasson appear before the Court of Appeal. The public prosecutor portrays them as liars and thieves who deserve their sentence. Maître Joseph Béziat, pleading for Malraux, sets the case on legal ground. Banteay Srei is a property with no owner, *res derelicta*. Decisions based on Indochinese heritage are therefore not applicable. Maître Béziat moreover objects to an example being made with the recommended sentence: in the past, higher residents should then have been condemned for appropriating works of art from the public domain. Like André Breton, Maître Louis Gallois-Montbrun makes ironical statements about the sudden interest of so many people in archaeology. He pleads for "two young lives" that "must not be wasted."

On October 28, 1924, a new ruling from Judge Gaudin, who directed the appeal with impartiality, condemns Malraux to one year's imprisonment, Chevasson to ten months, both suspended sentences. The judges have taken into account the expert's correction stating that there were two temples of the same name. Malraux behaves and speaks as if he had been declared innocent.

The following year—by coincidence?—the temple at Banteay Srei is cleared piece by piece by Parmentier and Goloubow. Then from 1931 to 1936 it is restored by Henri Marchal using anastylose, a technique employed in Java by Dutch archaeologists. Would so much attention have been paid to this "precious jewel" of a temple if Malraux hadn't looted it?[14] Did this thief not, finally, save Banteay Srei?

On November 1, Malraux sets sail with Chevasson on the *Chantilly*, taking some pieces of Khmer art with him and dropping them off in various locations, some with Louis Dideron, a sculptor in Marseille.[15] On November 14, Georges Groslier addresses a letter to Louis Finot, the head of the EFEO:

> Of course, thirty-six hours after arriving in Paris, I fell feet first into the frog pond from which Malraux, the young and sparkling dolphin, had leapt. The secretive little so-and-so had hidden from us that he was a decadent man of letters in order to pass himself off in our eyes as a well-informed archaeologist. And the *Nouvelles Littéraires*, that most active journal, had trumpeted in protestation, announcing a manifesto and a collection of lamentations signed by twenty mandarins with showy names, Gide in the lead, fresh out of *The Vatican Cellars*, followed by the Surrealist Breton, the comical Max Jacob, etc., etc., and not forgetting the good and candid Ed Jaloux, who is decidedly not having much luck with things from the Far East. A whole literary world, fooled by Malraux [and they would be again], marching in step with torches aloft. But I did eventually manage to make them understand that things were not as Malraux had communicated them. . . . Anyway, I was counting on finding out a great deal about Malraux in Paris. But not a bit of it. His friends know nothing about him. He turned up at all the private views and was in with all the avant-garde cliques. Everyone knew him in the gaudy village of the late Apollinaire, Salmon, Rosenberg, etc., talking on the Negro arts, the metaphysics of Greenland, the literature of the day after tomorrow. But of his means, his past, his family, nobody has the faintest idea. Oh, the charm of Paris! Oh, the indulgence of these natives! A well-cut suit, a pair of deep eyes, and anything goes.

CHAPTER FIVE

A True Revolutionary?

Malraux, back in France, has just turned twenty-three. He is sure of himself, and thinner. He and his wife move into a small apartment at 39 Boulevard Edgar-Quinet, near Montparnasse cemetery, in the same building as his mother's family, Berthe, Marie, and the retired Adrienne.

Malraux brought back some Indian hemp from Saigon. It triggers compulsive confession in Clara. She tells him of her infidelity. He is not amused. André refers pointedly to Clara's lover aboard the liner: "Just imagine what that chap thinks now! He probably despises you."

"I know he doesn't despise me," Clara answers.

"I know what a man thinks of a woman he has had."[1]

While on his tour of thanks, Malraux sees some Freemasons who worked for his cause before the trial went to appeal. Breton also helped Clara unreservedly. Malraux resents her having seen the surrealist but nonetheless goes to express his thanks. The two men do not hit it off. Both come away with the impression that the other is intolerably full of himself.

Malraux gets moving again: with Clara and the lawyer Paul Monin, he plans to publish a newspaper—in Indochina, no less. Monin is always ready to defend a "native" and often pleads for no fee in Saigon. In parliamentary elections he stood as a left-wing candidate against Ernest Outrey, backed by colonial authorities. Outrey received 15,049 votes to Monin's 624, with a "native" candidate getting only one. Monin has edited several short-lived papers, including *La Vérité*. He hates Maurice Cognacq, the governor of Cochin China.[2] And he detests, as does Malraux, Henri Chavigny de Lachevrotière, the editor of *L'Impartial*. Malraux shows himself receptive to the lawyer's militant, bellicose suggestions. A free press, thinks Monin, could act against the authorities' schemes and the misap-propriation of public funds by local businessmen. Industry in Indochina and the lucrative activities at the port of Saigon (transit, shipping, loading and unloading of ships) are being monopolized by a few.

Pascal Pia is told about the project and says he's ready to leave for Indochina. Marcel Arland likewise. The former would bring technical help, the latter intellectual collaboration.[3] Monin would like to publish two editions of the same paper, one in French, one in Vietnamese. Mal-raux has scores of his own to settle since the bas-reliefs business. Monin audaciously demonstrates to him that, in this adventure, he and Chevas-son were in fact victims of colonialism.

Clara and André meet Fernand Malraux in Orléans. The father admires his son and his daughter-in-law (a "good little woman"). He will invest 50,000 francs ($2,600) in the paper, which has a working title, *L'Indochine*. Malraux goes on a pilgrimage to Saint-Benoît-sur-Loire. He wants Max Jacob to accompany him to Indochina; he offers him 15,000 francs ($785) plus expenses for a lecture tour in China. The two men talk literature and Eastern philosophy. Malraux is fresh back from Asia. Jacob himself is not overly concerned with politics but is surprised that his young friend talks neither of past famines nor of revolutions to come.

In Paris, Malraux canvasses publishers—Arthème Fayard, Payot, the Messageries Hachette—asking for funds in exchange for advertising. This money allows him to buy the rights to articles from *Le Canard Enchaîné*, *Le Merle*, *Le Petit Écho de la Mode*, and *Le Miroir des Sports*. Malraux thinks big and demands exclusive reproduction rights.

Why go back to Indochina right away? Why throw himself into such a risky venture? Exoticism also urges him on. He did not see much of Asia. During his enforced free time in Phnom Penh and Saigon, he observed the colonial system close up. He wants to fight its injustices alongside Monin; he wants to act in order to be. Words are weapons to Malraux. He aims to take his revenge on papers like *L'Impartial* and its editor, Lachevrotière. Clara agrees with the idea of a militant newspaper. Moreover, Malraux is looking—more or less consciously—for a setting, an atmosphere, and characters for stories. He still envisages a book published by a well-known publisher, a door into the world of literature.

Malraux, without a large audience, still has a useful address book. Three days before leaving again for Indochina, he receives a message from the publisher Bernard Grasset. François Mauriac, already famous, has put in a good word for Malraux; during the trials, Malraux benefited from some striking publicity. Grasset is a skilful salesman, not a philanthropist; he knows how to make the most of the climate surrounding an author. Malraux must step into the breach with a novel or narrative story, not one of his recondite texts. The editor proposes a contract: 3,000 francs ($155) in advance and 7,000 francs ($365) when Malraux delivers the first of three planned books, each to be printed in 10,000 copies. Grasset knows how to bet on a writer, to encourage him, to exploit him as needed.

The Malrauxs almost separated. Now they are reconciled and have sold paintings to finance their journey, including several fakes: two "Picassos" and two "Derains." The couple sail from Marseille on January 14, 1925—only ten weeks after leaving Saigon. They travel third class to Singapore, second on the train to Bangkok, then first on the boat to Saigon, where Paul Monin is waiting for them.

Malraux finds himself back in the Hôtel Continental, with its patio, spacious rooms, ceiling fans, rum-and-sodas, and absinthe. From February to May, he travels around Cochin China. Malraux is not a passive tourist. He likes the bustle, the growing hum of the mornings and the buzz of the evenings in Saigon, and dislikes the customary siesta. He likes the port, the sampans sliding between rusty cargo boats, the scent of peppery sage sold on the pavements by women crouching under conical hats. He is not so keen on the colonial villas, their facades disfigured by the humidity, behind bougainvilleas or frangipani trees. Exploring villages and hamlets around Saigon, Malraux takes in the poverty of the peasants among the straw huts and in rice fields lacquered by the sun. Their wretchedness and that of the inhabitants of the Saigon slums, where rats run between the children's feet, strikes him more than the picturesque bamboo shoots and the street peddlers. He had his share of the exotic in Cambodia. In the shadow of the "French mission," he sees disorder created by injustice. About ten thousand civil servants and fewer than thirty thousand whites rule over seventeen million Indochinese. Malraux prepares to launch his daily paper. Sitting on the terrace of the Continental, facing the theater, he makes contact with the reality of colonial rites: no Annamese may drink alone on the terrace without being accompanied by a "white." Beneath Saigon's charm, Malraux watches the daily humiliation of the "natives."

Malraux and Monin are to run the paper together, without the help of Arland, Max Jacob, or Pia. It is to be a social and political daily, with no hypocrisy. Malraux does not admit to any ideological conviction: he even writes an enthusiastic preface to *Mademoiselle Monk* by Charles Maurras, who is extremely right-wing and loathed by Monin. But Malraux now has a heightened sensitivity to justice.

The production team gather at the coeditor-cum-lawyer's house, 12 Rue Taberd, near the Continental on the way up the Rue Catinat. Monin recruits seven collaborators; one of them, the young and enterprising Dejean de La Batie, is of mixed race and is made managing editor. The printer Louis Minh prepares to run 5,000 copies of the paper. Clara goes to Singapore to sound out the advertising market, without much success. Why should English speakers be interested in an obscure French publication from Indochina? Clara negotiates reproduction rights for the *Straits Times*, one of the better dailies in Southeast Asia. Malraux is received in Hanoi by a lower civil servant who refuses the publication of the paper in Vietnamese.

After several postponements, the first issue of *L'Indochine* comes out on June 17, 1925: six pages on paper of superior quality to that of *L'Impartial*. For four days, the paper is distributed free. Issue No. 1, price ten centimes, date missing by mistake, bears the subtitle "Journal quotidien du rapprochement franco-annamite" (A daily newspaper of mediation between France and Annam). The two editors in chief define the program as a "paper with no constraints, open to all, with no ties to banks or commercial groups." The moods of the collaborators will be respected by the editors. "Polemicists will write harshly, moderates with moderation." The former turn out to be more numerous than the latter: Malraux and Monin are not good at striking a happy (or not-so-happy) medium.

The first article, an interview with Paul Painlevé, the new president of the French Chamber of Deputies, concentrates on Annamese rights. "The natives," explains Painlevé, "will gain in effectiveness as they assimilate the French way of thinking." The government of Indochina "must make a more noticeable effort."

As early as the second issue, which is less woolly, Malraux, pastiching Anatole France, attacks the governor of Cochin China, Maurice Cognacq: "First letter from Jacques Tournebroche to Jérôme Coignard." (For "Coignard," read Cognacq.) *"Monsieur le gouverneur,* sin is within you, pride is pushing you to the most disastrous resolutions. And you will regret it keenly." The tone is set. Issue No. 4 attacks Mr. de La Pomeraye, a powerful businessman: "You accuse us of fishing in murky waters. To each his own." This wheeler-dealer had bought thread at 30 francs a meter to sell it at ten times the price, in piastres, to the Indochinese administration.

In their effort to bring together the French and "native" populations, Monin and Malraux launch a campaign to help the Annamese who want to go to France. "The candidate wishing to emigrate or simply travel," writes Dejean de La Batie, "first addresses a request . . . to the communal authorities of his village of origin. They, respectful of the hierarchy, transmit it, forwarding their views, to the head of the canton. He sends it . . . to the administrative delegate . . . to the head of the province, and so on up to the governor of Cochin China." Malraux also gives some advice: "There are no Annamese technicians. In twenty years, many will be needed. Turn your sons into engineers, foremen, doctors. . . . Above all, agricultural engineers. . . . Send them to France. If they don't want to let you do that, then we will see."

In issue No. 5 of *L'Indochine*, the news in brief on the first page announces, "We have just learned from English and Chinese sources that the British government has forbidden the export of all Chinese rice stored in Hong Kong. The exasperation of the Chinese is at a high point." *L'Indochine* follows events in China closely, as workers occupy buildings or demand the departure of foreigners, and police from international concessions open fire on demonstrators. Paul Monin, signing himself "member of the colonial council,"[4] denounces France's attitude to the conflict in China: "Each time one of the world's larger nations has started the glorious project of unification and independence, it has been France's natural vocation to offer material aid or moral guidance."

Monin and Malraux set the Indochinese problem in its Asian context. Monin hones his vision of a French political approach in the Far East that hardly coincides with that of the Ministry of Foreign Affairs. In issue No. 26 of *L'Indochine*, the lawyer advocates "a narrow but at least moral rapprochement with Gandhi's India, and with a China whose consciousness grows steadily." Monin is an Anglophobe and considers that beyond its moral logic, his rapprochement would have the advantage of protecting national interests. There are more French than British exports to China, he claims. The member of Parliament who beat him in the elections, Ernest Outrey, and the unspeakable Cognacq support Great Britain. Paul Monin finishes off his editorial with a punch: "If by any unhappy chance the severe economic quarrel that continues between France and England were to turn into an armed conflict, logic would demand that the political career of His Lordliness Mr. Outrey, being guilty of trying to deny his country two powerful, necessary and natural allies, should finish like certain others in the ditches of Vincennes."

The administration reacts. Monin and Malraux inform their readers that the authorities have launched an official campaign against *L'Indochine*: "The administrator has summoned those Annamese who are guilty of having subscribed . . . and has vehemently reproached them for it, not forgetting to denigrate us in the process." Malraux questions the governor of Cochin China, whom he nicknames "Mr. Je menotte" (Mr. I Handcuff): "You will not succeed in forcing a boycott of a newspaper that you do not like. . . . Such a course of action befits a valet: it is completely beneath a governor. Do not do it." "A.M." threatens to incite reactions in France. Does he have the means?

To pull themselves back from an uncomfortable and dangerous marginality, the editors of the paper encourage others to express their views, even cautiously. Monin presents an interview with the Socialist Marius Moutet that is favorable to French naturalization and native representation in Parliament.

"Indeed, I am not opposed to the idea of very wide-ranging natural-ization," declares Moutet—with inherent caution, as in reality, only an elite minority will ever either request or fulfill the necessary conditions for naturalization. "Those who are naturalized will have their hearts and minds turned toward us rather than toward a native nationalism, which is dangerous both for us and for them."

L'Indochine also calls on Rouelle, the mayor of Saigon, who has a repu-tation for integrity. Monin and Malraux compare the administration of the city of Saigon with that of Cochin China as a whole, contrasting the elected assemblies, on the one hand, to the appointed senior civil servants, on the other. How does the mayor see the Annamese question?

"Speaking as the mayor, I can't answer that. The council abstains from all political issues. As a private individual, I can say that, while these things must not be rushed, a certain amount of reform would seem to me to be welcome."

Maître Gallois-Montbrun, the most senior member of Saigon's Bar Association, states in *L'Indochine*:

The natives are not content. One only has to read the indepen-dent papers to realize this. Their elite is divided into two groups. There are the egotists, the immediatists . . . who are on the side of the strongest, whose suspect loyalty quickly earns them superb land concessions, ownership of profitable bars, and decoration. Then there are the other Annamese . . . (who can blame them?) who are watching us and observing all our faults.

The paper also lets well-known "natives" have their say. There is an interview with Phan Chau Trinh, a progressive nationalist who was con-demned to death, pardoned, exiled to France, then allowed to return to Indochina thanks to the Socialist Moutet and to Monin.

L'INDOCHINE: "What is your opinion of the French in metropol-itan France and those here?"
PHAN CHAU TRINH: "The French in France? There are good and bad. . . . They are, however, in general, better than most of the colonials we are given as governors. My sympathy is with the members of the Left and with those who think like them. I owe a debt of gratitude to some among them."

Other Annamese contribute anonymously to the letters page. From a reader in Soc Trang: "I am keen to know what is happening throughout the world, so I would like to buy *L'Indochine*. But faced with the threats

of . . . Mr. Le Phu Diem, who says that he will do all he can to have all
buyers go to prison, I am compelled to turn to you to fight for the freedom
to buy." Other readers write, "This is the first time in Cochin China that
a newspaper of the importance of yours dares to attack the authorities."

Monin and Malraux emphasize in their columns that the authorities
are there to serve the country and not the other way around. Monin provides updates on the occult workings of the Chambers of Commerce
and Agriculture, the town council, and the Colonial Council, of which
he is a member. Truong Nguyen, another collaborator with *L'Indochine*,
denounces despotism and favoritism "under the government of Dr.
Cognacq, radical Socialist as he would have it in France, Freemason, as
they say in Rome, staunch bloc-nationalist as we can see in Cochin
China." Throughout Indochina, states Monin, you will find "those who,
through real work, are creating something, but also those who will address
some senior civil servant as follows: 'So, my old chum, you want to build a
railway. This is a fine sentiment that does you credit. You can count on
me. I am completely behind such a highly French venture, which will
bring order and prosperity to this country that I came here to civilize, with
my simpleton's air and the natural grace that characterizes me. You will
give me materials . . . a workforce . . . and . . . you will subscribe for 90
percent of the shares, by way of a subsidy.' "

The paper is opposed not to the French presence in Indochina but to
the widespread system of exploitation and corruption, covered with a
layer of hypocritical and condescending propaganda toward the "natives":
"The French did not come here to civilize but to make money by their
work. There is nothing in that which need be hidden," writes Malraux.
The "government may forbid you to be involved in political and religious
issues, but it may not prevent you from freely expressing legitimate
protest, nor from working for the greater good of the two peoples called
to live here communally," stresses Truong Nguyen to his compatriots.

Malraux and Monin do not advocate radical measures. For what is
known as "the native question," they do not propose mass "naturalization." With hindsight, the republican universalism the two editors claim
to adhere to sounds like a quiet and gradual reformism. Any yellow, black,
or brown person could potentially make an excellent French citizen,
but . . . not right away. In Paris, as in Saigon and Hanoi, liberal minds are
not thinking of independence for the colonized countries.

In Indochina, where all progressivism is taken for communism, this
reformist critical position is enough to provoke furious reactions. The
popular press of Saigon, from *L'Impartial* to the *Courrier Saigonnais* and
Saigon Républicain, bombard Monin and Malraux, describing *L'Indochine* as
anti-French, antipatriotic, and unwholesome. The controversy about
Banteay Srei is revived and gives Malraux's enemies something to chew

over. The Court of Appeal cancels the decree of October 28, 1924, and the same court (with different magistrates) "suspends the case and the parties." Malraux behaves as if the case had been closed. But after continued niggling from *L'Impartial* and *L'Opinion*, which portray him as an overconfident adventurer and a looter of temples, he finds it hard to establish an honest and valiant picture of himself. He answers at first with irony: "I am not only a thief of bas-reliefs. I also steal old scissors, unused false teeth, rusty nails . . . not to mention the towers of Angkor Wat. That is why the greatest writers in France intervened on my behalf." Then Malraux turns from amusement to irritation and from political criticism to personal attacks.

Monin chooses his target, the governor, and Malraux his, the editor of *L'Impartial.* Monin offers Cognacq a job at *L'Indochine* in the "propaganda department. . . . I shall buy you a nice cap: on it, like on a little boy's Sunday best sailor's beret . . . the three words that sum up your administration: Disorder, Inequality, Anarchy." Malraux portrays Lachevrotière as a specialist in "pistol duels with the shortsighted, and sword duels with the one-armed." He builds up a hefty dossier on Lachevrotière's military non-career. Monin willingly countersigns as a "voluntary conscript for the duration of the war." Malraux claims that the virtuous editor in chief of *L'Impartial* has a tendency to abandon his children. On the terrace of the Hôtel Continental, the Saigonese amuse themselves over drinks with the exchange of fire between *L'Impartial* and *L'Indochine*, trying to sort out rumors from facts.

The main body of the paper continues to concentrate on serious inquiries into local public life. *L'Indochine* publishes a thick report on a scandal in the province of Ca Mau, at the extreme south of Indochina. A consortium of settlers wants to snap up land that the Annamese cannot afford because it is to be auctioned off in parcels of more than five hundred hectares. Some Europeans talk to *L'Indochine*; others support the paper without getting involved. Many work for the government and must think of job security. *L'Indochine* runs the headline "CA MAU: FOLLOWING OUR CAMPAIGN, 4,876 HECTARES RESERVED FOR 'NATIVES' INSTEAD OF 117 HECTARES." *L'Indochine* has thus effectively defended the Annamese here. For once, corruption did not prevail.

Many in Saigon would like to get rid of the manic Monin. The intelligence services get to work on the two editors in chief of *L'Indochine*. An encoded telegram from the Hanoi authorities warns the Ministry of Colonies:

Inquiry cannot yet establish origin of capital used to create daily "Indochine." Information from your 542 seems nonetheless corroborated by anticipation [*sic*, but doubtless meaning participation] in form of open subscription . . . to Newspaper "Indochine" by Chinese affiliated to Cantonese Kuomintang Party whose close links to Bolshevik agents I have often mentioned before. Malraux has links with anti-French Annamese, and his codirector, ex-lawyer Monin, appears to be the conseiller du comité of the Cochin Chinese section. Monguillot.[5]

They would like to bring a charge against Monin. The public prosecutor, Colonna, refuses to play along. The coeditors of *L'Indochine* publish a letter to the prosecutor: "Despite insinuations, allusions, proposals and entreaties, you refuse to place the Bolshevik Monin under arrest. . . . You have been given valid grounds: the Bolshevik possesses up to three perfume-throwing revolvers and is in correspondence with the shadows of Lenin and Sun Yat-sen via the seance tables. . . . You are a bad judge; you belong to that particularly odious class of magistrate who concerns himself with knowing whether or not the accused is guilty."

L'Indochine announces the nomination of the Socialist member of Parliament Alexandre Varenne to the post of governor-general of Indochina. Malraux and Monin are counting on him to get rid of Cognacq in Saigon. Varenne is a lawyer and journalist, like Monin, and wrote for *La Lanterne* and *L'Humanité* while it was a Socialist, not a Communist, paper. Monin describes him as an "adversary of the scheming born of monopolies and arbitrariness." Varenne appears to be a strong character.

In Cochin China, *L'Indochine* is much talked about but little bought. There are large numbers of returns, up to 2,500 copies out of the 5,000 printed. The Cochin Chinese government subsidizes 4,000 subscriptions to other papers for the administration. In this way, *L'Impartial* sells 1,600 advance copies, *L'Opinion*, 1,200, *Le Courrier Saigonnais*, 400. *Le Réveil Saigonnais*, *Le Progrès Annamite*, and *La Voix Annamite* share 800 subscriptions. Throughout the French Empire, "suitable" daily papers benefit from the same financial protection. Not so, of course, for *L'Indochine*. Numerous sanctions can be applied against newspapers that are out of control. They can be temporarily, or definitively, cut off. The principal rival of *L'Indochine* is still *L'Impartial*, whose circulation fluctuates between 12,000 and 20,000 copies (those are the official figures presented to companies publishing ads in the paper).

L'Indochine leans on its advertising resources. The firms canvassed in France by Clara remain faithful, despite the paper's ferocity: Dr. Rasurel's hygienic underclothes (Lyon), Bonnefond Mushrooms (Issy-les-Moulineaux), the perfumer Guerlain, Latrille & Ginest vintage Bordeaux wines. Even *L'Exportateur Français*, the producers' and buyers' newspaper, values its advertising in *L'Indochine*.

The daily paper stands out because of its tone, the subjects it broaches, and certain sections not often seen in Saigon: "The Elite Page" is a literary section, printing Parisian theater news to keep the conversation going over dinner in Saigon, as well as short stories by known authors such as Montherlant and Gorky, or stories sent in by readers. *L'Expédition d'Ispahan* by "Maurice Saint-Rose," a dreamlike account of a walk across Asia, stands out from the other texts. At the head of a regiment of Cossacks, the hero meditates among splendid ruins. He waits for night and with a friend roams the lanes lined with delicate palaces decorated with crumbling mosaics, disfigured statues, and frescoes. He fasts for forty-eight hours and loses all sense of time: "Every day, we felt more lost, then alone, among the illustrious dead and the invisible insects." Maurice Saint-Rose is a pseudonym of André Malraux.

Another idea of Malraux's is to devote a whole page to photographs of interesting, not always amusing, subjects: sugar refining in the Philippines, steelworks in Manchuria, the infrastructure of roads in Laos. Monin admires Malraux's choice of photographs.

Both would like to enrich the "World News" section, which, despite Clara's hard work, is superficial. It is something of a hodgepodge: they would like it to be truly international, but the newspaper cannot afford foreign correspondents. Nobody in Hanoi or Saigon thinks of inviting the editors of *L'Indochine* to the official "exchange of views" dinners, where integrity slides into compromise, is even surrendered completely, in the name of superior French interests and the inferior interests of the "native" masses. The most upright local journalists are engulfed, sooner or later, by the colonial machine. Monin is too well known an opponent, and Malraux's reputation is no better.

Efforts to revive the paper, even the lure of pieces on cinema stars, have little effect. The coeditors are not sure what to do. Having tried the cheery approach, should *L'Indochine* be more serious? For reasons of salability as well as conviction, the codirectors cook up a series of articles digging deeper into the colonial question. They come up against the permanent triple problem faced by a paper specializing in commentary when it wants to be serious and reasonable: how to inform without being boring, how to entertain without making concessions, and how to present political analysis in a way that is accessible to a sufficient number of readers to keep the accountant happy? How, especially in Saigon in 1925, can they increase their audience within a conservative readership? They could do with some party money behind them, but that would forfeit the paper's independence. Gifts and the subscriptions from sympathizers of *L'Indochine* in the Annamese and Chinese communities are never enough. Some readers are also becoming tired of Malraux and Monin's personal vendettas.

Malraux doesn't give up. He is enthralled by the excitement of evenings at Monin's, putting the paper to bed amid the noise of the type-writers. The smoking, the eating, the drinking as they cut or add to the articles. Anonymously, Clara puts together her collages from foreign newspapers. For the first time, Malraux is rubbing shoulders with work-ing-class people. He loves the smell of the paper and the lead at the print-ing works, the exchanges with the Annamese compositors who set the type by hand. Some of them cannot read French, but they make up their lines faultlessly.

Then disaster looms. The typographers go on strike, and the police authorities blackmail the printer Minh and his staff, threatening to prose-cute them for taking part in the production of a "subversive" publication. The print workers give in. Malraux considers acquiring materials from other print works to publish *L'Indochine* elsewhere. Clara takes him to an opium den and tries to calm him down. Monin suggests setting up a press at his place and getting hold of some type. In Saigon, nobody wants to sell them any. First in Phnom Penh, then in Saigon: Malraux is not about to be beaten twice in Asia. And whatever they say, he came out on top in Cambodia, he maintains. In Saigon, too, he will conquer.

Syable du Journalisme

CHAPTER SIX

A Farewell to Arms

CLARA AND ANDRÉ disembark in Hong Kong. Some English Jesuit priests sell them boxes of type, but without any accents. Not an *à*, *é*, *è*, or *ê* to be found. They forward the type to Saigon and devote a few days to tourism, admiring the commercial power of Hong Kong. In Macao, they appreciate the Portuguese architecture and the gaming houses.[1]

André returns to Saigon, ready to fight. But on the governor's orders, Customs at first refuses to deliver the crates of type and, a few days later, delivers only half of them. The paperwork is apparently not in order. The pugnacious Malraux and Monin follow up *L'Indochine* with a twice-weekly publication called *L'Indochine Enchaînée*, a "temporary edition of *L'Indochine* appearing on Wednesdays and Saturdays, waiting for the doubtless distant day when the authorities agree to give us back the printing type that belongs to us but that they deemed necessary to entrust to their own safekeeping."

The codirectors no longer preside over a folio-size newspaper but a small octavo biweekly, price 20 centimes. It looks like a review. A woodcut of a butterfly graces its white cover. The eighteen issues come across as a long pamphlet with many voices, expressing a stronger political philosophy than that of the forty-nine issues of *L'Indochine*. There is no advertising in *L'Indochine Enchaînée*. With regularity, display spaces announce that "this paper" is temporary. The real one will soon be revived. Malraux, the buyer and seller of rare books, comes back to life to tempt hypothetical Saigonese collectors: "In the meantime, *L'Indochine* is a bibliographic . . . rarity for our type set is far from complete—to be able to appear at all, we have replaced missing lead characters with wooden ones—as in the sixteenth century." Who but Malraux would find this argument enticing? The magazine's contributors are sometimes optimistic, sometimes despairing, and tend to reflect upon information rather than present it. Stories are reduced to a hundred lines, the print runs are small (1,000 to 2,000 copies), and sales are bad.

Malraux writes several articles for each issue in moving and prophetic tones. His lyricism prevails over the misprints:

> I say to all French people, this error [*sic*, for terror] rising from all parts of Hanoi's soil, this anguish, a repository for resentment and dispersed hate, concentrated over recent years, may, if you are not on your guard, become the field of a fearsome harvest. I ask my readers to try to know what is happening here. To those who come to Indochina asking where is the justice, ready to make it if it cannot be found, let them dare to say that they do not support, that they have never supported those whose only standard raised in the name of France and of Annam, in protection of their position, is the double mask of the fool and the knave, the sneak and the traitor.

Torture is practiced in the police stations and criminal investigation offices. Malraux makes good use of sarcasm:

> Constable M. . . . is an Indian police officer whose gentle morals have earned him a certain celebrity with the Annamese. I do not say that the profession of police officer is one to be exercised by little girls. Indeed not. But tying the Annamese to trees and beating them to death is a treatment of which, while not contesting its high administrative value, I would say that the necessity is difficult to detect. France may have requested the governors of the colonies to do all they can to build ties with the population, but it has not talked of tying by the feet, contrary to what is considered normal by the government of Cochin China.

The growing feeling of failure about the paper is coupled with disappointment at the first decisions taken by the new governor-general. In issue No. 5 of *L'Indochine Enchaînée*[2] the editors fire a warning shot: they explain Indochina to Alexandre Varenne. This man was a member of the committee on universal suffrage in the Chamber of Deputies. Clearly, then, voting in France and in Cochin China are different activities. *L'Indochine Enchaînée* takes apart the colonial electoral mechanism: "There are 600 Indians in Saigon, French citizens[3] who, living only off the authorities or from aid, bring about 2,500 votes to every ballot, including the most important, the legislative elections: 600 votes for the governor's candidate, whoever that may be." Monin has seen this administrative setup at first hand. Varenne must be naive or badly informed: the two directors propose to enlighten him. The man made a good impression on arrival, preferring a suit to the white uniform of a governor-general. Malraux and Monin want to convince him that Mr. Chavigny de Lachevrotière was elected president of the Colonial Council on Cognacq's orders. That there is an opposition within this council, starting with Monin. They again accuse Lachevrotière of being an informer, an agent provocateur, a spy, an embezzler of public funds. This style shocks Varenne even if he is used to the excesses of the press. The two lecturers in political science also challenge the second center of power in Saigon, the Chamber of Agriculture. Its presidency, they remind him, was bestowed on "Monsieur Labaste," again under instruction from Cognacq. Varenne, law LL.D., should be aware of the legalities: Labaste, points out *L'Indochine Enchaînée*, has been in the post for eighteen and a half months longer than prescribed in the regulations. He is also confusing the treasury of the Chamber of Agriculture with his privy purse. Where are the 130,000 piastres he owes to the Chamber of Agriculture? According to the editors in chief of *L'Indochine Enchaînée*, all elections and almost all nominations in Cochin China involve injustice and fraud.

De La Pommeraye, president of the Chamber of Commerce, organized a theater season with 80,000 piastres in subsidies. Offering plays to the people of Saigon is hardly reprehensible. Malraux and Monin, here, go too far.

The editors recognize that in the past, at least, an interim governor-general, Monguillot, protested against the administrative subscriptions that allow the political powers to obtain a benevolent neutrality from the press. But he was met with apathy from his departments. Varenne should imitate Monguillot, say the directors of *L'Indochine Enchaînée*, but more effectively.

Monin and Malraux beg Varenne to listen to the reactions of a "native" elite. Cognacq's entourage calls it the "false elite." "Where, then, is the real one in Cochin China?" asks Malraux. "Among the few well-read members of Chinese civilization, who hate us? Among the servant boys to whom he [Cognacq] has given pretty medals? . . . It is with this educated elite alone that France can create a stable government in Indochina. . . . The people are still passive and are not moving now, but hate us because we are foreigners. The sway imparted by their natural intermediaries, those with qualifications and citizenship, will determine whether they stay passive or rise up against the French."

In 1925, Monin and Malraux preach for the delegation of power, education, and the naturalization of the Indochinese. Malraux believes in the influence of men. Varenne is not a great man. In the "Annamese Questions" section, under the signature of a threatening and sentimental Le Thi Vinh, the conclusion of an article hits hard: "Ungrateful sons of *la belle France républicaine*, the liberator of enslaved peoples, you whose mission here is to protect us, instruct us and civilize us: be frank, loyal, and honest or go away."[4]

Léon Werth, an occasional contributor, writes "Notes on Indochina." In several issues, he suggests that the system across Indochina adds up to slavery—a word Monin and Malraux avoid. They prefer the term "exploitation." The colonial system, Werth states, pushes "a people with democratic ideas into complete servitude." Guided in his travels by Monin, Werth sees despoilment, theft, and crime everywhere. The paper's editors have never taken it so far. He attacks the settlers in a tone that offends most of Cochin China's bourgeoisie. Some sympathized with *L'Indochine* but are more doubtful when reading *L'Indochine Enchaînée*. The daily kept both moderates and liberals happy.

L'Indochine Enchaînée turns radical. Rioting breaks out in Cambodia. Some foresee trouble in Cochin China—or hope for it: an exemplary repression would bring the "natives" back into rightful submission. Malraux and Monin never call to arms.

Alexandre Varenne is a great disappointment to them. In Paris some people would like to have him thrown out of his party, the SFIO.[5] *L'Indochine Enchaînée* wonders about the real powers of a governor-general. Is the impotence at a structural level? This Varenne certainly has the "best intentions in the world," but he cannot innovate, especially not without the agreement of the Cartel des Gauches[6] government.

The Indochinese economy is developing, admits *L'Indochine Enchaînée*, but not its social and political regime. A small industry is set up in the south, a large one in the north, but there is no social legislation. Clara is insistent about this aspect of colonial reality. Where are the new freedoms they are hearing about? The rulers and administrators do not know the "native ways": government officials do not stay for long.

L'Indochine Enchaînée demands that a permanent committee on Indochina be set up in Paris, in order to recommend a political status to fit its economic development; a constitutional charter bringing it toward the rank of a dominion. *L'Indochine Enchaînée* seems to believe that only Paris can establish democratic institutions. The "natives" should be represented in the House. Only 2,000 citizens, including 1,200 government employees, elect the members of Parliament in Cochin China. The paper's campaign is not without consequence: in France, *Paris Midi* quotes *L'Indochine Enchaînée*. Didacticism pays—but not very much.

Paul Monin receives threats. He was awakened by a noise; he sat up in bed and struck a short aggressor who was rushing at him.[7] His servants are attacked. *L'Indochine Enchaînée* reports these events: "A zealous policeman gained entry to my abode, struck one of my servants, claiming that his wife, a market stall holder, had not displayed her trading license when asked to in French, a language she does not understand, and arrested the poor unfortunate and booked him for rebellion. . . . Some are so full of hate that they have to take it out on my servants. What grim cowardice! P.M." Some Europeans and Annamese—and a number of Chinese—express their sympathy to Monin.

Encouraged by Clara, André Malraux pursues his political, economic, and social education. He listens almost as much as he talks, and more than he writes. The PCF (French Communist Party) exists, but far from his political horizon. With the paper coming out only twice a week, Malraux works less and thinks more. He studies demographic figures on infant mortality. In the whole of Indochina, teachers are as scarce as doctors: "No work on infant care exists in Cochin China." Malraux discovers that description can be the strongest criticism.

Monin and Malraux are cast as ghastly Bolsheviks. However, important Annamese figures such as Nguyen Tan Duoc, colonial councilor and member of the Chamber of Agriculture, proclaim that "the Bolshevik threat does not exist here, it cannot exist for whoever knows the mentality of the natives, however remotely, such is their attachment to their ancient customs"—a point of view that, in the long term, is less perspicacious than Malraux's, given that fifty years later, Stalinists were occupying Saigon. Malraux and Monin pass their favorite themes to each other like a football. The lawyer contributes a history lesson in the form of a requiem for the colonial system. He describes "Varenne (Alexandre), Socialist member" as "proconsul verbosus, humdrumusque." The governor-general is "soaked by the downpour of Annamese disillusionment. He will not even open his umbrella." Monin points out that Varenne has enthroned the kings of rubber: the Michelin brothers, who have moved into the hevea plantations in Cochin China. Monin also criticizes "Varenne (Alexandre)" for leasing alcohol and opium. The gaming authorities should control these domains.

Beyond his efforts to understand the structures of colonialism, Malraux's criticisms often have a personal slant. He returns to his troubles when referring to the riots in Cambodia and summary justice. He knows that a "native" defendant can be prevented from talking, whereas he, Malraux, talked plenty during his trials.

To revive their readership, in the twelfth issue, the editors bring the price of *L'Indochine Enchaînée* down to 10 centimes. Varenne becomes "comrade Varenne" by derision. During a discussion of the colonial budgets in Parliament, Monin's adversary the member Ernest Outrey expresses approval at Varenne's nomination. "My enemy's friend is my enemy!" Monin thunders, while Malraux ponders.

Having obtained funding from some friendly Chinese, the editors announce that the paper will soon be coming out every day. They accept two-month subscriptions.

Maître Gallet, a liberal lawyer, falls victim to a poisoning, perpetrated by either a thug or an intelligence informer. The authorities fail to react. Malraux, with schoolboy inspiration, makes an excursion to Cambodia to cover a police case and proposes a revised penal code for the colonies: "1: The defendant shall have his head cut off. 2: He shall then be defended by a lawyer. 3: The lawyer shall have his head cut off. 4: And so on. To which one could add, 5: Any stenographer employed by a lawyer shall have the little she has confiscated and her contract canceled. 6: If she has children, she will pay the poor Monsieur de La Pommeraye the sum of one thousand piastres per child in damages and interest. 7: Her husband shall have his head cut off. Which brings us back to no. 1, see above."

Monin writes that they could introduce a new section,

OUR GREAT BOSSES: I have just met a loathsome salaried employee (all salaried employees are more or less loathsome, precisely because they demand a salary, whereas the bosses make do with profits). This loathsome employee had been working for seventeen years for the same firm and had never taken a day's holiday to breathe the air of France. His average working day? At least twelve hours, half of which was night duty. He has just been liquidated. The firm in question is rich to the tune of millions. Do you know what they gave the man who had devoted seventeen years of his life to them when he arrived at the age when retirement calls? . . . Two thousand francs!

Georges-André Malraux now signs himself Georges Armand Masson and speculates upon the nature of the colonial system. Malraux will not, like Marx, find positive aspects in colonialism, but he isn't far off. He tackles fundamental problems: What is the value of the administrative doctrines in Indochina? What benefit, if any, has colonization brought? For what crimes is it responsible? Has mainland France brought peace to Indochina? "Well . . . it must be admitted that many Annamese . . . would prefer war, so they say, even constant war, to the domination of foreigners."

Procolonial opinion would have it that French authority is the only thing maintaining unity in Indochina, linking together Cochin China,

Tongking, Laos, and Cambodia. Malraux does not agree: "This is not strictly true. French domination does unite Indochina, but it would not necessarily be divided without it. Essentially, it would break up into a republic or a constitutional Annamese empire, comprising all the Annamese-speaking countries and a kingdom of Cambodia. This would perhaps be a calamity for the map of Asia: Indochina is a lovely shape. But the Annamese and especially the Cambodians might not see that as a drawback." This is a farsighted Malraux, developing a taste for prediction without lapsing into prophecy.

L'Indochine Enchaînée, whose publication on Wednesdays and Saturdays disconcerts potential buyers, is sold in Saigon and Cholon. The subscriptions do not come. The paper's Chinese helpers become reticent. Paul Monin has several bouts of malaria and feels exhausted. In issue No. 16, a notice to subscribers announces that "our director, Monsieur André Malraux, being forced to return to France to deliver a series of talks to seek the intervention of a number of French individuals, in order to obtain from the government the freedom demanded by the Annamese, the leadership of *L'Indochine* will provisionally be taken up by Messrs. Dejean de La Batie and Le Thi Vinh." Malraux writes a cymbal-crashing editorial: "The great voice of the people must be raised and come to ask of its masters, in the face of this severe punishment . . . will we obtain freedom? We cannot yet know. At least we will obtain certain freedoms. That is why I am leaving for France."

Monin and Malraux no longer agree on which line to follow: in Indochina, should a reformist movement be encouraged or should a revolutionary program be adopted? In the first long editorial after Malraux's adieu (not an au revoir), the new editor in chief, Le Thi Vinh, puts a stop to all that. His headline: "Will we see the Indochinese revolution?" The Annamese journalist starts with a statement: France is not managing to restore its finances, is pursuing a colonial war in Morocco, and is putting down the Druze Revolt. Elsewhere, the Chinese "are making rivers of their blood run for the freedom, independence, and unity of China." Le Thi Vinh shelters behind a plural: "Some are wondering if the time has not come for the Annamese to raise the standard of revolt . . . and to set their country free from the Western imperialism that holds it in its grasp." Le Thi Vinh, who had planned to assassinate a senior government official, asks two questions never raised by the European editors of *L'Indochine* and *L'Indochine Enchaînée*: "1. Do the Annamese have the necessary arms such that the people may decide to sacrifice themselves to make their country free and independent? 2. Is the current state of mind of the popular masses such that the people may decide to sacrifice themselves to make their country free and independent?" The revolution is still a way off in

Indochina: the relationship between the "material forces" is unequal. Only the rich, notes the Annamese editor, have the right to own arms.

Malraux has not toiled for nothing. On December 23, in Hanoi, the governor-general signs a complete pardon for Phan Boi Chau, who has returned to Hue. Using available means, Monin and Malraux's newspaper fought a campaign to clear his name. In France, the Chamber of Deputies will be voting on a bill presented by Gaston Doumergue, the president of France, and Édouard Daladier, the minister of colonies, on the granting of French citizenship to "natives of the colonies" and countries of the protectorate within the Ministry of Colonies' jurisdiction: one small step forward toward limited equality. The first article stipulates that a native, to obtain the status of French citizen, must (1) formally renounce his current status; (2) be able to read French—which, in Indochina, eliminates 98 percent of potential candidates. An Annamese, Tonkinese, Cambodian, or Laotian native must not have been convicted of any crime, misdemeanor, act of hostility toward the French cause, or political or religious preaching likely to undermine general security. A university qualification, the Legion of Honor, having been a commissioned or noncommissioned officer in the French Army, or being married to a Frenchwoman—all will help to obtain citizenship. It will be more or less obligatory to have occupied an administrative job for ten years "or have rendered important services to French interests recognized by the local authorities." Citizenship for the "natives" is opened up in theory, only to be closed to the majority in practice.

In issue No. 17, *L'Indochine Enchaînée* wishes a happy New Year for 1926 to its readers. A minieditorial by Monin awards "twelve out of twenty to the student Alexandre Varenne for his French composition, perhaps even more." From now on, Malraux and Monin have less to do with the design and content of the paper. Three factors come together to interrupt publication for a month from January 2: money problems, technical breakdowns of the printing press at Monin's, and opposition from Mme. Monin. She returns from a journey and finds her villa invaded by contributors, a number of friends, and heaps of files, newspapers, and cigarette ends. Five issues are in preparation, for February 2, 6, 10, 20, and 24, 1926. Malraux, defeated as a journalist, more so even than Clara, feels discouraged by the resistance of the colonial machine.

More fascinated than his colleague with the wind of revolution blowing from Shanghai to Canton, Monin prepares to leave Cochin China for China. It's a sad Christmas for the Malrauxs. They share more meals with their Chinese friends than with Europeans or even Annamese. Malraux had been planning to go back to Paris from October 1925. He has almost finished a manuscript. His book will be called *La Tentation de l'Occident* (The Temptation of the West). On October 4, he announced to Louis Brun of Éditions Grasset that "half of it has already been translated into

Chinese and published in various periodicals and papers in Shanghai and Peking." Wish, once again, becomes reality for him. "It is a collection of letters exchanged between a young Westerner and a young Chinese man, annotated by one of their Indian friends, about spirit, art, and passions as perceived by East and West." Malraux also declared himself "already assured of significant foreign criticism." Henri Massis was to publish a volume of essays whose theme might overlap with his *Tentation de l'Occident*. Malraux contemplated "taking up [his] position opposite Massis." "The right-wing critics will certainly pay a lot of attention to these two literary events," he predicted. Aware of the publicity value of his activities, Malraux added, "Not to mention past fantasies, nor my current political role as head of the Young Annam Party."[8] The imaginary head.

The Malrauxs leave Saigon on December 30, traveling second class. Chinese associates finance their return to Paris. Not everybody is fooled by the arguments justifying this departure, even if some feel that Malraux will be more useful in Paris. He has also promised that he will argue with the relevant persons to obtain permission for the creation in Cholon of . . . a casino. On the boat, he works on his manuscript in the first-class saloon, forgetting Cochin China as he forgot Cambodia. He bequeaths leftover bits of articles to his moribund paper. The new editors do him no favors by publishing them. An "interview with the *gouverneur de la Chinoiserie*" (the governor of red tape) appears in issue No. 19 of *L'Indochine Enchaînée*, dated Tuesday, February 2, 1926. The Chinoiserie is Cochin China. Malraux verges on bad cabaret:

> "Would you care, Monsieur le Gouverneur, to point out the main principles behind your actions?"
>
> "Absolutely. A man of action must have principles. Colonization, as you know, can use two auxiliary devices: texts inspired by the desire for justice, on the one hand; and the whip, on the other. 'Before using the whip, it is advisable to wrap it carefully in the legal texts. Thus it is justice which strikes the Native . . .' "

Shortly afterward, *L'Indochine Enchaînée* wishes its readers a happy Vietnamese New Year. In February, the pages of the newspaper-cum-review offer the reader an imaginary interview with the president of the Chamber of Commerce of Saigon, again by André Malraux, now gone for some weeks. This document deals with the childish way in which the Chamber has been abandoned by smaller tradesmen, especially the "natives." "It seemed to be the right thing to do," writes Malraux, "to show the Annamese the effects of the tropical heat on French institutions." This final contribution is not typical of the tone of Malraux's articles.

In Paris, he does nothing about Indochina, which irritates Clara. He has turned the page, but the stored-up sensations, emotions, images, and ideas remain. Politically, he is incubating. He has broken with Monin, who did not see him off at the dock.[9] Malraux knows how to break a thing off. Weary of personal adventure in Cambodia and political action in Cochin China, he matures. With no reference to the theorists Marx, Lenin, or Kautsky, and more by intuitive stabs than by analysis, centering on experiences from Hanoi to Saigon, from Dalat to Ca Mau, he sounds himself out about communism, revolution, socialism, and reform. To some, his convictions are still too prudent. To others, they seem sensible and in advance of left-wing options during these dangerous 1920s. Malraux saw and felt more than he read during his stays in Asia. He was a rebel, not a revolutionary.

For future books, he is still looking for a subject and a tone. He has not taken his sentence seriously. Before leaving for Saigon, he was assured that "the matter would take its natural course." Did he fear an unfavorable decision, hence his quick return to France? The case is to come to a public hearing on May 11, 1926, in the Court of Appeal. From Paris, André will hide behind a medical certificate: he cannot, for health reasons, return to Indochina. Chevasson writes a letter to the public prosecutor asking for a transfer—same reasons. The court upholds the offenses but grants the accused extenuating circumstances because they have no previous criminal record. The case files are "forgotten."

Malraux often mentions to Clara his admiration for Gabriele D'Annunzio:[10] for his personality, not his ideas. Like D'Annunzio, Malraux likes pensive photographic poses. Where is the common ground with the Italian writer, now over sixty? An appreciation of Baudelaire, Dostoevsky, Nietzsche, and Barrès. Malraux leans on the personality of D'Annunzio, who tries to model his life into a work of art. Malraux admires the *condottiere*, the infantry and aviation commandante who occupied Fiume, getting there before the British and French, a feat that filled Benito Mussolini with enthusiasm. Malraux does not share D'Annunzio's interest in the superman, nor his erotically based morality and aesthetics. Malraux admires Napoleon, but he would not, like D'Annunzio, build him a chapel.

"I shall sculpt my own statue," André tells Clara, however.

At the moment he has a small pedestal. D'Annunzio held Fiume for a time. Malraux did not take Saigon. His sympathy for the Indochinese "natives," though keen, is no longer active. Words have ceased to be political weapons. Some obvious practical failures can lead to intellectual successes.

Malraux could say that he had a good shot with *L'Indochine* and *L'Indochine Enchaînée*. He grants himself a break and invests more in literature than in journalism.[11]

t . . . above the lacquered bay, the whole town, wearing its
vith pagodas as flowerets, emerges in the rising sun." A
postcard and a Chinese print; perhaps Malraux still feels
abodia and Cochin China to use images registered over
marks that Malraux is not keen on realistic description.
es not support the post-Nietzschean ambitions of an
ts to come across as a thinker. Does Malraux realize that
movement of literary exoticism after Loti, Segalen, and
ly. These writers know China. The deep meaning of the
ntly postponed promise, which comes unwillingly from

explain himself in interviews. "What the youth of the
for is a new concept of man. . . . Does Asia have some-
? I do not think so. Rather, it can offer us a distinctive dis-
we are."⁴ Taking a Chinese version of his book as a fait
ux declares, "If the title of the Chinese translation of *La
cident* were retranslated literally back into French, you
osition of the Orient.' "

of it, Malraux's book is about China and Western Europe.
is talking about himself: "All the nineteenth century's pas-
d developed into a vehement affirmation of the impor-
Well, this mankind and this self, built on so many ruins,
sway over us, whether we like it or not; and we simply
interesting." The royal "we" sounds suspiciously like
rate dissociation. "It has been said that none can act with-
ues Malraux. "I believe that the absence of all conviction,
self, incites certain men to passivity and others to extreme
ngkor and in Saigon, Malraux engaged in extreme activi-
ays that this self does not interest us, he is hiding. The
lf" are also Malraux standing back, feigning a haughty dis-
pection.

Europe "a carefully ordered barbarism." His Chinese
esponds to an idea that some Westerners have of Asians,
ties mixed together. He introduces binary themes: passiv-
being and doing. Ling is a reflection of Malraux but
im too: it is "not necessary to act," he says; "the world
ch more than you change it." In Cochin China, Malraux
colonial world. He was half beaten—but was changed.

sprinkles his book with seductive and commonplace
g, the nice Chinese man, Rome is a "beautiful antiquary's
andon." Or again: "All erotic interplay is there: to be one-
er; to experience one's own sensations and imagine those

CHAPTER SEVEN

Exotic Parisian

ANDRÉ MALRAUX SPENT two rewarding years cramming in experiences: unhappy but fortifying ones in Cambodia; and in Cochin China, first happy, then disappointing. Back in Paris, his elliptical thought and terse turns of phrase are striking. He expresses himself with saccadic gestures, moving his arms about and punctuating his sentences with silences, sneezes, exclamations, firstly . . . thirdly . . . Joking! *Bon* . . . Anyway . . . *Bon*. His presence in a room is impressive. He appears older than he is.

He works on raw material brought back from Asia. But he has no money. With Clara, he moves into a boardinghouse on the Quai de Passy. From their window, they can just see the elevated Métro and the Eiffel Tower. Paris is theirs! Clara is more imbued than her husband with a sense of the obligations contracted toward their Indochinese friends and returns to the attack. She pushes André to talk to parliamentary deputies and senators.

Three months after their return, they move into a three-room apartment at 122 Boulevard Murat, on the edge of the Sixteenth Arrondissement, near the Bois de Boulogne. By chance, the Lamy and Goldschmidt families—the latter now penniless—have moved to the same block. Malraux is surprised to find the Lamy ladies as attentive as Fernand Malraux. Mme. Goldschmidt stays away from this scandalous son-in-law, whom she doesn't understand, at least for a time. Then comes reconciliation.

The immediate problems are buying furniture and signing a lease. With Louis Chevasson—still in the disinterested service of his friend—André starts a publishing house to exploit his old and profitable seam: luxury books. His company, À La Sphère, occupies two rooms at 12 Rue de la Grange-Batelière in the Ninth Arrondissement. Malraux often goes to the auction rooms at the nearby Hôtel Drouot. He wants to earn his living in intelligent and artistic independence and keep a free mind. The little publishing company is admirable, certainly, but not always sensible. Malraux remains a brilliant, irrational gambler, just as Fernand was a reckless speculator. In life as on a ship, one must travel first class. À La Sphère publishes known authors: François Mauriac, Paul Morand, Albert Samain. Galanis illustrates some of the works. The market for collectors and investors is no longer what it was after the war.

Malraux lands a text by Valéry, but it gets him into debt to the tune of 20,000 francs ($1,050 in 1926). It will take months to recoup. Unable to pay the printer, Malraux and Chevasson go into voluntary liquidation. Malraux starts another publishing company, Les Aldes. The registered office is in his apartment. He hooks up again with Pascal Pia, who introduces him to Eddy Du Perron. Du Perron is two years younger than Malraux and declares himself Indonesian by education, Dutch by language and habits, and French from an atavistic point of view. A novelist, essayist, and poet, he has, says Malraux, "been ruined by an inheritance" managed by a careless mother. One of his later pseudonyms is Duco Perkens.[1] His father committed suicide, as Fernand Malraux later would. Du Perron freely compares Malraux's risk taking with Montherlant's footballing and bullfighting. For Du Perron, historical reality takes second place to art. In a description of Malraux, Eddy refers to André as Héverlé:

> It is easy to criticize Héverlé, I say, but every time he has been criticized in front of me, I have found him enhanced in my eyes. Does it bother you that he never lets himself go in confidential matters, does that seem to you a lapse of friendship? Héverlé only confides on impersonal grounds, on a sort of high plateau where all things float in the winds of the history of civilizations and philosophy. But that does not make him any less himself, for he is one of those rare individuals who may look like an actor, at a first, superficial glance, but who in reality is concentrated on the creation of his own character. . . . When he is criticized, I am always aware of a desire to see what the critic himself has to offer, by way of a character.[2]

Revisiting his interest in pastiche, Malraux encourages the ingenious Pia to publish what is allegedly Baudelaire's journal, *Années de Bruxelles.* Eddy Du Perron has supposedly discovered a manuscript of about forty pages by the poet. The work, printed in 150 copies, sells well. Clara can do little to contribute to the couple's finances. Malraux also uses the engraver Alexeieff to illustrate his books. Bernard Grasset buys out Les Aldes.

Things are looking up: Grasset publishes the first properly con-

structed, original, and acce
dent.[3] His two journeys to
cosmopolitan, but an intern
temple at Banteay Srey," rea
to cover up his Cambodian
adventurer.

La Tentation de l'Occiden
eration, just like Pierre D
Halévy's). After the war, G
through the book, affirmed
demise of God, seasoned wi
the spiritual and intellectual
eccentricity, Malraux the phi
lary essay, but one can sen
Frenchman of twenty-five (A
His correspondent, Ling, a C
twelve of the eighteen letters
ture from which a number of
is purely theoretical." Malrau
China is limited to his expedi

The book's *indication limi*
sound grander than "preface
should not be seen as a symbo
ages the reader to consider A.
The author states that these a
hai and Canton, and by Ling
many breaks in tone and an
both through Ling and throug
mer criticizes the West for its
latter, the Chinese, and Asi
questionable Eurocentric notio
and happiness; they share a co
Europeans—Clara and André a
In *La Tentation de l'Occident*, th
André Malraux's remarks in his
of Asia corresponds to a partia
America: Asia as the continent
determinism.

A.D. and Ling ceremoniou
experience, referring to each oth
Malraux draws very little on hi
local color to this allegedly two

ports at first lig
crown of walls
cross between
too close to Ca
there. Clara re
Such veneer
author who wa
he is joining
Claudel? Prob
book is a con
the text.

He does
West is looki
thing to teach
covery of wh
accompli, Ma
Tentation de
would get 'Pr

On the fa
But above all
sion for mar
tance of the
continue to
don't find t
denial and d
out faith," c
like convicti
action." Ne
ties. When
"we" and th
interest in i

Ling se
refinement
with all nat
ity and act
diverges fr
changes yo
tried to ch

The
images. Fo
garden lef
self and th

of one's partner." Some phrases are would-be metaphysical: "At the center of the European man, dominating the major movements in his life, is an essential absurdity." Malraux does not develop the meaning of the word "absurd" but this indefinite notion stays with him. Was his activity in Saigon absurd or disappointing? Can one assert that the Eastern mind "attaches no value to man himself"? Admittedly, the Western mind in the twenties—and ever since the Renaissance—"has wanted to draw up a plan of the universe, to make an intelligible image of it, in other words, to establish a series of links between things unknown and things known, to discover those that were obscure until then." One senses the influence of Chateaubriand and Barrès. Form is still getting the better of content. One character, Wang-Loh, whose "hatred of the whites" is his whole life, could be a product of the radical and revolutionary Annamese Malraux has met.[5] The author uses the freedom of the epistolary genre to air certain prejudices, regrets, and resentment. He leaves it to Wang-Loh, under cover of a letter from A.D., to denounce fools inebriated with university idiocy. In Paris, Malraux alludes to his university studies at the École des Langues Orientales, and at the same time to the stupidity of higher education.

He indulges in a few grandiose truisms: "There is no China," writes Ling, "there are Chinese elites. The well-read elite is now only admired as one would an ancient monument. The new elite, that of men who have undergone Western culture, is so different from the first kind that we cannot but think that the very conquest of the empire by the West has begun."

Far from the journalistic banter of *L'Indochine Enchaînée*, the writer wavers, groping for and finding a tense style. The facts, to which the editor that he once was devoted himself, are forgotten, as if he could not master sentences, ideas, and breathing at the same time.

The last letter, sent by A.D., turns into lyrical fancy. A.D. is no longer addressing Ling but himself: "God has destroyed everything. Man can find only death." A.D. slides about on notions of country, justice, greatness, and truth. "We can sacrifice ourselves to no ideal," he writes, "for we know everybody's lies, we who do not know what truth is." Malraux does not define truth any more than he does absurdity. Life is apparently absurd; therefore truth, one of the objectives of existence, also seems absurd. Taking serious risks in Indochina, Malraux lived a militant ideal and came up against social and political lies. He seems tired but not disheartened: rather, he is waiting. The final lines of the book describe in novelistic, romantic tones a young man taking stock of himself and the recent years of his existence: "O shifting image of myself, for you I am without love. Like a wide, unclosed *wound* [my italics] you are my dead glory and my living suffering. I gave you all, and yet, I know that I will never love you. Unbowed, I shall bring you every day an offering of peace. O eager lucidity, I burn still before you, a lone, straight flame, in this heavy night where the yellow wind cries, as all these foreign nights where the wind off the water repeated around me the proud clamor of the sterile sea." Malraux is not sparing with grandiloquence. Admire himself he may not, but sometimes he really does love himself. His first two journeys in Asia wounded him. Is he still suffering a little, or even a lot? He was more lucid in Saigon than when he was making his way to Banteay Srei. The dates at the end of the narrative, 1921–1925, indicate that what Malraux is expressing in his first finished book is a summary, emotional if not intellectual, of his existence from twenty to twenty-four years of age.[6]

He does not return to his political combats. To the detriment of the narrative, he includes a cultural tour of Asia. He draws little inspiration from what he experienced, referring instead to his fanatical and muddled reading. This explains the importance of the form and the weakness of the content, the overuse of vague abstractions, the sentences thrown out in bursts. A.D.'s journey in Asia and Ling's in Europe are striking in their dryness. To explain the erosion of old and new values, the writer juxtaposes action and dream. His indistinct philosophical reflections, based more on rhetoric than reason, do not make interpretation of his theses any easier. There remains, scattered throughout the book, an attempt to analyze the crisis of values that is more applicable to the West known to Malraux than to an imagined East; it is less clear than Valéry's pages on the "Crisis of the Mind." Malraux feels his way, overcoming the Spenglerian idea of a worn-out world. This little book with which the writer hopes to make his mark is a rough work. He had to hurry to finish, as evidenced by the surviving feverish fragments of manuscript: a patchwork of alterations, bits pasted onto writing pads, sheets of squared paper from an exercise book, and a cut-up accounts ledger.

Malraux has boundless energy despite painful attacks of rheumatoid arthritis. Seeking advice and support from Jean Paulhan, he launches his book with a selection of three letters in an installment of the *Nouvelle Revue Française* (*NRF*) of April 3, 1926. When *La Tentation* appears, the author announces not only the publication of the complete Chinese text (again), in Shanghai and Peking, but also an essay that is "in press" and a novel whose title has already been chosen, *Puissances* (Powers). Malraux confuses an imagined potentiality with a tangible reality. *La Tentation de l'Occident* is better received in the French provinces than in Paris; it doesn't take off well in the bookshops. Not one of the sixty-odd articles in the press is a dazzling review from a Paris weekly. The author is proud but not conceited; this is vexing for his self-esteem, but he manages not to show it. Ramon Fernandez, in the *NRF*, publishes a sweet and sour review of the book, conceding that there arises from it a hymn "that charms and dazes us." The author's poetic ambitions "spoil the clarity of the views he exposes." Fernandez does not dwell on the writer's cutting expressions. Malraux is talked about, but his book is not a success. However, in Paris, at least in Saint-Germain-des-Prés and Montparnasse, he is talked about as if he were already a successful author. The young man carries more weight than his work. The attitude of publicity experts such as Bernard Grasset confirms Malraux's own impression: he is a future great writer,[7] his feet squarely set between a slender present and a future that is sure to be broad.

He wants to travel again, to make the world his own, and to write. He is looking for fame. He no longer prefers "he who appreciates the garden" to "he who makes the garden." Clara encourages him. Together, they believe in his *genius*, a word Malraux likes. Despite stormy weather, the fiery couple's marriage holds together. They quarrel in front of friends; Clara is agitated, and André can freeze her with his coolness. She stamps her feet. On one point, they agree: in order to create, Malraux must feed his imagination with expeditions, with renewed experiences. Short of money? They'll find some.

Clara sometimes smokes opium with the literary figure Maurice Magre in his bachelor apartment. They live in the same building. André much prefers alcohol.[8] He puts his literary strategy back into practice in reviews and newspapers. At Paulhan's request, and backed by André Gide and Marcel Arland, he gives some notes to the *NRF*: a review of *Défense de l'Occident* by Henri Massis and one of *Bouddha vivant* by Paul Morand. Then he moves on to *L'Imposture* by Georges Bernanos and *Journal de voyage d'un philosophe* by Hermann von Keyserling. After the French publication of *La Tentation de l'Occident*, Arland compares Malraux with Keyserling. Both express the fears and aspirations of young Europeans. The comparison goes too far: Keyserling travels as much as Malraux but offers a "philosophy" that combines spiritual values, all-purpose unicorns, nationalism, and the dangerous beauty of industrialization. At twenty-five, Malraux steers clear of nationalism and is at best equivocal about modern technology.

He also publishes studies elsewhere. For *Formes*, he writes "notes on tragic expression in painting" regarding recent works by Rouault. He also writes an article on the idea of eroticism in D. H. Lawrence, later used as a preface to the French edition of *Lady Chatterley's Lover.* His output follows the principle of communicating vessels: the more books he finishes, the fewer articles he writes. His work gives a false impression of facility. Whenever an author lures him beyond his own personality and prestige, Malraux proves vigorous and clear, as with the favorable review of *Hyméné*, a novel by Louis Guilloux.[9]

The *NRF* accepts Malraux with reticence. He lacks the classicism and correctness expected of its contributors. At best, isn't he more of an adventurer, more like Raymond Radiguet or Maurice Sachs than Jean Cocteau or André Gide? The latter has a huge weak spot for Malraux, who often irritates or disconcerts him by his assurance. There is no hesitancy or caution in the author of *La Tentation de l'Occident*. Malraux's defenders, Arland in particular, explain that his curiosity, his knowledge of the visual arts, and his love of literature outweigh his arrogance. Malraux wants the *NRF* to take him on as an in-house literary critic. He is passed over: he is still pretty green, and the top editorial staff, in their eclectic wisdom, judge that the function and power of literary chronicler should be shared between several contributors. The founding father of the publishing company, Gaston Gallimard, claims not to have enough influence over the review to get Malraux the job. The capital's literati observe this young wolf with watchful mistrust. Some writers, Louis Aragon and André Breton, to name two, clearly dislike him. He refuses to yield to the demands and rites of the dadaist and surrealist sects; despite denouncing the established order, they take care to maintain their social and editorial networks. Against the prevailing current, Malraux does not feel himself obliged to get into bed with the French Communist Party. He has his own idea of independence. Some concessions are acceptable, but he will not stoop to hypocritical compromise.

Gaston Gallimard reacts with amused indulgence. He gives Malraux a job on account of his technical proficiency and the books he must have in him. André and Gaston, little crocodile and big crocodile, watch each other. Malraux's presumptuousness sometimes displeases Gaston, but the fellow seems efficient. He, at least, realizes that one cannot always publish at a loss. Too many authors are convinced that their publisher is there to be milked, for no return. Gaston likes Malraux for a connoisseur, a scout, a rascal, and one of the rare potential writers to know the printer's trade and the price of paper. From time to time, Malraux loses track in his estimates: his business sense is not always good, and his generosity is costly when it comes to advances. But he is interested in the production and selling of a book. Gaston doesn't mind losing money on an author such as Marcel Jouhandeau, but his publishing house is not a charity.

Gaston was not impressed by *La Tentation de l'Occident*; he detects in Malraux primarily a promise to be kept. The writer in him is not ripe, but, according to Gaston, he has editorial qualities. Malraux will at first be artistic director with Gallimard. He has an eye for typography and layout. His writing? That will be for tomorrow—or a few years' time. At any rate, Gaston has managed the publisher's trick of getting his hands on Malraux's future books in advance. They woo each other, with Malraux the more interested party.

Exotic Parisian

A NDRÉ MALRAUX SPENT two rewarding years cramming in experiences: unhappy but fortifying ones in Cambodia; and in Cochin China, first happy, then disappointing. Back in Paris, his elliptical thought and terse turns of phrase are striking. He expresses himself with saccadic gestures, moving his arms about and punctuating his sentences with silences, sneezes, exclamations, firstly . . . thirdly . . . Joking! *Bon* . . . Anyway . . . *Bon*. His presence in a room is impressive. He appears older than he is.

He works on raw material brought back from Asia. But he has no money. With Clara, he moves into a boardinghouse on the Quai de Passy. From their window, they can just see the elevated Métro and the Eiffel Tower. Paris is theirs! Clara is more imbued than her husband with a sense of the obligations contracted toward their Indochinese friends and returns to the attack. She pushes André to talk to parliamentary deputies and senators.

Three months after their return, they move into a three-room apartment at 122 Boulevard Murat, on the edge of the Sixteenth Arrondissement, near the Bois de Boulogne. By chance, the Lamy and Goldschmidt families—the latter now penniless—have moved to the same block. Malraux is surprised to find the Lamy ladies as attentive as Fernand Malraux. Mme. Goldschmidt stays away from this scandalous son-in-law, whom she doesn't understand, at least for a time. Then comes reconciliation.

The immediate problems are buying furniture and signing a lease. With Louis Chevasson—still in the disinterested service of his friend—André starts a publishing house to exploit his old and profitable seam: luxury books. His company, À La Sphère, occupies two rooms at 12 Rue de la Grange-Batelière in the Ninth Arrondissement. Malraux often goes to the auction rooms at the nearby Hôtel Drouot. He wants to earn his living in intelligent and artistic independence and keep a free mind. The little publishing company is admirable, certainly, but not always sensible. Malraux remains a brilliant, irrational gambler, just as Fernand was a reckless speculator. In life as on a ship, one must travel first class. À La Sphère publishes known authors: François Mauriac, Paul Morand, Albert Samain. Galanis illustrates some of the works. The market for collectors and investors is no longer what it was after the war.

Malraux lands a text by Valéry, but it gets him into debt to the tune of 20,000 francs ($1,050 in 1926). It will take months to recoup. Unable to pay the printer, Malraux and Chevasson go into voluntary liquidation. Malraux starts another publishing company, Les Aldes. The registered office is in his apartment. He hooks up again with Pascal Pia, who introduces him to Eddy Du Perron. Du Perron is two years younger than Malraux and declares himself Indonesian by education, Dutch by language and habits, and French from an atavistic point of view. A novelist, essayist, and poet, he has, says Malraux, "been ruined by an inheritance" managed by a careless mother. One of his later pseudonyms is Duco Perkens.[1] His father committed suicide, as Fernand Malraux later would. Du Perron freely compares Malraux's risk taking with Montherlant's footballing and bullfighting. For Du Perron, historical reality takes second place to art. In a description of Malraux, Eddy refers to André as Héverlé:

> It is easy to criticize Héverlé, I say, but every time he has been criticized in front of me, I have found him enhanced in my eyes. Does it bother you that he never lets himself go in confidential matters, does that seem to you a lapse of friendship? Héverlé only confides on impersonal grounds, on a sort of high plateau where all things float in the winds of the history of civilizations and philosophy. But that does not make him any less himself, for he is one of those rare individuals who may look like an actor, at a first, superficial glance, but who in reality is concentrated on the creation of his own character. . . . When he is criticized, I am always aware of a desire to see what the critic himself has to offer, by way of a character.[2]

Revisiting his interest in pastiche, Malraux encourages the ingenious Pia to publish what is allegedly Baudelaire's journal, *Années de Bruxelles*. Eddy Du Perron has supposedly discovered a manuscript of about forty pages by the poet. The work, printed in 150 copies, sells well. Clara can do little to contribute to the couple's finances. Malraux also uses the engraver Alexeieff to illustrate his books. Bernard Grasset buys out Les Aldes.

Things are looking up: Grasset publishes the first properly constructed, original, and accessible book by Malraux, *La Tentation de l'Occident*.[3] His two journeys to Asia have made Malraux an exotic Parisian; not cosmopolitan, but an internationalist. "To you, Clara, as a souvenir of the temple at Banteay Srey," reads the book's dedication. Malraux is not trying to cover up his Cambodian excursion: on the contrary. Yes, he was that adventurer.

La Tentation de l'Occident sets Malraux up as a spokesman for his generation, just like Pierre Drieu la Rochelle (whom he met at Daniel Halévy's). After the war, God was dead in the West. One idea running through the book, affirmed rather than demonstrated, is that this certified demise of God, seasoned with Nietzsche and Spengler, must bring about the spiritual and intellectual death of man. Emerging from a chrysalis of eccentricity, Malraux the philosophizing butterfly opts here for an epistolary essay, but one can sense the embryo of a novel. A.D. (André), a Frenchman of twenty-five (André Malraux's age in 1926) travels to China. His correspondent, Ling, a Chinese man of twenty-three, is the author of twelve of the eighteen letters. Ling is "struck by the curious Western culture from which a number of his compatriots are suffering, a culture that is purely theoretical." Malraux's own direct, nontheoretical experience of China is limited to his expedition to Hong Kong and his trip to Macao.

The book's *indication liminaire* (introductory indication—these words sound grander than "preface" or "foreword") advises that "Mr. Ling should not be seen as a symbol of the Far Easterner." But the text encourages the reader to consider A.D. as a representative of the Far Westerner. The author states that these are selected letters sent by A.D. from Shanghai and Canton, and by Ling from Rome and Paris. He allows himself many breaks in tone and an aphoristic style. Malraux expresses himself both through Ling and through A.D., two sides of the same coin. The former criticizes the West for its cerebral rationality and dryness. For the latter, the Chinese, and Asians in general, have a cosmic mind (a questionable Eurocentric notion). Their detachment brings them wisdom and happiness; they share a common bond, as with plants and animals. Europeans—Clara and André after their misadventures?—are less serene. In *La Tentation de l'Occident*, thought seems to be in fusion, like some of André Malraux's remarks in his mind-boggling conversations. This vision of Asia corresponds to a partial or false idea widespread in Europe and America: Asia as the continent of acceptance, home of a certain fatalistic determinism.

A.D. and Ling ceremoniously avoid physical contact and real-life experience, referring to each other as "Cher Monsieur" and "Cher Ami." Malraux draws very little on his recent travels when adding touches of local color to this allegedly two-handed account: "They come into the ports at first light . . . above the lacquered bay, the whole town, wearing its crown of walls with pagodas as flowerets, emerges in the rising sun." A cross between a postcard and a Chinese print; perhaps Malraux still feels too close to Cambodia and Cochin China to use images registered over there. Clara remarks that Malraux is not keen on realistic description. Such veneer does not support the post-Nietzschean ambitions of an author who wants to come across as a thinker. Does Malraux realize that he is joining a movement of literary exoticism after Loti, Segalen, and Claudel? Probably. These writers know China. The deep meaning of the book is a constantly postponed promise, which comes unwillingly from the text.

He does not explain himself in interviews. "What the youth of the West is looking for is a new concept of man. . . . Does Asia have something to teach us? I do not think so. Rather, it can offer us a distinctive discovery of what we are."[4] Taking a Chinese version of his book as a fait accompli, Malraux declares, "If the title of the Chinese translation of *La Tentation de l'Occident* were retranslated literally back into French, you would get 'Proposition of the Orient.' "

On the face of it, Malraux's book is about China and Western Europe. But above all he is talking about himself: "All the nineteenth century's passion for mankind developed into a vehement affirmation of the importance of the self. Well, this mankind and this self, built on so many ruins, continue to hold sway over us, whether we like it or not; and we simply don't find them interesting." The royal "we" sounds suspiciously like denial and deliberate dissociation. "It has been said that none can act without faith," continues Malraux. "I believe that the absence of all conviction, like conviction itself, incites certain men to passivity and others to extreme action." Near Angkor and in Saigon, Malraux engaged in extreme activities. When he says that this self does not interest us, he is hiding. The "we" and the "self" are also Malraux standing back, feigning a haughty disinterest in introspection.

Ling sees in Europe "a carefully ordered barbarism." His Chinese refinement corresponds to an idea that some Westerners have of Asians, with all nationalities mixed together. He introduces binary themes: passivity and activity, being and doing. Ling is a reflection of Malraux but diverges from him too: it is "not necessary to act," he says; "the world changes you much more than you change it." In Cochin China, Malraux tried to change a colonial world. He was half beaten—but was changed.

The writer sprinkles his book with seductive and commonplace images. For Ling, the nice Chinese man, Rome is a "beautiful antiquary's garden left to abandon." Or again: "All erotic interplay is there: to be oneself and the other; to experience one's own sensations and imagine those of one's partner." Some phrases are would-be metaphysical: "At the center of the European man, dominating the major movements in his life, is an essential absurdity." Malraux does not develop the meaning of the word "absurd" but this indefinite notion stays with him. Was his activity in Saigon absurd or disappointing? Can one assert that the Eastern mind "attaches no value to man himself"? Admittedly, the Western mind in the twenties—and ever since the Renaissance—"has wanted to draw up a plan of the universe, to make an intelligible image of it, in other words, to establish a series of links between things unknown and things known, to discover those that were obscure until then." One senses the influence of Chateaubriand and Barrès. Form is still getting the better of content. One character, Wang-Loh, whose "hatred of the whites" is his whole life, could be a product of the radical and revolutionary Annamese Malraux has met.[5] The author uses the freedom of the epistolary genre to air certain prejudices, regrets, and resentment. He leaves it to Wang-Loh, under cover of a letter from A.D., to denounce fools inebriated with university idiocy. In Paris, Malraux alludes to his university studies at the École des Langues Orientales, and at the same time to the stupidity of higher education.

He indulges in a few grandiose truisms: "There is no China," writes Ling, "there are Chinese elites. The well-read elite is now only admired as one would an ancient monument. The new elite, that of men who have undergone Western culture, is so different from the first kind that we cannot but think that the very conquest of the empire by the West has begun."

Far from the journalistic banter of *L'Indochine Enchaînée*, the writer wavers, groping for and finding a tense style. The facts, to which the editor that he once was devoted himself, are forgotten, as if he could not master sentences, ideas, and breathing at the same time.

The last letter, sent by A.D., turns into lyrical fancy. A.D. is no longer addressing Ling but himself: "God has destroyed everything. Man can find only death." A.D. slides about on notions of country, justice, greatness, and truth. "We can sacrifice ourselves to no ideal," he writes, "for we know everybody's lies, we who do not know what truth is." Malraux does not define truth any more than he does absurdity. Life is apparently absurd; therefore truth, one of the objectives of existence, also seems absurd. Taking serious risks in Indochina, Malraux lived a militant ideal and came up against social and political lies. He seems tired but not disheartened: rather, he is waiting. The final lines of the book describe in novelistic, romantic tones a young man taking stock of himself and the recent years of his existence: "O shifting image of myself, for you I am without love. Like a wide, unclosed *wound* [my italics] you are my dead glory and my living suffering. I gave you all, and yet, I know that I will never love you. Unbowed, I shall bring you every day an offering of peace. O eager lucidity, I burn still before you, a lone, straight flame, in this heavy night where the yellow wind cries, as all these foreign nights where the wind off the water repeated around me the proud clamor of the sterile sea." Malraux is not sparing with grandiloquence. Admire himself he may not, but sometimes he really does love himself. His first two journeys in Asia wounded him. Is he still suffering a little, or even a lot? He was more lucid in Saigon than when he was making his way to Banteay Srei. The dates at the end of the narrative, 1921–1925, indicate that what Malraux is expressing in his first finished book is a summary, emotional if not intellectual, of his existence from twenty to twenty-four years of age.[6]

He does not return to his political combats. To the detriment of the narrative, he includes a cultural tour of Asia. He draws little inspiration from what he experienced, referring instead to his fanatical and muddled reading. This explains the importance of the form and the weakness of the content, the overuse of vague abstractions, the sentences thrown out in bursts. A.D.'s journey in Asia and Ling's in Europe are striking in their dryness. To explain the erosion of old and new values, the writer juxtaposes action and dream. His indistinct philosophical reflections, based more on rhetoric than reason, do not make interpretation of his theses any easier. There remains, scattered throughout the book, an attempt to analyze the crisis of values that is more applicable to the West known to Malraux than to an imagined East; it is less clear than Valéry's pages on the "Crisis of the Mind." Malraux feels his way, overcoming the Spenglerian idea of a worn-out world. This little book with which the writer hopes to make his mark is a rough work. He had to hurry to finish, as evidenced by the surviving feverish fragments of manuscript: a patchwork of alterations, bits pasted onto writing pads, sheets of squared paper from an exercise book, and a cut-up accounts ledger.

Malraux has boundless energy despite painful attacks of rheumatoid arthritis. Seeking advice and support from Jean Paulhan, he launches his book with a selection of three letters in an installment of the *Nouvelle Revue Française* (*NRF*) of April 3, 1926. When *La Tentation* appears, the author announces not only the publication of the complete Chinese text (again), in Shanghai and Peking, but also an essay that is "in press" and a novel whose title has already been chosen, *Puissances* (Powers). Malraux confuses an imagined potentiality with a tangible reality. *La Tentation de l'Occident* is better received in the French provinces than in Paris; it doesn't take off well in the bookshops. Not one of the sixty-odd articles in the press is a dazzling review from a Paris weekly. The author is proud but not conceited; this is vexing for his self-esteem, but he manages not to show it. Ramon Fernandez, in the *NRF*, publishes a sweet and sour review of the book, conceding that there arises from it a hymn "that charms and dazes us." The author's poetic ambitions "spoil the clarity of the views he exposes." Fernandez does not dwell on the writer's cutting expressions. Malraux is talked about, but his book is not a success. However, in Paris, at least in Saint-Germain-des-Prés and Montparnasse, he is talked about as if he were already a successful author. The young man carries more weight than his work. The attitude of publicity experts such as Bernard Grasset confirms Malraux's own impression: he is a future great writer,[7] his feet squarely set between a slender present and a future that is sure to be broad.

He wants to travel again, to make the world his own, and to write. He is looking for fame. He no longer prefers "he who appreciates the garden" to "he who makes the garden." Clara encourages him. Together, they believe in his *genius*, a word Malraux likes. Despite stormy weather, the fiery couple's marriage holds together. They quarrel in front of friends; Clara is agitated, and André can freeze her with his coolness. She stamps her feet. On one point, they agree: in order to create, Malraux must feed his imagination with expeditions, with renewed experiences. Short of money? They'll find some.

Clara sometimes smokes opium with the literary figure Maurice Magre in his bachelor apartment. They live in the same building. André much prefers alcohol.[8] He puts his literary strategy back into practice in reviews and newspapers. At Paulhan's request, and backed by André Gide and Marcel Arland, he gives some notes to the *NRF*: a review of *Défense de l'Occident* by Henri Massis and one of *Bouddha vivant* by Paul Morand. Then he moves on to *L'Imposture* by Georges Bernanos and *Journal de voyage d'un philosophe* by Hermann von Keyserling. After the French publication of *La Tentation de l'Occident*, Arland compares Malraux with Keyserling. Both express the fears and aspirations of young Europeans. The comparison goes too far: Keyserling travels as much as Malraux but offers a "philosophy" that combines spiritual values, all-purpose unicorns, nationalism, and the dangerous beauty of industrialization. At twenty-five, Malraux steers clear of nationalism and is at best equivocal about modern technology.

He also publishes studies elsewhere. For *Formes*, he writes "notes on tragic expression in painting" regarding recent works by Rouault. He also writes an article on the idea of eroticism in D. H. Lawrence, later used as a preface to the French edition of *Lady Chatterley's Lover*. His output follows the principle of communicating vessels: the more books he finishes, the fewer articles he writes. His work gives a false impression of facility. Whenever an author lures him beyond his own personality and prestige, Malraux proves vigorous and clear, as with the favorable review of *Hyméné*, a novel by Louis Guilloux.[9]

The *NRF* accepts Malraux with reticence. He lacks the classicism and correctness expected of its contributors. At best, isn't he more of an adventurer, more like Raymond Radiguet or Maurice Sachs than Jean Cocteau or André Gide? The latter has a huge weak spot for Malraux, who often irritates or disconcerts him by his assurance. There is no hesitancy or caution in the author of *La Tentation de l'Occident*. Malraux's defenders, Arland in particular, explain that his curiosity, his knowledge of the visual arts, and his love of literature outweigh his arrogance. Malraux wants the *NRF* to take him on as an in-house literary critic. He is passed over: he is still pretty green, and the top editorial staff, in their eclectic wisdom, judge that the function and power of literary chronicler should be shared between several contributors. The founding father of the publishing company, Gaston Gallimard, claims not to have enough influence over the review to get Malraux the job. The capital's literati observe this young wolf with watchful mistrust. Some writers, Louis Aragon and André Breton, to name two, clearly dislike him. He refuses to yield to the demands and rites of the dadaist and surrealist sects; despite denouncing the established order, they take care to maintain their social and editorial networks. Against the prevailing current, Malraux does not feel himself obliged to get into bed with the French Communist Party. He has his own idea of independence. Some concessions are acceptable, but he will not stoop to hypocritical compromise.

Gaston Gallimard reacts with amused indulgence. He gives Malraux a job on account of his technical proficiency and the books he must have in him. André and Gaston, little crocodile and big crocodile, watch each other. Malraux's presumptuousness sometimes displeases Gaston, but the fellow seems efficient. He, at least, realizes that one cannot always publish at a loss. Too many authors are convinced that their publisher is there to be milked, for no return. Gaston likes Malraux for a connoisseur, a scout, a rascal, and one of the rare potential writers to know the printer's trade and the price of paper. From time to time, Malraux loses track in his estimates: his business sense is not always good, and his generosity is costly when it comes to advances. But he is interested in the production and selling of a book. Gaston doesn't mind losing money on an author such as Marcel Jouhandeau, but his publishing house is not a charity.

Gaston was not impressed by *La Tentation de l'Occident*; he detects in Malraux primarily a promise to be kept. The writer in him is not ripe, but, according to Gaston, he has editorial qualities. Malraux will at first be artistic director with Gallimard. He has an eye for typography and layout. His writing? That will be for tomorrow—or a few years' time. At any rate, Gaston has managed the publisher's trick of getting his hands on Malraux's future books in advance. They woo each other, with Malraux the more interested party.

Malraux has fun in his letters to Gaston, taking care to draw more friendly seahorses than mysterious cats in the margins. He treats Gaston like an ambassador met at the Quai d'Orsay: "Cher Monsieur et Ami. My seahorses are getting hungrier and hungrier. To keep them quiet I read to them from *La Révolution Surréaliste* [the review], which has Benjamin Péret listing his amorous performances in order—which is pretty lively stuff, when you imagine his face—but they refuse to listen. They are underfed and resistant to all literature; the ten seahorses are abandoning themselves to daydreaming, which is, as you know, the beginning of unhappiness."[10] In this correspondence, Malraux is amiable and obsequious. The two men talk books and percentages. Malraux starts on a *D'Artagnan* that he has already proposed to Grasset: "Starting is the important part."[11] Gaston suggests that André tackle a life of Edgar Allan Poe.[12] "I think Paulhan has made a mistake," Malraux replies. "I do not wish to write a Life of Edgar Allan Poe, I believe I would write it badly." Might it not be because Malraux cannot read English? "Of all curious individuals, there is one whose life I would perhaps write well," he says, "and that is my own, but given the title of your collection ('The Lives of Illustrious Men'), that would perhaps be premature!" Gaston Gallimard forwards the letter to Paulhan, who stamps "Yes" in the margin.[13]

Malraux does have an undertaking in mind: a *Tableau des poisons* (Table of Poisons). Gaston likes the idea. They work out the details: "Monsieur Malraux undertakes . . . Monsieur Gallimard undertakes . . ." One thousand francs on signing, 4,000 on handing over the manuscript, 3,000 when it is put on sale (the contemporary equivalent of around $300 overall). Malraux puts himself forward for a preface to *A Young Girl's Diary*, with its foreword by Sigmund Freud.[14] Clara wants to translate it. Then Malraux declines.[15] He does sometimes feel the limits of his competence. He can also take on an original and complex project and see it through. He plans the first volume of an encyclopedic *Tableau de la littérature française*, from Rutebeuf to the nineteenth century. He imagines Georges Bernanos writing about *La Satyre Ménippée*,[16] Gide tackling Montaigne, Paulhan covering the Grands Rhétoriqueurs.[17] Maurois? Malherbe. Romain Rolland would do Rabelais, Molière, or Voltaire. Malraux contacts the potential contributors, even if he doesn't know them: "The work is to be composed of studies by living writers on the great writers of the past. We ask each of our contributors for about ten pages on the writer—or writers—he has chosen, leaving all didactic intentions to one side. . . . We are calling on all the writers who, outside of the Sorbonne, currently represent values in France. Our intention is to establish a text that is free of all association with academic teaching." Malraux writes with a savvy hand, manipulating his cursive writing to make one word shine out in the head of the recipient. Writers do not live on spirituality alone; Malraux sets out the fees: "150F per page [$7 in 1927], sent on receipt of the manuscript." Malraux's outlook, like Gallimard's, is broad: he also calls on Pierre Mac Orlan and Edmond Jaloux. For his second volume, he would like François Mauriac to write on Pascal, Paul Valéry on Montesquieu, and Charles Maurras on Chénier. The eroticists must not be forgotten, nor must the remarkable memoirists, nor the great travelers. Malraux can see Paul Léautaud writing on Chamfort.[18]

Malraux reconciles extremes in a Gastongallimardian way. There is Romain Rolland on the left, and on the right, a Charles Maurras. They mustn't know that they are on board the same ship. Or they must pretend not to know. Gaston's ecumenical politics mean publishing all tendencies. He admires Malraux's deftness when diplomatically defending the interests of the publisher. They both have their hearts and heads on the left. The publications themselves must be all over.

Little by little, Malraux makes friends with the mysterious and precious Jean Paulhan, who becomes his critical but constant ally. Paulhan knows that Malraux wants to make a name for himself. When Malraux says to him, as he does to so many others, that he was "commissar in the Kuomintang Party in Cochin China at the beginning of 1925 and in Indochina in June, then member of the Kuomintang's Central Propaganda Committee," Paulhan does not believe him.[19] Paulhan likes truth but accepts that some writers build a legend for themselves. He encourages Malraux the writer: he has a style, lots of ideas and sensibility. When he is with him, Malraux desists from his scintillating monologue and engages in dialogue: "Perhaps we are both wrong, you for admiring the Sade myth too much and me for running the marquis down." With Paulhan, Malraux has almost no reserve: "I am also reading *Nadja*. Here is a prediction for you: Breton's next discovery will be Maeterlinck." Paulhan proves frank with him, and Malraux opens himself up: "When—on vacation—you go to the trouble of defending Valéry against Claudel, are you sure you are really defending V. against C., and not one form of poetry that you don't really like and, overall, one myth against another?" Faced with Paulhan, Malraux, unusually, grows modest: "I don't in the slightest think I am right about this, but I would say that Valéry seems to me, above all, a creator of myths and that if his myth makes no impression upon me, I am incapable of admiring anything else except his intelligence."[20] Malraux surrenders bit by bit; he does not willingly lapse into personal anecdotes, but he does seem at ease chatting with Paulhan, who backs him and, broadly, trusts him. He tells him that he likes cats: "Arland asked me for two days to look after a gray lizard-shaped cat called Chat-Boum (what a name . . . anyway! Chatoufu would be better, as my wife says). I advise you to get this cat lent to you too: he murmurs in a very curious way and, given his young age, I think he will soon be talking."

As editor, Malraux sees through a complete edition of the works of Gide, whom he admires, and a luxury edition of *L'Autre sommeil* by Julien Green, whom he doesn't much like. Malraux the professional editor knows how to say, "I don't like this manuscript, but we have to do it."

When Gaston Gallimard wants to counter *Candide*, a right-wing newspaper started in 1924 by Fayard, Emmanuel Berl launches the weekly *Marianne* in 1932, and Malraux collaborates. Drawing on his experience in Saigon, he helps Berl design a mock-up. Berl relies on him to choose photographs and come up with clear page layouts. Malraux sees himself as an artist and a gifted craftsman. On *Marianne*, he does nothing new but adopts "front-page" principles of photomontage. His technical input is greater than his contribution as a writer. In five years, he publishes five articles in *Marianne*.

When he returned to Europe, he enlarged his circle of acquaintances; some of them have become solid friends. Malraux now talks to the old hands as equals. With Mauriac, he reaches a level of intimacy.[21] Mauriac sends him *God and Mammon*. Malraux, speaking from the height of his future oeuvre, knows how to affect his correspondent: "It is clearly the most confidential of all your books, the most characteristic; and it constantly gives me the impression of an undeniable truth. . . . Being Catholic and writing novels are two things which, in themselves, seem no less surprising nor less compatible than being Catholic and living in this century. However, there is something plaintive in your book because it is really about something else; and clearly you are very much defending yourself against yourself." Malraux knows this struggle, on several fronts: so many Malrauxs coexist within him. He is twenty-eight.

Gide's pull on Malraux increases; Malraux visits him in Rue Vaneau near the Hôtel Matignon. They work together for Gallimard. Gide often comes away exhausted, wearied, and puzzled from conversations with his young colleague, "more overwhelmed than exalted." Gide is a complex man, Malraux a difficult character. André and Clara unenthusiastically go to pay their respects to Julien Green and while they are there meet Morand and Berl. They even talk about eroticism. Malraux, never short of a theory, even a banal one, proposes that eroticism is at its strongest in countries where there is a concept of sin. Gide wonders: Of Berl and Malraux, which is the more eloquent and obscure? Malraux, just, on points.

Such are the requirements of France and the age: literary figures, whether known or unknown, must give interviews on all subjects. Thus, some become famous before being published. Malraux was "born a writer," according to Berl; he refuses very few interviews.

La Revue Européenne sends out a questionnaire on Eisenstein's film *The Battleship Potemkin*,[22] banned by the French authorities. Its revolutionary propaganda is considered subversive. Malraux takes a position: "I think it desirable that not only 'professionals' but all those who care about art should be able to see a film about which they are curious. In a country with no censorship of the press, film censorship would simply amount to buffoonery, if it were not used as a means of defense by certain enterprises that you doubtless know as well as I do."

The newspaper *Monde* is exploring Zola; it asks Louis Guilloux, André Chamson, and André Malraux for their reactions to the writer's epic approach and social outlook. Malraux admits that Zola's work has never interested him. But he does wonder about the art and the function of the novelist: "The principal effect a novelist has on me—as with any sort of artist—is not the world he portrays but the particular transformation he is obliged to impose on this world in translating it. Balzac's work says less about the Restoration than the efforts that someone starting from where Bonaparte started would have to make, incapacitated by circumstances and forced to remain within a class or a profession in order to be fulfilled within that class or profession. [César] Birotteau and [Eugénie] Grandet, on their way up, are portrayed as miserly, foppish Bonapartes. Remove the Napoleonic spirit from the 'Comédie humaine,' and the work is not the same. The particular accent this spirit gives to Balzac's work seems to me poor and inconsequential when you find it in Zola." "Why is *Monde* interested in Zola? Clearly," Malraux answers himself, "because Zola portrayed workers. He was working with an idea of 'the people' that I think is valueless today. In France, some of the workers rally with the middle classes; the others constitute the proletariat, which is quite another thing from the people." Malraux's rhetoric often uses formulae of the type "*x* is not *y*, which is quite another thing," without his defining *x* or *y*. Who knows where that might take us?

Malraux participates in the Décades de Pontigny, organized by Paul Desjardins. The second seminar[23] centers on French youth after the war. Malraux is not the worst placed to talk on this subject. The organization suits Malraux: seminars and conferences are followed by discussions in which champions can stand out, as Berl does against Malraux. From time to time, Clara chides André for not always staying within his audience's reach. His hermetic turns of phrase, his twitching, his hair lying across his forehead like a windshield wiper; Malraux disconcerts, surprises, and annoys his audience. He fills them with wonder. He improvises, forging ahead with a labyrinthine plan in his head. The participants are leading lights such as Roger Martin du Gard, students from the École Normale Supérieure, Rue d'Ulm, politicians, novelists, and poets. At Pontigny,

Malraux builds on his friendship with a young philosophy teacher he met in Germany, Raymond Aron, who is giving a paper on Proust. Malraux respects but does not relish Proust. Aron always expresses himself with a didactic clarity that Malraux finds impressive. Aron (at least) has read the authors he talks about: Husserl, Max Weber, and Spengler. Malraux skims through books. Aron never holds it against him. Early on, he gets the feeling that this writer is on an imaginative and artistic level that he, Aron, could never reach. If Malraux is poetry, Aron is prose. With his aura of exoticism as well, Malraux dazzles Aron—sometimes—although the philosopher is the epitome of reason.

Suzanne and Raymond Aron and Clara and André Malraux see more of one another. Even if he finds her invasive, Aron appreciates Clara's intelligence. She often takes a backseat when her husband is present. The public disagreements between Clara and André embarrass and ultimately shock their friends. Clara adores allusions to free love and threesomes. When she accuses Malraux of Puritanism, he stiffens. Clara follows through by singing the praises of her husband's prodigious intelligence. She is not taken in by his legends. But she pays him homage and protects him. He has an excuse: he is a creator. Clara also needs to exist in her own right. But how, without appearing as a rival? She thinks André is a misogynist. She is allowed to talk, but not too much. She would like to be accepted by him, with her differences and, above all, with tenderness. She remains loyal and rebels at the same time. André talks of the proletariat, the people, the middle classes. Does he know them? No better than she.

Networks of friendship and fidelity form around Malraux. Louis Chevasson is always present, reserved, following his friend from childhood and later misadventures. Marcel Brandin and Pascal Pia are also around but do not stick to Malraux's career as Chevasson does. Pia places himself next to Malraux, not in his wake. The Left Bank, the offices of the *NRF*, Rue de Grenelle, then Rue Sébastien-Bottin, the restaurants and cafés of the Sixth Arrondissement, the printers in the Gobelins quarter, negotiations with the authors, their sometimes stimulating, sometimes disappointing company: Malraux is not fulfilled. Much may be expected and obtained from a work and little from its author. The Malrauxs would like to travel. André wants to make the world his own—and master it.

Le Démon des hippocampes

CHAPTER EIGHT

Asiatic Paths

S EPTEMBER 1928: André Malraux publishes his first novel, *Les Conquérants,*[1] in Bernard Grasset's elegant "Cahiers Verts" collection, a
3,800-copy print run. In November, Grasset's rival Gallimard does a
minilaunch of 572 copies of the little book eventually finished by Malraux,
Royaume farfelu. Two years later, in October 1930, *La Voie royale,*[2] another
novel, is published by Grasset.

Daniel Halévy, a writer and Nietzsche's biographer, holds literary Saturdays where he contemplates the rift between the generations separated
by the Great War. Halévy respects André Malraux and gets a long text out
of him, *D'une jeunesse européenne* (On European Youth). In good faith, he
introduces its author as a "young writer-philosopher," who wrote the
essay after "his return from China, where he stayed for two years."

In an extension of the thinking in *La Tentation de l'Occident,* Malraux
states that "European youth is more moved by what the world can be than
by what it is." Malraux is still digging over the theme of the death of God,
and he starts from a basic premise: "From the outset, the concept of the
divine was an essential characteristic of Greek and Christian cultures."
Christianity is a splinter in European flesh, for "our first weakness comes
from the inevitability of seeing the world, from where we stand, through a
Christian 'grid,' even if we are not Christians."

When discussing the nineteenth century, the essayist talks of others in
weakly general terms, but also of himself. Belief in progress, he suggests,
must be rejected. Taking up a basically antipositivist refrain, he claims that
"since our civilization lost hope of finding a meaning to the world through
science, it has been denied a spiritual goal."

Malraux's text, as a stylistic exercise, is more developed than *La Tentation de l'Occident* and establishes him as an essayist. The previous year,

Pierre Drieu la Rochelle, who fought during the war, wrote in his *Jeune Européen*: "A man of these times . . . lets a dreadful monologue grow in his heart on the strange beauty and the deathly glory of this rotting civilization, and that which is killing it, and may replace it, is merged with this." For Drieu, *La Tentation de l'Occident* was too "literary," too brilliant, and too accommodating. Malraux and Drieu claim to speak for a generation. With a hectic timetable, but one he can handle, Malraux transforms himself.

Had he continued in the vein of his first little works, Malraux might have fluttered about in the Parisian literary cage as a second-rate Max Jacob. Instead, he is recognized as an original novelist. In its intrigue and characters, his novel *Les Conquérants* maintains a flexible classical structure, to the benefit of a romanticism in its atmosphere. Malraux is not bothered about being avant-garde. The way the scenes are put together, along the lines of the best reporting, makes *Les Conquérants* very modern fiction. At the same time, Malraux is banking on Asian exoticism. This book is the first good *roman engagé* of the decade. Its violent tone carries a new subject: in the China of 1925, the Kuomintang Nationalists, once allied with the Communists, are now confronting them. Here is a meeting of East and West that is far beyond the convoluted letters of A.D. and Ling. European leaders are training Chinese revolutionaries for the Communist International. China boycotts trade with England and especially with Hong Kong, a cancer in the country's side. *La Tentation* was no more than a vague, pseudophilosophical backdrop. *Les Conquérants* is a novel with political substance. The Chinese government must prevent cargo ships from coming in at Hong Kong: the members of the Communist International, the Comintern, would like to impose a decree to this end, and their allies in the Kuomintang hesitate. The characters, almost all male, oppose each other like so many symbols; the climate is that of a good detective novel, complete with trickery, spies, daggers, and poison. Politics makes history from blood and heroism.

Malraux's temptations sneak into all the characters, but especially into Garine, the revolutionary, the intelligent pessimist, contrasted with Borodine, the mechanical servant of the Revolution. Malraux is still his own favorite hero in life, but not always in his fiction. He embodies a thirst for carefully directed power and passes this on to his characters. Malraux was not born in Geneva of Swiss and Russian parents like Garine; he did not inherit a fortune on his mother's death; he did not pursue literary studies in Paris like Garine; nor did he confabulate with anarchists in Switzerland. It is a novelist's privilege to award himself diplomas by proxy. Malraux is starting to know publishing companies, as Garine does in Zurich. But Malraux was not in the Foreign Legion. He did not advise Sun Yat-sen, nor help found the military academy of Whampoa, nor organize a general strike in Canton. For every one of Garine's credentials, Malraux, perhaps, harbors a suppressed wish. The writer lets Halévy and others repeat that he played an important role in the Kuomintang. He could have, he should have . . . Garine squanders a fortune; Malraux liquidated Clara's dowry. Garine and Malraux both talk with a jerky rhythm. Garine is mixed up in an abortion affair, as Malraux was in his apartment on Boulevard Murat.[3] Garine is the victim of a trial that he finds unwarranted, like Malraux in Phnom Penh and Saigon. In the first version of Les Conquérants, Garine was called Stavine: Staline + Stavroguine (Dostoevsky's Stavrogin). By name, a Dostoevskian Bolshevik crossed with Saint-Just and Nietzsche. Then Garine became Garine, probably because of Galen, the adviser at the military academy at Whampoa in 1925 with the real Borodin.[4]

Malraux adopts an apophatic approach: a being or a thing is defined by what it is not. "But Stalin means nothing against Dostoevsky, no more than the genius of Mussorgsky." This Malrucian tic gets more noticeable. In his narrative, he sometimes succumbs to flat clichés: "Individualism is a middle-class disease," "To judge, quite evidently, is not to understand, since if one understood one could no longer judge."

Les Conquérants opens on a telegram pinned up on a ship: GENERAL STRIKE DECLARED IN CANTON. The plot unfolds over a few short weeks, from June 15 to August 18. In his first books, Malraux stays within the limits of a restricted time frame. The narrative accelerates, punctuated with more telegrams, dates, and times thrown in here and there, like shorthand symbols. The novelist projects himself into Garine, "a type of hero in whom aptitude and action, culture and clearheadedness are united,"[5] but he does not express himself completely through him. Then he kills him off: a good way, for a novelist, to prepare for rebirth.

Malraux doesn't set out to analyze Marx or Lenin—not too much, at least. Carried along by the time, he admires them. They, like Garine, believed in energy. In this respect, Malraux is exceptional. From Paris as from Saigon, he sees Marxism (as does Garine) not as a scientific socialism but as "a method of organizing workers' passions, a way of recruiting shock troops from the workers." Once out of Cochin China, Malraux enters China in his imagination. In this he is a reformist Bolshevik and a revolutionary Menshevik, if such creatures exist.

Borodine is an industrious underling, open to compromise with the Kuomintang Nationalists, who plans the Revolution as he would prepare a meal. Borodine is a Stalinist, Garine isn't. Under a classification more literary than political, Malraux's Garine would be a "conquering" Communist, and his Borodine a Communist "in the Roman style." Garine has a taste for revolution and insurrection, not social organization. He is

opposed to Borodine's doctrinal dogmatism, and he likes certain abstractions more than human beings: "I do not like men, I do not like the poor,
or the people; those, in short, for whom I fight." He resembles Malraux.
Passion, rather than compassion, is what consumes Garine. Why, then,
side with the people? "Only because they are the vanquished. Yes, overall
they have more heart, more humanity than the others; the virtue of the
vanquished." Malraux belongs to the age of the Good Poor, the proletariat
as the vehicle of History. Through Garine, he lapses into a sonorous and
empty sentimentalism. Faced with the exploited—*les misérables*—Garine-
Malraux's pity echoes Victor Hugo. His proletariat resembles Jules
Michelet's people. But on balance, Garine's skepticism, even cynicism,
submerges the whiffs of sentiment.

Garine considers the bourgeoisie a fantasy, catchall notion, cherished
above all by the left-wing middle class; he hates it, more than Malraux but
less than a certain Bernard Groethuysen. Malraux's friend and mentor
Groethuysen undertook a monumental work, *Origines de l'esprit bourgeois
en France* (Origins of the Bourgeois Mind in France). Twenty-one years
older than Malraux, Groet (pronounced Groot) was born in Berlin,
though his family is from Luxembourg. He is a sort of bearded Socrates
with bushy eyebrows, a "stormy" and "violent" face, Paulhan said, though
others found him serene. He offers Malraux a refrain: questions are often
preferable to and richer than answers. Wittgenstein claimed that there are
no insoluble problems, only badly worded questions. Groet has no
impressive body of work behind him, like Gide or Valéry, but his willingly
shared erudition impresses Malraux. Groet and Alix, his militant partner,
are fascinated by the great light coming from Moscow. They are Communists: he of the Roman and scholarly sort, she of the barbaric, fanatic sort.
Through them, homeopathic doses of Marxism and great slices of communism come into Malraux's life. More a man of action than of theory,
Malraux discusses with Groet: How is the enigma of the world to be
solved? Why is the world? How can we explain death? How has the West
approached the question of the individual? How do we define the bourgeoisie? Technology? Science? The French Revolution? Collectivism, as
regards the individual? Groet has a technical approach to social and historical problems. Malraux sometimes tires of Valéry or Gide, but never of
Groet. With Raymond Aron and Groet, his esteem seems to be unre-
served. In their eyes, he remains the creator, the prose poet of action. One
of the things Malraux likes about Groet is that he dispenses myths onto
which he can tack his own apocalyptic syntheses. Groet disregards Malraux's inventions, such as his participation in the leadership of the Kuomintang. I know you know. And you know I know. In friendship as in love,
the best form of proof is the pardon of offenses against truth. "Mutual for-

giveness of each vice / Such are the gates of paradise," as William Blake put it.

Psychology, political economics, and the history of art are passions with Groet, as much in museums as in Hegel. In the summer he lectures in Berlin on French thinkers, spending the winter and spring in Paris. Generous with his time and ideas, he listens to Malraux and, miraculously, knows how to have him listen back. Groet is as good at dialogue as monologue, which is not the case with his turbulent friend. He chats with Clara in German, which annoys Malraux, as he is no good at foreign languages. Groet also knows Greek, Latin, English, and Russian culture.

"What if you awoke from death to find yourself faced with a Christian God," Malraux asks Groet, "what would you say to him?"

Groet answers wryly, " 'Lord, I didn't think it was as dumb as that.' "

Groet is a figure of the Enlightenment and of German philosophy, an explosive combination; he evokes Pierre Bayle, Kafka, Saint Augustine, and Pico della Mirandola. For Malraux, he becomes a selfless intellectual father figure. He takes psychoanalysis seriously, which Malraux doesn't. He is a philosopher who readily calls on writers: Shakespeare teaches us more about "emotions" than Descartes and the psychology manuals devoted to "passions." Groet forgets Spinoza and Kant to quote poets and novelists. Leaving Germany, he ended his last lecture on a vibrant note: "Intellectuals of all countries, unite."

Then he aligned himself with an approach which, from the Renaissance to the Encyclopedists, had been dreaming of an international meeting of minds to unite East and West.

Admiring the French Revolution and the Russian one, Malraux-Garine in *Les Conquérants* makes a prophecy about revolutionaries: "I know they'll become despicable as soon as we have triumphed together." He does not say that all revolutions become unacceptable or totalitarian. Malraux rejects Manichean oversimplification: "Lord! Deliver us from saints." He feeds his reader with excellently turned phrases like advertising slogans: "I have also learned that one life is worth nothing, but nothing is worth one life." Again in *Les Conquérants*, Malraux picks up a thread from *La Tentation de l'Occident*, the absurdity of the world, but the absurdity becomes that of society: "I do not take society to be bad nor capable of improvement; I hold it to be absurd. That is quite another thing." To escape the absurd for the duration of the insurrection, Garine puts his faith in a brotherhood that evades him. He aspires to "a hard but fraternal seriousness." Absurdity and fraternity: Garine grabs hold of the revolution as his last hope: "Anything else is worse, we must admit that, even when we are sick and tired of it."

Malraux avoids turning his novel into a didactic, theoretical work.

The book never defends an orthodox version of communism. When it is banned—so they say—in the USSR, Bernard Grasset is delighted. Without waiting for confirmation of this information, he has the work surrounded in bookshop windows with the sign "Banned in Russia and Italy." Malraux is apparently as much in Mussolini's bad books as Stalin's. Grasset hopes for the Prix Goncourt with *Les Conquérants*, before Malraux passes over to Gallimard. The editor respects a good contract: 3,000 francs on signing, 10,000 on publication ($500 overall). He also gets him good press coverage: for a beginner he would distribute 150 review copies; for *Les Conquérants*, it is 400. In a friendly salute to suicide, Malraux dedicates the book to his friend René Latouche, who killed himself. He surprises some Parisian critics. Where is the aesthete, the dandy? Malraux kept an eye on the preprints in the *NRF*: one of the first commentators on the novel was Groet. He puts the work into historical and political perspective, drawing attention to the writer's merits: "*Les Conquérants* is a very good novel: the novelist has sided with life." To Groet, this is a book of a new genre, showing that there is no inherent conflict between the novelist and the historian: "It is the novel itself which is engaged in a struggle with History, since it takes sides with the particular man whose distinctive life it re-creates." Malraux accepts the Hegelian (and Groethuysian) idea of history, but not a history that is overly predetermined by economics. For Groet, a historian of ideas, this novel unfurls in a China where "events of worldwide significance" are developing. As a Communist, Groethuysen understands the demands of discipline and political activism. As a friend of Malraux, he grasps the hero's standpoint: "If Garine had merely been a stranger among the men of his time and the bourgeois class to which he belonged, he might perhaps have lived on his own and become a poet. Had he only known the *libido dominandi*, perhaps he would have become a banker. But it is by combining both that he turns into what he is." Some people criticize Malraux for historical inaccuracies. Groet does not see the necessity of speeches about the class struggle, historical materialism, and the dictatorship of the proletariat; he absolves Malraux: "The novel meets requirements that the Party does not know." Groet's article devotes four pages to this novel and twenty-two lines to *Royaume farfelu*. Groet feels obliged to keep quiet about what he thinks of *Royaume*, published by Gallimard.

The East also makes an appearance in *Royaume farfelu*, peopled not with workers and policemen but with dragons and mermaids. The Ispahan that Maurice Saint-Rose—alias Malraux—portrayed in *L'Indochine* comes up again. *Royaume farfelu* now looks like a hiccup in the author's literary output. The almost simultaneous publication of the two books, *Les Conquérants* and *Royaume farfelu*, could give the impression that the writer is wavering between his robust neorealist vein, committed within the context of its period, and the soppiness of his youth. With *Les Conquérants* he has found a tone and a style. He stuttered through *Royaume farfelu*, bringing back to mind his *Lunes en papier*.

The writer often doubts his own talent, even if he does pose as a genius. He is attentive to critics. What a pleasure to be congratulated by Roger Martin du Gard! Malraux quickly replies:[6] "Thank you for your kind note. I attach enough importance to your opinion of *Les Conquérants* not to let you off quite yet. You are better off writing *Les Thibault* than talking about my book, but you are better off talking about my book than about many others." The two men met briefly at the Décades: "I hope to have the pleasure of seeing you again, if only at Pontigny. You may well be curious as to how I saw you: as somebody who is sure in all senses of the word, and believe me that, although rather young, I have lived a violent enough life to know the value of that, as much in intellectual terms as otherwise." Malraux clarifies, "I do not say 'sure of himself.' " He assures his correspondent of his "respectful friendship." Patrons such as Martin du Gard reassure Malraux, as do friends such as Emmanuel Berl, who writes:

> I consider *Les Conquérants* to be an event of the utmost importance in contemporary moral history. I am surprised . . . that so much should have been said about aesthetics, when there is something at stake far beyond aesthetics. . . . For me, Garine is a new sort of man, whose mere existence resolves many problems and difficulties. It also raises new ones. Bourgeois readers who are won over by Malraux's art will understand, tomorrow if not today, the danger to which Malraux is exposing them, and they will stop looking for information about China, scenery, a chronicle, or insights in his book.[7]

For the first time, Malraux's reviews are laudatory; the book is reviewed about a hundred times in six weeks. Grasset thinks he has his Goncourt. Forgetting Malraux's Indochinese escapades and the high-flown publicity orchestrated by the editor, some literary pundits are all over him. Albert Thibaudet, in *Candide*, recommends a "curious, lively, and subtle" book that offers "a bulk presentation of hinted impressions." André Thérive, in *L'Opinion*, gives three columns to a "remarkable writer . . . unparalleled narrator." Thérive adds, "An eye that chooses as well as this is obviously in the service of a strong and intelligent brain." Paul Morand, a reputation maker, starts an article in *Les Nouvelles Littéraires* on Mauriac, Maurois, Montherlant, Giraudoux, and Julien Green, and ends up with Malraux. Among the influential critics, Paul Souday of

Les Temps is almost alone in dispatching the "half novel" *Les Conquérants* in one paragraph. Souday does not like fictionalized politics. *L'Humanité*, now Communist, denounces Garine as a dilettante and labels the novel "definitely counterrevolutionary." Look out, comrades![8]

Morand writes that Malraux "can be permitted dangerous works because he has lived dangerously. He had already won our sympathy; now, with *Les Conquérants*, he has attracted the attention of today's wider public, who are hungry to understand and learn, and who can draw more than entertainment from the new approach to the French novel."

Malraux doesn't get the Goncourt, but his book sells well, allowing the couple to move from a three- to a five-room apartment. Edmond Jaloux expresses his regret at the absence of *Les Conquérants* among the winners of the sales-boosting literary prizes. He talks of the "most beautiful of all the books by young writers this year, the most audacious, the strongest, and the most intelligent." Malraux takes the French literary stage. He is translated in Germany, Spain, Great Britain, and the United States. He allows it to be said, he encourages it to be said, that he was a revolutionary leader back in Canton.

The mass of favorable articles, along with his personality and his work, bring about a public debate organized by the Union pour la Vérité.[9] The participants, under the benevolent presidency of the philosophical patriarch Léon Brunschvicg, are, among others, Julien Benda, Gabriel Marcel, Malraux's pal Berl, Pierre Hamp, and Jean Guéhenno, another friend of Malraux. The whole thing amounts to a coronation. Contemporaries old and young salute the beginner by their presence alone. With proud modesty, Malraux points out in his polished introduction to the debate that a novel rarely gives rise to so much passion. Historical accuracy? "There is not a single point in *Les Conquérants* that is not defensible from a real and historical point of view." Garine exists, since he met him while creating him. To those who would like to see in his book a recruitment tract for the French Communist Party, he replies, "*Les Conquérants* is not an apology for revolution as such but describes an alliance . . . a group of men who have a clear conception of the revolutionary ideal, bound to a historical doctrine that is Marxism; and these men act according to an idea of the Party that they have been obliged to modify several times to be able to apply it to China. On the other hand, there is Garine and his lot."

After his conversations with Groet and Berl, Malraux defines the bourgeoisie according to his heroes. For Borodine, it is a historic reality that must be overcome. For Garine and Malraux, it embodies a human attitude. In the course of this debate, more than in his novel and more than in *L'Indochine Enchaînée*—then he was merely a rebel—Malraux does his best to define the revolutionary: "For me, [he] is born of resistance. A man may be aware of certain injustices and certain inequalities, be aware of an intense suffering: that will never be enough to make a revolutionary of him. Faced with suffering, he may become a Christian, he may aspire to sanctity or discover charity; he will not become a revolutionary. For that, at the point when he wants to intervene in aid of this suffering, he has to come up against some resistance."

Malraux makes references to Gandhi, who has haunted him since his first trip to Asia. He also evokes the revolutionaries described by Michelet, strangely associating them with the Cheka (whose archives, he rashly predicts, will "soon be published in France"). Garine, he concludes, does not have to define the revolution but make it. Like Malraux. "The fundamental question for Garine," he suggests, "is much less knowing how to participate in a revolution than knowing how to escape what we call the absurd." Revolution, to the young writer, more than the desire for social change, becomes the absolute weapon against anxiety and absurdity.

Before a respectable audience, the row of middle-class figures in stiff collars analyzing revolutionaries appears a little barmy, somewhat *farfelu*. Gabriel Marcel presents an objection—or rather, what is to him a question: "The revolutionary, as you have defined him in Garine, has, in a sense, long done away with the myth of a goal. I don't think we could say the same of his brothers in arms?"

"Garine," Malraux answers, "does not mean that he has finished with action, but with the myth of Heaven on Earth. Could we not say the same of his brothers in arms?"

Marcel senses misunderstandings about Garine's actions. The essential thing for his hero, Malraux hammers out, is not to know what the end of the revolutionary action will be but what the responsibility will be at that end: "I myself [Garine-Malraux], who am chiefly responsible for my brothers in arms, I must act in this way, because I am linked to them."

Brotherhood defends the revolution against absurdity. Professor Léon Brunschvicg intervenes: "What part does personal choice play in this attitude?"

"Personal choice comes mostly in his [Garine's] previous life," Malraux replies. "From the moment there is fighting, the choice is dictated by the enemy."

The discussion gets bogged down. Brunschvicg makes a conciliatory defense of evolution as opposed to revolution:

"To see the Russian Revolution as a normal revolution, that is to say, as the substitution of a normal capitalist regime by a normal socialist regime, would obviously be an injustice."

Toward the end of the discussion, Malraux reflects further:

But how can we imagine the move from the world of the tsars to the Bolsheviks' attempts at collective life without a revolution? In Russia, what I have called a sacred art is struggling to be reborn, an art that calls on everyone. Birth or rebirth ... Will it endure? ... The essential question seems to me to be this: Are we to continue to look on the life of a divided humanity, where each continues to act in a private domain, or will we, on the contrary, see the birth of a great collective spirit that will sweep away all the secondary problems and reinstate humanity in a domain of quite different concerns?

Despite his pessimism, Malraux falls for utopia. For some readers, the echoes of this debate catapult him into the revolutionary camp. The misunderstanding sticks. For observers on "the Right," Malraux is a nefarious Bolshevik, a claim contested by offended orthodox Communists.

Author with Grasset and editor at Gallimard, Malraux has launched a collection, "Mémoires Révélateurs" (Revealing Memoirs), comprising Byron's *Private Diaries* and *A Life of Napoleon*, reconstituted from texts, letters, and proclamations.[10] Malraux compiled this biography of Napoleon himself while working on his novel. In Saint Helena, Napoleon said, "My life is quite a novel." If a life develops like a good novel, it becomes a work of art. Malraux explores books like a jungle, devours them, and exploits them. His memory is still wholly abnormal, capable of remembering chunks of pages, and, if necessary, inventing a few sentences. For his Napoleon, he drew from the *Mémorial de Sainte Hélène* and the *Correspondance de Napoléon Ier*, including unpublished letters, in the archives of the War Ministry. The antiques dealer, the book lover, the editor, and the author come together; they like to think of themselves as being beyond academic erudition. In a delightful serialization, Malraux's false autobiography of Napoleon rebounds off incidents, anecdotes, and keywords that echo from page to page: glory, victory, greatness, honor. Malraux loves both Bonaparte and the emperor, the conqueror of Europe, a great man, a superman, who, according to the writer, did more to shape the world than to torment it. "One of the first principles of war, Napoleon said, is to exaggerate one's forces, not understate them." Malraux fully adopts this principle in his life. After his excursion to Hong Kong and Macao as a quasi tourist, he set about translating, embellishing, and illustrating his experience. He dreamed of being, and therefore was, a revolutionary leader. Doesn't his character Garine exist so much more than so many living, mediocre subordinates who disappeared in the Chinese revolutionary night?

From August 1930, the conservative *Revue de Paris* publishes extracts[11] of a new novel to appear by André Malraux, *La Voie royale*. Before Malraux really visits Canton, Shanghai, and Peking in the spring and summer of 1931, the serialized preprints start, and they continue until October. The book is to be published by Grasset. It will be, Malraux announces, the first volume of a collection, "Les Puissances du Desert" (The Powers of the Desert), this part being the prologue to what will be a "tragic initiation." The writer's talent, his clarified experiences, and his success produce stunning progress: his characters are no longer symbols but powerful personalities. In *Les Conquérants*, despite their strong presence, they were often symbolic; in *La Voie royale*, they are unusual and cannot be reduced to a handful of concepts. Throughout the first novel, the heroes carry ideas of bolshevism, terrorism, and moderation around with them. In the second, they carry their stories, their unique lives. *Les Conquérants* was written in the first person and expressed successive points of view of the author; *La Voie royale*, in the third person, frees its heroes from abstractions.

The first part is inspired by Malraux's experience in Cambodia. The plot unravels the adventures of a man faced with a destiny shaped by tragedy and, of course, the absurdity of life. Claude Vannec, the archaeologist, remembers his grandfather, an "old Viking," a mythical Alphonse Malraux. A qualified architect, which Malraux isn't, Vannec leaves to discover lost temples in Cambodia. Malraux's manifest curiosity and hidden anxieties are expressed in him. On the liner taking him to Asia, Vannec meets Perken, more of a stateless adventurer than an internationalist, who emerges like a pith-helmeted carnival figure, a blown-up image of the expats Malraux had seen in Saigon and Phnom Penh. Perken works for the Siamese government, but mainly in his own interest. He is looking to buy some machine guns to defend the minikingdom he has carved out for himself in Indochina. How much would he make from temple bas-reliefs? The sum of a few hundred thousand francs evoked by Perken and Vannec—shameless coincidence—is exactly the same as that with which Malraux lured Clara. The two men set off on an expedition to satisfy Vannec's aesthetic sense and Perken's cupidity.

Claude Vannec has most of Malraux's pleasant qualities, but Perken doesn't have all his faults. Perken is looking to find a friend kidnapped by a minority tribe from a high plateau in Indochina. Malraux follows the two men's progress, with their escort, through Rousseauesque landscapes, rare descriptive passages for the author. As if against his will, he dwells on absorbing description, pieces that have been extremely popular choices for university translation exams: "Above the trees, large birds took off heavily; the men had hacked their way up to a wall. It was now easy to find the door and thereafter one's bearings. They could only have strayed toward the left; following the wall on their right would do it. Reeds and thornbushes came in against his foot. Claude jumped to his feet." The sun is shining. The men advance through the triple-layered jungle; a dark light filters through. Fear becomes absurd, and absurdity becomes frightening. The sweating world around Vannec and Perken makes their path difficult, far more than it was for André, Clara, and Louis Chevasson. Malraux embroiders on his experiences. Perken is in no way Louis, and there is no Clara. Indeed, she takes it badly, not appearing in the book. Malraux still seems incapable of including a real or imagined feminine character in a work of fiction. He finds it hard enough to place them in his own life. Malraux's naive conscience pushes him to write a provocative confession: "any adventurer is born of a compulsive liar." The young Vannec has achieved more than a contemporary Malraux has: he has published articles on Asian art, the same scholarly works that Malraux claimed as his own in interviews during his trial. In the confrontation between the author and his creation, there are moments of lucidity. Malraux describes Vannec as having "a way of thinking so concise that it becomes obscure." Concise, imprecise, or confusing in Malraux's case?

The novelist settles certain grudges. In a justification of Malraux's Banteay Srei expedition, Vannec has a discussion with members of the École Française d'Extrême-Orient in which he is more aggressive than Malraux was in Hanoi. "In twenty years, your department has not explored this region," Vannec says. "Doubtless you had better things to do, but I know the risks and I want to face them." Malraux drags along the accusations held against him, but the risks he took justify his bending the rules of legality or morality. The novelist projects his future into Vannec's past; Malraux is still thinking of constructing a great work on painting and sculpture. He has abandoned the idea of a history of art, an activity that often sounded ludicrous to him and to which his patience is not suited. He has heard Groet talk of a class he gave in Germany on the psychology of art. Malraux-Vannec has finely honed ideas about the places where works of art are exposed: "I see museums as places where the works of the past are sleeping; they have become myths, living on a historical life as they wait for artists to bring them back to some real existence. And if I am directly touched by them, it is because the artist has this power of resurrection." This absolute view includes relativism: "Deep down, any one civilization is impenetrable to all others. Objects remain, but we are blind to them until our myths concord with them somehow." Isn't this Vannec something of a Spenglerian?

One of the novel's leitmotifs is "You know as well as I do that life has no meaning. Death is there, like the irrefutable proof of life's absurdity." Malraux is convinced that the sentence "life has no meaning" *has* a meaning. What if it is simply the expression of deep but muddled feelings?

What if life, as such, does not exist? Perhaps, outside religious minds, the meaning of life comes down to the meaning that each man or woman gives to his or her own life. But what is the meaning of meaning? Human beings have a right to ask all questions which do not harm others. The undertaking might seem vain or vital. What is essential here for Malraux is the combination of death, life, and absurdity, of fate and inevitability. One cannot disprove the irrational. The world is not absurd in itself, any more than it is blue or is sugary: it just is. Life has a deep meaning for a believer applying or breaking a code of conduct, the Gospel based on the words of Christ, or the precepts of some other religion. A believer is often convinced that from the phrase "God exists," all morality can be deduced. But for some logicians "God exists" is not a proposition, not a meaningful statement. Or again: from a complete description of the world, nobody can deduce a logical or illogical system. Some would also claim that there is not just one proposition from which all true propositions can be deduced.[12] Malraux does not think like a logical positivist. He pecks at Nietzsche: "what is important is not eternal life, but eternal liveliness." The fact remains that, logician or not, a human being can say to himself: my life does not have, or no longer has, a meaning. Even those who deny that there can be an expressible "meaning of life," wonder about it.

In the first part of *La Voie royale*, Malraux takes his adventure in Cambodia and molds it into stirring fiction, through an effective transposition of his experiences. In the second part, the plot turns to the improbable, the theatrical, and the fantastical. Claude and Perken fall into the hands of a rebellious tribe and find the adventurer Grabot tied to a millstone, his eyes gouged out. Claude and Perken are afraid that they too will become slaves like Grabot. They escape. The novel has some gruesome scenes. Perken is wounded by a poisoned dart. Far from a competent doctor and effective medicines, he will die, confronting his death hour by hour, trying with opium to forget it. His "kingdom" has been invaded. He can hear mines exploding, proof that a railway line is eating into his territory. Despite a few purple passages, the ending of *La Voie royale* takes after bad opera.

Malraux gets carried away, but does he carry the reader away? He didn't live through anything resembling his characters' latest adventures. In 1930, in this second part, his imagination is not persuasive. Nevertheless, his book amazes readers and critics alike. This time it's the Goncourt, they think at Grasset. Malicious newspapers mention the misadventures of the "looter." In his choice of subject, Malraux has issued a challenge to his audience. His novel goes far beyond the now-stale anecdotes. In private, he expresses irritation and sometimes doubts, not about his work but about his characters.

René Lalou, English teacher by day and literary critic by night, writes a commentary on *La Voie royale* in *L'Europe Nouvelle*, revealing a work that demonstrates "the authentic power of the human being." "I would have answered you sooner," Malraux writes him, "if I hadn't been pestered by stories about some statues. . . . First of all, you have given a loyal account. I don't suppose you care about that, but I do: it's the first one in about forty articles. May I talk to you seriously? Of course, all it is really about is the matter of myth. There is an objection that you do not make, but you make me make. . . . I wonder if the myth of Perken will be as effective as the myth of Garine. I did not make Perken sympathetic—deliberately— perhaps that's dangerous." Malraux ranks his heroes pretty highly: "Mind you, Julien Sorel, Rubempré . . . I would like to know when we will see each other, what you think about that. And Nietzsche and Dostoevsky. Yours."

With René Lalou and others, Malraux corresponds as he talks, using pithy phrases and allusions: "Mind you . . . the fundamental difference seems to be in this, that Nietzsche accepts history, whereas Perken (what a daring comparison) speaks only for people who are forever separated from the world." How can you mind about an author who compares himself to the greats but describes himself as "daring"? Malraux has the vanity of his pride and the politeness of his own excesses. As if speaking aloud, he follows with general ideas and names: "With Dostoevsky I don't notice it as much, because Grandet pays no attention to time or the future. All the same, I'm wary." Malraux is thinking of posterity: "What's more, if these characters carry on living, it will, alas, be more like Julien Sorel than like Zarathustra. It's a strange question, that of mythical figures who express not a philosophy but a state of sensibility (as in Stendhal, Gide, Fromentin, Barrès . . .). This again. I'll stop—if I were to carry on, I could write another twenty pages and still not be finished. I notice in writing to you that I scarcely know what I really think of myself." Malraux likes Lalou: he gets a doodle of a cat on his letter.

"I scarcely know what I really think of myself": Is that just a coy joke? An attempt to sound himself out? Does Malraux think too fast to know the meaning of what he says, especially when talking about himself? Is it an intriguing half admission? Is Malraux sometimes conscious of his own lack of clarity when turning to face himself? Of an immaturity that is the counterweight, or perhaps the cause, of a creative maturity?

The novel finds a quite respectable place between Joseph Conrad and Jules Verne. Those who like *La Voie royale* do not always differentiate its first part, made out of believable experience, from its second, of imagined savagery. In *Candide*, the right-wing weekly, Auguste Bailly takes a swipe at one of Malraux's obsessions: "The idea of death and man's attitude to death is the basso continuo on which all the orchestration of the work is based; and it is what transforms this adventure novel into a tragic study of an adventurer's soul. Much more than asking for justification of the presence in the world of riches or power, it demands that justification of unknown fathers." Perken achieves neither power nor glory. Vannec has a potential for glory, like the artist who imagined him. He survives for a second part that is never written. In *Le Matin*, Joseph Kessel, a writer who has been around, regards each page as "nourished with the bitter, powerful juices of adventure."

However, despite the preprints in the *Revue de Paris*, the absence of political references in *La Voie royale*, coupled with the tempting presence of communism in the preceding novel, impels some conservative and reactionary critics to condemn the novelist. *L'Action Française* denounces "an approximate style." Some settle into the custom of confusing the writer with the man. Some, bearing old grudges, bring up the attack on the EFEO again. Others explain that there is no Moï tribe on the right bank of the Mekong as the writer claims or scornfully point out that the Stieng are not traitors. Beneath Malraux's luxuriant style, some critics discern an irksome condescension.[13]

Three weeks before the Goncourt is to be awarded, André Rousseaux publishes a venomous interview with the author of *La Voie Royale*:[14] "Is it because I know that André Malraux is an anarchist that I imagine I can confirm his character from his way of receiving me?" Rousseaux starts. "In the same way that some writers represent pure poetry, one could say that pure anarchy is expressed in Mr. Malraux. No faith and very little love. What does that leave?" Without actually holding a red flag in one hand and a bomb in the other, Malraux has "swept away religion, country, morals, society." In the room where Malraux sees him, the shrewd critic spots, "on some wooden shelves, sculpted Greco-Buddhist heads like the ones in the Guimet Museum." Rousseaux wants to talk about Malraux's excavations but is interrupted:

"What do you think of my book?"

"That it's a jolly good adventure novel."

Malraux explains, "I wanted to tell the truth about adventure. First of all, a truth that is simple accuracy. Just as the last war needed to happen before literature could reveal that war is dirty, in the most material sense of the word: mud splashes under your feet . . ."

The writer and the fledgling critic, having talked of adventurers—disinterested and otherwise—of the missionary and of the gold digger, go on to America and Russia, capitalism and communism. "Mr. Malraux declares that if Ford and Stalin, at the end of their day, were to ask themselves what they were here for, they would each be as incapable as the other of giving an answer. I say to him, 'And what about you?'

" 'I have no idea . . .' "

At Rousseaux's insistence, they go over Malraux's trial and his Cambodian misadventure. *La Voie royale* is forgotten. "I break off the interview, I run away, I leave Mr. Malraux, my heart heavy with disappointment. I thought for a moment I was in the company of pure anarchy, and I admired its lucid, dark despair, its horrible and sublime beauty, despite myself. I am afraid now that pure anarchy does not exist—or only in Mr. Malraux's books, but that's literature."

Where is the anarchy in *La Voie royale*? Worried rather than exasperated, Malraux challenges Rousseaux. *Candide* publishes part of his letter; Malraux, who has an elephantine memory, responds three months later in the *Nouvelle Revue Française*, giving his own complete account of what was said.

Pierre Drieu la Rochelle, though younger than Groet, also fought in the war. Eight years older than Malraux, he comes into the author's life in a friendship always surviving political disagreement. A poor student at the École Libre des Sciences Politiques, Drieu fed himself on Barrès and Nietzsche, like Malraux. He was wounded, and in his poems celebrated the brotherhood of heroes, beyond nationalism and nation. He is more tempted by surrealism than Malraux and has flirted with communism. He is obsessed with the idea of a French decline, which he explores in his essay "Mesure de la France." For Drieu, the world has come into an era where the masses are hostile to old civilizations.

He likes to like his friends' works, while retaining a critical stance. In "Malraux, the New Man" he writes one of the best articles, however pompous, to summarize Malraux the writer in a literary context, without leniency. Malraux, he says, "appeared on the European horizon two years ago." He is a member of the international human movement and the international movement of the picturesque. How does he place man, both new and timeless, in his humanity? Man has constant problems: "action, sex, death, which are rejuvenated by each new season; action and death are certainly present in Malraux's work." Drieu is thinking more about himself than about Malraux: sex plays hardly any role in Malraux's books. In *La Voie royale*, sexual references are rare: " '. . . cerebral types,' continued Perken . . . 'there is only one sexual perversion, as fools will tell you, that is the development of the imagination, the incapacity for satisfaction.' " Elsewhere: "An erotic pleasure built up like a slow combat . . ." Not enough to claim that Malraux deals with sex as much as with death. Nor to deduce anything about his sexuality. Drieu published *L'Homme couvert de femmes* five years before *La Voie royale*. "In each generation," states Drieu, "there are some men of this [Malraux's] sort who take the most direct and shortest route to the fundamental questions. The idle discuss whether they are romantic or classical, novelists or not, whether they write according to the rules or don't. But the hungry readers jump on them without prevarication." For Drieu, Malraux remains "a born writer, with a sense of style, with a personal mark—and yet he has an enormous fault, his conciseness, which makes for obscurity."

The relationship between the two writers seems lopsided. They like each other a little or a lot, depending on the year. Drieu admires and, most important, reads Malraux. Malraux reads Drieu little and manifests nowhere his appreciation of his admirer-cum-friend's work. "His novels," Drieu states about Malraux, "are fast, rousing, spellbinding stories, but they are narrow and have one track." In Malraux, Drieu sees a sincere character in whom "the function of writer is subordinate to his concern to be, before anything else, a man. . . . Malraux looks for and finds his balance above all between the fact of being a man and the fact of being a writer." Drieu summarizes those years better than anybody else, Malraux's meteoric course across "philosophical and historical speculation, Asia, Revolution." For Drieu, Malraux "will always lurk in these diverse provinces replenishing his loot; but he will not settle in any of them. Politics, perhaps? Archaeology?"

Drieu is often in the Gallimard offices; he is more accurate than others when he ponders over Malraux's "business activities." He ventures, "I do not know what Malraux did in Asia. I do not know what he was up to, but I believe he tried his hand at many things." Does this refer only to some stolen statues exported from Cambodia? Drieu is no fool, but he is not an informer either. He also addresses Malraux's literary mutation, the disappearance of the dandy and the aesthete. Drieu is not keen on *Royaume farfelu*, "a collection of prose poems smelling of literary opium."

The writer in Malraux no longer wavers. He still talks of Max Jacob with affection but has moved on from poetic prose in white, black, or fairy pink. Malraux no longer seems to be a literary dilettante. Leaving the affectation of *La Tentation de l'Occident* behind him, he has found a style, a tone—even several—and, with *Les Conquérants* and *La Voie royale*, a certain mastery. There is an unquestionable violence in his writing, which Drieu has not failed to detect. Even though obscurity remains—still according to Drieu—Malraux's experience has become "clear and ordered."

On December 2, 1930, Malraux is awarded the first Prix Interallié. For Grasset, this is small consolation: Malraux and his potential Goncourt are leaving for Gallimard.

Less than three weeks later, on December 20, Malraux's father commits suicide on Rue Lübeck in Paris. Malraux claims that a Buddhist text lay at Fernand Malraux's feet and that, on his father's instructions, he slit open his veins to make sure he was dead. Storytelling still? During his father's wake, Malraux leaves. Why not? Clara is appalled. He later says that his grandfather committed suicide. Mistake or wishful thinking? And why did Fernand Malraux end his own life? Behind his jovial, lighthearted appearance was depression: the source of all his tall stories, at which he was never as talented as his son. Since the 1929 crisis he had been using up his capital. But most important, he had committed a double error: he had courted, with his usual success, the sister of his second wife. Then he gave up the affair. The neglected mistress threatened to "tell everything." She was also involved with a high-ranking official in the Parisian police department. In her own tactful way, she threatened to reveal to the police that Fernand Malraux, while still married to Berthe, had illegally given his name to André's half brothers, Roland and Claude. Fernand got scared.

Tragic lack of forethought, he turned on the gas, without thinking of the risk to the whole building. Fernand Malraux almost failed his death as he had his life. The suicide encouraged his son to respect anyone's choice to take his own life.

CHAPTER NINE

Commercial Traveler

F ROM 1928 TO 1932, Malraux wrote sumptuous novels. Until May 1938, he sat at the oval table of the prestigious *NRF* reading committee, its youngest member, next to Gaston Gallimard, Robert Aron, Benjamin Crémieux, Ramon Fernandez, the commercial manager Louis-Daniel Hirsch, Georges Lecoq, Brice Parain, Jean Paulhan, and Georges Sadoul. Louis Chevasson, towing along, also working for Gallimard, attended meetings as a consultant.

As artistic director, Malraux does his job well, braving writers' moods and respecting Gaston's goodwill. He endures the moaning of the poet Paul Claudel, who complains to Gaston, "Mr. André Malraux promised me in the most definite manner that *Christophe Colomb* would be ready in June. It is now July, and I have heard nothing! I am starting to think that you have abandoned the whole idea of the volume. I have sent you the plates; the American publisher completed the publication in a few weeks; I can only conclude that the *NRF* is not in a position to carry out the publication of this book."[1] Gaston reassures Claudel, "Not a week has gone by without Malraux or myself being in contact with the printer." The publisher tries to calm the poet: "The plates you supplied were in fact tailored to the English text, which explains how the American edition could be finished in a relatively short time. But the length of an English text never corresponds to that of a French text. It has therefore been necessary to make adjustments to the typography and the position of the drawings, which has forced us not only to create a new layout but make a considerable series of revisions . . . three-color printing requires very delicate registration; paper of the form that we are using very rarely falls in exactly the right place on the machine, and the printer has to examine the sheets carefully one by one, to avoid, for example, the black dot of the characters' eyes being even slightly out of place, which thoroughly distorts the expression on their faces. Such meticulous work can be entrusted only to skilled staff, thus Massol has insisted on printing the work entirely himself." Before a considerable author like Claudel, the great publisher deploys all the diplomacy he can muster, pouring out explanations. Malraux, alone, would not yet be up to it.

Malraux contributes to *Marianne* and is constantly in charge of several works; he proves to be an effective beater. He contacts Céline, the now-famous author of *Voyage au bout de la nuit:*[2] "I have received a note from Berl—would you have any objection to letting *Marianne* have the text of the speech you gave on Zola? On another matter, I am sending you *The Artificial Silk Girl,*[3] which I mentioned when we saw each other. Would you agree to write a preface to this volume? I would have done it myself if it hadn't been translated by my wife. If it doesn't interest you, it would help if you could answer soon."[4]

Despite commitments in Paris, Malraux cannot stop traveling. On April 4, 1929, he boards a cargo ship in Marseille with Clara; the voyage is cheaper, and bothersome busybodies are less likely to pop up. Most of all, Malraux knows, a long journey will let him concentrate and write. The first part of the trip, after a short stop in Naples, will end in Persia. In his *Royaume farfelu,* Malraux imagined domes and mountains of amethysts. He says he is obsessed by the Middle East. André and Clara do not just want to browse through ruins and explore museums: they are planning on trading. They keep quiet about that in Paris. In literary circles it is admitted that patrons such as Doucet and writers such as Tristan Tzara, André Breton, Paul Éluard, and Louis Aragon buy and sell pieces, even publicly at the Hôtel Drouot, to expand or complete their African collections. Speculative art trading is part of Parisian literary culture.[5] Malraux plans to make a profit by going directly to the source. Clara too sees nothing wrong with the speculative trading of works of art after difficult research. She approves of this expedition, retrospectively condoning the excursions to Cambodia and Cochin China. Malraux also has to take his revenge: to him, the French justice system stole his pieces from him, no less, after the unfortunate Cambodian expedition. To collect art is to participate in a cultural adventure. To one with no personal fortune, a collection can grow as sales bring profits. The Louvre, the British Museum, all museums have built up their collections more or less by pillaging. This trip should also allow Malraux to deepen his artistic knowledge. Arland is still pushing him to compile a work on painting.

Neither André nor Clara is impressed by Istanbul. The Soviet port of Batoum stinks of vodka and tobacco. The Malrauxs take the train. In Baku, the burgeoning oil industry suggests an idea for a novel. The Mal-

rauxs cross the Caspian Sea and disembark in Persia, hiring a car and
driver. They cannot drive, and they will need a guide. Ispahan charms
them. By day they go on tourist trips. In the evenings they look for sculptures in antique shops. Malraux gets into theological discussions with the
French consul, Brasseur, who is interested in Sufi mystics. The Malrauxs
cover Iraq and Syria. They leave again for France with more than just
memories: actual souvenirs. They place their objets d'art in storage. One
year later in the spring, with the same intentions, Clara and André pass
through Turkey and find their way back to Ispahan. They engage in
the same artistic and commercial activities. They seem to go together
perfectly.

The Malrauxs have seen the Indian Ocean, the Red Sea, and the
Persian Gulf, and they send their news to Louis Chevasson: "There are
no postcards in Batoum or Tiflis or Baku or Tehran or Ispahan. . . . We
didn't go to Trebizond. . . . In Ispahan, the dyers' market is full of white
cats with yellow, blue, or red heads. . . . And the lambs are dyed pink, with
pompoms."[6]

The same year, Gaston Gallimard opens the NRF Gallery. The headquarters are moved to Rue Sébastien-Bottin with the publishing section of
the company; the main warehouse is on the Boulevard Haussmann. The
gallery presents an exhibition of "Gothico-Buddhist" art with the pieces
brought back by Malraux. A cryptic notice by the writer intended for public consumption indicates that the forty-two heads exhibited without body
or torso come from three sites in the Pamirs. Nobody can check that from
Paris. The Malrauxs did not spend any time in the Pamirs. How could
they have gotten hold of these pieces? Awkward customers from archaeological circles reckon that forty-two pieces—mostly heads, Buddhas, faces
of women or young men—is a lot for one amateur archaeologist to discover. But, as Gertrude Stein would have put it, Malraux is Malraux is
Malraux. Repairs to a forehead here, a nose there give the collection a
stamp of authenticity. In his notes, Malraux comments on the works. He
makes stimulating but daring comparisons between European Gothic art
and Chinese or Japanese Buddhist art, which leave the experts doubtful
and the uninitiated enchanted or amazed.

A columnist for *Comœdia*, Gaston Poulain, asks Malraux about his
finds.

"I left in June with my wife," explains the writer. "I thought there was
something out there. I looked. I found it."

Poulain: "Have you undertaken any special studies?"

Malraux, without hesitation: "I read Sanskrit, and I'm studying
Persian."

"Did you stay long on the Pamir plateau?"

"Three and a half months."

"And you found all that? . . . Do you think that a scientific mission would discover many pieces?"

"Why not? But it is a terribly dangerous area. Sixty kilometers outside Kabul, you would need machine guns."

"But would you?"

"For me it's not the same, I was a commissar in Canton . . . the armed nomads of the Pamir recognize a man who can handle a revolver or a machine gun."

The journalist presses him. What he really wants is proof. The brilliant archaeologist Malraux was helped by "natives." Poulain is surprised: the heads in the exhibition have all been severed in the same way.

"They were separated by the wind," explains Malraux.

"But they have been removed from the bodies."

Malraux's learned response: "They were destroyed by the Hephthalite Huns."[7]

Did Malraux bring back any photographs of himself on site?

"No, unfortunately not," says the swindling archaeologist.[8]

In university circles and newspapers, to which Malraux refuses to provide further explanation, questions are asked. The writer takes the offensive in a short text: "The exhibition of the objects I brought back from Central Asia has set the mercury climbing, which was predictable. There are those who are surprised to see so many heads without bodies (whereas the Guimet has fewer bodies than we do), those who explain the archaeology while misspelling the locations of the finds. A Monsieur Hiver, better known as a season than an art critic, explains all the relevant geography of the wrong Pamir. Never mind . . ." Malraux presents himself as a distinguished amateur and a known artist. He sweeps away objections: "Those interested in the scientific considerations and the problems they pose will find an account in the works of the French Delegation in Afghanistan on the excavations at Hadda Al-Hadda by J. Barthoux, their director." Malraux mounts a counteroffensive: "Behind the entertaining ghosts who talk of fakes one day and of buying in or looting the next, more vicious adversaries are readying themselves, and I await their arrival with curiosity. It is claimed that these pieces come from the Kabul Museum, which was destroyed by the Revolution. Yet the pieces from Kabul have been photographed in the work I have just quoted." Here is a good technique: an erudite, Hephthalitic allusion followed by a laugh. "As I have already said, if there are only heads, it is because I am still making the feet; and the places I dug in were revealed to me by a seance table. But next year, I'll take a bailiff with me."

The NRF Gallery, a public limited company with a liability of

1,000,000 francs (almost $40,000 in 1931) and shares at 1,000 francs each, is launched by this exhibition. The capital of the publishing section of Gallimard at the time is 2,500,000 francs. The gallery is not messing about. Of the fourteen shareholders, Gaston, Jacques, and Raymond Gallimard hold 80, 60, and 80 shares respectively. The Gallimard bookstore holds 250, and André Malraux holds 20.[9] The goal of this ambitious company is "commerce in all countries, of all art objects, the organization of all exhibitions and public sales," and, in a natural extension of Gallimard's activities, "the publication of artistic reproduction prints of all genres." Malraux has convinced Gaston of the great future of black-and-white and color reproductions. The gallery's statutes also allow for "real estate, movable property, and financial transactions." Malraux effectively becomes the paid secretary, a sort of banking executive with the authority to countersign invoices, both large and small.

The gallery wisely stocks a considerable number of pieces picked up or commissioned by Malraux during his trips: sketches, frescoes, Persian paintings, Mesopotamian objects, Chinese statues, even items of "Far Eastern abstract art," modern watercolors and drawings, and examples of African art. Twenty-nine Persian sketches are held in storage. "Nomadic objects" have been bought for 37,200 francs ($1,475). A profit of only 500 percent is anticipated on those. The gallery's warehouses also hold two imperial bracelets, twenty modern Persian paintings, an Assyrian bas-relief, three protomes, two Hittite Chaldean lions, a Hittite snake, seventeen Babylonian, Sumerian, and Chaldean plaques . . . The gallery is waiting to receive thirty more Persian frescoes and twenty-five seventeenth-century Chinese drawings, items paid for in Mossul. The gallery also invests in Jean Fautrier, a painter Malraux admires, and, from 1934, in some Soviet painters, without counting on making a profit. These works are used in the exhibitions with a more prestigious, less commercial orientation. As of December 3, 1931, the stock includes sixty-two "Greco-Buddhist" and "Gothico-Buddhist" items, valued at 920,000 francs ($36,500). The gallery is counting on a profit of half that again. But the crisis of 1929 has shaken collectors and the art markets as a whole. If the stock had to be put up for public sale, the company would make a profit of only 200,000 francs ($7,900).

To make substantial profits, one must invest skillfully and balance out one's stock.[10] Three categories of objects must be established: first of all, low-priced items, which may be used to make up a collection and exhibited abroad; then pieces of diverse value, exhibited, then deposited with foreign agents, usually Americans; and finally pieces of great value, salable "only to museums of the highest importance or at public auction." For tax reasons, the NRF Gallery must not allow profits to show in its accounts, a common practice especially in the art-trading world. Auditors, including the helpful Louis Chevasson, see to it that the books are kept correctly and the balance sheet is coherent. The bank allows an overdraft. A company headed by Gaston Gallimard must remain solvent. The gallery's shareholders receive no dividends, but crates of objects appear and disappear. The shareholders can be paid in kind. French Customs has little control over what comes in and what is sent out. Malraux is practically required to remove some pieces. He is, after all, the gallery's pioneer, and he has some knowledge of archaeology.

Most of the pieces are sold abroad by partners, "the French market being too limited to be considered on its own." The system is widespread and, at the time, legal: you bid high at a sale of your own items, boosting their quoted value, and buy them back; then later they reach more impressive figures at auction. The gallery doesn't always succeed. It has to postpone projects to exhibit in South America and hold off an exhibition planned for the Palais des Beaux-Arts in Brussels. One aspect remains sunny throughout: sales of heads from Asia. For quite some time the gallery's accounts devote particular attention to the Gothico-Buddhist, Greco-Buddhist, and Indo-Hellenic pieces. The dimensions and asking price of the objects are always specified, along with the unofficial reserve price at which the gallery or its honorable correspondents may part with the object. For a Gothico-Buddhist head of twenty centimeters, offered at 27,000 francs, it is advised to let it go, if necessary, at 24,000 francs. But even with these "secured" values, there are risks. A sale is considered final only when a head is paid for, sometimes eighteen months after delivery.

The principal intermediaries of the NRF Gallery abroad are the Stora Art Gallery and the Furst in the United States, and the Flechtheim in Berlin. The financial channels are routine, very respectable: the Stora, for example, goes through the Westminster Forest Bank and the Hanover Bank.

The Stora organizes prestige exhibitions in New York; one features Afghan stuccoes from the Parisian collection. Ninety heads and some statuettes are shown. J. Strzygowsky, art history professor at the University of Vienna, is asked to write a preface for the catalog. The scholar is careful in his digressions on Chinese Turkestan, the Greeks, and Buddhism.[11] He does not write a preface supporting Malraux. The explicit backing of a reputed art historian would have been useful: it might have silenced the "entertaining ghosts" who dare voice suspicions as to the origins of the heads in the exhibition. Strzygowsky talks coyly of pieces "found by Mr. André Malraux." Aesthetically speaking, those brought back from Al-Hadda by Mr. Barthoux are not superior, admits the specialist. Strzygowsky also gives his version of the famous decapitation. These heads were probably cut off by "some tribe or other." The expert devotes him-self to interesting descriptive analyses but does not conform to the Malru-cian Gothico-Buddhist theory. In these squabbles, Malraux protects himself well enough but defends his position badly.

At the end of December 1931, after a successful exhibition organized for Fautrier, Clara and André Malraux return to Persia and Afghanistan. They stop in Moscow and Tashkent. All along the way, they pick up money sent by the gallery. They decide to go around the world, pass through Kabul, and cross the Khyber Pass, so dear to Kipling. They pur-sue their artistic, touristic, and commercial activities in Peshawar, Srina-gar, and Rawalpindi. India amazes Malraux; he is gripped by Benares, Calcutta, Delhi both new and old. They take pieces out of the country, avoiding Customs with or without baksheesh. Malraux also does some tenuous artistic reconnaissance in Burma and Malaysia. He goes back to Hong Kong and eventually visits Canton, Shanghai, and Peking. Signifi-cantly, at the Hôtel des Wagons-Lits in the capital, Malraux works on a novel set in China. The Malrauxs receive 30,000 francs ($1,176) from the gallery for expenses and advances. Business, culture, and creativity go hand in hand like realism and abstraction in the works chosen during this trip.

The Malrauxs hesitate. They decide not go to Korea and head for Japan instead.[12] André has a huge appetite for culture: he wants to see the country and learn from it, enjoy himself and collect drawings and paint-ings from contemporary Japanese artists. The gallery envisages an exhibi-tion in Paris. Malraux makes friends with the painter Kondo. Patient for once, the writer admits that he has neither a general impression nor an all-embracing thesis about Japan. Visiting a Zen temple, he disconcerts his guide by asking if there is a devil living in it. Malraux is interested in Zen and the Ch'an, a "very elaborate" form of Buddhism, according to him.[13] His Japan, his China, and his India are not those of Victor Segalen, Paul Claudel,[14] or Saint-John Perse. He will prove it.

In Paris, the exceptional energy Malraux expends on the gallery's behalf impresses Gaston Gallimard. The writer earns his fee as a tireless prospector and organizer. His journeys entail costs. Between 1931 and 1934, not counting bonuses, he receives 3,000 to 5,000 francs ($100 to $200) each month and benefits from letters of credit of up to 90,000 francs ($3,500). He helps his grandmother Adrienne while out of France by hav-ing a check sent to her from the gallery account.

The richer authors for the *NRF* often have independent means. Mal-raux remains discreet about his resources. But he no longer travels second or third class and no longer takes the Métro or the bus. He eats at good restaurants on the Left and Right Banks of the Seine and munificently takes friends and writers out to lunch or dinner when Gaston suggests he lure them to Gallimard. To close friends, Malraux will sometimes also offer a little Gothico-Buddhist head, like a very big box of chocolates.

More of an amateur than a collector, Malraux does not line the walls of his apartments. His chests of drawers and tables are not covered with statuettes. He likes to vary his decor. When he moves to 44 Rue du Bac, in the Seventh Arrondissement, the few objets d'art that grace the walls are mostly from Southeast Asia. Two or three high-quality pieces stand out better than dozens piled up on top of one another, as in the display cabinets of a museum.

His trade—or traffic—in works of art allows Malraux to clear his debts, some of which date from the two publishing companies he started with Chevasson. Maurice Martin du Gard reports what Valéry told him while looking at a wonderful Gothico-Buddhist head in his living room: "Malraux . . . is a Byzantine barfly. Very curious, and very shady. He was my publisher. He did that awful edition of the *Odes* that didn't sell very well. At least I suppose it didn't, for he was never able to pay me. In the end, after I complained, he gave me that, one of the things he stole in Indochina, I suppose."[15]

The gallery cuts its salaried positions, and Malraux devotes less time to it.[16] As soon as he is no longer the driving force, its sales decrease. He thinks of putting his artistic skills to use in other ways, in publishing again. He no longer has those annoying cash flow problems. Above all, serious literary concerns spur him into action.

Le Roi Coq

CHAPTER TEN

1933

THE CHINA ONTO which Malraux grafts his current work is no longer that of the 1920s, the era of the first battles between the Communists manipulated by Moscow and the Nationalists of the Kuomintang. In January 1932, Japanese warships threaten the Chinese government. As a journalist Malraux perceived—from Saigon—the substantial significance of Asia. The Japanese are advancing, reaching the Great Wall, occupying a part of Shanghai. The League of Nations, Malraux observes, protests to no effect. Gandhi, much admired by *L'Indochine Enchaînée*, has been arrested in India. Nonviolence doesn't seem to be working. Malraux talks less of Gandhi, now on the verge of a hunger strike to protest against an electoral law concocted in London that excludes untouchables. Every time he returns to France, Malraux notices that Europe is no longer the center of the world. The balance of the continent is shifting: in Germany, the National Socialist Party—the "Nazis"—gain 37 percent of the vote and 230 seats in the Reichstag in July 1932, as compared with 133 Social Democrats and 89 Communists. A tripolar Europe is emerging, "Fascist," Communist, and democratic. On one side, the Italian Fascists are thrown in with the Nazis, although the word "Fascist" characterizes an ideology that is repugnant but different. Fascism—Italian fascism—is less harsh than Nazism. In a Germany formed by the Treaty of Versailles, of which Malraux, like Keynes, Bainville, and others, sees the damaging effects, there is confrontation between the Socialists and the Communist Party. Violence becomes the standard medium of political dialogue. The Communists oppose the Nazis, but they also attack the German Socialists, Social Democrats, and democrats, denouncing them as "social traitors." The same sort of thing is happening in France. Aragon, a fanatical Communist sympathizer, proposes to "fire on Léon Blum"; Malraux has sympathy for the Socialist leader.

The French Left regards Germany with dizzy disquiet. As a result, hardly any attention is being paid to the opposition attempting to unite in the USSR. Malraux did protest when the poet Mayakovsky was insulted by the official Soviet press. But along with other noteworthy writers in the orbit of a heterogeneous Left, he fails to react when about twenty Soviet dignitaries, including two companions of Lenin, G. Zinovyev and L. Kamenev, are excluded from the Communist Party, then eliminated— morally and physically—by Stalin. Germany seems close to Paris, while the USSR seems far away and hazy; the former decipherable, the latter enigmatic. Adolf Hitler seems more dangerous than Joseph Stalin.

German intellectuals are fleeing Germany. Thanks to his friend Groethuysen, Manès Sperber, another exile, and Clara (very sensitive to political developments), Malraux follows events in Germany closely, especially after the fire in the Reichstag, for which Communists are blamed. He wants to defend Dimitrov, arrested by the Nazis. He goes to Berlin with Gide. They both ask to see Hitler. They are not even admitted to see Goebbels. Their move has more of an impact on opinion in France than on German leaders.

In March, the first concentration camp, not yet an extermination camp, opens in Germany at Dachau. In Prussia alone, the Nazis arrest 15,000 opponents. Jewish shops are boycotted everywhere. Like all foreign tourists, Malraux has seen the posters on several trips to Germany: DO NOT BUY FROM THE JEWS, KAUFT NICHT BEI JUDEN. The Nazis are obliging enough to post their slogans in several languages: ALLEMANDS, DÉFENDEZ-VOUS CONTRE LA PROPAGANDE JUIVE. The Führer instates his gauleiters and marches on toward dictatorship. Malraux admires the director Fritz Lang for his films and for his refusal to collaborate with the Nazis, despite advances from Hitler.

In Asia, after another fast, Gandhi eventually forces the British government to take measures in favor of the untouchables. A weak consolation for Malraux: nonviolence can then obtain results in the Indian subcontinent. But not in China; nor in Europe, where, underpinned by memories of the butchery of 1914–18, it takes the form of pacifism.

Malraux feels he is a writer in his own right. In Germany the Nazis are burning books in public squares in the name of "moral order." Soon a single party will be governing in Berlin: this shocks French opinion, especially in the center and on the left. A single party has been governing the USSR since 1917, but that doesn't seem to register. The German economy works and is preparing itself for war. The Soviet economy has been enervated by the regime and can neither satisfy the citizens in peacetime nor prepare effectively for conflict—even though the military industry has remained a priority internally. In Germany, there is violent and courageous Communist opposition to the Nazis. Many democrats conclude that the Communists are potential allies of democracy.

Malraux finds the strength he drew on in Saigon: he is ready to fight, sustained by his literary energy. He has worked hard on his new novel, *La Condition humaine*, the third part of his Asian trilogy. The concept of the "series" in itself is all but forgotten; *La Voie royale* was supposed to be the first volume. The Georges Duhamel–Roger Martin du Gard genre of sequel novels does not suit Malraux. He gives this latest work, his most ambitious to date, to Gallimard. A preprint appears in the *NRF* from January to June 1933, ensuring a buildup for the work.

Malraux talks little to Clara or anyone else about his recent bereavements: his father and his mother, who died from an embolism on March 22, 1932. In his own way, he loves his half brother Roland, who thanks to him becomes André Gide's secretary and general factotum. Nothing becomes of Claude. André forgets him. He is sporadically interested in his aunt Marie Lamy; sometimes he sends her a check. He is a public figure, a *voyageur,* he hardly has time for his "nearest and dearest." His attention is turned more toward Humanity in general than close relatives.

In his political life he is drawn into the activities of "anti-Fascist" associations but is reluctant to become a card-carrying member. Chairing a meeting, raising a clenched fist, speaking in the Pleyel and Mutualité political meeting rooms in a resonantly emotional voice, sometimes incomprehensible when he improvises, all this is well and good. But he will not be labeled. Malraux, the unclassifiable, solitary individualist, will stand in solidarity, but he will stand alone. He allows the progressive wave to carry him, but not to carry him away.

In France, he participates in the activities of the Association des Écrivains et Artistes Révolutionnaires (Association of Revolutionary Writers and Artists, or AEAR). Malraux and others are unaware that the demonstrations are organized by infiltrators sent from Moscow, with wily Willy Münzenberg at the head. Münzenberg organizes a conference in Amsterdam, bringing together eleven hundred members. An International League Against War and Fascism is speedily formed, including two totemic figures of French communism, Henri Barbusse and the editor in chief of *L'Humanité,* Paul Vaillant-Couturier. The AEAR recruits more than five hundred members in a few months. André Malraux is not officially one of them.[1] With the help of his brother Roland, he persuades Gide to chair the first large meeting of the AEAR on March 21. The sixty-three-year-old Gide adapts his manner to the circumstances: in the French Freemasonry hall of the Grand Orient de France, with his presence and thanks to his work, he makes a strong impression.[2] Gide liberates many readers, and he seems a corrupter to some critics. His political career has been steady. There are political and social questions in the hedonistic *Les Nourritures terrestres*, as in the anticolonial *Voyage au Congo* and *Retour du Tchad*. In his *Journal*,[3] he says that he would be ready to give his life for the USSR. Malraux delivers a short speech "against Hitlerism." Gide is aware of "certain difficulties" raised by another totalitarian regime but declares that "even if the USSR also [as well as Germany] restricts liberty, it is to allow the establishment of a new society at last." In all the enthusiasm, Jean Guéhenno pronounces that "it is the duty of all artists and writers to state right away which side they are on." It goes without saying that there are only two sides. The audience, which includes the Soviet journalist and novelist Ilya Ehrenburg, is stunned by the theatrical way Malraux raises his fist, shouting, "If there is to be a war, our place is in the ranks of the Red Army!"

Malraux's dramatic phrase implies that they should be seeking closer links with the French Communist Party. Malraux has a staggering talent for inventing catchphrases. Does he really believe that the Soviets would accept volunteers? He uses an incandescent image to communicate an emotion to his already converted audience. His words seem coherent in a binary logic: it's either the Nazis—the "Fascists"—or us. Malraux attacks in a lyrical vein: "For the last ten years, fascism has been spreading its great black wings over Europe. With the exception of France and England, we can say that it holds almost the whole world, save Russia."[4]

Malraux fullfils a fantasy, imagining himself as a uniformed warrior. His taste for geopolitics and the eagerness of his anticipation are manifest. But he does not leave it at that for the rather weakly expressed "Russian difficulties": "André Gide referred just now to the comparison that can be drawn between the *terreur rouge* and the *terreur Hitlérienne* . . ."

To evoke a "Red terror" among Communists is tantamount to sacrilege. But then in France, the *terreur* of the French Revolution has a softening effect if that terror is associated with the Left.

"Yes! We must act," continues Malraux, "and before long take action in blood against blood."

On the right as on the left, blood, usually other people's, comes easily to French intellectuals. Malraux's opposition to Nazism reveals a desire for dignity, which is a theme of the current preprints of *La Condition humaine*. Then he proposes a curious choice of alternatives: "Every artist must choose between two possibilities: to be in the pay of others or to be at their call. Those who are here have chosen to be called, not paid."

When he denounces "German fascism," Malraux foresees war. Everything must be done to stop it happening. Like so many creators, he is at ease in a tragic universe; in denouncing and fearing the war, is he not unconsciously wishing for it? We must fight in order to crush Nazism, but also because, for a temperament of Malraux's sort, fighting is more inspiring than peace. Some adults, like children, think of war as a game. How many would exchange their civil troubles and unease, their personal difficulties for the danger and excitement of combat? Fernand Malraux was happy as a soldier. Life, for some, is simplified when they are called up. If it weren't for the dead and wounded, war would be "pretty," as Apollinaire put it: there are "songs," you get "lots of time off" . . .[5]

The June issue of *Avant-Poste*, a review with a small readership, inquires into the fascist danger in France. Could it take hold here in governmental form? What is Malraux's attitude toward democratic freedoms and their suppression? What are the most effective means of struggle against "fascism"? Malraux answers the questionnaire in writing: "I think that the capitalist system in France will always prefer democracy, as long as it is not threatened by the workers and forced toward fascism. Democracy pays more, pays better, and represents a lesser danger. The current relative weakness of the French proletariat seems to me, then, to rule out an appeal to fascism and allows us to foresee a government . . . of the Clemenceau type, centralized or radical." For Malraux, an element of the French lower middle class is inextricably linked to democracy. The proletariat and the petite bourgeoisie thus allied, he expects "the fighting masses to be set in conflict against fascism." Malraux the sociologist writer expresses no opinion on the elimination of democratic freedoms.

Clara is expecting a child.

"I hope it isn't a boy," says André. "I couldn't bear a caricature of myself."

Florence Malraux is born on March 28, 1933. The Malrauxs choose the name as a souvenir of their engagement trip to Italy. "Flo" is also given the names Adrienne and Berthe in honor of her grandmothers. She is spared "Fernande." Louis Guilloux receives a telegram from Malraux: "LITTLE GIRL. BRAVO SAYS CLAPPIQUE [from *La Condition humaine*]. ALL THE BEST, EVERYTHING IS FINE."

Clara has been causing more provocations and attempting more reconciliations. She is a great advocate of free love and practices (to some extent) what she preaches. At the very least, she needs to be seen with other men, against Malraux, a dangerous game even if her husband does not make women a large part of his life. When face-to-face with the theory, Malraux demurs; but he has his temptations and can give way to them. Throughout her affairs, Clara does not detach herself from Malraux. She accompanies him on his business trips to Switzerland and Belgium and on a cruise along the Norwegian, Scottish, and Icelandic coastlines to the

Spitsbergen Islands. But when Malraux indulges, he feels distanced from his wife.

Another questionnaire appears in *Le Droit de Vivre* in September, circulated by the Ligue Internationale pour la Lutte Contre le Racisme et l'Antisémitisme (International League for the Struggle Against Racism and Anti-Semitism). Calling on Henri Barbusse on the left, Henri de Kérilis on the right, and Malraux and others in between, the questionnaire focuses on the notions of authority, nation, and race. For Malraux, authority alone "does not entail anti-Semitism." It is not dictatorship as such that is anti-Semitic but its content: "Hitler is an anti-Semite, Lenin was not." He also supposes that "Anti-Semitism in France is a subordinate idea. . . . It is not because they were Jewish that the Jews were attacked during the Dreyfus affair[6] but because nationalist propaganda portrayed them as enemies of the army." The problem was apparently military, not racial. According to Malraux, "the only way the Jews have of fighting [racism] is to join loyally with one of the two forces that are opposed to the racial idea: democracy and the proletariat." Malraux shares a received idea, long held by the Left, that "the workers" are less racist than the middle classes. Opinion polls demonstrating the contrary come only later. He is as ready to believe in the proletariat as the vehicle of progress as he is in communism. Clara finds fault with his fast analyses. She can joke about it: "You can say a lot of things about Malraux, but not that he is anti-Semitic. And goodness knows I gave him enough cause."

Claudine Chonez arrives at Malraux's house on Rue du Bac to interview him for the July issue of *Le Rempart*. It is an old building with a tall gate, a minute away from the Gallimard offices. She remarks on the tall whitewashed walls, contrasting with the black of the library desk. There are "two or three admirable Cambodian sculptures," which she duly admires. Malraux walks with an elastic step, hair flopping over his forehead, a pale face with active features. He would look like a "romantic poet" if his clear, icy gaze was not fixed "well beyond himself." His tone is "deep and concentrated, his voice metallic." How does he carry off that "union of thought and action" going on within him?

"Thought does not feed on itself," he answers. "If thought digs down into thought, it finds emptiness, a Buddhist nothingness. No, outside metaphysics, the only valid thought is that which is built solidly on raw materials. . . . It happens that my own raw material is action, adventure. But I do not give it preeminence."

He continues, "For schizophrenics, it might be a dream; for a romantic . . . a love story. The source is not important. What interests me is what each man can make of it. And what he can make of it depends on the depth to which he has committed himself."

Which "lever" has acted on his "thought" with the most force? asks Claudine Chonez.

"Politics," answers Malraux, "in the wider sense, politics beyond France. I can't see myself as a member of Parliament, defending my electoral district in the corridors of the Palais-Bourbon."

No party card, no electoral district. During the interview, Malraux refers to the small Javanese island given to him by his friend Eddy Du Perron, to whom he has dedicated *La Condition humaine*.

Louis-Daniel Hirsch at Gallimard, assisted by Chevasson, orchestrates the launch of the novel. The first printing is big: 25,300 copies. By May 10, there are 8,130 books in bookshops and depositories, 1,200 in train stations, and 400 dispatched by the Overseas Department. In the space of twenty days, restocking demand rises from 81 to 276 copies a day: a good sign. Gaston Gallimard campaigns for the Goncourt, banking on Malraux. Gaston skillfully woos the members of the jury. He doesn't stint on personal notes, phone calls, and dinners. He is publishing an obviously indispensable recipe book by Marie-Claude Finebouche, wife of Jean Ajalbert, a member of the Goncourt jury. Gaston encourages Roland Dorgelès to appeal to Léon Hennique, the president of the jury. Hennique expresses regret at "Malraux's Communist leanings."

"He may not always be a Communist," interrupts Dorgelès, "but he will always be a great writer."

The jury meets on Thursday, December 7, 1933, at Drouant's restaurant in the Place Gaillon, in the absence of Hennique and Lucien Descaves, who vote by proxy. There is a four-round ballot. Malraux wins by five votes: Joseph and Séraphin Rosny, Jean Ajalbert, Roland Dorgelès, and Hennique.[7] Three votes go to Charles Braibant for *Le Roi d'or*, one to Paul Nizan for *Antoine Bloyé*, and one to René Béhaine for *La Solitude et le silence*. After the congratulations, the mediocre petits-fours, the excellent champagne, the rush of photographers, the lightning interviews, the "Mr. Malraux, if you don't mind, a little more to the left," after the small talk at Drouant's ("I knew it," "You look tired, Edmond") and at Gallimard ("It was a sure thing," "What a dreadful dress"), Malraux, looking tense, serious, and prophetic, reads a short speech, which is filmed:

It is customary, after receiving a literary prize, to explain why and how everybody will like the book one has written. I want no misunderstanding about mine. I have tried to express the only thing I feel strongly about and to show some images of human greatness: *having met them in my life, in the ranks of Chinese Communists* [my italics], crushed, murdered, thrown into boilers alive [a good old Malrucian claim, quite false], and destroyed in every way; it is for these dead that I write. Those who put their political passions before their taste for greatness should keep well away from this book; it is not for them.

Upon which the thirty-two-year-old prizewinner signs his piles of books, wrapped in the traditional paper strip bearing the words "Prix Goncourt." His statement is shown in newsreels. Malraux discovers the power the "talking pictures" can have to illustrate and serve a writer's career. His feverish silhouette is unsettling; a character is created by the halting delivery, the rough handling of cigarettes. Reinforcing his reputation as an adventurer and a man of action, he announces that he is preparing a "run" by air.

As a play—although the novel is more cinematic than theatrical—*La Condition humaine* would be in seven acts: I: In Shanghai, the Chinese Communists prepare an uprising. II: It happens. III: To keep Chiang Kai-shek happy, Moscow abandons the Communists. IV: The leader of the Kuomintang escapes from an assassination attempt and crushes the terrorist revolt. V: Organization of repression. VI: Repression, torture, massacres. VII: The survivors reflect.

Malraux is master of his plot, aided by a dense style and sudden, spasmodic developments. The filmic technique of the novel stands out; the rapid transitions from one location to another, like a sequence of shots, are more effective and give more pace than the techniques used in *Les Conquérants*. Movie producers and directors see this: adaptation proposals rush in, some from Moscow. Complicated negotiations begin with Eisenstein.[8] The projects come to nothing. There is more psychology in the book than the author realizes; the work's novelistic treatment of psychology wouldn't work on celluloid.

In *La Condition humaine* Malraux succeeds in synthesizing the symbolic psychology of *Les Conquérants* and the more individualistic psychology in *La Voie royale*. Not a lot of time elapses between the creation of the three novels, but the writer has gained years of experience in the trade. It is as if his skills have precipitated. He has chiseled out individual characters, yet they represent political types, basic but precise. There are the revolutionaries: Kyo, the young, virtuous Communist leader with a touch of Malraux's puritanism, and Gisors—G for Gide and Groethuysen. Paulhan and other elders are in there, too. Gisors the disillusioned aesthete, "conscience" embodied, an opium addict. Groet recognizes himself a little: "To make me believable," he would smilingly say, "Malraux transported me to China and gave me opium." There has to be a female character: May, Kyo's wife, a German doctor. Clara, with whom André's relations are becoming more than stormy, is of German extraction. Her forthright side comes out in May, but not her charm. May tells Kyo that she has been unfaithful to him, just as Clara admitted her infidelity on the boat back from Indochina. The scene of May's avowal takes a vaudevil-lesque situation and raises it to the level of tragedy. Malraux never liked people to talk about this overbiographical passage. He writes to Raymond Aron, "For me, the best passage in the book is not the scene between Kyo and May, it's Gisors and May in front of Kyo's body." Aron has criticized imperfections in the book. Malraux: "What is missing from this book . . . There is plenty missing. But a book is defined by what it is, not what it is not." It's the reverse of his usual apophatic method, the Malrucian mania for defining things by what they are not. "After all, it is a book . . . like the work of Grünewald, like *The Brothers Karamazov*."[9]

The secondary characters of *La Condition humaine* are important to the plot, especially Ch'en, Kyo's terrorist opponent, and Katov, the Rus-sian Communist: bureaucrat of the Revolution, brother of Borodine from *Les Conquérants*. Hemmelrich the Belgian deserter and the German König, Chiang Kai-shek's chief of police, also leave their marks. König's Germanness seems conventional. One protagonist, the clownish, eccen-tric night owl Clappique, reveals a dark and desperate humor in Malraux. Clappique is to Malraux's novel what Falstaff is to *Henry IV* and *Henry V*. The capitalist Ferral, the sympathetic cynic, shows his misogyny when with his mistress Valérie, a sketchy representation of Woman. They attain some level of fictional existence as light comedy characters. The picture of capitalism conveyed by *La Condition humaine* through Ferral is naive, very much of the period. The book finishes on a meeting at the Ministry of Finance in Paris: Ferral delivers a financial report, asking for support from the major banks and the French government. Malraux's socioeconomic thinking is here more crude than cruel. He doesn't use an ideological pile driver, but as a capitalist Ferral could be counted among the demonized "two hundred families" referred to by French Communists.

In his novel, Malraux admits that "Europeans only understand the aspects of China that resemble them." He uses historical and geographical lines to tie his book down. In writing it, he referred not only to stories sorted by Clara in Saigon but also to analytical works by (among others) Louis Fischer, the American columnist, and the Jesuit priest Léon Wie-ger.[10] An idea in *La Condition humaine* is fundamental to the understand-ing of Malraux: "*Ce n'était ni vrai ni faux, c'était vécu*": "It was neither true nor false but what was experienced." Malraux's China is neither true in its detail nor false overall, but it is nonetheless imaginary. Malraux cannot quite break clear of a conventional idea of China with coolies, bamboo shoots, opium smokers, destitutes, and prostitutes. Malraux does visit brothels in Paris with Drieu and Berl, as the fashion dictates. He also saw those in Cholon in Indochina. His Chinese brothel seems rather Parisian. There are not many truly Chinese characters in *Les Conquérants* or *La Condition humaine* either; they are often westernized or mixed race, like the Indochinese Malraux met in Saigon.[11] Malraux sometimes characterizes his Chinese by dressing them up in traditional descriptions: he gives Hong "little Asian eyes," and Ch'en "features that are more Mongol than Chinese." In *Les Conquérants*, his Chinese are often fat, as in many movies. Throughout *La Condition humaine*, they frequently rub their hands in unction. These clichéd views of Asians are rife in France at the end of the nineteenth century and the beginning of the twentieth. From *Les Conquérants* onward, his has been an urban China. He tacks Hong Kong and Macao, which he visited, onto Shanghai and Canton. He allows the reader to imagine a bucolic China with water lilies, abandoned pavilions, a "magnificent, mournful horizon." This is the lover of engravings at work. Malraux doesn't really like the countryside, either European or Chinese, whereas in *La Voie royale* he put superb stress on the jungle—sticky, overpowering, and teeming with insects. Nevertheless, his fictional, imagined China is captivating. His readers recognize the junks, the Chinese characters written in gold, the red signs, the silk, the braids, an expected feeling of exoticism. Malraux mixes revolution and drugs. To see that connection in the 1930s must not have been as easy as it would be today in Asia, South America, or Africa.

In *La Tentation de l'Occident*, Malraux talked of the "China of work," the "China of opium," and the "China of dreaming." Now the first of these arises, more symbolically than realistically. *La Condition humaine* is no tourist guide, it's not a travelogue: the China of work, in the form of actual workers, appears little. Malraux pays attention to the proletariat's demands, but he isn't a sociologist. He presents the magnified world of a revolution in preparation, its confrontation with the West, and its dealings with Chinese "collaborators," the Kuomintang. The latter are an embodiment of the bourgeoisie to fit the standard left-wing mold of the 1930s.

Since Indochina, Malraux's view of China and the revolution has evolved. From 1925 to 1927, he now realizes, China was working its way toward a revolution,[12] and he will impose the Chinese Revolution on the French public: "As for the discovery of the Chinese Revolution, I think that if they [the readers] made it, it is because I was coming back from China," he writes, unabashed, to Robert Brasillach.[13] He should have said, "because I was writing about China." What he describes or writes, he repeats to Clara, ends up coming true. The revolution he describes in his novel is anticipatory, going beyond a revolt, a riot, or a civil war. As coeditor of *L'Indochine* Malraux felt a reformist's reticence when faced with the idea of revolution. In *Les Conquérants*, revolution is used as a platform for the psychology of the revolutionaries, their political questions and answers, and their views of nationalism, terrorism, and communism. *La Voie royale* makes no space for politics or social themes. In *La Condition humaine*, revolution becomes historical and morally inevitable: Malraux adopts revolution, accepts the necessity of it and an obligation for him to march with the revolutionaries.[14]

Kyo's views run counter to Malraux's. Revolution, even if it fails, brings meaning to men's lives beyond absurdity. Kyo seems more human and optimistic than Garine. Man is the measure of man, states the novel; he must conquer his own dignity, "the opposite of humiliation." The writer, here, is ahead of the man: Malraux continues to allow people to believe that he was an eminent member of the Nationalist Kuomintang.

Unique among significant French writers at the time, Malraux is interested in the technical problems of revolution. Borodine, the psychologically inflexible "conqueror," strutted about as a professional revolutionary. In *La Condition humaine*, the qualitative treatment of feelings and theories is built on quantitative considerations of the means available. To transform a revolt into a revolution, Malraux states, count must be taken of one's armed units, cyclists, rifles. He describes in voluptuous detail three hundred revolvers to be seized from a ship and the millions of American and Chinese dollars destined for the Nationalists. Malraux the writer comes across as a specialist on the coup d'état and a technical expert on revolution, a cross between Clausewitz and Georges Sorel. In Saigon, he would only glance at the stories on events in China. The rebels, he knows, were adept at setting barricades, very ready with their slogans, but lacked weapons, grenades, and tanks—the appropriately mythical armament from Fernand Malraux's military service. "The disadvantage for the proletariat . . . most of the insurgents, with rare exceptions . . . do not know how to use the weapons . . . machine guns and artillery." It's the paradox of revolution: it starts as a civil venture and halfway through becomes the business of professionals.

As a novelist, Malraux's eyes are on the Chinese Revolution; as a French citizen, he looks to the revolution in Russia. Awareness of Stalin's "eliminations" has started filtering through to France. Malraux doesn't align himself wholeheartedly in one direction. Once he has decided which side he is on, although not a believer in half measures, he behaves with restraint. He talks in public of the "Red terror," but as a passing detail, certainly regrettable but inevitable. He does, however, stick his neck out to defend the exiled Trotsky. In *La Condition humaine*, the writer is inclined to favor Kyo, betrayed by the Comintern. Soviet critics see this as a symptom of revolt rather than sympathy for revolution. The novel also seems to them lacking in humanity, whereas, unusually for Malraux, there is a tenderness at the surface: "If one believes in nothing, especially if one believes in nothing, one has to believe in the qualities of the heart." Malraux's favorite heroes are driven to transform the world more by criticism than hatred. This is why he follows not Marxism and Communist theory but the Communist movement. Malraux comes fully into his own in seeking and offering comradeship. The paths he followed in Indochina, events in Europe, in his fiction and his life, are pushing him toward the Communists: men are still more important than doctrines, the brotherhood of combatants more fundamental than militant theology.

In a letter to the American critic Edmund Wilson,[15] Malraux unwisely revives his legend: "I went to Asia at twenty-three, as leader of an archaeological project. Then I abandoned archaeology, organized the Young Annam movement, then became commissar in the Kuomintang in Indochina and eventually in Canton." Malraux goes into detail: "In Canton in 1927 [more likely 1923 or 1925: things were different in 1927], there were noticeably more revolutionary adventurers than Marxists. And when Borodin talked with Sun Yat-sen there was never any question of the class struggle [implication: I know because I was there]." Referring to an article by Wilson in *The New Republic*, Malraux continues, "It is quite true that the role of objectivity in my books is not placed in the foreground and that *Les Conquérants* is an "expressionist" novel, like (with due allowances) *Wuthering Heights* or *The Brothers Karamazov*." Often more lucid about his books than about his life, Malraux concludes, "You say quite rightly that *La Condition humaine* develops certain ideas that are implicit in *Les Conquérants*. And also that it is a better book (at any rate, it is the only one I truly like). My way of constructing could not be compared to that of a writer like Morand: his types come from ironic observation, mine from the need to render a certain order of ethical values through the characters." The Paris correspondent for *Izvestia*, Ilya Ehrenburg, later declares that *La Condition humaine* is not a book about "revolution." It is, as Malraux explains, an X-ray of the author, "distributed by fragments in several passages."

The usual political divisions are disturbed by the book's critical success: Léon Daudet, squarely right-wing, says he is "enthralled by the beauty of the work." With *La Condition humaine*, Malraux reaches the status of a novelist who (almost) doesn't need reviews for his books to sell. Sixteen countries are planning translations. In the United States the novel is a success, more than in Great Britain.

André and Clara Malraux have been married for thirteen years, and the relationship is falling apart.[16] In addition to general wear and tear, Clara feels dispossessed of her self. She has served, encouraged, even sometimes ornamented her husband's impressive lies. Her activities seem to be subordinated to André's fame. Already in Cambodia, she accused him of misogyny. She contributed to the paper in Saigon, anonymously, then translated a few books. She has not yet written any. As much as Groet, she has influenced Malraux's political evolution. She feels "further to the left" than he. What can she do to draw level with him—or overtake him? After the supreme honor of the Goncourt, at which a certain pretty Josette Clotis was distantly present, a bad-tempered Clara attacked André:[17]

"You were the center of everything."

Malraux: "My dear, nobody's preventing you from getting the Prix Goncourt."[18]

The Berls, and those who take André's side against Clara, convince themselves that she has not forgiven him for writing *La Condition humaine*. What Clara cannot excuse is her husband's narcissism and selfishness. She can accept that he's a yarn spinner, because in her eyes he is still a genius. At the birth of her daughter, Clara remarked, "Now, that's something you can't do!"

Malraux is happy with his daughter, but not excessively so. Is he hiding the emotion of having his first child, typically for a man of his age and class? He does not give her the bottle, nor change her diapers. But with pride, he later helps "Flo" take her first steps.[19]

There are affairs. Why should Clara deprive herself? The Malrauxs do not play the "Who started it?" game. They do not, as Sartre and Simone de Beauvoir did, construct a pseudo-Kantian theory of necessary love and contingent affairs. Since his marriage, Malraux has cautiously had a few romantic flings, with more fling than romance, without Clara knowing or without her being offended. During his *annus mirabilis*, 1933, Malraux spreads himself thinner. He is attracted to two women,[20] both different from Clara, intellectual, cosmopolitan, and passionately committed. While traveling with Clara, Malraux writes to Josette Clotis in a playful mood, "If you want to see penguins,[21] don't go to the North Pole. You get to a great big glacial landscape covered in black rocks, in front of a mine with a hundred and sixty Russians doing not a lot, while listening to forty more playing the balalaika. . . . 'The auks [penguins],' you say very firmly. 'But sir,' says the chap, highly embarrassed . . . 'you've got the wrong pole. Here, we only have penguins. The auks are at the South Pole.' And it's true. Which just goes to show that disappointment is not limited to Beaune-la-Rolande." Josette's parents live there.

Josette Clotis sent a manuscript novel to Gallimard. Refused at first, it was mistakenly sent to Roger Martin du Gard, who thought well of it. It is to be published.[22] Josette has been courted by several writers at Gallimard and at the offices of the weekly *Marianne*, where she is assistant to Berl; she decides to go for the jackpot, Malraux. To her surprise, he notices her. Josette often talks about how essential it is for a woman to be a sexual being, how she should not be forced to wait, and of "this sham of keeping young women locked away." She will not be outdone by Clara. Down with frustration, down with the "tied-down woman"! Beautiful and soothing, unlike Clara, Josette takes Malraux to the Hôtel du Pont-Royal, then to the Hôtel du Palais-d'Orsay, handy for Malraux because the Rue du Bac and Gallimard are so close. They discreetly hold hands in taxis. The revolutionary author benefits from the convenience of adultery in a bourgeois setting and the tolerance of the French when it comes to hotel registration. He writes "M. et Mme. Perken" or "M. et Mme. Ferral." Josette still thinks about her novel but would much prefer to be in the movies.[23] Clara, the intelligent spider, judges it wise to catch her husband's mistresses in her web; she has no doubt that she will smother the Josette butterfly. Clara allows her to come to Rue du Bac. Gazing at Florence in her crib, Josette says, "I'd like to have a small child like that too."

Clara thinks of her brother-in-law: "Then go and see Roland instead."

Josette is awed by Clara but thinks her badly dressed. And Clara doesn't keep her apartment well. Ambitious and resolute mistresses consider themselves superior. Josette's detractors see a lower-middle-class girl from Beaune-la-Rolande.

The other woman in Malraux's life, Louise Levêque de Vilmorin, writes more masterfully than Josette Clotis. Louise comes from a family of famous seed merchants and claims to be of noble lineage. She is descended, she says, from Joan of Arc, a heroine to impress André more than herself. Antoine de Saint-Exupéry figures among Louise's lovers: some worship her from afar, some she sleeps with almost absentmindedly (men, poor oafs, are like that) or as the mood takes her. Louise's friends are conservative or reactionary and snobbish. They disapprove of her seeing this Malraux; he's talented, granted, and an adventurer into the bargain, but he's a friend of the Bolshevists. She finds André amusing when he reads her palm. Louise turns frivolity and flippancy into an art form. She met Malraux in the middle of the year.[24] Charming, beautiful, whimsical, with one eccentric side and another sophisticated, limping elegantly, she enchants Malraux. She also flirts with Gaston Gallimard. One shouldn't keep all one's charms in one smile. She has given an embryonic manuscript to Malraux: "I am very pleased," he writes. "You have a real talent. I skimmed through at first, and I wasn't sure. About the means, there is a lot to say [which allows him to say nothing]. Then I read it all: that first impression was not worthy (it was empty of content, the same impression I had from that painting at your brother's) [André de Vilmorin, the man closest to Louise]. But it is not that at all. There is a particular universe, without doubt. It's very good. I shall typeset a passage and send you a proof and you'll realize. . . . After adding some most necessary punctuation marks [Young lady, punctuation is not optional!], I had Drieu read it [Drieu has published *Une femme à sa fenêtre, Le Feu follet* . . .], and he also finds it excellent." In a flattering flourish, Malraux adds, "I will have Gide read it, preserving your anonymity—until you tell me not to. Don't go racking your brains for a plot, whatever you do. This dispersion is what makes it. . . . I shall have little practical things to tell you when you come back [Louise lives with her husband and daughters in the United States, out on a limb], but this is the only important thing: do not think that you can find what you have to say. It will get said, but only if it is not explained in advance. You have to have the same self-confidence as when you swim."

Louise's marriage with Henry Leigh Hunt, if it was ever really on its feet, is tottering on the ropes. She divorces, leaves Hunt and their three girls in Nevada, and comes back to Paris. Malraux is waiting for the last pages of her novel, *Sainte Unefois*. While Malraux and Louise de Vilmorin are still seeing each other, on and off, Louise forgets to mention—what can she have been thinking?—another lover, Friedrich Sieburg, German journalist and author of *Is God French?*, who stays permanently at the Ritz. A little before the Goncourt, there is gossip in Paris. Why should Malraux have it all? Some kind soul tells him about the Vilmorin-Sieburg affair. Free love? No thanks, and not with me: Malraux breaks it off. Three women to run away from, Clara, Louise, and Josette. Travel is a cure for women. Sometimes. Behind him, Malraux abandons an exasperated wife and two mistresses, one worried, the other indifferent.

On December 9, 1933, *Toute l'Édition* prints a declaration by André Malraux: "I am leaving on January 8 on a reconnaissance run to Africa. I want to try to pinpoint an unknown city, the capital of a lost civilization whose rough location I know."

CHAPTER ELEVEN

The Queen of Sheba

IN JANUARY 1934, the governor of the French coast of Somalia in Djibouti receives a letter from the Second Political Affairs Bureau at the Ministry of Colonies (Continental Africa and Madagascar), regarding two pilots, Chales and Corniglion-Molinier, and "the writer André Malraux".[1] It is stamped "Secret." They intend, on January 10, 1934, to undertake a "tourist trip by air toward Djibouti and possibly Addis Ababa."

The minister has looked into these individuals. Malraux has said that his "pilots will be Captain Chales [sic] and Cornignior-Hatigné [sic], the war companion of Guynemer."[2] The governor has "no particular comment to make about the two pilots, but as for Mr. Malraux, the most cautious reserve is necessary." It will not be necessary to keep the latest Prix Goncourt laureate under constant surveillance, but the governor "ought to know that Mr. Malraux's behavior was far from commendable during his stay in Indochina in 1924–5." Malraux is still a hot potato, ten years after the Cambodia episode. "Moreover, the writer made strong contacts with extremist groups." Malraux's reputation far exceeds the salons of the Boulevard Saint-Germain and the circle of Louise de Vilmorin's friends. The governor is to report on his activities. In Malraux's personal preparations for the expedition, there is no mention of any Chales or Challe. Political and police archives are often behind the facts, or ahead of them, their information rarely reliable or even plausible. At the Information Office, the Malraux file grows unintelligently and inaccurately.[3]

Malraux has many reasons to leave Paris, France, and even Europe. After his archaeological and journalistic adventures, he wants to turn a new leaf in his dealings with others—and himself. In his research, he needs to hold his own against experts. At home, the situation with Clara is now excruciating. Even with Florence's sweet presence, Malraux is maddened by family life. Clara runs off to Rennes and Bordeaux but is no calmer for it. Unfaithful but gentlemanly, her husband sends flowers to the Rue du Bac. Clara is furious. She threatens to commit suicide as if announcing her intention to go for a walk. But more conclusively, a trip abroad will feed Malraux's imagination. His will be the unknown lands, the unexplored ruins, the far-off revolts and unheard-of or failed revolutions. A writer such as he is always on the lookout for settings, characters, and atmospheres, a story or a novel. He does not see himself as an indoor author, wrapped up in a plaid rug like Gide. Moreover, he has a reputation as an adventurer to maintain. Jungle explorer yesterday, aviator today.

At the time, pilots enjoy understandable prestige: they are the conquerors of the earth and the skies, almost like warriors: Lindbergh conquered the North Atlantic in 1927; Guillomat, Saint-Exupéry, and Mermoz are called "crusaders of the South Atlantic." Hélène Boucher is referred to as *l'Amazone*. Saint-Exupéry's *Courrier sud* came out in 1928, *Vol de nuit* in 1931. Malraux's aerial temptations follow the trend, adding an original "archaeological" note. Malraux is looking for exploits and heroism.

Malraux stores up literary references, from the Bible to Flaubert and from that adventurer enthroned in unsurpassed legend, the English ex-colonel T. E. Lawrence. If *he* had seven pillars of wisdom, it's time for Malraux to build another for himself. He is fascinated by Lawrence and will often repeat the story of his meeting with the colonel in a famous hotel in Paris or in London or on a business trip—anywhere! He has never met Lawrence, but he has imagined him, so it is as if he has—neither true nor false, but "experienced" in the superior reality of historical fantasy. More and more frequently, his truth is catching up with and overtaking reality. He simply has to convince others and then himself, or vice versa. Lawrence also loved archaeology and Dostoevsky and Nietzsche via *The Brothers Karamazov* and *Zarathustra*. Gide and Malraux have discussed Dostoevsky many times. Gide feels that "Dostoevsky's novels, heavy with thought as they can be, are never abstract. They are rich in contradictions, they put mankind on trial." *La Condition humaine* also presents a breathless world, judged by communism and terrorism. Malraux's brief is to change the world by describing it.

Malraux is still obsessed by the Middle East and sees it as his literary hunting ground. He has mentioned to Gaston Gallimard a *History of the Persians* in several volumes.[4] He could be the architect of the work, with a few contributions from his own pen. But in the meantime, he has a less general and more concrete project. Jacobsthan, a German whom Malraux had met in Afghanistan, told him of buried treasures lying under the ruins of the supposed capital of the queen of Sheba, in Mareb, near Sanaa in Yemen; mountains of gold to be found. At the age of thirty-two, Malraux remains an adolescent who thrives on danger, that powerful aphrodisiac. It is not enough to kill off the heroes in his fiction, he must risk his own life. He refuses to be held back by the obligations incumbent on a Goncourt winner.

So off he goes, but not as a tourist on a cruise with wife and family. Guided by the Old Testament and particularly by the Koran, where the queen of Sheba is mentioned, Malraux thinks he just needs to get to Mareb. A recorded adventure, a successful discovery, would compensate for the failed semiadventure in Cambodia. To walk the desert, to experience hunger and thirst, physical exhaustion, and any number of trials, the temptation is irresistible. I am another, I am Lawrence, I am another Malraux. Lawrence could speak Arabic and dressed as a Bedouin. Malraux should do the same and organize the trip with more care than the chaotic Cambodia expedition. No point in applying for orders from the Ministry of Colonies. I don't trust administrative bureaucracy; sometimes I don't even trust myself. Malraux does the research for his expedition at the Geographical Society. There, a confirmed explorer and doctor, Jean-Baptiste Charcot, gives him a warning: the road to Mareb is strewn with the skeletons of amateur adventurers. In Hanoi already, an expert had warned Malraux. Very few who tried ever reached Mareb. One Thomas Arnaud, an eccentric army pharmacist turned grocer in Jedda, walked all the way to Sanaa. He survived and came back with notes on some forty inscriptions from the ruins of Mareb and, apparently, a hermaphrodite donkey for the Natural History Museum in Paris. He returned to Yemen and Arabia on an official mission, bringing back artifacts and publishing the articles in *Le Journal Asiatique* that catch Malraux's obstinate eye. One sentence in particular strikes him: "As I left Mareb, I visited the ruins of ancient Sheba, where nothing is left but mounds of earth." Malraux's imagination runs ahead of him. He would have liked to meet the man who discovered the "treasures of Mareb."[5] He takes it further: those "treasures" become invested not only with undeniable financial aspirations but also with almost magical hopes for literature and adventure. He is looking for Treasure Island. He loves being talked about but loves to write even more. Malraux consults Pliny and Strabo, as well as more contemporary historical and geographical accounts. None of the French and British maps are satisfactory: that *proves* the mystery exists. That is how Malraux works.

An overland expedition doesn't suit Édouard-Alfred Flaminus Corniglion-Molinier. This friend of Malraux's, "Eddy" for short, joined the alpine riflemen in 1914 at the age of sixteen and later became an army pilot. He shot down some Austrian planes. After the war he studied law, worked in aeronautics, and started flying again. There is no point in getting tortured and killed in the middle of the desert, he explains to Malraux. From a plane, they can take impressive photos of the ruins. Clara is fuming. She will be left holding the baby while Malraux sets off after fame again.

Malraux's royalties, both as an author and as an editor, satisfy his everyday necessities and luxuries, but planes don't come cheap. During the war, Corniglion-Molinier met Paul-Louis Weiller, executive of the plane engine manufacturer Gnome & Rhône. Some of the mountain peaks in Yemen reach 3,000 meters. The appropriate plane will need to fly at 4,000 meters and have enough range to cross the Rub'al-Khali Desert and go from Djibouti to Mareb and back again without having to refuel. A Scout's challenge: "Be prepared" to go higher and further, face more danger. A generous but skeptical Weiller lends his private heated airplane, a Farman 190, with a Gnome et Rhône 300-horsepower engine. He also lends them a qualified mechanic named Maillard. Malraux and Corniglion-Molinier, now friends, finish trials in February. Extra fuel tanks are added. In exchange for a series of articles, the high-circulation Parisian paper *L'Intransigeant* lends the quality photographic equipment they need. In Saigon, the shots Malraux handled for *L'Indochine Enchaînée* were poor.

Malraux, Corniglion-Molinier, and Maillard take off without communicating their flight plan to the authorities. There are stopovers in Italy, Libya, and Egypt. After visiting the museum in Cairo, Malraux gives a press conference, as befits a self-respecting—and self-regarding—journalist. Malraux is torn between his love of mystery and the appeal of publicity. With a mischievous glint in his eye, he can't help alluding to the fact that this is not a tourist trip; he discloses the archaeological nature of the expedition. In Cairo as in Phnom Penh, he has a talent for putting his foot in it. As a result, the Cairo correspondent for *L'Intransigeant*, Gabriel Dardaud, laughs his plans off as dangerous and ludicrous. There is a distinctly chilly atmosphere between Dardaud and Malraux, who hates to be taken for a fool.

"You obviously have no idea who the queen of Sheba was!"

"On the contrary. She was the Bedouin inventor of the best depilatory cream for lovely ladies."

Dardaud tells him how the queen seduced Solomon after using a special balm to remove hair from her legs. His advice to Malraux is to go to the Egyptian Geographical Society. There, Henri Munier,[6] a historian and archaeologist, reveals that the queen of Sheba left no trace:

"The queen of Sheba, Monsieur Malraux, come on . . . Why not Merlin? She was only a legend. Millions of men have dreamt about her for thirty centuries, but nothing, absolutely nothing—I'm talking historical fact here—has ever linked the woman who walked out of the desert to trade with Solomon to the Yemen where you seem to think you will find her capital, her palace, and her temples. She disappeared without a trace.

Unless, that is, you go for the Ethiopian tradition whereby the Negus is descended from Solomon, your queen of Sheba's temporary husband."

"But we know the Sabean people have a long history," protests Malraux. "They used to build temples for their gods and dams to irrigate their valleys. They had their own language, I am told, a sort of proto-Arabic, which has been deciphered on inscriptions."

"That has nothing to do with the legend of the queen of Sheba. She met Solomon at the time of his reign, in 900 B.C., but she is mentioned in the Bible only some three centuries later, in the Book of Kings. Three hundred years leaves a lot of time for dreaming, especially when one's aim is to magnify the wisdom of a long-dead monarch. Solomon was not the only one to meet the Sabeans; the Assyrians mention them in their cuneiform chronicles. Teglath-Phalazar in 733 B.C., then Sargon in 715, buy gold, silver, and particularly fragrant resins such as incense, laudanum, and mastic from them, but also horses and camels. As far as the inscriptions from southern Arabia are concerned, the earliest ones date only from the first centuries A.D. They give us the names of three Sabean kings, not that of a queen."

Malraux can't really bluff in front of the erudite Munier.

"But where can we find Mareb?" asks Corniglion-Molinier.[7]

Munier opens the latest issue of the *Revue de la Société Royale de Géographie d'Egypte*: "Here is an excellent paper on the journey to Mareb by the Jesuit priest Father Pedro Paez. He was captured by pirates and sold as a slave and followed his masters on the caravan trails of Arabia. He was the first European to see Mareb; he was later freed and described the ruins, but that was in 1590."

Later, at the bar of their hotel, Dardaud talks to Corniglion-Molinier: "How can you have got yourselves into this: flying over hostile lands, stretching your aircraft to its absolute limit, wanting to take pictures of the ruins of a town that has been dead for centuries and whose exact location you don't know? And neither one of you is a specialist. A simple sandstorm or layer of mist could wreck your plans."

Malraux doesn't let this get him down, no more in Cairo than it did in Hanoi. At the very least, Corniglion-Molinier and he will bring back pictures of a little-known civilization. Malraux is relying on his intuition, improvisation, luck, and destiny.

Diplomatic telegrams in French and English abound; word of mouth resounds. Cairo's cosmopolitan microcosm is buzzing. Giving a press conference in Cairo was about as smart as buying pickaxes in Siem Reap, thinking no one would notice him. Corniglion-Molinier is a replacement for Chevasson, with added panache. Malraux has a flair for securing the services of reliable and brilliant right-hand men. Hassan Anis Pasha, the head of Egyptian aviation, learns of the project. A well-known French writer will make a good dinner guest; everyone gets on well. Hassan Anis Pasha provides a map that is rudimentary but the best so far.

The plane takes off again on March 1, heading south. The three French travelers cannot understand why they receive a cool welcome at the British Royal Air Force base. The Foreign Office is suspicious of all French nationals to the west, east, or south of Suez. The French military in Djibouti are friendly. They are impressed with the plane and with Malraux. They do not share the reservations of the French Air Ministry in Paris, which is wary of creating difficulties with the local powers and the Foreign Office. Malraux is being watched by the authorities, as he was in Cambodia.[8]

The aircraft has to be made lighter, what with the ammunition and weapons on board. The fuel tanks? Essential. How about leaving Maillard—that's 175 pounds . . . But what if they have to land for repairs and face Bedouins armed with Mausers? Malraux prefers to take the mechanic and not have to come down. Malraux likes the plane, which is far superior to a Cambodian truck or buffalo.

The Farman takes off at 6 a.m. on March 7, following the coast of French Somalia, and reaches Moka on the other side of the Red Sea. In order to avoid checks by English and Yemeni agents, Corniglion-Molinier deftly avoids towns. Soon they come to the first mountains, Yemen, the valleys, then scintillating white Sanaa. At 10 a.m., the Farman has used up half its fuel. The explorers catch sight of an "expanse covered in colossal stones." There's no doubt about it, they decide, here must be what they are looking for, the city of the queen of Sheba. This is where it should be, so this is it. They take a few dozen photos. Some Bedouins shoot at the plane, adding spice to the adventure. The level of fuel is getting low: Maillard is worried and insists they go back. Malraux scribbles on a piece of paper the words "I believe we goofed up."[9]

The wind picks up. The plane's speed reaches 125 mph. Knowing they cannot get to Djibouti, they fly back over the Red Sea. A stroke of luck—they manage to land on a strip in Obok on the Gulf of Tadjoura. A French Colonial Infantry officer is delighted to welcome them. They get back to Djibouti, and Captain Corniglion-Molinier, at 7 p.m. on March 8, sends a telegram to *L'Intransigeant*: HAVE DISCOVERED LEGENDARY CITY OF SHEBA ON NORTH LINE OF RUB' AL-KHALI STOP TOOK PICTURES FOR INTRANSIGEANT STOP SINCERELY. Legend becomes history. Then all there is to do is to make this mixture palatable, without getting weighed down in geographical doubts, historical scruples, or fine geological distinctions. Taking serious risks warrants some simplifications. Neither true nor false, the city of Sheba, but experienced by a writer, a pilot, and a mechanic, the last having no opinion on the matter. The kite is intact; Mr. Weiller will be happy.

Then an improbable but delightful episode, straight out of the Bible, the Middle Ages, and the twentieth century: the Ethiopian consul contacts Malraux and Corniglion-Molinier. The king of kings, the Negus, Haile Selassie himself, wishes to see them. This flattering invitation is an order. According to official protocol and legend, His Majesty is the descendent of Solomon and the queen of Sheba. It takes between three and four days to get to Addis by train and only three hours by plane. Scenes worthy of Evelyn Waugh, shortly to be traveling around Ethiopia.[10] Why should the Negus doubt that his two guests have discovered his ancestors' city?[11]

A few ill-tempered and critical Europeans still have to be convinced. Unpredictably, as they stop over in Tripoli on their way home, Marshal Balbo's Fascist troops welcome them as brothers in arms—from the 1914–18 war. The three associates reach Algeria and Bône (now Annaba) as a storm hits the aircraft above the Aurès range. Hailstones pelt the cabin, the compass goes wild. The plane turns in the eye of the storm and loses altitude. They land in Bône. The Shakespearean tempest should yield plenty of literary material.[12] Malraux writes about it to René Lalou:[13] "I believed, for twenty minutes, that it was all over. For the first time in our journey, we had been taken by a cyclone, storm, or thing of that sort: it is a rare feeling. . . . It is thrilling in a thousand ways I won't go into here but that showed me without doubt that, as I had supposed, there is no experience of death, only a test of courage, which is far less interesting." In the same letter, Malraux declares that "one must risk death, not to die but in order to live. There is an ideology of human behavior, of which heroism is an expression, which remains to be found." Courage can be conquered.

The Farman leapfrogs from city to city. In Lyon, André Gide and Clara come to meet Malraux. Josette Clotis must not be seen there. The legitimate wife takes the limelight. Malraux has risked his life. He shines by his physical courage. He is going to need moral courage too. A question woven into his work and implicit in his whole life: Is a hero still brave if he is unaware of danger? Isn't the man who stands fast, feeling himself seized by mounting fear, more courageous? In 1934, Malraux is less interested in physical courage than in death. They are linked: courage reveals an attitude when faced with possible death.

Malraux creates the event before writing about it. He is attacked before his articles come out. No well-known archaeologists support his theory. John K. Wright, of the American Geographical Society, praises the "discovery of ruins in the southern Arabia desert which should be of

immense interest to archaeologists and geographers." But he concedes
that judgment should be withheld on whether the ruins can be identified
as the capital of the queen of Sheba. Malraux cannot conceive that he
might have mistaken a few hamlets for a whole city. He believes they are
"ruins covering an area five times as large as any of the known ruins in
southern Arabia and the only ones to remain standing." Malraux presents
himself as a champion, in all spheres. The photographic documents prove
the reality of his find, not just his good faith. He is not the sort of man to
mistake Sheba for Moka, "any more than the Acropolis in Athens for the
Champs-Élysées. We are keen to publish our paper within a fortnight, and
we ask people to read it before assuming that we are completely ignorant
of what we are talking about." William Albright, an archaeologist and
professor of Semitic languages at Johns Hopkins University, has visited
Mareb. Even before the publication of Malraux's articles, he has doubts.

Malraux writes seven articles for *L'Intransigeant*, Corniglion-Molinier
three.[14] Attractive titles ("Above the Arabian Desert") with appealing
headings such as "Flying over the Mysterious Capital of the Queen of
Sheba." Photographs illustrate the articles. Malraux showed his mastery
of the technique in *Marianne*. An architect, not an archaeologist, André
Hardy, provides clever and essential drawings, since the photos are disappointing. For *L'Intransigeant*, instead of journalistic stories, Malraux
writes lyrical essays. He embellishes, letting words carry him. The writer
takes the upper hand: "How many of those aircraft I saw, laid flat on a strip
of land disappearing into the water nearby, in a Muslim fragrance of burnt
grasses, pepper, and camels! Songs of southern Persia, the steppes of Central Asia, and the Russian pilots spending the night lying naked on swings
to escape the terrible heat at the foot of the Himalayas, in the scorched
gardens, under the wild, torrid perfume of burnt mountain lavender."

Malraux gets involved in his own game and soon starts padding. He
did not discover seventy temples or any treasure. He found desert, valleys,
ruins: an atmosphere and themes that induce the writer to flex his stylistic
muscles. In his poetic account, he discovers the Valley of the Dead and
brings in the Bible and Solomon: "For years, Solomon had fled Jerusalem. . . . The king, the author of the greatest poem of human despair, his
hands on the long staff he had walked with and his chin resting on his
hands, looked out onto the demons who had for many years guarded the
palace of the queen of Sheba." Astonished *L'Intransigeant* readers are suddenly faced with the author of *Lunes en papier* and *Royaume farfelu*: "Along
came an insect, looking for some wood. It found the royal staff and waited,
then became bold enough to bore into it. A few minutes later, both staff
and king fell to dust. The lord of silence, before whom even the birds
respected the protocol, had chosen to die standing so as to leave all his
slave demons to serve the queen." These interlocking, overlapping sen-

tences and images are presented as a descriptive report. "The shaken mind must choose among a web of dreams. If we are to follow the Bible and the legend, if this town was once that of the queen, it is the contemporary of Solomon, a gigantic monument, a kind of Notre-Dame from which a series of terraces tumble down to the petrified skeleton of a river. Was this the palace about which the Messenger says in the Koran: 'I saw a woman ruling over men from a magnificent throne; she and her people worship the sun, she is the one to whom Solomon sent the seal that can be deciphered only by the dead'?[15] Somehow Malraux establishes a genre, biblical reportage, interpreting the Middle East in his own way. The writer surprises himself, inventing or creating a world that doesn't conform to that of the archaeologist or the reporter. His writing is somewhere between Joseph Kessel's and Paul Claudel's: "Here starts the human landscape, here ends the world that was made to be seen by eyes other than ours: those of the red eagle we cannot see but whose shadow follows that of our plane; those of the fly, queen of these solitudes where even time burns, trembling in the heat."

One paragraph does not make the cut, though, proving that Malraux has some doubts about his discovery. "The queen of Sheba is known from two sources: the Bible and the Koran. In short, only the gods have written about her. We can reject her existence, regard it as a legend; but then what is this city, which is also only referred to in legend but does nonetheless exist? Whatever error might be made as to location under such conditions, this city is none of the known Shabean cities: neither Mareb, which has totally disappeared, nor Mein, in which only a small temple and a few boundary towers remain and which has no more than 400 meters of wall."[16]

In the United States, articles, maps, and pictures of the venture are published in newspapers. In France, there is a series of scathing attacks after the appearance of the pieces in *L'Intransigeant*. In *Le Temps*, for Mr. Beneyton, who has spent thirteen years exploring the Yemeni hinterland, Malraux has gotten everything mixed up. He and Corniglion-Molinier have probably "discovered" an oasis north of Mareb or a small village. Using his tested method of counterattack, Malraux responds, "It goes without saying that the town we discovered is not Mareb, which was discovered in 1843. It is not Tenna either." He continues, sarcastically, "If we run the risk, as anyone would, of getting it wrong when identifying a town we saw, what of the likelihood of our detractors getting it wronger when they attempt to identify a town they did not see?" Then a casual declaration: "At any rate, when we consider the amount of luck necessary for the success of an expedition of this sort, we can attach only a modest importance to this success. We are aware of the inconclusive nature of any identification that is not supported by appropriate epigraphic study, and we are obviously very much looking forward to seeing what is revealed by ground studies, whenever that may be possible."

Since his Cambodian peregrinations, Malraux has been used to academic criticism: those experts just can't see how the plausible can acquire the virtues of truth. As with poetry, in which Malraux perhaps sees a higher knowledge. Ever since Keats, beauty, to some, has been truth, and truth beauty. For Malraux, the beauty of what he sees and writes cannot be altered by facts. The controversy annoys and pleases him. Still, he wisely refuses to let his articles come out in book form. The quarrel dies down.

What Malraux actually flew over, as shown later by the historian and philologist Jacqueline Pirenne and others, was an oasis, some ruins, and the site of some inhabited dwellings: Asahil Rymen, Kharib, and Duraib.[17]

The man of the moment hops between continents, centuries, millennia. The intervention of the Negus is like a link between bucolic Old Testament times and the threatening, Nazified 1930s. On March 23, just after his return, Malraux joins the Anti-Fascist Intellectuals' Vigilance Committee, founded by Paul Langevin, Paul Rivet, and the philosopher Alain. In April, he attends a demonstration against the decision to expel Trotsky from the USSR. During that same month, he meets Manès Sperber, born in Galicia in Eastern Europe, who witnessed the atrocities of World War I and lived in poverty in Vienna. As a youngster similarly precocious to Malraux, Sperber studied psychology with Adler, whose disciple he became at the age of seventeen. He was briefly a Zionist and was imprisoned by the Nazis, then devoted himself to Marxism and communism. The Comintern sent him to work at the Institute for the Study of Fascism in order to study fascism in Paris. With vivacious Clara as an interpreter, he discusses history and injustice with Malraux. He draws his attention to the Nazi terror, telling him what he remembers, introducing him to German refugees, who are numerous in Paris. Abandoning the project of a Middle Eastern novel, Malraux thinks of writing something with Nazi Germany as a backdrop.

Malraux is bombarded by current events; his reaction is to use them and let them use him. This change of subject brings him back to the historical present, his favorite tense. In May, with Sperber, he meets André Gide at the Salle Bullier for a protest in favor of Ernst Thälmann, the Communist leader imprisoned by Hitler. Malraux throws himself into a campaign for Thälmann, attending meetings, including one in Belgium. He is applauded by a young Belgian Communist in the audience, Paul Nothomb. Back in Paris, Malraux often sees the Soviet journalist and writer Ilya Ehrenburg and his wife, Liuba. Ehrenburg was sent by Moscow to recruit sympathizers among Parisian intellectuals. Between Montparnasse and Saint-Germain-des-Prés, Ehrenburg turns out to be an excellent agent, smart and fast, good at hiding deep and ambiguous feelings. The Jewish Ilya, meanwhile, picks away at the Soviet Ehrenburg.

Events in 1934 give new pace to European history. In Paris, the Far Right denounces a "rotting" Republic, especially after the Stavisky affair. *Detective*, a periodical secretly owned by Gaston Gallimard, devotes a special issue to the crook Stavisky, who misappropriated 240 million francs (around $15.8 million at the time) from the Crédit Municipal de Bayonne. At the end of 1933, the authorities were accused of conspiring in the affair. Stavisky subsequently "commits suicide." Who is covering up for him? Left and right factions come face-to-face on February 6, 1934. The far-right paper *L'Action Française* condemns the "abject regime" and calls on war veterans to demonstrate at the Chamber of Deputies, as does the Communist newspaper *L'Humanité*: "Demonstrate! The Fascist organizations and governmental troops have mobilized against the workers." The skies above the Seine glow red throughout a night of rioting. Demonstrators set fire to a bus and attack the helmeted, armed riot police. The Far Right and Far Left have violence and antiparliamentary feeling in their blood: the Right hates the have-nots, and the Communists hate the bourgeoisie. By dawn, one mounted guard is dead and 255 of the governmental forces are wounded; there are 16 dead and 520 twenty wounded among the demonstrators. The "Great Capital" regime has not fallen.

Hitler is consolidating his power in Germany. He has made public a decree calling for the sterilization of criminals, sex offenders, and anybody suffering from a hereditary disease. The Führer initiates major building projects, such as a network of motorways, to reduce unemployment. He is also preparing for the rapid transportation of troops and equipment, trucks and tanks from east to west. During the "Night of the Long Knives" he gets rid of one of his possible rivals, Ernst Röhm, the head of the Sturmabteilung. Assassinations follow one another, and not only of Jews. Right-wing men such as Schleicher and Bredow are executed by the Gestapo. In Vienna, Chancellor Dollfuss is murdered. When the president of the German Reich, Field Marshal von Hindenburg, dies, Adolf Hitler achieves complete power, military and civilian, elected as both Führer and president of the Reich. Allegiance is sworn directly to him. Thirty-eight million Germans vote for him, 4,300,000 against. The citizens undergo a progressive indoctrination, from the People's Youth and the Hitler Youth to the Nazi Party, the army, and the Workers' Front.

Malraux prefers this modern history to ancient history: you can mold it and leave your mark on it. Yet in demonstrating a little with the Left, he has not paid full attention to the political and social movements going on in France, even when it came to rioting on February 6. For Malraux, Nazism is the danger in Europe. Not everyone in France is as perceptive. But the shrewdness of Malraux and others is politically shortsighted: their left eye has a large blind spot that prevents them from seeing the totalitarian Soviets.

CHAPTER TWELVE

Trotskyist Tropism

As AN ADOLESCENT, Malraux worshiped French authors whose aim was to make a difference to History, undaunted by the risk of losing themselves in politics: Chateaubriand, Lamartine, Hugo, Barrès. Malraux worshiped politicians who could write, such as Saint-Just and Napoleon. During his period of politically committed anticolonialism, Malraux never met anyone of that caliber. His support of the Left in 1934 is implicit, if intermittent. But who is there in France at the time whose actions and thoughts might seduce Malraux? Perhaps the head of the SFIO, Léon Blum, who might have wasted a career as a writer. During the Third Republic, nobody ruling from the Élysée Palace, governing in the Hôtel Matignon, or speaking in the Chamber of Deputies or the Senate seems cut out to be a historical hero. On the international scene, Hitler and Mussolini are not Malraux's style.

That leaves the more exotic heads of the Bolshevik Revolution, unconventional and bloodthirsty, co-opted or self-elected. The red glow coming from the East seems tempting to Malraux, but disturbing. Stalin, celebrated by Henri Barbusse in his 1935 hagiography, doesn't appeal to a lover of art, essays, and fiction like Malraux. Josif Vissarionovich Dzhugashvili saw himself as a theoretician. His *Principles of Leninism*, quite widely read in France, are unconvincing to a learned mind. Politicians' actions speak more to Malraux than their words. Lenin himself, to whom Malraux makes a few allusions (appropriately enough in the contemporary climate) died ten years earlier, leaving many written works. His texts on art and literature are still not well known in France. Malraux has perused a few booklets in translation: *What Is to Be Done?*; *Imperialism, the Highest Stage of Capitalism*; *The State and Revolution*. Malraux pays no attention to Vladimir Ilich's philosophical pretensions, especially not to the verbose nonsense of *Materialism and Empiriocriticism*. Partly through lack of information, Malraux hardly alludes to the police state whose first concentration camp opened under Lenin in 1918. He doesn't even seem to know—and he is not the only one—of Lenin's wish to eliminate the "harmful insects," that is, all his adversaries, real or supposed. It is Lenin's personality that inspires Malraux: the terrific charisma of the inventor of the one-party system and founder of the "socialist" state that is advancing, through mud, blood, deprivation, and concentration camps, toward a Communist utopia. But the programmatic and polemical side of Leninism is not to his taste. Malraux is not into historical materialism. Here and there he speaks of capitalism as having a negative impact, as always for the left wing of the 1930s. But he does not invoke the "power struggle" or the notions of superstructure or surplus value. Malraux is willful and self-centered and likes to keep his distance from the blind, overresolute masses. Although he makes collectivist noises in the name of socialism, he remains as individualistic as his heroes, from Claude Vannec to Kyo.

A revolutionary writer of Malraux's temperament needs a hero of the Russian Revolution: alive, powerful, dominating, an incarnation of historical legend. Trotsky appears to be tailor-made: an intellectual, one-third warrior, one-third thinker, and one-third prophet. He presided over the Soviet Workers' Council and was minister of justice. The Communist or Communist-supporting Left takes the Bolshevik coup of 1917 for a people's revolution, complementing the French Revolution of 1789.[1] To Malraux, who has been obsessed by military adventure ever since his father came back with tales of life as a lieutenant, Trotsky carries an aura as the ruthless creator of the Red Army. And he is a political theorist, which makes him more cultivated than most of the Soviet leaders. Malraux doesn't rate theory above practice—since the latter entails action—but knowledge and literary abilities do count. Trotsky is all the more alluring since his future looks bleak. At the start of 1928, the European Left was shocked to learn that Stalin had sent Trotsky and some members of the "left-wing opposition" into exile. The French Communists quickly and slavishly denounced the "counterrevolutionaries." The infamous label "Trotskyite" was used to brand anyone the Stalinists wanted to wipe off the political map. It was the start of the "lecherous vipers" period, allowing those who were accused to be dehumanized. The zoological vocabulary would be used from the time of the Great Trials onward.

At first, Malraux privately shares his sympathy for the exiled Trotsky with Clara. When André Breton heads a French protest group, Malraux has an idea: a bunch of writers, with the help of some intrepid types, could land in Alma-Ata and free Trotsky from under the nose of his jailers, who would (obviously) be mesmerized and paralyzed at the sight of a Goncourt laureate leading a literary commando unit. They can apply to the consulate in Paris for visas valid across the whole Soviet Union. They'd have to get to Trotsky's residence in Kazakhstan—perhaps through Kashmir or Turkestan on foot or on horseback, or they could drive or fly. They might be arrested when crossing the border illegally.[2] Malraux unfolds his commendable but preposterous plans to a few traveler types: Blaise Cendrars, Joseph Kessel, Pierre Mac Orlan, Francis Carco. Unfortunately, life is no novel. No one is infected by his enthusiasm, least of all Clara. Neither is Gaston Gallimard, who squarely refuses to finance the expedition. Never mind. International pressure, especially from the Left, is shaking Stalin's hold. Trotsky in exile becomes a martyr to be canonized. He gets into Turkey and starts his immigrant's journey.

The first appearance of the impressive Bolshevik in Malraux's life is not face-to-face. Trotsky sends the *Nouvelle Revue Française*[3] an article concerning *Les Conquérants*, something Stalin would never have done. Revealingly entitled "La révolution étranglée" (The Strangled Revolution), Trotsky's two-part critique makes a distinction between content and form. He appreciates the unforgettable "picture of the general strike Malraux paints" but thinks the underlying political analysis lacks color. Between Garine and Borodine, Trotsky chooses the former, without expressing great affection. The main point of his article is that Malraux's theoretical culture is insufficient. Malraux is a bad pupil who needs a "booster shot of Marxism" as political therapy. According to Trotsky, Malraux should have made it clear that the real "strangler" of the Chinese Revolution, way above Borodine, was Stalin.

Flattered by Trotsky's attention, Malraux publishes an extensive answer in the same issue of the *NRF,* with much detail about the 1920s "revolutionary situation" in China and the 1917 "Revolution." He believes that Trotsky is settling his grudge against Stalin, which seems accurate enough. A bloodthirsty ideologist himself, Trotsky has a soft spot for Hong, the terrorist. Malraux is cautious about that affinity: "I understand what can be captivating about this figure [Hong] in his resolve and savage purity; but I cannot forget that when Lenin and Trotsky met people like Hong they put the Cheka in charge of all communication with them." Well put.[4] Malraux is nonetheless indulgent about the Bolsheviks' methods. Dirty, bloody hands are purified in the long run, the end justifying the means. Further on, Malraux admires the "heroism, in its most realistic sense" of the role Trotsky requires of the proletariat. Then come some remarks on the positive effects that a "stronger Cheka" might have had in China. Our Father, give us this day more policemen and more victims, more accusers and more accused; our daily bread can come later. Malraux doesn't forget how detractors in the USSR were treated by the

Cheka but seems to think that a Chinese Cheka would have been useful. He again thanks Trotsky for seeing his characters Borodine, Garine, and Hong as "symbols," stating that "Trotsky extracts them from their time frame." The writer, with limited international political experience, courteously and loftily lectures the former chief of the Red Army on strategy. For his revolutionary realism and his apology for terror, Trotsky can join Saint-Just in Malraux's portable pantheon. Trotsky the man of action converses with Malraux the man of letters, a confrontation as original as it is surprising.

Trotsky eventually arrives in France. Malraux visits him[5] in Saint-Palais, near La Rochelle. He is guarded by some French militants and two German shepherd dogs, not by the police, since Trotsky is supposedly there incognito. Threatening letters from the readers of *L'Action Française* nevertheless manage to reach his address. Trotsky sometimes goes out for a drive. Malraux has two conversations with him, one in the afternoon, the other the following morning. Malraux is thirty-two years old, Trotsky fifty-four. They talk in French since Malraux doesn't speak Russian. Malraux faces a considerable historical figure for a few hours, and this extraordinary experience boosts his ego. Trotsky, an almost paternal hero and an affectedly kind teacher, is used to handling words and soldiers, ideas and masses alike. They cover countless topics. Malraux is comfortable with this, master as he is of the abrupt, logic-jumping change of subject. They talk of individualism and communism, postrevolutionary Russian art, the defeat of the Red Army in Poland, a possible war between the Soviet Union and Japan. Trotsky has read Céline's *Voyage au bout de la nuit* a few months earlier. Malraux is an excellent and cocky impersonator, making faces and imitating Céline, whom he knows from Gallimard. The writer and the former head of state talk cinema, an art for which Trotsky doesn't have much enthusiasm. Malraux thinks that Communist art is better incarnated in the cinema than in literature. Lenin, Trotsky says, was of the same opinion. What? Trotsky has seen neither *Potemkin* nor *The Mother*?

"When they were first shown, I was at the front," Trotsky explains. "When I came back they were no longer on, and when they were rereleased I was in exile."

Malraux, in his account of the meeting, starts inventing: How could Trotsky have missed films at the front when they had not yet been made?

Malraux and Trotsky walk in the vineyards. Jean van Heijenoort is with them. He takes note of their gestures: Trotsky's are "precise, controlled, didactic," Malraux's "jerky." The conversation is coming to an end. The two men touch on the issue of death. That is almost unavoidable with Malraux. That same year, the young Communist writer Paul Nizan said to Jean-Paul Sartre that he had discovered that communism had removed the problem of death, or at least of man's fear faced with his own end. In Saint-Palais, Malraux tells Trotsky, "One thing that communism will never triumph over is death."

"When a man has accomplished the task he has set for himself, when he has done what he set out to do, death is simple," answers Trotsky, for once the embodiment of common sense.

One of them has killed many characters in novels, the other has killed many men. They part company.[6]

Like many engagé writers at the turn of the 1930s, Malraux has a generous and very literary approach to political problems. To him, the international scene is an impressive, powerful backdrop for novels, not the focus of economic, political, or sociological analyses. His fiction is full of ideas: fraternity, dignity, efficiency. The novelist is interested in Trotsky's character but doesn't look into the ideological motivation of "the permanent revolution," the dictatorship of the proletariat. He is no Engels. He has neglected to study the living conditions of the working classes. The issues of prices and salaries are nothing to him. He can talk and above all write with more sensitivity about the fate of the Indochinese, of whom he knows little, or the Chinese of his imagination, than about the French in Lille, Paris, or Marseille. It matters little to him whether or not Lenin, Trotsky, or Stalin aligns himself with Marx. He accepts, without digging too deeply, a certain amount of Marx's economic and social analysis. But he has no time to discuss economics.

More than Stalin, Trotsky insists, theoretically, on the notion of democratic pluralism, the rich necessity of discussions between those with diverse opinions. But he doesn't reject the indispensable dictatorship of the proletariat, which is quite contrary to pluralism. In his essays and articles Malraux doesn't really grapple with the essential difference between Trotsky and Stalin. He hardly gives a thought to the strategies of the developing Third and Fourth Communist Internationals. Politics is not his job. Attempting to square the circle, he supports Trotsky without opposing Stalin; he denounces the Cheka, the offspring of these two great Bolsheviks.

Efficiency is very important to Malraux. The great threat in 1933 and 1934 comes from Nazi Germany. To him, even with its "faults," the USSR is the only possible ally against German Nazism and Italian fascism. And only communism, according to Malraux, can spearhead the great social revolution. Trotsky, the living critique of the current Soviet regime, wants to create a new worldwide revolutionary organization, yet he is an isolated, aging, almost embarrassing figure. In Malraux's eyes he is a modern revolutionary with no revolution, respected but beaten; a military commander without troops. His followers are a few thousand stubborn militants, persevering but often poor and inefficient. Malraux doesn't think the winners are always right. Neither does he think that Stalin is blameless. But he behaves as if some losers are wrong. Trotsky is a startling journey, a destiny at a standstill facing death. Justice is desirable, certainly, but efficiency perhaps more so.

Malraux distances himself from Trotsky and moves nearer to Soviet literary power. Benjamin Goriely proposes an anthology to Gallimard. Malraux writes, "The *NRF* refuses the project of an anthology of revolutionary poetry from which Russia would be excluded." Soon afterward, Malraux refuses to take up the defense of Viktor Serge,[7] one of Trotsky's supporters, whom Stalin sends into exile. Trotsky finds Malraux's silence indecent.

Malraux also shows reticence for writers representing the left-wing opposition to Stalinism. Boris Souvarine is working on a book about Stalin.[8] According to Souvarine, Georges Bataille reported Malraux as saying, "I believe you and your friends are right, Souvarine, but I will side with you when you are the strongest." Souvarine thinks that Brice Parain, the "qualified Russophile, very well informed about Soviet affairs," recommends the publication of his book. This is untrue. Parain advises against it, in order to protect Gallimard's interests in the USSR.

Nevertheless, torn between objective considerations and subjective sympathies, Malraux defends Trotsky's cause when the French government wants to expel him. He signs petitions and takes his place alongside Trotskyist militants from the Communist League and Socialists from the SFIO in a meeting at the Salle Albouy. He speaks alongside orators such as Pierre Franck and Marceau Pivert. In contrast to the French Communist Party, the revolution must be "as one," he declares. Malraux puts it elegantly: if one doesn't respect Trotsky, "one humiliates part of the revolutionary force that shook Saint Petersburg."

Malraux sides more and more with the Parti Communiste François (PCF), the bitter anti-Trotskyites. But he never considers joining the Party. He prefers to stay independent, a risky luxury: he does not see the Party up close, its Central Committee, or its pseudodemocratic centralism. He does not fully realize that it will never be like the SFIO, the Radicals, the Radical Socialists, or any other political party. Behind its front, its papers, its phrases and slogans, behind even the goodwill of its militants, the Communist Party is creating a countersociety in France. In order really to understand it, one has to be part of it, at least for a time.

Malraux is shortsighted about the Party, like so many left-wing citizens, but also when faced with Stalin's regime. There is dictatorship in Berlin and Rome, but he doesn't see it in Moscow. He doesn't wonder if, in reality (harsher than theory), the dictatorship of the proletariat has become a dictatorship of a stubborn, fanatical lower middle class. Neither does he ask whether political independence, the freedom of the working classes, of all classes, really constitutes an independent variable of economic freedom.[9] Nor does he question the necessity of nationalizing the means of production and distribution. Malraux doesn't assess real socialism. He does not—any more than Paul Nizan, a staunch Communist, or André Gide, a sly sympathizer—envisage a radical critique of Stalin's policies. If you want the end, you must accept the means. That supposedly realistic alibi will blind and sedate millions of minds. A socialist utopia is seen as the only possible future for humanity.

Malraux is not always convinced that history has just one irreversible, unavoidable direction. Too much of an individualist to believe in historicism, he skipped through Nietzsche and Spengler as he did Marx and Lenin. Still, he acts in public as if he believes that history, defined by revolution in the USSR at that point in the twentieth century, is indeed following a path prescribed by Stalinist Communists. Is this ignorance, opportunism, bad judgment, or carelessness? Perhaps he is playing the political dandy, as he did when entering the world of literature?[10] Of course, the period must be taken into account, with its blindness and confusion, its hopes and illusions, its ignorance. Malraux is no Trotskyite, but he has been drawn, for the duration of an article on one of his books and a few petitions for a man in exile. Just a brief tropism.

le dry abh dr falfalan

CHAPTER THIRTEEN

Soviet Comrades

O N May 30, 1934, Louis Aragon's muse, Elsa Triolet, her spite-fulness less in question than her talent, writes to her sister Lili Brik in Moscow, "The Ehrenburgs are leaving for London by boat around now, with Malraux. If you should happen to meet Malraux, for your personal guidance I warn you not to enter into friendly relations. He is bad and dangerous." In another letter on June 8, Aragon's partner points out to her sister, "The Ehrenburgs have left for the congress with Malraux. I believe I have already warned you not to become linked to him."[1]

After a weekend in London and a crossing on the *Dzerjinski*, a Soviet liner named after the founder of the State Security Service, the Malrauxs and the Ehrenburgs disembark in Leningrad on June 14. Ilya takes pictures with his Leica. The Soviet newspapers, *Izvestia* taking the lead, announce the arrival of the 1933 Goncourt Prize winner. Paul Nizan, graduate of the École Normale Supérieure, philosophy teacher, novel-writing member of the PCF, and journalist working in Moscow, author of "Watchdogs," a provocative pamphlet on conventional French academic philosophy, is there to meet them.

The Writers' Union and the VOKS (Society for Cultural Relations with Foreign Countries) are on the alert. Two days before the Malrauxs arrive, Nizan writes a skilful introduction to the author of *La Condition humaine* in *Literaturnaya Gazeta*: "Malraux is not a revolutionary writer . . . these young, famous writers . . . come from the bourgeoisie and foresee a natural death for this class, rallying with the proletariat. But this alliance has its portion of personal reasons that have nothing to do with the revolutionary cause." The authorities have cooked up a program. Four days after Nizan's article, the same paper publishes an interview with Malraux.

The conference in which he is to participate with fellow Frenchmen Jean-Richard Bloch and Vladimir Pozner should, in Malraux's opinion, concentrate on the problems of Western literature: "We must try to establish which form is most likely to allow revolutionary literature to attain its goal. Satire of capitalism, you might suggest. True, there is no shortage of fitting subject matter. . . . But there is always something conditioned and schematic about satire; we should be aiming for a complete artistic representation of reality, the creation of accomplished literary representations." Malraux limits himself to a few easily decoded remarks on Soviet novels. In France, Malraux explains, they are poorly served by translators, who are underpaid. How can work of a polished standard be produced in return for 2,000 francs ($130 in 1934) for two or three months' work? How, indeed?

The Soviets welcome Malraux with flowers and receptions. At the Hotel Astoria, he is introduced to the conformist author Alexei Tolstoy. Throughout this trip, Malraux takes notes.[2] On Alexei Tolstoy:

> The only one to be elegantly dressed. Platinum chain. They all seem to look on him with respect. Acknowledges that he is read by a great many readers, but acknowledges it almost with bitterness, and the tone of voice seems to say, "They swallow whatever they are given, there is nothing to be proud of."
>
> "The essence of art," he tells me, "is in the distinction between realism and naturalism. Naturalism is photography. It is not what is interesting. Realism is the conservation of real characters, but giving them something more (I could not tell whether he meant giving them a meaning, or making them into distinctive types). Naturalism is *Anna Karenina*. Realism is *War and Peace*, Flaubert, Balzac."
>
> M. [Malraux]: "It remains to be seen whether the photograph exists. For if it is Anna K[arenina], it is not convincing. I rather believe in the will of the photographer than in the ph[otograph] itself, in this will as a value. Who is that blond woman?"

Malraux, much in demand, writes articles and film reviews. On Dziga Vertov's documentary *Three Songs About Lenin*: "One of the eminent successes of Soviet cinema. . . . What we have here is a work of art of evident value. . . . Remarkable. . . . Strong, simple, virile emotion. . . . The impression of a great Russian tradition, from Pushkin to Tolstoy. . . . I was thinking of the famous scene in *War and Peace*: 'If you die, Prince Andrei, I shall suffer cruelly.' " Malraux concludes, "And the success of this film poses a considerable question that I can only touch on here: that of permanence across different civilizations. Vertov's art consists in expressing the greatest possible intensity with the fewest possible means. It is odd, almost poignant, to see a Soviet film director creating a great work and facing the same technical problem as Giotto or Piero della Francesca."[3]

In Moscow, as in Leningrad, a succession of meetings with writers' committees alternates between the productive, the banal, the boring, and the drunken. Clara and André stay at the National Hotel, reserved for celebrities. Nizan, posted in Moscow, is less well treated. Like almost all guests, the Malrauxs note (but do no more than note) the shortages; they miss the misery and the inefficiency of the system. Blindness, hypocrisy? Whether comrades or companions to the cause, often visitors do not want to see the reality of socialism. Yet Malraux writes in his embryonic journal: "At the zoo. The chimpanzee keeper, when asked, 'Does the monkey eat bread?' replies bitterly, 'Yes, but only the bread that's made for foreigners: not ours.' "

Malraux appears not to sense the permanent surveillance surrounding the conference guests. Nor that those close to him, who are to become friends, are "commentating" on his words and actions to the Soviet administration and the NKVD,[4] the successor of the Cheka. This surveillance is conducted via interpreters, members of the VOKS and the Writers' Union: those who welcome him and his "friends" are the ones who carry out the spying. Written and verbal reports delivered to the Party, the secret police (NKVD), or other departments are an essential, structural part of this totalitarian system: everything comes into the Party's possession by right. Informing is part of *Homo sovieticus*, the new man. In every Communist regime a management role can imply being a journalist, a diplomat, a writer, or an agent for a secret service. This multiplicity of interchangeable functions does nothing to enrich the level of competence, except in spying.

Ehrenburg and Koltsov are instructed to work on the famous, intelligent, often intuitive author. They are not only looking after Malraux. Koltsov, editor in chief of *Ogonyok* and of the satirical but careful *Krokodil*, also works for *Pravda*, which leaves him time to participate, as a deputy, in occasional meetings of the Supreme Soviet. He has the ear and eye of Stalin, who likes him—for the time being.[5] Ehrenburg has a fast hand. With Koltsov, he makes a better chaperone for Malraux than Babel, who has an unfortunate tendency to say what he thinks of the economic, political, and social situation in the USSR.

The average monthly salary of a Soviet worker is 125 rubles, multiplied by three for Stakhanovites. A schoolteacher earns around 120 rubles, a doctor, 200. Nurses earn 40 to 50 rubles a month. There are two selling prices, one for rationed food and one for the "free" market. Meat costs between 2 and 4 rubles a kilogram with coupons, from 5 to 12 without; potatoes, 20 kopeks or 2 rubles; a loaf of people's bread—so dear to the chimpanzee keeper—from 36 to 60 kopeks. In Moscow, supply seems better than in Leningrad or other cities. The daily bread ration of a Muscovite worker: a fifth of a loaf. In the favored restaurants and "palaces" such as the Grand Hotel and the Europa, three kilograms of meat per person per month is the norm. Foreign comrades are allowed nine kilograms of meat. The Muscovite population appears to regular visitors to be a little better dressed than a few years earlier. But clothes lack style, and the quality of the material is too poor for them to be exportable. The conference participants are spared these tiresome facts and superfluous details. Foreigners have special hotels, shops, and rations. They do not suspect—not all—that Soviet society is still living under worse conditions than some countries endured during the First World War.[6] Mostly, they do not want to know. They are mixing with the privileged and the converted. Purgatory leads to Paradise, that goes without saying. How could writers from the West know that enforced collectivization, the "removal" of the kulaks, their expropriation and their deportation had led to a dramatic decline in agriculture? Stalin's crazy antipeasant policy started creating famine in 1932 and continued into 1933. But the participants at the conference could, if they wanted to, have made telling calculations. In France many descriptive and critical articles and publications had appeared and been attributed to "counterpropaganda." Some visitors, such as Aragon, knew what was happening. Their false shortsightedness was either ideological or pragmatic.

Malraux talks about his plans: "I have started a novel about oil. The oil industry is an area where imperialist interests are in opposition to Soviet Russia. My novel will be set in Persia and Baku, where I mean to go. I intend to depict the worker in the Soviet oil industry."[7]

For Malraux, a book plan becomes a book that has been started; a manuscript that does not satisfy him is transformed into a book that has been lost. What is desirable has a truth that transcends what actually exists. Imagined essence comes before trivial existence and can even take its place.

Malraux talks a lot about cinema. The artists', workers', and students' cooperative Mejrabpomfilm waits on him. He announces that he is working on a screenplay of *La Condition humaine*. The film will be made by the Dutch cinematographer Joris Ivens or by Aleksandr Dovzhenko. Malraux is to meet Vsevolod Meyerhold, who is going to adapt *La Condition humaine* for the stage.

"If war breaks out," says Malraux, "I think that Japan will start it. I shall be the first to work on the formation of a Foreign Legion, and in its

ranks, rifle in hand, I shall defend the Soviet Union, the country of freedoms." Malraux swims in rhetoric when he envisages the formation of a
Foreign Legion. A theme is starting to develop.

Paul Nizan's wife, Henriette, and Clara Malraux get on fairly well, and
André Malraux and Nizan very well.[8] Nizan sometimes scoffs at the bosses
and the Party. For him, Malraux's political and philosophical culture is still
meager, but his experience is substantial. Malraux, only four years older
than Nizan, has crossed Asia; Nizan has not yet gotten any farther than
Aden. For Nizan, Malraux's inventions and wishes—I was an important
member of the Kuomintang, I founded the Young Annam Party, I will
command a Foreign Legion—outline a personality to be exploited by the
Communist movement. Over brochettes, the Nizans listen with pleasure
to Malraux describing a jade Buddha. Malraux loves good red meat, hard
to come by in Moscow, even for privileged guests. At the congress, an
excess of food hangs over the participants. Jean-Richard Bloch's liver gives
him trouble.

Henriette Nizan and Marguerite Bloch become friends. Marguerite
sends letters to her children:[9] "I am also getting to know Malraux's wife
very well. . . . They are a tremendously intellectual couple. He knows a lot
and doesn't hesitate to talk about it, but he is mostly interested in his own
psychology." Madame Bloch is appalled by Clara and André: "The Malrauxs are dreadful people. He talks exactly as he writes. Very tight logic
but discontinuous and very secretive; I find it terribly tiring. And he is so
horribly disdainful. . . . He has nervous tics that are painful to watch." In
Moscow as in Paris, a little alcohol calms Malraux's Tourette's, but a lot of
alcohol stimulates it. Henriette Nizan gathers that Clara wants to mend
their brilliant and broken couple. André is not helping her; he is very
interested in Boleslava Boleslavskaya, a young woman with gray eyes,
blackened teeth, and fantastic legs. She is a translator and Malraux's interpreter; she reports on foreign comrades. Boleslava is closer to Henriette
than Clara, who is keeping an eye on her husband. André and Boleslava
have a certain amount of difficulty in finding time alone together.[10] On
each floor of every hotel, a *dejournaya* sits in front of a table, looking after
the keys. She records the guests' meetings and times of arrival and departure for the police.

Malraux talks business with his potential Russian editors. To the publishers in Leningrad, he writes on July 5:

Comrades,
 I have been waiting to receive your contract before sending you
the preface. Two points are absent from it: first, that your initial
print run will be 10,000 copies; second, that the Moscow edition

will also be able to appear. I would be grateful if you would confirm these points separately, or send me a contract including them.

For the next novel, I think I will be able to arrange things with
Moscow for you to be the editor.

If you agree, you can start printing and thus be the first to come
out. I shall send you the preface in a few days at any rate.

Yours most sincerely.

Then, on July 13:

Dear Comrade,

No, it is not a question of rights, nor of money. In this regard,
as I have told you, I accept your contract as a matter of course.
What is important to me is the guarantee of a run of 10,000, even
if the rights were only for 5,000. For if the run in Leningrad must
be of an inferior quantity to that of Moscow, it is clearly absurd
that I should envisage dealing with Leningrad for the next novel,
since what matters to me is not to be paid but to be read.

Having said that, and my point of view being perfectly clear on
this, I am returning the signed contract so that there should be
nothing between us resembling bargaining. Do what you think
best and send me your draft contract for my next work.

Yours . . .

You will receive the preface in the course of the month.

The preface is never written. Malraux is not miserly like Montherlant,
but he has worked for Gallimard—he knows the tricks of the trade. The
USSR has signed no international convention on royalties: it simply pays
the writers it wants to cultivate.

As editor and snooper for Gallimard, Malraux discovers a book by Lev
Kassil called *Schwambrania*. He asks Henriette Nizan to translate it into
French with Vera Ravikovich. Malraux chooses the title *Le Voyage imaginaire*.[11] Two boys live through the Revolution by creating a private world
they call Schwambrania, peopled with symbolic characters who sometimes surface into the real world. To foreign guests, the USSR of 1934
appears half real and half imaginary.

For five weeks, Malraux frequents Moscow's intelligentsia. Ehrenburg
accompanies Malraux and makes sure the conference organizers are aware
of his importance. The two writers attend the presentation of a documentary film, *The Meeting of the Crew of the Icebreaker* Chelyuskin. Malraux
gives a speech on the architecture of literary texts, explaining how he constructed *Les Conquérants* and *La Condition humaine*. He attends a meeting

of the MORP, the Foreign Commission of the Soviet Writers' Union. Boleslava translates.

At the beginning of August, the Malrauxs leave for the west of Siberia. They visit Novosibirsk, Oirot, Stalinogorsk, and some model sovkhoz and kolkhoz farms.[12] They fly through this escorted visit and find it hard to keep their bearings. A guided visit of Siberia is a rare treat; it shows that Malraux is considered a good cog in the machine. He takes notes:

> Telegram from the government to the village: "Sexual relations between men and women are prohibited." Distinct feeling of unease. Then some clever sort (as in France) begins to understand. "It must be to keep all our collective energy for the harvest." One, who has said nothing, goes to the post office. The clerk there is a young peasant woman of sixteen, fresh out of school. He asks to see the telegram. "Oh," she says, "I threw it away. It came through all muddled and silly. Over there, they don't really pay attention to what they're doing, they send nonsense. Now, let's see, what did it say? 'Sexual relations between men are prohibited.' It was silly. So obviously I corrected it."

Little true facts, snapshots taken by Malraux's photographic eye while passing through:

SIBERIA
> The partisan with the rifle carrying the bayonet with which his son was killed . . .
> The chap who has to kill another so that the other can get the insurance money . . .
> The tall black firs on the thick yellow of the cut wheat [deleted word].
> The trans-Siberian abandoned like a boat in the middle of [deleted word].
> Streets that end up as tracks.
> Fields of potatoes in flower [deleted word].
> A monastery above a village of thatched roofs suddenly appears in the gap of a forest of fir trees [deleted word].

The Soviet authorities know how to build Potemkin-style villages. They make good use of Malraux, presenting him as an eminent French writer interested in the ethnography of Siberia and in ancient nomadic peoples. A Siberian newspaper reports how impressed Malraux is by some cannons cast by partisans. How were the Siberian Bolsheviks able to beat the White Army with such flawed weapons? During these excursions, Malraux is apparently fascinated by the breeding of silver foxes, or so claim the Soviet reporters. It takes an effort to imagine Clara—and André!—getting excited about day nurseries or ironing workshops. Malraux explains to invited journalists that he will aim to "present the image of new Soviet man with an awareness transformed through socialist enlightenment." The manipulated and manipulating Malraux here went as far as to say that neither France nor England had settled the nomadic peoples "in their Asian and African colonies." Did he really claim that only "the conditions of socialist work" could keep these people in one place? Did he really emphasize his passion for "the creation of new high-level managers"? Was he turned into a robot, conditioned by the messianic guides accompanying him, swearing that the new intelligentsia in Oirot, like all the intellectuals of the Soviet Union, "seems to differ from the bourgeois intelligentsia in many respects" in its strength of character? According to Malraux, or at least according to the comments attributed to him in the press, the Soviet Union had, thanks to Marxism, achieved the political and social union of different races. Like so many foreign guests, perhaps Malraux did not say what he thought but what they wanted to hear him say. The Siberian officials were satisfied by his amphigoric courtesy, as were the apparatchiks in their reports at each stage of the trip.

For a long time yet, most foreign intellectuals would not have a clear idea of the extreme poverty and backwardness of the Soviet working classes. It was clear, however, to workers and engineers who were posted to the USSR.[13] Malraux can see that foreign currencies are in demand on the black market. Not all the French, British, or American comrades change their currency on the "white" market, in the banks. Malraux and others do no more than look on. To use Bertrand Russell's distinction, his direct, "by acquaintance," knowledge of the USSR is even weaker than his indirect, "by description," knowledge. Malraux is still happy just to observe that privileges vary as prices do. He notes:

> The [deleted word] point of view. Everything the tourists think where the ruble is concerned is rubbish. The buying power of the ruble is linked not to the money itself but to the collective the person using it belongs to: one Soviet's cooperative will give a meal for one ruble that is five times better than in another cooperative. Thus to belong to a determined cooperative, to the determined Soviet, is more important than earning more or less money.

For two weeks, in Siberia, Malraux systematizes his vision of the USSR. Hovering outside the social and economic reality, he falls for Stalinist propaganda, especially about the massacred kulaks:

KULAK

At the worst point of the Revolution, when the starving towns were putting everything into construction, what was happening out in the country? The birth of capitalism. Among these peasants, an eternity of servitude was, at that very moment, molding the class of the most skillful or the most crafty into the souls of American farmers. We believe that the kulaks were rich former peasants. Not a bit. They were the new parvenus. . . . The amazing power of man, when he dares to govern. Periodically, a silent effort brings about the worst. Since Lenin, the history of the C.P. [Communist Party] has been that of a series of willpowers.

When he looks at the kulaks, Malraux does not see Stalin's bloody fantasies. The Soviets look after him well, almost as well as they look after Romain Rolland, the French intellectual they esteem most. All that suffers is his objectivity. Céline, less Potemkinized, fashions his experience into an awareness that has more to do with reality. Coming as an adversary, he attempts while there to counter the Soviet propaganda. As for Nizan and his wife, members of the PCF, they return "filled with enthusiasm"[14] after a trip into Central Asia takes them from the farthest edge of Tajikistan all the way to Stalinabad. The sympathizer or the militant often sees, in all honesty, what he is looking for. Or pretends to.

At last comes what the famous and the obscure, the corruptible and the upright, have been called to Moscow for: the Soviet Writers' Congress.[15] From August 17 to September 1, sessions sit from ten in the morning to two in the afternoon, then from six until ten in the evening, listening, more or less, to Soviet and foreign writers, workers' delegates, kolkhozians, pioneers. Seven hundred writers and as many officials from the Party and the police boil in the heat of the immense colonnaded hall of the Trade Union Building. Some admire the staging, the profusion of green plants, a bust of Lenin, the portraits of Stalin and Gorky. At the back of the stage, behind the enthroned Presidium, a huge panel of red canvas allows the spotlights, sweeping across the hall and the stage, to create varying lighting effects. Maxim Gorky is to open the first session. He appears. A spotlight blinds him.

"Get rid of that candle," protests the venerable writer.

The microphones don't work. No matter. Delighted and unperturbed, Gorky starts on a three-hour speech. Even in Stalin's USSR, it seems interminable. Participants slip out for refreshments. There are many buffets. When they want the hall to stay full, the organizers close the buffets. Listen up, intellectual comrades, hunger and thirst after righteousness.

The conference follows the instructions of the Central Committee.

Writers, Stalin declared in 1932, are the "engineers of the human soul." Andrei Zhdanov, the uncultured cultural ideologue, wants to impose a mutilating doctrine, socialist realism, on the novel, poetry, painting, and music. Seventeen years after the Revolution, artistic creation and creators are watched, encouraged, discouraged, and restrained, if only financially.

Two years before this congress, the intellectual associations were reorganized. Union leaders, designated by the Party, now manage the money and contracts for everyone from poets to theater directors. The aim is to build "socialism within a single country" and a single art within socialism. The socialist artist must represent life, not experience; sketch the radiant future as it should be, and not as it looms ahead, less and less bright. The subjects of novels and films must be drawn from everyday life, aimed at workers and accessible to all. This simplistic approach shores itself up with reasons of its own: the Soviet Communists are governing a nation and several nationalities of supposedly backward peasants. In the long run, they must transform workers and artists, prise them out of their mold with hammer and chisel, break them up and remold them ideologically. This induces an awful schizophrenia: since commissions come only from state organizations, some writers lead a double life to survive. They work according to the official line and keep the writing they value in a drawer. Cultural officials, themselves scared, sometimes terrorized, often incompetent and inflexible, instill a stifling climate. University research also suffers. Better to work on the medieval period than contemporary history. Academic work is peppered with protective quotations having no connection with the text. Footnotes referring to Marx or Lenin confer on university work a certificate of conformity and good Communist behavior. To some extent, science fiction escapes the vigilance of the censors.[16]

To the amazement of many Russian, Ukrainian, Byelorussian, and foreign participants, including Malraux, Gorky issues instructions. Boleslava translates for André. Part of the audience applauds Gorky's orthodox tirades. Nizan smiles an ambiguous, knowing smile. Some, such as Babel, become edgy. As Gorky goes on reading his speech, Malraux, racked with tics, grows impatient. Gorky repeats himself. As a materialist atheist, he explains, he scorns the church and all philosophies other than Marxism-Leninism. Malraux could perhaps accept that the old writer, paying court to Stalin, needn't have read the Kant, Plato, and Bergson that he is vulgarly vomiting on. But to claim that Dostoevsky was a product of capitalism or imperialism and understood nothing about human psychology, that's going too far.

"Comrades," says Gorky, "true literature, the authentic truth, is to be found in the popular heroes; the ancient heroes who are still there in the working classes."

Those present are made to understand that it would be discourteous to leave the room.[17] Malraux and others are particularly surprised, since fifteen years earlier, Gorky was opposing Lenin.[18] After he published *Untimely Thoughts*, Lenin and Zinovyev packed him off abroad to be cured. Gorky returned to the USSR each summer and eventually moved back for good. Are his words from the rostrum part of the price paid for the permission to take up permanent residence?[19] In 1934, Gorky seems to be in his servility period. Even Nizan, cynically speaking in favor of the demands of building socialism in the USSR, the "fortress under siege," thinks that Gorky is laying it on a bit thick. Gorky has lived in the United States. The detective novel, he declares, was invented by bourgeois capitalists to crush the proletariat's class consciousness. In bourgeois literature he finds assassins and thieves everywhere. Real literature, the right sort of literature, he concludes, must devote itself to the progress of socialism. For writers, there is only one hero, the working class. Gorky has discovered a law of literary dialectical materialism: in the Soviet Union, where there is neither governor nor governed, only men fraternally united in the construction of socialism, he asserts, the level of literary art can only rise as new techniques develop. Other speakers reiterate the same theme. Malraux grumbles, adding to the notes for his speech. An organizer asks him smoothly if he may look through it. Malraux refuses, saying that he has not finished it. The contribution of Karl Radek, a member of this conference's organizing commission, exasperates Malraux.

Nizan the sphinx smiles behind his glasses. Radek praises the realism of Balzac but pitches vulgarly into Proust, "scum incapable of action," and Joyce, a "heap of dung crawling with worms." The cultural underlings become drunk on insults. The German writer Gustav Regler and Ilya Ehrenburg try to calm Malraux down.

"If Radek thinks what he is saying, he's a bloody idiot. If he doesn't, he's a scoundrel."

Once on the platform, Malraux fires off directly. He would not be there if he did not feel linked to the Soviet Union.

"I . . . will talk to you as a man talks to men, about what unites them and what divides them."

In the USSR, intellectuals are not in the same situation as elsewhere: "You can already work for the proletariat. We revolutionary writers of the West are working against the bourgeoisie. . . . What is the fundamental character of Communist civilization for a Western writer?"

Malraux makes some concessions: "You have taken the oppressed women of tsarism and you have put your trust in them, and out of this pain and this hardship you have made Soviet woman. You have taken children and you have put your trust in them, even children who are beyond the law, and you have made them into pioneers."

In the streets, Malraux has seen children whose parents have been declared "enemies of the people." To avoid being arrested and sent to "colonies for children," they hide. These abandoned children are known as *bezprizorni*s. Before the conference, in his journal, Malraux noted:

> Mayakovsky's last poem, the one he was writing at the moment he died, "Comrade Government," etc., has become the song of the abandoned children. In Russian it has a grand enough rhythmic form for everybody to remember it, and they sing it, when it takes them, in unison, with a tone of bitter complaint, delighted by the rubles on the drawer.
>
> O destiny of Villon, if they sang these ballads at Fresnes! What of Lili! (She is living in the provinces, remarried to a Red Army general.)[20]

On the conference platform, Malraux hammers out: "You have taken saboteurs, assassins, and thieves and you have trusted them, you have saved some of them, and with them, you have built the White Sea Canal, and they will say, 'Through all the obstacles, through civil war and famine, for the first time in millennia, those people have put their trust in man.' "

The aggressive tirade, "I will talk to you as a man," is followed by a compliment. Malraux passes over the suffering of the convicts digging the White Sea Canal. To him there is a "misunderstanding" (a polite way of putting it) between the people from outside and those on the inside. Stunned, stupefied, mopping their brows in the thick heat, the audience hears Malraux attack socialist realism!

"Is the USSR expressed in the image its literature gives us?"

The orator dismantles his sentences: "In external facts, yes. In ethics and psychology, no. Because the trust you place in everyone, you do not always place enough in writers."

Malraux skillfully throws out a warning: "Take care, comrades, America shows us . . . that in expressing a powerful civilization, one does not necessarily make powerful literature and that photographing a great era will not suffice to give birth to great literature."

He drives the point home: "If writers are the engineers of the soul [essential Stalinist expression], do not forget that the highest function of an engineer is to invent. . . . Art is not a submission, it is a conquest."

This is a crime of lèse-Stalin. These Frenchmen are unpredictable! Communicating his speech to the press,[21] in case anyone should want to forget all about it, Malraux puts quotation marks around the phrase "writers are . . ." The clear allusion to Stalin is an incendiary bomb. For a Soviet citizen, it would constitute an offense punishable by imprisonment. Malraux could not be more lucid. He does allow himself a few opaque phrases, however: "Marxism is social consciousness; culture is psychological consciousness."

Are we to conclude from this that culture is not Marxist? Malraux relies on a cursory reading of Marx; Nizan has noticed this before.

"To the bourgeoisie, who were saying "the individual," communism answered: "man." And the cultural watchword used by communism against those in the greatest eras of individualism is the watchword with which Marx binds the first pages of German Ideology to the last draft of *Das Kapital*, that is: "more consciousness."

In a second challenge, Malraux dares to venture, "If you love your classics so much, it is chiefly because they are admirable; but is it not also because they give you a richer and more contradictory notion of psychological life than Soviet novels?"

Delayed revenge: "The works you admire the most, Maxim Gorky's, have never ceased, while remaining accessible to all, to present this character of psychological or poetic discovery that I am calling for here. What I call poetic discovery is the spectacle of the clouds in which prince Andrei Bolkonsky, wounded and lying on his back at Austerlitz, discovers a serenity above pain and the activity of men."

The French writer finishes his speech with a few barbed polite comments: new works will carry the cultural prestige of the USSR abroad. Malraux cites as examples Pasternak and Vladimir Mayakovsky, who committed suicide four years earlier. Stalin still likes Mayakovsky's poetry and lets it be known that "indifference to his memory and his work is a crime." It is not known whether Mayakovsky shot himself in the heart for sentimental or political reasons. In the course of the congress, Bukharin, representative of the Central Committee and editor in chief of *Izvestia*, heaps praise on him.[22] About Pasternak, Malraux writes in his journal, "A darkhaired Buster Keaton with long teeth, clumsy, stammering, but obviously inhabited by genius. As a Muslim, he would be a prophet."

With more shrewdness than sincerity, in words impermeable for the average participant, Malraux rolls out his last tirade, satirical treachery:

Dukes and picklocks listened to Shakespeare together. At a time when Westerners can no longer all gather to laugh bitterly at themselves before the figure of Chaplin, at a time when so many of our best artists are writing for different ghosts, like two hands of the same body, you are raising a civilization from which Shakespeares can emerge. Do not let them stifle beneath the photographs, however beautiful. The world does not just expect from you the image of what you are but also of what is beyond you, which soon only you will be able to give.

The auditorium reacts slowly, since Malraux is talking in French. Some participants move from surprise to perplexity, whether shocked or not. Marguerite Bloch judges that, for form, the majority of the contributors on the platform are no good. "Malraux . . . and his translator were the only ones to produce 'oratorical art' at the congress. There was also an old poet from Dagestan, but that was different; he did impressions of an old sorcerer, which was irresistibly funny; whereas with Malraux, it was in tragic mode, and most beautiful it was too; he had made a sort of prose poem in versicles, alternating with the Russian translation, and that was a great success, although he did include a verse about fear of the type of requirement we have here for the writer, which boils down to this idea: socialist realism risks crushing a naissant Shakespeare in the egg."

Malraux the picador has wounded some of the Stalinist bulls. Karl Radek takes the floor again as if picking up a weapon. Certainly, he acknowledges, Malraux is brilliant. The French writer is "recognized by our enemies," a worrying compliment since in Moscow's black-and-white world the friends of our enemies are our enemies. Radek attacks: "As for our comrade Malraux's fear that a Shakespeare emerging in our nursery will suffocate, it proves his lack of confidence in those caring for the child in this nursery. The better a baby is changed and fed, the more talent he will have."

Radek: "Why does not Malraux ask young Communists what they think of death? Why does he adopt this sterile attitude in a century in which the individual at last has the opportunity to fulfill himself in communion with others?"

Malraux, later, does indeed question some startled Soviet workers about death. Radek's conclusion comes out as a statement rather than a question: comrade Malraux, too, is a petit bourgeois.

On the platform, Malraux turns out to be the most vigorous of the opponents of socialist realism. Most of the speakers spin out a succession of predictable clichés. Yuri Olyesha is one of the few to support the right of an author to describe feelings beyond all political context. His contribution does not appear in the official report. Malraux's outburst, too conspicuous to be censored, is published. Besides, the organizers know that his speeches will be reproduced abroad. It is better to avoid open censorship and limit the damage. Malraux has created a feeling of unease. It must be dispelled by the gracious expedient of ramming the official line home with a pile driver. In turn, Nikulin takes up what Malraux said. For Malraux, he says, politics is situated below literature, which is an inadmissible idea for a socialist realist. Something the writer said after receiving the Goncourt shocked Nikulin: "Those who put their political passions before their taste for greatness should keep well away from this book [*La Condition humaine*]; it is not for them."

"Is this to say that he bows down in front of the dead without thinking of the living?" exclaims Nikulin. " 'The truth of this world is death,' Malraux has written. We say the truth of this world is life."

The next day, Malraux asks to speak and is allowed, which is not the case for all those who raise their hand in the huge hall. Trembling and impatient: "In the speech of comrade Nikulin, the broad outline of which I largely agree with, a misunderstanding has slipped in. For the fifth time already since I have been in the Soviet Union, I find myself faced with an incorrect interpretation of one of my sentences, a sentence about the relationship between literature and politics. . . . If I thought that politics were below literature, I would not be leading, with André Gide, the campaign for the defense of Comrade Dimitrov in France; I would not go to Berlin, appointed by the Comintern for Comrade Dimitrov's defense. And I wouldn't be here."

At the conference, Malraux's thought seems tortuous and difficult to follow. Elsewhere too. In the USSR, he is looking, he says, for "man who is in the process of being born," socialist man before Communist man.[23] Choices are emerging: "We have a new fact: we must no longer choose between democracy and communism but rather between communism and fascism. . . . I believe in the Soviet humanism to come, a humanism that is analogous to but not the same as that of Greece, Rome, and the Renaissance period."

He also has misgivings, which he does not always hide. Either a serious lack of forethought or a stunning audacity prompts Malraux to remark, "We have many abstract theories, but in my opinion we have one concrete subject—that of the purges. The publication of the most remarkable meetings of the Purges Committee would give us an image a thousand times more striking than all the theories that exist. And ten thousand times more novelistic."

It appears that Malraux charms those he talks to more often than he annoys them. Antonina Pirozhkova, Babel's wife, sees Malraux as "tall, very elegant, a little hunched, with fine features, large, remarkable, always serious eyes." She also notices the jerky movements and "smoothed-back hair with a lock" that often falls onto his forehead. When his tics come upon him, the writer turns voluble, intoxicating himself on words. He sets his sentences on fire. Malraux clears his throat and lets out a rush of twitches and sniffs, then calms down. An idiot suffering from Tourette's syndrome will repeat the same words in a monotone. Malraux's illness makes him lively, exuberant, and hyperactive; still, like the most "fragile" sick, he has a poor capacity for attention toward others.

Near Lenin's mausoleum, from the gallery reserved for foreign guests, Malraux watches a sporting parade on Red Square. Stalin can be seen in profile.[24] During a dinner at the National Restaurant, Malraux asks questions about the place of love in Soviet women's lives, how they see betrayal, their point of view on virginity. Babel translates. Malraux, looking serious, nods. He has told the Babels that "writing is not a profession." He is surprised: so many writers here who work only on literature own apartments or dachas or lounge luxuriously in convalescent homes. Malraux concerns himself with writers' physical conditions, not with their trials.[25] In 1936, Soviet power creates an authors' village near Moscow, Peredelkino. The leadership of the Writers' Union starts to make a list of key figures who are to have the use of a dacha. Babel and Pasternak are among the first on the list, as is Boris Pilniak, but not Mikhail Bulgakov or Osip Mandelstam, who have a bad reputation. Stalin understands that intellectuals are corruptible. To refuse a dacha takes moral and physical strength. They often have two floors, four or five rooms, verandas, and garages. Housing is still a serious problem. Sometimes the Russian writers seem to talk more of dachas than of literature.[26]

Those Malraux talks to are struck by his prodigious interest in film. In the *Moscow Journal* Malraux declares,[27] "Communist civilization—particularly in the cinema—has given to an art that draws its strength from the moment, its highest form, and its greatest intensity." Malraux is not blindingly clear: "There is a dialogue for Nietzsche and Napoleon, but there are only orders from Caesar or Augustus to the Roman writers." Where is the dialogue? In Malraux's head.

Although reserved when it comes to Soviet literature, in his conversations he often returns to the great Russian classics. He discusses the Communists' hostility to Dostoevsky with Ehrenburg and records the discussion in his notes:

> Eh.—It is often said, and it is true, that the Russian novel never used truly intelligent men, but almost idiots. Dostoevsky (whom I don't like) likes Dimitri, he doesn't like Ivan, who doesn't exist anyway.
> M.—But he would like to be him.
> Eh.—Yes, but that is different. And anyway Ivan doesn't exist. Dost knows very well that he is simply a vehicle for his ideas. French literature, on the other hand, always has intelligent people. At least the men. For women in French novels are attractive but stupid. A lot stupider than those in Russian novels. With you, in the novel, it is always the woman who is defeated; with us, it is always the man. Actually, the image of the Russian woman seen through Russian literature is idiotic.

Malraux writes on Dostoevsky:

> Adolescents to one side, those who talk of Dost, here, are almost
> all old men. The Communists hate him, quite understandably,
> and are well aware how far opposed his world is from theirs. They
> are so aware of it that they end up no longer understanding that
> Dost is a very great tragic poet. . . . The old people see in him a
> mystic poet, whose thought is based on the idea of the Antichrist,
> and are very surprised that a great French writer [Gide] should
> have written a book on him and that I know his work well. (They
> believe in Latin culture about as much as the Boulevard Montpar-
> nasse believes in the Slavic soul.)

The closer an intellectual gets to the Stalinist orthodoxy, Malraux
observes, the less he likes Dostoevsky: "The Communists detest him."

In this fragmentary journal, Malraux records real-life scenes. At the
National Hotel:

> HOTEL PROSTITUTE
> She lives in a Soviet apartment with a government worker com-
> rade, who believes she is an interpreter or a typist at the hotel.
> Member of the Public Food Union. Leaves every morning badly
> dressed, carrying a little suitcase with the "nice dress" in. Only
> speaks Russian. Has to ask foreigners to pay her first in gold.

Malraux loves gossip, "little truths" or falsehoods, anecdotes about
writers:

> When Gogol's body was moved, God knows why, a group of writ-
> ers stole the coffin. They take it to one of their apartments, open
> it on the table, and start getting blind drunk. After a few hours, all
> that's left in the room is a table with an open coffin resting on it—
> scattered sheets of paper, hair, dust, broken glasses or glasses full
> of vodka, and underneath, in pride of place, a load of shoes and
> boots. . . . The militia are called and arrive to take the coffin back.
> Half awake, the rogues head back to the police station (abandon-
> ing the guards from time to time to go back for a pillow), and
> Slanich yelling behind the coffin, which has lost its lid: "The lid,
> for God's sake, take the lid! Are you waiting for a housekeeper?" A
> few bones that fell out are gathered up in a handkerchief some
> chap is carrying (corners knotted into huge rabbit's ears). . . .
> Eventually it gets sorted out. But Slanich notices that there's a

vertebra missing. And he telegraphs Nikulin, who has been let off, one of the first to reach a neighboring town (N. is famous for his meanness). "Bastard. If Gogol's vertebra not returned immediately, will tell the Guepeyou." Missive is sent to said GPU, and Slanich spends the week in clink.

In the USSR, Malraux befriends Willy Bredel, a German Communist freed after a year in a Nazi camp. Bredel tells him of his experience in Germany, arrest, concentration camp, release. For Clara, the account of Bredel's captivity "served as a starting point" to a forthcoming book. Manès Sperber and Groet also supply Malraux with information. With this work, Malraux will evoke the near present.

In the France of the 1930s to which Malraux returns, a number of intellectuals are looking hesitantly at the three countries that appear to be disturbing the established order: Fascist Italy, Nazi Germany, and the Communist USSR. Some writers waver between the totalitarian Left and the totalitarian Right. In a bout of political teenage acne, Paul Nizan was drawn for a few months to a small extreme-right group. Pierre Drieu la Rochelle, the most hesitant, wavers for a long time. The era itself explains memberships and passing fancies. It seems natural to Drieu to go and visit the holy places: he has talked to Nizan of his wish to see Moscow. He knows of Nizan's "human approach" and knows how far removed his novels are from socialist realism. Nizan, at the time, thinks that Drieu can be reformed. Drieu is to make the pilgrimage to Moscow. It is not Nizan who gets the visa. "Malraux was able to do the necessary. And I am off," Drieu writes to Nizan. "However, I shall first go to Nuremberg to attend the Nazi conference."[28] Drieu seems to sense appetizing similarities between communism and Nazism. Malraux has never had the slightest accommodation for Nazism or fascism.

On his return from the USSR, he takes the role of coryphaean apologist for the USSR. The Soviets have promoted him to choirmaster of the intellectual companions to the cause. Every "fellow traveler" is a potential member of the Party. Malraux will be more profitable on the fringes of the PCF than as a card-carrying party member. The Soviet comrades speak of Malraux the man, at least what they remember of him, and very little of his work. Among the few thousand tourists and foreign pilgrims, Malraux seems one of the most promising in the eyes of apparatchiks, the Comintern, and the Politburo. This man must not be wasted. The most ingenious of the powerful agents, such as dear Ilya Ehrenburg, know that a few open disagreements on Malraux's part make him more credible, especially since the Sovietophile writer does not fall for all the waffle. This fellow traveler has style, looks, and talent but an unpredictable character. To be exploited with care.

For Malraux, as for millions of sympathizers, the USSR is the first country where a humanitarian and utopian ideal has served a revolutionary will. Malraux has glimpsed flaws and has brazenly attacked the fruitlessness of socialist realism. More complex than the exterior journey from cinema studios to writers' conclaves, from day nurseries to the model kolkhozes, there begins in Malraux an interior journey. He accepts the Soviets' cultural sterilization and their system of privileges in the name of unlikely but Shakespearean literary tomorrows. For a part of the European Left, the prospect of Soviet success is obvious, Capitalism being the incarnation of absolute Evil. With Malraux—half militant and a quarter millenarian despite his pessimism—an imaginary socialism gets the upper hand on socialism as it exists.

Dyable de l'exaspération contenue

CHAPTER FOURTEEN

Time to Choose

W HILE SOVIET INTELLECTUALS and critics were looking with admiration or suspicion into the writer's case, a text was taking shape: a long short story. The hero: a German Communist leader. Malraux is still receiving witness accounts from Nazi prisons and camps. In his text, he helps to reinforce a religiously leftist idea of Soviet communism: the Russian Revolution, "natural heir" to the French Revolution, is an assumption. Whatever leaders, the police, and the military may do in its name, revolution remains pure in its intentions. Communism could not make mistakes that it cannot rectify. It's not so easy to rectify deaths; but that's the price of history. The blindness, the self-inflicted nearsightedness, is understandable if not excusable: one cannot reproach Malraux for not having read in 1917, when he was sixteen, the lucid articles by the Russian correspondent for *L'Humanité*. When he returned to Paris in 1934, all the information he needed was near at hand and available, within Gallimard itself. Brice Parain, Gaston Gallimard's secretary, spoke Russian and had lived in the USSR, and not only in Moscow, having been active in the literary wing of the French Communist Party as a defender of "proletarian literature" and a combatant against "bourgeois literature." He then broke all ties with the PCF in 1933. He didn't go shouting about it, but he knew. Malraux, at best, did not want to know, or see, the appalling reality of the Communist regime, especially for the lower classes in town and country alike.

Malraux knows how to get a book into orbit. A first version of *Le Temps du mépris*[1] appears in installments in the *Nouvelle Revue Française*.[2] The old antique dealer's instincts complement those of the editor well. Malraux oversees the first edition: 8 copies on China paper, 11 on Japanese Imperial, 31 on Van Gelder, 297 on pur fil Lafuma Navarre vellum. Like Gaston Gallimard, André Malraux knows the artistic and commercial aspects of publishing, two sides of the same coin. *Le Temps du mépris* is issued by Gallimard in May 1935. There is no subheading: the word *roman* (novel) does not appear on the cover. The preface talks of a *nouvelle*, a short story.

Le Temps du mépris precipitates, in the chemical sense, the reports, secrets, and descriptions gleaned by Malraux from German friends. His imagination churns through the reality and filters it. He relives the suffering of the imprisoned German Communists: he identifies with them and with his hero, the leader Kassner. The Nazis are looking for the German Communist writer (Kassner echoes Sperber); the Gestapo is unable to prove his identity, and another prisoner sacrifices himself, pretending to be Kassner. The Party needs Kassner to be free. The writer reaches Prague, where he joins his wife and son. Man's condition in Germany since 1933 has not been human, but animal. Malraux becomes the first famous French novelist to write about the German concentration camps and torture; he has information about this from Germany. But what about torture in the USSR? Well, the camps over there are for "re-education." Western Communists and fellow travelers alike need to swallow this obscene nonsense. Malraux is no exception.

Despite the lessons on tone and style received in Moscow, Malraux has not adopted socialist realism. But his edifying work introduces a "positive, exemplary" hero, as Nizan points out in a review:[3] "We can sense here the profound accord Malraux has with Marx's greatest saying: we must give men consciousness of themselves, *even if they do not want it*." [My italics.] Make the people happy despite themselves, despite yourself, despite everything—a terrifying proposition. Nizan adds, "We appreciate this ambition for greatness in Malraux. He knows that communism is not just an economic or political thing but also a view of the world. . . . Communism lays claim to all aspects of a complete civilization." Complete—and totalitarian. Summing up, Nizan continues, "Malraux has moved on since *La Condition humaine*. He is one of the greats. . . . *La Condition humaine* is dominated by death, solitude, and escape: it was a novel for loners. *Le Temps du mépris* announces the age of 'manly brotherhood,' an entirely positive book, intent on affirming certain values that are less complex and stronger than in *La Condition humaine*." Nizan says a workman has written to him saying that Malraux's latest book seemed "more reliable."

To Gaëtan Picon in the monthly *Cahiers du Sud*, Malraux's vision of communism seems narrow. The personalist Emmanuel Mounier from *Esprit* describes the book as "a hiccup in an otherwise great oeuvre." A reader must emerge from the narrative with one firm moral and political conviction: that it is imperative to work with the German KPD and, failing that, with the nearest Communist Party. This wins Malraux the approbation of several Muscovite journals and reviews, and Aragon's indulgence. Malraux has done his duty. Yet Nizan and Aragon are too intelligent to consider this thin text excellent.[4]

The Communists in France are not entirely in step with one another, however. For the duty critic at *L'Humanité* (the PCF's daily mouthpiece) Malraux does not seem "reliable."[5] R. Gray is less enthusiastic than Nizan, with distant praise for the long short story that is not quite a novel. Gray quite rightly points out that manly brotherhood can become a value in itself, and just as easily on the Right, among fascists, French or otherwise, as on the Left. Malraux, he explains, will find socialist salvation for his soul and his works "by walking boldly in the path shown by Marx and Engels, the only one that will allow his great talent to show to its fullest extent." The Communists try to have Marx assume responsibility for socialist realism. The PCF had a duty to support Malraux, since he had taken the USSR line and defended Dimitrov, Ernst Thälmann, and the realism to come, that of communism. Dealings with him were to be conducted within the context of the battle fronts shared with the socialists and ongoing links with the Catholics. They were not to walk too far in his company—or rather, they were to overtake him, since it was predicted that in time he would overtake himself. In the eyes of the Party's watchdogs, Malraux is making progress. For sectarians such as Georges Cogniot and André Marty, even the dogmatic Nizan, like Malraux, is an object of suspicion without knowing it.[6]

The abundant reviews of *Le Temps du mépris* are on the whole favorable. One critic more than any other, instead of identifying the hero with Malraux, sees how much the legendary aspect of Kassner coincides with his creator: Robert Brasillach explains that Kassner becomes "a hero for Malraux before being a Communist." Could Germany, Nazism, and communism just be alibis? Malraux is constructing his own legend. Behind Kassner, is he himself more important than Thälmann?

From the start, the narrative gives the impression that the writer is lifting his head from a synopsis. The technique is cinematic: still shots and condensed dialogue come one after another.

> At the moment when Kassner was pushed into the waiting room, a prisoner under questioning was finishing a sentence, which was covered by the police noise of papers and boots [three shots]. On the other side of the table, the Hitlerian official, same jaw, same trapezoid face, same hair almost shaved above the ears, with little blond streaks on the top of the head, short and stiff [two shots, or three].
>
> "Party instructions."
> "Since when?"
> "1924."

"What has been the nature of your participation in the illegal Communist Party?"

"I know nothing about the illegal party. Until January 1933, my role in the German Party was a technical one."

Malraux uses journalistic methods, echoing American novelists. The psychology is behavioral. Malraux skillfully draws from his own life. The reader feels the heat of demonstrations and meetings, transposed from France to Germany, and an atmosphere of generosity, a widespread idea, often false, but comforting, that progressive discourse can influence history. Anna, Kassner's wife—at last, after May, another woman in Malraux's fiction—has Clara's green eyes. There is also a child. Following the death of André's parents, there are allusions to a mother and a father. Kassner loves cats, like Malraux. A vigorous descriptive scene with an airplane tossed about in a thunderstorm: the storm above Bône in Algeria that could have killed him and Corniglion-Molinier.

As if he felt *Le Temps du mépris* not to be as substantial as his novels, a third of the way through Malraux slips into the tremulous, fantastical style of his first texts, grafted onto a more linear story:

> Kassner felt himself move forward like a broken skeleton, rattled by the singing. Yet already—even as there rose with these voices from his stark contemplation the memory of revolutionary songs played on a hundred thousand men (and nothing in music is more thrilling than words spoken as one by a multitude), men separated and returned to the crowds like the glittering song of the wind on wheat as far as the horizon—already the imperious gravity of a new song seemed once more to draw everything in toward an immense slumber; and in the quiet of this army under shroud, the music eventually overcame its own heroic call as it overcame all else, as it is in its nature to overcome all things, to consume everything in the overlapping flames of a burning yet dispassionate bush; night set in on the entire universe, a night where men know each other in their walking or their silence, the abandoned night, full of stars and friendship.

It is as if Malraux is returning, despite himself, to the style of the books that came before his Asian trilogy. Past and present are mixed.[7] The unreal character of some passages comes out better in some fragments included in the *NRF* serialization[8] and later cut.

> A thousand memories, created by him, regrouped within to re-create him in turn, started to well up, summoned by a fascinated

self-satisfaction, by the same attentive abandon of children telling themselves ghost stories. Something subhuman was attracting him there . . . an unknown and yet intense danger in which he recognized, unmistakably, the intensity of death. This was the realm of the fever, the fascination with sacred terror that man experiences when he approaches his undoing. It was the primitive call with the resonance of a funerary trumpet, in which he recognized the delectatio morosa of sexuality and of death.

A curious association to make, between sexuality and moroseness.

Absurdity, unpredictability, and coincidence are consubstantial with the human condition: the Nazis free Kassner by accident. In the Indochinese trilogy Malraux distinguishes metaphysical death (*la mort*) from physical demise (*le trépas*). Here he adds an obsession with torture, all the more strongly when the author is identified with the hero. "In the throes of humiliation, as with pain, the torturer is very likely to be stronger than the victim." " 'If they were to force me under torture to give information that I do not have, I would not be able to do anything about it. Let us suppose, then, that I do not have the information.' His courage, at this moment, was busy separating him from himself, separating the man who in a few minutes would be in the power of these menacing sounds of boots, from the Kassner he would become again afterward." The eyewitness accounts of Nazi practices accumulate. Hitler's henchmen humiliate man himself, degrade him, hate him. In Malraux's story, the officer, the Communist militant, is transfigured into a symbol of humanity.

Malraux has no direct experience of life in a concentration camp. He makes efforts to root his character in the history of Germany and its Communist Party, going as far as to supply a "biog" such as Kassner might have put together for the Party bureaucrats or the Comintern, and such as Nizan and others gave to Moscow: "Miner's son; scholarship to university, organizer of proletarian theater; prisoner of the Russians, delivered to the partisans, then to the Red Army; delegate in China [like Malraux] and in Mongolia; writer, returned to Germany in 1932 to prepare strikes in the Ruhr against the Papen decree, organizer of the illegal information department, ex–vice president of the Secours Rouge." Malraux wants to be seen as a writer close to the Communists and pushes his relative orthodoxy as far as to quote the gurus: " 'One cannot conquer with the avant-garde alone,' said a haunting text by Lenin." The Comintern and its staging posts in Europe, the Communist parties and their satellites, are advocating "a wide front." This makes Kassner-Malraux a resolute devotee of the new party line: Kassner "had felt that it was impossible to create a workers' unit without being active in the Reformist and Catholic unions." Malraux sometimes seems ill at ease in his text and tends to embellish. Having met with some critical comments during the serialized preprint in the *NRF*, he begins his book with a defensive, sometimes condescending, and occasionally arrogant seven-page preface.[9] The choice of typography in the dedication is his own:

> TO THE GERMAN COMRADES
> who have asked me to communicate
> what they suffered and what they upheld,
> THIS BOOK, WHICH IS THEIRS

The "asked me to communicate" is interesting and somewhat pretentious. In the preface Malraux attempts to clarify his conception of communism. It is an individualism that has nothing to do with the Communist view of society: "In Kassner's eyes, as with a number of Communist intellectuals, communism restores the individual's fertility." It is humanism in solidarity. Rich in imperious comparisons, Malraux decrees that "with the Roman from the empire, the Christian, the soldier in the Army of the Rhine, the Soviet worker, man is linked to the collectivity surrounding him. The Alexandrian, the eighteenth-century writer, is separated from it." He once again mounts the hobbyhorse of Communist historiography, the continuity between the French Revolution and the Soviet Revolution. There is a certain amount of cymbal clashing: "One can wish the meaning of the word art to be the attempt to give men consciousness of the grandeur they are unaware of in themselves." Harking back to his Moscow speech, Malraux, an all-or-nothing theoretician, writes: "It is not passion which destroys the work of art, it is the will to prove," throwing out a fresh challenge to the extremist evangelists of socialist realism. The reader, whether sympathetic or not, finds passion in *Le Temps du mépris*; but also, in massive doses, a desire to prove. In fifteen years of writing, Malraux has never been more Manichean. Asserting the artist's right to individualism, Malraux slips in: "contempt for fellow man is common among politicians, but confidential." The Nazis' contempt for Communists in Germany, and that of the Soviet Secret Service for its fellow citizens, seems fairly public for whoever, among intellectuals, sees fit not to give in to the numbing temptation of totalitarianism.[10]

In this preface, he also returns to "manly brotherhood." Claude Vannec, Garine, and Kyo all end up in an uncertain solitude; Kassner is reunited with the world of mankind. The book ends with Kassner finding his wife and child, on a resonant, almost socialist realist note, like an image from a Soviet propaganda poster: "Now they were going to talk, reminisce, tell each other everything. . . . All of that was going to become everyday life, a staircase descended side by side, footsteps in the street, beneath a sky unchanged since the first human wills died, or conquered." In smoother tones, Malraux establishes a continuity by returning to the last words of *Les Conquérants*—"a hard yet fraternal gravity"—and the Malrucian melody—"this desperate brotherhood that drove him mad," the conclusion of *La Voie royale*. Malraux wanted to spare his reader the clutching solitude of Kyo's wife when confiding in old Gisors: " 'I hardly cry anymore, now,' she said with a bitter pride." In *Le Temps du mépris*, the heroes always appear proud, but they no longer feel bitterness, despite the wounds scarring their prisoners' dignity.

Finally, Malraux hits on one of his characteristic phrases: "The individual is in opposition to the community, but he feeds on it. And what is important is much less to know what he is opposed to than what he feeds on; like genius, the worth of the individual is judged by what he holds within him." Genius, again, as ever.

The Soviets like Malraux's book enough to publish it in 1936. *La Condition humaine* remains in serialized form in a review, with no one-volume edition and devoid of the scenes involving the characters considered "bourgeois": Ferral the "capitalist" and his mistress, Valérie.

Barely two months after the publication of *Le Temps du mépris*, Malraux takes part in the International Writers' Congress for the Defense of Culture, a follow-up to the Moscow Congress. Gide and Malraux are the stars, cultural agitprop agents cherished by Moscow. The congress runs from June 21 to 25, 1935. It could have been given the subheading "In Defense of the USSR." Hitler and Nazism are denounced as enemies of culture and freedom of thought. Stalin and communism, as we know, guarantee intellectual independence and stimulation. Sympathizers, Party members, essentials from Ehrenburg to Aragon, from Jean-Richard Bloch to Léon Moussinac, form into groups by affinity in the Mutualité meeting rooms. There are also liberals present: E. M. Forster, Aldous Huxley. Julien Benda and Heinrich Mann attend three of the five evenings. Nizan, Barbusse, and two foreign participants speak about "humanism" and Tristan Tzara talks on "nation and culture." Thanks to multiple maneuvers by Willy Münzenberg, the Soviet agent of genius, never have so many writers, painters, and sculptors been brought together in Paris to speak in favor of communism, defender of the Arts. Despite themselves, in many cases. Malraux talks on "the individual." In the aftermath of *Le Temps du mépris*, he delivers an ecumenical speech on man, humanism, communism, fertility, the will, communion, and difference.

The ceremony starts well in a progressive spirit of consensus. In the convivial heat of the plenary sessions and the corridors, the meetings in cafés and restaurants around Place Maubert, Münzenberg has managed to avoid the presence of party poopers, or so he thinks. The Soviets are counting on Malraux to avoid any incidents or ultimatums about dissidents imprisoned in the USSR. But, partly owing to the author of *Le Temps du mépris*, the impressive engine comes off the rails. The organizers know that André Breton, an awkward customer, backed up by Henry Poulaille—surrealism and populism hand in hand—intends to broach the subject of persecutions. Not in Germany and Italy, as intended in Münzenberg's planning of the ritual, but in the USSR: Where are the imprisoned Viktor Serge and Osip Mandelstam? The ever-present busybodies Aragon and Ehrenburg, each on instruction from his party, confer and take action: the congress secretary, the easygoing Louis Guilloux, "forgets" to put Breton on the agenda. Well, time is short, isn't it? Breton, excluded from the proceedings, wastes no time getting organized. He may be a surrealist, but he's not unrealistic. Important figures who know Viktor Serge are placed around the room: the Belgian writer Charles Plisnier, who has resigned from the Party, the Italian Socialist Gaetano Salvemini, and Magdeleine Paz. The British will lend their support. In short, it is a counterplot. Papa Gide, chairing the session on June 22, encourages Malraux to hand over to a troublemaker who has been sent by Breton. Who is the more unpredictable and dangerous for the Muscovite theoreticians and practitioners, Malraux or Gide? The microphone stops working: a technical hitch, naturally. Magdeleine Paz brings up the imprisonment of Stalin's opponents. Mikhail Koltsov replies from the rostrum: those imprisoned are counter-revolutionaries, he will not allow the honor of the Soviets to be . . . , etc. With the added complication of translation, people interjecting, delegates arriving and leaving in impatience or unconcern, the muddle grows. What's happening? Where are we going? Who said what? Who supports who? The Soviets get the feeling that in France, two plus two is five.

"An utter shambles," Paul Nizan tells his wife. "You can always rely on Breton . . ."

In the wings, there are moves afoot to pressure the Soviet authorities. Boris Souvarine has for a long time been telling his friends and his rare readers about the fate of "leftist" adversaries of the regime. Viktor Serge wants to leave the USSR. David Riazonov, ex-director of the Marx-Engels Institute in Moscow, has been in prison awaiting trial since 1931. Moscow thinkers accuse Riazonov of being a "talmudic connoisseur of Marxism." Souvarine mounts a bluff: from the telegraph office of the Paris Stock Exchange he sends a telegram to Stalin calling for the release of Viktor Serge. Souvarine signs, "Romain Rolland, Henri Barbusse, Charles Vildrac." These writers—these "comrades"—did not actually sign the telegram, but hey! They could have.[11]

Malraux concludes from all these protests and maneuvers that the

Soviets are underrepresented at the congress and are not giving a good impression, despite his friend Isaak Babel regaling the audience with anecdotes. What can be done to increase the Soviet presence? Gide and Malraux hurry to the Soviet Embassy: Moscow must send more cultural representatives. Dressed as a peasant, Boris Pasternak arrives under orders from Stalin himself. He reads a poem from the rostrum. Malraux reads the translation.[12]

Malraux has the honor of giving the closing speech. This conference, he states, has taken place in the worst possible conditions from a financial point of view. Yet the Soviets have forked out to pay for it. The participants have allowed "those who were gagged to express themselves and a solidarity to be shown." Let us return to the essential matter, comrades, companions: the defense of culture. It is not a speech of the finest Malrucian vintage.[13]

"This conference has shown that all artistic work is dead when love is withdrawn."

And as an echo of his great speech in Moscow:

"An inheritance is not simply passed on, it must be won."

And as if in reply to his preface to *Le Temps du mépris*: "Soviet comrades, what we expect of your civilization, which has preserved its old faces in blood, typhus, and famine, is that thanks to you, a new face will be revealed to us. . . . Every work becomes a symbol and a sign, all art is a possibility of reincarnation."

Serious political problems can gum up an audience like so much ideological maple syrup. Malraux, tense, his voice hoarse, feels understandably relieved when the participants leave. After the conference, the top authorities in Moscow express their dissatisfaction that these surrealists and Trotskyites were not kept quiet. Viktor Kine (aka Sorokin), writer and informer, explains in a report to Comrade Andreyev, the secretary of the Communist Party Central Committee: "Facts: we learned that the Trotskyites were preparing their intervention three weeks before the congress. Koltsov, staying in Paris, told us about the Trotskyite action for the liberation of Viktor Serge. Here are our actions concerning this matter. . . . (b) We made sure that this action would not take place in a large room in the presence of the public but in a small room for 250 people in camera (we had many difficulties and Malraux helped us a lot)."

Malraux's performance satisfies Johannes Becher: "Malraux is a great success for us." The intellectual stature of the author of *La Condition humaine* far surpasses that of other participants. "One notices immediately, when observing the best-known German writers, their lack of general knowledge. I refer to T. Mann, H. Mann, Feuchtwanger. They have literary training, but they lack a philosophical one. They have never read Marx, they have no idea about dialectics." Koltsov and Tcherbakov go further: "It is slanderous to accuse Malraux of 'gagging' our speakers. . . . After a short collaboration with the Trotskyites, Malraux left them abruptly and demonstratively to stay with us; he did us a great service throughout the congress. Nothing can be guaranteed for the future with Malraux, but currently this great writer and brilliant orator is essentially with us, despite the 'wailing' of the bourgeoisie. Such a person should be removed from the bourgeoisie instead of discouraged with discussions of his previous Trotskyism." So some Soviets are happy with Malraux. Koltsov is given the risky mission of tailing him:[14] a questionable gift for anyone dealing with this "target" writer, requiring culture and careful handling.

Malraux takes part—with Clara, not Josette—in a unitarian meeting bringing together Communists, Socialists, and Radical Socialists. Josette is not interested in politics, either French or foreign. She doesn't have the "what I think, comrade, is . . ." style familiar to Clara. When the Popular Front is formed on July 14, 1935, Clara marches with her husband from the Bastille to La Nation.

Malraux spends his summer holidays with Josette in Belgium, from Brussels to Bruges and Ghent. Then he picks up his political activities again with a look at colonial problems in the context of international politics. Having put French colonialism at its worst into the dock in Indochina, he writes a preface to Andrée Viollis's book *Indochine S.O.S.*[15] The fast, precise writing in Viollis's account comes across as a log. She has been through Indochina, from Cochin China to Laos, interviewing government employees, peasants, Asian officials, engineers, planters; she has followed in the footsteps of writers such as Roland Dorgelès and Luc Durtain, who described the mines he visited as "hard-labor camps."[16] In Hanoi, Viollis inspected the department of public health, going through twenty thousand files and fifty thousand documents. She interviewed a torturer. Some of the settlers and administrators she talked to are reminiscent of the despots denounced by Léon Werth in *L'Indochine enchaînée*. Viollis has conversed with young civil servants straight out of the École Coloniale, stuffed with theoretical knowledge, vain, preoccupied with their comfort ("ices, fans, servants"). The account moves Malraux: it is an Indochina known to him, with yet more men condemned to death or to a life of forced labor, with the horrors, the cruelties, the errors, the blunders of an almost omnipotent colonialism. According to Andrée Viollis, French colonial power is wiping out rebel villages everywhere, executing at random, terrorizing, and shooting. The journalist even meets with figures whom Malraux and his newspaper defended, such as Phan Boi Chau, who declares to Viollis, "Tell the French people that the old revolutionary Phan Boi Chau sincerely wishes to collaborate with France, but let us hurry, otherwise it will be too late!"

In his preface, Malraux lives again as journalist and editor of *L'Indo-*

chine and *L'Indochine Enchaînée*. He reminds the reader how the authorities forced his newspaper to stop appearing. With nostalgic melancholy, he evokes the Annamese compositor and the English type bought in Hong Kong:

> You pulled from your pocket a handkerchief knotted into a purse, with its corners sticking up like rabbit's ears: "These are just *és*. . . . There are acute accents, graves, and circumflexes. For the *i*s, it will be more difficult; but perhaps we can get by without them. Tomorrow many workers will do the same as I, and we will bring all the accents we can." You opened the handkerchief, emptied the characters onto the print bed in a disordered heap like jackstraws, and lined them up with the tip of your printer's finger, saying nothing more. You had taken them from the government print works, and you knew that if you were caught you would be condemned, not as a revolutionary but as a thief. When they were all laid out flat like counters in a game, you merely said, "If I am condemned, tell them in Europe that we did what we did for people to know what is happening here."

The story is corroborated by Clara, who is just as capable of making it up. But there is a convincing antique patina to it. Malraux hangs on to his ghosts, his dreams, and his fantasies.

The demands of the Annamese reported by Andrée Viollis are those Malraux was defending ten years earlier: freedom of movement, freedom of the press, the development of education, increased powers for the Indochinese assemblies. In the course of her work, Viollis wanted to prove with passion. Her book is packed with precise information, prices in piastres and in francs. The reader can hear shouts and music, smell the scent of the fruit and vegetable markets, the humid odor of the rice fields. Malraux always wants the distinction to be made between "the necessities of a colonization" and "the foolishness that goes on in its name." In France, the independence of the colonies still does not figure on the Left's agenda, neither with Communists, Socialists, nor Liberals.

Beyond the colonial problem, Malraux asks technical questions about writing, about the novel and what he calls "new journalism." As a defender of committed journalism, he claims that "reporting is weak in France inasmuch as it doesn't want anything." He hopes that in the better articles an element of revolutionary or at least rebellious protest can be found to give perspective to news. He thinks highly of Ehrenburg and Viollis's style. Malraux refers his readers back to *Les Conquérants* and *La Condition humaine*: "I think that there are few novelists of our time who have not toyed with accounts based on reportage collected into a volume, feeling that this was a new form of novel writing, and then fairly quickly abandoned their hope. Yet reportage continues. One of the strongest devices of the French novel, from Balzac to Zola, is the intrusion of a character into a world which he reveals to us as we discover it ourselves." Malraux sees ellipsis, more than metaphor, as an instrument to be used in the writing of "new" journalists. In a roundabout way, he explains himself as a novelist. Some have accused him of writing overlong reportages rather than novels. He perfects a technique found both in Andrée Viollis's book and in his own attempts. The journalist and the novelist are mixed together, to the disdain of literary purists. Viollis in turn seems inspired by Malraux's dramatic and cinematographic technique.

From *La Condition humaine*:	From *Indochine S.O.S.*:
"March 21, 1927. Midnight."	"Singapore, October 2nd. The same evening."
Or:	Or:
"April 11. Half past midnight."	"In the train, November 21; Huê, November 23."

The tool in the hand of the novelist-cum-journalist is as much a camera as a pen. Andrée Viollis, at the heart of her foreword, refers to an article by Malraux on Indochina, published two years before in *Marianne*. Like Malraux, she knows that over there, even Nationalists wanting to apply the democratic principles taught by France are called "Communists." Malraux writes, "It is difficult to imagine a brave Annamese as anything other than a revolutionary." But here, "revolutionary" does not mean "Communist."

Malraux forgets Asia and turns his attention back to Europe. He still starts from the same premise: there is a threat from a single main enemy, from Berlin to Rome. Mussolini has just struck Ethiopia. Right-wing contributors to *Le Temps* have published a manifesto defending the Italian attack in the name of a Western, Christian, "superior" civilization. Malraux responds by helping to launch *Vendredi*, a progressive weekly. Andrée Viollis is one of the editors.

La Corsienne

CHAPTER FIFTEEN

From Eisenstein to L'Humanité

ACK IN MOSCOW, the Soviet Writers' Union has been analyzing the trail left behind by the Malraux comet at the Writers' Congress. Reactions to his passage vary, as attested by the balanced, undogmatic discussion[1] presided over by Franz Chiller, historian of Western European literature. The introductory report is by Ivan Anissimov:

> Malraux is an original but typical artist. The issues he is concerned with in his works are very important to a great number of intellectuals. . . . It falls to us to understand this originality and typicality in his novels. He has broken free of bourgeois culture and found his own path leading to revolution. He is very close to a figure who has become his guide in many ways, André Gide. Malraux's premise is that bourgeois civilization is in decline.

Malraux could be seen as a Marxist extension of Spengler. The debate opens up. Abraham Efros, art critic and translator, sees Malraux as "the spiritual son of Gide." But he feels that *Les Conquérants* lacks objectivity ("his writing is surreal") and that *La Condition humaine* is full of "beautiful Chinese trickery." Efros doubts that Malraux's future novel, *Le Pétrole*, will illustrate socialism: "Malraux never says 'I'; he says 'yes' to our revolution, but in inverted commas."

The journalist Sergei Romov, who will be the first translator[2] of excerpts from *La Condition humaine*, steps in: "Malraux lacks ideas. I don't believe in his new novel on oil. He can criticize Chinese capitalism but not French capitalism. He is interested only in adventures involving people. . . . *La Voie royale* and *Les Conquérants* are fantastical, useless works."

Romov figures that Kyo is a Trotskyist because he isn't a Stalinist. He sees Malraux as a "complex" writer who cannot be "believed entirely." What is important about him is "his style and creative technique." The novelist Lev Nikulin (a favorite of Maxim Gorky) protests, "We cannot talk about [Malraux] like that. *La Condition humaine* is very popular in France. It sold 200,000 copies: only Céline's book has come close to being that successful."

Nikulin wants to understand Malraux's approach: "When he was in the Soviet Union, he was looking for characters out of Dostoevsky. He chose writers whose works evoke the 'Slavic soul' in the same way as Dostoevsky. Olyesha, Pasternak. When Pasternak speaks, Malraux thinks it is the voice of Soviet Russia."

Nikulin sees "Malraux and Céline [as] opposite poles." After all, "Malraux has managed to tackle a subject as large as the revolution in China. . . . Here, we are afraid of such far-reaching subjects." The Soviet writer believes that *La Condition humaine* should be published in the USSR. To Evgenia Galperina, the historian of European literature, Malraux "is one of the greatest French writers," but his past must be forgotten. "Céline and Malraux are extremities of ugliness and beauty. . . . Malraux is always changing. . . . His solitude is embodied in his opposition to the bourgeoisie; he does not see the proletariat at the heart of bourgeois civilization. His style is original. . . . One can hear the music of his writing. Very much like Dostoevsky."

Anissimov concludes the discussion: We must forget Malraux's past because "his entire life resembles a path toward revolution."

There was indeed a Malraux problem in Moscow. The Revolutionary Writers' Organization became interested in him again when preparing a gathering in Paris "for the defense of culture." Gide had refused the proposed program with a firm "never." Literature must not be dictated by a timid paracultural bureaucracy. But then he went back on his refusal. Becher sadly declares, "We cannot say that Gide is ours until he shows a willingness to get close to us. . . . We have not been able to explain the term 'Socialist Realism.' The association is theoretically very weak."

Becher adds candidly, "All of these writers must be led in such a way that they do not realize they are being led by Moscow. In other words, they must be made to say what we want to hear. . . . Malraux is a great success for us. Not only is he close to us in his works, but he is a very good organizer. No one can beat him in a discussion on Nietzsche. He speaks very fast French. Only Regler can understand him, but he is too young for him."

Becher ends on a regretful homage: "It is almost impossible to change the ideological opinions of people like Malraux."

Meanwhile in Paris, Malraux has raised the stakes. In *L'Humanité*, he proclaims that in the USSR "fears have changed a good deal, in content. A patient is no longer anxious about his own future but that of the collectivity, the kolkhoz, the factory, etc. Neurosis and psychosis are almost a thing of the past . . . because here, the future is not a threat. What is the main worry of the bourgeoisie? To secure their future. But here, the future is made secure by the collectivity, and because of that, man's activities have been almost transformed." Malraux is raving. Why these vaticinations? Because the readers of *L'Humanité* expect such excesses from witnesses returning from the potential paradise, the Mecca of communism? Something urges him to move closer to the Russian Communists when faced with a French journalist.

He declares that in the past, in Siberian Oirot, before the Revolution, pretty girls were sold to the rich and powerful. The relationship between a man and a woman was that of "master and slave." Now Malraux has observed over there "a young man" bringing "a little bouquet to a girl." This is supposed to demonstrate the progress of equality.

Malraux reports overhearing this highly edifying exchange with a little girl:

"What is it that you call 'before'?"

"Before was when men lived in trees and there were policemen."

Siberian girls as vehicles for the clichéd, elementary propaganda of the Party, but with an eccentric Malrucian twist.

When interviewed, Malraux puts on hold a critical sense that was not lacking in the USSR. In Moscow he attacked socialist realism and showed some nonconformism; back in Paris he becomes a conventional speaker of orthodox views with neophyte phrases. To *Pravda*[3] he had said that the most interesting aspect of the conference was the discussion on "the problem with socialist realism." Ten days later, he tells *L'Humanité* that he considers socialist realism to be a "viable and powerful method," since in the USSR this method is directed toward a romantic reality: the frontier guards, the autonomous republics, the civil war, and even—he adds in all seriousness—the five-year plan. He no longer sees stifled Shakespeares but an unprecedented hatching of Soviet culture: "The enormous strength of the Soviet force from the outset is that it is the type of civilization from which Shakespeares emerge; and it is all too obvious that no other Western country has ever come up with work similar to *The Battleship Potemkin*." He challenges those who suggest that the freedom to write is reduced in the USSR.[4] Malraux plays with the vague but practical notion of "the bourgeoisie," geometrical center of all vices. "For an artist, what is important is not the freedom to do absolutely anything but freedom to do what you want. The Soviet artist knows that it is not from disagreement with the civilization surrounding him but from harmony with it that he will draw the strength of his genius." The word *genius* appears more and more often in Malraux's vocabulary. He adds that one thing in particular struck him in the USSR, the "obvious brotherhood between the writer and the public." In Moscow, he never mentioned that fraternity.

The most striking thing about the USSR, Malraux continues, is "Soviet unity." He insists that

> it has become reality. Stalin's formula for minority culture, "socialist content, national form," has clearly taken shape. One hundred and fifty national minorities were represented; there were among them differences of sensitivity, not of thought. Marxism has enabled the Union to constitute its unity, in depth. There is now more that is picturesque in Moscow and indeed in Novgorod than in Samarkand. It is easy for those who are moved at the sight of a Breton traditional costume to laugh at Tadjik poets singing of the bringing of water to their desert.

Malraux's parallels are daring: "The inventory of the bourgeois world, one might say, is complete. The inventory of the Soviet world, on the other hand, is entirely still to do." And then a dead end: "There has been much insistence on the mistrust that Russian society—still under construction and so often threatened—has brought to bear on its fellow man. But let us take care to note that this mistrust affects only the individual. For mankind, on the contrary, the confidence invested by the Soviets is perhaps the greatest it has ever known." In short, the individual is crushed and mankind is free.

Thanks to his conviction, his passion, or his opportunism, Malraux satisfies all audiences. Based as it is on the hypothesis of a flourishing Soviet society surrounded by capitalist countries, his reasoning works well in the current climate of the Left. Malraux is not alone in the intellectual maze, but he is becoming the most noticeable fellow traveler to sing so out of tune. André Gide prefers to ruminate on his own observations and come up with more penetrating criticisms, even before going to Moscow.

Malraux returns to the USSR in March 1936. On the way he writes to Josette, "So I am definitively on my way to Moscow. I am traveling with Kysou (Roland's nickname—when he was little, he used to say 'quisourit quisourit')." Roland is in another bunk. He is to work at the *Literaturnaya Gazeta* and for the crypto-Communist Parisian daily *Ce Soir*, run by Aragon, where Nizan specializes in foreign politics. Malraux continues, "and when I allow myself to dream and believe that it is you [Josette] up there, austere reality brings things back into focus, despite the Polish stations where military music plays for officers getting off the train, making the cab horses' ears prick up in rhythm—they have such musical heads. I learn from day to day how wrong I was to have reservations, even slight ones, about your kindliness. The Polish girls line up and go to see national films on Chopin. I send you their dreams as well as mine, to send you dreams the color of travel."

Malraux has a few goals for this second stay in the USSR: to find interesting books to translate, to strengthen his contacts with the Soviet literary world and with the Writers' Union, and to visit Eisenstein. As one of the first French authors to consider the cinema as art, Malraux is keen to follow up his project of a film based on *La Condition humaine*. Like Pudovkin, Dovzhenko, or the Communist Dutchman Joris Ivens, like Paul Strand and Leni Riefenstahl, so admired by Hitler, he sees an instrument of propaganda in film that does not exclude its aesthetic ambition. Art and political ideas can progress, thanks to cinema. In France, the reputation of Soviet cinema is growing, strengthened by articles by Georges Sadoul and Léon Moussinac, Communist critics.

A few years earlier, Malraux had come to the defense of Sergei Eisenstein and *The Battleship Potemkin*. Director and writer met in the *NRF* offices in 1932. The polyglot Eisenstein judged at the time that this author was too proud in his knowledge of the arts in the USSR. Malraux, he thought, exaggerated about Dostoevsky. Nonetheless, Ilya Ehrenburg now tells Malraux that Eisenstein is toying with the idea of adapting *La Condition humaine*. Several other candidates have shown an interest, including Joris Ivens and Albert Gendelstein, a student of Eisenstein and Pudovkin. In Moscow, the manager of the Samsonov Studios introduces Malraux to Gendelstein: "We intend to make a film based on *La Condition humaine*. The management is putting you forward as director. If you agree, Sergei Eisenstein will participate as a consultant." Malraux values Eisenstein. Ehrenburg, the go-between, is the Soviet director's informant.[5]

In the Soviet capital, the writer also meets Dovzhenko, the director of *Earth* and *Arsenal*. In his rapid journey notes, he reports their conversation on cinema in general:

MALRAUX: Abroad, it seems that the momentum that made Russian cinema such an important art is slowing and that we are coming to a cliché where the cinema imitates itself indefinitely and simply exploits a certain number of artistic conquests born of the Revolution: familiarity with death . . . humanity, etc.

DOVZHENKO: We also have that impression. Russian cinema has to renew itself. But because of the same conquests you mention, it is understood here that cinema is inspired, intangible, etc. Which means that it is at the very moment when it would be most necessary to change it that it is the most difficult to touch it.[6] Obviously, something is not working! Let us look at our best directors over the last five years: Eisenstein—*¡Que viva México!* and then nothing; Pudovkin—two failures; Turin (director of *Turksib*)—nothing. It is significant. We are now facing an organization that wants to take demand into account, that is starting to want to "be commercial." What's more, our first films, the best ones, expressed a very strong idea or feeling with a very light plot. Today we are being asked to make films that are much weaker on content, with as much importance placed on plot as possible. Artistically, this is bad. Anyway, art in Russia has never been very good on plot; look at our novelists.

M: There are Dos[toevsky] and the Tolstoy of *War and Peace*. But on the whole, I think you are right.

D: And the novelist has means at his disposal that we do not have: the reader can pick up and put down the novel when he wants . . .

M: There is always the serial film.

D: But it is always bad.

M: The D[irectors] who have made serial films only ever made bad films up until then; one doesn't see why they would suddenly start making good ones. It should be tried with a talented D.

EHRENBURG: I think that it is not the same thing: individual reading can stop without danger; a show cannot, because it is felt collectively.[7]

Dovzhenko goes off to film in the Ukraine. He does not collaborate with the French writer. Malraux talks to Meyerhold. The writer explains to the director, with polite exaggeration, that Soviet theater is arousing great interest in France. They talk about *King Lear.* They listen to Prokofiev together and discuss Shostakovich, Stravinsky, Mussorgsky, and Bach. Malraux does not venture out too far on music. Meyerhold does not adapt *La Condition humaine* for the theater.

With Eisenstein, things fit together better. The great director is filming *Bezhin Meadow* in Kislovodsk. He invites Malraux to come over. Malraux notes, "Apartment for a Soviet. One bedroom in an apartment occupied by seven people. For him you ring four times, for the roommate next door seven times. We talk of the session yesterday at the Writers' House."

Eisenstein has for a long time been thinking of making an epic film on China (which he knows better than Malraux). He imagines the film in successive shots and makes numerous drawings.[8] Malraux shows him a draft synopsis, thirty-six typed sheets preceded by notes.[9] One can compare the opening of the novel and the beginning of Malraux's synopsis:

NOVEL[10]

Twelve-thirty midnight
Should he try to raise the mosquito netting? Or should he strike through it? [. . .]

The only light came from the neighboring building—a great rectangle of wan electric light cut by window bars, one of which streaked the bed just below the foot as if to stress its solidity and life. [. . .]

In his pockets, his fumbling right hand clutched a folded razor, his left a short dagger. [. . .] The razor was surer, but Ch'en felt that he could never use it; the dagger disgusted him less. He let go of the razor, the back of which pressed against his clenched fingers; the dagger was naked in his pocket. As he passed it over to his right hand, his left hand dropped against the wool of his sweater and remained glued to it.

That foot lived like a sleeping animal. [. . .]

What was the resistance of flesh? Convulsively, Ch'en pressed the point of the dagger into his left arm. [. . .]

SYNOPSIS

A hand emerges—slightly—from a pocket; a razor. Starts to open it. Closes it again. Drops it back in pocket.

Room in the night. A large rectangle of light comes from the open window, and projects the shadow of the balcony railings onto the bed, hidden by a mosquito net. [. . .]

Vague silhouette of a man in the night (Ch'en).

In the bed, under the mosquito net, we see only a foot.

The hand pulls a short dagger from the pocket, tosses it lightly several times as if to feel a resistance. Ch'en taps lightly on his sweater. Rests the tip of the blade gently against the wall.

The foot.

Ch'en sticks the blade into his arm. Gesture of the head (he bites his lower lip): I know. [. . .]

With a blow that would have split a plank Ch'en struck through the gauze. Sensitive to the very tip of the blade, he felt the body rebound toward him, flung up by the springs of the bed. He stiffened his arm furiously to hold it down: like severed halves drawn to each other, the legs sprang together towards the chest; then they jerked out, straight and stiff. [. . .]	Ch'en strikes, with full force. The metallic bedsprings push the body back against the dagger.

At this rate, the film would be at least twenty hours long, not the Chinese trilogy Eisenstein had in mind. In his notes, the director writes,[11] "Skimming through *La Condition humaine* thematically, reevaluating the author's ideology, modifying my own interpretation of his work with his input—he has strongly revised his conception of the facts, of the novel—we want to work together to remain visually faithful to the purity of his style. We must be stylistically sober, severe, and elegant, like his literary art. We must communicate the image of social passion, of death, of fighting, of self-sacrifice. . . . The idea that a town may be taken with 151 guns, if they are in the right hands." In the long outline of his project (not quite a synopsis), Malraux sacrifices most of his characters—not just the women—and large chunks of plot. He devotes more attention to the stage directions than to the dialogue. He has a sense of cinematographic language. This is a rush job, and he falls behind. He is not a professional scriptwriter, even if he does have a trained eye. Perhaps it is impossible to adapt *La Condition humaine* for the screen? That will be for the director to sort out! Before the word *Fin*, like a confession, Malraux writes, "Here, the very important scene between the capitalists and the police in connection with the capture of Shanghai by the town's revolutionary troops (see the novel: this would have to be an amalgam of a number of battle scenes, the general strike, etc.)." And also: "To be discussed with the director."

In the end, Eisenstein finds *La Condition humaine* too anti-Stalinist. He feels he will not get on with the author—and the authorities—from the beginning. He drops the project. Malraux is disappointed but does not give way to bitterness.

Roland Malraux accompanies André on his travels. Roland is interested in Boleslava Boleslavskaya, André's former interpreter. "Bosle" later escorts Gide, Romain Rolland, and Henri Barbusse.[12] Roland and Boleslava work together, translating texts into French, such as this "Letter from the Kyrgyz people to comrade Stalin":[13]

> Who revealed happiness to us? You
> Who made us blossom like flowers? You
> We have forgotten all our sorrows—with you . . .

The poem sings, "Stalin, the valiant fighter, the creator, the beloved father, the immortal." A quasi-religious vocabulary. The lines at the end of the poem become less liturgical:

> Those who from their stinking lairs
> Will try once again
> To advance their dirty paws
> Toward our glorious star
> Now it is not a bridle
> That we shall pass around their neck
> It is a good slipknot
> As on rabid dogs
> That we shall exterminate.

A warning to detractors and dissidents. Yet the politico-literary machine still mistrusts Roland, as well as André. Roland speaks Russian, and he doesn't tend to make silly mistakes. He passes at first for an agreeable sympathizer. Later, orders come down from the Comintern: his participation in publications must be limited, and, in particular, he must not be given political commentaries to make. It is not known "if his participation in the work on the review *Littérature Internationale* is useful." "New nuances" can be detected in Roland's points of view that "dictate to the editorial staff the necessity of using him with great caution." But they don't want to cut him off entirely: "It would not be wise to break off with him definitively, given his relationship with his brother, the great French writer." A solution is found: Roland is given "only works of art" to work on.[14]

Malraux conducts more interviews and puts his signature to manifestos. One is prepared by Louis Aragon (in Paris) and Vladimir Pozner and Paul Nizan (in Moscow), calling for the release of Antonio Gramsci, "brave leader of the Italian proletariat," and Karl Hofmaier, "Swiss revolutionary," both imprisoned in Italy. A Fascist court has condemned Gramsci to twenty-one years' imprisonment. Hofmaier is suffering from TB. He should be released, the declaration naively protests, "as the Fascist penal code allows for the release of sick prisoners" (which indeed it does). In keeping with contemporary taste, the text invokes the solidarity of intellectuals and the working masses and triumphant indignation from all and sundry. Stalin's jails are eclipsed by those of Mussolini and Hitler.

In Moscow, this time around, Malraux perceives a certain reticence toward him. Bah! It must be temporary. Putting socialist realism, Dostoevsky, and all the Soviet propaganda out of his mind, the sentimental and nostalgic traveler, impatient to get back to Josette Clotis, opens his heart:

There will be Monet's sun on the gardens and the suburban streets, and winter mornings not inhuman and magnificent like ours, but delicate and friendly like those by Sisley. Sometimes rain will fall on the stones of the town; it will be the rain of Baudelaire, and the drizzle will be nothing I have seen before because, like everything else, it will be something undergone by a great artist one day for his sadness or his joy. Courtyards by Balzac, streets by Victor Hugo, women by everybody! From the Renoir noons full of olive trees to the sculptures of Breton Pardons, this will be a country where only joy will live, and all this friendship I will offer in my heart to van Gogh, to Cézanne, and to Gaugin, to the madman, to the syphilitic, and to the poor petits bourgeois who have added their blood so that it should not just be rosy but also that it should be greater. . . . Paris! A warm river, almost pink when the sun goes down behind the Trocadéro, a river like a *bon viveur* lying on the stones that smell of women's scent, a slightly bitter scent, falsely wild. The same sun [gap] slowly the Champs-Élysées, slides onto the velarium of each café, on these large, plain canvases, royal blue, acid green, stretched out like royal tents in a theater where the spectator is somehow in the know. And the colors of the drinks are different in every glass; there is ice everywhere, a mist of condensation covers the glasses up to the curve of the women's red-stained lips. There are flowers that always need renewing and birds in glass cages. Around, infinitely far off, as far as the three seas, there are little villages in the setting sun, not green or wood-colored, like ours, but villages without isbas, covered with tiles or slates—mostly tiles, for I can see them to be pink—and they gleam by the rivers where the mist and the mosquitoes rise, like in the impressionist pictures.

Before returning to France, Malraux wanted to have a tête-à-tête with Gorky. On March 5, with his brother Roland, Koltsov, and Babel, he leaves from Kursky Station for Tesseli in the Crimea. Boris Pasternak

accompanies them to the station, smiling and awkward. The travelers analyze the blend of information and opinion in the Soviet newspapers. Bah!
Revolution demands that. Koltsov and Babel know the old writer to
whom they are going in pilgrimage. Gorky always spends the winter and
the beginning of the spring in the Crimea. Pushkin, they say, lived here.
Gorky likes to hear himself talk. Malraux, as a result, does not have time to
listen to Malraux. Gorky repeats himself. Some think he has aged.

"Stalin . . . yes, we must learn under his guidance . . . work," he
rambles.

Gorky embroiders his own opinion on the brevity of life; his sixty-
eight years (a stitch on the back), immortality, work, and thought (a stitch
on the front). The meeting threatens to turn bad. Malraux is wondering
about an article by Radek on Joyce published the year before. Radek qualified Joyce's books as a pinnacle of antihumanity, of strange forms of social
and individual corruption. Gorky has not read this article, but if Radek
wrote that, he agrees with him.[15] The unfortunate Gorky has the Pavlov-
ian responses of an honorary apparatchik and is sidelined nonetheless. He
has to judge a text according to the Party line, without prior reading.
Joyce, Malraux explains, represents an important stage in literature. Gorky
grumbles. He does promise to "reread" Joyce, even if this kind of literature
is unbearable to him.[16]

They talk about what is happening at the Writers' Association and the
publication of an encyclopedia that Gorky is thinking about. Time drags
on. Malraux tells Gorky a story composed of memories of Cambodia, Persia, and his queen of Sheba adventures. At the base of the Mongol steppes
(he says, to simplify) stands an ancient city where hundreds of wondrous
statues are gathered. From Paris, a route could be mapped into the city.
They would leave in a plane.

"In an airplane!" exclaims Gorky. "How long would that journey take?
What are these statues? . . . Very interesting . . . these statues, you must
get them, unearth them . . . study them! Show them to everybody!"

Babel pretends he is digging with his spoon in his cup. Gorky flares
up: "I would have gone in a plane! On my own, if I had to. There are airplanes in a squadron with my name on, you know! But there we are, never
mind, it's a bit late for me . . ."

The atmosphere calms down. They joke. They promise they will all
go to the desert after the writers' meeting in Moscow on March 11. Malraux cross his heart, will prepare a report for Gorky on the steppe statues.
And Gorky will forward it to the Russian Academy of Sciences. As the visitors are leaving, the old paternal writer gives Malraux a black fur hat:
"You will catch cold. . . . They say snow has been falling in Moscow. It's
chilly."

So many versts traveled, for not a lot. A conversation with Gorky was to be a substitute for speaking directly with Stalin. But Malraux's evaluation of the Stalinian love stakes is not up to date: Gorky is no longer in favor.

Returning to Moscow, Malraux has the calculated honor of attending a meeting of the Presidium of the Writers' Union. The meeting is to pave the way for a review by the International Association of Revolutionary Writers, to be edited by Gorky, Thomas Mann, André Gide, and, as main collaborators, Heinrich Mann, Karel Kapek, J. B. Priestley, Waldo Frank, Ernest Hemingway, Ehrenburg, Babel, and Alexei Tolstoy. Malraux also attends a screening of a film by Yefim Dzigan, *We Are from Kronstadt.* He is moved by its pathetic tone and especially a scene in which a bugler continues to play, surrounded by his dead comrades.

He sees a lot of Isaak Babel. Babel speaks French well and is passionate about the literary tittle-tattle from Paris. His novel *Red Cavalry* is still a success after ten years. Malraux likes Babel's excessive excitement, which tends towards cruelty; even his descriptions of summary executions. Babel calls Malraux "Andrushka." They both talk with the same intensity when examining the criticisms made against Shostakovich and formalism.[17] Babel's wife asks Malraux how he sees Moscow now, especially after the inauguration of the first Metro line (a must for all visitors).

"A little too much Metro," Malraux lets out.[18]

André returns to Paris, leaving Roland in Moscow with "Bosle." Two days before, in Karlsruhe, Hitler gave a speech: "I have made a grand call for peace in the name of sixty-seven million inhabitants . . ." In this spirit of pacifism, German troops had reoccupied the Rhineland a week earlier. The first Volkswagen, the VW30, rolls out of the factories. The gentle, peace-loving Germans approve the occupation by a vote of 90 percent.

After this second trip to the USSR, the relations between Malraux and Moscow, with all its cultural apparatus, change. Theoretical Marxism is the last of his concerns: he genuflects appropriately when in the company of the Left, exercises his prodigious charm and undeniable courtesy, and feigns admiration. But in his writing, nothing indicates an attentive reading of the sacred texts. He perceives no Marxist truth. He feels more of a general sympathy for the revolutionary current and for the country of communism than for Marxism itself.

To the Soviets, he still gives the impression of being scintillating, difficult to follow intellectually and politically. In Moscow, it is never forgotten that Malraux had dealings with Trotsky (two years before, he even toasted him during a banquet, to the astonishment of many present).[19] The Stalinists believe that this Malraux, a free electron, had "anarchist sympathies" in his youth. Yet up to now, his novels have often concerned

Communist individuals such as Garine, Borodine, or Kyo; not irreproach-
able, certainly, from the orthodox Marxist-Leninist-Stalinist point of
view, but promising nonetheless. Satisfactory student. Does not have a
feel for discipline or "proletarian vigilance." Could do better. Despite
Parisian rumors, nothing indicates that he is potentially a member of the
Communist Party.[20] Subtle orthodox players such as Paul Nizan,
tightrope walkers between credibility and cynicism, still see the uncontrollable Malraux as more useful outside the Party than in. He never
wanted to join anyway. Who manipulated whom, at the end of the day?
The nebulous politico-literary-Cominternian and his machine or the
French writer, attached to his independence and creative freedom?

In France, Clara and André quarrel and even shout abuse at each
other. In a train, André Malraux says provocatively to his wife, "I only
married you for your money."

Clara calls him a "thug" and slaps him. He grabs her wrists: "Try not
to be too stupid."

After corrosive insults, he returns to romance with Josette. Malraux
does not realize that Josette likes (let's keep it at that) many writers. She
turns on the charm with Drieu, who enjoys her advances; with Montherlant, disdainful; with Gaston, as amused as he is blasé about it—and even
with Gaston's son, Michel Gallimard.

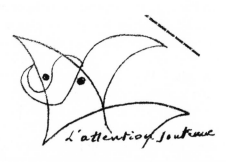

CHAPTER SIXTEEN

Stalinist Temptation

O N T H E O T H E R side of the Pyrenean border, in Spain, the Popular Front carried off an electoral victory in February 1936 with 4,650,116 votes and 267 members. The right-wing National Front received 4,503,505 votes.[1] Faithful to their principles, the Anarchists of the Confederación Nacional del Trabajo (CNT) and the Federación Anarquista Ibérica (FAI), numbering 1,577,547 members, presented no candidate. The Spanish Communist Party claimed to have 40,000 members. Internal reports of the Comintern numbered no more than a few thousand. The country was divided into equal halves around the two fronts, popular and national. In Spain, the mere word "front" (*frente*) had a military resonance, accelerating a brutal bipolarization. The electoral campaign left in its wake a picture of the future that was bound to panic the narrowly defeated faction. In a speech at Cádiz, Largo Caballero announced that "the dictatorship of the proletariat" was to be set into place, "which does not signify the repression of the proletariat but that of the capitalist and bourgeois classes."[2] Manuel Azaña, the left-wing Republican, formed a government.

The socialist and Communist trade unions start a general strike. Azaña wants to avoid confrontations in the streets. Officials on the Far Right are arrested. At the Cortes, the left-wing majority brings down the president of the Republic, Alcala Zamora. Azaña is to become head of state. Trade unionists ransack the headquarters of the right-wing parties. Throughout Spain, the radio becomes a rapid-firing weapon for the distribution of "news," true and false. The Comintern's policy of establishing a popular front from all the democratic, workers', and middle-class parties is relayed by intense propaganda. Malraux approves of this strategy. The Spanish Communist Party, like all the parties controlled by Moscow, insists on the necessity of preserving a "bourgeois parliamentary democracy" until its replacement by "proletarian democracy."

On May 17, with Jean Cassou and Henri Lenormand, Malraux goes to Madrid as a delegate of the International Association of Writers for the Defense of Culture. A tricky trip, since Clara accompanies André, who is after all still officially her husband, and Josette also finds her own way to Madrid. On May 22, Malraux gives a speech at the El Ateneo cinema. His main preoccupation is still the fight against "fascism," in its widest sense. There is a whiff in the air: that of the end of the Weimar Republic.[3] Malraux presents the problems of action to the Spanish writers: "In every country, we are systematically antifascist. There is no point talking about an action that is now absolutely necessary. We know that the differences causing us to turn against fascism must one day be resolved with submachine guns."

Malraux refines his definition to include Mussolini, Hitler, and the right-wing Spanish leaders. Before, he had declared,[4] "I call fascism a movement that, arming and organizing the lower middle classes, aims to govern in their name against both the proletariat and capitalism." As if no proletarian could be either a Nazi or a fascist.

Malraux gets onto culture: "It is not poets who need poetry, but the masses. . . . There are more than six hundred thousand writers and artists in the world who are with us." Malraux exudes statistics like images.

He looks into the relationship between artists and Marxism:

Nobody among us believes that Marxism is "a truth in itself." Just as nobody believes that Plato was truth in itself. . . . Marx thought that at the heart of any analysis there could be found an economic reality. But let us be clear on this: he did not say that at first. Marx himself always laughed at those who aimed to explain Greek art by citing nothing but the living conditions in Greek cities. It would not occur to a serious Marxist to explain Velásquez merely by invoking the coaches in Philip II's courtyard. We must rid ourselves of this misunderstanding.[5]

Malraux leaves for a series of lectures and protests in France. He has an almost physiological need to speak, at length, in private and in public, as if to rid himself of surplus energy and excess words. Different manifestations of "fascism" triumph throughout 1936. In Ethiopia, the Italians crush the Negus's troops, rifles against spears, and conquer the country by the middle of the year. Taking refuge in London, the Negus, who received Malraux among his peacocks and lions, starts to make his diplomatic rounds among the cowed and careful political crowd. At the Foreign Office, they hope to break the Rome-Berlin axis.

Hitler grants an interview to the French daily *Paris-Soir.* Germany, the Führer explains, intends to reclaim its colonies. He calls into question the balance of world power. The dictator has just opened the Eleventh Summer Olympic Games. As for the reoccupation of the demilitarized zone in the Rhineland, the League of Nations chatters and Paris and London talk of a violation of international law. Hitler won his referendum elections, without rigging them, on March 7, 1936.

In France, the Popular Front carries off the elections on April 26, 1936. The Malrauxs and the Nizans hear of this victory on the terrace of the Café des Deux Magots in Saint-Germain-des-Prés. The whole neighborhood bustles until dawn. "The people of France have voted for bread, peace, liberty," announces the front page of *L'Humanité.* On June 4, Léon Blum, not without hesitation, forms a government. The Socialist Party has 160 members or electoral allies, the Radicals, 111, the Communists, 72, the Right, 222. France enters a phase of festivities on the Left. The Communists support the Popular Front without participating in the government, which is fragile since the majority of the Radicals are rather centrist.

Unstoppable, Malraux goes to London[6] to defend a project developed with Gorky: an encyclopedia to outstrip Diderot's: "Not a battleship of an encyclopedia, like the *Encyclopaedia Britannica,* but a submarine of an encyclopedia. I mean a weapon of war that costs infinitely less than a battleship but can still sink warships."

Military comparisons, submachine guns, battleships, submarines come spontaneously to Malraux. The principle of this encyclopedia is almost unanimously accepted. It is never published.

On July 13, the highly conservative Spanish politician José Calvo Sotelo is assassinated. On the seventeenth at 5 p.m., in Spanish Morocco, army conspirators take control of the Melilla garrison and declare a state of siege. The next day, the military uprising spreads, taking Ceuta in Morocco. It reaches the peninsula on July 18. The seditious generals, some resolute, some nervous, advance. About fifty churches are set on fire in Madrid on the night of July 19–20.

In Spain, the Nationalists inform their supporters that it is "necessary to spread an atmosphere of terror. We must create an impression of mastery."[7] Insurgents emerge from the ranks of the three-year-old Falange Española, from the Carlist Party, and particularly from the heart of the army, the point of origin of the mediocre Francisco Paulino Hermenegildo Teódulo Franco y Bahamonde. They are carried along by a fear of illegal violence from the Left and by a strong conviction that God is with them. The Right talks of a necessary cleansing, *limpieza,* with an inquisitor's faith. Freemasonry, Marxism, the Jews, all threats to Spain, must be done away with; anarchy, communism, socialism, liberalism must be liquidated; religion, with Christ as King, must be defended. Sympathy for the Nazis and the fascists grows, although it is not the mainstay of the *movimiento*, the movement catalyzed by Catholicism.[8] In this climate, on the Right and the Left, large-scale terror is prepared. Many are ready to destroy and assassinate.

Throughout Republican Spain, in Catalonia, Madrid, Aragon, and Andalusia, convents and churches are attacked by fanatics, often Anarchists. With that part of Spain in the hands of the Nationalists, every gun has a hair trigger. On the Left, they talk with knowing smiles of *checa* groups in the loyalist camp. There are gangs beyond government control, "the Furies," "Force and Freedom," "Lynxes of the Republic." On the Right, the police, the army, and the civil guard, mostly Falangists and Carlists, attack not only members of left-wing parties but also those known or imagined to be their sympathizers. Before the events themselves, a civil war breaks out in heads and hearts. On both sides, murders are followed by executions. The more courts sit to examine atrocities, the more the atrocities are denied. The ritualistic sentencing is a celebration of summary justice. Prisons fill up, graves are dug. The violence shows more incompetence and irresponsibility on the government side than by the Nationalists, with their systematic terror campaign. Across the globe, journalists, whether conservative or progressive, emphasize whichever instances of plundering and abuse of power suit them. The greatest historical casualty is truth.

Malraux follows the events with passion from Paris. On the evening of July 18, he goes to the theater with Clara and their friends Léo Lagrange, the undersecretary of state for sport and leisure, and his wife, Madeleine. Pierre Cot, the air minister, is also there, in another box. Cot sends for Lagrange, who afterward tells Malraux about a military uprising in Spain. Malraux signs a telegram from a number of writers "to the Spanish people struggling heroically for the cause of humanity as a whole."

Madrid asks France for military assistance.[9] The Blum government, having disbanded the extreme Right leagues, is not faced with the sort of violence there is in Spain. French workers occupy factories, doubtless a breach of ownership rights, but they don't burn down churches. The French Popular Front came to power to the sound of accordions and harmonicas. Malraux is in permanent liaison with Cot and Jean Moulin, Cot's right-hand man. He calls a meeting at Rue du Bac, inviting his friend Lagrange, some Italian and German political refugees, and other foreigners, including Ilya Ehrenburg. According to Malraux, the essential problem, less than ten days after the Nationalist revolt, is the supply of military planes to the Spanish Republic and the shortage of pilots to escort them and take them into combat. At the beginning of the Franco-led uprising, the government had around four hundred planes, two hundred of them in good condition, four fifths of the available fleet.[10]

Cot and Moulin ask Malraux to go to Madrid to gather information. The writer wishes to go with Jean-Richard Bloch and Jean Cassou. He announces his departure for the same Wednesday, July 22, a few hours before the air bases are officially to close, and flies off in a French ministerial Lockheed Orion with Édouard Corniglion-Molinier, with Clara hanging on behind, resolved to play her part in an intoxicating adventure. There is a stopover for fuel at Forgas military airport, near Biarritz. The passengers sleep in the airport. The base commander announces that Madrid is in the hands of the "rebels." The terms "insurgents," "Nationalists," "pro-Francos," "nationals," and "Fascists" are also used. The travelers take off from Forgas on Saturday, July 25.[11] The right-wing press in Paris proclaims that the insurgents are closing from the north and are twelve miles from Madrid—wishful printing on their part. *L'Humanité* publishes a telegram sent from the Spanish capital by Malraux on July 27: "Arriving in Madrid, I must first of all refute reports that the city is surrounded and that Fascist groups are approaching the capital. Madrid is completely clear to the south right down to Andalusia, to the east all the way to the sea, and to the west as far as Portugal. It is only from the north that the rebel army has sent out small vanguards, which have been defeated and driven back beyond the slopes of Sierra [de] Guadarrama."[12] The press war of information and misinformation begins. *L'Action Française* retaliates, attacking the writer Malraux and Léon Blum's government. Pierre Cot, claims the far-right newspaper, is giving army planes to the aeronautics company Potez, to sell them on to Spain—which is true. A jumbled press campaign by the Far Right denounces Malraux as the special envoy of *L'Humanité*, a "thief" of statues in Cambodia, and a "Bolshevik."

Back in Paris on the twenty-eighth, Malraux has an idea: to buy these essential airplanes and recruit pilots. He telephones and meets politicians and announces he is going to fight in Spain. He has never used a weapon before, never piloted a plane. Yet Malraux manages to convince those he needs to, and no one is surprised. He is a born writer and a born warrior. What other writer could be as persuasive? Action is essential, both to life and to writing. Gide is disappointed: he neither understands nor approves. He is enthusiastic about Malraux, but with reservations. Often he admires the person, not the writer. For Gide, Malraux has "the makings of a great man," but he does not think that "he will become a great writer. His French isn't good, he doesn't instinctively know his craft, and what he ends up with, despite everything, is an artist's pseudowriting. One can always sense the intelligence of the author. For me, that cuts off the emotion it wants to produce." What's more, for Gide, writing and action are

incompatible. In his loyal but critical opinion, Malraux should have chosen between creating an oeuvre and waging revolution. Gide is thinking
about communism. Malraux is quick to take sides; Gide never does.

The great witness returns from war-torn Madrid. Malraux is given an
ovation at the first demonstration in support of Republican Spain on July
30, at the Salle Wagram. More than twenty thousand spectators gather
inside and out, shouting, "Long live the Popular Front! Solidarity! Long
live free Spain! Unity of action!"

They start singing "The Marseillaise" and other inspiring revolutionary songs. A collection is taken in aid of Spanish Republicans. Blum, Cot,
and Manuel Azaña, the president of the Spanish Republic, are honorary
chairs at the demonstration, as is Luis Companys, president of Catalonia.
A resonant rendition of "The Internationale" welcomes the fourth
speaker, André Malraux. This politico-literary orator has a way of grab-
bing an audience, like a wave covering a beach. Before him, politicians
have churned out insipid harangues about liberty, fascism, and the masses.
Blum, under the influence of the British Foreign Office, Chamberlain,
French staff headquarters, and his own Radical ministers, toys reluctantly
with the idea of a policy of nonintervention in Spain. Malraux's aim is to
persuade the public, and beyond them the readers of the newspapers carrying an account of this very debate in the Salle Wagram, that this apparently prudent and pragmatic policy is in fact a threat to France. He has
actually watched, in Spain, a popular army in training. A talented
preacher, he makes the most of "things seen." On July 17, he says, the
Spanish trade unions had warned the Republican government of the
forthcoming uprising. But the prime minister, Casares Quiroga, a "bourgeois," had refused to arm the working classes. Lyrical, but not quite fair:
Quiroga was afraid of a civil war. Malraux sets the Spanish conflict in its
international context for his audience, insisting on the legitimacy of the
Madrid government in power. This government has the ability and the
right to procure equipment. If democratic governments were to sell arms
to Madrid, he explains, totalitarian powers would jump at the chance to
supply arms to Franco. But Malraux sees no reason why "friends" of the
Spanish Republic should be prevented from sending volunteers and
"technical assistance." The specious argument is loudly applauded. The
orator's wave ebbs, revealing the odd rough patch.

"The French people demand that their hands be untied," says Malraux. "The Spanish need drivers, instructors, doctors . . . engineers . . ."
Malraux, pulsating with efficiency, sees himself primarily as an arms sup-
plier. But he doesn't say too much about it in public: Pierre Cot has given
him a lecture.

Everywhere, there is talk about civilian and military volunteers for

Spain. The Right and the Extreme Right become infatuated with the Nationalists, a little less noisily than the Left in favor of the loyalists. The ministries wait for the intervention, open or disguised, of Fascist Italy and Nazi Germany. The British are counting—too much—on the neutrality of the Italians. The French military fears a potential enemy on the other side of the Pyrenees.

Malraux would like to turn himself into a capable leader. How about a post as a brilliant second in command? Not on your life. He sees himself as an organizer, a buyer, and, above all, a combatant. A leader. Clara shares his excitement, Josette doesn't. For André Malraux at thirty-five, the world is no longer "absurd": it can be changed. He is never at a loss for a slogan: "Communism is not hope, but the form of hope." He likes to think he's a strategist. In Madrid, he explained to the civilians and some officers that they would not be able to create a popular army in three months, especially not with Anarchists who hadn't done military service (just as he hasn't). If they wanted to win the war, they would first need an air force. Some Republican officers, fully aware of the problem, found this French writer's assurance annoying.

Malraux overestimates the number of Communists in Spain, just as he underestimates their potential nuisance factor. At the time, Spanish Communists are far less powerful than the Socialists or the Anarchists, to whom the Republic owes its continued existence in Barcelona and Catalonia.

In Paris, Malraux is beginning to look like a conspirator. He stays in regular contact with the Spanish Embassy, the air minister, and the Office of the Président du Conseil. Blum holds him in high regard. But at the Ministry of Foreign Affairs, Malraux seems to be frowned on. What is this guy cooking up? Some semisecret competitive diplomatic action? His apartment is placed under police surveillance and serves as a hub for the Spanish Republicans. Malraux meets adventurers at the Rue du Bac and in cafés: some heroes, some creeps. The shifty types who emerge at the frontiers of all countries in times of civil war; a world connected with shady dealings involving the intelligence service, Jean Moulin, and the French Embassy in Spain. The French ambassador in Madrid is inclined to favor nonintervention; the military attaché, Major Cahuzac, who has no sympathy for Malraux, favors the Republicans.

Clara, determined to make history as well, wants to accompany her husband back to Spain. Malraux balks. Via Jean Moulin, he remains in contact with the minister of finance, Vincent Auriol, and a member of his staff, Gaston Cusin, from Customs. The Customs and the Criminal Investigation Department supervise airports and takeoffs. Throughout the Spanish Civil War, organization remains discreet.[13] It is a section of the civil staff[14] (the military offices sometimes grumble) that authorizes the firm of

Lioré-Olivier, the makers of Dewoitines, and the companies Potez and Bloch, to take delivery of airplanes destined for the French Air Force. These aircraft belong to the state, and the government can sell them to Brazil, Turkey, third parties, or the king of Hejaz. The third party is then well within its rights to dispose of them or convey them "in transit" via Spanish airfields within the Republican zone. Thus 129 aircraft, 83 of them equipped for military use, are delivered to the Spanish government. Some French reserve pilots fly the planes down to Spain in secret convoys. Cot's men encourage officers and NCOs of the French Air Force to request periods of leave in order to escort the aircraft. Victor Véniel, Jean Labitte, and Adrien Matheron are among the officers. By the time an official international embargo is in place, about 50 planes have been transferred. Jean Moulin says to his sister, "Nobody can prevent Finland, or any other country that hasn't adhered to this pact [of nonintervention], sending planes it has bought from us to Spain."

Between the Air Ministry, divided at the top, and the Interior Ministry, with ultimate responsibility for the Criminal Investigation Department, misunderstandings abound, inscribed for posterity on official circulars. Malraux is assisted in the recruitment of pilots by Ernest Vinchon and Adrienne Bolland. Jean Moulin works away for Republican Spain. Yet officially, France respects the embargo and does not intervene.

Clara treats the prospect of participating in an adventure with Malraux, or having a child with him, like therapy: let's stick the couple back together again with glue—or a war. A writer can make great resolutions, advance magnificent reasons, and thereby hide lesser motivations. Malraux goes to Spain to defend his conception of the world, the working class, the right of the masses to culture; but he also has no small desire to run away from Clara. He confides as much to Gide, who contemplates the shipwreck of the couple with his feet in the dry. What is to be done with the little girl, Florence? Various friends are ready to take her in, including the Berls, even though a political disagreement has turned Berl and Malraux against each other. According to the editor of *Marianne*, intervening in Spain would be to play Stalin's game.[15] Berl knows the secretary general of the French Foreign Office, Alexis Léger, aka the poet Saint-John Perse. The traditional ponderousness and circumspection of the *département* leads them to prefer the status quo, which in this case means nonintervention. Berl is with them.

Adding to the international confusion, at the Olympic Games in Berlin,[16] some teams, including the Austrians, Bulgarians, Italians, and French, raise their right arms straight. Is it an Olympic or a Nazi salute? The president of the International Olympic Committee, Henri de Baillet-Latour, ill-advisedly declares that these games can take place unperturbed by political difficulties, in a grand setting and a cordial atmosphere of "general friendship."

On August 1, Blum reluctantly chooses nonintervention. Malraux leaves again for Spain on the sixth, hope in his heart and a cloud above his head, because Clara's presence is threatening to spoil the adventure of war—and his escapade with Josette. His Potez leaves Le Bourget Airport and lands at Barcelona. Koltsov and Ehrenburg, correspondents for *Pravda* and *Izvestia*, respectively, both notice how much Clara embarrasses Malraux. He does not want her to be seen on the battlefield or the airfields. She might just be clever enough, militant enough, and brave enough to steal one of his roles.

The simple, official line of argument is that applying the principle of noninterference in Spanish affairs will avoid prolonging the war. The Western powers must remain neutral. The British government has placed an embargo on weapons; Germany and the USSR likewise. August 14, Nationalist groups combine at Badajoz. The west of Spain, including Pamplona, Burgos, Salamanca, Merida, and Seville, becomes "Nationalist." The east remains Republican, keeping Barcelona, Madrid, Toledo, Grenada, and Málaga. The *pronunciamiento* turns into a *reconquista*.

Against the background of bloodshed, noble sentiments, and sordid calculations in Spain, the trial of the "Trotskyites" in Moscow goes unnoticed. The accused have no lawyers. They admit their guilt. They are shot. Good-bye, Kamenev and Zinovyev. Malraux does not stumble. He will not be distracted from the fundamental danger, Francoism, the latest manifestation of fascism. Madrid is worth a few silences.

Malraux comes and goes between Paris, Barcelona, and Madrid. His novelist's mind is storing up sounds, images, symbols of hope, sensations, and arguments. In the Spanish capital, near the Puerta del Sol, he has observed civilians on carts loaded with kitchen cabinets, pillows, eiderdowns. The government sanctions loans to provide for the poor. Malraux is looking for brotherhood, and it exists. He finds this atmosphere "enthusiastic and intoxicating." He received a fine welcome from the president and the prime minister in Madrid.[17] Now here he is again, suddenly appearing with promises of planes and pilots. Republican leaders find him ready to fight. Simple words, here and there—¡Salud, compañero!—warm the heart. Malraux does not speak Spanish but has a feeling for the sonorous, moving, sometimes melodramatic beauty of the language.

Emotions, slogans, and propaganda to one side, Malraux has understood that a well-paid professional pilot, even without deeply held left-wing convictions, is more valuable than an inexperienced militant comrade who would crash his plane on takeoff. As long as that professional—or "mercenary"—does not turn out to be a Franco supporter and hand his plane over to the Nationalists. . . . In Madrid, they are informed by the Paris Embassy that Malraux is known to be liaising with Pierre Cot and Jean Moulin. Moreover, the writer knows some influential men in aeronautics, including Paul-Louis Weiller. The Spanish minister of aviation officially makes Malraux a lieutenant colonel. Malraux assumes the rank like he might throw a scarf around his coat collar. For someone who has never even been a basic soldier, this is doubtless excessive but accepted.

During the first few days of civil war, the Republicans get two hundred planes into the air, the insurgents about a hundred. Many army and air force pilots have joined Franco.[18] For a time, the Republican Air Force controls the skies, its fighter planes superior to those protecting the Nationalist bombers. Franco needs Hitler and Mussolini.

At first the pilots enlisted by Malraux and the planes bought thanks to him do not take part in delicate military operations. This squadron cannot afford to lose any planes just now; public opinion in France, in Great Britain, and elsewhere must not notice that nonintervention has been violated. So the squadron, christened "España," takes part in reconnaissance flights and bombs railway lines, power stations, and factories. Malraux gives an order: Avoid direct confrontations in midair with Franco's pilots. The right-wing press must not publish photographs of Republican planes piloted by the French.

Among the qualified "professionals" or "mercenaries" of the España, some have signed contracts of 50,000 francs a month, more than $3,000 in 1936, one hundred times the salary of a Spanish lieutenant. They have to take on experts, not washouts. The obligatory life insurance, from 200,000 to 500,000 francs, $12,000 to $30,000 dollars, has to be justified. At a recruitment center on the Boulevard Pasteur in Paris and another on Rue d'Alésia, two types of contracts are prepared for the candidates: the "political," with a monthly salary of 5,000 francs, for volunteers forwarded by antifascist organizations, and the much-higher-paid "commercial," designed for specialized aviators, such as fighter pilots. Other applicants turn up in Spain with no contract at all and even without having been requested. In the international squadrons, the salaries vary from 1,000 francs ($60) a month for an electrician/mechanic, Sarrigo Sauli, to 3,000 francs for an aeronautical engineer, Vicenzo Piatti, and the pilots Giuseppe Krizai and Filippo Matonti. Along with the French, the highest-paid foreign pilots are the Americans.[19] They alone get a bonus of $1,000 for every plane shot down (the same rate for a fighter plane or a bomber). Marx condemned piecework, not premiums, and anyway the Spanish Republican administration is not Marxist. In Paris, at first, it is difficult to distinguish mercenaries from volunteers, since at the Spanish Embassy they sign a contract that is completed only in Madrid. There are new arrivals every week. The strength of air and ground crews varies. At the start, Malraux's squadron has 5 members; at the end, 130.[20]

Malraux, welcoming his men, tells them, "Think of revolution as your second job."

He hates to be asked about the political affiliations of his aviators. With sincerity in his sidestepping, or perhaps doubt, he answers, "For me, the question doesn't arise."

To those who approach him, he often replies, "*Rojo, comunista no.*"

Or, Clemenceau-like, "I am fighting a war."

He picks out the leeches who were hoping for a bit of harmless sport in Spanish skies. His planes were in the air just four weeks after his return to Spain. A superb performance; he is the *fundador* of the España Squadron, its prestigious patron, its symbol, but not its operational leader. Aware of his limitations, he delegates this role to Abel Guidez. This is clearly a virtue in Malraux: the French are not good at delegating and tend to hoard information, mistaking it for power. Malraux knows how to share it. Guidez, of Catalan origin and something of an anarchist, is proposed— or perhaps imposed—by Pierre Cot's Paris office. There are mutterings that this serious man, a qualified pilot and officer in the French Army, is remote-controlled by the French Intelligence Service. He is not the only one. Another aviator is important later on: Paul Nothomb, alias Paul Bernier in Spain, who will be appointed political commissar.[21]

One of the pilots, Jean Darry, always impeccably dressed, naturally calm, fought in the First World War and brought down six planes.[22] Darry grew rich in the United States and was ruined in France; implicated in an affair of disguised cars, he had a taste of prison. He perfects a tactic for attacking bombers and brings down two of them: he avoids the forward and aft machine guns of the Francoist bombers by climbing fast beneath their belly to attack them. Another pilot, François Bourgeois,[23] a stocky, loudmouthed ex–airmail pilot, was imprisoned in North Africa. He pretended to be a tramp and amused himself smuggling Chinese immigrants into Canada and alcohol into the United States. Three years before, he took part in the war between Bolivia and Paraguay. Nobody knows on which side. Valbert, alias Paul Véniel, a member of the team, asks him what type of plane he knows how to pilot. Bourgeois answers, "Any kind with wings and an engine."

Is he kidding?

"Not at all," says Véniel. "This guy could fly a barn door."[24]

Véniel-Valbert, before leaving for Spain, was called in to see Jean Moulin, who detailed his mission: to feed the analysis of aerial operations. We need not only to help the loyalists, but also to see how the Spanish, German, and Italian opponents react.

Malraux stays on good terms with Captain Martin Luna, who shuttles between the international squadron and the Air Ministry, where Antonio Camacho, the undersecretary of state, countersigns contracts. From August to November 1936, for the defense of Madrid, thirty-two men pass through the squadron: seventeen pilots, one bombardier, three gunners, five mechanics, some all-arounders, and a few no-hopers.[25] Counting Malraux, twenty-two of the mercenaries and volunteers are French, five Italian, two Spanish, one Russian, one Czech, one Belgian, and one Algerian. The specialties are not rigid. A copilot often works as a navigator. Without discouraging the offers of help, Guidez and Malraux manage to avoid keeping the bluffers, the daredevils, and the kit wreckers. After his little trip to see the queen of Sheba, Malraux does not enjoy a solid reputation in Parisian aeronautical circles, where he has tried to win over professionals. Antoine de Saint-Exupéry is not free, nor are other pilots of the Aéropostale airmail service. (In Spain, Saint-Exupéry becomes war correspondent for *Paris-Soir.*) Well-known professionals decline offers. They do not want to take sides in the civil war, or else they do not trust Malraux. The Socialist Roger Beaucaire and Adrienne Bolland, who flew over the Andes, decline to take part. But Bolland, with Ernest Vinchon, is one of the recruiters for the España Squadron. Corniglion-Molinier stays close to the writer, but he does not always attract sympathy either.

As for bombers, at the start, Malraux finds four Potez 42s and 54s. The squadron eventually ends up with about twenty: first two more, then six Bloch MB 200 and 210s. There is no shortage of lame ducks, such as salvaged Douglas DC-2s, some of which come from the fleet of Lineas Aéreas Postales Españolas. One is "cannibalized" for parts. The Blochs are dangerous on takeoff and landing and worrying in flight for the crew; they don't fly much. Bloch and Potez used the same Gnome & Rhône engines. The writer-colonel rejects the ridiculous contemporary French tactic whereby a bomber works without a fighter escort. The "Foch" guidelines chose to overlook the superior maneuverability of the single-seat fighters. The squadron moves a lot in the outskirts, not far from Madrid. Little by little, it evolves an agreed-upon hierarchy, with no saluting or ceremony: Abel Guidez directs the pilots, Raymond Maréchal the gunners, and Marcel Bergeron the mechanics.

A brainteaser for Malraux: he gets hold of twenty-six Dewoitine B371s and B372s, but with no machine guns, something of a disadvantage for fighters. He finds some Spanish machine guns. He also finds five Loire 46s. The French Dewoitines are better and easier to handle than the German Heinkel HE51s; they can reach a speed of 205 mph, the Heinkels only 180. The Italian Fascists line up large numbers of Fiat CR32s, which perform outstandingly, which annoys Hitler, Italian engineers being, after all, halfway between supermen and subhumans. *Deutschland und Heinkel über alles.* The standard of enemy piloting is a significant factor in the conflict. The German Captain Molders also uses teamwork tactics: the first fighter attacks, the second protects the first one's rear. Later the Russians arrive with their satisfactory contribution: a biplane, the Polikarpov 115.

Over seven months, Malraux's squadron loses five planes in combat and eight on the ground. They receive French planes thanks to Pierre Cot, Jules Moch, and Jean Moulin, who is also the main liaison agent between the Office of the Président du Conseil and the Air Ministry. The Republican ambassador in Paris, de los Ríos, working closely with Indalecio Prieto, the Spanish air minister, keeps financial operations covered. French planes are the first to arrive in Spain, "straddling" the nonintervention deadline. One two-year-old Bloch 210, two three-year-old Dewoitines. The Potez planes arrive with their gun turrets empty. Some Loires: according to Véniel, "Piloting a Loire is a bit like driving a Ferrari." The old Vickers machine guns tend to fire one or two bursts and then jam. There's no bomb launcher on the first Potez 54s: they have to drop the bombs manually out of the cabin doors, which does nothing to improve their accuracy. There is a shortage of spare parts, even after ingenious makeshift repairs by the mechanics. The squadron rarely has more than eleven planes in operational condition. Adding to the collection, the squadron treats itself to a twin-engined Bréguet for reconnaissance, the BR460, negotiated by a Radical member of Parliament in Paris, Lucien Bossoutrot. For training, they use unwanted French tourist planes that have been flown across the Pyrenees.

The workers of the Blériot firm, in a surprising and touching move, buy a prototype light fighter, the Spad 91-6, more of a sports plane, that Guidez puts away somewhere. Possibly by mistake, the Spanish buy an American gem, the Boeing P26. On the first landing, Jean Labitte turns it over. On instruction from Paris, Air France starts to repair the military planes from Spain.

The squadron moves itself around in response to the fortunes or misfortunes of war. At first it sets up base at Barajas Airport in Madrid. Before the insurrection, the Republican authorities kept most of their aircraft there. Later the squadron stays in a castle near Valencia, much more agreeable than Madrid or Barcelona hotels. Hooray for orange groves, palm trees, even the odd hunting expedition. Germaine, the wife of the pilot Roland Claudel, looks after the household.

Malraux takes his orders directly from the ministry, which the loyalist general and field officers of the Aviación Militar and the Aeronautica Naval do not like. The squadron takes part in at least twenty-three missions. Yann Stroobant, pseudonym Croisiaux, nineteen years old, is with the squadron for several months and notches up thirteen missions as copilot, plus six on the backseat. These figures do not include reconnaissance missions or missions "aborted" after an error or counterorders.[26]

August 20, 1936: the squadron's first victory. Jean Darry and Jean Gouinet shoot down two Nationalist Bréguets. Two Dewoitines confront some Fiat CR32s. A draw: one plane down on either side. Four days before, on the sixteenth, the squadron bombed a column of enemy troops led by Colonel Castejon Espinoza, near Medellín and Santa Amalia, dropping clusters of bombs at four or five thousand feet to saturate the target. Colonel Espinoza's immediate superiors are General Yagüe and, at the top of the hierarchy, Francisco Franco. Louis Delaprée, a reporter for *Paris-Soir*, notices Malraux at the gunner's post in one of the Potez bombers.[27] Malraux is not a good shot. Nonetheless, the progress of the Espinoza column was halted for two days. The three planes from Malraux's squadron were carrying two thousand pounds of bombs. But there were three columnas advancing on different routes, gaining ground at night.[28] The Spanish Republican press celebrates this victory, although its real importance is more tactical and symbolic than strategic. This is no Battle of the Marne. "The disaster at Medellín," writes *Claridad*,[29] "is one of the largest that the insurgents have undergone." For *La Libertad* on August 19, "it is the best day *the Republican Air Force* [my italics] has had so far." The operation is chalked up to the "*gloriosa Aviación republicana*." The Escuadrilla España returns majestically from an operation, "*volvio majestuosamente a su base*." Pilots and planes are compared, with Hispanic enthusiasm, to "eagles." The Francoist military reports never mention Malraux's squadron, only "enemy aircraft."

Two men become very close to Malraux: Raymond Maréchal and Paul Nothomb. Nothomb wrote on foreign policy in the Belgian newspapers *Le Drapeau Rouge* and *La Voix du Peuple* under the pseudonym Paul Bernier. The son of Pierre Nothomb (a Catholic baron, senator, and supporter of Mussolini, a sort of Belgian Barrès), Paul Nothomb graduated from the École des Cadets as a navigator bomber—and a Communist. Five feet eleven, handsome, and cultured, with an aquiline nose, he dresses in the German style in boots and a flying jacket. He is a Stalinist: democracy is not important to him. To Nothomb, there are two types of Party members, the "clerical Communist" and the "action Communist." There are elements of both about him. After six months in the United States, he returned to Europe. His partner, Marguerite "Margot" Devenler, also a Communist, has been through a Party-run school in Moscow. She joins him in October. Nothomb-Bernier often talks about Nietzsche with Malraux. At the time, Nothomb sees his friend as a "revolutionary socialist." The writer-colonel abhors labels, not least the one applied by the writer José Bergamin to himself, of "anarcho-Catholic."

Malraux first met Nothomb[30] at the Hotel Florida in Madrid. Amazed and delighted, the officer bumped into Malraux, whom he had heard speak back in Brussels. The bar and restaurant at the Florida are meeting points for members of the squadron and *the* place for writers, journalists, politicians, trade unionists, and single, double, and triple agents. Some come to see, others to be seen. Part of the tragedy and comedy of the Revolution is played out there. The conversation ranges from geopolitics to small talk. The men of the España Squadron are noticed. They scorn classic dress, preferring what Malraux calls their "Mexican" uniforms: red-and-black neck scarf, peaked caps or sombreros, flying and other jackets in army drab or all sorts of colors. Malraux the dandy has achieved a carefully neglected look, gracefully combining civilian and military clothes.

Nothomb has told Malraux that he is a Communist. That does not prevent him—on the contrary—from noticing the disorder, the shambolic *balumba* of the Republic's military affairs. The Anarchists cover Madrid with a charming but not very warlike slogan: "Let's organize indiscipline." How wise is it to bray about the inevitable chaos of combat? Malraux is not careful: at the Hotel Florida, where informers are bound to be at large, the squadron's missions for the next day are often written on a blackboard. Ten languages are used. Malraux, expressing himself in French, seems to be understood by everybody. He hypnotizes a good many of his listeners, whether he is talking about strategy on a sierra or Velázquez at the Prado. Louis Aragon passes by without stopping to fight, as does Ernest Hemingway. Both turn out to be allergic to the Malrucian charm. Hemingway thinks this Frenchman indulges in pompous predictions. Malraux gets on better with the Spaniards José Bergamín and Rafael Alberti, or the French who pass through, Paul Nizan and Georges Soria, or the Chileans, including Pablo Neruda, and his favorite Russians, Koltsov and Ehrenburg. These intellectuals are resolute ideological fighters. Malraux fights physically and in a respected, almost mythological corps, the air force, not just the supply corps or the Meteorological Office. His mates forgive him his tirades, affectations, and somber expressions. Some are there to observe history in the making. In the tradition of Lord Byron, Lafayette, Garibaldi, and D'Annunzio, Malraux is making it happen.

Clara is there, making things awkward for *el coronel*, often preventing him from seeing Josette. The warrior cannot live on planes and speeches alone. Ostentatiously, Clara cultivates a romance with a pilot from the squadron. She annoys Malraux. He talks about efficiency as a necessary prevention against chaos, which distances him from the Anarchists and Trotskyists and is more in line with the Communists. Clara accuses her husband of submitting to the Stalinists and trying to impress them. Everybody notices the strain between the couple. Malraux leaves Madrid for his airfield with relief.

The squadron—or the two squadrons, since men such as Gisclon, a fighter pilot, consider that their squadron is commanded not by Malraux but by Guidez, Véniel, and Darry—chugs on through incidents and accidents. On August 20, Darry and Gouinet shoot down two Nationalist Bréguets. The next day, a Nieuport fighter piloted by "Thomas," escorting a Republican Bréguet, goes down. August 22, Gisclon and Véniel clash with three Fiat CR30s. Gisclon brings one of them down. Véniel goes to Valencia to pick up a plane that has landed on a beach without opening its undercarriage. It is a rebel F132 Junker. The squadron's ground crew paint over the Francoist white crosses with Republican red bands. Véniel flies the Junker toward Barcelona and is shot at by loyalist antiaircraft guns. He discovers that the ground crew comrades have forgotten to paint over the rebel markings on the underside of the plane. On August 23 and 24, seven Dewoitines out of the twelve are damaged by Francoist attacks.

August 28: Adrien Matheron and Jean Gisclon get hold of a Nationalist plane near Talavera.[31] On the way back, they open fire on a group of loyalist militiamen, near the village of Gredos. The two airmen clearly saw a priest being chased by Republican militiamen and decided to help him get away. The story causes quite a stir. The French ambassador is informed. The pilots claim they thought they were firing on Nationalists. They did not kill anyone. The priest gets away. Bad press for the squadron at the Air Ministry. Malraux's rating goes down when Hidalgo de Cisneros becomes commander in chief of the Republican Air Force. A newly minted Communist, Cisneros takes an instant dislike to the writer-*coronel*.

August 30: The squadron bombs Navalmoral de la Mata.

September 1: A peasant farmer crosses the lines and tells them of the existence of a clandestine Nationalist airfield at Olmedo. A Potez and three Dewoitines take off to attack this Francoist airstrip. The farmer, on board the Potez, loses his bearings. The bomber, piloted by Gontcharoff, blows up a fuel storage tank and an ammunition depot and destroys three enemy bombers on the ground. At the controls of the fighters, protecting the Potez well, are Guidez, Darry, and Hallotier. The incident stays with Malraux.[32]

September 2, 4 and 10: The squadron bombards Talavera de la Reina. A small victory.

On the seventh, a hard knock: Junkers destroy six planes from the España. Malraux never has more than five bombers and six fighters ready for flight after that point. He hears this news in France, to which he often returns.[33] His private life in Paris is almost as dangerous as his military life in Spain. Malraux navigates between Clara in the Rue du Bac and Josette at the Hôtel Élysée Parc. He shows his face at Gallimard. A naughty rumor says he has a uniform made for him by Lanvin.[34]

September 30: To the west of Madrid, where the Nationalists are approaching, Malraux's squadron loses a Potez in combat with seven men on board. Three are wounded and three killed, including an anonymous Spanish mechanic. Only the pilot, Dushuis, is unscathed. Koltsov keeps a diary. He notes, "In the international squadron very few aircraft remain. Fifteen men work in turns." The same day,[35] Guidez confides to him, "Men we have. The problem is, we have more gunners than guns and more pilots than planes."

In Paris, with his friends from the *NRF* (not in hearing of the staff of the Spanish Embassy), Malraux talks away as if at 5 a.m. the next day he would be taking on the politico-military command of all of Republican Spain: "His hope is to rally round . . . at present he has the power to do it; his intention, as soon as he returns, is to organize an attack on Oviedo." Malraux never attacks Oviedo.

At Albacete, the airmen spend time at the Hotel Regina, where a number of International Brigade volunteers pass through. Malraux makes a bucolic return to the country, among the orange trees of La Señera airfield near Valencia.

All over the world, the right-wing press is talking about the "mercenaries" in the España Squadron; the left-wing press talks about the "volunteers." To Nothomb, Malraux was very wise to go for efficiency. Whenever anyone tries to talk to *el coronel* about revolution, he repeats, "Later. We have a war to win."

Malraux is indisputably a leader, even if he cannot fly and is no good with a machine gun. He is charismatic for many of his men; he is flexible on discipline, having only one sanction: any navigator or member of the ground crew who crosses the line, he will send back to France. Under his headband or braid-embellished cap, the writer-*coronel* delights in his compelling influence. He can be mocking with his men or friendly and familiar, playing the Parisian lad and imitating old-fashioned career officers. Or distant and mysterious, disappearing off to meet with Spanish ministers or diplomats or the Soviet ambassador, Marcel Rosenberg. Next minute he's talking Plato with Nicolas Chiaramonte, a bomber and gunner.

Malraux's role is a perfect fit for him, and playing it satisfies his need for action. His knowledge dazzles the men, even when they don't understand what he's talking about. He is their equal when it comes to "guts." The head of a squadron doesn't necessarily have to fly. While in Spain, Malraux leads several lives: that of the combatant on the ground and in the air, and that of a potential politician. He talks to civilian and military officials and takes care of the squadron's public relations. He navigates among Clara, insistent and fearsome when she is there, various female admirers, male fans, and critical or jealous detractors. He takes notes in exercise books, on cards and loose sheets. The colonel gets drunk on work, gulping down the "manly brotherhood" in long drafts. The navigators share a dormitory; sometimes Malraux sleeps there. Often he gets up at four in the morning, awakened by the telephone: the War Ministry giving orders or information about a mission. Reconnaissance. Attack aerodrome at Salamanca at 0600 hours. Visibility bad. The pilots get black coffee, rye bread, and eggs inside them. They are not short of food.[36] Sometimes Margot makes them breakfast. The atmosphere is warm, convivial, and worried.

During the first months of the war, British airmen from the 2nd "Lafayette" Squadron were billeted near to "the Malrauxs." Six of them are killed in combat in August and September. The press and the left-wing parties in Great Britain cover this, but less than the progressive press in France does the Malraux squadron.[37]

Nothomb-Bernier observes and records the "scrapping." The navigators are having an aristocrat's war: they are called out three or four times a week. They do not see the horror of the struggle close up except when faced with their own wounded and dead. Enemy human beings, seen from on high, look like ants on the roads and in the fields. Nothomb notes the enthusiasm as well as the atrocities. True, you can't make an omelet . . . But men are not eggs. Many churches are burned and looted by the Republican side. In Barcelona, convents are broken into and coffins in the cemeteries opened, to expose the nuns' skeletons. It is these same unearthers of Carmelites, Nothomb-Bernier notes, who gleefully organize a competition for the best female postal worker.

A Packard limousine is delivered to the squadron: "Where are the owners?"

The delivery driver points a finger to the ground: "Gone for a walk . . ."

To their execution. No need for a trial. The owners are quite dead.[38]

The colonel zips between Madrid, Barcelona, Valencia, and Paris. Dropping in at Gallimard,[39] he learns that Aragon and Ehrenburg are campaigning to prevent the publication of a little book by Gide: the anti-Stalinist, deadly precise *Retour de l'URSS* (*Back from the USSR*). Malraux mutters. This book does not come at a good time, now that the USSR is taking sides with the Spanish Republic. The international antifascist movement must not be hampered. First of all, Malraux encourages Gide "not to be pushed around." Then he advises him to keep quiet. This old man embodies an imposing conscience. How could he be neutralized? He is a slow-burning rebel, not a revolutionary who can change tack just like that.

The Russians set up a parallel police body in Republican Spain, the Grupo de Información, a tentacle of the Information Department,[40] under the direction of the Soviet ambassador, Rosenberg, who saw Malraux shortly after his arrival.[41] The grupo tracks Trotskyists and Anarchists on instruction from Henrik Yagoda, head of the KGB. The writer Gustav Regler is dragged to the headquarters of the International Brigades, where the Frenchman André Marty sits in power,[42] with close links to the grupo. Marty is pathologically mistrustful and sees "Fascist spies" everywhere, not least among the volunteers flocking to Albacete. He likes to carry out interrogations himself. If he has any doubts, he has the suspect shot. Better to kill an innocent man than let a guilty one go free. Marty fires questions at the German novelist. Where have you been? Will the Republicans win? Who do you know in Paris? Malraux? Have you met any Anarchists?

Regler holds out a letter to Marty accrediting him in Spain for the German newspaper *Deutsche Zeitung*, published in Moscow. Regler is released by Marty, meets Malraux in Albacete in a café, and tells him about his arrest. Malraux tells Regler about Gide and his *Retour de l'URSS*: "He is asking us for advice on whether he should publish or not. It is quite a problem, with the help the USSR is giving in Spain. You understand."

Sensible forethought to some, opportunism or follow the leader for others. Malraux, in the end, declares himself hostile to the publication of Gide's pamphlet: "I think it would be better to put this publication off until the end of the war."

Whereupon the obsessional Marty brings Regler in again. Marty—as Malraux well knows—detests intellectuals in general and the writer-colonel in particular. For a Communist hierarch like him, any difference of opinion is turned into treason. The traitor automatically becomes a "Trotskyite," just to keep it simple. Marty writes in a report on the air forces in Spain:[43] "The few aviators remaining in the España Squadron are [here Marty crosses out the words "under the supervision of"] surrounded by Mexican officers." Marty has been told of the untidy, colorful "Mexican uniforms" of Colonel Malraux's squadron. He does not seem to know that there is not a single Mexican in the squadron. "Nevertheless," he continues, "there is an argument for liquidating Malraux as well as [here Marty crosses out "probably"] his assistant Guides [*sic*], who offers no political security." Marty also thinks that Malraux has been involved in a plot to prepare for the seizure of power by the Anarchists.[44]

Marty, in his brutality and crudeness, does not perceive Malraux's evolution as he plays the Communists' game in Spain for his own reasons. *El coronel* observes that the best-organized military units, such as the legendary 5th Regiment, trained and supervised by the Communists, respect discipline; they fight and stand firm. For Malraux and others, these Communist units are the embodiment of the ideal of the people's revolutionary army; the Anarchists are just too anarchistic to carry off the victories the

Spanish Republic needs. The Communists are realists, Malraux thinks, and have put social revolution off until another day. True, they do come with a number of drawbacks when it comes to matters of the mind and literature. But we'll see after the victory. "Every man carries within him a civil war," Malraux will later say. Marty's sort is incapable of understanding a Malraux.

The writer receives a manuscript of Gide's *Retour de l'URSS* from Pierre Herbart, who has come to Spain. Herbart is awakened at his hotel and questioned by a Russian.

"You're in a tricky spot," Malraux tells Herbart. "Are you absolutely sure Gide won't publish that while you're out here?[45] . . . And even if he doesn't publish . . . the mere fact of finding that on you . . ."

Herbart goes to Madrid to see Koltsov. The Soviet writer is preparing Gide's trip to the USSR: the manuscript is a threat. Herbart is questioned again, by a mysterious Russian who offers him champagne and confiscates his revolver. Malraux suddenly turns up, intervenes, and proposes (to Koltsov's relief) to send Herbart back to Albacete, where *el coronel* will find him a plane.

Gide does indeed publish *Retour de l'URSS.* Herbart goes to see him as soon as he gets back. The writer, jiggling with excitement, welcomes him with open arms: "My *Retour de l'URSS* is causing a hell of a stir!"

"You almost got me shot."

"Oh, what nonsense! Clearly, since you are here, you must admit what I did was for the best. And believe me, I did think about it, a very great deal."

Gide's narcissism seems, in this case, as staggering as his intellectual courage. "I doubt that in any country, today, even in Hitler's Germany, the mind is less free, more bowed, more fearful, more reduced to a vassal state," he has written.

Malraux also helps out Paul Gérassi, a friend of Jean-Paul Sartre, who has his problems with the Spanish secret police. The *coronel* carries the tragedy of Spain inside him, an internal war of conflicts and choices. He formulates perhaps his best justification, or explanation. "If one does nothing, one is always innocent."

When accompanying a crew as a gunner, Malraux recites Racine and Corneille out loud.[46] He goes to many bullfights, where the arenas are segregated into *sol y sombra*, the sunny side and the shady side. During Malraux's corrida in Spain, he walks in his own sun at its zenith and goes through some muddy puddles of shade too.

To celebrate the anniversary of the Russian October Revolution of 1917, the members of the squadron invite some Soviet pilots to a banquet, in Malraux's absence. Nothomb-Bernier stands up and makes a solemn toast in Spanish: "To the one we are thinking of!"

To whom? Nothomb-Bernier, the political commissar, gets specific: "To Comrade Stalin!"

He feels the disapproval of the Spaniards present and senses fear from the Russian pilots, who must think that this Frenchman is spying for the secret service.

October 16: One of the Potez bombers, now nicknamed "flying coffins," escorted by three Dewoitines, destroys some DCA gun batteries in the towers of San Martín de Valdeiglesias Castle.

From October 18 to 20, volunteers from the International Brigades arrive en masse in Albacete, where Marty is writing his reports for the Comintern and a Captain Mazay, an "emissary" from Jean Moulin, is writing his own for Paris. The members of the brigades are in transit. Malraux sets up an office to recruit competent men from among these volunteers. Nearly 45,000 brigadistes are registered, including 10,000 French. Eighteen thousand take part in the fighting, almost all of them volunteers. On the other side, the Germans line up 17,000 men, the Italians, 75,000. Some powers intervene more than others. Some Portuguese and 75,000 mercenary Moors fight under Franco's orders.[47]

Malraux, swinging between optimism and pessimism, slips off again to Paris for forty-eight hours, hoping to buy some planes from the Czechs. When he and Clara have company, she talks more of *el coronel*'s supposed female conquests than of his tactical victories or his strategic planning. Knowing yet greedy to know more, captivated but keen to encapsulate with his own commentary, Gide observes the Malraux couple as much an entomologist as a friend:[48] "Clara tells me that for a long time now, he has never slept more than four hours a night. But when I see him next he doesn't look too tired. His face is even less scarred with tics than usual, and his hands are not as feverish. He speaks with an extraordinary volubility that often makes him so difficult to follow. He describes their situation to me, which he would find hopeless if the enemy forces were not so divided." Gide is well informed about the USSR but less so about Spain, where the Republicans seem to be as "divided" as the Nationalists.

Inexhaustible, Malraux prolongs his diplomatic mission. In Geneva, the Spanish foreign affairs minister is pleading before the League of Nations: democratic states should abandon the nonintervention policy. In Spain, regular Italian and German troops are involved in air and land operations. At the League of Nations diplomats work on the paragraphs and punctuation of virtuous motions. Malraux swims for a while with the entourage of the French minister of foreign affairs, Yvon Delbos, but does not convince him of the necessity of a massive public intervention.

Early on October 27, three of the five Potez bombers the squadron now has, piloted by Guidez, Darry, and Véniel, take off in the dark. The crew of the last one includes a Spanish copilot and an Italian bombardier.

The Potezes attack Franco's headquarters at Talavera de la Reina yet again, damaging the runway and the camp.

At the end of the month, a worried Malraux gathers together some of his pilots near Albacete. "It is my duty to inform you," he says, "that Marty has done everything in his power to sabotage our unit, for it to be placed under his control. I have responded to General Cisneros, on whom we have always depended. All he could give me was a very evasive response. I then went to Valencia to the War Ministry to speak with Prieto. . . . Prieto reaffirmed his gratitude for all we have done for the Republicans. . . . In view of Marty's demands and pretensions, he offered me the following choice if we do not want to be incorporated into the International Brigades: to be assigned either to a Soviet squadron or to a Spanish squadron. I chose the second solution. For most of you, your contracts are nearing their end. The Spanish government does not intend to renew them under the same conditions." On November 2, Malraux inquires about the pilots' decision. Guidez and Darry say they are ready to serve in a Spanish squadron. Guinet and Matheron are to let them know on the 15th. Five pilots, including Gisclon and Véniel, return to France. In mid-November, the mercenaries leave the squadron and the last fighter aircraft join Spanish units. Republican headquarters transfers what remains of the España to Torrento and reorganizes it, imposing army discipline, army ranks, and army pay.

At the beginning of December, Nothomb renames the squadron "André Malraux." The less there exists of the squadron, the more it is made myth by the grace of these two words, "André Malraux," carving out a place for it in History that engulfs legend; legend resurfaces in History.

Near Valencia, where the Republican government has fallen back for the last few weeks, the squadron moves to La Señera, in Chiva.

December 27: The "S," a Potez from the squadron, takes off from La Señera and breaks down. On board, Malraux is shaken. At Valdinares, Heinkel fighters attack "N," another Potez, which crashes in the mountains, near Mora de Rubieros. Only Marcel Florein, the pilot, comes out unscathed. The Algerian mechanic, Jean Belaïdi, was killed before the plane went down. Four are seriously wounded: the bombardier Taillefer and the gunners Georges Croizeaux, Maurice Combias, and Raymond Maréchal. The last, proud of his successes with the ladies, knows he has been disfigured and wants to commit suicide with his revolver. Florein stops him. Malraux gets together a rescue expedition. Perched on a mule, he goes off to find his men.

The death of Belaïdi moves Malraux, all the more so since the writer has noticed the anti-Arabic racism on both sides of the conflict. The Francoist North Africans, poor devils, are the very symbol of colonial exploitation. Among loyalists also, the Arabs are often looked down on. Dolores Ibarruri[49] talks in her speeches of "the Moorish hordes, wild and drunk with sensuality." Moroccan workers are press-ganged by the Republicans to defend Madrid.

The mercenaries have left, the volunteers have scattered; Malraux gives up his uniform. The Republican authorities are toying with another project for him. In Spain he has seen Soviet guns, planes, and tanks. When he gets back to Paris, he is given an account of his squadron's latest mission: the protection of the inhabitants of Málaga, who are fleeing in a horrendous exodus. Two Potez bombers were sent in. "P" made a forced landing near Dalias. "B" crashed near a beach at Castel Ferro near Motril. These aircraft were brought down by Fiat CR32s. One dead: one of the latest to arrive, the Indonesian Yan Frederikus Stolk. Five wounded: Paul Galloni, Maurice Thomas, Albert Dewerts, Jan Ferak, and Paul Nothomb. The latter limps for the rest of his days.[50]

Malraux is more and more convinced: only a discipline of steel can save the Spanish Republic. Who can impose it? The Communists. The USSR delivers 362 T26 and BTS tanks, heavy Maxim and lighter Tokarev machine guns, Katioucha and Moskito bombers.[51] This is the heart of the Stalinist temptation for *el coronel*, in the form of a strategic justification. Viktor Serge asked Malraux in Paris if he accepted the Barcelona trials of the Anarchists, just as he had swallowed those in Moscow.

"I would do nothing against Stalin at the moment. I accepted the Moscow trials, and I am prepared to accept those in Barcelona."[52]

A civilian again after seven months of war, at thirty-five, Malraux has managed to combine dream and action. And in combat, not in a print room or an office, where a militant intellectual can raise impressive shouts and be wounded or killed by proxy. Mechanics from his squadron, irritated by the visits of zealously loyal foreign journalists, would say, "At least Malraux has balls."

Never had Malraux lived with such intensity. The Republicans' cry of war and of hope is taken up by their supporters all over the world: "*¡No pasarán!*"

The loyalists' songs are poignant, but the best choruses, alas, do not win wars.

CHAPTER SEVENTEEN

Agitprop

THE SPANISH WAR, Malraux quickly understands, is taking place in the international arena as much as on the battlefields. In the USSR and in France, he has shown his talent for political agitation and propaganda. He now prepares to leave for the United States with Josette. The more distance he puts between himself and Clara, who loved to torment him in Spain, the better he can breathe. New York, San Francisco, and Montreal are farther away from Rue du Bac than Barcelona or Madrid. And in America he can use a weapon in self-defense against a deserted and furious wife: the telephone.

When he speaks in public, despite the waves of applause, Malraux does not charm all his listeners. François Mauriac has observed him without charity at the Mutualité: "Against a reddish background, the pale Malraux hieratically offers himself up to the clapping. . . . As soon as Malraux opens his mouth, his magnetism weakens. Not that he does not have what it takes to be an orator, even a great orator; but the literary figure in him takes the wind out of his own sails. The images he comes up with, instead of heating up his speech, freeze it: they are too complicated, one can sense the man of letters in them. . . . Malraux's weak point is his disregard for man—this idea that one can intone any old rubbish to a biped, and he will listen agog. Whatever stories he may have told about himself, we have never completely believed him. There is a big talker behind the bravado, but a nearsighted one with no sense of what is beyond, who puts too much trust in our stupidity."

Malraux seems dangerous to the American State Department. The U.S. Consulate in Paris at first refuses him a visa, then grants it. The American government adheres to the nonintervention policy, although American volunteers still find their way to Spain. On February 24, 1937, André and Josette board the *Paris*. On board ship, Malraux writes.

Louis Fischer, the journalist and essayist, with support from the Spanish consulates and Malraux's American editor, polishes up a schedule for the trip. Between February 26 and April 4, 1937, eighteen lectures are planned, and as many interviews as the papers want. Not much fighting over Malraux by the radio stations: he doesn't speak English. The circuit passes through New York, Philadelphia, Harvard and Princeton, Los Angeles, San Francisco, Berkeley, and so on.[1] Local left-wing organizations set up meetings. Nimble preparations are carried out by *The Nation*, the American League Against War and Fascism, the Medical Bureau, and the North American Committee to Aid Spanish Democracy, the Canadian League against War and Fascism, various writers' associations, and the minute American Socialist and Communist Parties. Malraux is introduced by a teacher here, by a minister there, somewhere else by a writer. *El coronel* does not request arms or make collections personally. His friends advise him against trying to obtain military equipment: he would risk immediate expulsion. The police and the FBI are tailing him.

He appeals to humanitarian feelings. The Republican camp, he points out, has urgent medical need for anesthetics and X-ray plates. His audience is sophisticated, mostly left-wing; it knows the author of *Man's Fate* and *Days of Wrath*. Malraux denounces nonintervention. His words are both concrete and abstract, down to earth and poetic. He is well trained as a public speaker and has a Latin taste for the Romanesque and the emphatic. His mimicry and his tics surprise, fascinate, and charm his lis-

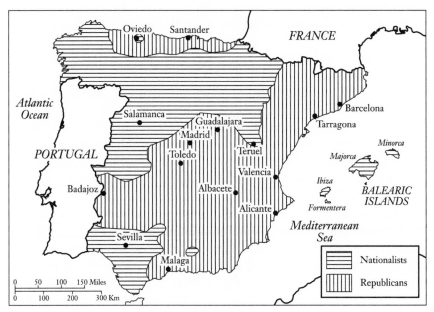

The two Spains in July 1936.

teners. He holds their attention with anecdotes punctuated by ideological remarks. He uses more or less the same ones wherever he goes, as would any itinerant slave to the lecture circuit. He uses a basic framework but adapts his speech to fit the audience, whether public, popular, lower middle class, or university. In speaking, he is writing, and he rewrites as he speaks. Across the United States and in Canada, he works on an outline reportage, or novel. On his first day in New York, at a banquet given by *The Nation* at the Roosevelt Hotel, he tells the story of the war:

> On December 17, one of the planes in my squadron was shot down in the region of Teruel—behind our lines. It landed in the mountains, about two thousand meters above sea level. Snow was covering the mountains. In this region, there are very few villages; several hours went by before the locals arrived and started making stretchers for the wounded and a coffin for the dead man.[2]

At the Sir Francis Drake Hotel in San Francisco, Malraux makes an impression as a raconteur:

> In Madrid, on January 1, toys sent from all over the world were handed out to the children. . . . For an hour, the children passed the piles of toys in silence; it was as if all the generosity of the world had been accumulated there. Then the sound of the first bomb. A squadron of Junkers was bombing the city.

Sometimes Malraux exaggerates, as at the Berkeley University Club:

> I am well aware that war is violence. I also know well that a government bomb could miss its military target, fall on a town, and wound civilians. But I want to draw your attention most emphatically to one point: we destroyed the airport in Seville, but we did not bomb Seville. We destroyed the aerodrome in Salamanca, but we did not bomb Salamanca. I destroyed Alvida Airport at Olmedo [not true], but I did not bomb Olmedo. For months now, the Fascists have been bombing the streets of Madrid [true].

He is preaching to the converted, those who already sympathize with the Spanish Republic. In private conversations and in public, Malraux alludes to an injury. Nothomb-Bernier observed "some bruises on one leg" after a bungled takeoff: Malraux was the gunner on board Potez "S" when an engine gave out. The pilot, Darry, "stashed" the plane, and the front part of it exploded. Malraux would surely like to have been wounded, in soul as well as in body. He doesn't trouble himself with dates.

At the Willard Hotel in Washington, he takes up the same theme and images he presented in New York:

> Early in the morning of December 27, we left Madrid and flew very high, with snow-covered mountains below us. There were seven men in my plane, airmen of five different nationalities, volunteers to help the Spanish people. . . . In the mountains above Teruel, our plane was shot down; one propeller and one wing blew up under the fuselage. . . . Six of our men were wounded.

In New York, the plane above Teruel was from his squadron. In Washington, Malraux is in the plane. He identifies with his subject, the characters, his comrades. Once again, imagined experience wins over veracity—Rimbaud-like. I am another, and the others are me. For his American public, the writer describes vividly scenes he has witnessed and reported or imagined events. He wants to have them share the experience. In short, he economizes on the literal truth.

> Coming back, as I passed near the lines, where the Moorish machine guns accompanied the noise of our ambulance in the heart of the night, I thought that something was happening here, something much more important than these wounded, even than the people following behind the stretchers; something for which there had been no precedent since the wars of the French Revolution: worldwide civil war had started.

Malraux often turns out to be a good prophet. Moved, he talks in religious tones of Jean Belaïdi, who died in his bomber: "Our comrade flies with us still. With the help of foreign troops supplied by Mussolini and Hitler, Franco may win military victories. He will never be able to conquer Spain."

This time his prophecy is less good.

F. W. Dupee interviews him for the Communist paper *The New Masses*:[3]

> "Are you working on another book?"
>
> "Yes, about Spain."
>
> "You know Gide's *Retour de l'URSS*, and you know that enemies of the Soviet Union are making use of it. What do you think of this book, and what is Gide's position now?"
>
> "Gide's opinions in this work were not definitive. . . . He is quickly preparing another book on the same subject, as far as I know to be called *Retouches*, which suggests that he will be revis-

ing his points of view, but I can't say, we'll have to wait until it is published."

Gide, contrary to what Malraux says to defuse the question, has hardened his tone: "There is no question of a party—no party will hold me back or prevent me from preferring truth to the Party itself. As soon as lying is involved, I am ill at ease; my role is to denounce it. It is to truth that I am attached; if the Party departs from that, then that's when I leave the Party." Malraux can't leave the Party; he doesn't belong to it in the first place, even if he does stick closely to the line of the Third International.[4]

In the United States as in Spain, when it comes to the USSR, Malraux (unlike Gide) chooses what he sees as efficiency over truth. Relative truth or absolute truth? The ending of *Retouches à mon retour de l'URSS*[5] is cruel: "The USSR is not what we hoped it would be, what it had promised to be, what it is still attempting to appear to be; it has betrayed all our hopes. If we do not want them to fall flat, we must pin them elsewhere. But we will not turn away from you, glorious and painful Russia. If at first you were our example, at present, alas, you are showing us the sands into which a revolution can sink."

Malraux cannot, will not, betray the Spanish Republic.

In the interview with F. W. Dupee, Malraux advocates the "organic unity," in France, of the Communists, the Socialists, and "other truly progressive forces." In Spain, the Communist Party also wanted to fuse organically with the Socialist Party—that is, to swallow it up. Shifting back into his snapshot style, which he does so well, Malraux has no qualms about making it up as he goes along:

> Several members of our squadron were shot down behind enemy lines; we had no means of knowing, back at base, what had happened to them. We quickly found out. A piece of enemy land fell into our hands. We discovered the bodies of some of our comrades. They had been mutilated and several had been tortured.

The War Ministry, Malraux maintains, has photographs. He mixes the true and the false to convey a powerful impression of personal experience. Spanish airmen were indeed tortured, but not those from his squadron. Let's just simplify; something is bound to remain. Malraux is getting closer in practice to a Leninist conception of truth and morality with all its inherent dangers: what is true is what serves the Party, and what is false is everything that harms it. Once this principle is accepted, the necessity, explanation, and justification of the slippery slope—as well as (although not for Malraux) any crime—follows.

The outlawed Trotsky, exiled to Mexico, is no stranger to violence or revolutionary lies. Still he attacks Malraux, the young, charming intellectual he formerly defended. Long gone are the days when the famous Bolshevik recommended to an American editor the publication of *La Condition humaine*, a novel, according to Trotsky, "exempt from all philosophical didacticism . . . from beginning to end a true work of art." Since the beginning of Malraux's American trip, which he has been following in the press, Trotsky has been getting more and more annoyed. No sooner does he arrive in New York than Malraux pronounces phrases (at the banquet given by *The Nation*) inexcusable to the founder of the Fourth Communist International: "Trotsky is a major moral force in the world, but Stalin has restored dignity to the human race. And just as the Inquisition in no way reduced the fundamental dignity of Christianity, the Moscow trials in no way diminish the fundamental dignity of communism." Malraux is answering the expectations of the numerous sympathizers with the USSR in the world, intellectually paralyzed by their faith and their hope. He speaks in public of the trials, more openly in the United States than in France. According to his logic, Stalin is associated with human dignity! In its report, *The Nation* drops the parallel between Christianity and communism.[6]

Malraux agrees to see a Mexican correspondent for *El Nacional*.[7] The journalist brings up the Moscow trials and Trotsky. Malraux rarely loses his cool. The future of humanity, he insists, is being played out in Spain. All "intellectual considerations" must be put to one side. It would be almost criminal to waste hours, whole months, discussing points to be dealt with later on. A week later, Trotsky, isolated and a little paranoid (not without reason), reads this interview. The Old Man sends a communiqué to the Mexico United Press Agency.[8] After agreeing with Malraux's favorable assessment of the Cardenas government currently in power, Trotsky moves on to his essential preoccupation: "New York," he writes, "is the center of a movement intending to re-examine the Moscow trials, which is the only way to prevent more legalized assassinations." All over, progressive intellectuals are worried about the Moscow purges; detainees are accused of having put screws into the butter of Soviet citizens, to sabotage the regime. Even Nizan says to his wife that there must be limits to ideological stupidity.

Trotsky goes on to Malraux's political role of ten years before, factual or fictional. In 1926, this writer was serving the Comintern and the Kuomintang in China, wasn't he? According to Trotsky, he is responsible for stifling the Chinese Revolution. Trotsky too is contaminated by the legend of a Malraux with high responsibilities in the Kuomintang. He attacks in a polemical vein: "Malraux is organically incapable of moral independence; he was born biddable." The writer is in the pay of the

Comintern, therefore of Moscow, therefore of Stalin. Trotsky draws his conclusions: "In New York, [Malraux] is making an appeal for everything to be forgotten except the Spanish Revolution. However, Malraux, like other diplomats, talks least of what concerns him most." In his thoughts, the exiled Trotsky is living in the USSR and Malraux, the propagandist, in Spain.

Trotsky comes to what is disturbing him: "Malraux's concern for Spain has not prevented Stalin from exterminating dozens of old revolutionaries." The Old Man, who himself, when in power, had more than a few dozen nonrevolutionaries exterminated, loses his temper: "Malraux left Spain to carry out a campaign in the United States to defend the judicial work of Stalin and Vishinsky [the merciless Soviet public prosecutor]." With his taste for historic synthesis, his fixation on Stalinism, Trotsky says, "It must be added that the policy of the Comintern in Spain completely reflects its disastrous policy in China." It is an absolute condemnation of Malraux by the Trotskyists. Objectively, as Trotskyists and Stalinists alike would say, the Old Man pushes Malraux toward the Communist parties, at least for a time. An unexpected mutual admiration on the part of both men is followed by a feeling close to hatred with Trotsky and near exasperation with Malraux. The exiled Soviet is all the more disappointed since, four years before, he had liked the hint of an anti-Stalinist line in *La Condition humaine*.

The left-wing press joins in the argument.[9] All the Communist parties, especially the expanding Spanish party, see here an opportunity to denounce Trotsky once again. The national secretariat of the Spanish Communist Party, well below the figures declared by the Comintern, was claiming in September 1936 that it had 254,000 militiamen. This year, 1937, it has 328,547.[10]

Hardly able to control his contrition, Malraux answers with irritation and loftiness, "Mr. Trotsky has devoted several works to the study of the Chinese Revolution. He has personally attacked all those he took to be responsible for the Chinese defeat; up to now, he has never attributed an important role in this revolution to me. For ten years, I occupied no place in the history of the Chinese Revolution; suddenly I have become the most important character in it." A clever defense: Malraux lets it be understood—without actually saying it—that in his time he did play a political role, not in the foreground as Trotsky insinuates and (oh, modesty) that he no longer has, at least not over in China. Afterward, he attributes his disagreement with Trotsky to a difference of opinion over the collectivization of land in Spain. This he believes to be "currently unworkable"—the position of the Spanish Communist Party and the Comintern. That allows Trotsky to transform the writer into an opponent of the Spanish Trotskyists and "the leaders of the POUM [Workers' Party of Marxist Unification]." Malraux clears himself of the Old Man's unjust accusations: "Mr. Trotsky declares that I came to the United States to emphasize the accusations made against him in the Moscow trials. If he had taken the trouble to read the papers, he would have noticed that none of the interviews I granted to the press contain any allusion to this subject." Duly noted. But that is just it: the Malrucian silence at the time seems deafening. "But Mr. Trotsky," continues Malraux, "is so obsessed by his destiny that when a man who, after eight months of active service in Spain, declares that aid to Spain must come before everything, he thinks he must not be trusted." Six, seven, eight months? What's the difference? Six would be closer to the truth. No point quibbling about it, although a whole run of silly little mistakes can end up constituting a major falsehood.

During his time in Spain, Malraux decided that the primary goal, the struggle against Francoism and the various "fascisms," must indeed "come before everything." The nonintervention policy, he observes, is working mainly in Franco's favor. At first Stalin decided to invest cautiously with munitions and weaponry. Now Soviet tanks, planes, and pilots are arriving. And the International Brigades organized by Moscow—Comintern circulars show it—are in Spain. At times, Moscow, which had wavered about Spain, seems as worried about the prospect of a revolution that is not Communist as it does about the prospect of carrying away a victory over the opponents of Republican Spain.

Francoism was not, at its outset, mistakable for fascism or Nazism. But it became their ally and ended up resembling them. When the war broke out, Hitler did not even know who Franco was. The doctrine Franco developed was not Hitler's or Mussolini's. Franco's vision incorporated clericalism, ultraconservatism, monarchism, and a chunk of fascism. Franco saw himself as defender of the Western Christian world. This mediocre man did not have the scope, dare one say, of Hitler or Mussolini. Like it or not, almost half of Spain supported the generalissimo. While Malraux is in the United States, Franco proclaims the Falanges the only party and becomes its leader, the Caudillo.[11] At the beginning of 1937, from a military point of view, nothing in Spain is settled yet.[12] German Heinkels bomb Guernica and Bilbao,[13] where an autonomous Basque government sits, loyal to the Republic. Incendiary and explosive bombs cause about 1,500 deaths and 2,000 wounded. The German fighters gun down inhabitants of the cities who try to run away. Malraux is right: all-out war against civilians is starting.

In Paris, an uneasy Clara feels as though she's out of the game. Josette, accompanying André in the United States, doesn't get involved in politics or polemics. Her silences comfort or absolve her partner, who knows that

Clara is harshly critical of his position. On tour with André, Josette prefers writers and actors to militants and politicians. In Hollywood, she hopes to meet Joan Crawford or Greta Garbo. She settles for Boris Karloff and Edward G. Robinson.

As if not sure of the soundness of his political line, a repentant Malraux becomes more and more vehemently anti-Trotsky and gets carried away in his interviews: he even convinces himself. In the course of one interview,[14] Robert Edward Knowles of *The Toronto Star* throws in a "colonel" here and there. Malraux tells Knowles that he is to see President Roosevelt in Washington. Wishful thinking. There has never been any suggestion of such a meeting, save in Malraux's head. He predicts to Knowles that there will be a general war within the next two years. Well spotted.

"Which nation, do you think, is closest to the true ideals of a great democracy?"

"Russia," Malraux replies.

Not so well spotted. Yet in Spain, Koltsov and Ehrenburg did put him in the picture on this. Babel was even more precise in his descriptions of the limits of Soviet democracy.

"And who," continues the Canadian journalist, "again in your opinion, is the exceptional man leading to this ideal?"

"There are three: Stalin, Blum, and Franklin Roosevelt."

Malraux is casting his net wide. Two days later, he gives a speech to the press in the Montreal Presbyterian Church.[15] There he is understood in French. He answers the numerous questions as if he were wielding a submachine gun:

"Are there Russian combatants in Spain?"

"There is no Russian infantry. There are airmen and technicians, same as the Germans."

"Are there large numbers in the International Brigade?"

"It reached fifteen thousand men, but now sixty percent of them have been killed or wounded."

"How long do you think the civil war will last?"

"Perhaps three weeks [a very optimistic Malraux], perhaps two years [a prescient Malraux]. Everything will depend on the assistance received and the success of our troops. Our victory is indivisible from the participation of the country people, who are coming over to us more and more [propaganda]."

A plane has been shot down in Spain with Louis Delaprée, a reporter, on board, whom Malraux knows and likes. Robert Brasillach, in his newspaper *Je Suis Partout*, accuses Malraux of being responsible for the death. A Quebecer journalist barges in:

"Can you shed any light on the death of the journalist Louis Delaprée?"

"No. If I accused you of having killed your grandmother, what would you say?"

"What is the nature of the wound that forced you to leave the front?"

Malraux improvises:

"The day after the battle of Teruel, my plane came down. I could have been killed. I received only minor injuries, really, to the throat, the nose, the chest. No broken ribs. Previously, I caught a bullet in the arm, nothing too serious."

Malraux, we know, was "bruised" during a failed takeoff. For the first time, he alludes in public to a bullet wound in the arm. Not a single member of the squadron, nor the French newspapers, have heard anything about this wound. In short, was Malraux discreet in Paris and verbose in Montreal? Some wounds of the soul or the mind are harder to bear than physical injuries.[16] Probably. Malraux's bullet wound is an amalgamation of the wounds of his heroes: his comrades. He bears the wounds of the squadron's Christs.

On April 19, back in Paris, André drops Josette off at the Hôtel du Louvre, then returns to his marital home in the Rue du Bac. André Gide meets him. His friend and landing neighbor, Mme. Théo, asks him questions. Gide is appalled: Malraux seems to have turned into a "complete Stalinist even in the matter of the trials.... He calls Trotsky a madman"—although, in mitigation, Gide notes that Malraux seems "caught up again by literature." All he is thinking of now is writing a book on Spain. While he was spouting a bit of nonsense in the United States, Malraux was already writing. Gide had implored him to concentrate on the novel he had started and not to go back to Spain. Malraux interrupts him: "You obviously haven't understood that one of the reasons for being in Spain was to get away from my home."

With her friend Suzanne Chantal and a third semiforsaken woman, Josette moves into an apartment in Paris. Malraux names it "Zenana," after the Persian harem. He dives into his novel, which Josette types out for him. Malraux comes and goes among Clara, their daughter, and the Zenana. Josette taps away on the typewriter, but Malraux talks about the novel to Clara, who has a political mind. Malraux wants to write *and* to get away from Clara, but he needs her judgment on what he writes. She knows his previous books; Josette doesn't. Malraux hesitates. If he were to go back and join his squadron, which now consists of volunteers and has been incorporated into the regular air force (where not all of his acquaintances are friendly), it would be as second in command, and he'd be a thorn in the side of government headquarters. Clara keeps her eye on

Josette; Josette keeps hers on André. He still campaigns for Spain and tells the story of his journey to the United States and Canada with a leitmotif: "If the democratic powers do not want to intervene militarily, they must at least provide peaceful assistance, economic assistance, medical assistance," he declares to *Ce Soir*, the unofficial evening paper of the PCF.[17]

Ten days after his return, Malraux attends a May Day demonstration, devoted to solidarity with the Spanish people. Collectors advance, holding out white sheets horizontally between them, with a poster in the center showing dead Spanish children. As they approach, workers lower their tricolors and red flags.

"That," says Malraux, "was perhaps the greatest emotion of my life."[18]

An opportunity arises to get back on the campaign trail and away from the hysterical Clara. Picking up on a project that has been in dry dock for a long time, the Spanish government is organizing a writers' congress. Josette, like Clara, would like to accompany Malraux. Malraux solves the problem by taking neither. He dashes off to Valencia, where the Republican government has been based for eight months. Madrid is holding out against the Nationalists, but the Republican government does not want to remain in the capital.

The prime minister, Juan Negrín, in the presence of his ministers, including Álvarez del Vayo and José Giral, inaugurates the conference on July 4. Eighty authors, representing twenty-eight nations, have made their way to Spain, not without difficulty in some cases: certain countries judge that sending writers, like dispatching arms, constitutes an intervention in the civil war. The Francoists muster by far the fewest literary figures. The English poet Stephen Spender travels with a false Spanish passport under the improbable name of Ramos Ramos.[19] He spends part of his time looking for a gay friend, to get him out of prison, where his desertion from the International Brigades has landed him.

Malraux goes first to Barcelona via Port Bou.[20] He symbolically hands over the sums collected in the United States to President Azaña.[21] Malraux's tour of the United States was a success for the Spanish Republicans. The two men have an idea for a film about the civil war that the ex-*coronel* would oversee. The government would finance the film, at least in part, promises Azaña. Headed by the famous French writer, it would certainly be useful and might even be good; that wouldn't do any harm.

In Valencia, the assembly of authors opens like a comedy. A pity Buñuel didn't film it. At the frontier, the Spanish hosts bundle the writers into Rolls-Royces and other proletarian cars. Everywhere, novelists, poets, essayists, and dramatists are welcomed with wild gratitude. Among the Spanish writers are Antonio Machado, Rafael Alberti, and José Bergamin, who is close to Malraux. Asked later if Malraux understood

Spain, Bergamin replied, "Better than any writer of his time, like Théophile Gautier in his own era."[22] Which isn't necessarily a compliment. Of all the French writers taking part in the Valencia conference, Malraux is the best known in Spain. Accompanying him from France are André Chamson, Julien Benda, Claude Aveline, and Denis Marion. Pablo Neruda, Octavio Paz, Alejo Carpentier, and Nicolás Guillén represent South America; Louis Fischer and Malcolm Cowley, North America. Although invited, Ernest Hemingway is remarkable by his absence. Among the Germans, Anna Seghers, Heinrich Mann—not his brother, Thomas—and Ludwig Renn, a former officer. Ehrenburg and Koltsov, with Alexei Tolstoy and Aleksandr Fadeyev, two Stalinophile courtiers, lead the Soviet delegation. The efficient help the USSR is giving the Republic casts a flattering light on the writers from Moscow.

The conference mulls over a short-term optimism and a justifiable pessimism about the outcome of the war. The conference's heavy motif is the role of the writer and his relationship to the masses. At times, the excitement thickens: that way some participants get the feeling they are fighting. Words are weapons. Ludwig Renn exclaims, "The role of writers who fight for liberty is not to write stories but to make history."

In the good-humored rowdiness, in an atmosphere of molten propaganda, the participants visit Madrid to pay their respects to the capital. Late into the night, they drink and talk. They raise their clenched fists, shout out, "¡Salud!" Any excuse will do to start them off singing "The Internationale," especially when a Soviet is speaking. Then an arresting interlude: uniformed officers arrive to report on operations at the front. The conference participants observe minutes of silence in memory of comrades killed in combat. The Soviet Embassy has transmitted instructions to its compatriots: Gide and his *Retour de l'URSS* must be demolished. On the platform, Tolstoy and Fadeyev, apparatchiki and prebendaries of orthodox literature, condemn him. José Bergamin too, who sees in Gide a "Trotskyite," the label at the time being more and more defamatory. There's no one quite like a Catholic progressive such as Bergamin to take things too far. In public Malraux keeps quiet on this point, but later he gives Bergamin a one-on-one lecture.

While the conference is in session, Japan openly invades China, without declaring war. In the USSR, with a somewhat marred sense of timing, Stalin treats himself to more purges. This time, it's the turn of Mikhail Tukhachevsky, the assistant minister of defense, along with several generals, including Uborevich and Yakir. The main charge is having betrayed the Soviet Union by maintaining regular correspondence with foreign powers, not least Nazi Germany. The writers in Spain refer to this little problem in private, never on the platform.

In France, the Popular Front is on its last legs. Léon Blum stands down. After the ritual ballet of a Third Republic crisis, a round of intrigues, rumors, and bargaining in the corridors of power, Blum advises the president, Albert Lebrun, to choose as his successor the centrist Camille Chautemps, who does not share Blum's sympathies for loyalist Spain.

Malraux takes the floor several times during the conference. In an account of his trip to the United States and Canada, he says that "this war has a meaning: the defense of culture. . . . Any intellectual must automatically feel himself to be at your sides."[23] Surrounded by the aura of his *coronel*'s prestige, Malraux joins in the discussions on tactics and strategy. The Republic cannot die. This war is becoming a struggle between civilization and barbarism, humanity and bestiality, a legitimate government and a military rebellion. The Republicans are fighting a just war. In Madrid,[24] Malraux gets up onto the stage of the Salamanca Cinema. Too much has been said about culture and the masses, peppered with abstractions and tiresome generalities. He makes a ritual condemnation of nonintervention but quickly moves on. Malraux does not talk of governments (they are booed by the audience); he conjures up the supporters of the Spanish Republic he met on the other side of the Atlantic. He tells a touching story, well tried and polished before this conference. A Canadian worker, he says, put an old family watch into the collection plate after a meeting, then came up to Malraux: " 'I don't know anything about politics . . . but . . . I understood that there were men who'd rebelled so that people like the poor all over the world wouldn't be humiliated anymore; and there were men, whatever their political opinions, who were fighting right now so as we shouldn't be allowed to look with scorn on mankind and so as we can trust them.' That is why he put this 1860 watch on the collection plate."

That's a stroke of luck, this Canadian worker talking about humiliation and scorn, just like Malraux.

Malraux grows impatient. The warlike fervor of his nonfighting colleagues wears him out. Who has actually joined up? George Orwell has been a corporal, then a sergeant, in a military section of the POUM, has even been wounded, but he is still an unknown[25] and isn't in Valencia anyway. In Madrid, the conference hesitates, then valiantly declares itself a "touring congress" and heads for Barcelona. There, before Stephen Spender speaks, out of politeness and deference the participants stand and sing "God Save the King"[26] with clenched fists held high. In the wake of this ecumenical development, why not go on to Paris, since the first International Writers' Conference is to take place there? French, Germans, Soviets, British, Americans, and Spanish head off on the sleeper, without

Malraux. The English poet Julian Bell, a volunteer ambulance driver, has only contempt for this Madrid congress. He is killed a few days later, during the tough Brunete battle, followed by the young philosopher Maurice Cornforth.

Aware of some ridiculous or pathetic aspects of the conference, an exhausted Malraux crosses the Pyrenees to join Josette. His book is taking him over. It will be called *L'Espoir*. Malraux writes, Josette types. He prepares to hand over his completed manuscript to Clara. Over the whole summer, he works on it ten hours a day with his usual technique: going back over passages, drinking Pernod, cutting up sheets, pasting and repasting, changing the order of paragraphs.

He goes with Josette on an excursion to Provence, to Aigues-Mortes and Les Baux. Clear of the Spanish drama and with personal tragedies and comedies yet to come, Malraux finds himself in this book. For some, war is a long-term stimulant, even when they are no longer in the action. Writing ripens a writer; it is what he does best. And a book can turn into an action. Words are weapons. Malraux stands firm and advances on what is perhaps his best front, literature.

Clef de sol
Limitée par la colère

CHAPTER EIGHTEEN

What Hope?

What's your proposal? To build the Just City? I will,
I agree. Or is it the suicide pact, the romantic
Death? Very well, I accept, for
I am your choice, your decision: yes, I am Spain.

—W. H. AUDEN, "SPAIN 1937"

MALRAUX WORKS ON his manuscripts in blue and red ink. He scribbles down notes on maps. One set of annotations is made in March 1937, after the Battle of Brihuega, in Guadalajara to the northeast of Madrid. The battle ends in disaster for the Italian troops, who leave behind about 3,000 dead and 800 prisoners. The Republicans' toll numbers almost 2,000 dead and 400 prisoners. Malraux is not in Spain at the time. His notes:

Macaronis [the Italian Fascists] open fire
Civilians in the cellar
Men brought . . .
. . . Phase II—no snow
2 days later after action against Ibarra
prep. air force, artillery
Garibaldi [International Brigade] and Franco-Belgian against Ibarra
. . . The carabineers of Alcaruda on hill 940
1:40—bomb—artillery
2:10—air action—leave Dombroski . . .
3 shelled throughout the night
6:00 the heights around Brihuega are taken . . .

The day before the attack on B brings mulled wine.
. . .
Brihuega besieged—all from Brihuega go from km 80 to 96
taken toward 7 p.m.
move in at 10 a.m.

Malraux draws determined red pencil lines on the map. His writing and rewriting, passages overhauled only to be crossed out, cover sheets of paper of every sort. He does not write at the first attempt; he does not have Aragon's stunning capacity. Malraux overfills his typed versions, working on his manuscript as a potter kneads his clay and draws up a vase, like a painter preparing a collage. Often he slips from the first to the third person or vice versa: I am the others from my camp. In the early drafts of the novel (written, as witnessed by the Hotel Pennsylvania writing paper, in the United States), he even crossed out the name "Garcia" and replaced it with "Malraux," not hesitating to set himself into the scene. Headed paper of the Compagnie Générale Transatlantique shows he used the return journey from the United States on the SS *Normandie* to get a firm hold on his novel. A sea voyage has become a ritual. The isolation of a ship can inspire and liberate him. He remains still, working in the saloon or his cabin, while the ship moves around him.

He flees Paris and Clara, the furnished apartments and the hotels of the Sixteenth Arrondissement.[1] In the calm of a chalet hired at Vernet-les-Bains, near Perpignan and not far from the Pyrenees, Malraux produces fifty chapters and ultimately one hundred and fifty scenes or sequences. He gets up late, works without stopping, often into the night, eats, drinks a lot of pastis and white wine. He suffers when writing, but not from writer's cramp. By writing about it, he keeps the Spanish war at a distance, yet keeps it close: on the other side of the Pyrenees, the war is still going on.

Malraux's imagination is seized by a machine: the airplane. After experiencing civilian tourist craft in the Middle East, Malraux has discovered in the warplane a symbol of the twentieth century. The airplane distorts time as well as space and changes civilians' and soldiers' lives. France was hit by the consubstantial myth and reality of the airplane and the aviator ten years earlier, with Antoine de Saint-Exupéry. Malraux avoids the "knights of the air" approach, where daring heroes are pitched against German fighter aces. Instead he shows a team of seven men, united by a fraternal solidarity surpassing that in the infantry. The novel, entitled *L'Espoir* (Hope)—Malraux has a knack for great titles—places pilots, mechanics, intellectuals, and proletarians side by side.

The refining and purification of a text is a literary and a technical undertaking, but with Malraux there is also a political dimension to it. A line written before he really got into the novel: "The optimism of myths (communism and many others) goes very well with the pessimism of methods." Malraux is no utopian: when it comes down to it, he does not believe in the millenarian end to history that is stereotypical of Marxist thinking. For the final version of *L'Espoir*,[2] in lucid acknowledgment and retraction—which readers will not see—Malraux cuts scenes about communism in the USSR and references to the very recent trials and disappearances in Moscow. In his notes for *L'Espoir*, there are remarks about Spain: "At any rate, the terror doesn't affect everybody." Malraux is aware of the activities of the NKVD and of the Grupo de Información. With the novel in full flow, Malraux steps back and stays quiet about the fate of thousands of non-Communists on the loyalist side.[3] Not a public peep out of him to condemn the legislation outlawing the POUM in May 1937. Nothing against the suppression of its paper, *La Batalla*. No protesting either when Gide, François Mauriac, and Roger Martin du Gard telegraph Juan Negrín asking for legal guarantees when the POUM comes to trial.[4] In the preparatory work for his novel, Malraux does, however, seem close to the Anarchists: "Always, in the foreground with them [the Anarchists of the FAI], this notion of brotherhood . . ." The word "brotherhood" comes up again and again throughout the book.[5]

In *La Condition humaine*, dignity was "the opposite of humiliation." Now a hero of *L'Espoir* proclaims just as loudly that "the opposite of being offended is brotherhood." But as Malraux knows, brotherhood is not the basis of an efficient army. There is another civil war being waged between Communists and Anarchists, within the civil war against the Nationalists and their allies; one question Malraux does not ask himself in his novel is whether this is contributing to the weakening of the government side.

Malraux sticks to a unity of place: Spain. As for time, *L'Espoir* takes place over eight months, beginning on the night of July 18, 1936, at the dawn of the civil war, and finishing between March 18 and 20, 1937, at the end of the battle of Guadalajara, an obvious success for the loyalists. All hope is not lost: a brigade from the government army drives out the Francoists and makes it to kilometer 95 on the Madrid-to-Zaragoza road. Hence the title of the book. "The greatest strength of the revolution is hope," as one of the characters, Guernico, puts it. In the novel, hope seems to be independent of success or failure. It survives adversity. Malraux, the novelist of the absurd in *La Condition humaine*, becomes the narrator of hope, the reverse of absurdity.

He does not write about events in the heat of the moment: instead he works with burning materials, the embers of events that took place a few months before the novel was written. In *Les Conquérants* and *La Voie royale*, he kept his temporal distance, and in the former he took liberties with history.

The syncopated structure of *L'Espoir* denies classicism, even in its proportions: 223 pages for its first part, "Lyrical Illusion," 103 for the second, "Left-Wing Blood," and, as if running short of time, 75 pages for the last, even if it is the title of the book, "Hope." The narrative is brisk, full of jolts, bumps, and noises, stuffed with characters but controlled, despite its sometimes excessive speed. Like any diamond, its faults are apparent under the magnifying glass. The reader is captivated within the first twenty pages and carries on fast until the end, as breathlessly as the author. This is also a military adventure novel. Malraux plays his scene-chapters like cards. He pauses on pessimistic tableaux of wounded and dead airmen being brought down the mountain with their cortege of locals, before the lyrical finale of the book. The last pages seem almost pastoral but barely believable: Manuel, against a backdrop of trucks rolling on toward a Republican victory, comes across a record of Beethoven, the rather cheery *Les Adieux*, Piano Sonata no. 26. Hope must not be dark.[6] Manuel-Malraux stands up in the last sentence of the book, and we imagine him raising a fist: "He felt this presence in himself, mixing with the noise of the streams and the prisoners' feet, permanent and deep like the beating of his heart." The music and the distant trucks answer to the "uproar of the trucks" at the start of the novel. Finishing as he does on Manuel's beating heart, shortly after the tuneful passage with the phonograph and its music, is Malraux thinking of the end of his latest, fairly recent work of fiction, *Le Temps du mépris*? There, Kassner, Manuel's Communist counterpart, was thinking of the music he had "tried" to use to keep going in prison. When reunited with his wife, Kassner felt freed, but amid the overall defeat of the German Communists. Manuel is free and can spy Republican victory on the horizon. Another heartbeat.

Gide, keeping politics and literature apart and forgetting their political differences, tells Malraux,[7] "You have never written anything better; nor even as good. You achieve, seemingly without effort, an epic of simple greatness. You must have been helped by events." Gide does not like history; he also considers that *L'Espoir* throws light on certain conversations that "were somewhat obscure" or "explain somewhat the position that [Malraux] took." The political threads of the novel are kept in the background. Justified or not, true or false, the desire to prove a point does not destroy the work of art here, as it does sometimes in *Le Temps du mépris*. Marxism appears here and there, but never didactically or to the detriment of the novel as such. Malraux keeps away from themes and expressions that kill a novel (the workers' party, historical determinism, dictatorship of the proletariat, history as a science). On the other hand, some of his characters' outbursts give us the tone of his convictions, or rather of his political emotions in 1937: "When a Communist talks in a meeting, he puts his fist on the table. When a Fascist speaks . . . he puts his feet on the table. When a democrat—American, English, or French— speaks . . . he scratches the back of this neck and asks himself questions." Malraux noticed it in Spain: "The Communists helped the Communists and the Spanish democracy; the Fascists supported the Fascists; but the democrats did not help the democrats." Why?

Malraux writes with insight, "As democrats, we believe in everything except ourselves. If a fascist or Communist state had the strength of the United States, England, and France put together, we would be terrified of it. But because it is 'our' strength, we don't believe in it. We should know what we want. Or else we say to the fascists: get out, or you'll have us to deal with! And the same thing the next day to the Communists, if need be." The author does not conform in the way *el coronel* did or the confer- ence speaker on his American visit shortly before. With caution and clear- sightedness, he puts a certain distance between himself and the official Stalinist line. One of the combatants in *L'Espoir* nevertheless says, "Eco- nomic servitude is a heavy load to bear, but if to destroy it we must increase political or military servitude, or religious or police servitude, then so be it." And Malraux repeats himself sixty pages later: "And if, to liberate them [the workers] economically, you have to make a State that will enslave them politically . . ." At least he's being thorough. The jour- nalist Shade: "In your country, anyway . . . everybody is starting to have a swelled head. That's why I'm not a Communist. I think the Negus [Anar- chist character] is a bit of an asshole, but I like him."

The Negus declares to the Communists that they are "eaten up by the Party; eaten up by the discipline, eaten up by their complicity. For anyone who is not one of you, you no longer have any honesty or duty or any- thing." To explain his pro-Communist position in *L'Espoir*, Malraux writes twice that "what is difficult is not to be with one's friends when they are right but when they are wrong."

Of course, Malraux shows through in his heroes. One of them, who fits him like a glove without reflecting him entirely [*Ma*gnin, *Ma*lraux], comes out with "I was left-wing because I was left-wing . . ." This tautol- ogy describes the Malraux of before the civil war and the Malraux of fight- ing Spain. Magnin-Malraux continues, "And then, all sorts of links were made between the Left and myself, loyalties; I understood what they wanted, I helped them achieve it, and I became closer and closer to them every time an attempt was made to hold them back"—a tortuous summary of his apprenticeship between Paris and Moscow from 1934 to 1936.

Luckily for his readers, the theoretical and practical problems of the

Communists are woven into the plot of *L'Espoir* without the stifling sluggishness of a heavily weighted down *roman à thèse*. What prevails is the sixty or so characters and the other, more eternal themes of war and death. Malraux detests war in theory, but in practice, without getting bogged down in it, he is attracted and obsessed by it. It is difficult, if not impossible, to start writing a novel while commanding a squadron. Malraux needed time and space to step back, to construct what was to become a novel of political adventure like *La Condition humaine* and psychological adventure like *Les Conquérants*, but more convincing and realistic than either of these. Hypnotized by opposing ideologies, Malraux seems to be less sensitive in his text to the savagery of the Spanish war than his competitor Hemingway, who later writes a very different and even more famous novel on the same theme, *For Whom the Bell Tolls*. It tolls for thee, democrat!

"They are wonderful when they are good," says Hemingway's hero, Jordan, referring to the Spanish. "There is no people like them when they are good and when they go bad there is no people that is worse." Malraux, the militant partisan, accentuates "fascist barbarism" almost to the exclusion of any excesses on the part of the Republican side. In the novel, Scali interviews an Italian Fascist pilot who has been taken prisoner and thinks the Republicans are going to execute him. Scali shows him photographs of Nationalist atrocities, including one of a pilot with his eyes gouged out.

"What . . . proves . . . that this photograph is not . . . that it wasn't sent to you . . . after having been doctored?"

Scali answers sarcastically, "Well, yes, it was. We poke out the eyes of Republican pilots to take photos. We use Chinese torturers for that, Communists."

Malraux the narrator continues, "Faced with these photographs of 'alleged Anarchist crimes,' Scali, too, initially supposed fakery: it is not easy to believe in the abjectness of those with whom one is fighting." Here Malraux is a propaganda merchant and is generous with his use of "alleged," leading the reader to suppose that the loyalists were guilty of no such crimes. Scali himself attributes them to the Anarchists, not the Spanish or Soviet secret service agents. The word "alleged" makes these supposed atrocities vanish into nothingness. For Malraux, all errors, blunders, crimes, and atrocities are a direct result of orders on the Francoist side. When it happens with the Republicans, surely it's always the result of uncontrolled spontaneity and is quite accidental. Just how spontaneous is a Republican secret service?

Malraux and Hemingway are both "antifascists," but the American is never an admirer of Stalin, Trotsky, or Lenin. Jordan, Hemingway's hero, talking to himself: "You're not a real Marxist, and you know it. You believe in Liberty, Equality, and Fraternity." For Malraux and his hero Magnin, Liberty and particularly Fraternity win the day. Malraux should know that some sort of fraternity is often what also binds Nazis, Fascists, and Francoists together. Jordan-Hemingway: "You believe in Life, Liberty and the Pursuit of Happiness. Don't ever kid yourself with too much dialectics. They are for some but not for you." Jordan-Hemingway is thinking about after the war. He will leave the Communists he has fought with, giving priority, like Malraux, to efficiency: "Here in Spain, the Communists were offering the best discipline and the most reasonable and healthy way to run a war. He accepted their discipline for the duration of the war, because they were the only faction whose program and discipline he could respect." Through Jordan, Hemingway probes his own political convictions: "What were his politics then? He had none now, he told himself." Malraux does not examine himself in this straightforward way.

The two writers watch each other jealously. They met briefly at the Hotel Florida in Madrid and in New York, where, Malraux says, Hemingway talked to him of Shakespeare, in striking terms, just as he speaks "of life in his best writing." Malraux later says that he considers *A Farewell to Arms* to be "the best love story written since Stendhal." Bitchiness, perhaps: really, nothing more than a love story?[8]

Hemingway has no philosophical pretensions. Malraux uses the word "metaphysical" a lot. For Hemingway, "Comrade Malraux" is a poser; to Malraux, Hemingway is "a false hard man" and "a madman who has delusions of simplicity."[9] But the two literary adventurers do have points in common. They have a physical and intellectual need to see history at first hand to write about it. War is one of their powerful literary drugs; they have great admiration for physical courage and are themselves brave. This admiration leads to exhibitionism. I am wounded, I handle guns, I fly in planes, I harpoon big fish, I hunt for biblical ruins, I get to the top of mountains, I hack a path through the jungle where statues sleep . . . therefore I am. Spain satisfies both writers' appetite for bravery, blood, and death—the raw material of two novels that leave their mark on the period. They saw different Spains. Malraux pulls the duvet over to his side: "Hemingway had spent more time than I in Spain before the war, and he spent less time during it. In short, he knew a great number of civilian Spanish and I knew a great number of enlisted Spanish. Example: his heroine is a woman [*sic*]; I do not think I knew a single woman in Spain with the exception of a few cultural officials and of course our nurses."[10] Seriously! Hemingway understood and spoke Spanish better than Malraux. In *L'Espoir*, numerous dialogues show Malraux communicating with the people more through pictorial art than with language. But the two novelists are alike in their reverence for simple people. Malraux knows the

Spanish people even less than Hemingway. In *L'Espoir*, the local who shows the Francoists' secret airfield to Magnin and his crew is very moving but hardly developed.

George Orwell had a balanced, perhaps more humane and objective view of the workers and enlisted peasants during the civil war. Orwell fought in the trenches, working his way up to sergeant; a private and NCO and an officer, an infantry sergeant, and a *coronel* in the air force do not experience the same war. Orwell noticed flaws that escape the Frenchman and the American in their novels. He noticed the "pathetic reverence that illiterate people have for their supposed superiors."[11] Another sad conviction on the part of the lowly in Spain, according to Orwell, is that "foreigners knew more of military matters" than the Spanish. Malraux will not venture out onto this terrain, with good reason. Orwell does not believe it is possible to turn the Spanish Republicans into titanic warriors: "The Spaniards are good at many things, but not at making war. All foreigners alike are appalled by their inefficiency, above all their maddening unpunctuality. . . . In Spain nothing, from a meal to a battle, ever happens at the appointed time." A charming characteristic common around the Mediterranean. Malraux, like his Scali, thinks that "no country has the gift of style like this one [Spain]. Take a peasant, a journalist, an intellectual; give him an official job to do, and he'll do it more or less well but almost invariably with a style to teach Europe a thing or two. . . . When a Spaniard loses his style, all the rest is already lost." The cliché of a national essence would seem a little too convenient.

Malraux doesn't make much use of humor in *L'Espoir*—nor in life, come to that—save the occasional association of tragedy and irony. He would never write, as Orwell does, "This is not a war . . . it is a comic opera with an occasional death." Long periods of waiting filled up the timetable of the squadron's foreign pilots, just as that of the infantrymen in their everyday lives; but the time is not the same. Malraux does not try to give a fully authentic, everyday account of war but instead draws together his most intense moments of action and emotion, concentrating on themes dear to him.

A romantic leitmotif emerges, the theme of the dehumanization of the leader. A Communist, Manuel (*Ma*nuel-*Ma*lraux), exclaims, "With every step up the ladder, as efficiency increases and the command improves, I get farther away from the men. Every day I am a little less human." Roland later says to Clara, talking about André, "Didn't you understand that he was inhuman?" As a writer, Malraux tends toward psychological Manicheism. A leader is able to keep his distance and not be affected by his mood. Must he necessarily become a butcher like André Marty?[12]

Malraux puts himself into almost every one of his heroes, as is his right, even his duty, as a novelist; but he never gives a full portrait of himself in just one. Here and there, he comes out with a piece of self-criticism. Of Garcia, who is otherwise a likable character, he writes that he "seemed all the more intelligent to part of his audience, since they were guessing, rather than understanding, what he said." Up to this point, Malraux has never admitted as clearly in writing his readiness to lose his audience in his monologues by talking above their heads.

As in all his novels, in *L'Espoir* he also introduces historical figures. *Les Conquérants* offered Borodine (small fry, really); *La Condition humaine* featured Chiang Kai-shek, from a distance; in *L'Espoir*, in the background, we come across Franco and Azaña as nonspeaking extras. The greats of this world, real or imagined, fascinate Malraux, even if it means giving them silent roles.

For the majority of his fictional heroes in *L'Espoir*, Malraux mostly draws from the men who were his friends or comrades. Golovkin is a blend of Ehrenburg and Koltsov; Shade, of Hemingway and Herbert Matthews. Guernico comes out of Bergamin, Gardet from Raymond Maréchal, Leclerc from François Bourgeois. Saïdi, feature for feature, is Jean Belaïdi. Never has Malraux transferred as much reality onto fiction as quickly and with as much vigor. He starts with Nicolas Chiaramonte to create Lopez, the painter and sculptor, and to sketch out Alvear, the art history teacher, proprietor of a gallery in Madrid. Alvear sells the work of painters such as El Greco and Picasso, no less. Not Greco-Buddhist statuettes. Chiaramonte can also be detected in a secondary character, Captain House, who reads Plato in the text.[13] The world of *L'Espoir* is overflowing with "manly brotherhood": there are no striking women.[14] The novel says that "war makes you chaste." It does indeed impose celibacy, but soldiers on leave in Madrid, whether Spanish or foreign, Malraux included, did not live the lives of monks.

Should we mind that most Malrucian heroes are, under their various masks, intellectuals or artists? Malraux mixes them with his own image— his several images. These he knows better than anarchist factory workers or socialist peasants. There are important figures from his squadron that Malraux does not use. One such is Jean Darry. To what can this absence be attributed? Would his transposed presence have harmed the dramatic progression or held back the narrative? Darry is an ex-NCO, a dandy, a fine specimen—perhaps too close to home? He later committed suicide while looking in a mirror. Did he reflect Malraux's hidden anxieties too much? That remains a secret of literary invention. The question remains open too for Deshuis, the Communist *conseiller municipal* from Saint-Denis, on whom *el coronel* depended for discipline in his absence. An excellent pilot and administrator, the oldest member of the squadron; perhaps he was also too perfect for a novel.

One Spanish character fascinating for a French reader, but apparently rather improbable for a Spanish one, is the old Republican Catholic, Colonel Ximenez. He fights alongside the Anarchists—Malraux can't get over it either. The writer's surprise gives the colonel a rare freshness.[15] Ximenez, having just shown immense courage, is saluted by Puig the Anarchist: " 'You were lucky crossing the Plaça Catalunya.'

"The colonel, who loved Spain with a passion, was grateful to the Anarchist, not for his compliment but for showing the style of which so many Spaniards are capable and for answering him as a captain of Charles V might have done, for it was clear that by 'luck' he meant 'courage.' "

Malrucian trumpet call: "For Ximenez as for Puig, courage was also a country." For Malraux, without a doubt, the Left was too. Ximenez was inspired by Colonel Escobar; Malraux's admiration for him is moving.[16]

Malraux, as *el coronel*, had the intelligence to take on mercenaries, while allowing the idea to spread that they were outnumbered by volunteers and that the volunteers were more important. In his novel, he caricatures a mercenary, Leclerc, comparing him to a "great ape with clown's hair and hands that are too long." Malraux turns him into a coarse, odious, and even, at one point, cowardly character. Thus the mercenaries in the book wane, to be outshone by the volunteers. The requirements of propaganda still need to be met. And Malraux, as in *Les Conquérants* and *La Condition humaine* with his Chinese characters, does not escape Spanish, or even French, stereotyping.

In the last ten years, there has never been such equilibrium between Malraux and the world around him. His oeuvre, for the first time, coincides with his life, even if, in imaginative terms, it goes beyond it. His escape from Paris to Spain is matched by and surpassed in the writing of his novel.

He is determined to separate from Clara. Yet he needs her. The passive Josette is good for typing, but the very active Clara is a far better judge of his work. In September, Malraux arranges to meet Clara in a hotel in Toulon to hand over his manuscript. For Clara, this novel is the Spanish war seen through inflexible, orthodox Communist eyes. Clara would always tend to sympathize more with the Anarchists and the angels of the POUM. In her critique of Stalinism, she is not far from Arthur Koestler's stance at the time. Both of them are ahead of André Malraux. Partly thanks to Clara, Malraux avoids the worst, a preaching novel in which a Communist strategy is presented as the only defensible one. Clara later said that she suggested numerous corrections and that Malraux accepted them.[17]

The relationship between Clara and André has been execrable for more than a year. There is no hope for their marriage. At dinners and with friends such as Gide, the Arons, the Arlands, Groethuysen, Alix Guillain, Drieu, the Nizans, the Lagranges, Clara has been making herself impossible. She kept talking about how dangerous it was for Malraux in Spain, in planes and in the hotel. She is quick-tempered; she wants to leave André and to stay with him. She finds Josette's (apparent) prevailing serenity hard to bear. She knows that Josette is going with him to the United States: "She's joining you in Southampton."

Josette has a miscarriage. Clara hasn't given up on the idea of a reconciliation. Malraux can't see it happening and consults lawyers. Their friends are required to choose between them. Raymond and Suzanne Aron prefer André. Marcel Arland and Emmanuel Berl manage the feat of remaining on excellent terms with both. Clara the *tragédienne* appears pained and dark. When Malraux runs off to Josette, she responds aggressively or takes refuge at the Arlands' in Rue Marbeuf. Florence, four years old, witnesses scenes between her parents. Malraux does not trouble himself with considerations of whether a divorce would harm Florence or whether, on the contrary, it might be beneficial, sparing her acrimonious rows, her mother's shouting, and the corresponding silences from her father. André's father left his wife when his son was four. Clara has to move out when she finds herself alone in the Rue du Bac and unable to afford the rent. From inclination or for provocation, she starts an affair with a Scottish lecturer, Allan Bose, who has introduced her to the work of Virginia Woolf. She talks to him about Malraux. Clara acquires a lasting specialty: that of talking endlessly about André to her lovers. Some even develop his nervous tics. Clara is brilliant but exhausting.

Josette and Clara share one conviction: that Malraux seems to be himself when he is writing. He escapes with his literature. *L'Espoir*, despite its tragic and romantic tone, expresses possible happiness with life. One can sense the artist fulfilled as a man of thirty-five, impetuous and calm, a Malraux in full possession of his literary faculties, using his stylistic resources to the full. Why are Malraux's good qualities, rather than his most exasperating flaws, precipitated at that precise time? First because, like Manuel, "for the first time, he [is] facing a brotherhood that [takes] the form of action." Malraux is not cheating anymore—or hardly at all—condensing some scenes from real life. His heroes are combatants, not cinema walk-ons. The characters of *Les Conquérants* and *La Condition humaine* had depth and substance but less tangible reality. Malraux was playing with them in a Chinese setting that he did not know well, or in an overly melodramatic atmosphere. Despite his skill as a craftsman and his artistic savoir-faire, his first novel sometimes felt like veneer and plywood. *L'Espoir* is solid wood.

Malraux expresses the brotherhood he felt in the Popular Front marches, in the streets of Madrid, on Barcelona's *ramblas*. His imagination rides on the crest of the mass of the combatants. His fighters are concrete, whereas his Chinese workers were abstract. Malraux does not describe his proletariat in a populist or socialist realist way, yet they still urge him on and inspire him by their fraternal presence. He shows them as if using a film camera, shot after shot, sometimes idealized, in a 1930s lyricism that harks back to Victor Hugo's *Les Misérables* and Jules Michelet:

> Still in civilian dress but wearing army shoes, with their stubborn Communist faces or intellectual's hair, an old Polish man with a Nietzsche mustache, a young man out of some Soviet film, Germans with shaved heads, Algerians [*salud*, Jean Saïd-Belaïdi . . .], Italians [*salud*, Nicolas Chiaramonte] . . . , some English, more picturesque than the others [cliché], Frenchmen looking like Maurice Thorez or Maurice Chevalier . . . with the memory of the army or that of the war they had fought against each other; the Brigade men pounded the narrow street, which resounded like a corridor; they approached the barracks and started to sing: and, for the first time in the world, men of all nations mixed together, in combat formation, sang "The Internationale."

Malraux's presence in Spain, the creation of his squadron within the first few weeks of the conflict, prove that he perceived the importance aviation would have in a conflict to come better than many French generals, including Major Charles de Gaulle, who was more of a proponent of grouped tanks. *L'Espoir* is the novel of the airplane. Malraux does not have Saint-Exupéry's flying hours, but he has absorbed the psychological atmosphere in the cockpit of an old bomber. He composes a classic passage:

> As if it had slipped between the white snow of the ground and the dirty snow of the clouds, the first Republican plane appeared. Then, one by one, oddly, like wounded soldiers, there appeared the old planes that no one had seen since August: the little avionnettes of the señoritos and the transport planes, the couriers, the liaison planes, Leclerc's old Orion and the training planes; and the Spanish troops welcomed them with a troubled smile, a smile perhaps inspired by their feelings at the time. When the apocalyptic assembly had arrived, snow-hopping to avoid the Italian machine guns, all the battalions of the people's army, waiting still, received the order to advance. And despite the low sky and the menacing snow, three at a time at first, then squadron by squadron, bashing

against the clouds like birds against a ceiling, then dropping down, filling the whole of the visible horizon, now nothing more than a horizon of battle, with a rumbling which set the snow lying on the ground and on the dead a-throbbing, it struck against the desolate line of sidelong plains as dark as the woods: strung out like an invasion, the combat formation of eighty Republican airplanes."

What Malraux brings back from Spain, as an intelligent and sensitive reporter, grabs the reader so much more than what he pulled from his bag after hunting for the queen of Sheba's treasure. *L'Espoir* contains gripping passages, written and rewritten, finely chiseled, mixed with dry, lofty, sometimes pretentious discussions. Some pages will move readers deeply, such as those devoted to the death of Captain Hernandez, taken prisoner by the Francoists, as he advances with the other condemned men.[18] With a surge of emotion, the epic rhythm starts to soar: "Hernandez is walking once more in the streets of Toledo. The prisoners are tied up in twos. . . . A little boy is watching them. 'They are old!' he says. How rude, thinks Hernandez. Is it death that gives me irony? A woman in black passes by on a donkey. She had better not look at them like that if she doesn't want to show she is with them." Malraux's stirring style.

> Here it is, what has so often haunted him, the moment when a man knows that he is going to die, without being able to defend himself. . . .
> Apparently, the prisoners are no more bothered about dying than the Moors and the Falangists are about having to kill them. . . . One of those leading the prisoners in front of the firing squad is leaning over into the ditch, revolver out in front, fishing about. The sky is shuddering with light. Hernandez thinks about how clean the shrouds are. . . . They're taking so long, arranging the prisoners as if for a wedding photograph, in front of the rifle barrels, pointing horizontally. The ditch. The raised fist. "Hands by your sides!" shouts the officer. The three prisoners shrug beneath their fists in the air. Three more, including Hernandez, go up into the smell of hot steel and dug earth.

Here is Goya's *Los Fusilamientos del 3 de Mayo*, reinforced by the weight of the present.[19] The ultimate present of Hernandez's death corresponds to the present of Malraux's existence. The writer is walking in his own footsteps. He writes with force and simplicity, bordering sometimes on grandiloquence. He is of his era. Hernandez-Malraux says, "I do not attach great importance to death, but I do to torture. . . . Even torture is a small matter compared with the certainty of death. The great thing about death is that it makes irreversible all that preceded it, forever. Torture, rape, followed by death, that is truly something terrible." Images of torture have been with Malraux since he was in Saigon. The confidences from the German immigrants for *Le Temps du mépris* piled them higher.

Further on, Malraux has Scali declare, "Death is not such a serious thing; but pain is. Art is not much compared with pain, but unfortunately, no painting can hold its own against bloodstains." Those who get past Malraux's wall of propriety know him to be obsessed, after death and torture, by the idea of pain. If he suffers, he does not admit it, as if he were the owner of a body anesthetized by his mind and his bravery. Faced with Hernandez the prisoner, Malraux writes firmly in his manuscript, "The . . . tragedy of death . . . turns life into destiny . . . from there on, nothing can be compensated."

Malraux finishes his book at the end of the summer of 1937, just as Japanese troops break through the Chinese front and advance. The Japanese show a complete lack of humanity. The Nanking massacres are perhaps the most hideous war crime of the twentieth century. Hitler welcomes Mussolini in Berlin and opens a huge camp at Buchenwald. In Spain, the Francoists take Gijón. The Nationalist troops have control of the northwest coast of Spain. Picasso's *Guernica* is being shown all over Europe. Communist critics and the Spanish government don't like it; it must be excluded from the loyalists' hoped-for victory. Songs and paintings do not make a war; they bear witness, no more.[20] Malraux doesn't trouble himself with the categories currently in vogue. He doesn't ask himself whether he has written a *roman* (novel), a *chronique* (chronicle), a *reportage romancé* (novelized report), a *récit* (account), or a *témoignage* (testimony). He feels he has constructed a book of a new genre, a cousin to American works, rather than a legitimate son of the French classics.

Now that he's a veteran of the Spanish war, armed with . . . a book, Malraux knows how to go about organizing the publication of a novel. The new crypto-Communist daily *Ce Soir* serializes *L'Espoir* from November 3. After a gap of a few days, the parts continue to appear until December 7. At the same time the weekly *Vendredi* prints fragments of the novel on November 12. Malraux also gets some extracts of his book into issue 290 of the *Nouvelle Revue Française* in November. The readership he can reach via Gallimard's monthly is fairly discriminating; with *Vendredi*, intellectual; more popular with *Ce Soir*. There is not much to be hoped for from the Right.

He wants a divorce. At the time, adultery is often recorded by a visit from the police, so he is careful. He moves into the Hôtel Madison for the winter, opposite Saint-Germain-des-Prés, and moves Josette into the Royal Condé, Rue de l'Odéon, five hundred yards from the Madison. Malraux also has to rid himself of some irksome female individuals swarming around his celebrity.

Bookshops put *L'Espoir* on sale on December 18, 1937. The writer gave the printers the go-ahead eight days before. He is not surprised by the reviews. He no longer needs them to sell his books. The extreme Right, of course, slams him. Robert Brasillach in *L'Action française* thinks he's being vitriolic:[21] "Between ourselves, had this novel been by a Hitlero-Japanese writer, by a vicious snake, a Trotskyite dog, a jackal of the POUM, or an anarchofascist, it couldn't have been more harmful to the cause it aims to defend. If that is how Lieutenant Malraux [*sic*] of the Brigade [*sic*] España thinks he can support morale on the home front, then we're in a fine mess." Brasillach reproaches Malraux for not showing any Francoists, Fascists, or Nazis: "Veracity to one side, wouldn't he have done better to grant some heroism to the combatants on the other side?" Brasillach later feels it incumbent upon him to write a pseudonovel in which Nationalist Spain comes across as rather dull: the author stuffs in documents, press cuttings, Falangist songs, crude tones. Pierre Drieu la Rochelle will also introduce Francoists in his *Gilles*. André Rousseaux of *Le Figaro*[22] slow-cooks his opinions in an unchanging stupidity: "The truth is that Mr. Malraux is a complete anarchist who has made a clean sweep of all values and now believes only in himself." But Henry de Montherlant, a remarkable man on the Right, writes for himself, "Of all the books to have appeared over the last twenty years, one would like most to have lived and written this one."

Workers and Spanish peasants, as Marcel Arland remarks, do not make much of an appearance in *L'Espoir*. Paul Nizan in *Ce Soir* sees a text that takes part in the combat of the Left: "There is no doubt that *L'Espoir* is a great book. A great book because of what the novelist achieves and by his fidelity to a subject that approaches the sublime. Malraux has for a long time been wondering if it is possible not to separate the action from an action novel: he has just answered himself." Nizan believes what he writes. He had to force himself to applaud *Le Temps du mépris*.[23]

On January 6, 1939, Claude Malraux, nicknamed "the Nho" ("kid" in Vietnamese) by Clara, is arrested crossing the border at Port Bou by Spanish Republicans and taken to Figueras for interrogation. Claude, nineteen, says he is an "assistant cameraman." He is carrying a pass for six days' leave signed by the colonel of the 1st Spahis Regiment at Medea. The pass is dated December 14, 1938. The "kid" gets into a muddle with his explanations, claims he is not a French soldier, writes a letter:

Figueras, January 8, 1939

To the Spanish Authoritys [*sic*]:

I, the undersigned Claude Malraux, requesting the Spanish Authoritys not to turn me back to France and not to hand me over to the French Military Authoritys.

Having left Banyuls by Foot [*sic*], I came to Port Bou through the mountains, being arrested by the carabineros and carrying on me French Army papers.

I made up a story so they wouldn't send me back to France, but afterwards having told the truth and having deserted I came to Spain, Firstly because of my Antifacist [*sic*] ideas and wanting to defend Republican Spain against the facist [*sic*] invasion, secondly, in coming to fight I made all proceedings against me stop and did not return to Algeria and the Army.

For I do not want to go back into the Army where there is nothing but humiliation and base insults, an Army where you lose all personality, all the character of yourself, where you are criticized for everything down to the name you carry. Why?

Simply because my Brother defended a Decent and Strong cause that of Governmental Spain, that is Why I ask the Spanish Authoritys to keep me in Spain so that I can fight for her and so that I am not handed over to the French Authoritys.

I hope that I will be understood and that Republican Spain will help me not to return to France.

The examining magistrate of the Ministerio de Defensa Nacional concludes his report: "We propose that C. Malraux be released on condition that he does not circulate on our territory wearing French military uniform."

André Malraux pulled strings in Paris for the young and wayward Claude not to be considered a deserter. It may be grueling to be André Malraux's half brother, but it is sometimes useful. And more so for the immature Claude than for Roland, a more balanced personality. When things get serious, André has a sense of brotherhood.

The critic André Billy exclaimed, "Malraux, with *L'Espoir*, has literally won the Spanish war." Could that be a misprint for "literarily"?

CHAPTER NINETEEN

Sierra de Teruel

S OME CRITICS THOUGHT *L'Espoir* was structured "cinematographi-
cally," like certain American novels of the 1930s.[1] Malraux often uses
film-related comparisons in his text: "Moreno has a movie face,"
Scali "the look of an American comedian in an aviation film," and the
Poles in the International Brigades have "mugs from Soviet films." While
in Hollywood, barely having started to write *L'Espoir*, Malraux was thinking about a film with Spain as a backdrop. The cinema reaches a larger
audience than books. In 1937, a well-known novelist might expect to have
tens of thousands of readers; a film director, hundreds of thousands of
spectators. Malraux's idea of a good film is also one that would reach millions of Americans and Europeans.

Producers weren't interested in a documentary on the Spanish war.
Joris Ivens, a "fellow traveler," made one using texts by Dos Passos, Hemingway, and Lillian Hellman. Boring, badly received, it lost money. Malraux eats with friends in restaurants in Los Angeles, on Wilshire
Boulevard, and in Santa Monica, amazing them with his film knowledge
and speeches on Chaplin and transcendence. To him they explain that
documentaries have no chance of succeeding. An action film is what
would really rake in the spectators. Malraux knows this: in France too,
stories with characters and a plot, a beginning, a middle, and an end,
preferably in that order, do better than documentaries. *L'Espoir* contains
several good, dense stories. Malraux could build a film around one of
them. After interviews with Azaña, Negrín, and Álvarez del Vayo in
Barcelona, Malraux thought he had found the money he would need. The
Republican powers had envisaged a budget, cars, extras, planes, studios,
hotels. Malraux had already proved himself by collecting dollars for the
Spanish Republic.

His novel takes off in the bookshops, with several translations on the way. But an excellent novelist does not necessarily make a good film director. Even the exceptional do not have every gift. Malraux wouldn't be content just overseeing the shooting: he wants to be the director, the chief, the creator. No suitable candidate comes forward. The Spanish film industry is faltering. Malraux has never directed a cameraman before. So what? He never flew a plane and still managed to become leader of a squadron. How much more complicated can it be to be a movie director? And if he fails, well, he'll fail in style.

Once the framework of the film has been decided—a plane from a squadron of international volunteers crashes in the mountains—how to find the money? Malraux asks Gaston Gallimard; his response is lukewarm. The resourceful Corniglion-Molinier also starts asking around. Malraux spends nine months working on his film project and making a number of trips between Paris, Madrid, Barcelona, and Valencia, with detours via Perpignan or Banyuls. Working titles suggest themselves: *L'Espoir, Espoir, Les Paysans* (The Peasants), and the one he eventually chooses, *Sierra de Teruel.* Malraux refuses to leave Gaston alone, and eventually, grudgingly, he comes up with some money. Louis Chevasson works as an intermediary. Gaston is happy with his author (a Goncourt winner is sometimes forgotten within six months, Malraux is still famous) but knows his financial habits. His personal needs are one thing; shoveling large sums of money into a film is something else. But Gaston is a suppressed writer and perhaps a would-be adventurer.

At the end of June 1937, Malraux's account at Gallimard is in the red, showing an advance of 147,222 francs, the contemporary equivalent of $5,955. From July 1, 1937, to June 23, 1938, the company pays him 169,470.81 francs, "to be deducted from his author's account and expense account." With his total royalties coming to 116,605.40 francs, his deficit ends up at 190,098 francs ($7,690). Gallimard does not see itself as a philanthropic institution. Malraux talks of possible American rights to *L'Espoir.* He is overstretched: Clara's maintenance allowance, his grandmother, the rents, taxes, "That is, all the things one cannot do anything about," he explains to Gaston. Malraux is also helping some friends: Manès Sperber, for example. If he is asking for an arrangement, "it is not so [he] can go off on a jaunt," since he's working on his film. He will "be in a fine mess" if Gaston does not help him out.

Malraux first of all sketches the outline of a screenplay, then writes a more substantial and precise one between January and May 1938. Looking for money and partners doesn't leave him much time to finish it. The writer creates a production company and has some headed paper printed in Barcelona:

PRODUCCIÓN A. MALRAUX
AVENIDA 14 DE ABRIL, 442 BIS

His company has the use of three and a half rooms on the ground floor of a building, a gift from the propaganda commissioner for Catalonia. The Republic is short of currency, but the *producción* is allowed unlimited use of the telephone. In the intersecting worlds of Spanish Republican bureaucracy and cinema, with their respective predispositions toward neurotic outbursts, Malraux holds a trump card: he never shouts. Another advantage is that he likes teamwork. He has the admiration of his French and Spanish collaborators, from the civil angle as Great Writer and from the military point of view as *el coronel*. One disadvantage when making a talkie: Malraux is no better at Catalan than he is at Castilian Spanish. But he knows how to charm and get a "yes" without having to repeat his request. He convinces all his assistants, technicians, secretaries, and actors that cinema is an art, not a tenth-rate form of entertainment.[2] Along with Cocteau and Giraudoux in France, he is one of the few creative literary types to take the cinema seriously in those days, not just see it as a technique, at best, or, at worst, an industry. Before shooting begins, he says that a film "comes up against a civilization in its entirety: comic films with Chaplin in capitalist countries, tragedies with Eisenstein for Communist countries, war films soon in Fascist countries."[3] Western cinema is, he thinks, too oriented toward laughter.[4] No danger of that happening with Malraux. He sees a continuity among paintings, reproductions of paintings, and the movement of cinema. Out on location on the plateaus, he talks about Velázquez and Picasso during breaks. His attitude to cinema is not (at the time) theoretical.

Once he has set up in Barcelona, the novice cinematographer chooses assistants quickly, as in Angkor and Saigon. Corniglion-Molinier and Roland Tual manage finance and administration, handling the logistics from Paris. The dramatist Max Aub is first assistant and, helped by María Luz Morales, the movie critic for *Vanguardia*, translates the screenplay. Denis Marion, writer and critic, becomes an important assistant, mixing together scenes and sequences. A remarkable cameraman, Louis Page, is part of the team; Boris Peskine fine-tunes the technical editing, Page works with Manuel Berenguer. Max Aub holds auditions, scouts for locations, carries film between Barcelona and Toulouse. Aub keeps up the morale of the film's troops with encouraging speeches. Public opinion in America, he explains, is a force to be reckoned with. Malraux has been offered a circuit of 1,800 cinemas, each with an average of 2,000 tickets sold per day. Aub's enthusiasm is contagious. A successful film will influence the American people.

Aub also chooses the extras. People are saying that Malraux's squadron was composed entirely of volunteers; this is not true. Later some claim that amateurs acted in the film; also not true, except in the crowd scenes. José Sempere, who plays the national aviation captain, alias Magnin, alias Malraux, already has a minor career. The local peasant farmer who leads the airmen to the objective, José Lado, is also a professional, and superb. Several of the actors are known in Madrid. They are badly paid and exhibit a Spanishness that Malraux cannot always tone down. He trusts his cameramen to judge whether a take is good enough. Sometimes he asks the secretaries what they think, as well as Raymond Maréchal, his squadron buddy with the messed-up face. When Malraux is worried, his tics get worse.

He drops his name in the tortuous negotiations with subcontractors and ministries. He does not get the tanks he wrote into his first screenplay. He needs them, but so does the Republic on its remaining fronts. Malraux cuts the scenes. It takes talent to stick to a screenplay but still more to improvise. Malraux comes to terms with the way things turn out. The film can't be processed in Barcelona; other reels are already being developed and there's a power cut . . . Aub leaves for Toulouse again. The celluloid is damaged in the fixing bath. They need the help of laboratories in France. Pilots with the commercial Paris-Dakar airline help out the moviemakers during their stopover in Barcelona. They can't get a single military plane? The plane is a vital character in the film. The head of aviation, Hidalgo de Cisneros, has more time for Malraux the film director than Malraux *el coronel*: he sends leftover bits of planes used for spares to build the cabin of a bomber. Much better than a set made of plywood. Malraux shoots above Cervera in an old Latécoère plane with no guns; just Aub, two cameramen, and crew. Good shots. Three Italian fighters appear. They are not in the script. The Latécoère dives and skims the ground. Fearing the antiaircraft artillery, the fighters do not give chase. Sitting at the forward gunner's post (so swears Aub), "Malraux was reciting Corneille."[5]

The director employs as a secretary Elvira Farreras, a young woman from a good family who speaks French, Italian, and English. She sees Malraux the whole day long; he is good-humored and concentrated. The crew works faithfully under exceptional circumstances. Food in Barcelona is poor: lentils, worm-eaten chickpeas, and rarely any meat. The Barcelonians have invented *tortillas vegetales*, omelettes made of yellow flour. The film crew samples pea pods and cauliflower stalks in the atmosphere of manly brotherhood (and womanly sisterhood) imposed by shortage. There is no tobacco. Some of the French amuse themselves by voting for the best steak and fries in restaurants around La Villette in Paris, like prisoners recalling unforgettable meals. Can't wait for a leave to Paris! The technicians stand in line amid morose crowds outside shops at three in the morning, to buy—if they're lucky—some coffee or condensed milk. American parcels arrive. Corned beef! Tears of joy. The crew are not so keen on the mock chocolate made from carob fruit. Human relations stay good, even when the Anarchists in the team are shocked to discover that some of their comrade artists or extras are not—can you believe it—union members.

André and Josette stay at the Barcelona Ritz, Max Aub at the Majestic. Josette follows the shoot. André seems happy. Elvira Farreras is startled to receive a curious telephone call from Port Bou: "Have a car sent to pick me up. I am Clara Malraux."

"Monsieur Malraux, there is a Malraux lady on the telephone," says Elvira.

"Yes," replies the writer-director without missing a beat, "it's my wife. She's here to talk about divorce."[6]

Well behaved, Clara spends two queenly days at the Majestic, but then she leaves, convinced: separation is unavoidable. Malraux carries on filming. Between Barcelona, Perpignan, and Paris, some film gets lost, then found, then lost again.

There are no comic interludes in the film, only off the set. At the Majestic, Malraux meets Theodore Dreiser. Another power cut: a candlelit dinner for the two writers, the poet Ernst Toller, Louis Fischer, Herbert Matthews, and Miss Boleslavskaya, who has come over from Moscow as a journalist for *Pravda*. A drunken Dreiser starts mouthing off: the Catholics and the Freemasons are responsible for the war in Spain! he yells. It's a plot! Down with the Pope! Boleslavskaya translates the English into French for Malraux. Josette can feel her lover's annoyance and wants to hold him back. Malraux holds up his hand. "Dreiser is wrong."

After making a few passes at Josette, Dreiser declares that Malraux was bound to say that, being a French Catholic. The American novelist hugs his French colleague and staggers up to his room.

The power cuts at the Orfea studio increase in frequency. Italian planes, Savoia Marchettis taking off from Mallorca, attack Barcelona at night.

Malraux's team also shoots at Santa Ana and Montcada, at Canudas Airport, at the Prat de Llobregat, at Montjuich Park, in Cervera. There, nine years earlier, there was an exhibition with examples of dwellings from Spanish provinces. Could these ruins be useful? Transport difficulties make the answer "no": when the whole crew has access to cars, which is rare, it needs gas, which is rarer still. During bombing raids, Elvira and others go to the shelters. The bombs whistle down. Aub, Marion, and Malraux show an example of calm serenity. The smoke from burning

gasoline tanks blocks out the sun. The film crew waits. Malraux looks for
a match to the gorge at Teruel in the French Pyrenees, with mountain
streams and birds of prey. He eventually finds the ravine he is looking for,
at Montserrat, in a sublime setting. He gathers more than two thousand
extras to make up the line of peasants greeting the airmen, the dead man,
and the wounded. Josette makes a suggestion that the women should take
the children off to one side as the stretchers pass.[7]

Malraux is generous and sensitive when "at work": he allows leave to
the French technicians who want to get away from the war for a few days.
"Go and get me a filter in Paris," he insists. Elvira wants to accompany the
unit to Tarragona and see her brother, who works there at the military
hospital.

"I need you in Tarragona, Elvira," the director says kindly.

Here and there, an attentive, considerate Malraux pops up.

He is still fighting against circumstances. Spanish drivers, technicians,
and actors are called up. Malraux gets them posted locally. He corrects
the screenplay, taking out a shot here, putting it back there, and dictates
as he walks up and down. His writing is dry, clear, without adjectives or
long sentences. He does not do many takes, both to save on film and
because he is usually happy with the ones he does. If the actors do too
much—vocal outbursts, tragicoemphatic expressions, fencing gestures—
Malraux politely suggests, "Play it more from the inside."

At the hotel or in the restaurant, Malraux talks about Soviet filmmakers and *The Battleship Potemkin*, and about Rubens, Tintoretto, El Greco,
Ribera. If he loses his codiners, at least he understands himself and
impresses, disconcerts, and amuses others. Some days, the crew cannot
work because of lack of equipment or because of the bombing. Or because
an actor forgot he was supposed to be on set that day. Can we get him on
the telephone? No. Malraux remains optimistic. The unintentionally dis-
jointed feel of some shots gives a certain rhythm to the film.

Now it is clear that the war will end badly for the Republicans; it will
not even be possible to finish the film in Spain. A few clear days: Malraux
writes more scenes and an article, with no access to reference material, on
Laclos, for Gallimard's *Tableau de Littérature Française*. Then he continues
shooting, with concentration.

January 20, 1939: Refugees are rushing down the streets of Barcelona.
The Republican defenses on the Ebro front have fallen. The inhabitants
of the towns and villages, workers, farmers, lower-middle- and middle-
class loyalists teem onto the roads leading to France, in the sadness and
distress of exile. The roadsides fill up with cars, abandoned when gas runs
out, broken bicycles, pieces of carts, uniforms, even weapons. In the studio on the twenty-third, Elvira says good-bye to Malraux. In the distance

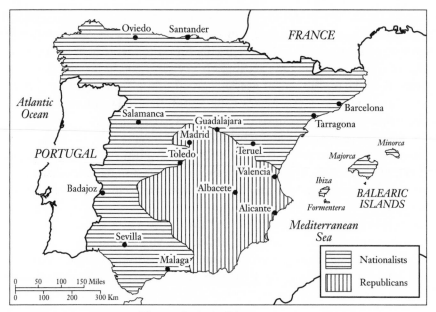

The two Spains in February 1939.

smoke is rising from villages that have been set on fire. Heavy gunfire comes closer: a prelude to the victorious arrival of the Tercio de Extran-jeros, the Francoist Foreign Legion, together with the North Africans and—who knows?—the Nazis and the Fascists. Malraux stares at the hori-zon of defeat and says to Elvira, "The Persians are here."[8]

More of an adieu than an au revoir. Malraux gets into a car with Josette, brazen, and some other French from the crew. Three days later, on January 26, Franco's troops march into the Catalan capital, bastion of anarchism. The Communists had been hunting down Anarchists to liqui-date them with a bullet in the neck. The Francoists follow up. Their secret service is looking for Communists, Anarchists, and just plain republicans. Arrests are made, judgments passed, detainees shot. The institutions of old Spain must be re-established: the Church, militarism, the respect due to the *señorío*. The Germans of the Condor Legion, young and mecha-nized, enter Barcelona on January 30. On February 1, a German military car stops in front of Elvira's house. She has worked for the well-known writer-director and leader of a Republican squadron. She is bound to be arrested. The Germans are delightful: "We need someone at the consulate who speaks German. We were told that—"

"Yes, I speak German."

"Come tomorrow."

The consul, Rolf Jaeger, never questions Elvira about her activities during the civil war.

In Paris, Malraux doesn't quite realize that in less than two years, he has written one optimistic novel, *L'Espoir*, and made a pessimistic film that could be called *Le Désespoir*. He protects himself from Clara, who is capable of starting a scene anywhere. His work is more important than anything or anyone else. He wants to finish his film.

On February 27, with diplomatic swiftness, Paris recognizes Francisco Franco's government. A month later, Madrid surrenders. The Republican government retreats to Figueras and, after a two-week detour in France, moves on to Valencia. One million civilian and military Spanish cross the Pyrenees. There is a split between elite and basic loyalists. President Manuel Azaña resigns, replaced by Dr. Negrín, who in turn is deposed by General Miaja. An awful mockery at the end of an abominable war: in Madrid, Communists, for once in league with the Anarchists, clash with the army. The Francoists are delighted. The French government sends Marshal Philippe Pétain as an ambassador to the Caudillo's de facto government in Burgos. They are counting on him to butter Franco up. French military experts want their hands free at the Spanish border in order to concentrate their forces on the Rhine. The Germans have invaded Czechoslovakia and created a protectorate of Bohemia-Moravia. Franco adhering to the anti-Comintern pact—now, that's worrying. Another anti-Cominternian, Mussolini, is about to invade Albania. These Spanish Republicans are all jolly nice, but they did lose the war: France can't be expected to ready itself on two borders. The British and the French have both signed the Munich Agreement with Hitler and Mussolini. Georges Bonnet, for France, has put his signature in Paris to a Franco-German treaty of "bonne entente."[9]

While he is editing his film, Clara harasses André with her last remaining weapon, the telephone. When passing through Paris, Eddy Du Perron sometimes sees a "distraught" Malraux. Fearing a scandal, the writer does not draw attention to himself in public with Josette. He swims around in his semiconjugal bowl. How can he get a divorce if Clara refuses? Friends and acquaintances, amused or upset (Louise de Vilmorin, Drieu la Rochelle, Jean Paulhan, Gide), are lavish with their advice. They need a legal separation. Malraux goes back to his film. He has watched some scenes at the studio in Joinville with Denise and Roland Tual. Corniglion-Molinier gets new funds. They are short of linking shots and short of money. Malraux shoots some necessary scenes at Joinville, then in April in front of the church in Villefranche-de-Rouergue, which "finishes off" the Spanish village of Linas. The last scenes are planned but never filmed, which for the audience leaves incomprehensible holes. Denis Marion inserts explanatory cards, silent-film style, so that the audience can understand the action.

First card:

During the Spanish Civil War, in 1937, a Republican plane returns after combat to the airfield where volunteers from all countries have come together to fight against fascism.

Last card:

The first plane has returned to base. The commander, informed over the telephone that a plane has been seen falling in the mountains, sets off to find his men.

This gives the film an unexpected melancholic charm. Malraux finishes the editing. He has spent more than a year on *Sierra de Teruel*, during which time he has also made a fair copy of some notes about the cinema.

On the evening of March 31, the Francoists capture the bastions of Almería, Cartagena, and Murcia, their final objectives. Crowds throw mimosas and roses. Women kiss their hands. In Burgos, when Franco's aide-de-camp announces the fall of Madrid, cool as a cucumber the Caudillo answers, "Very good. Thank you very much."

On May 19, 1939, the Nationalists parade through the capital. The Spanish war has lasted 986 days. Through his action and his book, Malraux has not ceased to be present. With his film, he prolongs the war.

In July's *Nouvelle Revue Française*—where André has friends who know how discreet he likes to be—Clara publishes "Le livre de comptes," a sixteen-page false short story–cum–true half confession, written more than four years before.[10] With Clara, great sorrow is not silent. In one attack, she shouts at her hero, Marc, "I shall come back! I didn't tell you when I left that I might not be back; but there are still things that I don't have to tell you for you to know them. I shall come back. Yet, having spent two weeks without you, I have acquired the certainty that it would have been better to accept everything than to do without you. What a funny declaration of love! I do not expect anything from you anymore." Further on, she reproaches Marc-Malraux for his "lack of tenderness." Clara admits she is beaten: "I accept my defeat, agreed, but I would like to know the reasons. They are in me, apparently. I don't mind that. But have I played badly because it was not possible to play well, or have I played badly because I did not know how to play? Sometimes, in moments of great rage, I have thought, 'You are playing badly because your partner is cheating.' I know that is not true. And anyway, does a man have to cheat to win, and does a woman have to play with a cheat to lose? It seems to me that all women have been beaten, even those among us who have been most successful—

even me!" Clara, if only in publishing this text, has not given up: "I would like the morning to come, Marc, and for you not to reject the one who fought with you, even if sometimes she wounded you in this uneven fight; she has more wounds than you."

Malraux does not flinch. Let Paris gossip! André has already cleared his slate without the aid of a "book." Clara won't stop settling scores.

The same day the British register their first "candidates" for conscription, June 3, 1939, a month before the Danzig Crisis, the first of a few private screenings of Malraux's film takes place. Nobody is surprised to see a feature-length film by Malraux. In the space of three years, he has been head of a squadron, author of a substantial and successful novel, why shouldn't he also be a filmmaker? Clara is not invited to the screenings. A copy editor for *Paris-Soir*, a certain Albert Camus, is present at one of them. He has read *L'Espoir* three times, he says. As an amateur actor in Algiers, he made a play out of *Le Temps du mépris*. Malraux and Camus exchange a few words. Louis Aragon declares that it's a masterpiece. The journalist Georges Altmann praises the film in *La Lumière*,[11] with reservations about the set piece, the journey down the mountain. To Altmann, the image is "inferior to the pages of André Malraux's astonishing book." Jean Cocteau, later on, is dazzled: "Saw Malraux's magnificent film. It is a triumph on the part of the writer-director. Ideas written directly for the eyes, on the screen." However, Cocteau does not like Malraux's literary work. Rereading *La Condition humaine*, he finds it journalistic and "like reading Claude Farrère. It's detestable."[12]

Critical articles are few and far between and dictated by the political opinions of their authors. Some see the film the way it appears on the screen, some the way Malraux conceived it. Malraux's intentions are sometimes contagious. He himself is not sure he has made the masterpiece he was dreaming of.[13] Under different conditions, he is sure, he would have equaled a Pudovkin or an Eisenstein.

Sierra de Teruel stands out in the output of French films in 1939, even amid Carné's *Le Jour se lève*, Abel Gance's *Louise et le paradis perdu*, and Jean Renoir's *La Règle du jeu*. Malraux could be a concentrated amalgam of German expressionists and Soviet films. Eisenstein inspired the long, majestic shots. One can also sense the influence of Swedish films of the 1920s and '30s. The plane in *Sierra de Teruel* is Victor Sjöstrom's *The Phantom Chariot*.[14] Some say at the time that it is the fact that Malraux was short of funds that gives his film its purity. *Sierra de Teruel* is no ordinary movie, in its theme, its treatment, and its mode of financing.

Malraux has shown his film to exiled members of the Spanish government at the Rex, a large boulevard cinema. The Republican leaders observed the on-screen homage to those who were defeated. Philippe

Pétain, now ambassador to Franco, asks the président du Conseil, Édouard Daladier, to prohibit the showing of *Sierra de Teruel*. Once it is banned, the film acquires the status of a legend, like the work of the accursed poet that the young Malraux never was.

The film is in black and white, has 39 scenes and 615 shots, and lasts, depending on the version, about 68 minutes.[15] It falls into a triptych of unequal parts, like the novel *L'Espoir*, but the other way around: the first two parts of the film are shorter than the last. The dramatic third part is in two sections and has touches of classical tragedy. Several scenes surround the death of an airman and take place in villages, showing peasants with furrowed faces. The action moves to a small town. A peasant crosses the "fascist" lines, tells the foreign airmen about the location of a clandestine enemy airfield. The peasant, in a wonderfully simple performance by Lado, contrasts strongly with the squadron commander, who is a little flabby. Two bombers take off. For thirteen minutes, starting with a shot of a dozen cars lighting up an airstrip until the moment when the Republican bomber crashes into the mountain, we follow and savor what is probably one of the finest war sequences ever made. Of the 615 shots, the aerial combat and the run into it take up 254, more than a third of the film. The peasant, disoriented under his beret, unable to recognize either Teruel or his village, becomes fixed in the viewer's memory. Thanks to the talent of the actor, the character's endurance, simplicity, and honesty personify the Spanish people, who are of secondary importance in *L'Espoir*. Malraux communicates a warmth in his film, perhaps more easily thanks to the interposition of the actors. Neither the Chinese workers of the previous novels, nor the Spanish militiamen of the latest had the depth of Lado. If to be a democrat is to like the people, with this film for once Malraux appears to be a democrat. The fascists appear, far off: they are the invisible bastards who fire at villagers through shutters or fighter pilots attacking the international side's bombers.

Also striking is the three-and-a-half-minute sequence where wounded and dead wind their way down the mountainside toward the plain. Brotherhood—although the word is never used—is expressed in these technically and aesthetically smooth scenes. It is the principal, strong link between *L'Espoir* and *Sierra de Teruel*. In the film, thanks to the presence of the peasants, brotherhood between the Spanish and the foreign airmen is even more marked than in the novel. Even beaten, the international airmen defend the cause of the people of the Spanish Left. Brotherhood and death, each as permanent as the other, are linked in the destiny of individuals. By saluting the airmen, by raising their fists, by escorting a coffin and stretchers, the peasants communicate more than a gesture of political belonging.

Despite the complications of the filming with planes in the air and on the ground, Malraux eventually removed the lumps and bumps from the last two parts of the film. He did not manage to do so for the first part; it was a while into shooting before he got a feeling for the rhythm of the piece. The film uses a symmetric structure: at the beginning, the viewer sees the corpse of a pilot and a recumbent statue, and, at the end, a dead man, a dying one, wounded men. Only some of those left at the end will survive, just as the idea of the Spanish Republic itself subsisted in the screening rooms where the film was shown during the summer of 1939.

From the first thirty minutes, the viewer is struck by the director's ideas: the luxury car carrying loyalists hurtling toward a Francoist cannon; armed villagers moving along a street with one limping along behind; sheep running from the machine guns; the wrinkled faces of the main and supporting actors. Malraux is as good at showing objects as human beings: massive bombers with Chinese dragon heads emerging from hangars at night; butterflies pinned in a box that fall out when the glass breaks. Throughout, with a touch of 1930s insistence, a poetic realism dominates. The dialogue is passable, if sometimes bordering on the pretentious. An elderly and crippled peasant decides to follow the escort.

"What can you do for a dead man?" a young man asks him.

"Honor him."

The lines spoken in Spanish sound beautiful and concise, gliding and metallic to a French ear. Spanish-speaking viewers sometimes find them pompous. There are some original elements that do not occur in *L'Espoir.* An airman, when asked why he is in Spain, answers, "I was bored."

Indeed, many men—and women—rush off to war out of boredom. Malraux travels, writes, and now films when he is bored. War is an ignoble but indisputable distraction. An old obsession of Malraux's returns: the right to suicide and the grandeur of the act; a disfigured airman, lying on a stretcher, asks the squadron commander for a revolver. This man is Raymond Maréchal. Malraux feels that certain lines or actions are right for the screen and not for the page.

As a director, Malraux knows how to use sound. The music by Darius Milhaud is less impressive than the actual sound track. Malraux resisted the temptation to make use of machine guns, exploding bombs, and throbbing plane engines, so overused in war films. He carefully measures out gunfire, birds flying off or singing, water dripping, popular songs. For a city man, Malraux seems more sensitive to nature, the sound of the grasses, the whistling of the wind. He filmed real, unreal, and surreal shots of the ground, seen from the plane by the crew and José the peasant. Malraux makes the most of the silences of a bomber with its engines cut. He does not use sounds to paraphrase the picture. He proves, instinctively, that the best commentary to a shot is not the strongest sound. He puts it well: "Modern cinema was born not from the possibility of being able to hear the words when silent film characters were talking but from the expressive opportunities offered by the combination of pictures and sound."

Malraux discovers the specific qualities of the cinema: a close-up of an ant on a machine gun. The writer-director steers clear of ideological discussions, which would paralyze the action. Not a word, here, on the Communist or Anarchist strategies. The question was no longer open by the time Malraux finished the film. Loyalist Spain lived with a cause; *Sierra de Teruel* is its requiem.

Slipping from practice into theory, Malraux finishes a short book, *Esquisse d'une psychologie du cinéma*. Despite himself, this is also a sketch, a fragment of André Malraux's psychology in 1937, 1938, and 1939.[16] The image, whether on canvas or celluloid, brings the author of *L'Espoir* back to the word, his preferred medium. The essay has six parts. Despite its title and Malraux's passion for the plastic arts—including the cinema—he talks mostly about literature here. Liberated by his film, he finds his fundamental inclinations again. The first chapter starts off on painting (Giotto, Clouet, Rubens, Delacroix), making penetrating observations and outstandingly foolish remarks. Dazzling so far as to blind even himself, Malraux comes out with daring assertions, in the manner of the aesthetic discussions in *L'Espoir*: "Chinese and Persians knew nothing of and had a profound disdain for perspective, lighting, expression." Or again: "Christianity introduced *dramatic representation*, which had hitherto been unknown." Then a stimulating phrase: "Europe substitutes . . . history for annals, drama for tragedy, the novel for the narrative account, psychology for wisdom, the act for contemplation: man for God." When writing as when speaking, Malraux has a machine-gun delivery. Sometimes, after a few tracer shots, his weapon jams. He subsists on generalities. Names, places, periods overlap in a turbulent kaleidoscope. A false proposition: "A man who is insensitive to painting as an art, visiting a museum today, finds himself facing a series of efforts quite similar to those of the sciences, to *represent* things." In a text by Malraux, often the italics are not there to underline an idea but to leave the reader in suspense, fixed to the spot by his own ignorance, terrified by the knowledge of the author. Malraux shows a certain scientific incompetence: the sciences have, for a long time, been "representing" less and less.

The following chapter returns to the cinema and some verifiable ideas. How did the techniques of photography and cinema, Malraux asks, become arts; means not only of reproduction but of expression? The film director, he remarks, in contrast to the theater director, chooses "his frame." Malraux talks about film directors at the beginning of the cinema as he would talk of the Italian primitives. Having examined shot sequence and editing, he starts on sound. In *Sierra de Teruel*, the writer-director sculpted it with his engineers, Robert Teyssere, René Renault, Archambault, and his editor, Georges Grace. The credits of the film, with no shortage of immodesty, announce that the editing is by "André Malraux assisted by Georges Grace."

The writer does not, alas, give an illustration of his own approach to cinema in this *Esquisse*. In true Malraux style, he limits himself to comparisons, often negative: "The talking film is no more an improvement on silent film than the elevator is an improvement on the skyscraper." Who said it was? Malraux throws in useful truths: "Already the most beautiful drawings can be reproduced with a forger's perfection; the same will certainly be true of paintings well before the end of the century." Followed by a banality: "But neither drawings nor paintings were made in order to be reproduced. They are an end in themselves." This is not only banal but false: Claude Vignon and William Hogarth made paintings, then cut engravings from their paintings. For Malraux, examples do not hold back his appetite for amplification. He moves straight from theoretical generalization to facts, as he does from the factual to the imaginary. In this text, the writer—it's not like him to quote sources—refers to the "remarkable work of Mr. Walter Benjamin" but omits to say where the reader can find the work in question.[17] More and more, consciously or not, Malraux practices an intellectual terrorism, reducing his reader or listener to a perplexed or frightened silence, whether it's Gide or a cleaning woman kindly questioned about pre-Columbian art while dusting a Cambodian statuette in the writer's study.

Malraux concludes his *Esquisse* with variations on theater and cinema. Here one can see that he neither likes nor frequents the theater. As a man of the twentieth century, he prefers film and film actors to theater actors. "A theater actor is a little head in a big room; a cinema actor is a big head in a little room." He points out the qualities of silence in cinema, used with artistry and discretion in *Sierra de Teruel*. The problems of theater and cinema are, for him, opposite: "The principal problem for the author of a talking film is to know when his characters should speak. In the theater, let us not forget, they are always talking." Well, actually, do let's forget that, because it isn't true. At the time Malraux was writing, silence was being used in plays. In years to follow, some theater directors even overused it. Ahead of others, Malraux draws attention to an aspect of twentieth-century civilization: talking cinema becomes text, and "its true rival is no longer theater but the novel." Malraux centers the penultimate part of his *Esquisse* on the novel and cinema. One can, he says, analyze the stagecraft of a great novelist.

In this essay, as he later does in numerous articles and interviews, Malraux evokes his favorite scene from *War and Peace*, where Prince Andrei contemplates the clouds after Austerlitz at night. After *Teruel*, after Madrid falls to Franco, what is Prince André Malraux contemplating? The last part of the *Esquisse* is largely padding, except for one point: the author discovers the cinema star, before other essayists. A star is not just an actress who makes films. With a little talent, she embodies a personality and a myth. Her face becomes a symbol to the collective instinct: "Marlene Dietrich is not an actress like Sarah Bernhardt, she is a myth like Phyrne." Malraux—perhaps out of nostalgia for his childhood in Bondy—returns to Chaplin: "In Persia I saw a film that does not exist, called *Charlie Chaplin's Life*. Persian cinemas are in the open air; on the walls enclosing the spectators, black cats sat watching. Some Armenian cinema managers had cleverly edited together all the Chaplin shorts. The result, a very long film, was surprising: the myth appeared in its pure state."

In 1939, *Sierra de Teruel* is neither a success nor a failure, since the film did not receive authorization to be released in cinemas. Commendably, Malraux doesn't complain. He appears to digest disappointment as easily as success. It is a form of courage, or at least "guts." "Besides," he slips in negligently, "movies are an industry." He could have added: and a product sensitive to political disturbances.

During the summer of 1939, Spain is teetering over the trapdoor of history and guilty consciences. The French want to forget all about it. Discussions among the British, French, and Soviets grind to a halt. On August 23, to the consternation of progressive thinkers in France, Spain, and beyond, a nonaggression pact is signed by Molotov for the USSR and von Ribbentrop for Germany, under Stalin's facetious gaze. A shock wave shakes the French Left. Paul Nizan resigns from the PCF. The party leaders Maurice Thorez and Laurent Casanova had kept him in the dark about the change of direction by the USSR. Nizan adopts a political point of view: "At bottom, I think I am in the right: only events will confirm or refute my position. But not arguments of morality. It is not because I thought the USSR's accord with Berlin was 'bad' that I took the position I did. It is precisely because I thought that the French Communists have not had the political cynicism necessary and the political power of untruth needed to get the best benefits out of a diplomatically dangerous operation. They didn't even have the Russians' audacity."[18] Malraux, in private, condemns the Soviets, both morally and politically.

He currently has a negative value in Moscow: the defendants' statements in the insane trials show that. To have been with Malraux has become a presumption of guilt. Vsevolod Meyerhold is holding on tight. To Second Lieutenant Chibkov, examiner for the NKVD, he declares, "Ehrenburg never told me that he was in regular contact with André

Malraux as a Trotskyite. I noticed the friendship between Ehrenburg and Malraux. I may add that during Malraux's first visit to the USSR, Ehrenburg and he tried hard to adapt Malraux's novel *La Condition humaine* for the screen, a work that is influenced beyond doubt by Trotskyite ideas."

On one point, the accused remains firm: "Neither Malraux nor Ehrenburg ever said to me that the Soviet system was short-lived, nor that the Trotskyites were going to take power, nor that fighting would be necessary . . . against the Communist Party, nor that the Soviet regime would have to be overturned."[19]

Meyerhold was later shot. Koltsov cracked after being imprisoned for a year. An extract from one of his interrogations:

"Among the agents of the French Sûreté, with whom, apart from Malraux, did you make contact?"
  "With Vogel."
  "Who is that?"
  "Vogel is a journalist. He is a spy who looks after 'Russian affairs.' He worked with Malraux."

Koltsov, too, was shot.

André Marty quickly took refuge in the USSR. Had Malraux ventured to turn up in Moscow, Marty would have found it easy to have him "liquidated."

CHAPTER TWENTY

The Phony War

MALRAUX ATTRACTED THE suspicion of the French police like a magnet. "We hear from a reliable source that Monsieur Serre, the manager of Air France, and Monsieur André Malraux have been hired to recruit pilots and aircraft technicians on behalf of the Chinese government." The French Sûreté also believed he had the intention of "flying to the help of various movements in South America."[1] And indeed, before the hostilities that were a *lentissimo* prelude to the Second World War, Malraux did propose to Paul Nothomb-Bernier to create a new squadron in Chile. A Popular Front down there, brought to power by the army, was in need of help.[2] On the other hand, whatever the French police might think, the writer had given up the idea of serving in China. Malraux settles into his myth: adventurer in the real world (or in a world of imagination), civilian-yet-military, Indochina-or-Spain, novelist-*coronel*, director of that brilliant film—that hasn't come out yet . . . a comet with a trail of legends, rumors, gossip, works, and feats of arms.

A man-myth still needs to earn a crust. Malraux had money problems. Over the winter of 1939, his deficit with Gallimard reached 178,491 francs. Gaston had payments made out of Malraux's account: 44,000 francs to Clara, 11,000 to Josette, and 5,000 to Grandma Lamy.[3] Malraux is banking on a substantial advance for a novel about another fabled character, the Baron de Mayrena.[4] *El coronel* is taking the conquest of Republican Spain as a personal defeat. He wants to run away from European reality into an Asian past. Gaston is irritated by his requests for money but makes good his debt. Malraux is a flagship he does not want to lose: he attracts other authors to Rue Sébastien-Bottin. What is good for him seems good for Gallimard. Gaston does not actually believe in this Asian novel, any more than in the Lawrence of Arabia biography Malraux talks about. He plays with too many projects without getting started. He leaves Rue Le Marois, near Boulevard Murat in the Sixteenth Arrondissement, and moves into a furnished ground-floor apartment on Rue Berlioz. With Josette. Malraux is taking a risk: Clara could send a police inspector to his apartment (in fact she never thinks of doing this).

Malraux sees Gustav Regler and Arthur Koestler, Communists who have cut their ties with the Comintern. Koestler was locked up in France, then released, but was not forced to join the Foreign Legion like so many other German immigrants. Malraux wonders. His self-confidence loses vigor. There's just time, he feels, to reorient politics in the Kremlin. At least, that is what he announces to a stupefied writer, André Beucler:

"Absolutely, you and I . . . take a plane to Moscow and go and see Stalin in the Kremlin. Once we're there, I'm sure I can get us in. I have the equipment, the staff, the funds, and everything the enterprise needs. If you accept—and I trust you will—we can fly off at the end of the week— in utmost secrecy, naturally."

This is a Malraux not changed by defeat. When war breaks out on September 3, most of his Communist friends do "their duty" and do not leave for Moscow as Maurice Thorez does. Malraux helps Nizan get an interpreter's job with an English regiment.[5]

Josette—to Roland "a long, blond, lazy dormouse"—gets pregnant in February 1940. Malraux would like her to have an abortion. Demoralizing visit to the doctor's by Josette.

Malraux was deferred in 1922, declared unfit for service in 1929, and finally accepted for auxiliary service: he has no chance of becoming an officer in France. T. E. Lawrence went from the rank of colonel to that of private. Malraux, too, starts again as a private (*deuxième classe*) after the intervention of General Chardigny, a colleague of Jean Giraudoux at the State Information Commission. Josette accompanies André to the Gare de l'Est. He leaves with other conscripts. On April 14, 1940, Malraux is drafted as a dragoon into the 41st Dépôt de Cavalerie Motorisée near Provins, fifty miles southeast of Paris. He sleeps in a twelve-bed dormitory, with nine Bretons and two other Parisians. It is, at first, a "phony war": an irritatingly quiet period, making barracks life monotonous when one is stuck in one place. As Malraux writes to Chevasson, "If this is not quite a holiday, it is still bearable." Courteous, keeping some distance, he drinks rough red wine with his roommates.

Josette comes to visit him. Should she keep the baby? Malraux again talks vaguely of divorce. He has consulted a lawyer, Maurice Garçon. Josette doubts André's intentions. The lovers quarrel. Through a thin hotel wall in Provins, Suzanne Chantal, Josette's confidante, hears her friends' row. Josette hates the idea of an abortion and, almost as much, that of having a "bastard" child. But she also dreams of having a child with André Malraux. He wavers and accepts the situation grudgingly. Josette returns to Paris. Posted to a platoon of NCOs in training, Malraux writes to her on April 17, 1940:

> Theoretically, we are here for three or six months. Basic training on tanks, armored cars, etc. Specialization comes later. So we can either sort out a hotel or rent something. We only get our uniforms tomorrow and have nothing to do until then. Then the work will start. At first sight, it all seems very bearable, human even. Very instructive as well. Intelligence, as artists understand it, is a very small thing on the surface of man, but what we find underneath, when there is no great collective or individual passion, is something like the prehistory of the human being. I shall try to write a 'journal for you.' "

Shades of Barrès.[6] "I am wary," he continues.

> There is no shortage of subjects for reflection, but no atmosphere in which the reflection would have any value, which must quickly become quite dangerous. And to move from one world to the other, from the barracks to a shadow of one's own place, must be quite difficult intellectually. We'll see. Still, tanks will be defended only by getting into them, not just by oiling and numbering them. I am writing in the soldiers' foyer, and the radio has just started blaring.

An admission:

> I have the impression, as a trooper, that I am learning the meaning that the word *happiness* may have had, when it was there and I could not see it. Especially since leaving for the station in the taxi. The instruction will have been worth the journey, if it doesn't all end in mindlessness. The canteen radio is broadcasting Cardinal Verdier's funeral. They have just sung Palestrina's *Kyrie* and are following it up with one of the most beautiful Gregorian chants.

Malraux does not even have time to become a corporal. At the end of April, armored vehicles from his unit, mostly tracked, set off for Dunkirk, without him. Haunted by the legend of tank officer Fernand Malraux, André wants to become a "*tankeur,*" as he puts it in his letters to Louis Chevasson. In the barracks courtyard, he contemplates a rusted tank.

Eddy Du Perron, he learns, has died of angina. Malraux and Du Perron had grown more distant since *L'Espoir*: for his Dutch friend, the novel was "Malraux versus Malraux."

Private Malraux is placed under the orders of Staff Sergeant Albert Beuret, a hairdresser in civilian life. "*Ils ne passeront pas*" proclaim the posters on the walls of France: "[the Germans] shall not get through." They do get through, and very quickly. Soldiers from the 41st, including Malraux, are involved in skirmishes. The Germans pick them up south of Courtenay. Prisoners! That was a short war! Malraux, his feet aching from ill-fitting shoes (he'll say it was a war wound), is looked after by Wehrmacht nurses. The Germans distribute biscuits to their *Kriegsgefangene*. Prisoner Malraux does not complain. He and his fellow prisoners are marched against the flow of refugees up to Sens. They are shut into the cathedral, then onward to an improvised camp, the Front Stalag 150, next to the Yonne River.

On June 17, 1940, after massive German progress onto French soil, Marshal Pétain forms a government, and the armistice is signed with Germany on the twenty-second. Germany annexes Alsace-Lorraine. France is divided into the Occupied Zone—north and west, down to Spain—and the "Free" Zone, where Marshal Pétain sets up a new regime.

Malraux and the other prisoners are as dazed as the French in general. They do not hear the eight speeches made by temporary Brigadier General Charles de Gaulle, broadcast by the BBC from London. On June 18, the unknown de Gaulle creates the organization France Libre. He has posters put up in England: "France has lost a battle, she has not lost the war."[7] From Sens, the war appears to be quite lost. On June 26, de Gaulle the rebel general addresses Pétain. He listens "not without emotion . . . to the great soldier that you are" before coming out with his verdict: "This armistice is dishonorable." There was no ambiguity in the positions de Gaulle took as he stepped unhesitatingly into political and historical legend. As Winston Churchill (who gave the unknown general a warm welcome) might have put it, this was "his finest hour."

André Malraux's aunt, Marie Lamy, having received a card from her nephew, visits and chats with him through the barbed wire. She reports that Josette, in the Ford V8 that André gave her, has driven down to Hyères, on the French Riviera, where her parents live. When she announced the good news of her pregnancy, her mother showered her with blame: "Josette, how can you have done that to your father!"

M. Clotis is not as shocked as his wife by the idea of having an unmarried mother for a daughter. A card from Malraux on July 17 informs Josette that life in the camp is tolerable. He says he has reworked a chapter of his *Mayrena* and has grown a mustache. Some prisoners escape.

Malraux shouts at another soldier, "You, over there, why have we lost the war?"

This private, Jean Grosjean, was recently ordained. Grosjean has read *La Condition humaine* but does not recognize its author. The two men talk. Why this defeat? And for the best army in the world! Was it unwillingness on the part of the officers? Fear of repeating the butchery of 1914? Were troops cut off from headquarters? They end up agreeing on the ineptitude of clauses in the Treaty of Versailles, the absurdity of the Danzig Corridor. They talk of Asia and Syria, where Grosjean has lived. They pace up and down the banks of the Yonne River. Perhaps they should run away. Go to London?

"More interesting to stay in France," Malraux says.

Then, with his gift for flicking from the immediate to the timeless, he asks, "When you are not doing anything, what do you do?"[8]

Three days later, Grosjean learns that he has been talking to André Malraux. Grosjean, Beuret, and the writer are part of a group of ten that includes a farm laborer, a garage mechanic, a painter, and a decorator. The Germans spread their prisoners around the surrounding countryside to work in the fields and be fed by French farmers. Malraux, Grosjean, and Beuret get sent to Collemiers, a village to the southwest of Sens, three miles from the cathedral. They depend on the goodwill of Mr. Courgenay, the friendly mayor, and on the affability of their German lieutenant. Oberleutnant Metternich insists that his prisoners must have better sleeping conditions than his horses do in Germany. The prisoners are barely watched over and could easily escape. But they don't want to run away; that would make problems for the mayor. Life is pretty soft. Seems there'll be no coal over winter. Right. The prisoners become woodcutters. The mayor asks them to catalog the books in the library. Malraux finds a Kropotkin. When school starts again in October, the prisoners—the Germans have not printed "KG" (*Kriegsgefangene*) on their jackets—give lessons to the village children. Rumors float about: all prisoners are going to be sent to Germany, all the KGs will be set free. . . .

Grosjean was a metal worker for a time, then went into retreat with the Jesuits and attended seminary classes. As a priest, the Bible fills him as much as God does. "What it says interests me," he says quietly. "What it doesn't say doesn't concern me." Hellenist, Hebraist, eleven years younger than Malraux, he's been around the Middle East with Christians, Jews, and Arabs. When he was drafted into the infantry, he was not a conscientious objector but remained a pacifist. Refusing to join the corporals' training course, he warned his captain, "Don't expect me to shoot."

There is more literature and religion between Grosjean and Malraux than politics. The prisoners roam freely around the village and are authorized to walk to Sens without guards. They do not feel the need to move, especially Malraux, who writes as if he were on a ship.

In the evening, they talk. That is, they listen to Malraux practicing his favorite sport, monologue. He comes out with subjects like a professor opening a seminar, which turns into a small-scale lecture. Let's talk about sunsets. Who believes in eternal life? Actually, what does Grosjean think about that? When I was shot down in Spain . . . They go to bed early. Metternich imposes a flexible curfew. Malraux strokes the cats. The birds sing. The days go by, the months go by. Malraux writes. He is a man of cycles: in Indochina and in Spain, he acted first, then wrote. He tries out fragments of the novel he is working on on Grosjean. Malraux is digesting two defeats, that of Spain and that of France. The time for arms in Madrid is in the past, the time for writing in Collemiers is the present. Malraux believes in words when he has no more weapons.

Beuret gets on well with his two pals. Beuret—father an architect killed in the 1914–18 war, mother died of cancer when he was seventeen— had to interrupt his secondary education to start working in a bank. Beuret and Malraux address each other familiarly as *tu*, Grosjean and Malraux more formally as *vous*. Sergeant Beuret admires *L'Action Française* and has never raised his fist. He likes coarse jokes. Grosjean is surprised by Malraux; Beuret is impressed.

Fall passes; the pals become friends. They must hang on, Malraux explains, they must wait. He predicts that the English will not be beaten. The pals let the writer, who is clearly not manually skilled, write. He is excused from household and village chores. He lives within his novel in progress, writing about the First World War through the Second. Malraux needs to transpose the present straight away, even if it means tacking it onto the past. At Collemiers, he plays with two titles, *La Lutte avec l'ange* (Fighting with the Angel) and *Les Noyers de l'Altenburg*[9] (The Walnut Trees of Altenburg). In a stunning scene in the book, he gets to ride in the tanks that were not available to him in June 1940, the tanks that Fernand Malraux did not take into battle in 1914 or 1915. For a few lines of writing, Malraux has his fellow prisoner Voisel, who was in a tank crew, produce "ten days of sketches."[10]

Josette comes up from the South, seven months pregnant. She crosses the demarcation line with an *Ausweis* and visits both André and Roland. The writer-prisoner goes to the inn to work in the afternoons. Josette spends her time in the grocery store–and–refreshment room or takes over from Malraux at the library. Beuret does the hair of the ladies in the village. Grosjean refuses to take this de Gaulle chap seriously. Malraux is neither in Collemiers nor in London, he is living in his novel.

On his second visit, Roland warns his half brother: there have been announcements on neutral radio stations, Swedish and Swiss: the Germans are looking for writers, including André Malraux, Georges André on his identity papers. Now the KG has to escape. Given his past, the writer has little chance of being released.

He thinks about North Africa. He informs his group that he is going to leave. During the All Saints festivities, the stations will be full of passengers; it will be difficult to check them all. On the eve of November 1, after five months as a model prisoner, Malraux spends the night at the inn so as not to get his fellow prisoners into trouble. Someone throws pebbles up at his window; Malraux comes down in pajamas. Beuret and Grosjean are there to give him the money from the kitty. Malraux refuses to take it. Roland appears with a pair of socks, which are too small for his big brother. The brothers walk to Sens. Roland has two tickets but only one pass. He bluffs his way past by addressing a Wehrmacht sentry in German: Would he be so good as to help him carry a suitcase to the train? Very nice of him. Roland says that Drieu will get an *Ausweis* for Josette in Paris so she can join her partner in the South.

The two brothers cross the demarcation line to the south of Bourges, with (so the story goes) a black cat that, meowing with happiness, becomes attached to André. They reach Montluçon and the coast, without the cat. Josette's family put up their pseudo-son-in-law in Hyères. On November 8, Malraux sends a few lines to Paulhan: "I have arrived in Free France, after a curiously comfortable escape. I have had news of almost everybody, but not Arland. If you know what has become of him, please tell me."[11]

Josette gives birth prematurely to a boy in a clinic in Neuilly-sur-Seine. The child is named Pierre (after Drieu) Guillaume Valentin, father unknown. He still takes the name Malraux: the single and generous Roland acknowledges him as his own. The Gallimards keep an eye on Josette. From Collemiers, Malraux asked Gaston to sell some statuettes to get money for Clara, Josette, and Roland. André writes to Josette from the South of France, "I await you in a pink house with a little wood of orange trees, a magnolia, and a cat."

On the coast, Malraux meets up with Parisians: Gide in Nice, Berl at Monte Carlo, the Sperbers at Cagnes-sur-Mer. Gide's friend Mme. Théo observes Malraux's "torrential gabbing."[12] It's impossible to establish a "human contact" with him. He is not at ease. Only Berl stands up to him. Berl, although Jewish, did something very stupid in putting his pen to the service of Pétain, however briefly. The undying phrase spoken by the octogenarian marshal, "*J'ai fait le don de ma personne à la France*" (I have given myself to France), was written by Berl, as were "*La terre ne ment pas*" (The earth does not lie) and "*Je tiens mes promesses, même celles des autres*" (I keep my promises, even those of others).

Malraux goes to the Monaco train station to welcome his one-month-old son and Josette. He drives them to Roquebrune. The villa, "La Souco," a cypress flame in the middle of the garden, belongs to the Bussys, English friends of Gide. They are lending—not renting—the house to Malraux. The living room has only five French doors. Italy on the left, Monaco on the right. Luigi, the resourceful butler, gets on his bike and goes to buy groceries in Italy. He serves at table in white gloves. Luigi nicknames the baby "Bimbo." Roland stops by. There is a shortage of butter, sugar, pasta, cheese, and, hardest of all for Malraux, cigarettes. When Roger Martin du Gard comes to supper at La Souco, he conscientiously sends food coupons on ahead.

Robert Haas, Malraux's American editor, sends dollars. The money passes through the hands of Varian Fry, whom Malraux met in the United States. Fry, working as a representative of the Emergency Rescue Committee, finds money, visas, and passes in Marseille for French intellectuals under threat. Malraux thinks about the United States. "I don't really know if I'll go to America," he writes to Louis Fischer. "It's not easy to get a French passport, and besides, it's not certain that here everything's over."

Josette wants him to devote himself to his family. He writes. The novel he's working on, he points out to Haas, will be "metaphysical." So far, it is a fragmented text in which the experiences of several generations of the half-German, half-French Berger family are piled on top of one another. The first-person narrator is a French Berger with no first name. Malraux asks Gide to listen to a reading. Gide protests: the text is hybrid and breaks too many grammatical and syntactical rules. Malraux gives the father Berger the diploma in Oriental languages that he himself never got. Delightful, the way characters can satisfy all the fantasies of an author. Berger senior has a "fanatical desire to leave a scar on the earth." Berger thinks that "intellectuals are a race." Is that what Malraux thinks too? A class apart, at any rate, or simply a social subgroup, with its prerogatives and privileges?

Malraux asks questions that are haunting him: "Does the notion of Mankind have a meaning?" Does this question itself have a meaning, outside certain university lectures? Perhaps it is the meaning that every man gives to his life. What is life beyond the sum of individual human, animal, and vegetable lives? Ah yes, of course, there's "the Cosmos." French intellectuals, well behind the Germans and long after the Greeks—and two thousand years of philosophy—have to ask themselves these painful questions: Why Life? Why not nothing, or Nothingness? Malraux refers back to his works and *La Condition humaine*: "Once more Pascal comes back to me . . . one imagines a large number of men in chains and all condemned to death. . . . Those who are left behind see their own condition in that of their fellow creatures." Malraux attempts to surmount the bitterness of some undeniable defeats and give a meaning to the fighting in which he has taken part. His consolation, his therapy, his justification, the meaning of his life, is to write. Yet that is not enough. He needs to know why he writes. To give meaning to his life: the thought bites its own tail. He wants to formulate the largest number, walk on the horizon, fix on paper the meaning of existence.

The novel's Altenburg Symposium is reminiscent of Malraux's Union pour la Vérité discussions. Walter Berger is not Paul Desjardins, but he does own a medieval abbey. Malraux provides some polished scenes, including one with a gas attack, where German and Russian soldiers fraternize during the First World War. European reconciliation? Malraux carves a few likenesses out of his walnuts. One is a portrait of Nietzsche—the man, not the thinker:

> The photographs do not communicate his look: he had a feminine softness, despite having the mustaches of . . . an ogre. This look no longer existed. His head was always still, his voice always set back—as if he were speaking not for my father but for the illustrious books and photographs in the shadows, as if no interlocutor were quite fit to understand him; or rather (my father's impression became clearer as he listened) as if those who might have understood what he was going to say were all from another time, as if nobody today would accept to understand him, as if he were talking only out of courtesy, lassitude, and duty. There was, in his whole attitude, the same arrogant modesty as was expressed in his little raised desk.

Malraux fashions a portrait of Vincent Berger, a wartime leader like himself, and a philosopher, which he would like to be. Berger, a political éminence grise, is inspired by Enver Pasha and the nebulous doctrine of Turanism. Some passages tie up well with *La Tentation de l'Occident*: the West "is in opposition to the Cosmos, to fate, instead of being in harmony with them." Or "Man knows that the world is not made on a human scale; but he would like it to be. And when he reconstructs it, he reconstructs it on that scale." Left to his obsessions and his rhetoric, Malraux mixes Plato and Saint Paul, the Hindu belief in the Absolute and the West's devotion to homeland and to death. In a novel, Malraux's style has never been so telescopic, with vast subjective descriptions and immense imprecise sentences. He writes about a Middle East and a Turkey that he does not know. To his American publisher, he again explains that this work will be "a book about this war, made of the same 'stuff' as *L'Espoir* but with a stronger metaphysical character and a weaker political one. I have given

Berthe Lamy.
*The sorrows of a father, a husband,
a son. You are ugly, André.*

Fernand Malraux.
*Discounter, manufacturer,
banker, captain, command-
ing officer, with his eldest
son, André.*

André Malraux. *Crafty and charming.*

Clara Malraux.
Let's get married. We'll get divorced in a few months. Nevertheless, Dostoevsky writes that . . .

With Louis Chevasson.
Always ready, always loyal.

From left to right: Arland,
Malraux, Supervielle, Paulhan.
In the foreground: Valéry. *Malraux
installs himself at the* Nouvelle
Revue Française, *among the
greatest.*

Josette Clotis.
*Malraux—I handled him like a
racehorse.*

Between Hemingway, on his right, and Robert Haas. *A rival writer, a genius, and his American editor.*

With Meyerhold and Pasternak at the Writers' Congress in Moscow. *It took much work to bring* Man's Fate *to the stage—and to the screen.*

A Potez. *A flying coffin for heroes.*

SOCIETE D'ENTRAIDE DES COMPAGNONS DE LA
LIBERATION

BULLETIN D'ADHESION (2)

NOM : MALRAUX   PRENOMS : André Georges   ALIAS : C' Berger

Date et lieu de Naissance : 3 Nov. 1901 Paris   Nationalité : F.

ATTENTION - Les renseignements suivants sont destinés à figurer dans l'annuaire en préparation , IL Y A LIEU DE LES REDIGER AVEC SOIN.

ARME :   UNITE OU RESEAU   GRADE :
F.F.I   Commandos   Brigade Alsace-Lorraine   C' Chef de l'Unité
Ensuite: 9   Lieutenant-Colonel

Adresse actuelle (téléphone):   Résidence familiale
19 bis av. V. Hugo (Mol 33-65)   fixe :

Profession civile :   Branche ou spécialisation :
écrivain, ancien ministre

Raison sociale et adresse professionnelle (Tél.) R.P.F, 19 B' de
                                                   Capucines (OP.93-32)

Mandat électif - (nature et lieu d'exercice):

Décorations : L. d'Honneur, Croix de Guerre, Off. Résistance,
D.S.O. — Commandeur Rép. Espagnol. Résistance tchèque.

Blessures : 3   Taux d'invalidité : 1

Marié ? oui   Charges de famille : 3 enfants

Prénoms et date de naissance des enfants : Florena 1933
                                            Gauthier 1940
                                            Vincent 1943

OBSERVATIONS :

Fait à Paris   le, 1° Nov 4.
Signature :

In the rear of a cockpit, the boss. *Yes, he flew, even if he wasn't great with the machine gun.*

Photo opportunity. *You are making me take this picture.*

OPPOSITE: A form filled out by Malraux. *One wound has become three.*

Eddy Du Perron. *I make you a gift of my friendship
and an island in Indonesia.*

up on the second Spanish book I talked about. Its themes will go into the French book; the problems of war, life, and death are not national. . . . Such a book will no doubt find an audience in America. So I should like to send it to you part by part, so that translation can start as soon as the first part has been received. . . . I would like you to keep me informed. To take a year to translate a book like this would, I think, be a pity."[13] Malraux does not listen to Gide's advice on how to untangle himself from his ambitious muddle. Out of obedience to his creative logic, he wants to—he has to—transpose immediate reality into a remote past. He wants to say everything in the same book; he is offended when *Life* magazine turns down one of the better-structured chapters. "I am less well known than Mr. Hitler, and less topical," he writes to Haas. " 'The Pit' is an average chapter; neither one of the less good ones, nor one of the best."

Malraux thinks again about going to North Africa and again of the United States. He writes to Haas in 1941, "It is quite possible that I may have the opportunity to shake your hand before the end of the year." The writer is living in France but does not want to commit himself to France. The family stays for a while at Cap d'Ail, in a villa called "Les Camélias," then returns to Roquebrune. Malraux sets himself the task of writing down his memories of a lost war, that of 1940. They are written—but in his head, therefore experienced. He refers to himself at the time as *le forçat de la plume*—the convict of the pen.

This long pause in the South of France brings him to no conclusions about action as such (although writing, for him, is action). He corresponds with Jean Paulhan: "I think that a philosopher is simply a man who can carry his thoughts through to a conclusion, can know their consequences, and can throw light on what they intersect with. I don't know if this definition is accurate for philosophers (and actually, who cares?) but it is right for you."[14] And right for Malraux? There's just not enough room on an interzone postcard for effusive outpourings. The writers write to each other. That's what writers do. Letter from Martin du Gard to Malraux: "I reckon that for seven tenths of Europe, the Communist peril is still the No. 1 nightmare. In attacking it, the Reich will win over not only all governments from Vichy to Madrid, from Stockholm to Ankara, but also a large majority of public opinion: the whole rural population and all the Christians in Europe. That comes to a lot of people (and I'm including England, and America even more so)."[15] Martin du Gard is a powerful novelist but is not good (here at least) at predictions. "As a result," he continues, "Hitler becomes again the old 'rampart' and cancels out the wrong done to him by the Germano-Russian pact of '39." The political and strategic Martin du Gard is floundering, like many of the French at this time, puzzled and ignorant, looking for the Pole Star in the southern sky.

Malraux keeps in contact with Pierre Drieu la Rochelle. Drieu, a collaborator, has been given control of the *Nouvelle Revue Française*. Gide hesitates for a while about publishing texts in this *NRF* under Drieu. Malraux does not; he categorically refuses. Drieu comes to see him and Josette on the Côte d'Azur anyway. He drives around in a Renault, thanks to Mme. Renault, who is very kind to him. Josette adores Drieu and dips into her provisions for him, particularly from the canned fish shelf. "I am very susceptible to this man," she notes, "his way of being, his way of writing. He is so handsome! If only all André's friends were like him." Drieu would like to win Malraux over to Vichy—or Nazi Germany. He does not lose all hope: "I regret that I did not see you for longer. I am assured that you can come to V[ichy] as well as here [Paris] without the least trouble. . . . If you need anything at all . . ." On a card sent from Switzerland after the publication of *La Lutte avec l'ange*, Drieu finds the work "very Germanophile" and its style "full" and "flowing." But in his diary, Drieu remarks that he does not understand "very much in this first volume. . . . What is Malraux thinking? Deprived of his aptitude, he seems to have lost his motivation. I detect nothing in *La Lutte avec l'ange*, but it is only a 'prelude.' " For Drieu, this novel is confused, often artificial, and dry, despite its pomposity. Malraux will pride himself on being one of the rare French writers not to publish in either the Free Zone or the Occupied Zone. He also often says that he is "the only writer to have fought in a tank division."[16] Yes, as a foot soldier.

Malraux lets Drieu in on Gaston's reservations: "Thank you for your card. I shall retain what it says. Gaston phoned and is coming down the day after tomorrow. Half of my novel (*Les Noyers de l'Altenburg*) was bad, and I am redoing it completely. May the God of Literature be with you, because the God of Action has gone stupid."[17] Malraux would nonetheless have been ready to give his manuscript to Gallimard for publication. Like the young Albert Camus and others, he makes a clear distinction between Gallimard's review, the *NRF*, and its book publishing. His friendly loyalty to Drieu carries no implications of political connivance.

The relationship between Drieu and Malraux is puzzling. They belong to opposite camps. Malraux knows Drieu better as a person than as a writer. Both men are fascinated and tormented by deception. For Malraux, Drieu is a crypto-Fascist, veering toward crypto-Nazi. For Drieu, Malraux is a crypto-Communist sleeping off an ideological hangover. Yet Malraux is grateful to Drieu for getting Josette an *Ausweis* and says to Gaston Gallimard that "if the situation were the other way round, I would have done the same for him." Drieu also protects Aragon and Éluard and in November 1940 asks the Francophile Lieutenant Gerhard Heller to protect Gaston Gallimard, Paulhan, and Malraux.

André, Josette, and Bimbo stay for a few days with Chevasson and his wife, Germaine. Louis has taken up a factory in the Allier region as cover for its Jewish owner. He is enthusiastic about Malraux doing a preface to Lawrence's letters: "Who will publish it? Relations being what they are, I'd be surprised if it was the *NRF.* By the way, have you got the *Seven Pillars?*" Then from metaphysics to mocha: "I've heard you can get green coffee from Portugal. Since you know some Portuguese people [the husband of Josette's friend Suzanne Chantal is Portuguese], perhaps you can get some sent over. We'd pay you back. . . . And we could take on the copying of all of Mallarmé's poems. Anyway, this is just to please Germaine [who also proofreads Malraux's work]. Don't go to any trouble."

Malraux ambles in the garden, strolls along the Promenade des Anglais, and walks around his head, where several projects jostle for attention. He has been amassing documentation on T. E. Lawrence. The preface to his letters is off, but the biography is on again. There are common points and interests between the colonel of Arabia and the *coronel* of Spain. One is archaeology: here, Lawrence's abilities outweighed Malraux's. In *La Voie royale,* Malraux wrote that "every adventurer is born a mythomaniac." On the Côte d'Azur, if you don't join the Resistance, the only available adventure consists of clambering up mountains to find butter, beef, and potatoes. For the moment, Malraux does not want to live on a diet of adventure; better to write someone else's. Thanks to a certain pride, a contempt for pedantry, and an undeniable talent, Lawrence becomes a character not unlike Malraux. Lawrence studied at Oxford; Malraux imagined he did at the École des Langues Orientales. Geopolitics fascinates them both, and they share a dogged determination to mark History with "scars," Lawrence in the Middle East, Malraux in Asia and in Spain. They imagine themselves to be, and are, writers and men of action. A love of Dostoevsky and Nietzsche, publicity and mystification, leads them to produce prose that is often tortured. Both are compulsive liars. It's a toss-up as to which of them is the most depressive. Malraux writes that Lawrence "had, in three years, read four thousand volumes and learned four languages." A little more than three books a day? These two insatiable spirits, positioned equidistant from literature, war, politics, and sometimes poetry, have one agreeable common trait: they are almost never mean or disdainful. They were both in armored vehicle regiments, Lawrence finishing as an aircraft man in the RAF, Malraux ending his war among "tankers," without a tank.

The English will emerge victorious, Malraux tells Chevasson, but not tomorrow. Pia arrives in the South of France. He wants Malraux to work on a review called *Prométhée* that he is to launch in opposition to Drieu's *Nouvelle Revue Française.* Roland escorts a manuscript by Albert Camus, living in Algeria, from Pia to Malraux; thanks to Pia, Malraux starts a very

moving correspondence with the as-yet-unknown Camus. Malraux turns
out to be a meticulous, kind, and enthusiastic reader of *L'Étranger*.[18]
Chevasson has also read it but is more reserved: "Pia made too much fuss
about it." Malraux pushes *L'Étranger* at Gallimard and responds warmly to
Camus, writing that he was "rocked" by the two typescripts, *L'Étranger*
and *Le Mythe de Sisyphe*. To Pia:

> I have just finished Camus's manuscripts. . . .
>
> I read *L'Étranger* first. The theme is very clear. . . . On the
> whole, I'd say that *Caligula* should be left in the drawer until
> *L'Étranger*—or something else—has familiarized the public with
> Camus. We can talk some more about this if you like.
>
> *L'Étranger* is obviously something important. The strength and
> simplicity of the means, which end up forcing the reader to accept
> the character's point of view, are all the more remarkable given
> that the fate of the book depends on how convincing this charac-
> ter is. And what Camus has to say, what he has to convince us
> about, is not insubstantial.

Malraux numbers his technical criticisms:

> 1. The sentence structure is a little too systematically subject-
> verb-complement-period. At times it begins to feel like a process.
> Very easy to put right, by changing the punctuation here and
> there. 2. It would be worth working more on the scene with the
> chaplain. It is not clear. What is said is clear, but what Camus
> wants to say is said only partly. And the scene is important.

Malraux concludes:

> I am not trying to tell you anything intelligent or penetrating, I
> am trying to say useful things, which sounds schoolmasterly.
> Never mind. As for the essential issue Camus has tried to address,
> he is not to worry, it is in there.

Camus receives the remarks from Pia, their mutual friend, and thanks
Malraux also for looking over the details of his contracts with Gallimard.
Camus is keen to read the book on Lawrence. Despite his own fame, Malraux treats Camus with a touching kindness, and as an equal. He keeps his
heart hidden away, yet he does love others—through their books. With
one foot floating in the metaphysics of his novel, the other firmly planted
in the necessities of printing and publishing, Malraux asks Camus for the

prices of paper and Esparto in North Africa, on behalf of Gallimard. Camus sends him oranges and books about Isabelle Eberhardt. The protégé and his mentor interact with a radarlike long-range sensitivity. With Gaston, Malraux maintains a friendly and commercial correspondence: "My dear Gaston, about the paper: 50 tons will be available; we will in theory get the rest, but I have to put something down in compensation . . . and if we lose another month, I won't have that to give. . . . André M." Malraux can be as good a businessman as Gaston. "A ton of paper is worth 370 to 400 F. . . . A freight car can hold 6 to 10 tons."

The French have been orphaned politically by the war. They don't know what to do about the armistice. Intellectuals file through the Malraux home, much to Josette's annoyance. She has no interest in current events and does not want the father of her child drawn away by them. André should be writing! She does not realize that he relies on experience for his inspiration. In *Les Noyers*, the war stories come out like waxworks (with notable exceptions). Josette is furious. What are all these disoriented or resolute people doing, coming to make demands on Malraux, pushing him into underground activism?

The young Roger Stéphane comes to see Malraux, the admired and retired *coronel*, his son sitting on his shoulders, and confides that he is going into the Resistance. Malraux mocks, "Well, if you want to play at soldiers."

Two authors Jean-Paul Sartre and Simone de Beauvoir also turn up. Their tiny underground movement, Socialisme et Liberté, cannot last. What can they do to fight the Reich?

To a succession of visitors—Claude Bourdet, Boris Vildé (representative of one of the first Resistance networks), Emmanuel d'Astier de la Vigerie, Francis Crémieux, Vital Gaiman, Corniglion-Molinier (who reaches London), the lawyer Gaston Defferre (whom an embarrassed Malraux asks for advice on a possible divorce)—Malraux poses the same question: "Do you have money, and weapons?" Where are the planes and the tanks? The Americans and the Russians have them: "serious" circumstances that implicitly explain Malraux's refusal to get involved. He tells Francis Crémieux that he has tanks in the mountains. Would Crémieux be able to provide fuel? Malraux is no Kantian: he does not ask himself what would happen if the principles behind his (in)action were applied universally. If every founder or member of an underground network or newspaper had done the same as he, the Resistance would never have gotten started. Where is the militant editor of *L'Indochine Enchaînée*, the charismatic leader of the España Squadron? He has nerve, usually too much: he can't be accused of not having guts. His visitors expect something different; not, between whinnies of derision, his "Seriously!" or "You must be joking!" All those geopolitical speeches ending up in a standstill! What has become of the old Malraux? He feels he lost the war in Spain in 1939 and the battle of France in 1940. He no longer trusts bravado.

Simone de Beauvoir is shocked by Luigi in his white gloves, the stylish furniture, and the "lavishly served" grilled chicken. Sartre remains ambivalent about Malraux, who is, after all, the author of *L'Espoir*, yet whose "book is . . . not good," "full of ideas and very boring." Sartre has confided to de Beauvoir that he is "irritated by a sibling resemblance between the literary processes" of Malraux and himself. The author of *La Condition humaine* has an international reputation. This man has explored absurdity, contingency, man's solitude—on a novelistic scale but never on a philosophical level. Malraux is four years older than Sartre and has a head start of nearly ten years as a known author.

Roland Malraux comes south, and he, too, talks of fighting the Germans. Josette does not forgive him. Paulhan and Pia, who joined the Resistance very early, do not try to influence Malraux. He is writing, and he does it well. Pia knows his friend to be profoundly anti-Nazi; that is enough.

Pia sends Malraux reproductions of paintings by Rousseau and Matisse. He is still thinking of a magnum opus on the psychology of art. Malraux can talk to Pia about his family problems. Josette wants him to get a divorce. "Divorce legislation," Pia writes to Malraux, "may yet be severely called into question by the Marshal [Pétain], whose opinions on the sacrament of marriage are those of Louis Veuillot."[19] The woman of the house would like Malraux to be both the man of the house and a man of letters. She pokes fun at his "homosexual and left-wing friends."

Often she is no more duped by Malraux's embellishments than Clara was: "He is more concerned about creating a work of art than saying things that are accurate," she writes. Like Clara, she venerates Malraux's intelligence, but she understands it less. To her, he looks "plump, meek, American, pleasant, young." But she can see another mask: "When the mouth falls and the look becomes sharp, it is that of a clergyman, a monkey, an old fossil." Clara liked to watch André, despite himself, get drawn into large-scale domestic quarrels. André and Josette live on the verge of suppressed arguments. In his cocoon, Malraux is tense; he may well be writing, but his boredom is showing through. He continues to think about divorce, but not without apprehension: during the German occupation, if your wife is Jewish . . .

Josette is not as silly as Clara thinks. She just likes her home comforts and cares about respectability. Malraux's cousin Pierre Félix is arrested for resistance and is deported, but Malraux has no contact with his family around Dunkirk. He writes letters to his Aunt Marie Lamy; she sometimes types up his texts for him. He makes up his mind to see Clara and Florence: the child turned seven in 1940. She is precocious and fragile and suffers from rheumatoid arthritis. Clara talks ceaselessly to Florence about André. She sees her as a stake in the game. The stake and Clara do not live in the same luxury as André does. Clara got out of Paris in May 1940, just in time: the Germans went directly to her apartment. Anti-Jewish laws have been promulgated by Vichy from October 1940. Clara joined Florence at Lozes in the Lot. They reached Toulouse and lived for a few weeks in a firehouse in the company of other refugees. Madeleine Lagrange's family welcomed them in. Clara started giving German lessons.

She meets André in a café in Toulouse, on Place Wilson. He has no manuscript to give her; he explains that he has to get a divorce. Clara declines. She wants to go to America with Flo: once over there, she will accept a divorce. Malraux refuses.

"You won't do it," he says.

"You can always use the new anti-Semitic laws against me, that would be easier."

"You are a bitch."

How, at the end of 1940, could André Malraux not have given Clara permission to leave with their daughter for the United States and escape Vichy and the Nazis? Was he as blind as the Jewish war veterans, who thought they would never be abandoned by Marshal Pétain? To hate each other so much, perhaps Clara and André must also have loved each other deeply.

The mother and daughter stay in a boardinghouse, then move on to new quarters in Toulouse, "the cellar," where Clara holds a salon. In Paris, Paulhan, Groethuysen, and Alix remain loyal to her. Clara has no links with Drieu. Like André, Clara talks about literature; but also about the Resistance, and it is not only talk. With a new love, younger than she is—Gérard Crazat, a German revolutionary and veteran of the Spanish war—she circulates among Toulouse, Montauban, Cahors, Lyon, and Paris, carrying tracts, documents, and false identity papers and taking great risks. She is in contact with a German resistance movement for Jews, Communists, and Protestants. The women talk to German soldiers in trains to extract information that they then transmit to London. Clara works with two French Resistance movements, the MRPDG (Movement de Résistance des Prisonniers de Guerres et Déportés)[20] and the FTP (Francs-Tireurs et Partisans) and also a little with two Communist German Jews, Dora and Hans Schaul,[21] the latter a former member of the International Brigades.

Clara also needs to find provisions. France is living on a diet of beets,

Jerusalem artichokes, and rutabagas. With a J2 ration card, Flo gets milk; with the lack of heating, she gets chilblains. Clara finds some cod-liver oil. Since Flo is Jewish via her mother, Clara has her baptized. André, aware of the problem, does his bit by sending a false certificate of baptism, drawn up by an understanding priest. After catechism classes, Flo asks her mother: Did the Jews really kill God? Why is there a God? How? Why an end, why a beginning? Her father could have given so many answers, but he is not there. The monthly payments he sends are intermittent. If Clara complains, she receives a Malrucian telegram: "Do as I do, and wait." When he sends money, Clara is never short of repartee, even telegraphic: "Our daughter is wrongheaded enough to eat three times a day." In a notebook, Clara notes, "The winter will be hard on 2,000 francs [$40] a month."

Despite his curiosity, his output, and his intensity, Malraux is looking less like a man of action and more like a prudent forty-year-old, settling back into himself, his work, and his food. In the Lawrence book, *Le Démon de l'absolu*,[22] he declares, "Exoticism is born when faraway scenes give birth to particular feelings." He is so unhappy with this book on Lawrence that he tells people (perhaps including himself) that he has lost it. Lawrence also mislaid manuscripts. It happens, especially if you don't like them—or never write them.

Why does the Lawrence biography fail? Malraux has difficulty getting under the skin of an Englishman living in the Middle East, which he knows only from books. He can get into another Malraux, such as Claude in *La Voie royale* or Magnin in *L'Espoir*, but he cannot exist fully as a writer if he has to project himself into real people, or "introject" them into himself, and throw them onto paper.

Malraux sees Jean Grenier, the philosopher and friend of Camus, who does not believe in the Resistance.[23] "This is the third defeat that I have seen: China, Spain, France," says Malraux, now suffering from rheumatism.

He makes prophecies, sometimes farsighted:

Americanism will triumph in its economic and cultural form. The American lifestyle is already all over the world, especially in Japan. Just twenty years ago, true American culture didn't exist. Today, Gallimard is much more interested in Faulkner and other American writers than in writers from Germany, England, or anywhere else. Capitalism will be transformed by better distribution of goods. For the first time the world will be united. After the war, a sort of capitalist Council of Trent will take place. Russia—already Americanized—will remain to one side out of dissidence, but there has always been an orthodox religion and a Slavic world apart. England is in liquidation. Continental Europe will perhaps be German for several years, as it was French during the Napoleonic period, but the United States will end up having the upper hand. Perhaps it will choose Germany (without Hitler) to organize Europe, as the only country capable of doing it. France will lose her colonies. We will talk of the empire when it is lost. Japan will be attacked directly; its structure is weak. The Asian peoples do not want Japanese domination.

1942: From September 15 to the end of October, Malraux recovers from "larvae typhoid." He watches over his oeuvre from afar. He imagines, with pleasure, publishing an edition of *La Condition humaine* illustrated by Picasso.[24] When teased about the Resistance, he gets angry: "I've had enough of fighting for lost causes."

In 1942, the war takes a turn. In Southeast Asia, the Japanese are advancing; they force the British in Singapore to capitulate. But the Allies land in North Africa, and in Stalingrad the Germans suffer a defeat that leads to a huge surrender. The Americans bring off a raid on Tokyo. Pierre Laval is returned to power in Vichy. The French police round up 13,000 Jews into the Vélodrome d'Hiver.[25] Joseph Darnand creates the armed collaborationist force La Milice, specialized in hunting down members of the Resistance. After the American landings in North Africa in November, the German Army "reunifies" France: the Free Zone and the Occupied Zone are no more.

Malraux decides to leave the Côte d'Azur, where he could easily be found and is in danger. He reaches Argentat in the Massif Central. Josette joins him in mid-December. Josette, in Berl's view, is "estimable" and "charming." Her value is strong in the Gallimard tribe: she has slept with Michel Gallimard, and probably with Gaston too. She writes better than she speaks but thinks less well than she writes. In the eyes of the young Robert Gallimard, she seemed "touching" but not dazzling. After Hurricane Clara, some friends find Josette to be a soothing breeze for Malraux. Which she is, for a time.

CHAPTER TWENTY-ONE

The War of the Phonies

AFTER THE MALRAUXS' strategic withdrawal from the Côte
d'Azur, Bimbo is looked after by a builder for a few days in
Beaulieu-sur-Dordogne. His parents stay at the Hôtel de Bordeaux. Then Emmanuel Berl introduces Malraux to Maître Franck Delclaux, a notary in Saint-Chamant, on September 8, 1942. Malraux rents
part of a little château for 2,200 francs a month—and often forgets to pay
his rent. He shares the corridors, the stairs, and the kitchen with "Aunt
Andrée," a relative of the owner.

Gaston Gallimard sells pieces of art for Malraux: Persian miniatures,
an Assyrian bas-relief, a Hittite lion, various Tibetan objects, and Fautrier
paintings. Gaston foresees an edition of Malraux's complete works, to be
published by Skira in Switzerland. One volume would contain *La Condition humaine*, *L'Espoir*, *Le Démon de l'absolu* (his Lawrence of Arabia), and
Le Règne du malin, the Mayrena novel that never was. A second volume
would combine, bizarrely, *Le Temps du mépris* and *Royaume farfelu*.

Malraux receives his mail at Saint-Chamant, in his own name. His
ration card is also in his name. A feeling of impunity, or is he just being
absentminded?

Josette corresponds with her "little Gaston." She pays Malraux's taxes.
She wonders. He just doesn't seem very conjugal. She writes (again to
Suzanne Chantal) that she must "not be much fun as a partner. . . . But
there must be somebody in the world who would approve of the way I
am." Where have the joyous times gone, Barcelona and Madrid before the
war? "When it was illicit, André loved me. Since we've been living
together, who can say if he still loves me? He doesn't even need to take a
step to be with me." She keeps a diary: "He likes to make love in the
morning. He likes to make love often. He likes to make love simply. Then

he puts his arms around my body, his cheek against my cheek; we move no more than two blades of grass."[1] She ventures onto "the strange Asian manners of this famously cold man, this edgy, sanguinary fiend, of whom there is no proof that he was not slightly homosexual." Is Josette projecting?

Malraux moves his manuscripts into the study in one of the towers. Josette writes to her friend, "I am writing to you from the terrace of my château, with guinea fowl dressed in tulle and my child dressed in red, all cackling about me. We are above a beautiful valley. . . . All of it is russet. It would move you. . . . Our bedroom is round, like the study, where we eat in front of a big wood fire. . . . For your dreams of coming here, our town is Brive [15 miles away]. Here we do not suffer from the rationing as on the Côte d'Azur. You cannot imagine our life in Corrèze. . . . It is peace, we never see any Germans. . . . Malraux doesn't look as if he will be tempted to fight." She continues, "We suffer from restrictions—no mushrooms, nor caviar, nor anything from Hédiard, but we make omelets with fresh truffles and armagnac, and gastronomy fills the better part of my life, I must say . . . I make all the recipes from *Jardin des modes*. Corrèze won't be bombed tomorrow." The *coronel*, the *tankeur*, can drink, eat, digest, doze, and write.

André and Josette grow close to Maître Delclaux and his wife, Marie-Françoise-Jeanne. Malraux calls her "Rosine"; she and Josette become friends. "She [Rosine] is no bright spark, but she has an intelligent understanding of material things, something direct, resolute, and nimble," writes Josette. Rosine and André go for walks in the woods. Bah! Josette won't know . . . or doesn't want to know. The "illicit" Josette works off her hate of the legitimate Clara: "I am happy that I can think of Clara and not give a damn. . . . I have never been more legitimate than here in this area." She wears a wedding ring. "We came here because of the Berls, and we never see them. We are alone in the world, without an intellectual in sight, so we get on famously." Josette is perceptive: "Obviously circumstances have allowed me to get things my way. After the war André wants to do more cinema. That means tears for us." Suzanne Chantal sympathizes. Josette has Malraux in her possession for the unforeseeable future—as long as she devotes herself to tinned fish and pâté. Malraux congratulates her. But does he mean it? She understands what Clara didn't: for André, one writer in a couple is enough. She repeatedly loses André and finds him again. "I love him very much, I count on him, I trust him for the serious things even though I think he is a bit of an oaf. But I like this naive oafishness, his enthusiasm, his Wallace Berry [*sic*] side. André trusts only himself." How deep does Malraux's self-assurance run, beneath the sharp composure? I have genius, he thinks, but where are my talents?

The less Roland Malraux comes to see them, the happier Josette is, for he has been seriously engaged in the Resistance. Roland, tall, thin, and casual, has light blue-green eyes and a romantic beauty and, like André, plenty of drive. But why must he keep going on about the Resistance? Roland has made a Malraux out of André's son by acknowledging him legally. Josette acknowledges his deed, but not from the heart. Roland, to begin with, hides himself behind an official "cover." He represents a supply outfit in Toulouse. He clowns around with André:

> And I work jolly hard, apparently. . . . Where is my former indolence? Getting up at a quarter past seven, nine hours of work a day, you wouldn't recognize me! . . . Still haven't seen Clara—no complaints there. I would have liked to send some toys and sweets to Flo, though. . . . I can't bring myself to like Toulouse. Perhaps because I feel more of an exile here than anywhere else yet. I don't know anyone, I don't see anyone, I'm not even sleeping with anyone. What I'd really like to do is come into a big inheritance, get married, have two children, and live in affluence and idleness in a property of 450 hectares. Life doesn't look as if it's headed that way.[2]

The flighty Roland is beginning to settle. He is more sensitive than André to music and falls in love with a young pianist named Marie-Madeleine Lioux. His older brother, the admired patriarch of the tribe, approves his brother's choice and advises him to marry her. To his future sister-in-law, Malraux seems "very tormented." Roland confides to Madeleine that his brother's morale always needs boosting.

Roland and Madeleine are married at Tulle on January 8, 1943. The witnesses are Berl, "*homme de lettres*," and Malraux, "*écrivain*." Josette stays away from the ceremony. Why should others get married and not her? The quasi sisters-in-law still confide in each other. Has Josette actually read André Malraux's books?

"I gambled on him as if he were a horse."

Roland and Malraux's younger (half) brother, Claude, gets into the Resistance full-time. After his desertion, Claude did go back to France. He does a bit of dealing on the black market. Fair enough, considering the existing pay schemes: Communists in the Resistance are paid badly, to deter adventurer types; Gaullist *résistants* more generously, to cater for the necessity of buying, say, a car, or a Vichyist policeman. The British secret service, for which Roland and Claude work, meets halfway: an agent gets officer's pay, plus expenses. Roland and Claude both belong to networks of the SOE, the Special Operations Executive.[3]

Roland is classified CM2, *chargé de mission* (project leader) with the Nestor circuit. His rank is equivalent to lieutenant. He then becomes head of the false papers department in the Hamlet circuit, with forty agents in his group. Claude, "the kid," becomes group leader and a specialist in sabotage. Claude turned twenty in 1940; the Resistance catalyzes his skills.

Roland thinks that André has multiple talents. He mentions to his young wife, Madeleine, "He has genius, but he can be really disappointing."

Josette gets pregnant in July 1942; Madeleine, in January 1943. Perhaps the anticipation of another child prompts Malraux to write one of his very rare letters to Florence: "My little cat, I would have written to you earlier had I not been prevented from doing so." By what? "I wish you all the magnificent things you would like to be wished and which I don't know, but you do. I would like to send you a present, but I have just come back to a little village where there is nothing: so I am sending you a money order; it is not such a pretty surprise, but you will turn it into a surprise yourself, like a magician." Malraux finds it particularly hard to give presents to people close to him. To give a present is to open oneself up. A check or a money order is a more distant move. Florence is ten years old. "I should be asking you things," adds her father, "because this is your first birthday in double figures and you are getting big. But I know that you are good, just enough, not too good, which is quite right. I know you are second or third [in class], and that is also very good. And everybody says that you can do it without trying too hard, that you do what you are supposed to, that you are intelligent, that you have a look like that of your papa, and I see from the photos that you are a pretty little-big girl. All you need to do to please me is carry on being little Flo." After signing off—"You are sweet and I send you kisses. Your papa"—Malraux adds one of his cats, in profile.

Flo never received this letter; Clara kept it.[4] She is possessive and torn between her wish for Malraux to manifest his affection for his daughter and her intention to show the child that he is a terrible father. She broods over things that were said. In Toulouse, Malraux asked for a divorce, saying, "I do not want Josette's child to be an illegitimate child." Clara, with her acute sense of retaliation: "I wouldn't care about having an illegitimate child myself, if only its mother weren't Jewish." Clara feels disillusioned and furious that Malraux would put convention before Florence's and her safety.

Josette and André's second child, Vincent Jérôme André, is born on March 11, 1943. Vincent, like a hero from *Les Noyers*. Josette was hoping for a girl, Corinne. If only Vincent could be legally acknowledged by a

Malraux, like his elder brother. Now that he is married, Roland is no longer legally allowed to step in. For Josette, this second boy is "unwanted and ugly." "That hooked, pointed nose, the absence of chin! . . . He looks like Pierre Renoir or Harry Baur or—Good God!—like Sainte-Beuve or Sperber. That thin, severe mouth and the glint in the eyes. It's too absurd. Born to be the family failure." Then this sentence: "It was almost as if I had a dead child."

A slogan reigns over Pétainist France (not one written by Berl): "*Travail, Famille, Patrie*" (Work, Family, Country). Josette, with her concern for respectability, finds herself an unmarried mother for the second time. She expects everything of André, and he gives her not enough. She herself is not acknowledged as his legitimate spouse. Madeleine sympathizes with Josette, shares her woes, but gets tired of her moaning.

Knocking back the local plum eau-de-vie, Malraux spends all his time with his second family: the Bergers, Goya, and Colonel Lawrence. He frowns with concern as he works. He borrows a typewriter for Josette from the greengrocer. He writes long epistles in the familiar tones of a man of letters living on the brink of posterity. To Louis Guilloux about *Le Pain des rêves*: "If it's a sort of *Maison du peuple*, good. Then it's your best book since *Le Sang noir*. It would do a great deal of good to cut a number of things: any description that does not concern the author." As well as occasional attention paid to the works of his friends, Malraux the writer is still corresponding with Haas in the United States. He sends manuscripts to him via Lisbon and Suzanne Chantal's husband: "Volume 1 of *La Lutte avec l'ange* (the novel that you are to publish)," writes Malraux, "is finished, as you know. I am publishing it separately in Switzerland, in a luxury edition with a very small print run. Could you think, when it is in your hands, whether you might consider publishing it similarly, that is, in a small run, or in an ordinary edition as a first volume (as they did with Romains's *Les Hommes de bonne volonté*, I think) or if you prefer to wait for the next one: two volumes at least. Of course I defer to you. The important thing is that the current situation should not continue, whereby you have sent me advances and have nothing in return; now you will at least have the text of the first volume." The writer writes and fools around with Rosine. Malraux practices what the Brazilians call "colorful friendship," *amizade colorida*.

Malraux is requisitioned to do guard duty at the transformer at Saint-Chamant with Henri Madeslaire, headmaster of the school. Available men are taken in alphabetical order. While waiting in their hut for unlikely attacks by maquisards, they have a bite to eat. Malraux asks the headmaster, "If I am a minister one day, what do you want me to do for your school?"

How could this man, already loaded with responsibilities to his family and his work, find the time to join the Resistance, even part-time? He announces to Haas the forthcoming conclusion of a second volume of *La Lutte avec l'ange*, which in fact he has not even started. "Before finishing Volume 2, for a breather, I am writing something else. It is called *Le Démon de l'absolu*, and it is a book about Lawrence of Arabia. It's difficult to sum up, but I think I can say without undue pride that this will be the most significant book published about him, since nothing of much importance has been published." Malraux does own B. H. Liddell Hart's 1935 biography of Lawrence and *With Lawrence in Arabia* by Lowell Thomas. On the latter he has scribbled, "It is not the man who makes the legend, it is the legend that makes the man." Malraux explains to Haas that his book will be completed by August. "When you get the text, decide to publish it or wait, as it pleases you. The book could sell very well, I think, and if you judge it best to wait for a more favorable time, please do so. The book should be coming out (later on) with Gallimard. (Of course, my share of the rights stays with you to pay off my debit.) But I have made sure that the American publication is exclusive to you. I will then get on with Volume 2 of *La Lutte avec l'ange*."

Martin du Gard takes Gide's place as Malraux's counselor. Malraux writes to him from Saint-Chamant: "I have started again on Lawrence. The situation I find myself in, whereby I either do nothing and am pretty unhappy about it or do something considerable and enter a realm of semi-deception, is at least useful for understanding the character." Is Malraux capable of understanding himself? As his friend Raymond Aron puts it, nobody is as "opaque" as oneself to oneself.[5] Malraux does not like psychology, and introspection still less. "My Lawrence is becoming a big book, and I am more and more drawn back to the novel since I have been separated from it. Its great strength is decidedly that it is the transcription of experience, the intermediate link between life and some abstraction. Thus I discover that the most subtle parts of Lawrence's adventure could be made much more intelligible through fiction than the analysis that I am pursuing."[6] Malraux is doing more to explore the author of *La Condition humaine* than to explain Lawrence.

He writes slowly, as if in a maze, unable to find the way out. At this time, he does not have the fire of the novel in him. Nor (at any time) the qualities of the historian, the taste for precision and assembled, analyzed, synthesized facts, patiently basing one's research on documents, witness statements, and internal or external criticism. In his defense, Malraux does not have access to the Bibliothèque Nationale in Paris or a suitable university library. This has never stopped him in the past, but in this instance invention does not compensate for lack of research. Later, he says to Martin du Gard, "What an odd sort of monster it is, a book where the only art is in the narrative, where nothing can be invented and where, above all, one is betting on the complete item. The book will be good or bad as a whole."

It's bad. The first part is entitled "Le Temps des échecs"—The Time of Failures. "There is no great art without a part of childhood, maybe even of grand destiny" is the last sentence of the final draft. Tucked away in the middle of France, Malraux did not delve into his childhood, nor his adolescence, nor even his manhood, in this thick manuscript of more than 2,600 pages at the final stage. He signs a contract with Gaston Gallimard for the book but keeps the manuscript locked away in a drawer.

Malraux gets interested in pataphysics:[7] he is fascinated by the irrational, the unreal, the surreal. He subscribes to the paper *Les Cahiers de la Pataphysique* and is thanked for it, later, by Lachenal, the editor: "We are happy at the college that you are continuing to pay for *Les Cahiers de la Pataphysique*."

Malraux does a double take: "But am I still paying?"

The writer is afraid of a "semideception" if he gets more involved with those who are fighting the Germans in France. Instead of acting he travels, making frequent trips to Paris. In the summer of 1943, Gaston Gallimard creates the Pléiade Prize, to be awarded by a few Gallimard authors to . . . a Gallimard author. Gaston approaches the big guns to form a jury: Sartre, Raymond Queneau, Marcel Arland, Paul Éluard, Jean Paulhan, and André Malraux. The last is pleased to be asked, but the collaborationist press attacks him as a "Bolshevist," an enemy of the French national Revolution and the European German Revolution. Malraux withdraws from the jury.

Josette is thinking about Drieu, one of the few intellectuals she worships. She writes to him, "You know that I have a second son. I hesitated to ask you this before, perhaps it is a little silly to care about titles or labels, but here: Would you like to be the godfather of this second baby? The children are not Catholic, but putting religious considerations to one side. . . . Could you look at this child with an eye which is not the ordinary eye—in a way I place him in your hands; if there are things which you consider should be taught to a man, I would like him to learn them from you. I would like there to be a somewhat isolated relationship between you, if he is worthy of that. And I shall not bring him up not to be worthy of it—this custom touches me." The letter exposes Josette's subconscious like an open book: "And André and I, who are without brothers, would like to give the children perfect uncles. If it does not put you out, there, I give you Vincent. For the moment, he is not a shameful godchild." Josette wrote "without brothers," negating Roland, who acknowledged her first

Madeleine and André at Boulogne. *A true musician and an amateur.*

With the first president of the Fifth Republic.
I will always have my ingenious friend at my side.

The minister of
cultural affairs
departs for China.
*For the cartoonist Tim,
the cleaning up of Paris
would go on without
Malraux.*

Inauguration with Nehru.
*In Peking, is it Marx or
Nietzsche who comes out on
top?*

With Raja Rao. *First official visit to India,
the land of spirituality.*

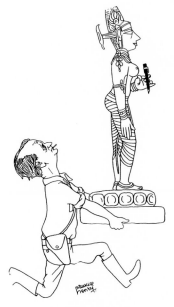

As seen by Maurice Henry.
The arts, Art, Truth, the Absolute.

ANDRÉ MALRAUX

With Mao Tse-tung. *That's how they deceive the masses with muddled methods.*

With Khrushchev. *This guy is starting to annoy me.*

Escorting Jackie Kennedy, at the Malmaison. *Josephine was a real handful.*

Florence Malraux. *If you had been a nurse in the FLN again.*

During a taping. *Television (along with computers) is the future of national education.*

With Shiva.
*Malraux associated
with all the gods
of Asia.*

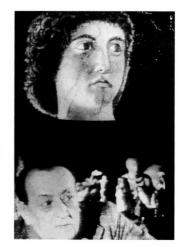

On television. *A star criticized from time to time, but indisputable.*

In his office at the ministry.
Raymond Mondon sat here before me.

Before the Arc de Triomphe.
Michel Debré, the minister of
state, Jean Bozzie, and in the
second row, Robert Poujade.
Vive de Gaulle! Vive de Gaulle!
Vive de Gaulle! . . . The ebb.
The Sixty-Eighters have lost.

In a ministerial DS.
Wasn't he born above all to write novels?

son. Drieu knows Roland. Josette, in one fell swoop, also wipes out Claude and offers Vincent as godson to the one friend of her partner who is a prominent collaborator.

Drieu keeps company with Otto Abetz, the Francophile Hitlerian German ambassador in Paris. Abetz produces a list, accepted by the willing French publishers, prohibiting the sale of 1,060 French and foreign works, including *Le Temps du mépris* and *L'Espoir*. Having taken over the *Nouvelle Revue Française*, Drieu publishes a premonitory article, "La Fin des haricots,"[8] in which he talks of Malraux: "M. is a writer who is committed to political action, as am I. If civil war breaks out, all he will be is a political leader, as, I suppose, will I. If he becomes a true leader, he will be a mortal enemy. So if I were to meet him in battle, I would have to shoot at him; and perhaps I would not be allowed to prevent his being shot, as a prisoner, in certain extreme circumstances. . . . If I do not think that, I do not take M. seriously, I insult him; and I do not take myself seriously. M. is transparent."

Josette's second son is growing on her: "He is pretty, chubby, and serious, and he has the greatest childish gentleness I have ever seen. We think that he will look more like André: he has his nostrils." Before signing herself "Josette Malraux," she invites Drieu to visit them.[9]

To Malraux, despite his excursions to Paris, the world of Josette and the little boys seems dismal. The odd quest for potatoes and chickens does not constitute an adventure.

Roland rents an apartment in Paris, on the eighth floor of a building in Rue Lord-Byron near the Arc de Triomphe. From Friday to Monday, Madeleine comes up from the conservatoire in Toulouse to join him. The rest of the week, it serves as a meeting point for English pilots and French or British SOE agents, including the young and enthusiastic Claude.

Josette is not really with it. She thinks mostly about after the war, placing immediate reality between brackets and hiding it behind her pots of jam. She predicts a role at Malraux's side, saying to Madeleine, "When we are at the Élysée Palace, we will put our feet on the table. We shall live in Rue Raynouard."

When he goes to Paris at the end of 1943 and the beginning of 1944, Malraux adopts the look of a conspirator, hat pushed down over the eyes and wrapped in a scarf. If he were an agent for the Resistance, he would quickly be spotted. In theatrical tones, he utters with a smile, "Do you not see it? I am he who plots. I beg of you, do not recognize me." A breath of humor, a point of self-criticism. Malraux does sometimes know how to mock himself.

Claude and Roland are in touch with Philippe Liewer, an important agent in the SOE. Having known him since 1942, André could have joined the Resistance in British or French networks, either in Paris or down at Brive. In the capital, Malraux stays at Albert Beuret's, who has returned from a prison camp in Germany. Then—the perfect cover—he stays at Drieu's apartment.

While Malraux was hesitating, Charles de Gaulle was reading Mauriac's *La Pharisienne* in a plane and talking to Captain Maurice Schumann.[10] The General confided to the captain, "The two finest novels between the two wars, in my opinion, are Bernanos's *Journal d'un curé de campagne* and *La Condition humaine*."

There is a proviso: "But if I had to award a Nobel Prize, it would go to Mauriac for his continuing work."

Having observed his two brothers' distant clandestine work, Malraux makes a few contacts but no irreversible decisions. In his eyes, the Resistance is, little by little, becoming "serious." It may have no planes and tanks, but it has machine guns, revolvers, explosives, and money. It could find him a suitable role. He starts to gather momentum. At Argentat, he declares to Berl, "An act of faith in the person of General de Gaulle is required."

Malraux was never—absolutely never—tempted to collaborate. Nor to support Pétain, in either a hard-line or a soft-boiled way. In his opinion, one could understand—Malraux did not say approve of—Pétain as French head of state, up until the Germans invaded the so-called Free Zone:

"His case," said Malraux, "became indefensible the night he [Pétain] did not leave [for North Africa]."[11]

Until 1942, at least, many French saw in Pétain the shield of France and in de Gaulle the sword; divided in appearance but, deep down, united. Berl reacted to Malraux's "profession of faith" with disbelief: "I thought he was having me on; then I saw that he was not joking at all. I turned on him. I told him, 'How do you expect me to make an act of faith in the person of General de Gaulle when I myself cannot answer for what I will do in ten minutes?'" Malraux was not discouraged. Why should Berl be touched by Gaullist grace when he didn't want to take sides with the Spanish Republicans?

Malraux's cyclical side comes uppermost again: there is a time for writing, a time for action, a time to be a *coronel* or a *tankeur*, a time to make a film. A time to hold back and a time to commit oneself.

CHAPTER TWENTY-TWO

Malrauxs in the Resistance

AT DAWN ON March 3, 1943, eight members of the Resistance under the command of Claude Malraux (known as "Cicéron" or "Serge") break into the premises of the Compagnie Française des Métaux in Deville, near Rouen. They neutralize the guards and the night staff. The factory makes alloys for the German Air Force. The Resistance fighters demolish press pumps, drop hammers, and a 1,200-horsepower motor. The factory is brought to a standstill for a fortnight, its production reduced to half for six months. On the same day, the singer Yves Montand starts a run at the ABC music hall in Paris. A few weeks later, Claude Malraux's deputy Maloubier and six other men blow up an electrical relay station, also near Rouen, with six kilograms of plastic explosive.

Claude takes part in several operations. He is made full lieutenant by London. There are 250 members in his network, some looking after "drop points" or depots for weapons and explosives, some attacking bridges, submarine sheds, or German troop trains. The leaders are not content merely to organize; they make sure they also handle the explosives. Claude's superior, Major Staunton, leads an attack on an armored train; another detachment derails a train in Corrèze. British sections of the Special Operations Executive in France (the SOE-F) have been set up almost everywhere in the country. The zone Claude comes under stretches between the lower Seine, Calvados, and the Eure. It has an English code name: Salesman. Other circuits have more picturesque names: Ventriloquist, Clergyman, Diplomat. The departments of the Dordogne, Corrèze, and the Lot are important for the "story" of André Malraux and the Resistance. The SOE hierarchy is complex.[1] In February 1943, Claude took the command of Salesman when Philippe Liewer, his predecessor, went to London.

In the fall of 1943, André Malraux is repeatedly approached[2] and requested to join the Resistance, but with the same result as when he was asked in the South in 1941 and '42. "It isn't time yet" is his response.

In November 1943, Serge Ravanel is the national head of the Mouvements Unis de Résistance (MUR) in the southern zone. Ravanel is sent by the Conseil National de la Résistance (CNR) to contact Malraux at Brive. Malraux suggests that he already has links with the SOE and could obtain parachute drops of arms for the Resistance. Ravanel's impression of the discussion with Malraux is that it keeps stumbling across "evasions." All Malraux can actually give is Roland, as a contact. Roland is no more capable of organizing parachute drops than André.

All of a sudden, Roland and Claude stop seeing each other. On March 8, 1944, a Gestapo agent turned up at the "Micheline letter box" at 74 Rue des Carmes in Rouen, supervised by a Mr. and Mme. Sueur. The Gestapo man claimed to be defecting: the Germans, he said, were looking for him. He gave the password (extracted from a resistant under interrogation) and declared that he wanted to join the Resistance. The Sueurs suggested he should come back that afternoon. Claude Malraux makes irregular pickups from the "box." What should the Sueurs say to the defector? Claude agrees to meet him at seven that evening on the cathedral square, dressed in a gray raincoat and carrying a scarf in his hand. At seven o'clock, the Gestapo arrives and arrests Claude. The same day, about forty members of the Resistance are also picked up in the Rouen area.

On March 12, 1944, the SOE-F in London receives a message from Mackintoshred, a circuit under the command of Harry Peulevé in Corrèze. He reports the arrest of "XLAUDEMALRAUX" as well as his radio operator, Pierre, and the seizure of eighteen tons of arms by the Germans. Claude's circuit was apparently broken up because a head of department had talked.

On March 22, Pierre Brossolette, a leader in the French Resistance, so as not to confess anything, throws himself off the fifth floor of a building occupied by the Gestapo, in Avenue Hoche in Paris. The day before, Roland Malraux was arrested along with his superior, Harry Peulevé, and transferred to a prison in Limoges. The prison register notes that he was in possession of a "clandestine transmitter" and that "his case is serious." Roland was denounced: a neighbor in the Milice believed that the house where he was staying in Brive harbored black-market runners. Roland had been traveling with suitcases stuffed with leaflets, weapons, and false identity and ration cards.

Some weeks afterward, Madeleine receives a courteous visit from two Frenchmen—possibly policemen or members of the Milice, in plainclothes. What does she do for a living? Teacher at the conservatoire. Married? "No." The visitors do not insist on examining her papers. On advice from Roland, Madeleine has kept her identity card in the name of Lioux. The policemen notice a switchblade knife.

"You are not allowed to have a weapon!" They make no allusion to the arrest of Roland. A case of good luck and bad policing.

André hears of his brothers' arrest. He decides to move into active service. He asks his correspondents not to send letters to Saint-Chamant.

At the end of March, Claude Gallimard (released from a POW prison camp with Albert Beuret and Jean Grosjean) replies by letter to Diffusion Industrielle Nationale, a company trying to locate André Malraux about outstanding payments on a car. Malraux considers himself "in a state of complete illegality," although only since March 1944.[3] So he moves on, to action. What job can he find for himself?

He adopts the name of one of his own heroes and starts calling himself "Colonel Berger." Fiction and reality penetrate each other. André is known at the SOE in London, thanks to his brothers. In Paris he had already met Philippe Liewer, who worked with Claude. André Malraux said he would like to join the Free French forces. Liewer was not the best possible sponsor, working as he did (and very well too) for the SOE, which was mistrusted by the Gaullist Free French.

For members of the Resistance in and outside France, April 1944 was a crucial month. Philippe Pétain came to Paris for the funeral of 642 victims of Anglo-American bombing on the Parisian areas of Les Batignolles and La Chapelle and was cheered down the Champs-Élysées. The same month, General de Gaulle became commander in chief of the armies of "La France Combattante." He appears to be the unique political and military leader among the anti-German French. He devotes a considerable amount of energy to ensuring his hold over the Resistance.

Thanks to Roland and Claude, André knows a lot of people active in the Resistance, both in the provinces and in Paris.[4] He also came across Peulevé when he was organizing the Author circuit in Corrèze. Raymond Maréchal (who went by the name of Mennisier in the Resistance and corresponds to the Gardet character from *L'Espoir*) was directing an Action group. André Malraux moves in March 1944 from a state of vague sympathy to commitment.

A crucial meeting takes place with an officer of the SOE, Jacques Poirier, nicknamed "Captain Jack" or "Nestor." He is French but pretends to be British so as not to get mixed up in the conflicts between the various Resistance movements.

Berger-Malraux has grand projects in mind, but so do the departmental and regional heads of the Resistance. The Armée Secrète (AS), mainly right-wing, has deep reservations about this Colonel Berger: he was in Moscow and worked with the Reds in Spain. The Communist officers of the Francs-Tireurs et Partisans (FTP) have a symmetrical mistrust of anybody not from the Party, especially intellectuals such as Berger, who is quickly known to be Malraux. Poirier, of all the Resistance officials, is the one who admires André Malraux the most. Malraux doesn't have the ideal profile for an anonymous Resistance agent: he is famous and therefore recognizable, if only by his nervous tics. He introduces himself as a military expert. Not everyone he comes across is duped by his repetition of "Seriously!" or his allusions to "this guy de Gaulle" or the "Churchill guy," suggesting a familiarity that just isn't there. Others are hypnotized when he lets loose a sumptuous monologue on Spain or Lawrence's feats in Arabia.

Captain Jack, alias Lieutenant (later Captain) Peters, alias Nestor, alias Poirier, is in charge of the new Digger circuit. He needs to lie low for a few days: the Germans and the Vichy authorities have his description and a photo of him. London lets him know that the Gestapo and the Abwehr consider him a dangerous terrorist. Poirier goes to Paris with Malraux, partly to try to get a member of the Resistance out of Fresnes prison. A military adventure becomes a literary outing. Poirier meets Jean Paulhan and Albert Camus. The Resistance poet Jean Lescure puts him up in a room in Neuilly. Malraux comes by to pick up Poirier and presents Lescure with two jars of pâté de foie gras.

"No, it's too much," says Lescure.

"Taken from the enemy," Malraux comments.

Malraux meets up with Josette, who has come to Paris with Bimbo. While at Gallimard she receives a mysterious phone call: "Métro Censier-Daubenton in twenty minutes."

She candidly tells André that she has a rendezvous with Drieu la Rochelle and that she has a new identity card in the name of Josette Malraux. Malraux is furious: "It's the worst thing you could have done."

Josette, recklessly, sees Drieu one afternoon and, the same evening, dines with André (with Poirier in tow) chez Prunier. The headwaiter immediately recognizes him: "Bonjour, Monsieur Malraux."

Josette and André part, to meet again, over the week, in Métro entrances, at the Tuileries, for dinner at the Tour d'Argent. Malraux sports a sombrero and wraps himself in a long overcoat. Poirier, meanwhile, has had the ludicrous idea of buying a cumbersome German shepherd. Malraux is amazed.

Poirier and Malraux leave again for the Southwest. The Dordogne is littered with châteaux, almost all of them beautiful. Josette and André leave Saint-Chamant, pass through Toulouse, then move on to the Château de Castelnaud overlooking the Dordogne.

In *L'Espoir*, Malraux explained that some men want to be and some want to do. He wants to be Colonel Berger and to act—at last. As long as he is a would-be member of the Resistance, he is not responsible for an area. Malraux wants to be a leader, *the* leader, the organizer, the recognized tactician, the admired strategist; specifically, the supreme boss of the R5 region in the Resistance hierarchy—certainly a commendable ambition, but not everybody is as willing as Poirier to be charmed by the self-proclaimed Colonel Berger. Those who have been in the Resistance for a long time have no intention of handing over their power, in whole or in part. Wanting and being are more than a sliver apart.

"When one has written my books," the writer repeats, "one fights."

And what great subject matter it would make, the maquis, armed resistance. There is no shame in living through an experience in order to write about it. *La Voie royale* and *L'Espoir* prove it: Malraux always writes better when he has experienced what he wants to describe. Single-handedly creating the conditions of this action, Malraux announces, "I have been instructed to take charge of the Resistance in this region by the Conseil National de la Résistance."

He met no members of the CNR in Paris.[5] He claims to have seen the head of the Gaullist mission and a mysterious colonel. Even better, Colonel Berger asserts that he has been vested with powers by General de Gaulle via General Koenig. Malraux seems to have gotten muddled: being contacted and being put in charge are not quite the same thing. Poirier receives a detailed explanation:

> I saw all the members of the CNR [Malraux claims]. I received a mandate from the Conseil National de la Résistance. I have to coordinate the action of the Resistance in the Lot, Corrèze, and the Dordogne. In essence, I have to harmonize relations among the different groups. You can help me in many ways: first by discovering the main objectives of our allies so that the maquis groups can be very efficient; then with your assistants, by setting up a sort of military training school; and finally, of course, by organizing parachute drops of arms. The other parachuting systems are nonexistent [allusion to the Gaullists]. You are the only one with the means to carry them out.

Indeed. Poirier does not spend his time kneading dreams and knitting schemes.

Malraux has gotten it into his head to federate three departments that do not come under the same region: Corrèze and the Dordogne are in R5, the Lot is in R4. The R4 and R5 regions have been sectioned off from each other, Serge Ravanel explains to Malraux. The division concerns all structures of the Resistance, at regional as well as departmental level, in both civilian and military matters. Ravanel does not have the power to alter them. What is more, such a change, with no justification, would entail unnecessary complications for the regional officials.

Malraux does not let go of his trinity of the Lot, Corrèze, and the Dordogne. Poirier thinks that Malraux's prestige could make him a unifying influence for the regional Resistance. Through Malraux, Poirier would help group together small, medium, and large structures, which, according to the London authorities, are getting in one anothers' way and doing nothing to ease the supply of arms. Malraux will be taking more risks than a maquisard staying in one place in the Barade forest.

So Malraux travels around with Poirier as an energetic door-to-door salesman of himself, visiting Resistance groups of the AS, the FTP, and the Vény group. Colonel Berger tells them (and himself) that he is inspecting these groups. A genius with words, he has a brilliant idea: he invents an "Inter-Allied Staff Headquarters" for the region: his own. In London there is an Inter-Allied Council. At the SOE, the letter *M* means Inter-Allied Mission. Malraux slots these expressions together and shifts seamlessly from the potential to the real. To justify this unofficial term, the Inter-Allied Staff Headquarters (*état-major interallié*) is formed around Malraux and some British officers of the SOE-F, including the Frenchman Poirier. Premises are found in Siorac by René Coustellier, alias Soleil, for Poirier and his English radioman, Ralph Beauclerk. Malraux and another Englishman, Peter Lake, stay at the mayor's residence. Malraux-Berger, like a king of France in search of a kingdom and troops, goes from château to château: Soleil moves him on to Castelnaud-Fayrac.

Malraux does not, at this time, appear to be in awe of de Gaulle. He sizes him up with Poirier: "I don't know him, I don't like his speeches, but if he can make a place for himself among the allies, we will have won the war. If not . . ." he says with a broad gesture.

Poirier, like Lake and Beauclerk and the other British officers in the area, manages to avoid the political quarrels of the Resistance. Some members want unity and discipline; others have long-term political views.[6] Poirier devotes himself to the needs of the maquis and organizing parachute drops, Lake to the handling of weapons and plastic explosives. Beauclerk works at his radio and sometimes plays the piano.

"You play the same pieces as my sister-in-law," says Malraux. "I would have liked to play an instrument."

The Nestor-Digger circuit carries out more than eighty drops. There is a trace of Malraux's influence in a message transmitted by the BBC: "*Les farfelus sont réunis*" (The eccentrics are united), and "*Le temps du mépris tire à sa fin*" (The time of scorn is drawing to a close). The British agents like Malraux, but none of them consider that he has any military value. Poirier just enjoys his personality. He thinks that some are made to act and others, usefully, to talk.

Colonel Berger's inward-looking "Inter-Allied Staff Headquarters" keeps radio contact with London thanks to Poirier and Beauclerk. This fantastical institution does not and will never figure on any Resistance diagram. What, in Malraux's mind, is the theoretical structure of his Inter-Allied (or sometimes interzone) Staff Headquarters? Number one, André Malraux; number two, Jacques Poirier. Special adviser, Lieutenant Roche Bouët, alias Aumale. Number three, Peter Lake, instructor. Radio: Ralph Beauclerk, on his B Mk II suitcase radio (with a speed of twenty-five words a minute, at the mercy of the German radio direction–finding equipment). Between ten and forty maquisards are involved in what Malraux sees as the staff headquarters. What does it matter if neither the British in London, nor the Americans, nor the SOE, nor Colonel Passy's BCRA, nor the CNR in France is aware of its existence? When the stakes seem to be getting a little high, "Inter-Allied Staff Headquarters" is downgraded to "the Inter-Allied CP," or command post. What exists, in reality, is the SOE Digger circuit: chief, Poirier; number two, Peter Lake; Beauclerk on the radio; and Major Robert Poirier under the orders of his son. Poirier never mentions the "Inter-Allied Staff Headquarters" to London. Thanks to Poirier and his men, Malraux, who has no command, enjoys a certain authority. When he meets officials, he comes out with "Over to you."

He makes blunders. When addressing some maquisards who are not Communists, he gets the film wrong entirely and raises his fist. In an odd sort of dreamlike coherence, he lives at this time not in Corrèze or the Dordogne but probably back in Barcelona or Madrid. He calls meetings, receives visitors, expatiates, promises to send messages to London, jerks his head upward, pushes away his forelock, rests his chin on his hands, staring at invisible points on the horizon of History.

Only a mobile group, mostly made up of refugees from Alsace and Lorraine, accepts Berger's authority. Their leader, Ancel (alias Antoine Diener, a schoolteacher), meets with Colonel Berger and recognizes the writer Malraux. Ancel needs weapons for fifty men. Malraux promises ammunition and plastic explosives. Where Ancel receives Colonel Berger, near a farm, his men stand at attention around a flagpole and hoist the colors. Malraux exclaims, "You want arms, you'll have them! You want to fight, you shall fight!"

He does not say, "I will give them to you."

Malraux returns delighted from that outing. Marvelous chap, that Ancel. At staff headquarters (or command post), Poirier, Berger, and the others listen to General de Gaulle over the airwaves of the BBC. The British Broadcasting Corporation was the umbilical cord between the Free French (the Forces Françaises Libres, or FFL) and the interior resistance (the Forces Françaises de l'Intérieur, or FFI). On June 5, 1944, at 9:15 p.m., the day before the Normandy landings, the BBC broadcasts instructions to the Resistance: "The giraffe has a long neck," announcing the Allied landings; "Her skirt is red," sabotage the telephone lines; "The postman is late," sabotage roads and attack German convoys.

Malraux does not join in the close fighting. He is a colonel, why should he? His responsibilities are too great.[7] Most of all, the colonel has no troops under him. The Resistance, as far as it can, carries out the orders from London and moves on to attack. The Germans have to get their elite Das Reich Division to Normandy fast. It takes them ten days: the maquisards hold them up by blowing up railway tracks. The Resistance forces are armed with a few bazookas, rare but excellent Bren machine guns, thousands of Sten submachine guns (inaccurate junk beyond twenty yards but cheap), Mills grenades, archaic shotguns, and hunting rifles. These men would not know how to attack the heavily armed German soldiers face on (even those not in the Das Reich Division). The FFI is equipped to dig antitank trenches, cut down trees, and blow up railway lines. The 2nd Panzer Division Das Reich has the latest model of Tiger tanks. It has one tenth of the German armored vehicles on the western front, guns, armored cars, 3,000 vehicles, including 359 equipped for attack,[8] and 13,421 men, including many young Russian and Hungarian recruits. The Resistance is facing whole battalions of infantry. Lake has five hundred yards of track blown. The German command signals to its troops on June 10, "All communications with Brive, Tulle, Périgueux are also disrupted."[9] The maquisards do not stop Das Reich but create a climate of insecurity and put the Germans in a defensive position.

Amid all this, Malraux does not forget about literature. Raphaël Finneclerc and Léon Lichtenberger, two liaison officers from the Communist FTP, spend a week with the writer. Malraux gives these young men the impression that they are "his equals." His reasoning, they judge, is "like a spiral," turning on itself but always climbing to a higher level. They ask him about literature, the past, the present, China, Spain. Malraux makes an effort to use, with them, "simple language interspersed with dazzling flashes."[10]

On June 11 in Domme, Madeleine Malraux gives birth to a boy, Alain. André Malraux goes to see the mother, as does Josette. The boss of the "Inter-Allied Headquarters" is not as careful as he might be. In a Citroën with Captain Jack, Colonel Berger suddenly finds himself facing German tanks. He brings out a 7.65 revolver and fires at the stupefied Germans.

"André!" says Captain Jack with a look of amused reproach.

The Citroën turns around and scrams. A headquarters, even one with no troops, must not be taken by the enemy. Malraux relocates. He moves into the house of Father Dufraisse at Limeuil, then to the magnificent eighteenth-century château at La Vitrolle. Two weeks after the Normandy landings, at tremendous risk, he continues his tour of the maquis groups. Differences of opinion set the groups against one another: the exact "borders" of their zones, questions of precedence, financial problems, squabbles about the sharing out of weapons, the political goals of certain leaders. The Resistance is a mix of heroism, jealousy, foolhardiness, stunning feats of derring-do and making do, strengths and weaknesses, courage and cowardice, tragedies with comic asides—in short, all that makes up a war. Malraux, the hero of the Spanish war, is brave enough, but he does not have the equipment of an experienced Resistance fighter, nor the seniority, nor the expertise. No false identity papers either. And what a pseudonym to choose, Colonel Berger! Luckily, the Abwehr and Gestapo men, miliciens, and Vichy informers are very unlikely to have read *Les Noyers de l'Altenburg.*

On June 25, a unit from the 11th Division of the Wehrmacht moves on Limeuil. Malraux and his colleagues scatter, to regroup at the beautiful chartreuse Château de la Poujade in the small village of Urval. There, they talk strategy, literature, and politics. Lieutenant Marc Gerschel (code name "Gilbert") is parachuted in on the night of the first of July. In the course of his comings and goings between France and England, Gerschel escaped from the prison at Eysses.

"Eysses prison?" interrupts Malraux. "I know it well. We sprang the main inmates."

Gerschel can't believe his ears: Malraux is taking credit, with his royal, omnipotent "we," for the escape of twenty-four prisoners, including himself. Shame, Gerschel thinks, that's how it should have happened. He hazards a judgment: "There are three writers in France who can pass for writers of action . . . Saint-Exupéry, an intellectual who thinks he's a man of action . . . Henri de Monfreid . . . a man of action who thinks he's an intellectual, and then there is you, who combine a bit of both."

Malraux is not amused by this sweeping summary. He strikes Gerschel as vain. Any allusion to someone who is not him seems out of place. Colonel Berger starts on a speech foreshadowing *La Psychologie de l'art.* Gerschel savors that performance.[11] Malraux turns up at Marcheix, at the command post of Colonels Georges and Hervé, hoping to run the Armée Secrète. Thanks, but no thanks: he is dismissed.[12]

Malraux promises arms to whoever asks him, or whoever will listen. Perhaps he can make an impression by announcing parachute drops. Poirier has been asked by London to find locations for a major drop. On July 9, at a local meeting to discuss preparations, Malraux meets Major Pierre Élie Jacquot. He knew him before the war, when he was military attaché to Édouard Daladier's Cabinet. A career soldier, he commanded the 40th Infantry Regiment in Brive but has only just joined the Armée Secrète. Malraux says he needs a French assistant who is competent in military matters. Jacquot accepts the job.

At dawn on the fourteenth of July (symbolically enough), at four points on French territory, the largest parachute drops of the war are carried out by about 150 American Flying Fortresses and 200 RAF fighters. Malraux goes to the first site at Loubressac, Poirier to the one at Moustoula.

Malraux now goes around in uniform, with fairly wide colonel's stripes and leggings or boots, like his father in 1915. He claims responsibility for the drop organized by Poirier. Thanks to this drop, thousands of submachine guns, pistols, grenades, ammunition, and some heavy machine guns and bazookas are distributed as far as Tarn-et-Garonne.

Although officially and practically unable to give orders to regional representatives of the Resistance,[13] Malraux summons some of them to his château in Urval. They, at least, agree to see him.[14]

"With war, real war," he tells them, "a theory means nothing, unless it is put into practice. When the largest armored division of the Third Reich is on your doorstep and it must on no account reach Normandy, that's what war is."

The Das Reich Division has been fighting in Normandy for a month already. Malraux also tells them, "You are chiefs; I will strengthen your command if you commit yourself to attack and fight when I give you the order to do so. . . . Those who do not obey, I will have executed."

All of a sudden we're in *La Condition humaine* or *L'Espoir* again, far away from the French maquis. Malraux does not even seem to be aware of the danger to which he is exposing them, and himself, by gathering area leaders in one place. He in no way replaces the FFI leaders of Corrèze and the Dordogne; neither the FTP nor the AS is under his orders. A more conciliatory label is required: it is as "Chief Inspector of the FFI for the Dordogne, the Lot, and Corrèze" that he now introduces himself—a diplomatic diversion from the main line into an honorable (but entirely honorary) siding.

So Malraux, in uniform, continues inspecting. On July 22, escorted by Colonel Vincent, "Vény," and an English officer, he visits a maquis group near Rodez. Vény's maquisards are still devoted to Malraux. On the route back to "inspection" headquarters, he refuses—despite advice—to take the country tracks. His front-wheel-drive Citroën shall drive on the roads: "The *routes nationales* are made to be used!" exclaims Colonel Berger.

Never mind about the Milice or German soldiers who might be lying in wait. Malraux's movement on this tour, on foot and by car, serves as a demonstration to himself that he is organizing and instilling order. To be, if one cannot do, is to seem. Across three departments, he pops up in woods and fields, in villages and châteaux, wearing a tunic or a jacket. The verbal virtuoso, braving these dangerous roads, does not pass unnoticed: rumors, flattering and otherwise, precede him. Berger is Malraux. Here's Berger, Malraux's coming.

The first-rate officer Poirier keeps control of the infrastructure of the SOE, overseen in theory by the gaseous Inter-Allied Headquarters, with some real elements to it and others imaginary, plenty of appearance but little actual substance. When things get complicated and confused, Poirier thinks some people count "more for what they say than for what they do."

On July 22, Malraux's black Citroën takes the departmental D14 road toward Gramat. Squashed into the back are George Hiller (British), Colonel Berger, and Henri Collignon. The Germans have set up a road-block made of tree trunks and branches. Toward 5 p.m., coming out of a bend, the Citroën comes face-to-face with German soldiers, who start shooting. The rear windshield shatters. The resistants scramble out of the car. Malraux falls. A bullet pierces one of his leggings, another grazes his right leg. The resistants run. Hiller is wounded but escapes and is later repatriated to London on a Lysander. The Germans take Malraux to a villa on the Figeac road, then to the Hôtel de Bordeaux in Gramat.[15]

He recites his name and rank to his captors. He says he is the military head of the region. This is in accordance with guidelines: if taken, a member of the Resistance should claim to be of the highest rank possible to avoid immediate execution. Then he must hold out for two days under torture before giving any information, in the hope that the network will have had time to disperse. Malraux later writes that he was stood in front of a firing squad.[16] By empathy, he has become Hernandez from *L'Espoir*, whose thoughts he almost shares: "What meaning did his life have, would it ever have? But I was sucked in by a tragic curiosity for what awaited me." This fantasy of "I was nearly shot, what joy, how horrendous" also captivated Maurice Blanchot in a little-known text, *Death Sentence*.[17] Blanchot would later write, "On returning to Paris, he [the hero, standing for Blanchot] met Malraux. The latter told him that he had been taken prisoner (without being recognized), that he had managed to escape, losing a manuscript in the attempt. 'It was only some thoughts about art, easy to make up again, whereas a manuscript would not have been.' " Malraux never claimed to have escaped. But the theme of a manuscript destroyed by the Germans solidified into another leitmotif.

Questions remain. Did the prisoner really allude to his reputation as a writer, really declare that he had taught and lectured at Marbourg, Leipzig, and Berlin? Did he really state that his unit was holding about a hundred German prisoners? Did he really have a cyanide capsule on him, like some members of the Resistance—and like one of the heroes of *La Condition humaine*? What are we to make of his dialogue with Oberstleutnant Traugott Wilde,[18] who is supposed to have interrogated him? Malraux, as he later remembers it, engages in high-level discussions. The officer asks Berger why the Resistance is destroying what the Germans can so quickly repair. Did they really talk of tanks, so dear to Fernand and

André Malraux? Did Wilde really go to the trouble of asking his French prisoner if the Resistance had antitank weapons, just so that Malraux could answer "yes"? Why didn't Malraux save time and follow Resistance guidelines and give information that was "usefully false"? Why isn't he executed, given that orders were to liquidate "terrorists"? Was he mistaken for his half brother Roland Fernand Georges? The writer, in civilian life, is still Georges André Malraux. The Germans look after him. "They put a makeshift bandage on my trousers," he later writes.

Malraux spends the day of July 23 at the Institution Jeanne-d'Arc school in Figeac. Nuns bring him real coffee and a New Testament: he wants to reread the Gospel according to Saint John.[19] He is bundled into a German ambulance and taken to Villefranche, where he is seen by a Dr. Dufour. He spends the night of the twenty-fourth at Albi, where—in his *Antimémoires*—another wonderful novelistic scene takes place, a beautiful fragment in a literary anthology of recollection. A sentry shows Colonel Berger photographs of Marshal Pétain and General de Gaulle. The German (supposedly) puts a finger on the photo of Pétain, saying, "Very good." Then another finger, with disapproval, on the photo of de Gaulle: "Terrorist." Then the soldier is supposed to have added, "Tomorrow . . . maybe very good" and, pointing at Pétain again, "Maybe terrorist." So an ordinary German private in these circumstances would have had a photo of General de Gaulle? Even in the Resistance, portraits of the leader of the Free French were hardly ever seen. Malraux himself had seen a photograph of Charles de Gaulle for the first time only a few weeks before. And the sentry's political vision seems very astute. Was he another Ernst Jünger, in the form of a private?

Malraux stays in Revel, on the ground floor of an abandoned villa. The next day, he is taken to yet another château. The prisoner is introduced to the commandant of the 2nd Division, General Wend von Wieterscheim. According to Malraux, the general sits behind a Louis XV desk, has dark glasses and white hair, and is polite. We can let the white hair pass (although it was in fact completely brown) and ignore the sunglasses (which the general never had). But the writer's novelistic account of the discussion is indispensable.[20] It is a magnificently resonant, classic Malraux dialogue; courteous, literary, and geopolitical. Malraux writes:

> "I would like to know from you," asks the general, "why you do not recognize the armistice. Marshal Pétain is a great soldier, the victor of Verdun. France committed itself, and we were not the ones who declared war. A nation does not commit itself to die by proxy."
>
> [Berger:] "Allow me a hypothesis: with Marshal von Hindenburg as president of the German Republic, a world conflict ensues

and Germany is beaten, as we have been. The marshal capitulates. The Führer (who isn't chancellor, obviously) makes an appeal from Rome for German fighters to continue the war. Which one elicits Germany's commitment, and who are you with?"

"Why is de Gaulle in London?"

"The heads of state are in London, except one, who is in Vichy. General de Gaulle is not commanding a French legion to serve the Allies."

"What purpose is served by what you are doing? You know very well that every time you kill a soldier we will shoot three hostages."

Colonel Berger explains that French intellectuals admire Hölderlin, Nietzsche, Bach, and Wagner, despite the fact that the general has not, in reality, read or listened to them.[21] *Bon.* Seriously. Malraux did not understand German. The real general needed an interpreter.[22] This brilliantly drawn tête-à-tête was not just improbable but impossible. The discussion quoted by Malraux has style, a certain tone, fantasy in its form and content. It is a theatrical scene that recalls the heroes' conversations in *L'Espoir*: Colonel Ximenez, for one. We have been happily cast off into a sea of literature.

Malraux is taken back to Revel and spends the night there before being transferred to Toulouse. Even here, everything reminds him of Spain: "Place Wilson, the Café Lafayette, where I so often sat during the Spanish war." Place Wilson does not remind him of his stormy discussion with Clara—that would be out of place in an epic story. Afterward, he says, his guards gave him "eggs and ham and a bottle of Bordeaux." All that's missing is the vintage. He is locked up for the night in a bathroom with a bed in one corner, adorned with a blanket and white sheets. This treatment proves just how important Malraux must be: Resistance prisoners were rarely if ever given these considerations.

Poirier and others attempt to bribe French and German officials to prevent Malraux from being shot. There is discussion of what capital is available to buy the freedom of members of the Resistance. On August 2, the Germans incarcerate Malraux in Saint-Michel prison in Toulouse, in cell 32, where the journalist André Culot is also being held.[23] Malraux states that he was "prisoner of the headquarters of the Armored Division Das Reich for three weeks." No part of Das Reich Division was in that area at that time. Malraux tells how he was taken prisoner:

"I was inspecting the maquis groups of the Lot, Corrèze, and the Dordogne when I fell into an ambush during a journey in a car with French and English flags flying in the wind. The chauffeur was killed outright, the car turned over. An English officer was wounded and was finished off as he tried to run away. As for me, I was lucky to get out alive. A bullet went through my thigh, and the Boche found me in the bushes where I had taken cover."

"Are you still in pain?"

"Yes, I only received very basic care. My wound is still oozing."

"You should go to the infirmary."

"I prefer to look after myself. The less I see of the gray-green uniform, the better I feel."

Pretty preposterous.

August 9, 1944, a large sum is set aside "for liberation of Colonel Berger."[24] Malraux continues to want to rank highest, even in cell 32. The prisoners shouted (according to him), "Berger, in command, Berger! Berger!" But did he, as he claimed, get up on a table and hold forth to his fellow detainees? His faculties for sympathy or empathy are intact: he confuses himself with J. Rouket, "Capitaine Georges," who did give a few orders. A colonel should have had precedence over a captain.[25]

Malraux was not rescued by a commando raid. Nobody tried to organize an escape, although Serge Ravanel thought about it. It would have had to be a large-scale operation. The Resistance had a lot to do. Malraux was liberated from Saint-Michel, along with the other prisoners, on August 19 at around 3:30 in the afternoon. He arrived at Madeleine's parents' house in Rue d'Alsace-Lorraine wearing pajamas and a pullover. Josette, who had been there for a few days, welcomed him in. The Germans evacuated the town. Two days later, Berger, in transit between history and legend, leaves to take up an imaginary post as interregional FFI leader—for the first time. He surfaces in one of his old headquarters at the Château de la Poujade, where the first to welcome him is Peter Lake.[26] Malraux moves on to Angoulême and Périgueux for meetings of the civilian and military Resistance officials, and to Limoges, where funds are distributed. Nobody invited him. He is not given the leadership of the 12th Military Region that he wanted. He, the unforgettable Berger, has been forgotten. He was expecting the resistants in Périgueux to swear allegiance to him that day.

The Vercors maquis, with no mortars or heavy guns, was crushed at the end of July. But Allied troops, reinforced by General Leclerc's 2nd Armored Division, eventually broke through the German front near Avranches. France is theirs, despite the Germans' fierce defense. Soviet troops are on the Vistula in Poland. Under the circumstances, the French Communists in the FTP and other Resistance movements infiltrated by them have no desire to let this Berger-Malraux play a role. The right-wing movements have no reason to accept him either. Once more, he is not wanted. A morose Malraux, like a kid shunned by his friends starting another game without him, heads for Paris. He stops off at Saint-Chamant, to which Josette has returned, and looks after Bimbo, Vincent, and Alain, his sons and nephew.

In Paris he has a lot of money in hand. He also has a tendency—perhaps this is a splinter under his skin since Bondy—to let himself believe that he is richer than he is. But he does have more money than would come from his royalties. A few days before his release, maquisards, including some from the Valmy group who were faithful to Malraux, attacked a freight car belonging to the Banque de France in Neuvic station in the Dordogne, getting their hands on 2.28 billion francs—the contemporary equivalent of more than $46 million.[27] Another convoy was attacked near Brive. Some members of the Resistance kept their war spoils. The banknotes were not exchanged before 1945. Others handed over large amounts to the Treasury.[28] Malraux does not appear on the lists of beneficiaries of the train robbery, at least not under the name "Berger," but he did receive money from the R5 region that is accounted for elsewhere. August 4, 1944: "Paid to . . . Colonel Berger 500,000 [francs]. 8th: Paid for the liberation of Colonel Berger 4,000,000 [total: $91,140]." Colonel Berger was no exception. Large amounts of money evaporated to the left and right in the mad, tragic gaming of the Resistance. The money was apparently conveyed to Paris by Josette's friend Rosine.[29] Malraux writes to Suzanne Chantal, "If you have money worries . . . don't hesitate. At the moment I am rich."

When he returned to Paris, Malraux visited Ernest Hemingway, a war correspondent at the time. He found him lounging at the Ritz, Armagnac and champagne within equal reach. The two writers exchanged weighty words.

> Malraux: "How many men did you command?"
> Hemingway: "Ten or twelve, two hundred at the most."
> Malraux: "I commanded two thousand."
> Hemingway: "Shame we didn't have your help then, when we were taking this little town of Paris."

Hemingway's armed FFI bodyguard, a maquisard cowboy, exclaims to "Papa" Hemingway, "Papa, shall we shoot this asshole?"[30]

The asshole in question, before attending this literary summit and after leaving the Southwest, where he had signally failed to make an impression, apparently addressed the members of the Resistance who were refusing him the eminent post he deserved: "Since you don't want me, you will hear all about Colonel Berger."

CHAPTER TWENTY-THREE

The Alsace-Lorraine Cross

INDEED THEY DID. September 9, 1944: the First American Army charges on Aix-la-Chapelle; General de Gaulle is in recently liberated Paris, consolidating his power there; Soviet troops, supported by Yugoslavians under Tito, move into Albania; and Colonel Georges-André Malraux signs a No. 2 Movement Order and some appointment papers—his own: "Colonel Berger takes command of the independent Alsace-Lorraine Brigade." Malraux also names his deputy, Major Pierre Jacquot, and gives the order for a battalion to move to Brive and Tulle. Three days earlier, Colonel Georges Pfister, "Marius," deputy commander of the FFI in the southern zone, signed orders requesting Malraux and Lieutenant Colonel Jacquot (quickly promoted) to create the Alsace-Lorraine Brigade. Pierre-Élie Jacquot abandons his nom de guerre, "Édouard." Promotion and self-promotion abound. Advancement is on tap for those with the merit, the cheek, the innocence, and the experience. Malraux has made a record leap from the rank of *cavalier de deuxième classe* to that of colonel.

Malraux-Berger bounces back with all the spirit of *el coronel*. Colonel Berger lets it be understood that he has a stock of munitions at hand, even though he doesn't. For a few weeks, his unit goes by various grandiose names: Groupement Malraux, Légion Alsace-Lorraine, Colonne Malraux, Première Demi-brigade d'Alsace-Lorraine.[1] The rubber stamps the unit uses say "F.F.I.," "Mission Régionale Corrèze," or just "République Française." At last the troops Malraux wanted to command pass from a state of essence to one of existence. Courageous bands of men are gathered into groups of maquisards and then into regular formations. Malraux surpasses himself—as he did in Spain—in the role of persistent organizer, now that he has a solid grip on the men.

A combination of circumstances, willpower, and luck placed him at the head of this unit. Malraux gave Jacquot a boost; he is pushed along in return. A few days after the Normandy landings, Malraux received Antoine Diener, "Ancel," at the Urval château. The cocksure Colonel Berger announced out of the blue that the British were going to parachute ten thousand men into the Dordogne. Desirable, certainly, but in fact only virtual; a bluff woven out of Malraux's own brand of *farfelu*. He had no power in the maquis, nor over the FTP of the Lot, nor over the AS in the Dordogne; but his imagination could convince others, as well as himself. When Berger announced, just as abruptly, that the drop was canceled, Ancel and two others, Bernard Metz and Father Pierre Bockel, were already in his pocket.

They gathered together the men from Alsace in the region. Metz had previously recruited for the "7th Alsatian column" and been part of the Martial Resistance Group. As a medical student, he was able to rally many decided and undecided students to Malraux's camp, some of them having maintained connections with Vichy headquarters until the Normandy landings. Toward mid-August 1944, Jacquot was chosen as their leader. A good diplomat, Jacquot negotiated the surrender of German troops at Tulle.

When Malraux arrived, Jacquot stood down from his brief command of the Alsatians. On August 30, Colonel Berger was enthroned unit commander elect by his friends and acquaintances, including Jacquot and the not-very-military Emmanuel Berl. Some of the volunteers were not too pleased to learn that Colonel Berger was Malraux, the Bolshevik writer. That communism should be any part of the unit's declared objective—to recapture Alsace—was unacceptable! The mobile Alsace group started off badly. Captain Peltre, Professor Baas, and others managed to dissolve some suspicions (wasn't Malraux a known personality, a famous novelist, a humanist, and an aesthete to boot?), and Malraux's own charm and assurance untangled the most hostile. Haloed with his arrest "by the Gestapo," the man had style.

Heroic times. The French are as staunchly behind "the Liberator" de Gaulle as the Allied soldiers. France participates, as far as it can, in the last thrust against Nazi Germany. A dizzying logistical chaos reigns, especially when it comes to amalgamating (under the orders of General de Lattre) regular soldiers from Italy and North Africa with irregular maquisards.

On September 19, 22 officers, 54 NCOs, and 218 privates arrive from Annecy and come under Malraux's orders. Not all of them are from Alsace or Lorraine. They belong, they say, to the "Mulhouse" Battalion, which is essentially composed of maquisards, some from the Toulouse area.

Malraux and Jacquot go to Dijon, to the headquarters of the flamboyant commander of the First French Army, General Jean de Lattre de Tas-signy. At the Hôtel de la Cloche, where de Lattre reigns, Malraux and Jacquot are joined by three more officers, Lieutenants Holl, Jessel, and Landwerlin. They have their own men.

In Spain, the *coronel* placed Gardet at his side. In France, Malraux has Jacquot. He sets up a command structure: Colonel Malraux, Lieutenant Colonel Jacquot (*adjoint-breveté d'état-major*), Major Brandstetter (*chef d'état-major*), Captain Schwarzentruber (*compagnie d'état-major*), Major André Chamson (*liaisons 1re Armée*), Second Lieutenant Metz (*liaisons Réseau Martial*).

Malraux grants an interview with *Carrefour*.[2] Colonel Berger paints a picture of his "two years" (surely a slip of the tongue for "two months"?) in the Dordogne maquis. Yes, he was there with Major Brandstetter, for-merly of the French Camel Corps, and with Jacquot. Yes, Malraux was a prisoner "of the Gestapo."

"We are short of everything," he says. "Granted, the Americans are generously offering me everything they can, but I don't want to and can-not keep on asking them."

Then comes one of his first declarations of allegiance: "France has at its head another man who has faith. I am sure of General de Gaulle. I am sure that he will fulfill his mission."

Nice of Malraux to give the General a character reference.

The Malraux unit will be called La Brigade Indépendante Alsace-Lorraine, the Independent Alsace-Lorraine Brigade. Sounds good. The word *brigade* seems imbued with hope, like the International Brigades in Spain. And it is independent: in Spain, the Malraux squadron dealt directly with the War Ministry. Ah! If only the Alsace-Lorraine Brigade could be answerable directly to General de Lattre!

In the middle of September 1944, the brigade moves from the south-west toward Burgundy. The "Metz" Battalion, under the command of Major Charles Pleiss, leaves from Montauban and Souillac in sixteen GMC trucks sent by de Lattre. The "Strasbourg" Battalion, formed from the maquis of the Dordogne and commanded by Ancel, leaves from Périgueux in gazogène charcoal-powered trucks. The brigade has a third battalion: the "Mulhouse," formed with men originally from Alsace and Moselle, gathered from the maquis in Savoie and Haute-Savoie, under the command of René Dopff.

At the end of September, Malraux's 1st Battalion has 19 officers, 99 NCOs, and 366 soldiers; three days later, the 2nd Battalion, 6 officers, 11 NCOs, and 43 men. That's too many officers. In military and political circles in Paris, this brigade is looked on favorably. When the time comes, it will help to win over the "natives" of the two provinces: Alsace and Lorraine will be seen to have liberated themselves. In fact, the brigade also includes combatants from Savoie, Anarchists from Spain, and others. Some of those Spaniards are good with a bazooka. There is a dilemma, however: Alsatian autonomy is not to be encouraged. Paris appreciates that Malraux has flanked himself with Jacquot and Brandstetter, two professional soldiers. The art of command, once again as in Spain, is also that of delegation.

From the outset, the brigade is short of trucks, radio equipment, clothing, and guns. It includes a mixture of recent and long-standing members of the Resistance, a few draft dodgers, deserters from the Wehrmacht, some repatriated French from Switzerland, some hardened maquisards, some *"malgré nous"*—young men from Alsace and Moselle drafted compulsorily by the German Army—and some Spanish Anarchists, who allegedly astonish the officers by preaching discipline without always practicing it. There are many officers in this brigade, but not enough men. Lieutenant Métivier is sent out as a recruiting officer and returns from Bordeaux with "about twenty promises to enlist." Some who do enlist are attracted by the prospect of joining a "commando" unit: the word smells of shock troops and adventure but in fact is just the brigade's name for companies.

Both the veterans and the greenhorns lack the necessary training for a conventional war. Half the new recruits have no helmet. The brigade has Bren guns, Thompson submachine guns, Lebel rifles, revolvers, Czech and Polish weapons. It is the writer André Chamson's job to find ammunition for all these, a task for which L'École des Chartes, the National School of Archival Studies and Paleography, has ill prepared him. They have no artillery, not even mortars. Luckily, the Americans like to swap and will happily exchange a modern rifle, the Garant semiautomatic, for a good vintage Lebel, a German pistol, or a bottle of fruit brandy. The extraordinary Malraux and his deputies manage to put together a combat unit in which most of the men are late additions and have neither theoretical nor practical training in combat situations involving tanks and aircraft. Some of the officers and NCOs make the best of what they have picked up from books or can salvage from rusty memories of 1940 or earlier.

De Lattre knows Chamson, which helps persuade him to accept the Alsace-Lorraine Brigade, despite a few conservative grumbles at staff headquarters. From September 27, 1944, for ten days, the 1,200 men of the Malraux brigade fight in the Vosges, an area that de Lattre says "is eating a lot of men." Until October 28, the brigade's three battalions are brought in to support the 1st Armored Division on the western foothills of the Ballon de Servance. Thirty-two men are killed. The brigade has to

back up tanks, a dangerous operation for infantrymen. The members of
the brigade quickly learn the rudimentary tactics: the tank is deaf and
blind, the foot soldier has mobility. . . . At least that's what they tell the
foot soldiers. To tank crews they explain that the pedestrians in the infantry are an easy target.

Lieutenant Colonel Jacquot blocks the German counterattacks. He
teaches his beginners the art of mopping up, but not without losses under
the dense barrage of German fire. The recruits have to get used to the
fearsome curved trajectory of enemy mortars. The men see many more
dead and wounded than in their maquis groups. After one engagement,
Major Diener (Ancel) realizes that out of a section of forty men, in the
space of a few minutes, five have been killed and six wounded without
even having caught sight of a German. "Rough stuff," he writes. Having
enough helmets to go around would have helped.

Malraux has the same problem as he did in Spain: How to transform
semicivilian combatants into professional soldiers? There are basic combat "classes," where they learn more than the art of saluting a superior; but
these are not sufficient. Morale is important: it must be carefully maintained. Thanks to two Catholic chaplains, Bockel and Bonnat, and two
ministers, Weiss and Frantz, morale stays high for most of the men. Some
three hundred choose to leave, calling a truce to this unforeseen war.
They are not deserters: no undertaking was signed committing them for
the duration of the war. Then the numbers are reinforced. On November
12, an order from the War Ministry allocates "600 men as reinforcements
for the brigade, including 10% officers." In the towns and villages they
pass, the brigade puts up posters.

DO YOU WANT TO SERVE

IN THE

ALSACE-LORRAINE BRIGADE?

YOU WILL FIND:

DEPORTEES, ESCAPEES,

PRISONERS OF THE GESTAPO,

REFUGEES,

MAQUISARDS FROM ALL

REGIONS OF FRANCE,

LEADERS,

ALL VOLUNTEERS.

Malraux allows boys of sixteen and seventeen to join, without
hesitation.[3]

His men do not have enough gloves, socks, shoes, or lined boots, and they lack transmission equipment for communications between battalions, "commando" companies, sections, and groups. Food distribution is bad: a hungry fighter, whether a maquisard or a regular, will quickly turn to looting. Malraux's headquarters requests, then insists, then begs. At the end of the year, General de Montsabert asks General de Lattre in person "for the 1,200 men of the Alsace-Lorraine Brigade, 150 complete sets of kit, 500 shirts, 300 pairs of shoes + 500 pairs of socks." In the margin of his request, Montsabert writes for de Lattre: "As per personal promise on your part." One officer cadet begs to be supplied with thirty-one rifles, two machine guns, and five submachine guns. He gets eleven rifles and five submachine guns. Compared with the troops of the First French Army, who are kitted out in the American style, Berger and Jacquot's men seem like heroic beggars or the international volunteers in Spain.

The fighting in the Vosges, at Bois-le-Prince, showed that the men of the brigade have plenty of enthusiasm but little know-how. Jacquot explains it in a report to Malraux: they have "brio in attack" but many losses are due simply to "being crammed together." Real training in the line of fire is better than rehearsing movements and firing blanks. But they have not had the apprenticeship that other Allied forces had in North Africa or Great Britain. They are learning on the terrain of the real war, confronting hardened German soldiers and miliciens. Moreover, the tanks the brigade is supporting are Shermans, which are inferior to the German Tigers. Some men of the Corrèze company fight in shorts or combat clothes and flat shoes. But they have strong discipline; they don't fire at random.

"*Le péril approchait, leur brigade était prête,*"[4] Malraux hums with them.

His men buzz around American depots. They siphon gasoline, swipe K rations, discover Spam wrapped in ingenious little greaseproof cardboard boxes, vitamin-enriched chocolate, packets of instant coffee, packs of five cigarettes—in short, the fundamentals of American militaroculinary civilization and its concern for the comfort of its soldiers. Often, if there is not enough time to sort through its contents, a whole Jeep or truck full of provisions will be stolen and sold: it's a lot quicker. The American soldiers are in a hurry. The brigade is referred to—with fondness or with irritation—as "brigade brigands" or "Colonel Malraux's very Christian brigade."

His soldiers know the colonel likes to drink, in a manly way, even ordinary red wine; more so the whisky bought from the Americans. When speaking to his troops, Malraux still has a taste for grandiose phrases: "I salute your dead, those of today and those of tomorrow."

That casts a chill among the ranks. Malraux is living at epic pitch.

The colonel often talks theology in the presence of his priests and ministers. He generally keeps off the military terrain with Jacquot and Brandstetter. At daily meetings of his majors and captains, he goes over the broad strategic lines, after giving a bulletin on what is happening politically in Europe and the rest of the world that helps to situate the brigade's battles in a wider context. He seems more at ease monitoring worldwide strategy than tackling unit formation for an attack on Hill 212. He leaves the tactical bread and butter to the professionals. The odd lecture about Wellington's strategy at Waterloo to one side, he seems to know where his military incompetence begins.

The brigade, with never more than twenty Dodge trucks, still has serious transport problems. The men march. A lot, like most infantrymen. The majority of them admire their colonel. Very few of them have read Malraux. In his tight fur-lined jacket, topped off with a beret, he seems to know no fear. He walks on the front line and even, with Jacquot (wounded three times), in front of the French lines.

From November 23 to 27, 1944, the brigade is sent, in a support role, to join the 5th Armored Division and strengthen the breakthrough of the First Army between Switzerland and the Vosges. A checkpoint on the Belfort-to-Mulhouse road costs them eighteen lives.

The brigade lines up its three battalions, Metz, Mulhouse, and Strasbourg, now numbering 1,400. Whatever their region of origin, the soldiers sing:

Vous n'aurez pas l'Alsace et la Lorraine!

But also, because of those from different provinces:

C'est nous les Alsaciens
Qui v'nons de loin
Nous v'nons d'la Haute-Savoie
Pour libérer l'pays
Roulez tambours
À nos amours . . .[5]

Officers smile and join the chorus. As with any military unit, stories are embedded in the brigade's collective memory. A former pupil of the Saint-Cyr Military Academy shouted out to his men (so the story goes):
"Come on lads, forward!"
"Go on yourself!"
He stood up:
"I'll show you how you die at twenty-five."
While charging toward a farm, he was shot by an SS who was pre-

tending to give himself up.[6] Captain Peltre was later killed carrying helmets to the soldiers on the front line.

On November 12, Malraux receives a telegram from Saint-Chamant. Josette, accompanying her mother to the station, has fallen under a train, crushing her legs. While waiting for Malraux in hospital, she put on makeup. Before she died, Josette apparently murmured, "Nasty Clara."

Malraux rushes to Saint-Chamant. On the way back he passes through Paris, leaving his two sons with the notary Delclaux and his wife, the beautiful Rosine. He sees his sister-in-law, Madeleine, and drops in at the editorial office of *Combat*,[7] where he chats with Pascal Pia, the editor, and Albert Camus, the writer of well-known columns.

Charles de Gaulle, accompanied by Winston Churchill, inspects the Lorraine front on November 13. Bernard Metz overhears a discussion between Malraux and Jacquot: Can the brigade parade in front of this right-wing general?[8]

The brigade fights fiercely. Against excellent German troops, it takes the town of Dannemarie. Novelistic history and historical novels seem to have a standing appointment with Malraux. Today, veterans from the brigade (their memories sometimes embellished like Malraux's) remember attacking an armored train, just as in *L'Espoir*. In fact, they came across a goods train, fitted with a few sheets of armor plating, defended by some Russians who had been conscripted with the Germans. The taking of Dannemarie costs the brigade eighteen KIA and more than a hundred wounded.

The nights are freezing: five below zero Fahrenheit. The watch is reduced to a half hour. These men deserve their pack of cigarettes at Christmas.

At the end of December, the Germans launch a counteroffensive between Luxembourg and the Rhine. To shorten the front, General Dwight D. Eisenhower, supreme commander of the Allied forces in Europe, wants to shrink the defense lines, move back on the Vosges, and evacuate Strasbourg—which is just another town to him. De Gaulle and de Lattre reject this decision. Strasbourg is too symbolic. Malraux comments (or was it de Lattre?): "We'll make it another Stalingrad, if that's what it takes."

Not a very appropriate image, considering that those surrounded in Stalingrad were wiped out, and for nothing.

The brigade is sent forward, on its own, as the avant-garde of the First French Army, to Strasbourg. General Leclerc's 2nd Armored Division, integrated into the Seventh American Army, is due to retreat from Strasbourg in accordance with the Allied plan of action.

Lieutenant Michel Holl's logbook gives an account of the climate in the "commandos" of the brigade:

Sunday, November 26, 1944.

On alert at 1300 leave 1400 to clear a wood on outskirts of Aspach, liberated since noon by a tank unit and the Legion. At 1445 at 500 m from Aspach on a minor dirt track the chasseur Zundel Henri blown up on a booby-trapped antitank mine. Originally from Thann, he was a few km from home. He had not seen his parents for 4 years. At the entrance to Aspach a burned-out tank and some legionnaires' corpses. The commando enters Aspach, strewn with abandoned German equipment. Takes up position beyond Aspach at the edge of the wood to be cleared at around 1500. At 1515, zero hour for the start of the maneuver, we receive counterorders and the order to return to Altkirch. Order is carried out around 1600.

State of alert still in force for the commando, and I must refuse requests for a few hours' leave to young soldiers who are a few km from home. Among others, Corporal Hell, who has not seen his mother for 5 years. He would fall the following morning, his head taken off by a shell explosion. New departure takes place midnight.[9]

Despite repeated attacks from about forty German tanks, including Tigers, Strasbourg holds out. Malraux gets to participate in the defense of Strasbourg. Intuition, savoir-faire, courage, luck, and glory. The Alsace-Lorraine Brigade has helped defend the honor of France. Even the general officers who are least sympathetic to Berger-Malraux—the adventurer, the amateur—acknowledge that his brigade fights well. A few weeks later, the advance almost turns into a pleasant stroll.

Saint-Exupéry is dead, having disappeared with his plane over the Mediterranean. Malraux becomes the most famous fighting French writer. In France, as in Spain, he is sought out by reporters and photographers. A noncommissioned officer in the brigade takes a picture of Malraux in a fur-lined jacket, beret with five stripes on the badge, cigarette in his right hand, with a serious look but the hint of a smile at the edges of his mouth. The colonel-writer is delighted with this photo. He asks the NCO to lend him the negative for his "press service." Malraux is quick to perceive the importance of such a service.

After the liberation of Strasbourg, Colonel Berger remains at the head of his brigade, which has seen 1,712 men pass through it from September 1944 to February 1945. In conversation, Malraux has a tendency to round that figure up. He attends the first Mass in Strasbourg Cathedral. Bockel reads the homily. Pleased though he is to enter Germany with the victory procession, Malraux soon seems to lose interest in military problems. At last he is part of a victory over Nazism. Politics claims him again.

From the time spent in his "Inter-Allied Headquarters," he drew at least one political conclusion: the Communists, via the FTP and the PCF, made a determined effort to infiltrate the Resistance bodies all over France, and now, when they can, they are penetrating those of the state. Returning to Paris on January 23, 1945, Malraux attends the conference of the Mouvement de Libération Nationale. The MLN wants to coordinate the activities of its constituent Resistance movements. The Communists within those organizations, in a generously ecumenical move—quite touching, really—want to melt down all the movements into one. The resulting physical proximity should bring about an ideological osmosis and, indirectly, obedience to the Soviet leaders, who insist on "national" fronts everywhere. Malraux can see what is happening. The USSR and the Red Army are highly rated at this time. Whoever shows a shade of doubt is immediately accused by the PCF machine of "blatant anticommunism."

Malraux finds himself speaking again in the Mutualité rooms where he spoke so often before the war. Now he is no longer a Communist sympathizer (which earns him a rapid disappearance from the Soviet encyclopedias). There are hardly any uniforms in the stalls or the circle of the Mutualité: Malraux, in his, is an imposing presence.

He would like to see a new party, which could benefit from "democratic" centralism, but without the Communists. The conference participants who have observed the Communists at work during the Resistance, and do not get Stalin and Churchill confused, applaud the orator-colonel throughout. Malraux doesn't explain how, in his new party, a level of discipline could be established to equal that of the PCF. In passing comments on the new press, where Right and Left have been engaging in personalized insults, Malraux calls for moderation from journalists and editorial writers: "We can attack doctrines as much as we like, but we must not attack people." This is no longer the polemicist of *L'Indochine* in Saigon. Politeness and firmness in elegance come, if not with wisdom, at least with age.

He broaches the principal issue of the conference. He thinks he knows that there is a crushing majority in the hall who are against the proposed fusion. General hubbub. There are protests from the auditorium: a vote will decide the issue. Malraux finishes his speech, addressing his audience as Camarades where he started with Messieurs and proposing a new watchword: "A new resistance is beginning." (Prolonged applause.)

The message for the participants is that the MLN must oppose the

Communists. A motion is proposed stating clearly that the MLN must proceed with "no organic fusion with a political movement or party." If the motion is successful, it implies a woolly federation at the national level in order to accommodate the Communist goat and the MLN cabbage successfully. Malraux's motion is carried with 250 votes to 119, no abstentions. The party executives at the heart of the management committee announce an unusual supplementary motion: in order to preserve their liberty of action, several members pledge not to seek a mandate from the voters. The clause suits Malraux, who is not interested in the electoral process. The unity of organizational action preached patiently by the Communists is thwarted. For the first time since before the war, Malraux has taken an extreme political position, in public. His maneuvering between political trends during his time in the Resistance has been useful. When he buttered up the Communist-sympathizing FTP in the departments he wanted to conquer (to no avail), they rejected him out of hand. Now he is resisting the Communists who resisted him.

At the Mutualité, he appears to be a firm Gaullist. After the conference, he distances himself from the MLN. He is usually absent from the meetings of the management committee and after a while drops out.

Returning to the front, Malraux begins six hours of conversation with journalist and essayist Roger Stéphane. During the Liberation, Stéphane had assisted in the capture of the Hôtel de Ville in the heart of Paris.[10] Malraux is on top form in the interviews. A few little untruths slip out: he states that the Germans stole from him the second volume of *La Lutte avec l'ange*, which he never wrote. On his Mutualité speech—Stéphane has the text, printed in *Combat* by Pia, in his hands—Malraux is clear. He could have been president of the MLN, he claims. The daily byline of *Combat* is "De la Résistance à la Révolution." Malraux says that one cannot wage war and revolution at the same time. He suggests with jovial pessimism that perhaps France should adopt "Anglo-Saxon" socialism.

"The best thing for the French would be a Labour Party."

When those who have been shut up in prison camps return, Stéphane asks, will they bring fresh revolutionary blood to France? Malraux's commonsense prediction is that "They will be too happy to be returning to their wives and bicycles."

And the big problem of the MLN conference, the Communist attempt on the MLN itself?

"I am not still wet behind the ears. Thirty Communists from the management committee of the F[ront] N[ational], plus eight concealed among us, makes thirty-eight out of sixty. I've nothing against an alliance, I just don't want to be robbed."

What is Malraux's perception of his officers from the Alsace-Lorraine Brigade? Intelligent? Eccentrics? Technicians? There is a bit of everything. Stéphane is concerned that Malraux might be slipping toward fascism. At this time, Stéphane is on the left and sees in Gaullism the threat of a Caesarist dictatorship. He quotes *L'Espoir*: "A man who is active and pessimistic at the same time is or will be a fascist, unless he has loyalty behind him."

Malraux: "I have this loyalty behind me: my loyalty is dynamiting."

The writer confirms that he does not keep a diary: "Diaries are for people who like to contemplate their past."

Poor Gide, author of the most famous French diary of the century. For the questionable benefit of biographers and textbooks, Malraux decrees that his *Le Temps du mépris* is, in his view, rubbish (*un navet*). When pushed by Stéphane, Colonel Berger returns to an obsession of his: torture. He describes the atmosphere of Saint-Michel prison in Toulouse, before his release. Stéphane wants details: "What do you call torture?"

"There were two sorts. The first was strappado. The arms of the victim were tied behind his back, and he was dropped from a gallows and flattened against the ground. If he didn't talk, it was the bath. . . . One day, a man was being ducked in the bath for the fourth time (the fourth session, you understand). His hands and feet were tied. They were about to push his head under the water when the German typist rushed toward him with this Dostoevskyan outburst, in a thick German accent: 'Schpeak, mister, schpeak! I gan't pear zis any more!' That man told me that even if it took him his whole life, he would find her. He hated her as I have never seen someone hate. Then one day the FFI came and liberated the prison. I had not yet been tortured." Should we infer from this last remark that Malraux was tortured? Or just that perhaps he was going to be tortured? The second interpretation is both less unpleasant and more likely. Apart from this occasion, Malraux never claimed to have been tortured.

The next day Malraux describes to Stéphane the Battle of Dannemarie. "What strikes me," notes Stéphane, "is that Malraux admires his men. He admires them even more than he likes them. One can sense that they have impressed him." Malraux confides that he is going to write a book on the Resistance. Stéphane, like his interviewee, is as much interested in literature as in politics.

"For me," says Malraux, "the three best writers of this generation are Montherlant, Giono, and Bernanos." He announces that he refuses to contribute to *Les Temps Modernes*, Sartre's monthly review.

"Do you know what they are going to do?" asks Stéphane.

"Yes, I saw the preview issue. It is going to be extraordinarily unliterary, antiliterary, and just very boring. For an article to strike Sartre as worth reading for the purposes of publication, it has to be at least four hundred pages long."

At Gerstheim, from January 7 to 10, two hundred men from the Verdun and Valmy groups, commanded by Ancel, fought for three days and three nights. They had to abandon the town to the Germans. With all its material weaknesses, the Alsace-Lorraine Brigade fought with all its might and held a front of about 25 miles from a point level with Erstein to Rhinau, south of Strasbourg. They had to face Tigers and Jagdpanthers, the best tanks in the war after the Soviet T34s. With the Battle of Strasbourg over, the First Army troops cross the Rhine.[11]

On February 23, the brigade has 78 officers and 900 NCOs, as well as the troops. On March 15, the Independent Alsace-Lorraine Brigade is quietly disbanded. In September 1944, the War Ministry had approved a clause whereby the brigade's volunteers were engaged only until such time as Alsace and Lorraine was liberated. Some men were demobilized and returned to civilian life; others re-enlisted in the 3rd Demi-brigade de Chasseurs, under the orders of Pierre Jacquot, promoted to colonel. In Spain, the Malraux squadron was absorbed by the Republican Air Force; in France, the regular army swallows up the Alsace-Lorraine Brigade. For the writer-colonel, the brigade has been a success. Without him, it would not have achieved the recognition it did, alongside so many units that remained anonymous. Colonel Berger was the impressive leader and impresario of his brigade, which allowed him—at last—to participate in a war as a victor.

Malraux appears again as a man of cycles. During his bungling adventure in Cambodia, he floundered like a literary fish on dry land; the experience, on a human scale, was a negative one. The positive period of *L'Indochine* and *L'Indochine Enchaînée* followed. In the same way, Colonel Berger's 1944 Resistance was, at best, ill defined, and at worst, a failure. But the battles of the Alsace-Lorraine Brigade have been an epic success. When all is totted up, the brigade did not suffer excessive losses: 63 killed, about 225 wounded, and around 60 prisoners taken. Malraux and his seconds did not waste the lives of their men. In Magnin-Berger-Malraux there appears over the years a manic-depressive character, with successive strong and weak phases. Writing, for Malraux, is worth as much as being, doing, and acting. What can the writer, at forty-four years of age, draw from the escapades, adventures, and Colonel Berger's finest hours?

Tous le Quant à Soi

CHAPTER TWENTY-FOUR

History, Legend, Novel

FTER THE LIBERATION, Malraux has his military service vali-
dated: his file consists of twenty-seven pages.[1] Malraux fills some
of it in himself, which is not the way it is usually done. For the
civilian part, under the heading "Education," he declares himself to have a
Ph.D.: "Docteur ès lettres. H.C. [honoris causa]." He does not claim, this
time, to have a diploma from the École des Langues Orientales. The
"Identity" section gives him a "two-part campaign, from April 15, 1940, to
August 20, 1944, and from the 21st of the same month to August 20,
1945." The document justifying this double campaign is a certificate of
membership of the Resistance, drawn up by Malraux himself, with annotations in his own handwriting, declaring that he participated in the
"Resistance from December 1940 onward." According to this document,
he was in "complete illegality" for fairly long periods. No details, just one
arrow labeled "November 1942" and another, "1943."

Under the heading "Organized Resistance," one reads "Nov 42 Combat Group" and "Maquis Corrèze-Dordogne-Lot (interregional delegate)." Then: "FFI, brigade of 400 to 4,000 men, depending on date."
The following feats of arms are mentioned: "Organization of dynamiting
of Central sector . . . Attack of Das Reich Division, Battle of Dannemarie,
commander of the southern sector of Strasbourg." In this file, which is
very lightweight for a superior officer, Malraux refers endlessly to his decorations. In support of the Legion of Honor pinned onto his uniform by
General de Lattre in person in Stuttgart,[2] there is a decree from General
de Gaulle dated August 19, 1945. Quote: "Organizer of the armed Resistance in the departments of Corrèze, the Dordogne, and the Lot." Malraux also has another significant decoration, the Distinguished Service
Order (DSO).

"January 1948. Promotion to the order of the DSO. Colonel Malraux organized guerrilla battles on a large scale against the German forces in his area, leading his troops into battle personally on all occasions [false]. His command and his courage under fire gained him the respect [half true] and the admiration not only of his own soldiers but of the British officers who fought alongside him."[3]

The passage detailing the grounds for Malraux's British decoration:

"This French officer was one of the first leaders of the French Resistance in South West France [false]. . . . In the Autumn of 1943 [false], he joined a British liaison officer and helped construct a powerful organization in Corrèze and the Dordogne: he also trained several groups in the Lot, where he worked with another British officer [Poirier, "Captain Jack"?].

"In May 1944, Lieutenant Colonel Malraux was appointed regional commander of the FFI [absolutely false]. Thanks to his tact, judgment, and personality, he triumphed over political rivalries and personal jealousies in the area, and in consequence his FFI achievements in Corrèze and the Dordogne were outstanding. [Here tribute is paid to Malraux the diplomat, who nevertheless did not manage to federate the various organizations.]

"He was wounded and taken prisoner . . . but escaped [false] three weeks later in time to direct final operations for the liberation of his region [quite wrong]. Having done this, Malraux took the leadership of a battalion in the Dordogne [the brigade seems to have melted into a battalion]. . . .

"This French officer merits the highest praise for his indefatigable efforts made in facilitation of the task of the Allied armies in France [quite right].

[The payoff:] "We heartily recommend that Lieutenant Colonel Malraux become a Companion of the Distinguished Service Order."

The Malraux legend is, in part, legitimized by his DSO; the British, despite themselves, are responsible. It is usual for facts to be "enhanced" in military mentions, but rarely to this extent.[4] The embellishment is not due to the British agents who were working around Malraux. The Americans didn't fall, it seems, for Malraux as a Resistance leader.

Malraux's file also details a lightning-fast retroactive rise through the ranks. A proposal dated June 1, 1945, has him made second lieutenant,

lieutenant, captain, major (*chef de bataillon*), and lieutenant colonel. Many officers from the Resistance were recognized in this way, their situation regularized, but few at that speed. Malraux is promoted to the rank of colonel of the FFI (No. 4465) by the Commission Nationale d'Homologation des Grades FFI on July 13, 1945. (This commission file has disappeared.) Malraux's rank is set at second lieutenant dating from January 1, 1939—which is before he was drafted as a private in the infantry. The same day, he takes the rank of lieutenant. He is promoted to captain on January 1, 1941, to major on January 1, 1943, to lieutenant colonel on June 1, 1945. A decree, countersigned on July 26, 1945, by Charles de Gaulle and War Minister Diethelm for the provisional government of the French Republic, makes the whole thing official. Malraux is appointed *Compagnon de la Libération*, nominated by Colonel Rebattet (alias Cheval), deputy to the commander in chief of the 1st French army, General de Lattre. Rebattet, an honest and naive man, cites three wounds Malraux supposedly received, allowing Malraux to return to these wounds as a leitmotif later on.[5] Rebattet also exaggerates the quality of Malraux's involvement, referring to him as "FFI Commando." The commandos, like the air force, paratroopers, and tank men, were considered elite troops.

Malraux is also decorated with the Croix de la Libération, the Médaille de la Résistance, and the Croix de Guerre.[6] There are complaints from high-ranking officers. Not just Pétain supporters, either: on December 7, 1951, the army corps general Jean Imbert, inspector of Defense Zone D, writes to the secretary of state for war, "I believe it to be my duty respectfully to draw your attention to the particular case of this FFI officer." Imbert points out that "the Resistance activity of Mr. Malraux took place not on a regional level but on an interregional level."

On December 20, 1951, Colonel de Bélenet, chief of the Sixième Bureau, asks André Malraux for "a certificate from a resistant of officer class and on whom the group that you commanded directly depended." On January 15, 1952, Malraux replies, "The only officer under whose orders I found myself, before being part of the First Army, was General Koenig. Lieutenant Colonel (now Major General) Jacquot will be happy to supply further documents, but he was at the time my deputy and not my superior. Moreover, I think that the mentions enclosed will give you everything you may need." Note in the margin of this letter: "Keep General Jacquot informed."

March 14, 1952: The same Colonel de Bélenet writes again to Malraux: "Following a telephone conversation with Major General Jacquot, it emerges that the first meeting of your interzonal headquarters apparently took place in May 1943." The secretary of state for war provides a certificate of membership to the FFI.[7] Nothing abnormal about that. Malraux is not the only one, in one way or another, to have joined the maquisards a few weeks before the Allied landings in Normandy. But Colonel de Bélenet, only doing his job, asks insistently for the exact date of a meeting mentioned by Malraux (that of May 2, 1943) and what it consisted of. The conscientious colonel would like to be in possession of the "names of those who were present." He makes several meticulous requests for "precise details." The writer refers to his medals: the authority method. How dare this flea, Bélenet, rummage through Malraux's lion's mane? It is in Malraux and Jacquot's best interest to throw a veil of doubt over the year 1943. They give each other predated mutual certificates of good conduct and membership in the Resistance.

Malraux's file, at least from the point of view of the military authorities, has huge gaps in it. Who authorized the writer to fill it in himself? Which British and French officials were unable or unwilling to correct some of the sizable errors? Why was Malraux promoted so easily despite these annotations: "Unable to determine due to lack of information" and "Still unanswered"? Was there one injury or several? Only Malraux's medical file—which has disappeared—could authenticate the injuries. Malraux, at any rate, is obsessed with his own nonexistent war wounds.

Malraux's autobiographical manipulations place him on a pedestal of decorated notoriety. First of all, this Compagnon de la Libération. He was honored by Charles de Gaulle. Who would dare, in public or administrative circles, to question the judgment of Le Libérateur? Malraux is a Compagnon de la Libération and received the Médaille de la Résistance, therefore, he must have been an exceptional liberator and an important member of the Resistance. They don't make just anybody a Compagnon. Here, effect precedes cause in a curious stretch of space-time where chronology is reversed.

Clara Malraux, thinking of Roland, Claude, and others who have been deported and never return, those who have not been showered with medals and commendations, says cruelly about André, "It is the others who get themselves killed."

But one cannot reproach the writer for not being dead. In Spain and on the Alsace front, he took risks. In Corrèze and the Dordogne too, but not the ones he said. In his military record, a few simple words, chosen out of haste or negligence, can suggest a fragment of an epic. The phrase "in the course of an ambush" refers to August 22, 1944, when Malraux was shot at and arrested near Gramat. Meeting the Wehrmacht by chance is not the same thing as falling into an ambush. An ambush, strictly speaking, is an active operation in which troops are hidden to surprise the enemy.

Even involuntary errors on dates help to set the Malrucian legend in stone, without those responsible having thought to rectify them. In his French military record, Malraux was "taken prisoner on August 22, 1944." For the English who give him the DSO, the Germans took him on "23rd July." One can only marvel that investigations to reconstitute a serious military career should have been undertaken so frivolously. In fact, the Gramat episode started on July 22. No matter.

Malraux himself distributes certificates liberally and kindly. He signs one for the husband of the charming Rosine, the notary Franck Delclaux. Malraux, "head of the interregional mission Corrèze-Dordogne-Lot," certifies that Mr. Franck Delclaux "was attached to [his] particular headquarters from before June 6, 1944, with the rank of second lieutenant, assigned to: departmental and interdepartmental liaison; organization and recruitment; parachute drops in liaison with the AS forces of Corrèze." Rosine Delclaux is Vincent's godmother. This certificate of accreditation is essentially a family matter. The notary had many qualities, but not military ones and not of this order.

Do all these attestations, decorations, inquiries, and contradictions count in the eyes of History? The essential point, for the writer, is elsewhere. To do or to have done is so much less important than to write, to create. Imagination on its own is an accreditation.

Following the success that his film *Sierra de Teruel* has had with the critics—it receives the Louis Delluc Prize after the Liberation—Malraux mutters that he would like to make a film about the Resistance. He tells friends and acquaintances, such as Marc Chagall, that he is going to write a novel about it. This novel, he says, "will be [to the Resistance] what *L'Espoir* was to Spain."

He has started the project several times without success. Novelistic inspiration has not turned up. The dense, ambitious *Les Noyers de l'Altenburg* is not as good as the prewar fiction. Malraux is no longer inspired in this genre. Yet he thinks on about this Resistance novel. The provisional title is *Non*—the response his men gave to Nazism and Vichy.

Malraux sketches six scenes, in which he talks a lot about himself. These fragments take place before the Liberation. The story starts in Paris, in a black-market bistro on the Left Bank. The author describes the scene hesitantly: "Below, a Métro entrance. Members of the Resistance will be alone in this room papered in black and garnet up to and including the ceiling in: a box."

Then this bizarre phrase: "The Resistance is often unreal [*irréelle*]." Can we, dare we interpret that to mean that "Malraux's Resistance was in large part unreal"? Semihistorical, semi-imaginary characters figure. Serge *Ra*vanel, who exists, becomes *Ra*guze. Malraux cannot quite manage the transposition, still immersed in the heat of the experience as he is.

The alchemy fails. These first scenes take place after the arrest of General Delestraint and, significantly, that of Jean Moulin, alias "Rex" or "Max," which was a great blow to the Resistance. In *Non*, we also come across Fouché, alias Marcel Degliame, a powerful member of the Resistance. Colonel Berger arrives in person, with his customary modesty: "The risks of the Resistance are familiar to Berger."

Malraux-Berger reflects: "Berger thinks: What if the Gestapo were to break in? We will be taken sooner or later before the landings. . . . The networks will survive, but not their leaders." And again from Berger: "I do not like to talk about what a man may say under torture."

Ever since Andrée Viollis told him about the heroic deeds of the French policemen during their interrogations in Cochin China, since *Le Temps du mépris* and *L'Espoir*, Malraux has been going back to "the problems of interrogation." Berger is told that he must make a request to the Gaullist organizations for cyanide for everybody:

> "Those of us who are friendly with the British, you, Berger, for example, should ask for some too."
> "Yes," says Berger, very reasonably.[8]

At least once in his life, Malraux sees himself as a reasonable man! Malraux-Berger is presented as a veteran of the Resistance. Rex (Jean Moulin) is arrested and needs to be replaced. It is clear that Rex's successor will be . . . Colonel Berger: "Berger will be there tomorrow."

Malraux's ambition in the Dordogne and Périgord was to be at the top. An honorable enough goal, and one he was conscious of harboring. From this point forward, for many years, he dreams of being at the top in France. A novel could get him there. In *Non*, Malraux wants to portray Berger as a boss: "Berger had given the order to his maquis leaders . . ."— notice the plural—"these men, under his personal command, attacked armored German divisions with bazookas." How many? Two? Three? Ten? In another scene, Malraux-Berger comes across Violette, SOE agent and heroine, who did exist.

Raymond Maréchal was killed during the Resistance. As Gardet, he was already used as a character in *L'Espoir*, and it is as Gardet again that he is resuscitated in a sketch of the second scene of *Non*. He visits "Tante Marie" in a housing estate. Marie is a common enough name, but André's aunt was called Marie Lamy and lived in a housing estate in the Fifteenth Arrondissement. Malraux worms himself into Gardet, who, in this draft, brought back textiles from Persia. Gardet manages a network and asks Tante Marie to take in "one of his chaps with a radio set."

Unhappy with this version, Malraux writes another. This time,

Gardet's aunt becomes Tatouche and Gardet an English agent named Jacques. Philippe Liewer, perhaps, or Captain Jack? The scene takes place this time at Rue des Saints-Pères in the Sixth Arrondissement, which is more chic than the Fifteenth. Malraux met an SOE-F agent at Rue des Saints-Pères before joining the Resistance. Tatouche has a lady's maid, and her husband has a racing stable. Malraux writes, "Jacques paces up and down the sitting room (should one say sitting room?), a glass of port in his hand." What a good nephew André is to give his aunt a social promotion.

The narrator says to the aunt: "If you were asked to house a radio transmitter here, what would you say?"

"What would you expect me to say? Go and put it in the café on the corner?"

Silence.

"Thank you," said Jacques. "All the same, are you still friends with Drieu?"

"Remember that I am proud of not becoming angry with any of my former lovers . . ." She laughs. "Drieu is all very well, but he thinks what he thinks, and I think what I think."

"You know the risks?"

Becomes tedious: "Just why are you with us? Because we are Jewish, you and I?"

Philippe Liewer's aunt, Alice Jean-Alley, lived at 7 Rue des Saints-Pères, and her husband was Jewish. They hid a radio transmitter under their roof.

Malraux, quite rightly, is not satisfied with these scenes. The writer in him resurfaces when he starts on a sequence in the maquis with the liaison officer Gardet and an English radio operator. Now Gardet comes directly out of *L'Espoir*: we hear that "he fought on the Ebro." He looks more and more like Maréchal: he has "a dip in his forehead as big as your fist." Snapshots from *L'Espoir* and *Sierra de Teruel*—where the disfigured airman was tempted to commit suicide—seem to overlap each other here but are out of focus, like bad photos.

The few surviving fragments of *Non* are touching. We can feel Malraux on the verge of taking off; then he breaks down, remains grounded, crashes onto the paper. His taste for grandiloquence returns. True, it is still at the stage of a rough draft, but he lets in clichés: "the secular night"; "the maquis have no past"; "the Romanesque church watches the evening fall as it has done for eight hundred years." Malraux is trying to do his job as a writer, churning through reality to create a rich and poignant literary universe. This time he fails.

He is always looking to bring characters from other novels back to life. When he published *Les Conquérants* and *La Voie royale*, he promised a trilogy. At the beginning of the Second World War, his baroque novel *Les Noyers de l'Altenburg* was supposed to be the first volume of a series, *La Lutte avec l'ange*. But—oh yes, that's it—the manuscript of the second volume was taken by the Gestapo.[9] Was *Non* going to be one of the volumes, lashed to *L'Espoir* or *Les Noyers de l'Altenburg*? At least three times in his life, he had a desire to complete novels organically linked to one another by resurfacing characters. His imagination is just not up to it; his lifestyle and his other literary preoccupations—needing to finish up works on art, also planned as a trilogy—do not lend themselves to it. Besides, he is not Balzac, Galsworthy, Tolstoy, Proust, Martin du Gard, nor even Georges Duhamel or Jules Romains: he is attracted by too many domains. What is missing most from *Non* is that he is not driven by a profound, authentic, lived experience, as he was when writing *La Voie royale* and *L'Espoir.* His Resistance experience was not real enough. He did not have a leading role in the maquis, and he arrived late on set. His was an excellent supporting role, a Pirandellian character bustling about in the middle of a play-within-a-play, where words about the Resistance replaced action. Is it surprising, then, that in this unfinished, barely started *Non*, he should qualify the Resistance as having been "unreal"?

For Malraux, two worlds are more real than the tangible world: literature and art. He asks questions and, more rarely, talks to others about them. Jean Grosjean:

> From 1951 onward, Malraux asked me many times over the years, at point-blank range, if after fifty years, one may write "I" without the reader thinking that it means oneself. . . . In fictional characters, one can put a part of oneself (the best or the worst, what one would like to have been or what one fears to become, and so on). These are fragments of a human truth that we give to the reader. But writing in the first person, even in the role of a spectator, is recklessness or bravery; one is never quite as one says. If you blacken your own character, you degrade the reader. If you raise yourself up, you cast yourself in the role of messiah (to resolve to do that, you need a storm inside you).[10]

Malraux often thinks of making a film about the Alsace-Lorraine Brigade, rather than the Resistance. He would doubtless have made more of a success of it than the stillborn *Non*. Fiction, through the novel or the cinema, remains his major creative temptation.

CHAPTER TWENTY-FIVE

Civilian Life

T HE WAR OVER, Malraux feels that army life is not for him. It's not
his style to occupy Germany or enjoy the beauty of Lake Con-
stance. A disordered purge among French intellectuals takes place
at the hands of the National Writers' Committee, in a move to seize intellectual power for the PCF. Malraux doesn't join in.

Drieu escaped the purge by committing suicide on March 15, 1945.
He may have asked Malraux to accept him in his Alsace-Lorraine Brigade,
possibly under a pseudonym.[1] A few months before, he noted in his journal, "I have always had confidence in Malraux." Paul Nizan had foreseen
that "Drieu will die alone." Malraux looks after his ex-colleague's work.
Armed with an expandable suitcase to carry manuscripts, he turns up at
Drieu's brother's apartment: "Come on, let's do the rounds of his lady
friends."

In April 1945, Colonel Malraux goes to Stuttgart to receive a fourth
mention for his Croix de Guerre from de Lattre (nicknamed "Roi Jean").
On May 8, still in uniform, Malraux attends the Te Deum in Strasbourg
Cathedral. In the first row of the congregation sits Charles de Gaulle, his
face impenetrably "closed," as at most ceremonies, religious or not.

De Gaulle's first meeting with Malraux happens not at Strasbourg but
later, in discretion and secrecy, after a priceless orchestrated misunderstanding. Three people conspire to bring de Gaulle and Malraux face-to-
face: Corniglion-Molinier, now a general and a veteran of the Free French
forces; Gaston Palewski, General de Gaulle's trusty political sidekick; and
Captain Claude Guy, de Gaulle's aide-de-camp. They have often whis-
pered to one another that this Malraux fellow could be useful to de Gaulle
as security on the left. François Mauriac says to his son, Claude, "Malraux
is just waiting for a sign." Claude Mauriac reports these words to Captain

Guy. Malraux then dines at Palewski's with Guy. The idea of meeting Le Libérateur appeals to the writer. De Gaulle is amused by Malraux's personality but grumbles, "He [Malraux] will never want to."

Who will make the first move? Malraux consults Léon Blum. The Socialist sachem sees a very promising project there. The first week of August 1945, the telephone rings at 19 bis Avenue Victor-Hugo in Boulogne, where Malraux is now living in a duplex apartment with his sister-in-law, Madeleine, and their respective boys. Claude Guy pulls up in an official car: "The General asks in the name of France if you want to help."

It's like Corneille or Victor Hugo. Alain Malraux, Roland and Madeleine's son, has an early memory of Corniglion-Molinier singing General de Gaulle's praises and Malraux responding with "What, that Fascist?" Malraux's Gaullism between 1942 and 1945 went up and down like a yo-yo. De Gaulle receives Malraux for half an hour[2] on either August 5 or 6, 1945. The war is winding up: America drops its atomic bombs on Hiroshima and Nagasaki, and Churchill, Truman, and Stalin declare it all over on August 15. With the occupation of Hanoi by the Viet Minh, the French have another conflict on their hands.

The General apparently makes a resonant start to the conversation with Malraux: "Let us begin with the past."

Then (again, according to Malraux) they talk flat out about Marx, Nietzsche, the Resistance, the West, Empire, Revolution, General Hoche, the International Brigades. The two men size each other up, and each finds the other to his taste. Behind their motivation, they both have ulterior motives: Without that, would they be de Gaulle and Malraux? The novelist sees, standing and sitting amiably before him, behind his little mustache, an unquestionable Great Man of history and legend. He thinks, perhaps, of how he wrote about Lawrence without having met him. Here is a great character: Would he slot nicely into a book? De Gaulle has the appeal of June 18, 1940, behind him; he has been the leader of Free France, disarmed the Communist militia, pardoned the deserter Thorez. He is a two-star general who gives orders to other generals with four or five stars; he annoys and endears Churchill, another Great. So dry and sure of himself in appearance, yet he can be as shy as Malraux. Maybe depressive like him, too. He has been called a fascist, but clearly he isn't: Malraux can feel that. Is this a hero to cram into a novel, to pull out of an article, this de Gaulle, neither "true" nor "false," but what he is about to "experience"? For all his embellished accounts of Stalin, Trotsky, and others, Malraux has never been close to a real live Great for a decent length of time. It is worth finding out in a subordinate job under the orders of this general. De Gaulle is président du Conseil; he hints that there will be a ministerial portfolio. . . . Malraux becomes a technical adviser on culture to the General's office on August 16, 1945. In this capacity, he is absorbed by three subjects: cultural policy, opinion polls, and the modernization of state education.

The trial of Marshal Pétain begins. At the Potsdam Conference, Stalin, Churchill, and Truman manage to get by without the presence of a mortified General de Gaulle. "My heaviest cross during the war was the Cross of Lorraine," Churchill said. The British electors vote for the Labour Party and Clement Attlee. According to Malraux, "certain great men show their full worth during a war." Is he thinking only of Churchill? De Gaulle was sublime in the storms of war; how will he cross the calmer waters of peace? Ho Chi Minh creates the Committee for the Liberation of Vietnam. In France, the Communists triumph at the French legislative elections in October. Three parliamentary groups rise to the surface: the PCF, with 161 deputies elected; the MRP, with 150 deputies; and the Socialists, also with 150. Since these three parties have obtained 461 seats out of 586, de Gaulle forms a tripartite Cabinet but decides not to trust the PCF with any of the three key ministries that govern foreign policy: "diplomacy, which expresses it, the army to back it up, and the police, who protect it."

De Gaulle pitchforked Maurice Thorez, the pardoned deserter, into a minister's job. On November 21, the General's office offers Malraux the post of minister of information. Malraux accepts and takes his friend Raymond Aron, the intellectual par excellence, as an assistant, and the dashing Jacques Chaban-Delmas for secretary-general. Aron makes sure that Malraux appears precise and competent, even if he does not come from the political inner circles where one learns the difference between a law, a ministerial order, and a ministerial decision.[3]

For Malraux, there is a link between information and propaganda. Radio belongs to the state and now depends on him as minister of information. He adds a register to his orator's craft, speaking for the first time in front of the deputies, presenting himself as more of a technician than a politician. From the parliamentary benches in the Palais-Bourbon, he declares, "It seems to me vital that culture should cease to be the privilege of people who are lucky enough to live in Paris or to be rich."

As a writer he wants to illustrate the art books he is working on. As a minister, he would like to have giant reproductions of one hundred masterpieces of French painting printed for museums or traveling exhibitions. Meanwhile he will be allocating paper, which is in short supply. The black market has flourished in this and every century. Presenting the Information budget to the National Assembly, Malraux explains himself:[4]

"If, tomorrow, a minister of information decides to give authority to the newspapers without giving them paper, what will happen? Quite simply, this: black-market paper will become king, and you know as well as I do that in practical terms, those who have the most money will be those who have the most paper. To abolish the authorization and the allocation of paper before we are able to re-establish its complete freedom would in fact be tantamount to re-establishing . . . capitalism in this country."

Malraux the adventurer turned minister navigates the government with pleasure, although at that level, he says in private, adventure no longer exists. *Coronel*, then *tankeur*, so why not leave some "scars" as a *ministre*? A time for arms, a time for words, a time for ministerial decisions. It is "too late," Malraux also says, "to act on things, it is time to act on somebody." On de Gaulle, that is, and it's a good idea not to say that too much in public.

In Vietnam, the Viet Minh are controlling the hinterland as far as the Chinese border. In Paris, there is hesitation between making an agreement with Ho Chi Minh and attempting to recapture territory.[5] Malraux reads up on the subject and puts two questions during a dinner given by Paul-André Falcoz:[6] "Firstly, do you think it possible for France to maintain its power in Indochina if she does not occupy the border with China? Secondly, how much time do you think Chiang Kai-shek will resist the push of Mao's agrarian revolution?"

Later, to his friend André Bourotte, a teacher in Indochina, Malraux writes, "My point of view is not that of absence of interest, it is that of pessimism. The fate of Indochina has never been in the hands of you-know-which dummies; it is no longer even in the hands of France."[7]

On December 3, 1945, Malraux dines with the British ambassador, Duff Cooper, and his attractive wife, Diana. Louise de Vilmorin, who is friends with the couple, is present at the dinner. Duff Cooper notes in his diary:[8] "Malraux, who is now Minister of Information, was extremely brilliant. He is a very remarkable man. He prophesied that the Communists would try to obtain power by force in the twelve months to come and that they would fail."

January 20, 1946: De Gaulle bucks. He will not accept what he calls "party maneuvering"; he abruptly calls a Cabinet meeting and announces his departure. "The cause is plain: it would be vain and shameful to assume to govern, now that the parties, having concealed their means, are resuming their erstwhile games." Do the French want a government that governs or an omnipresent assembly "delegating a government to carry out its wishes"? Like most ministers, Malraux was neither consulted nor warned.

Soon afterward, he is again at the British Embassy. Duff Cooper's latest installment:

"Malraux . . . as always very interesting and a little alarmist. . . . Convinced that France is marching towards dictatorship. I don't think he regrets this. The issue is knowing whether it will be a dictatorship by the Communists or by De Gaulle, and that will be decided by force. He says that De Gaulle's resignation is not the end but the beginning of Gaullism, which will now be a great movement across all of France."

Abroad, as in France, Malraux has a reputation as a plotter: he has been preparing to form an anti-Communist organization that would stretch "from the center to the extreme right," notes the information department of the U.S. Strategic Services Unit. He is apparently coordinating a "new political leadership." The department states that "Malraux, former minister of propaganda," and Claude Bourdet, director of French broadcasting, as well as others, including Generals Juin and Revers, are set to supply "sympathetic support." The Americans are not well informed here, to say the least.[9]

Duff Cooper, a few days later: "Loulou [Louise de Vilmorin] has seen Malraux. He may be getting involved in a Caesarist plot based on assassination. The Gaullists are mad. I saw Pierre de Bénouville this evening, he is a little less mad than the others." Two days afterward: "Loulou reports to me that Malraux says de Gaulle is now like a sleepwalker or a convalescent. His mind seems barely to be working and he appears incapable of making a decision." A few months later, in May: "Loulou arrived at the embassy at the same time as me. She had seen Malraux who told her that the General would be President of the Republic on September 1, and that he, Malraux, would be Minister of the Interior."

Malraux, for the moment, holds back his ministerial ambitions. Despite his Gaullist activism, all the more vigorous since it is quite fresh, he must devote himself to other activities. He found his way back to Gallimard immediately after the liberation of Paris. Gaston Gallimard, as always, treats Malraux well, but the climate has changed. When Gaston was criticized for having published the *Nouvelle Revue Française* under Drieu, Malraux stepped in. With Sartre, Camus, and others, he took the defense of the founding father: Gaston helped many Resistance writers. Malraux was especially grateful to Raymond Gallimard, who was always devoted to him: "Between us, it can only be a question of answering 'yes' to all your wishes, even if it is not about works in progress." Malraux sells well.[10] Gaston signs a "special dispensation" to the contract of April 12, 1928, giving the writer 20 percent after the first thousand copies sold. The more popular an author is, the more his percentages increase.[11]

Malraux has the huge honor of becoming, in 1947, the second living

French writer to have his complete works published in a Pléiade edition, after Gide with his journal. *Les Conquérants, La Condition humaine,* and *L'Espoir,*[12] without notes or commentaries, are published in the prestigious format. Claudel registers his vexation: "And what about me!" André Chamson slightly less: "I am the only one who deserves to be at his side." Some authors, if they are jealous enough, insinuate that once you're out in Pléiade, you're fit to be buried: "Malraux's getting old very quickly." He is forty-five.

André Malraux and Gaston Gallimard liquidate objects from the gallery. In recent years, Malraux has taken back fourteen Greco-Buddhist heads, fifteen Persian pictures, some Assyrian bas-reliefs, and some Fautrier paintings. He clearly needs a substantial amount of money: his royalties and his minister's pay cannot be enough. As minister, he was earning 500,000 francs, plus 100,000 francs, per year, the equivalent in total of almost $12,000. The career-end salary of a university professor at the time was 323,000 francs and that of an urban mailman, 97,000 francs.[13]

Malraux finds out what he needs to know about print reproduction processes in Europe and the United States. His appetite for typography and the plastic arts revived, he picks out paintings, selects Ektachromes, and does not hesitate to have a color modified here and there. There is no such thing as faithful reproduction: eyes vary in their perception of colors. Malraux's eye is average.[14] He uses the best printers of the time, Rota-Dedag in Geneva, Draeger in Montrouge, Georges Lang in Paris.

Claude Gallimard was a prisoner of war with Albert Beuret and Jean Grosjean. He takes them both on at Gallimard. Along with Louis Chevasson, they form a tight group around Malraux. Beuret works in the morning at Gallimard for Malraux the writer and in the afternoon for Malraux the minister. To Malraux, Beuret and Grosjean are "the only two who never ask me for anything, not even a manuscript."

Beuret has a basic principle: "I am there to make [Malraux's] life simpler, not more complicated."

Beuret the businessman and Grosjean the literary man are linked by their prisoners' camaraderie and memories of the Stalag in Pomerania. With one, Malraux talks finances and politics. With the other, he converses mostly about literature. Grosjean is one of the few to know that Malraux's first drafts are flat—or worse, incomprehensible. He submits his own works to his writer friend. Malraux asks Grosjean for his opinion and dusts his texts off, cuts and files them down, saying, "I am picking off the fleas." Malraux respects Grosjean as a man and as a poet. He confides to him that he suffers from insomnia and reads detective novels "for the pace." They have a writers' relationship, better for Malraux than an intimate friendship. From now on, Malraux writes fewer and fewer letters. He throws away letters from Clara without even reading them but keeps Grosjean's.[15] Malraux's third pillar at Gallimard, Louis Chevasson, fields certain requests on his behalf. The writer to Chevasson: "No, no question of being painted, even by somebody talented. It takes too long, and even if I had the time, I'd prefer to be doing something else: seeing my friends, for example."

Malraux has some enormous faults—perhaps inherited, perhaps of his own making—but he is almost never petty and almost never bears a grudge. This is especially true when it comes to writers, whom he sees as a class above the fray. When Jacques Chardonne clashed with the purge-mongers and Marcel Arland asked Malraux to intervene on his behalf, he did not hesitate. Chardonne had intervened for Paulhan, Mauriac, and Malraux during the Occupation. Malraux even later signed an appeal for pardon in favor of Lucien Rebatet, who had pursued him fiercely when Vichy was in power. Malraux may be stubborn, but he is never blood-thirsty. He writes to express his concern to Jean Giono, who is also on the guilty list, according to the National Writers' Committee, where Aragon rules.[16] "Do I have to tell you that you can count on me if the need arises."[17] Malraux knows talent when he sees it. He suggests to Gaston Gallimard that he take Louis-Ferdinand Céline, the tired horse, into his stable. "I believe that Céline has a great desire to come over to you. I also believe that what he was personally reproached for was false;[18] and on a literary level, amnesty now seems certain, whatever the result of the elections. . . . No need to tell you that I couldn't care less; I think he recently showered me with insults (which I didn't read), but even if he's a swine, he is a great writer. So if you want me to have him brought in, let me know."[19] Malraux readily does favors here and there: he proposes Louis Guilloux for the Légion d'Honneur and gets his wife a job.

He tells Beuret about his marital adventures and misadventures. Albert serves as a shield. Clara has not finished mourning their separation. She has said that she would replace Josette and bring up the two boys, Bimbo and Vincent. Malraux cannot get away from Clara. It took the Resistance—then, tragically, death—to escape from Josette. Clara sees in Malraux a man who will accept neither submission (Josette) nor revolt (herself). Malraux is her "beloved rascal." An article about *Les Noyers de l'Altenburg* by a certain "C.M." appears in *Action*, now a well-behaved Communist weekly. It is a mocking, spiteful review that makes an uncalled-for allusion to Malraux's situation when he wrote the novel: "That a man, after a particularly arduous military battle, should discover that he is striving for happiness at the deepest part of himself, this too is a capitulation and one that every convalescent knows." C.M.—Clara

Malraux—turns brutal: "May we say here, first of all, that the man about whom I am going to write is probably the most important writer of his generation, that he is the one who is most interested in the essential issues, that he is admirably helped in his task of evocation, for after all he is a novelist, by extraordinary artistic gifts." But Malraux disappoints his readers here because he "intellectualizes." According to the *Action* review, Malraux is no longer asking what man can do but what he is: "Suddenly we're in the realm of metaphysics." The book contains no real action, no conflicts.

Malraux went wrong in not planning and writing his novel at Clara's side, not even showing her the manuscript. Clara remains ravenous for crumbs of news about Malraux and never forgets him. Her life in Paris since the Liberation has been difficult. First of all, Marcel and Janine Arland put up Florence and her mother. Then they both occupied lodgings at 17 Rue Berthollet in the Fifth Arrondissement, with a nice view over the Val-de-Grâce, one double and a small single room, no bathroom or shower, an old tub for washing, a sawdust-burning stove for heat. Hawked from one scholastic establishment to another during the Occupation, Flo is now at the smart École Alsacienne in Paris. Clara writes bits and pieces for various reviews, *Action*, the *Tribune des Nations*, *Étoiles*, and *La Nef*. She has kept Malraux's name, but it is no use to her. On the contrary, sometimes: the Paris literary milieu is aware of her tumultuous relationship with the great man, he who must not be offended. When Malraux came into her life, Josette stopped writing. Clara writes more and more. She distances herself from Malraux by writing but keeps finding him in what she writes.[20]

Malraux no longer has any reason not to divorce. He lodges a request for *torts réciproques*—"reciprocal fault." Clara writes to her husband: "Do stop, my dear André, these childish games, which are worthy neither of you nor of me. . . . I do not mean that you must stop the divorce, but I really couldn't care whether it is you or I who starts, since it is obvious that we must divorce." A reproach: "I shall do nothing to stop you from using to your advantage the laws you scorned so when you were twenty." Another: "I have said—and I repeat—that all these stories of legality and money make me sick." Malrucian, down to the turns of phrase: "I was married with no guarantee, I shall divorce with no guarantee." When they met for the ritual reconciliation session, Malraux proposed his minister's salary as alimony.[21] Before the judge, Clara answered that she had married an adventurer, not a minister.

Malraux met with his daughter, Florence, for the first time after the war, while still a minister. He picked her up with his official car and took her to a luxurious restaurant, the kind she was not used to. Afterward, during their meetings, Malraux would ask, "What are you reading at the moment?"

"The Brothers Karamazov."

Satisfied, the father quickly sets out instructions for their future meetings. No chitchat. *Bon.* Let's talk. Seriously.

André has learned of the death of his two half brothers. Claude is missing, no doubt executed. Roland was killed in the *Cap Arcona*, a prison ship that was bombed off the port of Lübeck in northern Germany by an RAF plane. He was stacked in with other deportees, headed for Sweden, where the Germans were proposing to exchange their prisoners against Allied concessions. The British airmen spotted swastikas on the ship's flags.

André is now living with Roland's widow, Madeleine Malraux, with the three little boys, on the two floors of the Boulogne apartment. At first, Madeleine and the boys occupied the second floor and André the first, with his Greco-Buddhist statues and Fautriers. Now André and Madeleine are openly living together. The children play together in a garden behind the building. Yvonne de Gaulle, the General's wife, is known for not approving of these "situations." André and Madeleine are to be married—but not until March 1948. At Avenue Victor-Hugo, there are proper bathrooms—not an old tub in sight—two entrances (one for the servants), a laundry room. Malraux feels at ease in a light Art Deco ensemble with balustrades, a half landing, and alcoves. The main entrance looks out onto chestnut trees in the avenue. Malraux likes his Boulogne duplex so much that he insisted on paying ten years' rent in advance.[22] They have several servants: a valet, a butler and his wife, a cook, two maids, a chauffeur, a cleaning lady; the cleaning lady's husband helps out too. Malraux's lifestyle does not correspond to his minister's salary and his author's royalties. Malicious types murmur that many members of the Resistance got their hands on the organization's money.

Malraux appears happy, or at any rate relaxed. He receives a letter from the writer Roger Nimier, offering his services "should you one day be in need of a killer or a bodyguard."[23] Malraux does not reply. He catches up with old friends, going to see them rather than just letting them come to him. There is a correspondence with Roger Martin du Gard. He has "cash flow problems" and wonders if he should sell a house in the Seventeenth Arrondissement.[24] Malraux's a practical chap; can he advise him? Martin du Gard has a titillating piece of information: in "three years," Malraux will apparently be the "only candidate for the Nobel." Of course, the Nobel Committee is "worried" by the idea that Malraux might have abandoned the novel. Martin du Gard adds, "I do not know if the idea of being 'Nobélisé' is repugnant to you." One of the reasons Malraux has been rejecting proposals to join the Académie Française is precisely the possibility of being awarded the Nobel.

Martin du Gard writes again to Malraux[25] to tell him of the death of Gide in 1951: "We saw him sinking slowly, calmly, into the depths, without dread . . . exactly the death he had wanted; that we all wished for him, that must be wished for all of us." Malraux seems to be thinking less about death, but that of Gide, his irritated and puzzled admirer, touches him. When the collaborator Drieu committed suicide, Malraux—who threw away so many letters—kept the pathetic missives he left behind:

> I do not want to run away.
> I do not want to hide.
> I do not want to be killed by cowards.[26]

Drieu died alone; Gide, surrounded by friends, but not including Malraux. When Groethuysen is on his deathbed, Malraux does not go and see him because Groet and Alix are too close to the Communists.

Malraux remains at a studied distance from the so-called existentialists: Sartre, Simone de Beauvoir, Maurice Merleau-Ponty. Sartre takes his hat off to Malraux—or at least gives him a semiexcusatory nod in a footnote:

> If I have not spoken louder either of Malraux or of Saint-Exupéry, it is because they belong to our generation. They were writing and publishing before us [true], and are doubtless a little older than we are [Malraux is four years older than Sartre]. Malraux has the immense merit of having recognized, from his first work [probably, for Sartre, *Les Conquérants*], that we were at war, and of having made war literature when the surrealists and even Drieu were devoting themselves to peacetime literature . . . hope and the human condition [*L'Espoir* et *La Condition humaine*] . . . these will be the principal literary and philosophical themes of our day. When I say we, consequently, I believe I am also speaking for them.

With the arrival of the Cold War, relations between Malraux and Sartre take a turn for the worse. Both sides are just waiting for an excuse to break the links between them, which were never very strong in the first place. It arrives in the form of an article by Maurice Merleau-Ponty in *Les Temps Modernes*. Malraux finds the article offensive and makes a scene with Gaston Gallimard, demanding that he no longer publish Sartre's review. The publishing house needs Malraux as an author, and vice versa. Gaston asks Camus for advice: "Would it be better to keep Malraux or Sartre?"

Camus advises keeping the former. Malraux threatens Gaston Gallimard about *Les Temps modernes*, warning that certain files from the Occupation could come out. Gaston is infuriated by this remark: from that
point on, his relationship with Malraux becomes strained. In the end, neither Malraux nor Sartre has to leave Gallimard as authors, since Sartre
takes his review to the publisher Julliard, a hundred yards from Gallimard
in the Rue de l'Université.

Malraux's Gaullism is limited to the General in person. De Gaulle
would later claim that everybody was, is, or will be a Gaullist. Sartre
chuckles hoarsely when he hears talk of "left-wing Gaullists." Not Malraux. The author of *La Condition humaine*, to the surprise of Raymond
Aron, reacts more and more violently to the PCF. The man of war is wak-
ing and preparing to do battle. A passionate faith in de Gaulle, not always
realistic but always exclusive, is now an important part of Malraux's life.

CHAPTER TWENTY-SIX

The Militant Companion

G ENERAL DE GAULLE married France with a long-standing "certain idea," and Malraux, for the sake of his country, has divorced Revolution. Malraux the futurologist broods over pessimistic ideas. Either the USSR will attack Western Europe, in which case the Communists in France should be crushed first, or, better still, before the USSR can intervene, the Gaullists should seize the Chamber of Deputies, Matignon, the Élysée Palace. Colonel Berger reappears under the minister's double-breasted suit.

On April 7, 1947, in Strasbourg, de Gaulle creates the RPF, the Rassemblement—that is, rally, or gathering—du Peuple Français. A few days later, de Gaulle is entertaining guests at Malraux's apartment in Boulogne. The General is a little shocked at the luxury of the place, with its avant-garde paintings and statuettes. He asks his aide-de-camp, Claude Guy, "But where does he find all this money?"

"His author's royalties, probably," answers Guy.[1]

Malraux foresees troubles. The Communists will be looking for the "liquidation of General de Gaulle and the leaders of the RPF." The General doesn't believe it. Malraux sends Madeleine and the three boys to Strasbourg for safety. Sometimes the advice from Malraux and other RPF figures annoys the General: "I've had enough of these perpetual clumsy declarations from Soustelle, Malraux, Palewski, and Diomède Catroux! It has to stop! I am big enough to realize what my own intentions are at a given moment." When Claude Guy tells the General that Malraux is "in top form," de Gaulle retorts: "Naturally, they are all in top form! Because now they all think there's going to be a war. And they're right. They will have war . . . it will all finish very badly."

The RPF tests the waters: in the municipal elections of October 1947, it obtains 38 percent of the vote. For three years, the RPF is the second French party after the PCF.

Malraux spends long hours with his assistants, Diomède Catroux and Christian Fouchet, at the RPF headquarters at 19 Boulevard des Capucines, near the Opéra. He is the official "propaganda organizer." Malraux has been schooled in theatrical politics from Moscow to Barcelona and Paris. He takes hold of the ritual of the General's public appearances and modernizes it. Each meeting of the RPF is to feature a national speaker and a "local" one (unavoidable, alas). If the spectators are lucky enough to be granted the actual presence, de Gaulle, before he speaks, Malraux introduces him with a sonorous "*Honneur et patrie, voici le général de Gaulle!*"

The posters must not say "RPF meeting" but the more lyrical "for the Gathering [Rassemblement] of the French People, our companion such-and-such will talk to you about . . ."[2] Malraux coordinates the meetings like a stage director, demanding careful lighting and red, white, and blue drapery printed with the Lorraine cross as a backdrop. He likes to speak in meetings, where his tics serve a purpose: they may bother him, but they magnetize those listening and watching. A shiver runs through the crowd. When PCF militants heckle in the RPF meetings, Malraux quivers with excitement. The Gaullists expel the Communists. A very perky Malraux: "See, ladies and gentlemen, how the fascists have been kicked out of this meeting!"

His stance against communism appears "visceral" to commentators on the Left: his antifascism has turned into anti-Sovietism. Before he battled against the brown plague, now he is waging war against the red plague. There's nothing quite like an old fellow traveler from the PCF, unless it's a disenchanted card-carrying member, to metamorphose into a hardened adversary. He repeatedly taunts the "gilt-edged Soviet marshals"—an image he uses seventeen times over the course of his public appearances. Whether talking about culture or geopolitics, Malraux is quick to upbraid the Communists in front of his audiences: "Oh, my little Stalinist friends, I don't want to talk to you any more than you want to listen to me, but we have been waiting for you for such a long time! I waited for you for seven weeks in Spain—you were not there! You didn't come! I waited for you in Berlin when we went with Gide to petition Hitler to free Dimitrov. We were there on your behalf, and you were not. I waited for you in the Resistance for two years and you were not there!"

Is this provocation, thoughtlessness, or sheer impudence? Many Communists joined maquis organizations long before he did, even if the majority did wait for Germany's attack against the USSR.[3] Malraux enjoys the effect nonetheless, smells the incense of admiration rising from the immense spaces where he polishes his orator's art. The Vélodrome d'Hiver, where cycle races alternate with Gaullist and Communist meetings, is a favorite. Before one event, Jacques Baumel, a member of the Resistance from the first, comes into Malraux's hotel room to see him rehearsing and gesturing in front of a mirror.[4] In front of a diverse social and professional range of Gaullist audiences, he pushes his ideas to extremes: "Since the war, democracy has ceased to exist in Europe.[5] What is important is not to change such-and-such a minister but to change the system."

What de Gaulle can offer in place of Marxism, Malraux says, is a "profound ideology" and a concern for the "general interest." The democratic idea of the general interest must "provisionally, at least" take the place of the class struggle. He refutes the calumnies uttered against Gaullism: the General never said that he would dissolve the parties, he declared "that it was intolerable that a minister should obey his party and not obey France." Malraux is often bang on target in this area: "Let us just say that it is a little excessive to claim that General de Gaulle is against the right to vote for women, simply because he is the one who established it. That it is excessive to proclaim him an anti-Semite, because he repealed the Vichy laws! That it is excessive to say that he has destroyed the Republic simply because it is he who has rebuilt it."

As the party gains ground legally, Malraux gets cocky with the Communists: "We believe that the future of General de Gaulle does not lie in the grubby mitts of Mr. Jacques Duclos [well-known member of the PCF party executive]."

The great red light of the East, which shone with hope in the twenties and thirties, becomes worrying for Malraux: "The Soviet Union has arrived at a dramatic turning point for all those in France who desire peace. . . . It is an undeniable success on the part of Communist propaganda to have managed to convince so many people that the Stalinists are the Left and that we are the Right."

He makes a distinction between the PCF leaders and mere members of the Party: "The average Communist is a sincere man who believes himself to be a patriot. . . . If Soviet Germany can find unity, Russia is promising the possession of Austria, part of Hungary, and Alsace [Malraux is speaking in Colmar, which is in Alsace]. I would like to know what the Communist workers in Alsace, the real ones, think about that."

From its geopolitical strategy, the RPF would appear to know the intentions of the Politburo and the top brass in Moscow: Malraux is afraid that "France may become an advance post for Soviet fighter aircraft." The Communists may come to power in Marseille, but the RPF will win in Paris. From Lille to Marseille, from Brest to Strasbourg, Malraux always stresses the idea that Gaullists and Communists are not separated by the problem of social justice.

Malraux flings out slogans in meetings: "What do we want? We want to separate ourselves from the separatists [the Communists]." He borrows this and other slogans from de Gaulle. But he also makes himself a populist: "And France is starting to be truly weary, this France suffering from sleeping sickness, weary of the belief that one day we will stop the Soviet tanks with gatherings of chess champions and crossword enthusiasts."

At a meeting at the Salle Japy in September 1947, Communist workers from a Renault car factory break up an RPF meeting by throwing nuts and bolts: a Waterloo, from the militant Gaullist point of view. Less than a year later, the RPF has its Austerlitz in the same auditorium. The fighting is perpetuated into a gentle civil war. Despite the tense climate, this is a civilized country, and there are rules: a few wounded can be accepted easily enough, but there must be no deaths.

The press must be carefully looked after, especially that of the RPF itself. The comatose news sheet *L'Étincelle* is replaced by *Rassemblement*. Malraux has Pascal Pia work on it. The energy Malraux had as a journalist for *L'Indochine* and *L'Indochine Enchaînée* comes back to him. He finds in himself the vigor of Garine in *Les Conquérants*, inspiring Communist propaganda in China, the drive of the young Malraux when he claimed responsibilities with the Kuomintang. He also echoes Vincent Berger, who, in *Les Noyers de l'Altenburg*, is responsible for German propaganda.

Malraux responds quickly to the demands of Gaullist parishioners, hungry for their meetings and well-phrased homilies. He has a soft spot for students, teachers, and intellectuals. He likes to mention under his breath "a student . . . as I also once was . . ." In student halls of residence, he declares, "It is basically a matter of knowing if you want to accept the culture you have inherited or if you are going to want to change it."[6]

Malraux knows that the majority of the party members listening to him are either centrists or right-wingers, yet he still leans to the left. He is trying to find a "Gaullist socialism": a reformist, social democrat, neo-socialism with an acceptable public face. He is convinced that a "great dialogue" is starting between the General and France itself. Malraux sometimes addresses his audiences as "*chers camarades!*" (like the Communists) and sometimes (like the Anarchists and the Gaullists) as "*compagnons!*" Sometimes it is both. Crocodile eyes fixed on the red, white, and blue lines of his destiny, the General listens to Malraux. He never comments in public on Malraux's performances.

Politics are the prolongation of war by other means. The writer marks out the battle lines: "They are now defined by our enemies: we have one on the right, namely Vichy; we have one on the left, namely the Communist Party."

He repeats an absurd phrase: "What is there at the moment in this country? Us, the Communists, and nothing—or rather, the people who are vaguely linked to them and people who are vaguely linked to us."

This binary view of the French political scene at the end of the forties and after 1950, a false analysis, has more to do with wish than reality. Many voters choose parties other than the RPF and the PCF. But Malraux likes war: "There are no better posters than torn-up posters, there are no finer faces than faces that bear wounds."

The legislative elections of June 1951 are disappointing, both for those faithful to the General and for the "separatists." The PCF had 165 seats and loses 101 of them. The RPF hoped for 300 seats at best, 200 at worst; it finds itself with 117. Neither the Gaullists nor the Communists will be stepping up to a position of power via the ballot box quite yet.

Everywhere he goes to speak, Malraux calls for a genuine State, genuine social justice, genuine hope. When twenty-seven RPF deputies vote for the nomination of Antoine Pinay as président du Conseil in 1952, all but one of them have to hand in their resignation from the RPF parliamentary group. They move away to form the Groupe Indépendant d'Action Républicaine et Sociale.

"They have to make a living somehow," comments Malraux.

Malraux's fundamental idea remains that only the General can save France and that de Gaulle is neither from the right nor the left but from elsewhere. No other French writer at the time commits himself as far in public. Nobody else puts the same passion into his cause. Camus and Sartre make political speeches, but almost in spite of themselves and certainly not at the Vélodrome d'Hiver. Aragon is influential in the PCF but works in the background. Malraux is to be found not in the civilian zone but up at the front.

The writer makes allusions to his own life in press conferences and when speaking from the rostrum. The biography of the General, that of his erstwhile minister, and the history of France are mixed together. A journalist puts a question: Some say that General de Gaulle has already thrown his hand in once. If and when he comes into power, what is there to tell us that he wouldn't do the same again in a fit of temper?

Malraux: "Great men have never remained as great historic figures and kept a nice personality; the qualities that bring authority are those which imply a certain firmness in human relations. Obviously what you were referring to is political firmness. As far as the private character of General de Gaulle is concerned, I must tell you that I find this story of a gruff personality to be a legend. Inasmuch as my opinion may interest you, I find him extremely distant in his connections, but noble; and I have very often seen how he is with soldiers, sensitive in a restrained but very real way, and I have seen him, two or three times during the war, with people who were about to die. That's a pretty hard ordeal, and it is quite rare for a military leader to cope well next to a dying soldier."

Malraux has never seen Charles de Gaulle with wounded men who are about to die. But it is as if he has. He feels the General sitting at the bedside of the main casualty, moribund France.

Journalists ask for the text of a speech before Malraux gives it, as is the custom. Never mind if it is handed over hours later or the next day, after the morning editions have gone to bed. Spluttering, crescendoing for effect, joking around, sometimes, blowing into the microphone, with de Gaulle behind him, literally or figuratively, working history over with the plowshare of his formulaic phrases, Malraux hooks his public and makes them smile. Every public speaker is an actor. Actors in the cinema or on television can be attractive because of a different physique, complete with faults, a fascinating ugliness, even; a politician holds or charms his public with his expressions and his gestures. Malraux all the more so, since he is good-looking.

In the RPF offices, Malraux descends from the heights of his existential generalizations and astonishes colleagues with his practicality, when they are quite ready for him to be disorganized or muddle-headed. He wants local radio to broadcast the Gaullian Good News. He delegates as necessary and surrounds himself as he did in Spain and Alsace-Lorraine. Brigitte Friang assists him on press and radio matters; he is also ably assisted by André Astoux, Jacques Bruno, and Pierre Juillet.

Malraux has a methodical approach, whether it is a matter of reading a manuscript—*L'Étranger* during the war—or launching an operation such as the stamp campaign to support General de Gaulle. To fill the RPF coffers, the French are urged to buy 50-franc stamps and to send them to Colombey-les-Deux-Églises, where the General lives. Malraux presents de Gaulle as "the only Frenchman since du Guesclin about whom the famous phrase on Joan of Arc could have been said: '*Il n'est si pauvre fileuse en France, qui ne filerait pour payer ma rançon*' [No spinster in France is so poor that she would not spin to pay my ransom]." De Gaulle and Malraux both worship the warlike maiden Joan of Arc, loved by the French from primary school onward. Millions of stamps arrive at the RPF offices. At a press conference, the writer supplies details with the drawling Parisian accent he sometimes affects: "Three million people [who have sent stamps], that really means something. People don't like to write. Most French people find it a bit of a chore even to write to their own family." With a greengrocer's precision and a novelist's eye, he continues, "All this

mail looks like something that many of us have known: the mail for soldiers. The paper, ninety times out of a hundred, is squared paper. Many of
you will have seen the gathering at the Vélodrome d'Hiver. Did you see
the public that turned out? It was like the Métro exits at rush hour."

In a twenty-page memo to the party's regional organizers, Malraux
gives details of the preparation, financing, and distribution of responsibilities for "Rally" days (*journées du rassemblement*), taking his inspiration
from the Communist festivals. Malraux—always a confident negotiator of
contracts with his publisher—overflows with ideas to rake in the dough at
Gaullist jamborees. On his instruction, they are to sell badges and, when
the fete is over, sell all the remaining goods by auction, down to the children's balloons. "For the stallholders and storekeepers we will arrange
fixed prices." No pilfering, please. The collections will be taken in "lead-
sealed collection boxes" that will be opened by the lady president of the
women's committee. In the margin of his circular, Malraux specifies in his
own handwriting that these collection boxes will be of a uniform design.

Six pages of this note are devoted to the "national" part of the day: the
appearance of Charles de Gaulle. Malraux insists on the planned ritual
steps. 1: Announcements—the General is coming; music. 2: Arrival—here
he is, "*honneur et patrie*"; applause. 3: Address—he talks to the faithful,
who are to listen reverently and go wild (De Gaulle! De Gaulle!). 4:
Assumption—the General ascends into the sky of his solitude, returns to
the desert of Colombey-les-Deux-Églises (which is not without its oases)
or the Hôtel La Pérouse, where de Gaulle stays when he is in Paris.

Party brochures all over the world are of a similarly low standard.
There Malraux has to put up with "mediocrity." He tries to give those
who make up the brochures lessons in how to write, then gets tired of it.
But the party propaganda still needs to be disseminated.

Malraux often prophesies: "General de Gaulle will not do things perfectly: nobody does things perfectly. He will not do what everyone in
France wants; nobody does what everyone in France wants. [Malraux
often chants in this way in his speeches, which flow with the rhythm of
free verse.] But once he has taken what can be done into his hands and said
to this country, 'I take it,' the promises he has made will be kept, and that
will be the first time that has happened since he left." Malraux uses these
physical expressions, "between your hands," "bare hands," "hold out their
hands."

Malraux is often to be found at the RPF headquarters in Boulevard
des Capucines, opposite the Opéra, turning up at 9.30 a.m. to preside over
party propaganda. But his work there—interspersed with meals of high
calorific and intellectual content at excellent restaurants—does not prevent him from preparing the second volume of his *Psychologie de l'art, La*

Création artistique.[7] Madeleine types up his manuscript; he scores it with crossings out and corrections, then entrusts it to his secretary, who sticks on more pieces of paper with further sentences and paragraphs. For Brigitte Friang, looking on with amused affection, his scissors and glue pot are as indispensable to his creativity as his pen.

During these years, Malraux writes fewer and fewer letters. He dictates, and keeps them short. He expresses himself more clearly in his correspondence with foreigners. From the United States, Louis Fischer asks about Malraux's political shift. Why has the writer broken off with the Stalinists? "This split," writes Malraux,[8] "was somewhat enriched by the Germano-Soviet pact." During the war, Roosevelt discerned a future dictator in Charles de Gaulle. Malraux: "I do not believe that General de Gaulle's desire for personal power is any greater that that of President Roosevelt." The General's economic program is judged conservative by some Americans. Malraux answers, "The only structural reforms to have been carried out in France were made under his government." For Malraux, only the RPF will be "strong enough to stand up to the Stalinists." It is a matter of "publicly organizing the Left of the Party, as, for example, the revolutionary Left of the Socialist Party is organized . . . *precisely so that it does not become a right-wing force.*" Malraux jokes, "General de Gaulle is triply at fault for being a general, being noble [that's not true, but let's just simplify for the Americans], and being Catholic. The only serious problem is knowing whether we should try to constitute our Left within the Party or outside it." Malraux was apparently, for a while, thinking of joining a Trotskyist splinter group. *Bon.* Seriously. He has a certain disdain for the rank-and-file militants. He doesn't despise them, but those underlings just don't make History.

Louis Fischer asks for permission to publish Malraux's letters. Malraux refuses: he is writing to inform. Fischer claims that de Gaulle "is followed by reactionaries." Malraux: "If you mean by that, that the old mustached soldier in the provinces votes for General de Gaulle, of course that is true; but that doesn't really signify. If you mean that the real reactionary forces are behind him, you are wrong. The truth is that these forces detest us. They may not have a choice, in fact, but their relationship with us is so uneasy that there is absolutely no risk of them steering us. Any parallel with fascism is leading you up a blind alley." For Malraux, French opinion has been characterized by negative concerns over the last ten years, more than positive ones: "France was *anti*-Fascist, is in the process of becoming *anti*-Communist, and is, above all, antichaos."

Malraux knows that it is important not to forget about the Americans. He grants a substantial interview to one American who is making a name for himself at the time, James Burnham.[9] Malraux's interviewer—surprisingly—talks almost as much as he does: Burnham speaks mostly of the managerial society, organizers, inflation, the trade gap. Malraux is keen to change the subject: "Yes, this is a period of change, of metamorphosis." For Malraux, the word "metamorphosis" can be used to refer to the social, the political, and the aesthetic. He makes whirlwind comparisons: "Europe is suffering from a break in consciousness that is comparable to that which marked the end of Roman paganism."

Interesting, Burnham comments, that at a time when Malraux is becoming more and more involved in a battle of internal politics, he should be publishing his essay on Goya and the first volume of his *Psychologie de l'art*, *Le Musée imaginaire* (Museum without Walls).[10] Naturally, Malraux replies; Goya was one of the rare painters whose work went hand in hand with a struggle. He confirms that he started planning *Psychologie de l'art* before the war—which is true—and claims that the Germans destroyed his manuscript—which is not. Malraux sees no incompatibility between a life in Art and a life in Action. Sophocles, Dante, Bacon, and Cervantes were all men of action, and three of them were soldiers. The eternal prototype of the artist does not stop with Henry James and Flaubert. Malraux concedes that it is difficult to live as an artist and as a man of action. All art implies "a sort of obsession" in order to "distill" the world into the work of art. Action implies the "dissolution" of the world into action.

Can his illustrated essays on art be seen as substitutes for fiction? His activities with the RPF are less glorious and heroic than his actions on the Guadalquivir and the Rhine. Has there been a slackening of the sort of imagination that feeds on intense emotion? Malraux's face is still thin, his forelock still unruly. His behavior is more suave now, more official, more like that of a cardinal than a colonel.

Sensing that Gaullism is leaning toward anti-Americanism, Malraux writes a "letter to American intellectuals" for the weekly *Carrefour*,[11] where Pascal Pia has a literary column: "We want Europe to begin with what General de Gaulle has called 'an act of popular faith': every European should be targeted, called upon, concerned; by an accurate referendum, everyone should answer some essential questions that would permit both the establishment and the limitation of confederal action (you [Americans] have not destroyed your states) and allow us to avoid the Shakespearean spectacle of the inheritance of Rome being fought over by the powerless hands of unemployed heads of state." Malraux can't stop himself from coming out with a petty comment: "The best Gaullists are those whose names are on a list [whose? the PCF's or the CIA's?]; when the day comes, they will fight—even if they know that you will come too late or not at all." Like many Gaullists—and just as many Communists—

Malraux seems here to forget that in both world wars, after some isolationist hesitation, the United States came to the rescue of European democracies. The rise in anti-Americanism is actively fueled by both orthodox Gaullists and doctrinaire Communists, feeding on the same old myth: Paris and France itself having been liberated by the French. Ah yes, of course, they did receive support from the Allies, including the Americans. Many GIs went to war before Malraux did.

Out of concern and respect for the United States, Malraux takes a trip there. At the reopening of the Metropolitan Museum of Art in New York City and the bicentenary of Columbia University, he talks with his hosts not about technical and museum-related issues but about civilization. "Ours," he explains, "is attempting to found a primary universal idea of mankind . . . not as Greece did, through the creation of heroic or divine models, but through a search for the deepest element."[12]

Malraux is drinking—wine and whisky, and plenty of them. He uses amphetamines—Maxiton and Corydrane—to help him face his tasks. Alcohol on top of these multiplies the effect. To an idiot, these substances would give the impression of being intelligent; to the intelligent, the conviction of becoming talented; to the talented, the certainty of their genius.

De Gaulle gives Malraux practical problems to solve; he doesn't just talk to him about civilization. To regain power, they will need funds: Could the RPF buy such-and-such a newspaper? "The *Journal du Midi* business Mr. Malraux will talk to you about is an interesting one," de Gaulle writes to Pia. "If we can do it, let's do it." Beyond his good works as an activist, Malraux shows repeated acts of thoughtfulness to de Gaulle. When a work of his comes out, he chooses a limited-edition copy and perfects an inscription. If he's not happy with it, he takes another copy and starts again.[13]

Malraux sometimes has his doubts about the return of Charles de Gaulle to power, as does the General himself. When he skips meetings at the RPF summit conference—even though they are presided over by the Savior himself—Malraux receives his call to order:

Mon Cher Ami,
 There will be a meeting on Tuesday, May 1, at 5.30 p.m.
 Your presence at this meeting is, as is that of every member of the Cabinet, strictly indispensable.

The Cher Ami continues to forge electrifying phrases for the Gaullist activists, but his heart is no longer in it. Malraux can feel that the family of the non-Communist Left is moving away from him. How many intellectuals are confirmed Gaullists? Raymond Aron is slipping away. Who is left? Francis Ponge and—an immense consolation—François Mauriac. Critics on the left and in the center point out—sometimes coarsely—that some of the themes Malraux espouses are fascist ones: the strong State, hero worship, the denial of a Left–Right divide, the insistence on will, energy, and movement, a view of social justice tinged with paternalism.

The far Left attacks him. In the very first issue of *Nouvelle Critique*,[14] the monthly review of "militant Marxism," Malraux is condemned along with Sartre, Mauriac, and David Rousset: "With more or less cynicism, they are content to tag along behind the American industrialists." These adversaries are not in fact as homogeneous as the PCF would like to believe. Sartre and Simone de Beauvoir refuse an invitation to spend a weekend with Koestler. Malraux remains on good terms with Koestler, but not with Sartre. After repeated dinner invitations from Koestler, Sartre eventually replies through his secretary: he cannot maintain relations with a friend of Malraux, the toxic supporter of de Gaulle. Malraux still sees Sartre as a writer, politician, and philosopher: he recommends *Huis-Clos* and *La Nausée* to his daughter.

The municipal elections of April–May 1953 in Paris seem to push the RPF off the edge of existence, into nothingness. Of its fifty-two seats, it holds on to only twenty-one. De Gaulle decides to put a brake on the moribund party's parliamentary activities. He lets his deputies and senators go. After being a devotee of the General for almost six years, Malraux dives back full-time into his literary activities, or nearly. Has the Communist danger passed, then? Malraux seems to forget the RPF posters: "Watch out! The Communists are preparing civil war in France." A lost cause is a turn-off to Malraux. Or is that just what he needs to force him back to his writing desk? A new cycle in his life begins as he leaves his office as a top RPF official to work with regularity on his books in Boulogne. The warrior at rest. Studious days. The cashmere sweater where once there was a three-piece suit and, before that, a uniform. On vacation from his Gaullist revolution, Malraux dabbles in Art at home.

Ange matois

CHAPTER TWENTY-SEVEN

Family Life

O N THE SUBJECT of the Communists, Malraux said to de Gaulle, "There is a great deal to reproach them for, but when I see their enemies . . . they are so much more stupid."

Malraux's nephew, Alain, asks his uncle, "Papa [that is what the child calls him], what are the Communists? Are they baddies?"

"It isn't like that," answers André Malraux. "What they want is good; what they do is base."

The Communists have stolen from Malraux the hopes of his youth and the brotherhood he is looking for, and finding less, among Gaullists. He works off a nostalgia, regrets, but no remorse. The writer belongs, honoris causa, to the largest party in France: that of former Communists and fellow travelers of the PCF.

In civilian life, Malraux attends meetings of the veterans of the Alsace-Lorraine Brigade. But he sees himself more as a current combatant than a former one. Who is there to fight against, militarily, intellectually, politically? De Gaulle is clearly not going to get into power. Case closed. Might as well get on with sorting out the photographs of works of art.

Malraux works with Roger Parry, a production technician with Gallimard. Parry is always late and always lovely. He has lived in Tahiti as a painter and photographer. He can sketch a rose with the flick of a brush. Malraux spreads out his reproductions on the floor, filling his sitting room. *Paris-Match* and other publications photograph him there with his beautiful images. He is calm and would be happy if happiness were a category in his thoughts. When Emmanuel d'Astier de la Vigerie asked de Gaulle, "Are you a happy man, *mon général*?" he was apparently answered with "D'Astier, stop asking stupid questions." A passably Malrucian response.

The writer plays with his photos, his pasteups, and his layouts. Serene but still racked with tics, he meditates now on Mankind and Art, and not so much on politicians and politics—which still, for him, has not earned a capital letter, as History has. He has lived a lot, read a lot, seen a lot. That doesn't impress Blanche, the cook: "They say Monsieur has seen every-thing, but he hasn't seen my ass."[1]

Malraux sees less of literary friends and acquaintances than before, and without any great pleasure. They are present but distant: Arland, Sperber, Guilloux, Louis Martin-Chauffier, and a confidante in the form of Alice Jean-Alley. Malraux's character becomes more centripetal than centrifugal: others come to him more than he goes to them. He solilo-quizes more than he converses. In front of others, André loves to talk to Malraux and vice versa. He declines numerous invitations and tenders very few himself. He has no reason to see the political figures of his recent past. He used to like talking to Raymond Aron but hardly sees him any-more. Does he have any real friends? Faithfuls, without a doubt. He keeps an eye on Paul Nothomb, the Attignies of *L'Espoir* (aka Julien Segnaire in literature). Nothomb has left Brussels; Malraux gives him work doing research for his art books in Paris.

Others that are close to him are far off, dispersed around the world: Bergamin in Montevideo, Max Aub in Mexico. Malraux has excluded Corniglion-Molinier from his entourage after some blasphemous remark about de Gaulle. In the first circle there are still the regulars, the useful ones: Beuret—Iago to the Othello of Boulogne, say those who don't like him—Marcel Brandin, a touch cynical, and Chevasson, always discreet and self-effacing. These attentive and indispensable protectors are ever present at Gallimard and around Malraux. Beuret has no children and is very fond of Malraux's second son, Vincent.

Malraux's familial situation again resembles that of his father. André married his sister-in-law after the death of his half brother. Fernand Mal-raux opted for a sort of collateral incest by embarking on an affair with the sister of his second wife while still living with her. There are more striking resemblances: Fernand had a son from a first marriage, André, and from his second union, two sons (Roland and Claude), who were acknowledged, then legitimized. André Malraux has a legitimate daughter, Florence, and two sons from a later union. Pierre Gauthier Guillaume, the eldest, is still not legally André's son since Roland acknowledged him, but at least he has the surname Malraux. The place of the second son, Vincent, is less certain: in public records he is Vincent Clotis, born of father unknown. Josette's attentive and affectionate father obtained papers for Vincent in the name of Malraux from Hyères, where he would later be mayor and where both boys often go for holidays. In everyday school life, Vincent is called Mal-raux. Madeleine goes to see the teachers at the start of each year. Malraux does not attempt to clarify the situation. He cannot acknowledge his first son, Pierre Gauthier Guillaume, retroactively. He could take steps to acknowledge Vincent with the help of a decision from the president of the Republic, but it is hard to imagine Malraux bringing the subject up with the current president, Vincent Auriol. He never explains himself on this matter. At that time in France, illegitimacy was still a burden to carry. Is it surprising that there are hardly any children in the novelist's work? Kassner's daughter in *Le Temps du mépris* is hardly sketched.

The two boys and Madeleine's son, Alain, have different statuses at home in Boulogne. Gauthier is still his father's favorite, noticeably so. After Josette's death, he lived in the South with his maternal grandparents. His arrival at Boulogne was tough. He would often throw up after dinner. His father would go up to his room and tell him stories. Madeleine tries to help each of André's sons to forget the strangeness of their situation. She is affectionate and maternal with all of them, but Alain is her son, not her nephew.

As mistress of the house, Madeleine entertains guests and accompanies her famous husband. André Malraux depends on his wife when working on his art books. She wouldn't be able to help him if he were putting together a novel, but he doesn't write novels any more. When he is choosing a photo, working on a layout, deliberating about typefaces, she is there to help. She goes book hunting at Gallimard, Buloz, or Galignani, seeks out plates in specialized shops in the Rue de Seine, and looks for documents at the Bibliothèque Jacques-Doucet. Clara did not type Malraux's manuscripts; Madeleine, like Josette, does. How, then, is she to devote herself to her career as a pianist? She plays Brahms, Debussy, Satie, and the rare works by Nietzsche on a Pleyel 1937 with dual keyboards. Malraux makes comments. Madeleine doesn't even pretend to attach too much importance to his remarks. She has had lessons with Marguerite Long at the Conservatoire; music, she knows, is not André's forte. He makes too much of dichotomies: Couperin compared with Rameau, Braque versus Matisse, Japan against China. Madeleine protects the boys and, most of all, André. She becomes unobtrusively attached to the passions, interests, and whims of this solitary man, who loves to be surrounded by people; a genius, many say. Madeleine chooses the coffee chez Corselet, the tea chez Hédiard, the caviar and the lobster elsewhere. If they go shopping together, André refuses to carry the packages, even in the elevator.

"If the General carries packages," he states quite seriously, "he is no longer General de Gaulle."

Now a full-time man of letters, Malraux gets organized: "To the workbench."

In a moiré dressing gown with embroidered cuffs, he sits down at his desk before eight in the morning and writes by hand on unlined paper. At eleven, he bathes and shaves. The adults do not eat with the children. Malraux says that this way he respects them. They can have lunch or supper together on Sundays. One step further than some English families: in Malraux's presence children should be neither seen nor heard. In some ways he is loved by proxy: the children are fond of Grosjean, which pleases the writer.

He does not detest a siesta. At half past three, he gets back to work. He smokes twenty cigarettes a day: Camels in the morning, Craven As in the afternoon, and later on, Turkish cigarettes. Just a ritual or obsessive-compulsive behavior? Those around him consider that he drinks a lot of whisky. He loves luxury. Is he savoring a revenge on his childhood? Which was neither miserable, nor poor, but average? Does he know how most French people live? Grosjean notes that he prides himself on sometimes wearing mended shirts or darned socks. He often likes to eat his meals with Madeleine in their bedroom on a card table. He tells his daughter, Florence, "There is a room for you here." In theory: he does no more than say the words. Then Florence comes to stay. The three little boys are introduced to her by their governess, Julienne: "*Mademoiselle, vos frères.*"

It is a like a scene from the court of the king of France or a prince of royal blood. André chides the boys: "Don't get in the way!"

And to his daughter: "Stop playing with the little ones."

Malraux remains locked in; he is ceremonious in his affection. "Flo"—luckily—has a passion for literature. She looks like her father. Unfortunately, she also reminds André of Clara. Even after the divorce, Clara is still a blot on the landscape. She writes an article[2] in which she analyzes "the conjugal row": she explains that it "requires a secret and profound agreement, a harmony that allows the ritual development of fighting." She still questions anyone who has seen or heard André. It is implicit in this second "Livre de comptes" that Clara is living if not with, at least through Malraux. She publishes books that challenge him. *Par de plus longs chemins* (1953) is easy enough to decode: Bernard the archaeologist leaves for Persia, he is an incessant liar, and so on. Malraux claims that he does not read his ex-wife's novels any more than her letters or the biographical articles about him. He tells Grosjean, "You know what I think about the literature of my 'widows' [Clara and Josette]."

Clara has moved into an HLM—a housing project—near the Santé prison. She lives an intelligent, restless existence, carrying on a single-handed, one-sided dialogue, making "huge scenes"; in short, continuing to live with a man who no longer wants to talk to or see her. Florence listens to her soliloquies and hears her make repeated threats of suicide. One morning, her mother is rebuking André for being an ex-revolutionary turned Gaullist, for siding with the conservative camp. That afternoon, Florence sees this attractive, cultivated man, a genius in her eyes. André Malraux never utters Clara's name in front of his daughter.

After the Liberation, he took her to an exhibition. Picasso was present and made a remark, out loud, about Florence's fine features. The little girl was touched by his attention and said to her father that she found Pablo's way of seeing to be extraordinary.

"Be quiet, he is a clown," interrupted Malraux.

She was eighteen when her father remarked to her, "I warn you, all the men who court you will just be trying to get to me. You should know that."

Taken aback and not a little annoyed, she replied, "Perhaps I shall have some charm?"

"Yes, that is possible."

In the eyes of her father, Florence has a failing: she mixes with the intellectual Left, therefore with Communists. As long as they stick to talking about Tolstoy, Victor Hugo, Baudelaire, Racine, or Flaubert, it's fine. Having lived with Clara and then earning an independent living, Florence knows the price of a half pound of butter. Her father doesn't; he spends an awful lot of money and just doesn't mention the needs of others. For Florence, having money is pleasant and vaguely reprehensible. She enjoys the courtiers who mill around the writer, the inexhaustible respect and goodwill of Claude Mauriac, son of François. Florence observes the ceiling of the sitting room, the drapes, the satin, the works of art, the slightly showy side of the Boulogne duplex. Strange father. One can talk with him about Faulkner or Laclos but rarely about everyday events. This is his way of treating his daughter as an adult. The originality of her father's conversation, his singular brilliance, pleases Florence. Is André Malraux bothered by her little "trivia"? His daughter is dazzled by the richness of his culture and his monologues. You have to concentrate to follow him, to make the most of him, this man who is grandiose, even grandiloquent, yet vulnerable and shy, perhaps, behind his confident remarks. For Florence, André Malraux is never at peace. Indeed she detects a growing aggression, an unpredictability that she puts down to alcohol.

Since she has been at the École Alsacienne, Florence has become friends with Mlle. Quoirez, alias Françoise Sagan. Malraux mentions, "It would amuse me to see her."

Françoise Sagan is delighted, André Malraux is charmed. He declares, peremptorily, "She is the new Colette."

Florence does not let herself be overawed by lunch chez Lasserre or by Malraux's favorite, Château Pétrus. She watches her father eat thick, grilled red meat and gobble down mille-feuilles. Cheese he hates—so much that he won't have it in the house. *Bon*. Seriously. Not easy to be the son or daughter of this famous man. How many characters are fighting a civil war within him? Is it hard for him to be a father? He grew up in a neurotic atmosphere; Fernand remains an eccentric and hazy father figure to him. Out of the three boys in Boulogne, Alain, the youngest, seems most at ease. For a long time, the relationship between Malraux and his nephew-son remains good and balanced. Alain's problem is finding just where he fits in between the photo of Roland, his father, framed in his room, and André, the uncle who he cannot help calling "Papa." Gauthier and Vincent know that Madeleine is not their mother. Gauthier wants to be talked to about Josette. Malraux sidesteps. The child confides to Suzanne Chantal, "What my father told me about my mother would fit on the back of a postage stamp."

Gauthier, dark, serious, and pessimistic, adores and reveres his father. He has a Cross of Lorraine on his jacket. If only loving him were enough . . . How is he both to identify with him and break free from him? If he has a rendezvous with André Malraux on a particular day, Gauthier dashes out of his lecture and into the Métro or onto the bus: "You don't keep a man like my father waiting."

He keeps on and on about wanting the same dressing gown. He wears a coat thrown around his shoulders, like his father. Malraux rarely looks at a composition or essay of Gauthier's or a drawing of Vincent's, although he is very gifted. The boys do not dare to speak about themselves in front of, let alone to, André Malraux, the genius. He seems shut off, distant, inattentive: in short, the sort of father and uncle who is very much in touch—with himself. Don't get in the way! Odd words, brilliant or funny judgments about literary and political figures, stick in the children's minds.

"For Paul Morand," Malraux explains to them, "life is hard: when he dines with duchesses, he misses the bistros; when he eats at the bistros, he misses the duchesses."

Vincent is thin, tense, and very good-looking, and seems quite lost. Beuret suspects great unhappiness and pain in this little boy's head. He takes him out.

Vincent, the nervous, hostile runaway, finds himself sent away "for his own good," with the approval of Father Bockel, speaking for God, and Manès Sperber, speaking for psychology. Beuret thinks these two have not understood the drama of Vincent's situation. Who can he confide in? His elder brother, Gauthier, is clearly his father's favorite. Vincent still has his godmother, Marie-Françoise-Jeanne Delclaux, "Rosine." And his maternal grandfather, kind Mr. Clotis, who is even allowed to visit Boulogne (unlike Josette's mother, who is vetoed by Malraux).

Vincent bumps along the bottom for a time, then is blown off course to a boarding school in Alsace, under Bockel's close guard. Malraux corresponds with Bockel and brings up "the hypothesis of Vincent coming to Paris." The brothers must not be together. "If you decide to bring Vincent, it would be wise to send Gauthier off to work in the country during that time."[3]

Does André Malraux channel a love for his first, happy years with Josette through Gauthier, in denial of the later, heavier years when Vincent was born? Vincent revolts and turns against him. Can he sense that his father did not want him? He merely passes through the very chic École des Roches, escaping before long; he is put down for the Collège Saint-Clément at Metz. Bockel is chaplain for students in Strasbourg and gets him into the Lycée Fustel de Coulanges. Worried, Malraux follows from afar Vincent's misadventures as he verges on delinquency. In response to Bockel's descriptions of his pupil's highs and lows, Malraux answers,

"None of all that surprises me, although every relapse destroys a secret hope. . . . However, I have the very strong feeling that you have not intervened in vain, and you know how grateful I am to you. We shall talk about it when you come." Writing to the chaplain is easier, quicker, and less painful than talking to Vincent. Malraux delegates his duties as a father. Vincent shows a real talent for drawing and painting, and Father Bockel gets him into the École des Arts Décoratifs. Vincent stays there for a year. Bockel recommends that he be allowed to ride a motorbike. There are one or two minor accidents. Malraux writes to Bockel:[4] "Vincent seems to be intending to come to Paris on Sunday, on his own authority. An authority that is little justified by the stunning results obtained with the motorbike. I urge you earnestly to tell him not to put himself in this situation. No good will come of it. I know that I never write to you without asking for some chore." Malraux addresses his youngest son via a third person. Did propaganda at the RPF seem easier to control than the impulses and anxieties of a motherless and semifatherless teenager? His sons are starved for affection: they rebel. The smallest thing can become an excuse to pick an argument and unpick a relationship. At eighteen, Vincent attacks his father in an area where the latter did not want to clash with him. There is a violent disagreement. Malraux to Vincent: "If somebody said to you that a boy of your age was explaining to André Malraux that he has failed to understand Cocteau's latest film, what would you tell him?"

"I would tell him that anyone can make mistakes."

Vincent runs off. In front of Madeleine and Alain, Malraux murmurs, "I had to hold myself back just to stop myself throwing him out of the window."

Vincent gets on well with Florence and, once childish squabbles are past, better and better with his elder brother. While on the run, Vincent goes to eat every day with Gauthier, who is staying in a clinic. Gauthier understands his brother: there is a solidarity in their shared solitude, real or imagined. Whatever Madeleine does, she cannot replace their father any more than she can take Josette's place. Gauthier tries to reason with Vincent: don't mess up again! One of the minister's private staff is a former member of the DST, the equivalent of the FBI. He takes care of a few "problems" Vincent gets himself into.

Gauthier becomes conventional and conservative. He has followed regular studies at the Lycée Janson-de-Sailly. His father expects a lot of him. André Malraux has no apparent respect for scholastic results, as far as he himself is concerned, even if he does claim to have a university degree. As for his sons . . . He follows the results of his eldest from afar, as they suffer the swings of an irregular pendulum. In tenth grade, Gauthier's results are disappointing in French composition (he ranks twenty-fifth, fourth, and twenty-fifth in the class in the three terms) but rather better in history. In philosophy, Gauthier "is an intelligent pupil who manages well" and in English a "dilettante who does little work." He wants to write: not novels but "philosophical things." He gets a *mention assez bien* at the baccalauréat and goes on to the Institut d'Études Politiques de Paris to prepare for the civil service training institution, the École Nationale d'Administration. The name Malraux marks you out from the rest.

André Malraux is not close enough to his sons to advise them. His links with his daughter are no stronger but are simpler. She does not live with him so does not have to undergo his moods and dwell constantly in his shadow. Moreover, Flo is a girl and the oldest of the children. She cut the cord with him long ago, out of necessity. Most of all, she does not live through him, listening as the boys do for the return of the prodigious and not very prodigal father. She does not wait around for compliments from him. Malraux is not good at expressing his emotions and his (possible) affection. He does not push his children away: they move away from him. Gauthier demands a room in town. This is not his only move toward independence: he also wants to get married. He is twenty, his fiancée eighteen. The parents are hesitant. Malraux: "If they are conventional, we can ask for a religious wedding in Notre-Dame. I'll get it."

Malraux seems more flexible with his nephew-son, Alain, who objects to his behavior less. The writer withdraws, seems absent even when sitting with Madeleine and Alain listening to the radio. Or when Madeleine plays the piano. Could he have comforted and encouraged the tormented Vincent? Finalizing his art books is less disconcerting than examining Vincent's gouaches.

He devotes himself to the three volumes of *Le Musée imaginaire de la sculpture mondiale*. He writes a preface to a book by Major General Pierre-Élie Jacquot on world strategy. He watches closely over an essay by Gaétan Picon, *Malraux par lui-même*: a flattering, prettily illustrated hagiography. Malraux chooses the photos and documents with Picon and annotates the book. Opposite certain pages, Picon places forty-five plates of Malraux, some worked over with a feigned negligence. Malraux appears mummified by this book. His notes seem to come from beyond the grave. Here and there, he surrenders and writes as he talks. Where the word "unconscious" comes up in a paragraph, Malraux notes, "In 1910, we would rummage through the unconscious looking for demons; in 1953, we are starting to find angels (or heroes) there. Who knows where that might take us." Malraux begins to open up: "The word 'know' [*connaître*], applied to beings, has always made me dream. I think that we know nobody. The word incorporates the idea of communion, that of familiarity, that of elucidation—and a few others." The idea seems, philosophically and psychologically, distressingly banal, boiling down to saying that *A* is never *B*. Applied to Malraux, does it mean that he does not want to or cannot know others, including his children and those close to him? Or, further on, "Meditation on death at no point matches the fear of being killed: I have sometimes fought with indifference, and I am not the only one."

Malraux rewrites the final scene of an atrociously bad theatrical adaptation of *La Condition humaine* by Thierry Maulnier. At Gallimard, he eventually inaugurates the "Univers des formes" collection. Finalized by Georges Salles, with Beuret controlling the logistics, it should start appearing in 1960. The writing of *La Métamorphose des dieux*[5] also takes some time. Malraux accepts a few paraliterary tasks. He joins past winners of the Goncourt at a reunion for the prize's fiftieth anniversary. At coffee, Elsa Triolet proposes a toast to the many points the Goncourt laureates have in common.

"Although many things separate us, Malraux and me," she adds.

Malraux, loud enough to be overheard, says, "Yes, talent, for example."

Despite the lack of understanding among the members of the family, Malraux spends holidays with the boys and sometimes with Florence: at the Hôtel des Balances in Lucerne, the Minerva in Florence, the Hôtel du Golf at Cran-sur-Sierre, a villa in Saint-Jean-de-Luz, a hotel in an old convent in Taormina, Sicily. Some holidays are happy and harmonious. Madeleine, Florence, and Alain follow André, at a run, through the museums. Malraux still remembers pictures with impressive precision.

In 1956, he celebrates his fifty-fifth birthday. He is putting on weight, thickening out. He drinks too much. The children know, and Madeleine tells him off about it. He doesn't like this frank criticism. He behaves like a grand bourgeois with a literary career that, if not quite interrupted, has moved onto a track—a siding, perhaps—that is not that of fiction.

He appears to have forgotten politics. It doesn't forget him. In April 1958, four years after the beginning of the war in Algeria,[6] his daughter calls on him to sign a "solemn address to the president of the Republic," René Coty. The government has seized *La Question*, a book by the Communist Henri Alleg, describing and denouncing torture in Algeria. "Police operations" have turned into a war, in which thousands of French soldiers are getting caught up; not only the professional servicemen but conscripts too.

A settled André Malraux drops back into his art books, as if diverted from world events. At the invitation of the Cini Foundation, he goes to Venice to give a talk on "The Secret of the Great Venetians," like an emeritus professor who has chosen to take early retirement and contemplate his past. Venice in the spring, in an excellent hotel, is a timeless wonder, fixed in a bygone age unrelated to Malraux's History.

le couteau - unte - les - dents

CHAPTER TWENTY-EIGHT

Power

I N VENICE, MALRAUX was not expecting the chaotic events in Algeria. Those who have been plotting to bring de Gaulle back to govern
France mistrust Malraux and have not kept him informed. In May
1958, the General begins the process of seizing power.[1] He achieves it
with a coup d'état, not constitutional but democratic: the deputies set him
in place, and a majority of French voters count on him to get France out
of the Algerian conflict. In 1940, the National Assembly handed power
over to Philippe Pétain. Less than twenty years later, an Assembly that is
in almost as bad shape surrenders to Charles de Gaulle. The French, since
Bonaparte, have loved a man in uniform.

De Gaulle sarcastically explains to the journalists that he is a bit old
"to start a career as dictator." Aware of the gravity of the situation, Malraux abandons Veronese and Tintoretto and gets back to Paris.

He meets General de Gaulle in the Hôtel La Pérouse. Both talk of
State, a stable currency, Empire, but not Algeria. De Gaulle keeps his
plans for Algeria close to his chest. On June 1, having become président
du Conseil—a narrow title with a tight collar but one that will do for the
time being—the General names Malraux "*ministre délégué à la présidence du
Conseil*"—minister reporting to him. As in 1945, he gives the writer responsibility for information. For someone who was hoping for an important ministry, this perhaps strikes Malraux as something of a rehash. He
will also have responsibility for a vague mission, "the expansion and influence of French culture." But with his family, Malraux is chirpy enough:
"Right, my studious days are over."

He moves into temporary premises opposite the Hôtel Matignon and
de Gaulle and sends a few lines to Pia: "The ministry I am entering is a
graveyard. As soon as it has ceased to be one, I will ask you to come and

see me." He does not let his disappointment show. He would have liked to go to the Ministry of the Interior. He could have managed Algeria nicely from there. France has two last resorts, in Malraux's opinion: the General and himself. The former can shout all he wants and doesn't deny himself the privilege. The latter must keep quiet.

The minister in charge of information appoints Albert Ollivier head of television. For Malraux, whoever controls television has a hold on information, and information is, more and more, a part of power. Malraux leaves a note[2] for his successor in which he presents the ministry as "an apparatus intended for French information and propaganda abroad." He proposes a central reorganization, a regrouping of the ministry's departments, including one "solely with responsibility for the United States."

Malraux looks for handholds to steady his power and particularly that of the General. Radio is a "ghost ship that has not yet sunk," he says. It must cease to be "a dumping ground or charitable organization for the parties." According to Malraux, radio is an institution "where each party, on arriving in power, had added its creatures to those which it replaced without prejudice from a fairly extensive Communist infiltration." Redundancies must be made "for reasons of politics and reasons of incompetence." "Political purification" must urgently "remove all the technicians who belong to the Communist Party" and "put into place an apparatus capable of functioning in case of strike. . . . Information radio, which is the primary target in any political strike, can function with fifty technicians." According to the minister, we must "remove all journalists who have shown during the crisis [May–June 1958] their hostility to the national objectives and to General de Gaulle." Malraux explains: it is not a matter of "knowing if our adversaries of yesterday could be scared into behaving decently but of making sure that the government does not find them ready to betray it at the first obstacle that it meets." No matter the "howling provoked by the dismissals or transfers." Malraux is clear: "The apparatus I have prepared—whether it be called information management, current affairs, or something else—is a limited apparatus and easily controllable; its installation is entirely distinct from the reorganization of the fiction services (theater, etc.); in radio, the reorganization is much slower and of a different nature."

He places this political contraption under the direction of Louis Terrenoire, a hardened Gaullist. The "apparatus" consists of radio news, television news, and so-called current affairs programs; it also oversees the "psychological services in the army and . . . some others." Malraux does not want it to be subjected "to the fiction of objectivity currently professed by information broadcasting."

Malraux becomes the theoretician and practitioner of the Gaullist (and for a long time French) conception of information broadcasting on "public service" radio and television. He is interested in television technique. When he offers Claude Mauriac a job, he asks him to work on the General's television appearances: "Yes, it is at his [de Gaulle's] request; he has had enough of being shot from the front, with a complete lack of imagination. For example, you should go from a shot of the General to the statue of the Republic, when he's talking about the Republic, in Place de la République on September 4 [1958]. . . . They never show the Republic [statue]. They always make sure they don't when it's the General."

Malraux is asked questions about Algeria. Journalists suggest that the demonstrations of fraternization between Muslims and Europeans in Algeria, far from being spontaneous, were set up. Malraux does not deny it, as many Gaullists do. He answers, à la Malraux, "The Battle of Valmy [France versus Prussia, 1792] was paid for, and the French Army did not know it at the time. It is not certain that Danton, in doing so, was doing France a disservice." He adds, "We have seen more Muslims cheering General de Gaulle than there are fellaghas in all Algeria."

Some consider that Malraux represents the left wing of Gaullism, by virtue of his anticolonialist past. He claims that there have not been any more tortures in Algeria since the General came to power. He must know that he is lying, or else we have to grant him a dose of naive optimism. After the resignation of General de Bollardière, who refused to employ the interrogation methods of the French Army, Colonel Roger Barberot wrote to Malraux, "I think it indispensable that your voice be raised . . . the Bollardière affair is serious. Because he is the last spotless knight."[3] Malraux appears before the English-speaking press.[4] "If . . . you were a young Muslim, would you be a supporter of the FLN?" they ask him.

"If I were a young Muslim, I would perhaps fight with the fellaghas, but I would be happy to turn now to the man who has fought against torture, and I would put myself at the service of the man who has defended courage."

The government seizes the newspapers *France-Observateur* and *L'Express*, which have been attacking French policies and denouncing the use of torture in Algeria. When talking about another matter, Malraux clumsily (or hypocritically) declares, "These newspapers were seized at the request of the military authorities . . . the government does not intend to reinstate the violation of opinion and censorship. . . . If *Le Monde* was seized in Algeria, that is because it is in Algeria, not in France, that there is a state of war. . . . We are doing what we can, how we can, and when we can. It is not very good, but it is better than the others."

Malraux has his own plan for Algeria: it needs to be partitioned: one territory for the Algerians, the Arabs, and the Kabyles, another for the French. In short, they would be placed into peaceful competition for the happiness of the people. Who would get the Saharan oil that obsesses Malraux?

What is to be done with Malraux the minister? Pierre Lefranc, on de Gaulle's staff, suggests the General send him on a trip—a multiclient sales rep in literature, action, and politics for the firm of Gaullism, Inc. Malraux leaves for Guadeloupe, Martinique, Guyana, Cayenne. There, for the referendum on September 28, he helps to land 80 percent of the voters in the General's favor.

He considers himself a very special envoy, a self-styled "Minister of Urgent Affairs." Urgency can emerge everywhere. Some of the ministerial high-ups see Malraux as the General's dancer; gifted, brilliant, but too wild and unpredictable. Some of the senior civil servants of the Fourth Republic who have remained in place are none too keen on this new minister, especially when they do not like his books.

Article 1 of Government Decree No. 58630, dated July 25, 1958, specifies that André Malraux "deals with all matters that are entrusted to him by the président du Conseil and, if there is cause, proceeds in the study thereof with the ministers concerned." Nebulous and dangerous attributions, which officialize a mystical link between the General and the writer-minister, short-circuiting the ministries. At the Foreign Office on the Quai d'Orsay, Malraux's promotion and the text of this decree arouse angry comment: "This new mission of Mr. Malraux does not carry the signature of the minister of foreign affairs." Malraux is suspected of having previously arranged a transfer of powers. The wording of the decree is "equivocal." And the two words "diverse projects": they don't like the look of that. The minister of foreign affairs, Maurice Couve de Murville, and other worthies sense the presence of a large appetite here. The Foreign Office has one peculiarity: France is one of the only major democracies to have a foreign policy for culture. It immediately imagines, with the bureaucratic fantasy of which the department is sometimes capable, that this "delegate" will soon be asking the minister of foreign affairs to carry out projects for him—he will be giving him orders! "Proceeds in the study thereof . . . with the ministers concerned" . . . sounds deliberately hazy.

The *compagnon*-colonel-minister-Goncourt is awaited with administrative machine guns and cultural bazookas at the ready. A legal adviser prepares a note for the chief officer of cultural affairs at the Foreign Office, Roger Seydoux. As the lioness her young, the Quai d'Orsay will protect its territory and its historic political and cultural prerogatives. Malraux is alerted and sends a plenipotentiary, Alain Brugères, to reassure the department. In Note No. 2693, addressed to Couve, Malraux's envoy assures "that his minister never had the intention of dealing with cultural affairs." Come now, Decree No. 58630 "had no aim other than to prepare the takeover of youth services" without irritating the education minister. "I thought it best," writes the department man who receives Brugères, "to put together a certain number of arguments, in case Mr. Malraux should be tempted to become interested in our business another time."

Malraux travels again. He goes to Iran, India, Japan. A note from the Foreign Office, December 17, 1958: Action stations. The department passes from the defensive to the offensive. Sweet enough at first: "After returning from the East, where, with the Iranian, Indian, and Japanese authorities, he studied grand projects of artistic and cultural exchange . . . Mr. Malraux indicated that he judged it necessary, in order to put his projects into practice, to create a post of high commissioner for the Arts." Then the tone becomes plaintive: for the department, "the intentions attributed to Mr. Malraux are very worrying." Diplomats of all departments, unite! There is a "risk of the door being opened to further dismantling." Notes circulate among middle management, upper management, and the minister's private staff. Malraux's ambitions and pretensions must be crushed.

On December 21, 1958, Charles de Gaulle becomes the first president of the Fifth Republic. He moves quietly from the Hôtel Matignon to the Élysée Palace, taking ten minutes to speak with his predecessor, René Coty. Twenty-one cannon shots, and hey, presto! there he is on the other side of the Seine. De Gaulle reshuffles his government: "I have decided to take [Jacques] Soustelle in place of Malraux."

The General asks for "something to be found" for Malraux. Michel Debré, the new (and first) prime minister, does not appreciate the president explaining to him that Malraux's presence will give "depth" to his government. Georges Pompidou plays a role from the shadows as fixer of numerous nominations.

"Information is too narrow for you. Soustelle can do that," he says to Malraux. Pompidou and Debré explain to Malraux that the General wants to create a Ministry of Culture, an important ministry that would bring new dimensions to the actions of the state. You are the only one who can bring the necessary style and grandeur to this undertaking.

General relief: Malraux is delighted. A beautiful love story between the writer and de Gaulle is sealed.[5] As an honorary bonus, Malraux is named *ministre d'état*—minister of state—with responsibility for cultural affairs on January 8, 1959. Soon he will have an office with a view onto the gardens of the Palais-Royal. *Ministre d'état!* This title places him on the General's right in Cabinet meetings. Malraux is not prime minister, which he wouldn't mind, but he is one of the important ministers. And de Gaulle often writes it without a capital: *premier ministre*. In France, there is only one Premier: you-know-who.

Won't Malraux's ministry (they sigh at the Foreign Office) absorb department heads from other ministries into his own? But it will also attract more staff. Told you so: Jacques Jaujard, head of Arts et Lettres at the Ministry of Education, becomes general secretary of the unwieldy new Ministry of Culture. A founding decree of July 24, 1959, defines his duties: he has "the mission of making accessible the major works of mankind, and mainly those of France, to the greatest possible number of French people, to ensure the largest audience for our cultural heritage and to favor the creation of art and the spirit that enriches it." Malraux worded the decree himself. The General couldn't find anything wrong to say about it.[6]

Malraux sees what he is creating as an original and sovereign ministry. He must not end up (seriously) looking like the much-disparaged junior ministers in fine arts of the last administration—which would take us nowhere. Malraux takes control of architecture, Arts et Lettres, and the National Archives, which up until then had belonged to the Ministry of Education. He is also assigned the Centre National de la Cinématographie, previously under the tutelage of the Ministry of Industry. He would have liked to have, once again, supreme control over television. Michel Debré opposes that; so does the General.

Enthusiastic to start with, Malraux soon loses his innocence when faced with the arguments, sluggishness, and complications of French administrative bureaucracy. He has at his disposition 600 assorted officers in central administration and 3,500 in external departments. Progressively, he defines the main lines of his policy: the inception of regionalization, an inventory of France's cultural wealth, the endorsement of projects for the restoration of ancient monuments, an assessment of the status of artists, the establishment of a music policy in France, and, above all, the introduction of regional arts centers, *maisons de la culture*.

Malraux protects himself. As his principal aide, he takes on Georges Loubet, who, during the Occupation, shot Philippe Henriot, the Vichyist minister of information. That sort of hard action really impresses Malraux. The transfers, much feared by other ministries, take place at last. Malraux just manages to snatch some departments away from the high commissioner for youth and sport. He is no longer amusing to the ministers and ministries that find themselves dispossessed; just annoying. The Foreign Office changes tactic: perhaps the minister with responsibility for cultural affairs should take some responsibility for political affairs, since he already sees himself as minister of "urgent" affairs and minister plenipotentiary. The more he busies himself with politics, the less he will be tempted to swallow up the cultural services belonging to the Ministry of Foreign Affairs.

A battle is also being waged on the financial front. Those responsible for cultural affairs at the Foreign Office on the Quai d'Orsay want to keep an independent budget. The Quai d'Orsay is, after all, a permanent institution, representing French culture across the world; Malraux is just a fad of the General-President and an alibi for the Left, an intellectual diversion.

Malraux and de Gaulle have been planning a short voyage to South America for the ministre d'état. The Foreign Office is informed and proposes that Malraux visit not four but ten countries "to defend France's Algerian policy." The suggested destinations are Argentina, Bolivia, Brazil, Chile, Colombia, Ecuador, Paraguay, Peru, Uruguay, Venezuela— the works. On the plane, Malraux confides to one of his aides, Pierre Moinot,[7] "I am not going to sell a cultural policy, I am going to explain our policy of self-determination [for Algeria]."

"Does the General know?" asks Moinot.

"No, but it's in line with what he wants."

Malraux's mission consists of shaking the lethargy out of the inactive, putting some heat under those who are lukewarm, and convincing the hostile. Speaking in South America, the writer-minister is heckled by Algerian nationalist students from the FLN.

Whenever Malraux arrives in a capital city with a president or minister, the accredited French ambassador accompanies him, of course, then sends a report back to the Foreign Office. The growing pile of dispatches at the Quai d'Orsay exasperates and amuses the diplomats. Malraux does have his admirers and fans in the department. After all, he is a Goncourt Prize winner, supposedly a great member of the Resistance, and leader of the Alsace-Lorraine Brigade. Not every visitor from Paris to stay in a French ambassador's residence possesses his titles and prestige.

Malraux gives a speech at the launch of a son et lumière show at the Acropolis in Athens at the end of May 1959. He is accompanied by Maurice Herzog, the high commissioner for youth and sport. The French cruiser *De Grasse* sparkles from the harbor. Malraux is awarded the Grand Cross by Paul of Greece. Guy de Girard de la Charbonnière, the French ambassador, looks on at what is "in local terms, the most important event to have marked Franco-Hellenic relations since the war." Alas, the show is a disaster. The ambassador finds that "the *lumières* are as frustrating as the *son*, which is dreadful. The numerous sound sources placed around the auditorium on the Pnyx Hill seem to have no link between each other. Instead of the stereophonic effect promised by the technicians [Philips], the audience suddenly hears a blaring from its right, then a screeching from its left, followed by a howling from in front. All of which is incoherent and extremely disagreeable to the hearing. The 'sound effects' were, besides, as bad as can be imagined. The arrival of the marathon runner, for example, the intended highlight of the show, is, as one of my neighbors said to me, more evocative of 'a horse galloping on a sheet of metal and racing against a locomotive.' "[8] Not all diplomats are fawning sycophants. The ambassador nonetheless praises the depth of Malraux's speeches, referring to the "dazzling presentations" at which his listeners at the École Française d'Athènes were "filled with wonder."

"The Acropolis is the only place in the world haunted simultaneously by the spirit and by courage," Malraux said. As for Greece itself: "Never before her did art unite spear and thought." There's a fine quote for senior-year dissertations: Give examples other than Greece. The "major political problem of our time," Malraux stated, "is how to reconcile social justice and liberty." The word "culture" is "confused": for him, it is "the entirety of the creations of art and the mind." He adds that "culture is not inherited, it is won." According to this view, state education makes no contribution to culture. Malraux embellishes and perpetuates a chosen image of himself: "We have learned the same truth in the same blood spilled for the same cause, when the people of Greece and the Free French fought side by side in the Battle of Egypt, when the men of my maquis made little Greek flags with their handkerchiefs in honor of your victories, and when the villages of your mountains rang their bells for the liberation of Paris. Between all the values of the mind, the most productive are those which are born of communion and of courage." My maquis. Who's going to check?[9]

In Mexico, the ambassador Jean de La Garde reports Malraux's remarks to a colleague. He stated that "artificial rain is a process which is now fully ready." Having thus anticipated modern technology, "Mr. Malraux shows that . . . if Mexico wanted to call upon American companies to organize irrigation of the north of the country with artificial rain, it would need to pay these companies substantial fees. On the other hand, with a global plan, they could obtain the said procedure from France free of charge." Well, they sigh back at the Quai d'Orsay, at least for once Malraux didn't tell them "the General wishes . . ."

Once he is back, Malraux's missions often look costly. Some even hint—slander!—that the ministre d'état gets confused between old and new francs. Some Foreign Office departments think he "has his head in the clouds." It is down to them to keep the accounts firmly at ground level. Free of charge, the rainmaking machine? Paid for out of France's pocket, more like. In fact, it turns out that there is no such invention and Mexico has enough rain anyway. The department piles on additions and subtractions. In private, the minister of foreign affairs declares that Malraux is an "impostor" with Pharaonic projects. The General, France, national prestige, culture, transcendence, all very interesting. How much is it going to cost? De Gaulle is an excellent tightrope walker: he counts on Malraux to get France talked about throughout "the universe" ("world" being too mean a word[10] for the General) and leaves it to the state bureaucracy to limit the financial damage.

Malraux goes to Japan in February 1960 to inaugurate a new building at the Maison Franco-Japonaise. The Foreign Office is perturbed to hear that Malraux's mission has "received a mandate from the government to bring about and see through negotiations concerning the cultural exchange policy between the two countries and that they had the complete agreement of the department." French painting is bewitching Japan. The Japanese ask for specific paintings: the portrait of Zola by Manet, Van Gogh's *Chambre de Vincent à Arles*, a particular Delacroix, such-and-such a Toulouse-Lautrec. Not easy to negotiate with these delightful Japanese: You have to know their codes. A nod, which in France passes for "Yes, we agree," actually signifies "No, we'll have to think about it." Malraux, with superb arrogance, makes commitments in the name of France.

After this excursion—which is a media success in Japan, from the General's point of view—the cultural top dog at the Foreign Office, Roger Seydoux, sends a note: "To the knowledge of the department, Malraux received from the government no mandate of this sort." The Quai d'Orsay does not like nasty surprises. It has been paying in and paying out but would like to put the brakes on this impetuous minister. Japan is expensive in 1959 and 1960: 98,178,000 new francs, the equivalent of just under $20 million. Seydoux complains: even before being asked by his foreign counterparts, Malraux proposed to the Indians, the Iranians, and the Japanese that "their civilization should be presented to France," thanks to international exhibitions. Without the benefit of closely argued discussion, he acts as if money will be generated by cultural and political goodwill alone. Seydoux defends the department: "Mr. Malraux makes no effort to hide his desire to control our artistic policy abroad."

Roger Seydoux requests a disciplinary memo and a summit between Foreign Affairs and the Ministry of Culture. Malraux receives him. The two men hammer out conflicts of attribution. Malraux swears he has had approval for the idea of his "shock missions"; they have been entrusted to him by de Gaulle in person. They have "in reality a political goal." In order to keep them secret, if not discreet, Seydoux notes afterward, the ministre d'état is "sometimes required to give them a cultural varnish." So it wasn't to talk about Gide or Picasso that Malraux went to Tehran, Delhi, Tokyo, Rio . . . Seydoux does not emerge from the meeting convinced. But he doesn't telephone the General's office to ask for confirmation. When the General hears that Malraux and the Quai d'Orsay are bickering, he sighs, "Inevitable . . . Malraux . . ."

Malraux, at home in his ministry, often comes across as inaccessible. Backslapping isn't his style. He has chosen men he knows for his private staff and his department: Albert Beuret, Louis Chevasson, de Gaulle's niece's husband, Bernard Anthonioz, Gaétan Picon, and Pierre Moinot. Beuret shuttles between Malraux's private and public pursuits. He still oversees the writer's work at Gallimard, where he can argue with Gaston in person. The latter complains about the production costs of *Le Musée imaginaire de la sculpture mondiale*. Lang the printer is expensive: "Too many illustrations! We have to drop one in ten."

"You want to turn it into an *Almanach Vermot* for sculpture," says Beuret.

Gaston: "You're not working for de Gaulle here."

"I know that only too well," sighs Beuret.

Albert Beuret accompanies Malraux on a few trips. In Africa, an embassy adviser, seeing to what extent Beuret imitates Malraux in tone of voice and gesture, mentions it to him.

"That's better than aping some damn stupid diplomat," retorts Beuret.

Malraux is as active in France as he is abroad, at least at the beginning of his ministry. He goes through two periods. First, an intense creative activity lasting four years from when he comes to power. His ideas have a price: the budget for his ministry is upped from 0.3 percent to 0.43 percent of the national budget. In this conscientious phase, Malraux listens to his colleagues, even those he doesn't like, such as Valéry Giscard d'Estaing. Giscard sees him to discuss the Ministry of Cultural Affairs' financial problems.

"These *maisons de la culture*, what's that?"

The question does not amuse Malraux. In the 1930s, he was already talking about the idea to the League of Intellectuals Against Fascism. Even before forming his ministry, Malraux announced that within three years, each department in France would have a *maison de la culture*. Once a minister, he presented his idea to the National Assembly: "Three hypotheses dominate the domain of the arts in France. The first is totalitarian culture, and we reject that. The second is bourgeois culture, that is, in practical terms, culture that is only accessible to those who are rich enough to possess it . . ."

The third is culture à la Malraux: "If we accept neither the first nor the second hypothesis, noble or worn out though the word 'democracy' may be, there is then only one democratic culture that matters . . . in every French department, these *maisons de la culture* will be disseminating what we are trying to do in Paris: any child of sixteen, however poor he may be, should be able to have a real contact with his national heritage and with the glory of the mind of mankind."[11]

The Senate is treated to the Malrucian—and calamitous—formulation of what, in the vision of the writer-minister, is an essential doctrine: "It is the job of the universities to get their students to know Racine, but it is only for those who perform his plays to get them to be loved. Our job is to get the geniuses of mankind, and particularly those of France, loved; not to get them known." How can one love without knowing? By visitation? Who has not loved certain authors at university, thanks to or in spite of certain professors? According to Malraux's way of thinking, the culture presented in his arts centers runs counter to education. The minister is specific about this when inaugurating (with a sledgehammer) the *maison de la culture* in Amiens:[12] "University is there to teach people. We are here to teach people to love. Nobody in the world ever understood music just because he had the Ninth Symphony explained to him. Nobody in the world ever loved poetry because he had Victor Hugo explained to him." A *maison de la culture* does not explain, it "animates" in an atmosphere of liberty and versatility. "Each time we replace this revelation with an explanation, we will be doing something perfectly useful, but we will be creating an essential misunderstanding."

Moinot defines the objectives of a *maison de la culture* more clearly than Malraux: "To offer to every person, whoever and wherever he may be, the temptation of culture; it is there to bring about an encounter. From this encounter can be born a familiarity, a shock, a passion, another way for each person to envisage his own condition. Creations of the arts being, by their essence, the property of all and a mirror for ourselves, it is important that everyone should be able to measure their richness and gaze upon themselves in them." The *maison* "excludes specialization . . . and is home to all forms of culture under all their aspects. . . . It is not concerned with the organization of teaching, even of the arts, and always gives preference to the work. It gives rise to a direct confrontation that avoids the pitfall whereby [the work] is impoverished by a simplifying vulgarization."

The first *maison de la culture* opened in Le Havre in 1961, followed by Caen, Bourges, Thonon, and Firminy. These were set up within buildings that had originally been conceived for other purposes (a museum, a theater, a convention center, a cinema in the case of the Théâtre de l'Est in Paris). Amiens and Grenoble were purpose-built. New *maisons de la culture* opened at Nevers, Reims, Rennes, and Saint-Etienne, all (except for Paris) financed—in theory, at any rate—half by the state and half by the town in question. Exactly what would constitute a success was flexible to Malraux's assistant and friend, the writer Gaétan Picon, who said at an opening in 1966, "What the *maison de la culture* will be is not something we know so much as something we will seek out together." Individual *maisons* could, and can still, be judged on their own merits. In terms of the influence of the scheme's spirit, there are now sixty-three successful "national stages," even in small towns, which are rigorously faithful to the project's approach. Better still, a number of classical and even centenarian institutions have integrated the principle of plurality of artistic disciplines: libraries, municipal theaters, "specialized" festivals, museums, and art schools. The Pompidou Center, the Musée d'Orsay, and the Louvre itself offer concerts and film screenings throughout the day and have cassettes to borrow and buy; the Comédie-Française and the Conservatoire National have similarly diversified. Yet the concrete declared aims of the project were not met: the network of *maisons de la culture* was never established at anything like the intended scale. "If there has been talk of a failure of the *maisons de la culture*," wrote Augustin Girard of the ministry, "it is because this approach of broadened access to the arts, which was so immediately attractive to cultural leaders all over the world, from North America to the heart of India, was implemented here by Malraux himself . . . only in seven towns—and not in ninety-five departments as he had hoped."

Malraux's second ministerial phase runs up to 1965. He drinks more and more. Often, at the ministry in the Rue de Valois, Beuret fields inquiries from Malraux's entourage. How is the minister today? Beuret (to the initiated): "A bout of the old malaria."

Translation: Malraux has been drinking, better see him another day. He's snowed under, Albert also explains. He's working. Very busy with his oeuvre. When Malraux has a "bout of malaria," his tics become more visible. He slurs his speech slightly. He speaks so fast that his sentences are compressed. So it's better to communicate by note. A little alcohol calms him down; a lot overexcites him.

Between 1963 and 1964, the ministry functions without Malraux following the "details" too closely. His relationship with his staff and the heads of departments is distant but less hostile than before. Then, toward 1965, it is, for many, disenchantment time.

Malraux is used to living in style. He invites friends and colleagues to the Relais Henri IV or chez Taillevent or (posher still) chez Lasserre, his favorite restaurant. In conversation, he shines. Those who know him well—those he does not mistrust—feel that he is becoming distant. Where is the old Malraux?

If somebody leaves him, he feels betrayed; they have failed in their duty to him. André Holleaux's post implies military hours; *directeur du cabinet* is a twenty-four-hour-a-day job (especially when the minister is there for only a few of them). Holleaux would like to take over as head of cinema when the post becomes vacant.

"Consider it done," says Malraux; and although he replies to his letters, he never speaks to Holleaux again. He turns minor molehills into ministerial mountains, even in fields where his competence is not glaringly obvious. He lets Gaétan Picon go: Picon is required to resign because he has defended Pierre Boulez against Marcel Landowski when it comes to naming a head of music. Madeleine intervenes, but in vain. "The best thing is not to give a damn," Malraux responds.

He receives praise. He spreads embarrassment. He causes disappointment. He drinks.

"Tell me, Foccart," grumbles de Gaulle to his Africa specialist, "Malraux seems tired. He's not on dope, is he?"[13]

His sullen mood—he seems unhappy more than anything—pushes him to delegate not only ministry business but also his personal problems. Loubet is given "responsibility for Vincent" as he might have been given responsibility for historical monuments. He meets with Florence Malraux, who is supporting her half brother. Loubet holds forth: boys like Vincent have to be pinned down, taken in hand.

Having been punctual in the years up to 1965, Malraux now tends to arrive late. Or he relies on his secretary's excuses and diplomatic acrobatics to reschedule meetings. He no longer holds a group meeting of his department heads. He thereby loses contact with the senior civil servants, the link with the base. Those who do remain in contact with him—Pierre Moinot, Brigitte Friang, Diomède Catroux, Beuret, and Chevasson—are crestfallen, although they can still benefit from Malraux's good qualities. Drunk or not, when he escapes his state of torpor, it is clear that he has not forgotten his mastery of monologue. He believes in himself but is less and less inclined to take on anything big. He is protected and lamented by those around him. He who started as such a good pupil, studying his dossiers with diligence.

Less concerned with his ministry, Malraux remains nonetheless a brilliant and charming orator. At least up to 1965, the parliamentary assembly enjoys his eloquence (whereas Malraux himself is bored by his appearance at the Palais-Bourbon). Malraux, despite his worship of fraternity, is not much of a democrat; he does not like the parliamentary process, even as rehashed by de Gaulle. The opposition? A load of driveling whiners. Malraux does, however, behave respectfully toward the representative assemblies. In public, at least; in private, it's often "those stupid bastards!"

Despite the suggestions made by certain ministerial colleagues and even the president, Malraux refuses to present himself at the elections. He cannot see himself shaking sticky hands, kissing babies, presiding at dinners. The *coronel* has no reason to stand as a candidate. He derives his legitimacy from Charles de Gaulle, who derives his directly from French voters. Malraux's place at the top, as minister, remains assured, since de Gaulle has a system that allows him to appoint a minister, or even a prime minister, without that person being a member of Parliament. Malraux, however, without flagrantly courting Parliament, does behave tactfully. He does not frequent the bars of the Palais-Bourbon or the Palais de Luxembourg, but he speaks to the rank-and-file deputies in the corridors. Even with the most obtuse, he chats about Romanesque architecture or this or that *conservatoire*: yes, indeed, your town could really do with that. . . . When asked to intercede, he has his office reply and then signs the letter. He pulls some wires, with moderation.

Over ten years, the minister appears twenty-six times before the Assembly (barely the minimum required for a minister). Less often in the Senate. Sometimes he fills the House. There aren't that many compelling speakers. He amuses, delights, and tries his public. Whatever you say about him, he's original. As in Moscow or the Mutualité rooms or in front of American progressives, he lets loose his formulaic phrases. He strays from his notes and waxes lyrical about culture, history, and destiny. Many members of Parliament are convinced that he has a privileged relationship with de Gaulle. When the verbal vertigo seizes him, Malraux is neither Barrès nor Jaurès, just Malraux, with his slogans: "My ministry is not fine arts modernized, it is the State at the service of culture." Understand: I am an extraordinary minister with a ministry; not, I repeat, a junior minister.

"I am the only one who doesn't know what culture is." This joke delights deputies and cabinet ministers.

"Money is not everything." Not the sort of thing to come out with when presenting your budget.

Malraux's performances in front of the Assembly establish a ritual. Fernand Grenier, a Communist member and cinema lover, specializes in picking fights with Malraux. If Grenier is absent when the minister enters the chamber, Malraux is worried: without this expected interlocutor, the show won't be complete. A supporting actor should be there for the leading man.

Accepting, as is the custom, to answer for other ministers who are absent, Malraux appears one afternoon in the House when only five, then three, deputies are present. One of the speakers refers to "the Assembly."

Malraux exclaims, "What assembly? There are three deputies here!"

The chairwomen of the session tries to excuse the Gaullist members: "Monsieur le Ministre, there is the UNR convention . . ."

Malraux, barely mollified: "I know that! I will be there on Sunday. But today I am here."

Three or four spectators for an actor of his caliber—really! Especially when he has agreed to understudy for a less important minister.

Often Malraux charms the deputies: "We have just been told that each speaker regretted not having more than five minutes in this debate, whereas the speaking time allowed to the government was forty-five minutes. I have to respond to three report presentations and fifteen speakers, making a total of eighteen speeches. That therefore leaves me with two and a half minutes per answer. I think we can say that the score is even. [Laughter.]"

Some right-thinking (or unthinking) deputies attack Malraux: the state-subsidized Théâtre de France opens a production of *Les Paravents*[14] by Jean Genet in 1966. The themes of Genet's work—theft, homosexuality, crime, outcasts, and victims—its heretical heart and sumptuous style, are not within the reach of every conservative member of Parliament. Nor of those on the Left, come to that. Malraux prepares a long answer to those who were offended by this play.

"Liberty, ladies and gentlemen, does not always have clean hands: but when her hands are not clean, before throwing her out of the window, we must look twice. This is a subsidized theater, you say. I have nothing to say about that. But the reading we have heard is a fragment. This fragment is played out not on a stage but in the wings. They say that it gives one the impression of being confronted with an anti-French play. If we really were confronted with an anti-French play, we would be facing a fairly serious problem. However, anybody who has read this play knows that it is not an anti-French play. It is antihuman. It is anti-everything."

Malraux was perhaps never in such brilliant form in front of the Assembly before this day. In the same prepared speech: "What you call rot is not an accident. It is that in the name of which we have always stopped those we have stopped. I do not in any way claim—and it is not my place to do so—that Monsieur Genet is Baudelaire. If he were Baudelaire, we wouldn't know it. The proof is that none of us knew that Baudelaire was a genius. [Laughter.] What is certain is that the argument invoked, 'That offends my sensibilities, so it must be stopped,' is not a reasoned argument. The reasoned argument is the following: 'This play offends your sensitivities. Do not go and buy a seat. Other things are on elsewhere.' "

Oratorical pyrotechnics, perhaps, but he knocks them dead in the House: "I stress the words 'for no reason,' for if we ban *Les Paravents*, it will be put on again tomorrow, not three but five hundred times. We may have pronounced an excellent speech and proved that we were capable of taking measures of prohibition; but in fact we would have forbidden nothing at all. What is essential is not to know what we can do with three francs of public money but to know what we will ban or not, to be aware how much glory a shortsighted action would impart to a play whose influence we want to minimize. I don't think it is urgent. [Smiles.]"

In the Senate, Malraux flushes out a senator, philosopher, and hard-line member of the Central Committee of the PCF, the unpredictable Roger Garaudy.[15] Garaudy detects a rampant fascism in the minister of culture: "To democratic methods, you seem to prefer those of enlightened despotism. Your plans for *maisons de la culture* are subject to the same state of mind: the director of each *maison* is to be designated or approved by you, the amount of subsidy will depend on your agreement with the programs. It seems, then . . . that you want to create a cultural instrument for government propaganda. The *maisons de la culture* will be run not along democratic but authoritarian lines, like all the institutions in your regime. You are thus introducing a sort of cultural paternalism, bringing culture to the people like a simple inheritance."

As long as he doesn't talk about money too much, Malraux can do more or less what he wants (within the limits, alas, of the budget). Successive prime ministers do not want to quarrel with him. In July, the prime minister balances the budget. Malraux, defending his corner at the Matignon, from the start of play has a momentous tone: in my budget, there are three types of spending: those General de Gaulle wants, which are not open to discussion; nor are mine, otherwise I'll leave; for the rest, do what you want. Whereupon the grand French dignitary leaves the room and the Hôtel Matignon. Successive prime ministers—Michel Debré, Georges Pompidou, Pierre Messmer, and Maurice Couve de Murville—may have their doubts: the spending "the president wants" could be that of the minister. In Matignon, the General's hobbyhorses are well known: historical monuments, the restoration of the Marais area of Paris or of Tours, international cultural exchanges. Malraux accepts the barrage of incomprehension around him. Only the General really understands him.

Throughout his ministerial career, his irascibility increases. Madeleine Malraux tells him he should leave the government.

"Never!" he interjects.

"Go back to writing."

Almost every week, Malraux takes part in a Cabinet meeting at the Élysée Palace, a gloomy high mass, with the president, the prime minister, and a few ministers as officiants. On the president's right, the writer scribbles, smiles, grows bored, closes his eyes. He speaks up when he has to raise a question about culture or give a report on foreign travels. After a jaunt abroad, it is traditional at the Élysée to give an account of the trip. At the Cabinet table, what is expected of Malraux is not a constructive summary or verifiable information but a colorful account. Malraux transmutes reality. The General loves that. Why shouldn't they have a bit of fun?

De Gaulle can, on occasion, put his minister of genius in his place. After a trip to the Congolese capital, Brazzaville, Malraux gives an epic description of his entrance into the city in an open-top car, forging through an excited crowd.

"I'm not sure what they were cheering for most," he tells the Cabinet, "independence, me coming to proclaim it, or nickel-plated motorcycles."

De Gaulle: "Next time, the solution would be to parade on a motorbike."

Malraux also speaks up in a Cabinet meeting when the General addresses a problem by asking all the ministers for their opinion, in turn, from left to right. Seated at the right hand of the Father, Malraux gets to speak last. He has time to work on his answer. The question on the agenda: to devaluate or not to devaluate. Implicit drum roll, short silence, and Malraux majestically gives his verdict: "*Le Général de Gaulle ne dévalue jamais.*"[16]

Malraux again informs the General's close assistant, Pierre Lefranc, of his wish to change ministries. The Interior, Algeria, Foreign Affairs would suit him fine. Point-blank refusal. De Gaulle knows not to let certain intellectuals play with matches in the key ministries.

There are compensations that Malraux accepts with an adolescent, even childlike, pleasure. Malraux loves the pomp of the Republic. He attends dinners at the Élysée Palace, solemn affairs. He likes being among the men in tails and women in long dresses, with so many eyes fixed on him. He gazes at the circle of ladies around Mme. de Gaulle. He in turn is more an object of scrutiny than other ministers. The General entertains all France courteously; he is essentially there on duty. France at home. Who better to represent her than de Gaulle and Malraux? These two Frances have a damn hearty appetite.

De Gaulle and Malraux, with the RPF in its various manifestations, have not forged a party which is neither to the left nor to the right. They are not understood. They understand each other. At elections, each with his own specialty has been able to draw a large center vote and even supporters from the left. Malraux remains convinced of that: he himself is no stranger to the slide from the left toward Gaullism. Even in front of the Cabinet, they both propose "a certain idea of France." They are France's awareness of herself. They just have to accept the National Assembly and the stubborn Senate. Charles de Gaulle knows he already has a place in History and the textbooks. Malraux does not (so he says) take himself to be "a man of History; the General, yes." He has some doubts as to his own posterity. He sticks close to the General; the General keeps him close by. Governments pass, Malraux remains. They know how to joke together. When Nikita Khrushchev visits, De Gaulle acts as his guide.

"This is the famous Versailles parquet floor," he says to the Soviet leader.

"We have exactly the same at the Hermitage," says Khrushchev. "But ours is made of ebony."

De Gaulle murmurs to Malraux, "This chap is beginning to get on my nerves."

In public, Malraux never strays from his admiration for the General. At home, he allows himself to comment on de Gaulle's outbursts in Quebec ("Long live a free Quebec") or about Israel ("This proud and domineering people"): "Now he's going too far."

Malraux is convinced that de Gaulle will always support him on essentials. An annotation by the General on a project sent by Malraux: "I have read Mr. Malraux's note very closely and the comments of our secretary-general on the subject of cultural policy. It goes without saying that Mr. Malraux's projects are eminently justified."

One time, the General puts his foot in it during a Cabinet meeting. They are talking about Mauriac.

"Our greatest writer," says de Gaulle carelessly.

The other ministers see Malraux tense up. The General wriggles out of it. He stares at the ministre d'état: "One of our . . ."

The job of minister is chaotic, full of surprises, obligations, and constraints, but it also offers delightful moments of satisfaction. Eminently. It goes without saying, Malraux needs to be appreciated and reassured by de Gaulle.

CHAPTER TWENTY-NINE

Jackie and La Gioconda

J ACQUELINE KENNEDY MADE an official visit to Paris and was impressed by Malraux.[1] He showed the president's wife around the museums. For a long time, "Jackie" had been wanting to meet Malraux and de Gaulle. Her requests reached the Quai d'Orsay, the Élysée Palace, and the Ministry of Cultural Affairs via Nicole Hervé Alphand, the wife of the French ambassador in Washington. President Kennedy's wife was insistent. She had admired *The Conquerors, Man's Fate,* and *Museum Without Walls.* Their author was, for her, a "Renaissance man."

Malraux steered Jackie through the Jeu de Paume. Malraux explained Manet, Cézanne, Renoir. He had prepared for the occasion: he had Bouguereau's *Birth of Venus* placed below Manet's *Olympia,* the former having won the Prix du Salon in the year that *Olympia* was refused. At the Musée National de la Malmaison, Malraux moved from history of art to history. Jackie was rooted in front of a portrait of Josephine: "What a destiny! . . . She must have been an extraordinary woman!"

"A real handful," retorted Malraux.

Jacqueline Kennedy, née Bouvier, expressed herself well in French. The minister and the first lady could talk without an interpreter. At Malmaison, Malraux held forth about the tumultuous relationship between Napoleon and Josephine. Three weeks later,[2] he sent a book to "Jackie" in a diplomatic pouch, *Le Louvre et les Tuileries.* Thanking him, Jackie sent him a work by himself that her sister had given her for Christmas seven years before. Would the minister be so kind as to sign it for her?

Jacqueline Kennedy flirted with the dark and handsome minister of cultural affairs, and with the writer too. Ah yes, Goya . . . Hegel, of course; all of Malraux's heroes combined in one eyelid flutter, emphasizing Jackie's charming, carnivorous smile. What an interesting man! She knew about the Prix Goncourt. She also knew well her own place at the center of John Fitzgerald Kennedy's cultural mechanism. The Kennedys had—as a couple—a sense of efficiency, of manipulation, and of publicity. A bit of literary admiration from the first lady could be politically useful to America. Washington had mistrusted Gaullist France and the French General-President for some time. No question of helping him out in his atomic research as long as he was wanting to push the United States out of Europe. Paris, watching the young Kennedy, saw a clever and endearing man, but the United States? Cold monsters. They gave him the benefit of the doubt, pending a fuller inventory and estimation of future benefits. If it couldn't have American military atomic secrets, the SDECE (the French CIA) wanted to obtain from the CIA the information it had on certain Soviet atomic "recipes."

Jacqueline Kennedy accepts the honorary presidency of the Société des Relations Culturelles Franco-Américaines. Bilateral relations with France are tense at the White House and the State Department. The General is not an easy client. That is the problem: he refuses to be a client. It is thought nonetheless that André Malraux could be used as a bridge between Paris and Washington. The State Department suggests that he come to the United States to speak at the Seattle World's Fair. This strikes Paris as a very provincial offer, coming after the Acropolis. The ministre d'état regrets that his schedule will not permit . . . They want Malraux in Washington. The request is matched on the other side of the Atlantic, and André and Madeleine Malraux are invited to spend a few days in the American capital. The visit will serve as a booster rocket; at least, that is what some in Washington are hoping. Nobody there knows what weight Malraux really has at the Élysée Palace. The French Foreign Office see no obstacle to this trip: it can't do any harm. With a bit of luck, it might oil the works, or at least defrost the atmosphere. Malraux's presence doesn't have to commit the Quai d'Orsay or the Élysée.

Before he leaves, Malraux talks about the trip with the ambassador, Hervé Alphand. Kennedy has been to Paris, but de Gaulle doesn't want to go to the United States. Malraux says this to Alphand about the General: "He doesn't mind sending his tanks in first—that is, ourselves—and having them set on fire to light up his way."

One can understand the first part of this remark, but the rest is rather obscure. "Set fire to his tanks"? Since his childhood, the tank has been part of the Malraux bestiary. In Washington, he will talk politics with the president, of course, and talk culture with Jackie Kennedy. These general surveys are usually "broad" and the "exchanges of views" usually "detailed."

So André and Madeleine leave for America in May 1962. On May 15, Malraux gives a speech for the fiftieth anniversary of the French Institute in New York. Then the Malrauxs are welcomed by the Kennedys in the American capital almost like kings, presidents, or prime ministers. Jackie has been preparing for this visit for five weeks. In her turn, she serves as guide. She would like to take her guest around the National Gallery of Art. She has had catalogs and photographs of the works in the Mellon Collection sent to Malraux, the connoisseur: Could he choose what he would like to see, so as not to "waste any time"? The White House Press Department makes sure that the Kennedys and the Malrauxs are photographed together and have television coverage. The coupling suits Malraux: he hopes to take on his true international political dimensions.

The White House press secretary, journalist Pierre Salinger, multiplies the classic stops for photo opportunities; we see the Kennedys and the Malrauxs together on the lawn, in the Oval Office, in the Rose Garden, André smiling next to Jackie. He seems enraptured. Jackie bewitches, simpers, and bubbles with sophisticated banter. The Kennedys' "New Frontier" slogan gives a social and cultural aura to the White House. Film stars and singers, but also writers, musicians, and artists are invited: Bob Hope for the man in the street, Robert Frost for the one in the ivory tower. In Paris, de Gaulle invites Brigitte Bardot as well as François Mauriac.

"André Malraux must not be bored, and since he doesn't speak English well, we should invite French speakers to the White House," the first lady said to Nicole Alphand, the ambassador's wife. The watchword at the White House for Franco-American dinners: don't mention Lafayette. Out of respect to Malraux, we have a duty to avoid platitudes. The Kennedy Machine has no need of clichés.

JFK is happy to welcome so many American artists: "This place," he jokes, "has become a restaurant for artists. But they never invite us back."

Jackie has decided not to invite five American Nobel Prize winners. When it comes to the Nobel, she knows that Malraux is touchy. But the White House draws together for the occasion the Lindberghs, rarely seen in public, and 160 celebrities, including the choreographer George Balanchine; film director Elia Kazan; two Pulitzer Prize winners, Archibald MacLeish and Robert Lowell; three playwrights, Arthur Miller, Tennessee Williams, and Thornton Wilder; and painters Mark Rothko and Franz Kline.

Kennedy has learned his cue cards, material supplied by the U.S. Embassy in Paris: "Malraux carried out an archaeological expedition in Cambodia," he states. "He has had 'connections' with Chiang Kai-shek and Mao Tse-tung." Therefore, the American president wishes a warm welcome to a minister and friend of General de Gaulle. Monsieur and Madame Malraux, Kennedy has no doubt, will return to France and put in a few friendly words "in favor of the United States and their president." Malraux oozes courtesy: he has been greeted by the masterpieces of the world, and, better still, they have been shown to him by Mrs. Kennedy. He salutes the brotherhood that exists in the United States. According to Malraux, it is the first time in millennia that a nation has become number one in the world not by pursuing conquests but by looking for justice: "I raise my glass to the only country in history to occupy the first place among nations without having sought it."

The ministre d'état and Madeleine Malraux are invited to Hyannis Port, the private residence of the Kennedy clan. JFK, as King Arthur at Camelot, and his wife, as the queen, handle the whole operation. There is a run of dinners, cocktails, polite small talk, press conferences, all resembling one another; but during an interview in which Malraux talks to journalists, one last question is fired off: "If we expressed a wish to see the *Mona Lisa* in the United States, what would you say?"[3]

"Yes, without hesitation," answers Malraux. The idea comes back to find him and the Kennedys before long.

Malraux has no clear image of America. What he knows is American literature. He does not share de Gaulle's Americanophobia. On the Côte d'Azur, at the beginning of World War II, Malraux predicted decisive intervention from the United States in the war. He goes out of his way to pay homage to a helpful continent. He can take the General's anti-American tirades without batting an eyelid, but not those of the Communist (and non-Communist) Left. He has noticed that the migratory flow from France tends to go toward the United States, not the USSR; never from America toward Europe. Interested as he is in film and the detective novel, he feels that the United States is, little by little, imposing cultural norms. Or that Europe and Asia are attracted by these norms. There is no supply without demand.

"It is, when you think about it, the first time a country has suggested romantic themes to the entire world; its underground universe, its lovers, its thieves, and its assassins," says Malraux. "I believe that a new culture is in the process of being formed, that we have felt it welling up for quite a time (and we would feel it more if we had fewer prejudices against it): it is Atlantic culture."

When Malraux is visiting Washington, American policy about Vietnam—Indochina—is not yet distinct. Malraux finds the interior policy of the young president disappointing. To him, the New Frontier does not look like a New Deal. Jack Kennedy, despite all the noise made by the information (and misinformation) services, is no Roosevelt.

Kennedy and Malraux spend almost three hours together talking politics.[4] Factor out the translations, the polite remarks, and the time given to photographers, and you have an hour and a half. Kennedy would like Malraux to take a message to General de Gaulle: there is no fundamental difference of opinion between the two countries. Three times he repeats that the United States is ready to leave Europe, if that is what the Europeans ask for. The American tradition, he stresses, is isolationist. Do the French accept Great Britain in the Common Market? The American president says that it is difficult to force a man (Great Britain) to choose between an old wife (the Commonwealth) and a new mistress (Europe). Ambassador Alphand remarks that the man can keep both. Malraux adds that organizing your life around both is a difficult endeavor. He diplomatically recognizes that "it is not impossible" that de Gaulle "may mistrust England," a double-negative euphemism. Kennedy does not understand France's attitude. He thinks (at least says) that de Gaulle is 80 percent right in the contention. If only he could recognize that Washington is also 20 percent right! Alphand jokes that the numbers could be reversed. The aim of the conversation is to dispel "the misunderstandings"; it doesn't. France does not end up accepting the atomic triumvirate of the United States, France, and Great Britain, nor a multilateral force. De Gaulle does not want Polaris missiles for France. He stands his ground, retaining two convictions: "England has become a satellite of the United States" and "We will detach ourselves from the Americans while remaining good friends."[5] Well, Malraux did what he could.

Via his go-between, Kennedy wants to have de Gaulle understand, once again, that the Soviet military threat is still substantial but that the big problem will be Mao's China. De Gaulle and other European leaders should think about what they are going to do when China becomes a nuclear power. Mutual deterrence plays a part, but in the case of China that doesn't really work: the Chinese would be ready to sacrifice hundreds of thousands of lives in order to push their aggressive policies through. Malraux draws President Kennedy's attention to North Vietnam: even though it is small, the Americans should see it as a nationalist country, vigorous, independent, anti-Chinese, that could put up a barrier against China. Kennedy does not go for this idea. Malraux accepts the analysis of Ho Chi Minh as more of a nationalist than a Communist. He explains that the Great Leap Forward left China in an economic slump. The country does not have foreign adventures in mind. The French minister repeats, "One must know one's enemy."

Kennedy sums up his feelings about his difficulties with his allies: "I feel like a man carrying a sack of potatoes": others around him do not have the same burden, and they keep telling him how to carry this weight.

Malraux is satisfied to have been taken seriously on both art and politics. He finishes the trip off with Robert Kennedy in northern Virginia.[6]

Children mill about them. The language is still a problem for Malraux. He lectures his host: "The war in Vietnam is against American tradition."

Malraux is aware, particularly when visiting Washington, of the importance of television, the way it can not only give an account of an event but amplify it or suppress it by not talking about it. Personalities' "media coverage" becomes the essential element of their movements, at the expense of the substance of what they say. One photograph taken with Jackie is worth any number of statements released to the press. Malraux has known for a long time what an image is, in all senses of the word. Television is becoming more powerful than radio or cinema.

When the curators of the Louvre learn that because of a pledge made by André Malraux, the *Mona Lisa* will be crossing the Atlantic, they are worried. The chief curator of the department of paintings and drawings stresses "the exceptional fragility of this work." Madeleine Hours, the head of the Louvre laboratory, is sent on a reconnaissance mission:[7] "It is quite clear that we have not been able to foresee all eventualities and that the behavior of a fragile painting that has been used to French soil for more than five hundred years is unpredictable. This picture was painted on a panel of Lombardy poplar and is very sensitive to atmospheric variations."

Malraux does not dwell on these questions. To the astonishment of curators—not only those of the Louvre—he goes further: after the air crash at Orly that plunges Atlanta into mourning on June 3, 1962, he lets Jackie Kennedy know that France will be pleased to lend *Whistler's Mother* to the cultural center of the South. Letter from Malraux to Jackie: "Just as one places on a tomb the flowers that the dead would have liked, France wishes to place in the Atlanta Museum, for whatever period it may suggest, the work that it would perhaps choose among all others." In all these maneuvers, Malraux presents the French government officials with a fait accompli. The General remains confident: "He must know what he is doing. He's doing the right thing."

The journey of *La Gioconda* entails abundant correspondence among the French government, its minister of cultural affairs, the Smithsonian Institution, its director, John Walker, the White House, and Jackie Kennedy. The painting is to be entrusted "to the President of the United States." They could hardly announce that it was being handed over to his wife. Who has the better smile, Jackie or the *Gioconda*?

Malraux omits to mention that the cult painting is in a sorry state. The pigments are disappearing: some of the colors just aren't there anymore. *La Gioconda* already has a wooden brace on the back to tighten up a split. Over the years, the binding agents have partially broken down. No painting on wood travels well. The *Mona Lisa* is not more fragile than an altarpiece, but it is also not less.[8]

The picture is not granted military honors—despite France's request for warships, no less—but its journey still resembles a military maneuver. Experts have looked into the technicalities with Walker. The *Mona Lisa* arrives in her sealed, unsinkable container made out of inert material (required temperature, 18°C, ambient humidity 50 percent). She has crossed the ocean in her own cabin on the good ship *France* under personal bodyguard, accompanied by Mme. Hours of the Louvre and by Jacques Jaujard from the French Ministry of Cultural Affairs.

At the Smithsonian, the *Mona Lisa* is locked in a chest, surrounded by police and FBI agents. President Kennedy attends the reception at the French Embassy as if he were receiving a head of state. A delighted Malraux is escorted by Lyndon Johnson, Secretary of State Dean Rusk, and Congress leaders. Rusk comments to him, "In a domain where we are unarmed . . . that of the intellect and the mind . . . your influence is considerable. You will be opening Latin American minds to a path other than Marxism or Castroism."

Malraux nods with a look of solemn intensity. It is impressive yet comical that an Italian picture should serve as a link between the United States and France. The enigmatic smile does not hide the political disagreements. France does not see Europe becoming a third power to be directed against the United States and the USSR, Malraux declares. No, France has never had any intention of questioning the Atlantic Alliance. No, France has absolutely no objections to Great Britain's entry into the Common Market. Hervé Alphand wires to Paris, "Mr. Malraux's statements to journalists helped to appease minds."

Cultural hugs and kisses are not enough, however. Malraux, in the course of all his political discussions, does not manage to convince his interlocutors of the validity of the General's positions, nor even of his sincerity. *Gioconda* or no *Gioconda*, Malraux knows that the General will refuse France's participation in the nuclear agreements being concluded between Great Britain and the United States in Nassau. Malraux also knows that de Gaulle is opposed to Britain's entry into the Common Market. But why spoil the party in Washington? Both sides may say, with Malraux's voice or with Kennedy's, that the two revolutions, the French and the American, have defined democracy and liberty; nevertheless, their political viewpoints in the second half of the twentieth century are different. De Gaulle remains convinced that the United States would be ready to embark on a nuclear war without consulting France. If the Soviets attacked Europe and swallowed up France, would the Americans make a move?

Malraux returns to his *Gioconda*. On January 8, 1963, three thousand guests are crammed together for the inauguration at the National Gallery of Art. The elevator doesn't work. Kennedy has a bad back. He has to take the stairs. The microphones go wrong. The guests can hardly hear the three speeches by Rusk, Malraux, and Kennedy.

The previous day, at 11 a.m., Madeleine Hours noted that the curvature in the back of the precious painting was "very slightly more accentuated" than after the examination of October 16, 1962 . . . "it seems therefore that the panel has warped very slightly." No need for a press conference on this minor detail. . . .

Kennedy, having digested his notes and listened to Jackie, says that Malraux has revived the ideal of the Renaissance. General de Gaulle's minister is "a writer, a philosopher, a statesman, and a soldier." In Kennedy's entourage, historians and economists such as Sorensen and Galbraith have their doubts about such hyperbole. But reasons of state carry their own weight, and Kennedy is not entirely humorless. During the preview ceremony (and after the Nassau summit) he remarks, "This painting has remained carefully under French control . . . and I want to state clearly that, while we are very grateful to receive this painting, we will continue to move forward in an effort to develop an independent artistic force and power. . . . [So much for the General and his French bomb.] [Malraux] has demonstrated that politics and art, the life of action and the life of thought, the world of events and the world of the imagination are one."

John Kennedy does not believe a word of what he says. But it is designed to please Malraux, who answers Kennedy the day after the preview, with a less down-to-earth speech. Some of his ideas escape his audience:

"Here, then, is the most famous painting in the world. A mysterious celebrity that is due not only to genius. . . . Other illustrious portraits can be compared with this one. But every year, more than one poor madwoman believes she is Mona Lisa, whereas nobody believes himself to be a figure by Raphael or Titian or Rembrandt. When the *France* left Le Havre, among the bouquets sent . . . was one with an anonymous card bearing the inscription 'For Mona Lisa.' "

The American (and French, Australian, and Brazilian . . .) magazines love this story. After the anecdote, Malraux sticks to aesthetics: "Antiquity, which the Italians brought back to life, offered an idealization of forms, but the people in statues of the classical period, being a people without expression, were also a people without a soul. Expression, soul, spirituality were Christian art; Leonardo da Vinci had found this illustrious smile in the face of the Virgin, and used it to transfigure a secular face. Leonardo idealized the soul of woman in the same way that ancient Greece idealized her features."

Vice President Johnson gets bored. Malraux knows that the *Mona*

De Gaulle concludes, "It is a considerable operation and altogether beneficial. It is not finished, since *La Gioconda* will remain in the United States for several more months. But when it gets to New York, for God's sake, don't let the United Nations cash in on it."

During this Cabinet meeting Malraux explains (according to Alain Peyrefitte) that Kennedy is a "novelistic character" with a rare "span of openness." "Probably only you, *mon Général*, have as planetary a vision as him." After the meeting, the General murmurs to Peyrefitte as an aside, with a tone almost of tenderness, "Malraux was dazzled by Kennedy; as always, he gets a bit carried away. It is true that Kennedy is a gifted young man. He is not a provincial politician. He has wide views, and his mind is turned toward the future. In the Cuba affair, he showed that he had national instinct and guts. . . . He will go far, if he doesn't take a fall. He is sometimes a little reckless."

The ministre d'état resumes his routine activities, abroad or in France, and now often seems absent, broken, or altered. He makes appearances in Canada and Switzerland. He commissions Marc Chagall to paint the ceiling of the Paris Opéra and André Masson to decorate the ceiling of the Théâtre de l'Odéon. A depressed Malraux consults numerous doctors. His relationship with Madeleine is turning very sour.

On her return to France, *Mona Lisa* gets a clean bill of health: "No alteration during travel." Five myths have crossed paths: the genius Leonardo da Vinci, the *Mona Lisa*, Kennedy, Malraux, and, behind him, the General himself. Isn't that worth taking a risk with the painting? No, it isn't, say the art historians and museum curators, if only because it set a dangerous precedent. Yes, it is, say the politicians. Malraux has pulled it off.

Lisa's expedition is provoking criticism in France. Kennedy has spoken o a "historic loan." Malraux goes for a preventive strike: "When, on m return, certain sour faces ask me in the House, 'Why have we lent *La Gio conda* to the United States?' I shall answer, 'Because no other nation woul have received it as it has.' "

Malraux plays a card to trump the Americans' feeling that they ar misunderstood and not well liked in France: "Much has been said abou the risks taken by this painting in leaving the Louvre. Though exagger ated, they are real. But the risks taken by the boys who landed one day a Arromanches—not to mention those who preceded them twenty-thre years earlier—were much more certain. To the most humble among then who are perhaps listening to me now, I would like to say, without raisin my voice, that the masterpiece to which you have paid tribute this ever ing, Mr. President, a historical tribute, is a painting they saved."

The American press and television give more coverage to this con ment than to Malraux's ponderings on the soul, spirituality, and Goethe Since the General's return to power, the Americans, leaders and peopl have not been used to being thanked like this. At last, a waft of friendl fresh air. Malraux is sincere in his compliments. He has fulfilled his mi sion and Jackie Kennedy, hers.

The United States is seized by *Mona*-mania: *La Gioconda* turns up o birthday cards, comic strips, advertising for food products. The amba sador, Hervé Alphand, gets excited: "It is almost no longer a painting bu a talisman. . . . The *Mona Lisa* is more than an extraordinary painting, sl is the ideal woman, as well as the ideal work of art." Twelve hundred jou nalists come to see the painting, and 1.7 million visitors, including or thrown out for hiding a dog in his jacket. "I wanted him to be the first do to have seen the Mona Lisa," he explains after his arrest.

The line of visitors advances, three abreast; each person is allowe twelve seconds to gaze on the painting. At the Ministry of Cultural Affai in France, some savor this success. Beuret, now Malraux's deputy chief staff, declares that it is "the most brilliant testimony that this painting h ever received." Malraux maintains his paraministerial contact with tl Kennedys. Jackie respects and admires him and, like Jack Kennedy, us him. Malraux is an iron in the political fire.

On January 16, 1963, Malraux delivers his account to the French Cal inet. He refers to some unfortunate interpretations of his speech: "Tl French press has portrayed this ceremony in an absurd manner. I had fu ished my speech by saying that the arrival of American soldiers in Fran allowed *La Gioconda* to be saved, which was true, because the Germa wanted to seize it. The papers had me say that the Americans came France in order to save the *Mona Lisa*. Which, obviously, is idiotic."

CHAPTER THIRTY

Crises

N OT ALL OF Malraux's initiatives are as successful. He makes
well-intentioned political gestures about Algeria that, given that
he is cut off from the realities of the war, are misguided and inef-
fective. Malraux offers to three French Nobel Prize–winning writers,
Mauriac, Martin du Gard, and Camus, a trip to Algeria on an investigative
mission—during the war. They hesitate, Camus especially, fearing that
the means of inquiry at their disposal will be unsatisfactory. The project is
visibly a failure.

Malraux's own position on Algeria wavers, even when Aron demonstrates to him that these "three French departments are a financial bot-
tomless pit." He waits for the General to state his position before
deciding. Above all, from 1958 to 1962, the writer-minister does not want
de Gaulle paralyzed by Algeria. The problem of torture resurfaces, this
time in *La Gangrène*, written by four FLN militants. The work is seized.
Malraux reacts negatively. According to him, the accounts of torture in *La
Gangrène* have been fabricated by the Communist Party. Malraux functions on a lopsided syllogism: the situation in Algeria is complicated; the
General has outlawed torture; therefore the French Army is not using
torture.[1]

The clear division between Malraux and the intellectual, non-
Communist Left dates largely from these Algerian years. The novelist
Graham Greene (who passes at the time for "progressive") writes an open
letter to Malraux in *Le Monde*, reproaching him for his silence. Malraux
has a reputation for having been a revolutionary before his time in French
Indochina. When it comes to Algeria, he appears not even to be a
reformist. He protested against torture in the past, why not now? Sartre
gets more deeply involved, denouncing the "dirty war." He turns into the
Anti-Malraux and Malraux into the Anti-Sartre.

"I was in front of the Gestapo," says Malraux, "while Sartre was putting on plays in Paris." The assertion is far from being irrefutable and in any case has no logical connection with the Algerian War.

A young philosophy teacher in Morocco, Maurice Maschino, refuses to join the French Army and publishes a shattering book, *Le Refus*. He explains how a conventional young man like himself has become an outlaw. How many drafted Frenchmen subsequently refuse, like him, to join their regiment? Only a few handfuls. But in the wake of the book, in September 1960, 121 intellectuals, including Sartre, Simone de Beauvoir, Marguerite Duras, André Breton, Alain Resnais, Alain Robbe-Grillet, Jean-François Revel, and Maurice Blanchot, sign a manifesto for the right not to defer to the draft. The declaration is aimed at young people who are likely to be called up: "We respect, and consider justified, the refusal to take arms against the Algerian people and the behavior of those French who judge it their duty to provide help and protection to the oppressed Algerians." It is also an appeal for desertion and an invitation to support the FLN in both Algeria and France. A few days before the "Manifeste des 121" is broadcast by the press, Florence Malraux sends a note to her father, warning him that she intends to sign it. Malraux pays no attention to her letter. He reads the text of "121" in Boulogne in front of Madeleine and Alain and stares at the signature Florence Malraux.

"This time I have seen enough of her," he announces. "What books has she written, what pictures has she painted to sign this? When we have made peace in Algeria, how will they look then, these great revolutionaries who are always explaining to me what I should be doing in the name of what I have done in the past?"

Occasionally *La Condition humaine* or *L'Espoir* is thrown at Malraux. He is rarely petty but in this case is capable of bearing a grudge: Florence has wounded her father. He stiffens. Perhaps the more so since his conscience on Algeria is not entirely clear. The young André Malraux would probably have signed the "Manifeste des 121." The prime minister, Michel Debré, tactfully suggests to his ministre d'état that he should have seen to it that his daughter was "better brought up." Debré would like all the signatories of "121" to be taken to court and those who are civil servants deprived of their jobs. An example must be set! The General manages to calm Debré. Signatories who are well-known teachers are temporarily suspended from their jobs; for others, the authorities just drop the matter.

Malraux also feels that Clara is getting at him through Florence. Although she has not signed the manifesto, her sympathies are known to lie with the Algerian "rebels." Malraux thought he had found his daughter again. He had encouraged her to work at *L'Express*. The weekly paper is making peace in Algeria one of its crusades and takes up a position opposing General de Gaulle. When Malraux offered his daughter a job at the ministry with him, he understood that she couldn't accept.

Malraux applies the principle of governmental solidarity. His silences in France are more striking than his declarations abroad and make him, in the eyes of many critics, jointly responsible for the policy in Algeria. In private, he murmurs that the men of the FLN who have taken up arms have courage. But courage is no proof of the justness of a forbidden cause. When a minister's sympathies go no further than this in public, they confirm the status quo.

During the generals' putsch[2] on the night of April 23, 1961, Malraux hurries to the Ministry of the Interior in Place Beauvau with a few friends. The prime minister has made a grotesque and pathetic appeal on the radio, asking the mainland French "on foot, on horseback, and in cars" to prepare for seditionary parachutists to fall from the skies at Orly Airport and elsewhere. Malraux waves his arms about at the ministry and declares himself ready to command a tank unit, his persistent fantasy. Malraux at the age of fifty-nine in the role of counterinsurgent is a moving—or perhaps just embarrassing—sight. He seems to be reviving a part in a play not quite written for him.

For a brief moment, Malraux is in favor of bombing the European rebels. But a week later, he is back in his double-breasted suit and—instead of a tank—his ministerial Citroën DS. Battle dress is no longer for him. He returns to his cultural projects.

His two sons, Gauthier and Vincent, have been studying for exams at a friend's house on the island of Port Cros off the Côte d'Azur. They drove south in an Alfa Romeo Giulietta given to Vincent by Clara Saint, the young woman in his life. On the evening of May 23, 1961, Madeleine and André receive a telephone call; it is Albert Beuret. Gauthier and Vincent have been involved in a car accident on the way back from the South of France, near Dijon. It doesn't appear to be serious, Beuret says at first. One of the boys is wounded, he doesn't know which one. Yes, Vincent was probably driving, without a license.

In fact, both the boys are dead.

After the quarrels, the misunderstandings, and the provisional separations, Malraux has lost his two sons for good. Florence had been working on the set of Truffaut's *Jules et Jim* in Alsace. "Do you mind my coming?"

"No."

She arrives at Boulogne.

That night, Malraux talks to his daughter about Egyptian funeral rites. He sighs, "What a tragedy my life is!" Is he thinking of his father's suicide, his two brothers deported during the Occupation, Josette's mortal accident? Now Gauthier and Vincent. The day after the accident, André and Madeleine arrive at the Hospices de Beaune to see the bodies. The same day, a letter from Clara arrives at Boulogne: "André, I hope that our Flo, so gentle, so fine, can be for you if not a joy, at least a comfort." Madeleine does not give André the letter. General de Gaulle and his wife, Yvonne, come. The General hugs Malraux. His wife says to Madeleine, "You must keep everything."

Mme. de Gaulle means objects, souvenirs filled with meaning. She has lost a daughter. Letters arrive at the ministry and at Boulogne. Some are unexpected and sympathetic: there is one from Léon Degrelle, founder of the Belgian Rexists, exiled in Spain. Others are dreadful and upsetting, sent by far-right fanatics, expressing their satisfaction at the accident. Malraux decides that his two sons will be buried near their mother, in the little cemetery of Charonne to which he had Josette's body transferred after the war. Pierre Bockel takes the Mass, as if, faced with death, Malraux felt the need for a ritual: "Like when we used to bury the comrades who fell at our sides."

As an unfortunate consequence of the death of his two sons, a misunderstanding also deprives him of one of his oldest friends and colleagues, Pascal Pia. Pia telephones Chevasson to ask where the funeral is taking place. Chevasson says that Malraux wants an intimate ceremony, just with the family. Chevasson stays away from the funeral, but more than 150 people attend. Pia finds out, refuses to listen to an explanation, and never sees Chevasson or Malraux again. Shortly after the funeral, Malraux attends a reception at the Élysée Palace. His impassivity astonishes the other guests. Everybody is looking at him and his wife. He whispers to Madeleine, "We're scaring them."

Malraux has denounced the Liberals and the Left. On the Algerian issue, the extreme Right sees him as a defeatist because he is a Gaullist. According to the extremists in Algiers and Paris, everybody who is close to "the giraffe"—as they call de Gaulle—wants to sacrifice French Algeria. After noon on February 7, 1962, a plastic explosive bomb placed near a ground-floor window of the building where Malraux lives goes off. The minister has already left for his office; Alain is practicing his scales at the piano. A shard of glass lands in the left eye of four-and-a-half-year-old Delphine Renard. The child loses this eye.

At Évian-les-Bains, the French government and the Provisional Government of the Algerian Republic (GPRA) sign agreements recognizing Algerian sovereignty. A clause makes provision for a referendum, however, to choose among three options: preservation of the three French departments in Algeria, autonomy, or independence. Malraux has no doubt that the final outcome will be independence. Meanwhile, the OAS, the last refuge of the rebellious *pieds-noirs*, bathes Algeria in blood. On April 8, the General obtains an immense success at the referendum: 90.7 percent of the votes cast approve the Évian agreement; Malraux can be satisfied with that.

On April 14, 1962, in accordance with the hypocritical ritual, Michel Debré hands in his "resignation" to General de Gaulle. Georges Pompidou becomes prime minister. Malraux's post at Rue de Valois is renewed. The eternal ministre d'état sits—still—at the General's right hand at Cabinet meetings.

"Nobody is brave enough to tell you, but somebody has to," Madeleine stresses, "If you want to save yourself, you have to stop drinking."

"I was waiting for that one," answers André. "Well, if I drink, it's because of you."

"No, because you were already drinking with Josette. She complained about it to me. She told me you finished writing *L'Espoir* running on Pernod."

Madeleine takes refuge in music. In Malraux's eyes, she has an irremediable fault, like Clara before her: she knows André too well. After more than fifteen years of life together, there is nothing she doesn't know about the tragedies he has been through and the comedies he has staged. She has seen the creator up close, the depressive, the man of projects, of visions, of ornamented lies and camouflaged truths. Often, the man of myths lapses into outright megalomania. He will, for example, never answer the telephone in person: "Nobody disturbs General de Gaulle on the telephone," he explains.

He pushes the identification further: "The General has only one real successor: me. Only I can't tell him."

Malraux spreads a rumor: de Gaulle has written a secret will. Were there to be an accident, according to this improbable, hypothetical document, André Malraux would succeed him. As if Charles de Gaulle would have allowed himself to write a codicil to the constitution. As ministre d'état he would anyway have to leapfrog the president of the Senate, the president's natural temporary successor. If this anecdote is mentioned in front of him, Malraux smiles inscrutably: I'm not saying anything, it goes without saying, don't make me laugh. De Gaulle—always—identifies himself with France. Malraux—sometimes—believes he is de Gaulle. But is Malraux still Malraux?

He has slowed and subsided; his progress is now automaton-like. Sometimes he is so vain as to be beyond arrogance: "Who has done as much as I?" Yet sometimes humble: "I am good for nothing." Crossing Paris, he can see the results of his efforts: everywhere monuments are being restored and numerous private houses are being whitewashed. The idea was not his: in 1956, the prefect of the Seine, Baylot, gave Parisians ten years to clean up their facades; but it was Malraux who found the financial wherewithal.

Years of ardent efficiency are followed by years of lifeless bureaucracy. Attentive and precise until 1965, Malraux seems now to have switched to automatic pilot, flying on nighttime instruments. He represents France, de Gaulle, Culture, everything except himself. He bobs to the surface here and there, at UNESCO for a conference, at Lambaréné in Gabon with Dr. Albert Schweitzer, another great actor, writing an introduction to an exhibition catalog, chaperoning a visiting head of state, making departmental appointments, it is all one. Malraux bores his listeners by repeating himself, pointing out that his office in Rue de Valois was used by Le Roi Jérôme,[3] that his lamp is believed to have belonged to Napoleon. Visitors hear the minister exclaim, "Sometimes I have a rush of pride just being able to touch it."

In the same hour, he points out a window that overlooks the Palais-Royal: "Alexandre Dumas worked there when he was secretary to the duc d'Orléans."

The curves of his highs and lows are getting higher and closer together. Between two "bouts of malaria" (when he is drinking again), a manic-depressive Malraux murmurs: "What I want is mad. What I can do is nothing."

He takes stimulants, and when they keep him awake, sleeping pills on top. He sends Madeleine to Switzerland to buy his tablets. About the brand, he says wildly, "Get the Hitler ones."

When he wakes up he is distinctly pasty. Uppers followed by downers followed by uppers is a dangerous diet; a punch under the chin, a punch on top of the head . . .

Alain Malraux gives his "parents" two Siamese kittens, Olympe and Octave. They are distant and mysterious, as André often is. Is it easier to love cats than humans?

Malraux is jumpy and irritable. He smokes a lot. Beyond his apparent successes—the inaugurations, ceremonial fêtes and journeys he undertakes to fill an emptiness—those who are closest to him perceive his ill-being. His health is deteriorating. The more brilliant, if not more successful, his public life appears, the more his private life falls apart.

He doesn't mind a bit of militant activism on the side. He launches an association, Pour la Vᵉ République, in the run-up to the legislative elections in November 1962. There is a high abstention rate: with 31.9 percent of the vote, it is a Gaullist landslide.

Malraux has a job to do. He walks Konrad Adenauer, the chancellor of the Federal Republic of Germany, around the Louvre. He inaugurates the Maeght Foundation at Saint-Paul-de-Vence. He is the object of pity from some quarters: all these books on art are very nice, but he's not really writing anymore, is he? Malraux enjoys—at best—a condescending, disenchanted sympathy. The writer is publishing nothing that appeals to the general public. He is institutionalized, a permanent fixture, a mummy. His compulsive traveling, his need to escape, comes upon him from time to time like hiccups. Travel intoxicates him and allows him to become intoxicated away from the journalists. But where are Malraux's noble causes? He seems to be running away from his own life.

At Boulogne, Malraux gets drunk. There, with the heavy movements of a deep-sea diver, he can emerge from within himself. He soliloquizes and splutters. The energy and responsiveness are not there. He floats. Only close friends and family know what role alcohol plays in his life. When the General is informed, he shrugs sadly. Some ministers sleep around, this one drinks.

He has to leave Boulogne. Georges Pompidou offers him one of his official residences, La Lanterne, a pavilion at the Palais de Versailles. If the Gaullists play it carefully and avoid making too many big mistakes, Malraux judges, they will remain in power for a long time. He shuts himself away and starts taking stimulants again.

Ten times he has refused a seat at the Académie Française. He deserves the Nobel, he thinks, so much more than Hemingway. There's no doubt in his mind: he is the top writer among those who are living, the survivors. Sartre and Aragon are important, but they come after him. And in politics, ephemeral prime ministers may come and go, but he, Malraux, is number two in France, after You-Know-Who. Others may have their doubts, but Malraux is in line—in secret line—for an absolute inheritance. Only he cannot talk about it or tell Him.

When John Steinbeck gets the Nobel Prize in Literature, Malraux just shrugs. He seems slightly less disdainful when the Stockholm jury crowns Georgios Seferis. In the run-up to the Nobel in December, as the rumors start to spread, so often to be contradicted by the final vote, it is better to keep quiet around Malraux. He gets impatient. When Camus was awarded the Nobel, in 1957, he had the good taste to say to the press, "It's Malraux who should have had it."

Why on earth does Malraux care so much about the Nobel? In his eyes, the Académie Française is provincial, or European at best. But why not . . . the Nobel, there is a prize on a planetary scale.

After coming and going for a while, he separates from Madeleine.[4] She has been with him for twenty years. With no family, Malraux becomes more solitary than ever. Megalomania reinforces his isolation. The writer-minister neither asks for nor accepts advice. He has no sons anymore, and despite the affection she showed him at her brothers' death, Florence remains distant, at her father's behest. Malraux keeps one parent by proxy, a symbolic father: de Gaulle.

A sick man, deep in mythomaniac and megalomaniac depression, can push suffering to extremes, in himself as well as in others. Malraux lives alone at La Lanterne, at first, until Jean Grosjean and his wife join him there. In the fall of 1966, Malraux organizes the Picasso retrospective at the Grand and Petit Palais. Bureaucratic oversight: no invitation is sent to the painter. A telegram reaches Malraux: "Do you think I am dead? Picasso." The reply: "Do you think I am a minister? Malraux."

Malraux first consults Professor Jean Delay about his depression and

le 7/juin 66

Mon V

Au moment de quitter Marly, permettez-moi de vous remercier d'avoir eu l'attention de m'y abriter.

Il y a dans le jardin un lapin de garenne apprivoisé. Je lui ai conseillé de rester là, pour le cas où vous reviendriez ...

Je vous prie d'agréer ... de mon div. affet. reconnaissant drinking. Then, on the advice of a general practitioner, Dr. Laponte, he goes to see Louis Bertagna, who treats him with antidepressants. Malraux ditches Delay after the latter proposes an IQ test.

General de Gaulle has let Malraux have the use of Marly, another residence belonging to the Republic. Before moving on again, Malraux sends him a few lines:

> Mon Gl,
> On leaving Marly, allow me to thank you for your thoughtfulness in letting me stay here.
> There is a tame rabbit in the garden. I have advised it to stay put, for when you return . . .

The letter is dated June 7, 1966. To have a date at all is rare for a handwritten Malraux letter. But this is a letter to Charles de Gaulle.

Before Christmas 1966, Malraux takes part in the discussion of a parliamentary bill on historical monuments, and the following week, he meets with his nephew, Alain, for lunch. Malraux tells him he wants to "cast out some of his fears." He abruptly comes out with "So, we shall not see each other ever again."

Thus Malraux blows his bridges. He hates being alone but forges his own solitude.

The Paris intelligentsia look on at Malraux's metamorphosis. Once a veteran adventurer, then a decorated combat veteran, now settled into steadiness and fast becoming a bourgeois old fuddy-duddy. Despite a few flashes of intensity—such as his speech for Jean Moulin—he provides minimum service. He has commissioned Olivier Messiaen's *Et Expecto Resurrectionem Mortuorum*, a musical work commemorating both world wars: the ministre d'état attends the first performance in the Sainte-Chapelle. He has also founded the Orchestre de Paris, with Charles Munch as first artistic director; he has erected nineteen sculptures by Maillol in the Jardin du Carrousel. But he no longer enjoys his minister's job. He is less and less accessible, even to Grosjean. To be, to do, to have are concerns of former days: the stumbling Malraux now seems mostly to seem. They say that he is writing. A novel, memoirs? Often in the past he has announced books that never appeared or lost manuscripts that never existed. He appears more in the gossip columns than in the literary chronicles. He is featured in weekly magazines such as *Elle* or on Radio Luxembourg. He even starts to have a solid reputation as a television star. You can't understand what he's saying, but doesn't he say it well? And what a presence!

Bertagna, a specialist in brain chemistry, tries Malraux on different protocols. The range of available antidepressants, neuroleptics, and tranquilizers is not, at the time, huge. Some, however, seem to suit him.

His voice becomes croaky. His tics are still with him. What is starting to be referred to as stress also aggravates his condition. Malraux knows that hyperactivity can have a palliative effect, but he faces some activities with dread. Sometimes, before a television broadcast, his doctor prescribes Haldol. But it can have unpredictable side effects, can deaden the patient's mind. They drop Haldol.

Malraux, clearly, is not well. He is losing his grip in his professional and private lives. Repercussions of his illness and his behavior now often reach the Élysée—by way of certain ministers feigning concern about their colleague.

The General strongly advises rest. A long trip should provide an explanation for the absences and outbursts of the ministre d'état. So goes the malevolent whisper. Malraux is good only for inaugurating exhibitions and giving speeches. Malraux is no longer in Malraux. Where is the novelist? It is blindingly clear (some murmur with a spiteful pleasure, others with genuine regret) that as a writer, Malraux is finished. He's sixty-four, after all. Malraux makes up his mind to travel, alone. His staff can look after day-to-day matters. They can do without him for a few months. Besides, exhausted as he is, staggering about, mumbling sometimes, what use would he be to them right now?

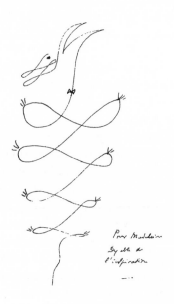

CHAPTER THIRTY-ONE

Mao, Memoirs, Antimémoires

AT THE BEGINNING of 1965, urged by his doctors and encouraged by de Gaulle, Malraux decides to take a sea voyage. A string of embassies on the route from Marseille to Japan are forewarned. China is foremost in Malraux's mind. No dates are specified, but wherever he decides to surface, the ministre d'état will be given a welcome befitting his rank. This is not to be an official mission: neither the Élysée nor the Matignon nor the Quai d'Orsay wants that. At best it will be an opportunity to "influence" and at least a chance to convalesce. The minister of information, Alain Peyrefitte, doesn't make the expedition sound glamorous: "Mr. Malraux's voyage," he announces, "is a private trip but is not without interest from a general point of view." In short, instead of taking the waters at Vichy, Malraux is going to Asia for a cure. There are murmurings that he is getting over a nervous breakdown. He is still in the middle of one. He will roam, without Madeleine, as the fancy takes him, with Borodine, Garine, and Kyo, conversing ghost to ghost.

The Sino-Soviet schism has been developing nicely for the last five years. The USSR has recalled its experts working in China. Against the thoughts of Chairman Mao, the Ninth Plenary Session of the Eighth Central Committee has adopted a policy of economic liberalization. Liu Shao-chi voiced his criticism of the Great Leap Forward, and therefore of Mao Tse-tung himself. The People's Liberation Army has occasionally, almost absent-mindedly, bombarded the Taiwanese islets of Quemoy and Matsu. The Nationalists respond with sweet little bomblets filled with candy and toys. The Chinese Communists have overindulged their internationalist enthusiasm and waged a minor frontier war with India. The Indian Army took a beating.

Malraux wants first of all to stop off in Red China to see Mao and talk with him. Paris and Peking have recently re-established communications, a move that Malraux sees as pragmatic. This has a twofold effect: First, de Gaulle has officially recognized a country—a continent, almost—that opposes the "two hegemonies," the USSR and the United States of America. Second, the restoration of diplomatic relations annoys the Americans. Franco-Chinese trade is no better for it, nor is cultural exchange. But the outlook is "promising."[1] The French Foreign Office is hoping that if Malraux is headed east he will avoid Communist China, given the complexity of the situation. It is not just that he might do a cultural deal with the Chinese and bring back one of those costly exhibitions to Paris in his luggage, as he has done (or will do) with the Iranians, the Indians, and the Japanese. He might also say something really irresponsible.

He is clearly too exhausted to travel alone. Several friends are asked, including Bockel, and decline. The steadfast Albert Beuret boards ship with him in Marseille, on June 22. The *Cambodge* carries 539 passengers, 117 of them in first class. It has air-conditioning and a Denny Brown stabilizer to reduce roll. Malraux appreciates the luxury but still spends more time in his cabin or on deck than in the saloon or the sycamore-paneled bridge room. He is writing.

There is a stopover in Port Said. Malraux and Beuret visit Cairo. At the foot of Cheops, Malraux looks up at the pyramid and contemplates himself. It is an appropriate setting for a grand decision: he tells Beuret of his intention to write "memoirs of a sort." He has not yet decided on a title.

And this is what he works on while at sea, as he did for part of *La Tentation de l'Occident* and the beginning of *L'Espoir.* They put in at Karachi, Bombay, Colombo. Malraux toys with the idea of stopping in Vietnam, seeing Cambodia, inhaling his youth. The Quai d'Orsay, on advice from its outposts in Saigon and Phnom Penh, insists that Cambodia would be unwise (the pilfering of his younger days has not been forgotten) and that Malraux's presence in Saigon would appear to support the United States' policy. The minister is effectively refused entry for diplomatic reasons.

On the night of July 12, a Dutch oil tanker rams the *Cambodge.* Beuret emerges from his cabin: "What's going on?"

"We're sinking," says Malraux, almost jubilantly. The *Cambodge* is immobilized for a month in Singapore, which in Malraux's view lacks exoticism, despite the squabble between Indonesians and the British and Singaporeans next door in Borneo. President Lyndon Johnson, successor to John F. Kennedy, authorizes American troops in Vietnam to begin attack operations. The American military is no longer just there to advise and fly helicopters. In a few months, 25,000 men will have landed; soon afterward, half a million.

Malraux has been interested in what was Indochina on and off since his youth. In August 1964, he heard from Russian sources that Hanoi wanted to talk with Washington. He transmitted this information to Charles Bohlen, the U.S. ambassador in Paris, and took it upon himself to suggest a line of cease-fire. What could be more natural than military advice for the Americans in Southeast Asia, coming from the French minister of culture? Bohlen explained to Malraux that President Johnson was not willing to negotiate; even if de Gaulle were to sponsor talks, the United States would not participate. In April 1965, before leaving on this trip, Malraux made some remarks about Vietnam in a Cabinet meeting. In his judgment, the Americans did not want to enter into negotiations just yet: they would negotiate from a strong position after they had dropped more bombs. When the North Vietnamese Communists had been punished and started to give way, conversations could begin. Malraux commented on the steady escalation: "The United States wants to see Ho Chi Minh and his advisers ponder over a country that has been razed." General Curtis LeMay later offered to "bomb North Vietnam back to the Stone Age."

The writer-minister thinks that he can influence the war in Vietnam and make his mark on the history of the former Indochina. An idea takes shape: since he is not allowed to make peace in Saigon or Hanoi as a senior minister, he will prepare the ground as senior statesman in Peking.

In diplomatic circles, Malraux's excursion is followed with interest, caution, or amusement. The CIA is keeping track of French reactions and initiatives:[2] the French appear to believe they are the only ones able to communicate with Peking and Hanoi. They "are engaged in a long-term exploratory effort. . . . André Malraux, in the course of his current travels in the Far East, will meet with Mao Tse-tung" to find out "how China sees the world situation, its role in world affairs and under which conditions it could agree to participate in a peaceful solution in Southeast Asia." Still according to the CIA, the French government does not want to take a position on the war in Vietnam, either on one side (with Hanoi) or on the other (with Saigon and Washington). The belief of the French is apparently that only secret diplomacy can result in a solution. Which is Malraux's element, and he is swimming in it.

Beuret and Malraux reach Hong Kong by plane. About forty years earlier, the writer came here with Clara to buy type for his newspaper *L'Indochine*. On July 17, he receives an official invitation from the Chinese authorities. It does not say that Mao will see him. Malraux considers Mao's struggle to be "an example for all of humanity." Before leaving Paris, he could not stop himself from coming out with a Malraux-ism: "Vietnam is Spain in '38, without the Fascists." But he has his instructions:

under no circumstances is he to offer services or act as East-West mediator in the Vietnam War.

Malraux and Beuret cross the bridge linking Hong Kong to China on foot, amid villages and hills that seem suspended in the vaporous air of an engraving. They reach Canton on July 19 and visit the Revolution Museum, like good little tourists. They arrive in Peking on the twenty-first. A timetable is falling into place. To the ministre d'état, Chinese protocol seems to be distinctly lacking in consideration. Two years before, Edgar Faure had been sent by de Gaulle to cement the restoration of relations; he was received the day after he arrived by Prime Minister Chou En-lai, and a week after that by Mao himself. Malraux sits and frets at the French Embassy. These days, the French ambassador, Lucien Paye, assures him, Mao hardly ever gives interviews. Malraux sulks. The Élysée is bombarded with requests from the embassy to intervene.

Embassy dinners, often boring, are utterly dreary in the company of a minister suffering from Great Man Deprivation. Malraux sought no specialist advice in Chinese affairs before leaving Paris and does not appear to have read the dossier prepared for him by the Foreign Office. Brigadier General Jacques Guillermaz, the military attaché to the embassy and a brilliant Sinologist, talks with Malraux. Commenting on the way the regime has reorganized Peking with devastating results, he understands from Malraux's silence that the city is not familiar to him. Guillermaz also gathers that Malraux has had no contact "with known Chinese Communists" in the past. At the embassy, Malraux does not question the diplomats present about China or the Chinese. Ambassador Paye tells the story of how he met Mao a year before, in Hangchou. When he saw him, Mao was propped up by a young nurse. The Great Helmsman was suffering from a "slight trembling of the hands that could be the beginnings of Parkinson's." Mao was a "strange character, worrying yet attractive. . . . No magnetism emanates from him, but he is still interesting. . . . The future he seems to think of as something external to him, with a sort of detachment." The ambassador also describes Mao's "intellectual cruelty." Malraux listens to Paye. He waits, fidgeting with impatience. No plans have been made for one of those elaborate and tedious banquets usually reserved for Grand Guests. Haven't these Chinese read *Les Conquérants*, *La Condition humaine*, or *L'Espoir*? Don't they know who André Malraux is? He feels like a television star abroad, recognized by nobody.

At last, on July 22, the Chinese minister of foreign affairs, Marshal Chen Yi, Chou En-lai's successor in the post, receives him. Malraux proposes . . . a Chinese exhibition in Paris with numerous cultural events. A shudder from the Quai d'Orsay. Malraux suggests having high-relief sculptures cut out to be shown in Paris. The Maoists are not particular when it comes to destroying works of art, but this time even they are shocked.

Marshal-Minister Chen, "fairly moonlike" in Malraux's notes, is a narrow-minded apparatchik. The main part of their interview relates to Vietnam. Malraux asks if "a negotiation on Vietnam would take place after an undertaking to withdraw or after an effective withdrawal of American troops." The Chinese minister does not want to compromise himself: the decision belongs to Hanoi. He imagines that withdrawal would be a prerequisite.

Why do the Chinese not want a negotiation?

"Because we do not want to help the United States," says the marshal simply.

Malraux's Vietnamese project seems to be stuck in neutral. What is more, he knows that in Chen Yi, he has met an underling. He is discourteously informed that there is no objection to his sticking around until August 1. The French Embassy sends a request to Paris that the General himself intervene to get Mao to see Malraux. The only weapon in his possession on his arrival in China was a letter from the General to the president of the Chinese Republic, Liu Shao-chi.

> Mr. President,
>   I have asked Monsieur André Malraux, Ministre d'État, to attend to Your Excellency and President Mao Tse-tung and to stand as interpreter for the feelings of friendship on the part of the people of France for the great Chinese people. Monsieur André Malraux will be pleased to engage in detailed exchanges of view on the substantial problems concerning France and China and, consequently, the future of the world. I attach in advance a great price to whatever information he may bring back to me, having, I hope, gathered it from you and the leaders of the People's Republic of China.

Eventually, Chou En-lai sees him. Chou has traveled abroad, where much is made of his merits. In a land of plains, Marx said, hills look like mountains. Chou churns out predictable speeches about the United States, saying that it is aspiring to worldwide domination. Malraux interprets Chou's thought: "It is not a matter of evacuating Saigon, which it will never do, but evacuating and dismantling all the American bases, including in Cuba, Santo Domingo, and the Congo." The Chinese prime minister considers that "only the [National Liberation] Front and Hanoi have the right to come to a decision, but the Front first of all." As if both these entities were not as one, dependent on military aid from China and

the Soviet Union. Malraux's impressions are carried via Paye, his colleagues in Peking, the head of the Asia Department in the French Foreign
Office, and some visiting American diplomats to the CIA. In its report,[3]
"Malraux was surprised by the hard and cold attitude of the Chinese
regarding possible negotiations on the situation in Vietnam."

Malraux is at last received by Mao on August 3, 1965, at the People's
Palace.[4] His impression is roughly that the minister Chen Yi is the "record
tester," Chou En-lai is "the record," and Mao is "History." You get waffle
from the first two and the Communist Truth from the Great Man. Present
on the Chinese side are the interpreter, a nurse in the background, and
two "records": Chen Yi and a new one, Liu Shao-chi, the president of the
Republic. On the French side, accompanying the ministre d'état, is the
ambassador and interpreter Georges Yacowlievich.

For two years, with his movement of socialist education in the rural
areas, Mao has been opposing his own bureaucracy and preparing the
Cultural Revolution. He has already launched his "four cleansings" campaign; in order to regroup the average and poor peasants into associations,
the local officials must be purged. The enemies of socialism in China want
to restore capitalism, Mao thinks; the hierarchy is infected with corrupt
individuals; he is considering seizing power forcibly by arming the peasants. Mao sees anti-Party maneuvers everywhere. He wants to press on
with campaigns against "mandarins," the intellectuals.

Beyond a few irreducible differences, Malraux and Mao have points in
common. They are both self-taught, cultivated; they may or may not be
geniuses, but they mistrust academics, or "mandarins." They both believe
more in the will than in the economy. They have a penchant for pithy
phrases and a taste for glory. Malraux has known one great man at length,
de Gaulle; one great man of the past, briefly, Trotsky; and one potential
great, John Kennedy. In Mao, he meets another who is assured of a place
in textbooks.

The interview lasts one hour in all. Taking into account translation in
both directions, Mao and Malraux each speaks for about a quarter of an
hour at most.[5]

Malraux jumps in first with "I am very moved to find myself sitting
today next to the greatest of all revolutionaries since Lenin."

The emotion is doubtless genuine and perhaps explains, without
excusing it, the adulatory tone. When he gets the transcript back in Paris,
Étienne Manac'h, head of the Asia Department at the Foreign Office, cuts
this toadying, unworthy of one of General de Gaulle's ministers, before
circulating the document.

Mao answers, "You are too kind."

The interview gets off to a sticky start:

"Er, you have been to Yan'an," says Mao.

"In Yan'an," replies Malraux, "I saw how difficult life was before; people lived in caves. I also saw a photo of Chiang Kai-shek's house. Comparing the two, I understood why the Chinese Revolution was a success."

Mao: "It is the law of historical development. The weak always end up winning over the strong."

An observation worthy of the *Little Red Book.* Mao declares shortly afterward, "There are bound to be defeats, but the important thing is to have fewer defeats and more victories."

Such brilliance!

"That is also what I think," Malraux follows up. "I also in the past led Resistance units, but what I saw at that time cannot compare to your experience."

No, indeed.

"I heard that you had been in the Resistance," replies Mao.

Malraux: "It was in the center of France. I was leading peasant units [*sic*] in the struggle against Germany."

Malraux styles his military identity. As is his wont, he mixes literature and politics: "I went to Russia, and I talked about this problem [of cities] with Gorky. I talked about Mao Tse-tung with him. At the time, you were not yet president. Gorky told me that for the Chinese Communist Party, the greatest difficulty was not having big cities. Then I asked him if he thought that the Chinese Communist Party would succeed or fail because it did not have any big cities."

That, in 1934, was impossible. One of the few French to have even heard of Mao at the time was the writer René Étiemble. This is the first time Malraux claims that he alluded to Mao when talking to Gorky. He is functioning on free associations, autonomous in relation to facts.

Mao: "Did Gorky answer you? [Malraux shakes head] He did not know the situation in China. That is why he could not answer."

QED. Malraux does not seem to realize that he is being snubbed by Mao.

Malraux always refers to Mao in the third person, using the obsequious form "the president." Such a courtesy is not called for by Chinese custom.

Malraux is dazzled, perhaps shy. He seems to be bothering Mao. The president in return tangles the minister up in tautologies and banalities: observing, for instance, that since the re-establishment of diplomatic relations between Paris and Peking, China and France have been friends. But he keeps his distance too: "We have all sorts of friends. You are among them, as is Aidit [the president of the Indonesian Communist Party, visiting Peking at the time]. We have not met with him yet. We have points in common with Aidit. We also have points in common with you."

Malraux tries to get onto the subject of Vietnam. If he could bring back to Paris a proposition formulated by Mao himself! What a diplomatic step forward that would be!

"In practice," says Malraux, "only France is opposed to the American escalation in Vietnam."

Apart from a large chunk of public opinion in Europe, the Americas, Africa, and the whole of the developing world, that is. Anti-American demonstrations are multiplying. Where, in fact, can one find any pro-American manifestations outside the United States at that time? Mao doesn't take the bait. He lets the others present chip in. There follows a succession of clichés. The Chinese tinkle away at variations on the theme of Great Britain's support of the "American aggression" in Vietnam. Malraux states that General de Gaulle has a policy of decolonization. He agrees wholeheartedly with Chinese ideology, even anticipating Mao: "If the Sovieto-American double hegemony [Malraux uses the vocabulary of de Gaulle and the Chinese Communist Party to flatter the Great Helmsman] were to establish itself in the world, there would then be no chance for China to become the true China and France, the true France."

Here we see the Gaullo-Malrucian idea of an essence of France and China to be made flesh. The discussion laps at the degeneration of the USSR: "The Soviet Union," says Mao, "is looking to take the path of capitalist restoration. Which is well received by the United States and by Europe, but not by us."

"Does the president really think that they [the Soviets] intend to take the capitalist route?" asks Malraux.

Mao: "That is correct."

"I think," explains Malraux, "that they are looking for a way to distance themselves from communism. But where do they want to go? What are they looking for? They themselves do not have any clear idea."

"In this way they mislead the masses with confused methods," Mao replies. "You have your own experience. Is the French Socialist Party really building socialism? Does the French Communist Party really believe in Marxism?"

Malraux, still aiming to please: "In your opinion, Mr. President, what will the goal be of the next stage in the struggle against revisionism? I mean in terms of interior policies."

"Well, it will be the struggle against revisionism," Mao answers.

Malraux refers again to this next step and, unwisely, says that he has the impression that the industrial problems have been settled in China: "Or at least that you are on a very healthy track in this domain."

Either Malraux is unaware of the lamentable state of the Chinese economy, or he is laying his compliment on a bit thick. It falls flat, in any case: "Neither the industrial problems nor the agricultural problems are resolved," Mao retorts.

Despite the state of his health, doesn't Mao wonder just where this clown, this *ch'ou chüeh*, is coming from? The president is at the limits of politeness here. More seriously, without Malraux noticing, at the time or afterward, Mao hints at momentous events in the making: "We have a socialist layer who would like to follow the revisionist path. The problem is to know how to treat it. . . . Some of the writers are ideologically opposed to Marxism. Doubtless, there are some inconsistencies."

Mao is hardly more friendly when the ambassador makes a contribution: "I have the feeling," says Paye, "that the youth of China is orienting itself in the direction indicated by its president."

An almost clairvoyant intuition. Mao: "How long have you been here?"

In other words, what do you know about China? Paye mentions his fourteen months in the country. Malraux, picking up the ball again, cannot resist relating his visit to a model textiles factory, ending up on a question: "Are you now thinking of launching a movement with a greater influence than that of the people's communes?"

Mao's disastrous people's communes have, at this time, already been abolished. When Malraux asks how much of the country is under cultivation, Mao stops the interview: "What is most important is to improve the yields. . . . That is all for today. On your return, pass on my regards to your president."

End of the official version. Four final sentences exchanged by the two greats are blue-penciled out of the transcript by Manac'h at the Quai d'Orsay:

"I received a French parliamentary delegation," Mao said.

"I'm very mistrustful of what parliamentarians say," Malraux answered.

"Their attitude on America was not as clear as yours."

"Perhaps that is because I have more responsibility than they do."

Malraux has no responsibility in the domain of foreign policy, certainly less than the president and members of the Commission on Foreign Affairs received by Mao. Malraux's efforts in the course of the interview have gone unrewarded. His interviewee has kept his responses to a minimum. Like an inexperienced journalist, Malraux has made his questions too long. Mao hardly replied and certainly didn't ask Malraux about France or General de Gaulle.

Neither Malraux nor Paye noticed that Mao alluded to possible persecutions of intellectuals. It is not fair to expect Malraux to have made detailed predictions about the Great Cultural Revolution, which would cause 20 million deaths. One can, however, criticize him for having been impervious to the few pointers let out by the aging dictator during the interview. Why this lack of perspicacity? Partly because his first concern when faced with Mao was his own image. Reading the transcript of the dialogue, one feels embarrassed for Malraux as he labors his platitudes in front of the Great Helmsman. Did he have to go to China to learn that the French Communist and Socialist parties were not revolutionary in the Maoist sense? That the Soviet regime was changing? That France was antagonistic enough toward America to work together with Mao's China for a while?

Arriving in Hong Kong on August 7, Malraux tells the press that he spent three hours with Mao. "I feel that my conversations with President Mao Tse-tung were a dialogue on the most important problems of our time, with a man who appreciates them fully, one who has been an intellectual all his life." In the plane, Malraux writes a succinct summary in his notebook: "France is de Gaulle, China is Mao."

Using his twenty-five pages of notes, Malraux gives his traditional travel report to the French Cabinet on August 18. With the tacit agreement of the General, the trip to Peking becomes a "mission." The Chinese, he says, are intrigued by France: "The Chinese are the French of Asia." A flattering formula, but an empty one. Malraux, for once, is clear, not as enigmatic as he often is in Cabinet meetings. He paints for his colleagues a portrait of Mao as a "bronze emperor"—the first use of that phrase—omitting to mention any details that might suggest that Mao is sick. He sketches a hero in whom minor details take on a sublime symbolic value: the "famous wart on the chin" is like a "Buddhist sign." Mao has a "serenity all the more unexpected because it appears violent." On the nature of his power, Malraux impassively conveys that "He leads the Party, and everything in China is done by the Party or under its leadership. . . . The Party is merely applying the principles that have guided Mao for more than forty years. Mao is setting out to conquer power." A phrase that perhaps, unconsciously, predicts the "Cultural" Revolution.

In Hong Kong, on the way back to France, Malraux also spoke about Vietnam and the "mistakes made by France in Asia in the past," suggesting that he had made policy proposals in Peking. This is denied both by the Chinese government and by Alain Peyrefitte for the French government. But Peyrefitte adds that the information and impressions Malraux has brought back are "considered by the president and the Cabinet to be of very great significance."

Not everybody in France is duped. "Some commentators," writes *Le Monde*, "have considered it reasonable to draw conclusions from the remarks made by Mr. Peyrefitte about Mr. Malraux's impressions of his trip. The vagueness of these remarks is in contrast to their formality and leads one to think that either the ministre d'état brought back nothing very new from his meeting with the Chinese leader, which would tend to prove that there was no talk of the restoration of peace in Vietnam, or that General de Gaulle has judged that these problems are too important to inform the citizens about them now."

At the Quai d'Orsay, the Cultural Relations Department is dismayed to learn what Malraux did bring up with the Chinese in Peking: an exhibition of Chinese art in Paris. The partial result of Malraux's trip to China is a cultural accord, planned by the Foreign Office before Malraux even left, involving French teaching, audiovisual exchanges, and future medical missions.

After his two-month trip in Asia, Malraux seems transformed, thinner, calmer, rejuvenated almost, and less disfigured by tics. His absences at the ministry are excusable.

"He is writing," confides Albert Beuret with a happy smile.

Malraux is coming alive again. His new big book is neither a novel nor an art book, nor a standard volume of memoirs. The chosen title, *Antimémoires,*[6] signifies that chronology and accuracy, as a historian might see them, do not count. Acrobatics in the introduction: "I call this book *Antimémoirs* because it answers a question that memoirs do not ask and doesn't answer those that it asks." Again: "And also because one finds in it, often linked to tragedy, an undeniable and slippery presence like that of a cat slipping by in the shadows: that of the Farfelu whose name I have, unknowingly, revived." Just as interesting, in the opening bars of this symphony, Malraux states insistently that there *"are no grown-ups* [his italics]." Is that a way of saying that he is still a child? Still in his introduction, he formulates his technique: "The memory . . . does not revive a life in sequence. Lit by an invisible sun, nebulae appear and seem to prepare an unknown constellation." Malraux is interested in a "past that emerges like lightning." He is like an actor watching a film in which he played and jumping through the screen to place himself in the film and carry on in the plot. With his talent and use of skillful special effects, Malraux plays in all his old films.

He breaks up the chronology and, throughout the book, constructs chapters out of rehoused or recycled pages from previous works. Critics hostile to the old Malraux, the new Malraux, or both may judge his inspiration and imagination to be on the wane. Yet he makes no secret of it: "I include here a scene previously turned into fiction." In including extracts from *Les Noyers de l'Altenburg,* at least he goes about it like a collage: he corrects details and adds linking texts.[7] Throughout *Antimémoires,* he combines appearance, the ephemera of stories and History; he mixes novelistic truth and the novel of his truths, all lying with the same implicit logic: what should have been, was.

The passage in *Antimémoires* devoted to the meeting with Mao is pure fantasy. The writer finds the inebriation of words again. Malraux wants to carve Mao and Malraux out of marble. He is not looking for what is true, nor what is false, nor what was experienced: he wants what is written. His aim is a beautiful page. One only has to compare the twenty-six printed pages in *Antimémoires* to the eight typed sheets bearing an account of the Malraux-Mao summit to appreciate the verbal craftsman at work. Malraux draws on the French and Chinese shorthand transcriptions; he even allows them to be published in part, which shows either an admirable candor or a remarkable lack of concern on his part. It says something for his partial honesty but much more for his lack of interest in the truth and his passion for the swell of language. The account in *Antimémoires* follows the real interview—it includes, for instance, the contributions of the other people present—but it doesn't reconstitute it. At best, Malraux romanticizes; at worst, he makes it up. Of course he does not portray himself as a sycophant, rebuffed by Mao, the mummified Pharaoh figure, the secular saint, the great among greats. On the contrary, Malraux suggests an intimacy that the events do not justify: "Mao cordial and curiously familiar, as if he were about to say 'To hell with politics.' "

Mao, apparently, confided in Malraux that he had always believed in de Gaulle's victory. Malraux says, or might have said, or should have said, "I remember the words of General de Gaulle: 'When did you think that you would regain power?' 'Always.' " Malraux identifies Mao and de Gaulle. Later, Mao repeats, "I am alone." Like you-know-who.

In this transfigured interview, Malraux is also inspired by his novels. He practically introduces Mao into *L'Espoir*: "Revolution is a drama of passion [Mao 'said']; we have not won over the people by appealing to their reason but by developing hope, trust, and brotherhood." Malraux goes a long way to re-create a Mao who expresses himself like the writer: "Faced with famine, the desire for equality takes on the force of a religious feeling." Mao becomes a novelistic character. "Imagine the life of the peasants," says the Malrucian Mao. "It was always bad, especially when the armies were living in the country. It was never worse than at the end of the Kuomintang's power. Suspects buried alive, peasant women who hoped to be reborn as bitches to be less unhappy, witches invoking their gods by singing, like a song of death, 'Chiang Kai-shek is coming!' " The author of *La Condition humaine* shows through. "The peasants have hardly known capitalism: they found the feudal state before them, strengthened by the machine guns of the Kuomintang." Gisors might have said that, sitting smoking an opium pipe.

Mao is a man of culture. Malraux salutes his qualities as an artist ("your poems") and here talks to him as if the Great Helmsman had skimmed through the writer's art books. He gives the tyrant an epic dimension: "The man who is walking slowly at my side is tempted by more than uninterrupted revolution; by a huge thought that neither of us talked about [that's a shame]: that underdeveloped [countries] are much more numerous than Western countries and that the struggle started as soon as the colonies became nations." Malraux, self-promoted Third World expert, adds that Mao "knows that he will not see the planetary revolution. The underdeveloped nations are in the same state the proletariat was in 1848." Historical comparison may be very thought-provoking but is also, here, false: the English workers whose inhuman living conditions were described by Engels had a standard of living superior to that of Ethiopian or Pakistani workers in 1965.

The writer builds up to his final cadence: "Behind all our conversation, poised on the lookout, the hope of a twilight for the world." It remains to be shown that Mao, despite the abundance of his complete works, was this original, "giant" theoretician.

Malraux involuntarily turns himself into an apologist for the Chinese regime with a lyrical description of the bewitching Long March, which he decants from other works. We learn that "the passage of the Red Army across China was more powerful propaganda than all that the Party had conceived: all along this trail of corpses, the entire peasantry rose up when the day came." Since the battle of Alsace, or perhaps since his finest hours with the RPF, Malraux—like Mao since 1949—hasn't seen one peasant or one proletarian close up, except when opening the front door to the gas man. But he allows himself the popular appeal of this line. Does Malraux believe what he is writing? Is he responding to some irresistible impulse? Perhaps he simply sees the meeting as an opportunity to show himself in a good light, egged on by the page in front of him, allowing himself to be swept along by words. He poses one of the problems of the half century: How could so many minds have gone so far astray and come out with such inanities?

In *Antimémoires,* reality is invaded by Malraux's fantasies. He turns Mao from the master of a mysterious continent into a superman who cares deeply about culture, intelligence, and poetry. Despite one negative allusion to socialist realism, we find ourselves steeped in romanticism and blinded by its "redness." The reader will learn nothing about what is going on in contemporary China from *Antimémoires.* Malraux skimped on the recommended reading and advice on his trip. He does not want to see the reality of the current situation in China. What is essential is that in his book, Heroes and History are met. Alexander the Great, Saint-Just, Napoleon, a discredited Stalin and a still-accepted Lenin, Gandhi, Nehru, de Gaulle, and finally, this sublime Mao. To hide his more contemptible features, Malraux needed to use a mask, that of the hero of History.[8] The minister has traveled physically, but it was the art lover who went on the journey and the novelist who did the writing. From the Mao he did meet, there remains at least (or at most) a vase: a copy, not an original antique, presented to the writer by the dictator.

Malraux copes more or less well with the day-to-day affairs in his ministry but very well with events that are out of the ordinary. Just two weeks after his return from Asia,[9] for the funeral ceremony of Le Corbusier, in the Louvre's Cour Carrée he stood and knitted an exceptional funeral oration. Le Corbusier built the new town of Chandigarh, which Malraux had seen on a trip to India in 1958. Malraux turns the funeral into an Indian voyage. He was hoping to have some Indian witnesses. The day before the ceremony, he telephones Arajeshwar Dayal, the Indian ambassador in Paris: "You have to come with some water from the Ganges."

"But I don't have any."

"Somebody at your embassy must have some. [pause] Surely."

The ambassador duly turns up in the Cour Carrée with a silver tumbler containing "water from the Ganges."[10] Could it possibly have been Vittel, Evian, or the highly prized *eau du robinet de Paris*? Everything is in the symbol. Neither the ambassador nor the minister is duped.

Is the ministre d'état starting to doze? Is his life drawing to an end? It becomes clear that Malraux is not finished as a writer when Gallimard publishes *Antimémoires* in mid-September 1967. In three weeks, it sells 200,000 copies, escorted by largely laudatory and literary reviews. For the facts, Malraux seems to benefit from rights of extraterritoriality: literary critics look more at the form than the historical detail. Exaggeration sublimates errors and untruths. *Antimémoires* should be downed in one torrential poetic draught. No room here for historians and their methodological prejudices.

Malraux has a copy of *Antimémoires* sent to Florence and is reconciled with his daughter. The "Manifeste des 121" is in the past, and they scarcely refer to it again. Malraux explains that if Florence had become a "nurse" in the Algerian National Liberation Army, he would have understood.

In his private life, André Malraux has taken up again with Louise de Vilmorin.

CHAPTER THIRTY-TWO

Temptation of the East

INDIA HAUNTS MALRAUX. It is omnipresent in *Les Voix du silence*,[1] in the two first volumes of *Le Musée imaginaire de la sculpture mondiale*, and in *La Métamorphose des dieux*. It also crops up in into his *Essay on Goya*.[2] Malraux is clearly fond of dialogues between civilizations. All civilizations for him are equal, but India is more equal than some. He is fascinated by Mao but not particularly by China. More and more, he is possessed by India. He has taken to saying that he is a religious mind without faith. India seems to be obsessed with a sacred time, real or unreal, and by death. India made fleeting appearances in *Royaume farfelu*. Gandhi preoccupied the journalist of *L'Indochine Enchaînée*. The Mahatma also appeared between two paragraphs of *Les Conquérants*: Garine criticized his ineffectiveness and received the answer "If Gandhi had not intervened, Mr. Garine, the India that is giving the world the highest lesson that we can possibly hear today would be no more than a rebellious region of Asia."

Before his trip to India in 1958, in a five-page note to Charles de Gaulle (then prime minister) about his mission to Asia, Malraux defined his ambitions: "If it is appropriate to have the largest audience possible for what the diplomats call a goodwill visit, and to establish by this visit new and relatively durable links between France and another nation—links that are deliberately limited in the cultural domain but likely to facilitate diplomatic or political action—then India seems appropriate for such a mission. Both objectives are combined; one can reach her people only in the spiritual domain [*le domaine spirituel*], and the links I must attempt to establish with her government are primarily (even they if are to change later on) in the domain of the mind [*du domaine de l'esprit*].

Some demands surprise both French and Indian Foreign Affairs officials:

I shall visit, rather than the current universities, the great centers of art and thought that in India play the part of our medieval universities: the Institutes of Indian Culture in Bangalore and Bombay, the Institute of Oriental Research in Poona, the Music Center in Madras, the Bose Institute, the Sanskrit college in Benares, etc. In each of these cities, *I will receive* [my italics] the principal writers; up to this point Europe has made contact only with those of Bengal and Delhi. (Doubtless it would be good to visit the new capital of the Indian Punjab, Chandigarh, built by Le Corbusier and dominated by the 'Hand of Brotherhood.') Finally, it is probable that Pandit Nehru will ask me to talk about India at Santiniketan, in memory of Tagore.

Malraux did not appear to know that India also had physicians and mathematicians of a very high level.

When he left India for Japan, Malraux left behind him a message that was broadcast on national radio. Nehru had it translated into the Indian languages and dialects after polishing up the English version himself. Malraux spoke more as a guru than as a minister:

This old land of spirituality is also, for many men who will never see it, the young land of hope. She who found her independence only in the name of justice, she who will conquer her poverty and regain her greatness, but only in the name of liberty. These are great dreams, but what is the face of Gandhi, seen everywhere here, if not proof of what can be created by invincible patience in the service of a great dream? And perhaps in the face of Jawaharlal Nehru, and in some of those who are looking to one of the most onerous tasks of our time, history will be surprised to recognize the figure of wise men following the figure of a saint.

The treatment of India in *Antimémoires* stretches over three chapters, more than 110 pages. The book's epigraph is a text about the successive incarnations of the Buddha: "The elephant is the wisest of all animals, the only one to remember his former lives. Thus he stays still for long periods of time, meditating on them." Malraux does not see himself, apparently, as a Buddha, but he superimposes his previous lives, laying them across one another, and meditates upon them. He spends more time on his 1958 trip to India in this work than on his recent, formal stopover of 1965, which he found frustrating.

His expedition in the summer of 1958 was better prepared, and what he experienced was more worthy of inclusion in a novel. France on the whole looked on India, its neutral stance on Algeria, and its nationalism without too much annoyance. Relations between the two countries were quite good. The French trading posts, from Pondicherry to Mahe, had been handed back to India, even if the treaty of retrocession was still awaiting ratification. Count Stanislas Ostrorog, the French ambassador in New Delhi, prepared Malraux's trip. Malraux himself, ignoring diplomatic custom and sensitivity, announced his intention to stop over in Pakistan. The Foreign Office, on the lookout for blunders, pointed out that whichever country was visited second out of Pakistan and India would be offended. Malraux avoided visiting both countries on the same trip.[3]

Coming from Persia, accompanied by Madeleine, his chef de cabinet, Pierre Juillet, Albert Beuret, and one other, Malraux arrived in New Delhi in the evening of November 27, 1958. He stayed at the Hotel Ashoka. Two days later, Nehru invited him to stay at the Capitol, one of the palaces belonging to the Republic. Malraux yielded willingly to the ballet of meeting the president and vice president, the visit to the two houses of Parliament, and the homage to the memory of Gandhi. This was at the start of Malraux's career as minister. He was waiting for his main course, a planetary figure, a Great Man, Nehru. Malraux met a French specialist in Indian music from Benares, Alain Danielou. Bad vibrations between them.[4] Danielou did not appreciate the wave of "pseudo-Oriental philosophy" in which he found Malraux's guides to be steeped, especially his friend Raja Rao.[5]

Nehru received Malraux at his official prime minister's residence, an exquisite colonial building that had been the headquarters of the commander in chief of the British Army in India.[6] The two speakers each had his great man: Gandhi on the one hand, dead and a martyr; de Gaulle on the other, very much alive and returned to power. Nehru had been to Harrow and Trinity College, Cambridge. Malraux's universities were the cafés of Montparnasse and Montmartre. Both were men of culture. Nehru liked social history, Malraux just History. They both wrote. Nehru's writing in English was influenced by Walter Pater; at his worst, he tended to lapse into solemnity. He was not a magnetic or prophetic orator. Malraux and Nehru both largely respected the traditions of Anglo-Saxon democracy. Nehru had helped forge the concept of nonalignment in 1955, which didn't displease the General (although he tended to see in it an inclination on India's part to align with the USSR). Malraux aligned himself with de Gaulle. Malraux and Nehru were both as immodest as they were proud. They had both waited a long time for power.

Ambassador Ostrorog would translate. As with the meeting with Mao, the reader should really filter the account in *Antimémoires* through Ostrorog's dispatch to the department. Alas, there is no transcript of the interview.

"So you're a minister now?" Nehru asked. Allegedly. According to the

Malraux of *Antimémoires*, this meant "That is your latest reincarnation." After having embraced as if they had met a month before (whereas they had not seen each other since meeting briefly in Paris twenty years earlier), Nehru said, or may have said, "I am happy to see you again. The last time, it was after you were wounded in Spain; you were coming out of hospital, and I was coming out of prison."

As "quoted" by Malraux, Nehru validates a fairly serious injury demanding at least a stay in hospital. Even in his most inventive moments, Malraux had never claimed, up until then, that he had been hospitalized in Spain; only that he had visited his wounded airmen. A fine example of an indirect, retroactive, and literary trauma to the leg. The two men exchanged platitudes on the future of the world. Who can tell the distressing vacuity of so many exchanges between politicians? Malraux was quick to raise the idea of a big Indian exhibition in Paris. It would be shared among the Grand Palais, the Opéra, the Louvre, the Collège de France, and the Sorbonne and would include sculpture and painting. Indian music would be played. Teachers and spiritual leaders would attempt to communicate the meaning of Hindu philosophy. Malraux wanted to put across the "soul" of India. In his report, the ambassador points out, "An imaginary museum of all Indian values is just the thing to charm Nehru." With one eye on Malraux, the other on the Quai d'Orsay, Ostrorog continues, "The answer was therefore immediate, and with no reservation other than the material conditions to be agreed." Malraux makes the offers, the Quai pays for them. Then, in 1958, the department was just starting on that long, hard, Malrucian road. Ostrorog continues, "Mr. Malraux . . . got right to the heart of it: When reaching for the spiritual order, what are the places and who are the men in India that the foreign visitor should see?"[7] Malraux seems to be asking Nehru for philosophicotouristic advice. The ambassador reports that at this question, "Nehru's face froze as if the light were failing." Nehru was not accustomed to being taken for a Who's Who of the saints.

" 'The places of pilgrimage, you know of their existence. As for men of this order, how are we to tell them apart and choose them? I am looking for them myself; I cannot answer you. . . . But the immediate needs of India are so great, the misery so general, that I must, out of priority, see to material problems.'

"Mr. Malraux replied that a solution to these problems, with the immediate importance they have for whoever is directing the fate of India, does not imply the exclusion of spiritual values. The prime minister agreed, but the indigent masses, deprived of essentials, would not listen to him if he were to preach resignation primarily—and further appeals would be made to engage the struggle along another path. It is to avoid such subversion that the renewal of India and its adjustment to the current state of the world must be accomplished without delay—if not, other methods will be called upon."

Then arises one last question that does not figure in *Antimémoires* but does occur in the ambassador's reports. It certainly sounds like Malraux: " 'In the Russian Revolution, Nietzsche prevailed over Marx. How will it be in China? . . . What are your thoughts on this subject?' "

Ostrorog notes cautiously: "Nehru remained pensive. How to answer such a question?" Indeed, what do Malraux's words mean? His sense of the summary condensed into incomprehensibility, which had bemused Gide, perplexed Nehru. The Pandit, according to Ostrorog, acquitted himself well: "History shows that China, in her periods of power, manifests her desire for power. Under the Communist regime, this desire is taking more fearsome forms. But I hope that some values of the past are not dead, only sleeping, that one day they will break through anew to allow not indeed a return to the past, but an integration of permanent values into the new order."

Not one geopolitical or bilateral problem had been raised until that point. Ostrorog concludes, "Between these two men the dialogue could have gone on indefinitely; but the prime minister asked Mr. Malraux to continue the interrupted conversation after his visit to the South."

Malraux spent five days in Madras and the south of India with Madeleine. He visited, among other places, Mathura and Bombay, inspected the Bakhara Dam and Chandigarh, the new capital of the Punjab created by Le Corbusier.

Standing before the nine stories of Madurai Temple, their guide introduces a married couple to the Malrauxs: "This is the minister of France." The father of the groom orders his son to fall at the writer's feet. The mother prostrates herself as well.

"That will bring you luck," says the father to his son.

Raja Rao is the guide. "Is it the sun that lightens the solidity of this tower, or is it the architecture that alters its dimensions as I look at it?" asks Malraux.

"A man stares at an object and it dissolves," replies Rao. "The tower is there to indicate space. The sun is there for the ground to be cool. The absurd is there to reveal that for which there is no answer."

Later, Malraux says, "What strikes me here is the silence despite so many people."

After Coimbatore, the Malrauxs went to Ellora. In his memoirs, Rao notes the "facility . . . the familiarity . . . the intimacy" of Malraux with the gods. "One might believe that by some magical means, he knows the gods and their attributes." Malraux asked hundreds of questions. Rao was stumped by some of them. The French minister seemed to have the "dictionary of divine biographies" off by heart. From Bombay, the Malrauxs took a boat to the caves at Elephanta, perhaps the jewel of Hindu statuary.[8]

Rao had prepared an excursion for Malraux to Trivandrum in Kerala and a meeting with a Vedic master. The meeting was canceled. Perhaps time was short. Rao thought that the writer grasped that he would "find himself facing the teaching of the absolute."[9] Was the friendly guide succumbing to an Indian temptation: the desire to convert Malraux, a non-believer? Perhaps the writer had no need at that point to confront an incarnation of the "absolute."

Returning to Delhi, at a dinner with the prime minister, Malraux presented his host with an edition of Villon's works as a souvenir of the time when Nehru, imprisoned as an opponent of the British Empire, had read *Le Grand Testament* in his cell. To this personal memento, Malraux added a twelfth-century Romanesque statue of the Virgin Mary, a present from the French government, not a copy. André and Madeleine Malraux chatted with Nehru in the company of Ostrorog and Rao. After this quasi-familial dinner, Malraux and Nehru withdrew to talk in private.

Ostrorog was captivated by the allure of these two great charmers juxtaposed. In a fresh dispatch, he wondered "How to reproduce the touch of genius?" The diplomat pointed out that the "immediate political problems were not broached. Neither the [French] settlements . . . nor Algeria arose." Which should satisfy the Quai d'Orsay. Ostrorog again: "The themes developed dealt with the respective share attributed in India to spiritual values and to material evolution." At the embassy, the ministre d'état is advised to avoid giving a press conference because "The Indian journalists are indiscreet." Which translates as: they do their job.

In India, Malraux, like many tourists, did not see the outside world. He "went deeper," as the wife of the former Indian ambassador in Paris, Susheela Dayal, puts it. Deep down, Malraux had changed: at Sens in 1940, Private Malraux was inquisitive about the behavior of his fellow recruits. A quarter of a century later, the minister was not particularly aware of the fate of the Indians: he had no "experience" there to transform into "awareness." Less susceptible than the Dayals, a Sikh writer and journalist, Kushwant Singh,[10] who interviewed Malraux in 1958, judges that the interest shown by Malraux was no thicker than the "varnish on so many Westerners. Malraux's phrases were often like firecrackers. Lots of noise and sparks when lit, but afterwards only smoke. During his travels in India, Malraux reassured some Indians who were living in confusion, searching for a virulent assertion of their identity. The Hindu absorption realizes he does not grasp well. His only grip on the human India is via its great men, Gandhi and Nehru.

He turns back into a traveling aesthete. Beyond the coquetry and rambling discussions with Nehru, India itself stimulates the author in him, much more so than his experience of China did beyond the brief meeting with Mao. Despite the official figure he has become, the writer works more by suggestion than by witness account. Between voyages, his style changes. In 1929, he visited the religious capital:

> At last at Benares, with its hotels closed at this time of the year, its rest house where the old women have been pulling the panka the whole night like before the Sepoy Revolt; its lanes, between high walls of gray stone. . . . All that in a mist of Tibetan steps, their sticky clouds loitering around the tended flames of the idols. The world to which these unreal stairways led is, in my memory, a world of high, lichen-covered walls, like those of the abandoned ruins under the great forest, at whose feet small lights burned endlessly, with glimpses of sacred animals passing through the fog.

And so on. In 1965, Malraux likes the town just as much but sees it (and more importantly, shows it) better with distance. Less vaporously, without the sfumato:

> At this hour, Benares was the Ganges. A sparrow hawk followed our boat between the constantly renewed fires of the funeral pyres and the piles of wood for cremations. In the slapping of a river the color of hemp, like the city, a silent voice quoted, "Here are the waters of the Ganges that sanctify the half-open mouths of the dead."

What if Malraux were not a metaphysician of the Absolute, a thinker on Destiny, but above all an agreeable travel writer?[13] He chooses to overlook the filth and grime. If we refuse to accept the intrusion of the character of Malraux himself into his exotic world, we must refuse to follow him. Otherwise, we can get on well enough, through his *Antimémoires* and his abstract, spiritual obsession with India.

Nehru died before Malraux's last trip to Asia.[14] The writer finds himself in New Delhi in 1965, with sprays of flowers for Gandhi and for Nehru's tombstone. "It has not yet been placed: its position is marked by a square of grass," writes Malraux in *Antimémoires*. "The tombstones are symbolic, since they do not cover the body. The man who, last time I came to Delhi, held India between his shivering hands is now a square of

in the self corresponds to the preoccupation of the writer with l
When writing, eight years later, the account of his first meeting
Pandit, Malraux used this trip to prolong the unity and continu
Self. Of his overdeveloped ego, some might say.

Malraux sticks to his uniform view of India, its metaphys
gious, and spiritual reality.[11] He is looking for the reality tha
"already in the Vedas."[12] "Of this civilization," the author's *Ani*
asks on his behalf, "what did I really know? Its art, its thought, it
The same as for great dead civilizations, except that I had heard
I had met men of the Brahmin caste but not priests, intellectu
diplomats. . . . Not a single shopkeeper, no peasants." No q
Malraux becoming Hinduized, going into an ashram, like the c
women he mocks. In his youth, Malraux had read the philoso
Guénon; he had contemplated the Indo-Buddhist works of
Guimet Museum. Almost thirty years later, we find him rela
Breton's declaration that "It is from the Orient that the light (
today." Reading Malraux at the time, no one would suspect th
age Indian's income is no more than $150 per year, that there
telephones in total for 500 million inhabitants, that 80 per
inhabitants live in rural areas, and that a child born in 195
expectancy of forty-three years. In 1958, epidemics wer
endemic illnesses such as tuberculosis, smallpox, and dysente
quent. Above all, there is not a word from Malraux on th
social cancer, the abominable caste system. Is that out of dipl
ary, or philosophical politeness? Or simply blindness? In 196
he could have made the short trip from the rather bourged
hood of Defense Colony to old Delhi, which is both picture
did. The best Malraux does is to mention the 0.8 percent o
go to what could charitably be called university. He fails to
lutions, negative or positive. Does he notice them? He ign
tence of a quality free press and a tightly controlled radio
service in the hands of the government. He does not report
the disappearance of famines, or the drop in infant morta
that concerned him long ago in Cochin China. He does n
"mixed economy" as a marriage of socialist hobbyhorses
practices. His eyes fixed on abstract nonviolence, Malraux
the manifest violence of the infanticide of little girls and
widows doused with acid. From 1958 to 1965, he has not
knowledge. When he was dealing in statuettes before th
Gandharian head in two and displayed the two profiles no
ing at each other. In *Antimémoires*, the writer saws India i
tic and metaphysical India contemplates the other India,

turf, where the already warm wind sets rippling the short grasses growing between cut flowers thrown there by joined hands." "Some of our dreams," says Malraux, "have no less meaning than our memories." He had dreamed of a privileged relationship with Nehru. Their relationship was superficial, devoid of the sumptuousness that Malraux—as a writer—drapes it in. Memories concerning Nehru, in Malraux's antimemory or paramemory, perhaps indicate a desire to build a bridge between the West and the East. But the spirituality invoked by the writer had no effect on the Pandit. Malraux did not understand the "Brahmino-socialist"[15] Nehru, his obsessions with planning and the iron and steel industry. In 1965, Malraux recollects a saying of Gandhi's: "If cowardice is the only alternative to violence, it is better to fight." For the former combatant Malraux, nonviolence cannot be a universal technique, but it does tempt him. Not as much, however, as certain Indian concepts that satisfy his cosmic aspirations, such as the Self, or the universal Being in all beings.[16] He does not set out to compare one civilization with others but to explore an eternal India, to advance "in obscurity toward the light of the torch she carries." To his friend Dileep Padgonkar, he said, "For the first time in her long history, India is India," just as France is turning back into France under de Gaulle; they are realizing their essence.

Malraux returns to Paris, a politico-literary Janus: he works on his oeuvre and seems fortified by it; and he forgets about the Absolute just long enough to participate in the presidential electoral campaign.[17] Although he usually avoids getting personal in his political outbursts, now he fervently attacks François Mitterrand for daring to oppose the General. In a speech at the Palais des Sports,[18] speaking for the Association pour la Ve République, Malraux sees in Mitterrand "a man who has never liberated anything." Malraux has never been this violent about a politician before: "You have dreamed up the Left . . . since you do not symbolize in any way a real action on the Left, since you do not symbolize the Republic. . . . What do you symbolize? First of all, a combination of touching aspiration and predictable demagogy implicit in an attitude of eternal intention, as opposed to political action. It is easier to get the voters to agree about their wish to go to Heaven than to give them the means to get there."

François Mitterrand never forgave these cruel attacks. Were they fair? In Malraux's eyes, Mitterrand was at that time promising the people "history fiction, as there is science fiction." In his summing-up to the Assembly, in front of Gaullist militants (half of whom he doesn't rate), party executives, and de Gaulle–abiding deputies, Malraux evokes the heroes from the book he is currently working on: "For Mao Tse-tung, as yesterday for Nehru, France is the revolution of General de Gaulle." All on the same shelf: Napoleon, Saint-Just, de Gaulle ... Not Mitterrand—he is not a successor to the General but a predecessor. "It is time to choose between a man of history who has taken France in hand, the like of whom France will not find again tomorrow, and politicians, who can always be found."

Political scandal, in Malraux's view: Mitterrand pushes de Gaulle to a second round. Speaking four days before the ballot, Malraux fears the worst. De Gaulle is re-elected with 55.1 percent of the vote, 44.8 percent going to Mitterrand. The writer returns to his desk and to History, which nearly overturned before his eyes, in the ballot boxes of the fickle French people. He shifts back again from reality to dream in his book.

He has been carefully kneading his literary dough. When Beuret insists that some very "farfelu" passages that clash with the rest of the book should be cut, he at first resists.[19] And just as he is in the middle of corrections to the first volume of *Antimémoires*, Malraux brings out his militant left-wing Gaullist costume and steps into action again as an irregular, devoted servant. He lends his support to Louis Vallon, the most markedly left-wing of the Gaullists, in the legislative elections for Sarcelles.[20] Vallon and Malraux have two passions in common: the General and whisky. In his short speech, Malraux proclaims, "We must work out whether France is decided that it is vital that left-wing Gaullism should be in place, or whether we really need another Communist deputy in the Assembly."

While Malraux has been diving back into politics, de Gaulle has been diving into literature. The president finishes reading *Antimémoires* on board the *Colbert*, a warship. To thank the author, he sends a coded telegram, 01/CT-HRANT1909072:

> finished first reading stop wonderful book in all three dimensions stop very best wishes stop.[21]

What are the three dimensions? The novel, history, and politics?

Letters and telegrams between Charles de Gaulle and André Malraux are rare, in both directions. They are better at writing about each other than to each other. De Gaulle sends Malraux his regards, his "deep admiration," his "profoundly sincere and affectionate wishes."[22] Despite the depth and the affection, they remain distant from each other in their correspondence. They are cramped in their exchanges, almost official, reserved, little inclined to outpourings, shackled by a mutual intimidation. Malraux sends a book. De Gaulle replies, "My dear friend, thank you for having written *Le Triangle noir*. ... I thank you for signing it for me, with your immense talent and your extreme loyalty. Believe me, my dear friend, your devoted . . ."[23] Malraux, on his side, struggles with the simplest of letters. When writing to the General, he seems paralyzed; he makes rough copies, like a schoolboy. He starts to sign off with *"le témoignage de mon affection et de ma . . ."* (the expression of my affection and my . . .).[24] As if taken aback by the audacity of the word "affection," he crosses it out, negating its commitment, and finishes anyway with *"respectueuse et affectueuse fidélité,"* in evidence of his boundless respect.

On the publication of Charles de Gaulle's speeches, Malraux writes to him, "They are monologues, supreme and sometimes secretly desperate." The writer perfects his literary criticism, also rediscovering his propensity for negative definitions. The General's speeches establish "a form, not like one school follows another but like Cézanne follows Claude Monet: another domain is born; these speeches break with tradition because they are not of that tradition."[25] When the General publishes his *Mémoires d'espoir,*[26] Malraux tells him that the real title should have been *La France, c'est moi.* Obviously, he says to de Gaulle, "you clearly can't use it." He is moved by the famous paragraph on himself, starting "On my right [in the Cabinet], I have and will always have André Malraux . . . friend of genius." The letter continues, "To have had the honor of helping you has been the pride of my life, all the more so now as I face nothingness." In his polished passage on Malraux, the General claimed that the writer's presence had prevented him—the president of the Republic—from descending from the heights. In their correspondence, each takes up a position on a high peak. When they address each other, they seem to have difficulty breathing, let alone writing.

Not so Marcel Arland, who, writing to Malraux about *Antimémoires,* tells him, "It is clearly your book, this long dramatic, and solid song, this incantation, lucid and passionate in its scope—of the only debate that counts: that between man and oblivion. It is your essential course, fully rendered, and in that, these are your real memoirs." Pierre Jean Jouve sees in *Antimémoires* "when all is said and done, a meditation between action and pain. . . . There is everywhere . . . a bravura of the mind that belongs only to you." Romain Gary, writer, diplomat, and ex–Free French airman, who reveres Malraux, writes to him, "What is really mysterious in the book is the calm creation of something unformulated." The writer-minister understands but doesn't like a critic to suggest to him that his book is fictionalized. On the other hand, he states, with his usual self-restraint, that to say "it is written with the means at the novelist's disposal is absolutely true, for the very good reason that it is also true of [the eighteenth-century memorialist] Saint-Simon: Saint-Simon's means were also those of the novelist."

Sometimes Malraux judges his own books for those close to him.

L'Espoir is "excellent"—or a "failure." *Le Temps du mépris* is always bad, according to its author. He does not sustain such doubts with *Anti-mémoires*. Either proud and naive or pathologically pretentious, Malraux murmurs to his daughter and others, "I am the only writer who counts."

Today, that is, in France. That goes without saying. Or does he mean the only writer in the world? Who knows where that might take us? Seriously.

CHAPTER THIRTY-THREE

The Orator

AFTER SO MANY meetings organized, gatherings presided over, *maisons de la culture* and exhibitions inaugurated, Malraux, with accents of Jean Jaurès, Jules Michelet, and Maurice Barrès, produces a number of miniatures of his oeuvre, in the form of funeral orations. Oratorical exercise is sometimes a way for him to catch his breath. December 19, 1964, holds a particularly striking moment for him and many onlookers (including a uniformed Charles de Gaulle) as Malraux gives his most ambitious funeral oration, for Jean Moulin. At Malraux's insistence to the General, Moulin's ashes are transferred to the Panthéon in Paris. Malraux as Berger, as if frozen by the cold in his greatcoat, speaks in a cavernous voice about Moulin—or "Rex," as he was known in the Resistance—and addresses him directly.

Whether dedicated to Le Corbusier or Jean Moulin, to the painter Georges Braque, the Resistance, or deportation, his orations are fashioned not for a pulpit in Notre-Dame but for the Acropolis, the Cour Carrée of the Louvre, or the Panthéon. Television is becoming the means of distribution par excellence. Live broadcasts are moving. A death cannot be put back by a day or a month at the speaker's will. Malraux's elocution is closer to a prewar Comédie-Française style than the minimalist theater of the 1960s. Even if he irritates some and makes others laugh, he is incomparable. In the same lineage as Demosthenes, Saint-Just, Jaurès, Briand, and de Gaulle: he stands trembling, the delivery is jerky, the breath hoarse, the sentences broken up, but his paragraphs roll like waves over shingle. Years of training in conferences, antifascist meetings before the war, the grand RPF rituals. And when he speaks, most often, his tics subside.

The funeral orations deserve to belong to the Malrucian corpus. He does not just throw them together, and he no longer improvises as before the war—a strategy informed not by age, but by technique: each line uttered will be a line written, publishable, published. Even so, clichés creep in: "The funereal night" always seems to come to hand and is just about as worthwhile as "somber dejection" or "gloomy despair." But the agile charmer emerges, when necessary, from beneath the skillful politician. If it's a Greek audience, Greece is the center of the world. An Indian auditorium? Then it's India. *Bon.* Not too seriously. Malraux gets the job done. And through these stylistic gymnastics, it is often the General that he is addressing more than his French or foreign audiences. The ideal listener, de Gaulle remains there as a watermark behind Malraux's words, a stern father admiring his gifted child.[1] Beyond the crowds and the television viewers, Malraux's incantatory monologue is an endless communion with de Gaulle.

A religious funeral oration would usually include a panegyric and lead to meditation. Malraux is agnostic or atheist; a religious person but a faithless one. He replaces the religious content with personal witness, thereby adding a chapter to the autobiography dispersed throughout his works.

Listening to or reading the end of the short but heartfelt speech for Le Corbusier's funeral, one senses a man who is deeply moved: "Adieu, my old master and my old friend, good night. . . . Here is the homage of epic cities. . . . Funeral flowers from New York and Brasilia. Here are the sacred water of the Ganges and the earth of the Acropolis." The verbal landscape artist builds a waterfall and controls its flow. What of his sincerity? Who can say.

When talking of Georges Braque, politics and propaganda lurking in the background, he stresses, "Never has a modern country paid homage of this sort to one of its painters at his death." He plugs away at the exceptional, the superlative, the prodigious, the stunning. All the more so since he often finds a place in an oration for his own amazing life. Taking part in the commemoration of the Liberation of Paris at Montparnasse station a little after the General's return to power, Malraux finds his novelist's accents, recalling the "deep manly brotherhood and the humiliation" just as when he was writing *L'Espoir* and *La Condition humaine.* He has regrets; he does experience nostalgia. But public remorse is not his style. Without naming him, he evokes his brother Roland and the extermination camps, which "laid out, as far as the Baltic, a strange retinue of shadows waiting for the vanquished to arrive." The Baltic occurs in his first and last oration and, with it, Roland. What guilt does the writer-minister feel for having survived his two brothers in the Resistance? When referring to the Resistance, none of his texts escapes a conventional use of "we"—"We fought a guerrilla war"—which anchors Malraux himself and identifies the orator and his listeners with the Resistance fighters.

The personal backdrop is very obvious in the most famous of his orations, for Jean Moulin on the Place du Panthéon.[2] The ministre d'état, having made an inventory of those whose remains have been laid to rest in the Panthéon, judges that a lot of them are worthless unknowns who simply cannot be put anywhere else. Jean Moulin will help to make up for the second-raters. Malraux, in top form, pays homage to the only living being who counts for him: "Monsieur le président de la République." Not a word for the other VIPs. Nor for Jean Moulin's sister, who is there. Holding on to his sheets of notes, feeling the cold of December despite his thick coat, the orator throws a bridge between his own Spanish war (Moulin was "a friend of Republican Spain" and helped the *coronel* obtain planes and pilots) and the Resistance in France (Moulin transformed a "brotherhood" into a "combat" thanks to a "courageous disorder"). He recognizes himself in Jean Moulin. His remarkable delivery, captivating and pathetic, is carried by the weight of two lives, Malraux's and Moulin's. The writer-minister has now told more than one person that two political figures are evidently emerging in France, himself and de Gaulle. Malraux could, would, and should have been Jean Moulin, he should have been at the head of the whole Resistance. In his three departments, Malraux didn't control much of anything. In the role of the General's deputy, he has apparently added an intellectual and "metaphysical" tinge, a tone of "transcendence." Somebody—Destiny or God—must have messed up.

With this speech, Malraux gives another sketch of himself on the stage of History. Later, when he wants to publish his funeral orations, he proposes a title for the book, "The Seven Historic Speeches." Jean Grosjean suggests instead "Gods. Saints. Heroes." Gallimard doesn't use that line either. Malraux keeps a close eye on the publication of his anthology. To Claude Gallimard:[3] "I do not wish to publish *Oraisons funèbres* at just any time, but on May 15 [1971] at the latest. It is on their link with *Les Chênes* [*Les Chênes qu'on abat*] . . . that I am counting on to ensure their audience, in the same way that the link between the General's speeches and his memoirs ensured an audience for his speeches." More insistently, a week later: "I don't want to be boring about this, I just want to convince you. I have, for a number of years, been not completely incompetent in matters of publishing. The way I see it, publication [in September] implies the death of the book. Speeches do not sell. (Look at those of Gambetta and Valéry.) Our only chance is to pull this car along with *Les Chênes* as a locomotive, just as the General's speeches were pulled along by the memoirs." *Les Chênes qu'on abat* is published on March 17, 1971, and the coal cars, *Les Oraisons funèbres*, two months later, on May 15.

Malraux experiences a rebirth, thanks to two books (*Antimémoires* and *Les Chênes qu'on abat*), one doctor, and a woman. When Malraux left Madeleine, Florence asked him about the reasons for the breakup.

"I don't know what came over me," he answered.

Malraux also tells his daughter later on, "The women of my life, I have loved them all."

Malraux left Madeleine for good before *Antimémoires* was published. Nobody, at the time, could have spotted the embellishments in that book better than she. Clara and Madeleine carried and supported Malraux, which he cannot bear any longer. Madeleine does not say, as Clara did to Florence, "I fell in love with your father the day he left me."

Living at La Lanterne, the lodge on the grounds of Versailles, Malraux had Jean Grosjean and his wife for troubled witnesses and, for confidante, Louise de Vilmorin, rediscovered and reconquered, if such a woman can be said to be conquerable. At the beginning of the 1950s, Malraux sent Louise "a four-leaf clover . . . those that truly bring luck and happiness." Mme. de Vilmorin is also a writer; he said nice things about her books. Louise took the compliments with caution: in her opinion, he says nice things "to everybody."

Lively and funny, spiteful and, especially when she drinks too much, the first sense of "Loulette" is seduction. In her blue drawing room at Verrières, she receives Jacques Prévert and Maurice Druon. In 1967, at sixty-five, she is one year younger than André; she has humor, grace, and a sense of the ephemeral. Up to 1969, she sees Malraux two or three times a week. Then she goes to La Lanterne every day. Eventually, she asks him to move into Verrières-le-Buisson, the Vilmorin family home, built in 1680. She gives him a study on the ground floor, two adequate—not luxurious—upstairs rooms and a bathroom. That part of the house is known as "les bateaux" because of the prints hanging on the wall. Also living at Verrières are André, Roger, Sosthène de Vilmorin, Louise's nephew, and his wife, Corinne Godfernaux, who is also Malraux's secretary.

The unlikely literary twosome get talked about in the papers. André and Louise send each other cuttings announcing their marriage. Malraux's is from *L'Est Éclair*:[4]

"To make you laugh—despite the staples, we look good."

The incomparable Louise: "Who bothers to get married these days, apart from priests?"

Malraux does not divorce Madeleine. Her demands, he says, are excessive. He claims she wants to share everything; out of exasperation, he offers to cut every book in his library in two. They could also divide the debts. Madeleine has the well-known Maître Badinter for a lawyer, Malraux has an unknown. He writes to his wife, "To twenty-five years of generosity, you respond with provocation." Malraux is never in a hurry to divorce, from Clara or from Madeleine. Divorce implies mourning.

Louise has had a few husbands, and more than a few lovers. Now André Malraux, this grand figure, has shacked up in her life, then moved well and truly in. Louise's favorite man is still André de Vilmorin (nice first name), one of her four brothers. The Vilmorins like to joke and collect things. Malraux and Louise de Vilmorin show each other off to advantage. Two lines from a poem by Louise could be an idyll to sum up their relationship as portrayed in the popular press: "L'écho du rire / Est un sanglot" (The echo of a laugh is a sob).

The fact that they are a couple provides romantic stories for a readership that does not, on the whole, know their books. Photos in *Paris-Match* show them walking hand in hand in the grounds at Verrières. When Malraux came back into Louise's life she was well known but her reputation was fading. In the arms of her minister, Louise de Vilmorin becomes famous; she no longer feels she is on the wane. Two monsters, two mirrors: she, the reflection of the unconventional, *farfelu* side of them both; he, the grave and serious image. André arrives on time, Louise is late. The play is cast.

Her false triviality contrasts with the frequent solemnity of her companion. She knows how to make him laugh. She loves flowers, he loves Goya. They have in common a taste for words, the approach of old age, and alcohol, a powerful link. If Louise de Vilmorin were a pretty hourglass in the sun, Malraux would be a large sundial in the shade. They support each other, she pulling him toward comedy, he pushing her in the direction of tragedy. She puts on the brakes with all the resistance her wit can muster. André and Louise: partners in an odd alliance, like many couples. She says she is delighted about Malraux's reconciliation with his daughter. She does not understand much of what he writes. Has she really read his work? She likes to have him within reach; he likes to have her on his arm.

Later, Malraux has his study "done" by a modern decorator, Henri Samuel. Louise, laughing: "I know what Malraux is like. Nobody has taste as bad as his."

He urges her to read. She resigns herself: "I'm following your advice. I am reading Thomas Mann."

"You've just gotten to page two."

The writer accepts Louise's society dinners and enjoys them. The wines at Verrières are excellent. There are champagne and whisky. She dines by candlelight: it suits a woman's complexion. That of aging men, too. Louise imposes some principles and bans certain subjects: politics, religion, opposition to Napoleon, Victor Hugo. Malraux gets fidgety when Brigitte Bardot (herself terrified) arrives in a black cape. He is always happy to see the sculptor Jacques Zwoboda, the actor Paul Meurisse, the singer Guy Béart, especially when Louise comes out with "Guy, get your guitar, I didn't ask you here for nothing."

At Mme. de Vilmorin's table—for a change—Malraux holds back a bit on the monologues. The guests are also sometimes allowed to speak. Malraux pretends not to be the center of interest at dinner. Other writers—Maurice Genevoix, Dominique de Roux—drop in. Malraux still prefers his friends, René Clair and his wife and the old faithfuls. He likes the tales of who's sleeping with whom that are peddled at the table. Louise and André spend without counting the cost. Louise always finds a way to pay, borrowing here and there, especially from her first husband. She says, "In money matters, Malraux is worse than I am."

For someone who is the epitome of unfaithful giddiness, Louise has some serious loyalties. Every week she writes to the artist Jean Hugo. Her brother André de Vilmorin talks to her every morning at eleven. He has accepted Malraux, but not before telling his sister, "He is not a man for you."

The Vilmorin clan takes Malraux on as one. They are a family to him. He intends to descend from his pedestal but doesn't quite manage it. The two monsters undergo a double convalescence. They offer Paris another literary couple: Aragon and Elsa, Sartre and Simone de Beauvoir. Malraux and . . . nice photos. The questionable period of "celebrities" is beginning, where writers can be in, irrespective of their books, and cinema actors stars almost in spite of their films. Do André and Louise love each other? Some are convinced they do. Others, like the writer Jules Roy, are not. Malraux resumes some of his literary activities and lunches between visits to the ministry. Louise encourages him, in all domains: "But why don't you court the Comtesse de Karolyi?" Catherine de Karolyi, or "Gogo," is a friend of Louise.

Out of necessity, Malraux becomes spontaneously amiable again. Ever since his misadventures in Cambodia, he has known how to handle journalists. An interviewer only needs to come and see him and, if he is not a fool, he will come away with a copy of the book they have been talking about bearing a personalized inscription. Malraux knows the vanity of the milieu. He peppers every interview with "As you know." He is always in demand, on all sides. Press conferences and interviews are part of his oratorical art; they call for an artificial intimacy that Malraux finds it easy to slip into. He will start the day at the ministry, maybe give an interview, a speech, a meeting over lunch at Lasserre, an interview, a spot of writing, another interview . . . *Bon.* Another speech?

Malraux speaks at the Palais des Sports in 1967. The concept of nation, he declares, "is the capital discovery of the century," "organic across the world." He is setting the General's libretto to music. He also stages a scene with one of his favorite heroes: "Mao Tse-tung, who had forded the eleven rivers, passed through the snowy mountains of Tibet, crossed rivers and bridges on fire; when he had no more than his immense chains drawn tight across history, when he had arrived with seven thousand men, had conquered seven hundred million Chinese, I said to him, 'Well then, Mr. President, will old empires now be reborn?' Mao Tse-tung simply replied to me, 'Yes.' " The idea is generally accepted within France: Malraux must have conversed for many hours, several times over the course of the years, with Mao. He returns to this tale in writing and in speeches.

He has made good use of photography over the years, starting with Gisèle Freund; radio, likewise. He perceives the possibilities of film and television. He doesn't like to see himself on the small screen. From September 1967 to 1976, he speaks or appears eighty-seven times on the radio or television. He refuses to allow the transcription and publication of his several hours' worth of programs on art. His hands and arms, his body lurching forward, the index finger raised and aimed like a little springboard, do not always obey the advice of the directors. "Don't move too much. Try not to hit the table!" The noise is magnified by the microphones. It suggests the presence behind him of tempests, thunder, and lightning. He appreciates compliments. "I couldn't have done better," de Gaulle says to him after one program.[5]

The first episode of *La Légende du Siècle* starts with a forward-looking shot: Malraux—very much alive—in the vestibule of posterity that is the Panthéon. Shooting goes on for months. On one day Malraux, perhaps under the influence of medication, seems absent and incomprehensible. On another session, he shines and clings to transcendence. To some television viewers, Malraux seems possessed, a visionary; to others, muddled and recondite. It is by these programs more than anything else that the majority of listeners and viewers form their opinion of Malraux. Many who come to film or interview him arrive in raptures. See Malraux and die. (Or survive.) From time to time, the writer abandons the oracular style and opens up. But despite a few familiarities and jokes, this is Malraux playing Malraux. Indeed, a little bit of informality is what allows an institution, a myth, to speak like you and me. Malraux puts on masks. His silences when he is thinking are moving; chin on his hands, forehead creased in thought, eaten up by who knows what inner fire, on the edge of what gulf of inexpressibility, sometimes expressed by words that do not bear analysis. "That would take us too far . . ." Where is it that Malraux does not want to go or cannot go? Prose poetry for some, pretentious nonsense for others. But either way, imbued with passion.

For the written press, Malraux places himself on a level with everybody.

"Are you happy, André Malraux?" asks Victor Franco in the *Journal du
Dimanche*.

"As much as the next man."

"How do you see your contemporaries? . . . What have you brought
to them?"

"I don't see them very often."

Malraux quickly gets onto Malraux: let's talk about something interesting, let's talk about me.

"What I have that is special? Let us say an artist who has participated
in the History of his time and who expresses it with astonishment."

By now Malraux comes across more as a French writer than as a
Parisian politician. Politicians are afraid of tape recorders and often—in
France—ask to reread their interviews. Not so Malraux; he is decent
enough to accept cuts and patched-up passages. In interviews, he per-
forms himself in front of himself, watched by journalists, sound engineers,
cameramen. Nobody can stem his flow. Many writers can switch on the
charm. Malraux does it more than most. His exquisite way of welcoming
journalists seems to say, "You are the one I have been waiting for" or
"How is it that we haven't met before?"

CHAPTER THIRTY-FOUR

Clouds in May

T HE EFFECT OF *Antimémoires* is subsiding. In literary and political circles, there is a widening split in attitudes toward Malraux. He is not liked by his own, the Gaullists, but they know how close he is to the General. Those who oppose Gaullism feel uneasy. They start to think that Malraux has changed camp and personality. While the minister is taking care of the business in hand, forging ahead with promising or doomed projects, his *maisons de la culture* are attacked, more from the right than from the left.

Malraux has tried to depoliticize official appointments. Ministers will persist in believing that they govern. When they do, it is often against their faction and their bureaucracy, the permanent substance that long survives the evanescent minister. The executive figure is often dragged down by the administrative burden and sometimes resigns himself to strutting about. Malraux lasts ten years as a minister and endures.

On February 25, 1968, François Mitterrand, in a written question to the National Assembly, asks why Malraux has "evicted, in particularly shocking conditions, the director of the Cinémathèque Française [National Film Archive], to whom, for the last quarter of a century, cinema has owed the safekeeping of its creations"? The archive's director—and cofounder—is Henri Langlois, and he is defended by Jean-Luc Godard, François Truffaut, and battalions of film lovers. Malraux, in fact, has helped Langlois: his subsidy has been doubled since 1958. A modern screening theater was built for him at the Palais de Chaillot. Film warehouses have been agreed on. Twenty million new francs—$4 million at the time—have been spent over the last ten years.

Langlois has no flair for administration and no sense of bookkeeping. He is not interested in the day-to-day running of the archive: if he is asked for the number and titles of films in his possession and what their legal origin is, he cannot answer. Sometimes he does not even know where his copies are. Malraux explains that thousands of reels of film stored for conservation "in the blockhouses at Bois d'Arcy are often in a deplorable state." Rusted cans are piled up in no particular order; some films are damaged. A bohemian or arbitrary approach to order places copies of no interest next to pieces of value. One and a half thousand copies have been made since 1963—where are they? Langlois does not want his films to be worked on. He won't allow technicians and some researchers into the blockhouses. Cultural Affairs has tried several times to reason with him: Would he be so kind as to collaborate "with a senior official . . . charged with administrative and financial responsibility for the Cinémathèque Française"? Langlois is a taboo totem for young filmmakers, a master in his field, but he is temperamental. Malraux thinks he should keep his post as artistic director, with "the most complete liberty," but hand over the administrative reins.

Guerrilla war ensues. Langlois draws admirers and supporters. Malraux answers Mitterrand, the momentary film enthusiast: "A collection of books does not become the Bibliothèque Nationale without a decisive transition. The same is true of the Cinémathèque. Mr. Langlois has rendered an eminent service. What he likes doing, he does very well. What he doesn't like he does less well, and he hasn't let anybody else take responsibility either; the list is starting to get long. For the very future of the Cinémathèque Française, it has become vital to secure its management in a less personal and more accountable way."

In short, it is a clash of two "geniuses": Malraux in a "right-wing Gaullist" dunce cap and Langlois with a "left-wing and the Arts" shield.

The left-wing press protests. Langlois called some senior civil servants philistines because they were curt with him. Malraux finds this unacceptable and sends him packing, with the brutality of those who doubt the form and content of their decision. The writer's popularity rating falls. Clearly (to some), Malraux is showing his true totalitarian colors. Demonstrators shout, "Malraux, fascist!"

At the beginning of 1968, Malraux said in front of his new director of theaters, Francis Raison, "There's going to be a squall in this country."

On Thursday, May 2, at Nanterre University near Paris, an unknown Franco-German student named Daniel Cohn-Bendit organizes an "anti-imperialist" day. Weeks of "meetings" and "happenings" with nocturnal barricades and diurnal scuffles follow. Malraux is not the only one at the heart of the government—or in opposition—to look to the "events" of May 1968 for some kind of perspective on what Raymond Aron called a "revolution that could not be found." Malraux is concerned but disoriented; he has no connection with these youths. He passes a strange few weeks, unable to get a grasp on events. As ministre d'état he has no role to play. The prime minister and the president listen to his opinions—which aren't even advice—with half an ear.

Malraux does not participate in any of the conclaves of Gaullist moderates, who think the General is definitely looking past it and ought to go. The ministre d'état asks to see de Gaulle several times but is not admitted. Having met with two members of the U.S. Embassy, Malraux writes to the General. He tells him of the NATO allies' anxiety. He receives his answer in the form of a note in the third person: "The president of the Republic regrets . . ." De Gaulle, meanwhile, is probing his staff: Should he be attempting to regain the confidence of the French people, or should they be trying to obtain his? The General disappears, without even warning Bernard Tricot, the Élysée Palace general secretary, who usually knows everything. Malraux was not consulted or warned either. De Gaulle has left by helicopter for a secret meeting with Generals Massu and Hublot in Baden-Baden.

Malraux is no worshiper of youth as such. He often reproached Gide and Sartre for paying too much attention to adolescents. Nevertheless, when the students crowd onto the Tomb of the Unknown Soldier at the Arc de Triomphe and sing "The Internationale," he is not deeply shocked. It's just not in very good taste. He has often sung it himself. There are barricades, fires, fights: right-thinking editorial writers and readers experience panic and express disgust; Malraux doesn't. But when a night of troubles finishes with more than seven hundred wounded, almost four hundred of them seriously, and at least a hundred burned-out cars, he does raise an eyebrow. This is not an acceptable revolution. For Malraux, de Gaulle is still the rebel, the incomparable revolutionary.

The minister-writer talks to an American diplomat of his pessimism about the situation: "Your students want reform; ours just want to destroy. On the whole, yours are not nihilists in the Russian sense of the term. At least, not for the moment. Ours are. You can talk with a Communist. Not with a nihilist. . . . Our problem with young people is deeper and more serious than yours."

"A morose observation for the author of *La Condition humaine* and *L'Espoir*," notes the diplomat in the margin of his report.

Malraux's judgment of the students and their leaders changes with his mood. He confides to Jacques Chaban-Delmas that he doesn't know if he likes or hates them. He is not the only one in Paris to nurse this ambivalence. José Bergamin ("Pépé") tries for several weeks to "live" May '68, and Malraux, in Bergamin's opinion, tries to "understand" the events. They have lunch together. The ministerial limousine, a Citroën DS, waits for Malraux to take him to the National Assembly. Where can he drop his friend (or is he an adversary)?

"At the Sorbonne [the focal point of the student movement]," says Bergamin.

Malraux, with a smile: "You are heading for the irrational, I for the unreal."[1]

Malraux flounders about, out of touch and out of play. He cannot act. Prime Minister Pompidou does not consult him. The writer notes "the absence of hatred on both sides." The students shout out in the streets their far-fetched comparison of Parisian and Nazi security forces: "CRS: SS!" De Gaulle calmly declares himself ready to have the security forces open fire on the ministers' sons among the demonstrators. But there is hardly any violence; Grimaud, a prefect and the chief of police, holds back his exhausted men and forestalls any irreversible action. Hate is indeed absent, and there is little bloodshed. Malraux gathers his heads of departments at the ministry to try to make sense of the situation.[2] To Malraux, the situation is not revolutionary because nobody is looking for arms. But it does appear to be openly rebellious since it is an attempt "to break down a structure": to topple the government. Pierre Moinot watches as Malraux pictures himself in the Louvre, facing a riot crowd, rushing to the stairway next to the Classical Department: "Let them come in that far, none of those statues on the lower level is very fragile. There are lots of copies. They can come in that far. But from that staircase onward, I'll be in front of *Samothrace*, in the middle of the steps, and you'll all be behind me, we'll be there, with our arms stretched out."

Has Malraux been at the Maxiton?

The man whose job it is to play the trump cards of power—or discard them—is the prime minister, Georges Pompidou. André Malraux is no longer close to him, far from it; gone are the days when he wrote to the future prime minister, "We both need to work together in a certain brotherhood."[3] There is, on Malraux's side, a personal grievance: Pompidou and his wife have remained on good terms with Madeleine. And another reproach, which has more to do with psychology than politics: Malraux has the feeling that Pompidou sees him as a possible competitor for the Matignon, or higher still. He is wrong about this. Pompidou admires the writer, but to him, Malraux is a tightrope walker, especially in internal politics, an amateur, and sometimes even a dangerous one. He is too fond of secret service plotting and panache. Pompidou has heard from Claude Mauriac what Malraux confided to Claude's father, François: "There are only two men in France, de Gaulle and me."[4] Pompidou published an anthology of poetry; Malraux comments that the compilation is not worth bothering about.

Malraux does, reluctantly, appear in the events of May 1968, in a petty role unworthy of Colonel Berger. The minister has entrusted the Théâtre de France, based at the Odéon, to the actor and director Jean-Louis Barrault. The building is occupied from May 13 by students: real and wannabe beatniks and *katangais* (hooligan, tough-guy drug addicts armed with clubs, knives, and one or two revolvers). Militants have been sweeping the Latin Quarter, recruiting: "Everybody to the Odéon!"

As at the Sorbonne, the debates at the Odéon are tumultuous and confused. The protestors announce that "the actors want to take control of the Odéon," which is far from the truth. Bourgeois residents from the neighborhood, whether progressive or not, pop in at the beginning of the evening. What fun! Should we dine at Brasserie Lipp afterward, darling? Daniel Cohn-Bendit spoke on the first evening at the Odéon, making fun of "Chagall's graffiti on the ceiling." The decoration is in fact by Masson: Cohn-Bendit was getting mixed up with the ceiling of the Opéra, also commissioned by Malraux. The students declared the Théâtre de France morally dead and its director devoid of interest. Barrault dashed back to his theater from London and got up onto the stage. With conviction—or perhaps just testing the waters—he announces, "So be it! Barrault is dead, but he is still a living man."

He is met with more jeers than cheers: "You bastard! You dine with Pompidou!"

"Have him play for free!"

Madeleine Renaud, Barrault's wife, a great actress but not the finest political mind, cries out, "The Théâtre de France, which put on *Les Paravents* [the Genet play Malraux defended], is not a bourgeois theater. . . . If you want to take it out on bourgeois theater, go to the Comédie-Française or the Folies Bergère."

The next day, the minister of cultural affairs announces the "profound discontent in high places provoked by [Barrault's] unfortunate pronouncement." Glancing at the newspapers, de Gaulle apparently remarks, "If he is dead, we'd better bury him."[5]

In a Cabinet meeting on May 18, de Gaulle turns to Malraux: "They took the Odéon from you?"

"It won't do them any good," replies the minister.

The Sorbonne, the Odéon, that's too much. It's time to get this under control.

So Malraux participates. The situation at the theater is deteriorating; little bands are stealing props and stage weapons from backstage. Technicians block the safety curtain. Under orders from the Élysée and Matignon, Malraux decides to evacuate the theater. On May 20, the actors and theater staff receive a succession of orders and counterorders. The minister of culture's office instructs Barrault to have the theater's electricity and phone cut off. Barrault refuses. The actor puts himself onstage for the benefit of the newspapers and history, to declare, "Servant, yes. Lackey, no!"

It's as good as Hugo—or Malraux. But stupid. Barrault requests an audience with the minister: "I am anxious to maintain with you, on noble terrain, the relationship that we have always had." Malraux steps out of his car; Barrault comes toward him. The ministre d'état shakes his head, gives a sour smile, and leaves. At the end of August, Barrault receives a letter from Malraux: "I have to inform you that after your various declarations I judge that you cannot continue to hold the post of director of this theater, whatever its future vocation may be."

Malraux meditates on the facts he has at his disposal and on those he doesn't, and he finds something to say about the events of May and June 1968: "It is a crisis of civilization, and it concerns all the students in the world. . . . What are the students doing? They write phrases, words, letters on walls. Now, what religions did, of course, was not to write letters on walls but inscribe things in the hearts of men. And you can sense the discrepancy. Our civilization, the first to be what we might call an agnostic civilization rather than a religious civilization, poses the problem of religion more brutally than any other civilization."[6]

On May 23, the Cabinet discusses various ideas, including that of a referendum. Would it give de Gaulle back the legitimacy he has seen disputed and damaged by recent events?

Malraux to the president: "Yes, a referendum is imperative; nothing else will do it. The choice must be made by the country: it's either reform, which only you with your government can bring about, or revolution. It's simple, and the people will understand. Reform must on no account be prescribed by the opposition. The government must not dance to the strikers' tune. What will come after the referendum will be the establishment of something fundamental, a systematic new deal."

Malraux returns to a position on the forestage, at the head of a Gaullist procession on the Champs-Élysées on May 30. Gaullist leaders and 500,000 to 700,000 supporters of the General proceed up the main thoroughfare. The streets are theirs now. Malraux, at the head of the demonstration, looks utterly convinced but ultimately lost, hysterical, both exhausted and energized as he advances among the fifty- and sixty-year-olds in suits and ties. He turns to the onlookers and protestors in the side roads, and yells, "*Vive de Gaulle! Vive de Gaulle!*"

Malraux gives a speech to the Gaullist masses at the Parc des Expositions on June 20, 1968, in the run-up to the legislative elections. His public includes Gaullist dignitaries, party members at every level of the bourgeoisie, white- and blue-collar workers. "Capitalism" does not carry us in its heart, says Malraux, but General de Gaulle and Mr. Pompidou will defend capital and the franc better than Messrs. Mitterrand and Mollet.[7] Which is not necessarily all that convincing for the top members of his audience: there is a certain enmity toward Pompidou, which Malraux savors. He is standing up there to assure the General of his unfailing commitment, not to reassure the Gaullist rank and file or top brass.

On May 31, de Gaulle appoints an interim government. André Malraux remains on the General's right. He sees to the ordinary business of his ministry, congratulates Marcel Arland when he is elected to the Académie Française. On June 30, following the tidal wave of the Champs-Élysées demonstration, a seismic electoral aftershock gives the General's party 358 seats out of a possible 485. Election on a majority basis has helped, but France has also reacted to the events in Paris seen by the whole country on television. A bit of a bust-up with the CRS and the cops, at a push, is understandable; young people will be young people. But images of fires, property and cars burning, have been arriving in people's homes. A Gaullist future is outlined on the political horizon; it could be in place for twenty, thirty, perhaps a hundred years. The non-Communist Left is stunned and crushed and finds it very hard to recover.

On a trip to the USSR at the beginning of the year, Malraux observed that nothing there had changed: the Moscow regime was still totalitarian, ideology was still its dominant feature. On August 20, 1968, Russian, East German, Polish, Hungarian, and Bulgarian troops and T54s roll into Czechoslovakia. Malraux says he has been "expecting nothing else" of the Soviets and their satellites. In his report to the Cabinet after his trip, he described a "weighty stability behind the Iron Curtain." The USSR is now weighing down upon the so-called popular democracies and "stabilizing" them. Why didn't de Gaulle summon him to the meeting about the events in Czechoslovakia? Malraux is not included in the most important privy Cabinet.

General de Gaulle bites the hand that fed him by dismissing Georges Pompidou, or rather, places him *"en réserve de la République"*—at the Republic's disposal. On July 10, 1968, Maurice Couve de Murville becomes prime minister.

"Couve," says Malraux amiably, "will be sure to obey the most questionable orders." On June 20, Foccart and de Gaulle, in their almost daily conversation, discussed a forthcoming assembly of the CDR (Comité de Défense de la République). De Gaulle: "As for Malraux, plan on a replacement speaker. I find him tired these days."[8]

In September, the general meeting of the International Assembly of French-speaking Parliamentarians is due to take place. Foccart tells de

Gaulle that Malraux is supposed to give a speech but that at a dinner, he again found him weary.

"Yes, I've noticed," says the President. "But what's the matter with him?"

"Some sort of generalized fatigue."

"He's not drinking, is he? He hasn't started to drink?"

"No, *mon Général*. At least, I don't know."

The ministerial routine starts up again. Malraux gets back into certain projects. He has felt some of the shock waves of May and pays attention, where it concerns him, to some of the students' demands. He addresses the Cabinet on December 4 about the notion of reform in the teaching of architecture: "The architect of the last centuries was an individual who was building an object (a palace or a house) for a client who was also an individual, even if it was the king."

Malraux suggests putting an end to the Prix de Rome architecture prize and proposes the creation of special grants to send students to "the countries where modern architecture is being made": Finland, the United States, Brazil, perhaps Japan. The minister criticizes the teaching in France as "excessively centralized," "traditional," and "lacking in means." Then comes a reputation-making declaration from the point of view of established architects (those who have the power, the veterans of May '68 would say): there is "no architectural research in France."

Malraux approves of the proposed reforms in further education, more so than de Gaulle. But rather than pluridisciplinarity or the relationships between teachers and students, he prefers to meditate on the "planetary crisis of civilization," which, according to him, has been revealed by the events of May. He has to settle for his ministerial projects; useful, certainly, but mundane, everyday tasks. This bill to introduce commercial film theaters run by small businesses . . . what a good idea. There are thirty-two people sitting around the Cabinet table while our civilization and the cosmos itself are in crisis—it's ridiculous! At every meeting of ministers, Malraux finds himself sitting opposite Couve de Murville, who is not his type. The feeling is mutual.

More writer than minister, Malraux picks up his literary work again. De Gaulle carried the day, but France, on the left at any rate, is suffering from a hangover. So, as regards politics, is Malraux.

Richard Nixon arrives in Paris. General de Gaulle welcomes him in person at Orly. Nixon seems to be negotiating a bend on the path of American foreign policy: Europe is apparently one of Washington's priorities. With Nixon, Malraux has a less intense relationship than with Kennedy. What is more, Pat Nixon is less attractive than Jackie. Nixon is apparently much less cultivated than Kennedy, and he doesn't appear to belong to History's Greats. Does he have a destiny? Paris is waiting to see how the new American president's political and military strategy in Vietnam will develop. Still, a man like Nixon—who is obviously respectful of Charles de Gaulle—deserves to be shown prudent sympathy.

Malraux is approaching seventy. He wedges his feet into posterity. He protects his legend down to the most derisory details, perfectly ready to play with his biography for the sake of glory. He cannot read Greek (he can decipher so many other signs, after all), but he answers a questionnaire from a Professor Le Gludic of the Lycée Montesquieu in Bordeaux, who is concerned about the drop in the number of pupils studying Greek:

1. What led you to study Greek?
   André Malraux: The study of philosophy.
2. What is your favorite work of Greek literature?
   A. M.: *The Orestia.*
3. Who is your favorite hero from Greek literature?
   A. M.: *Antigone.* [Malraux used to say to his daughter: "You should play Antigone."]
4. What has Greek given you? How has it helped to shape you?
   A. M. [a typically Malrucian, almost apophatic response]: By all that, in the Greek world, opposes the Latin mind.[9]

Is Malraux a victim of social and cultural terrorism by his contemporaries? Access to the higher echelons is generally by inheritance or education; members of the elite have been to the École Normale Supérieure, the École Polytechnique, or the École Nationale d'Administration. Malraux, the talented autodidact, still claims to have been a pupil at the École des Langues Orientales. Who would doubt that he reads the Greek classics in the original, along with Sanskrit and Persian? Only himself. Childish and touching, the little boy from Bondy.

CHAPTER THIRTY-FIVE

Literature Still

ON FEBRUARY 1, 1969, Malraux is in the South of France inaugurating a building that is to enshrine the seventeen paintings of Marc Chagall's *Message biblique*. An amateur painter and enthusiastic protestor named Pierre-Émile Pinoncelli sprays water at Malraux.

"I wanted to take this opportunity," says the aggressor, "to manifest my disagreement publicly. . . . I do not approve of Mr. Malraux nor of Chagall. . . . Chagall has been 'dead' as an artist for thirty years. . . . As for Mr. Malraux . . . he too has been 'dead' as a man since the Spanish war. I only wanted to attack two ghosts. . . . Having no water pistol, I made do with a pear syringe. When Mr. Malraux's car arrived . . . and he got out, I went toward him and I squirted him. . . . He pulled the bulb out of my hand and squirted me back."

Malraux refuses to bring charges. Neither dead nor doddery, he has inner resources and, when he is not depressed, a rare capacity for work. Working helps him fight depression. He takes antidepressants to ward off relapses. International and national politics bore him, and so do the problems of his ministry. What can happen to him now?

In spite of the advice to the contrary from some of his ministers, including Malraux, de Gaulle wants to hold a referendum. The General is proposing relatively minor changes, based around regionalization and a reform of the Senate. On April 10, in a televised interview with Michel Droit, a complacent journalist, the General specifies that if the "no" vote wins, he will abandon power. The referendum doesn't look good. The leader of the independent republicans, Valéry Giscard d'Estaing, urges not to vote "yes." Georges Pompidou also campaigns, though quietly. If the dauphin Pompidou would only state that he would not be a candidate for the presidency if the General were to go, the referendum would appear in a different light, say the Gaullo-Gaullists to the Gaullish Pompidolians.

On April 23, Malraux enters the arena of the Palais des Sports once again.[1] He does not bother to tease out the legal threads of the proposed law: "As in so many other circumstances, a 'yes' is simply a show of trust in de Gaulle; a 'no' is no more than the wish for his departure. If a part of the old Left rushed to attack the election of the president of the Republic at universal suffrage, wasn't that because it was General de Gaulle? If the Senate's most constant adversaries want to keep it the way it is at any price, is that not in order to set it against General de Gaulle?"

On April 28, 52.4 percent vote "no," 47.6 percent, "yes": the General is rejected. Charles de Gaulle hears the results at his residence at Colombey-les-Deux-Églises.[2] He leaves power.

The General savors his political suicide; it justifies his historical pessimism. In the France of 1969, Charles de Gaulle is just not in any more, like high heels. But the void that occupies the writer is a cosmic abyss. Alain Poher, the acting president, intermittently sees himself at the Élysée for good.[3] A majority in France desires continuity in a Gaullist changeover, a moderate variety of Gaullism without the General. In June, Georges Pompidou is elected with 58.2 percent of the vote.

"Gaullism is finished," Malraux says in private. He stays in his post for a brief interim period to finish off projects in hand. Then he ceases to be minister for cultural affairs even though Pompidou has insisted, for the sake of propriety, that Malraux must, with his prestige, his task unfinished, and so on, keep his ministry.

The writer stays with Louise de Vilmorin at Verrières-le-Buisson and buys a duplex apartment on Rue de Montpensier, overlooking the gardens of the Palais-Royal. He plans to move in there with Louise. From his windows, he would be able to see those of his successor. And who could succeed him? Have you seen who is succeeding de Gaulle! France is carrying on like a happy widow, forgetful of General de Gaulle, to whom she owes so much—everything, according to Malraux. The former minister seems half orphaned.

On December 11, the General invites Malraux to La Boisserie, his private residence. They have a one-to-one conversation of thirty-five minutes, before dinner.[4] On the way home in the train, Malraux takes notes and writes them up as soon as he gets back. Corinne Godfernaux types up thirty-one pages.[5] First sentence, incipit: "Snow falling on all of France. In the Basel-to-Paris train, our ambassador Geoffroy de Courcel, who was the General's aide-de-camp in London, his current aide-de-camp, and me. . . . At Bar-sur-Aube, his [the General's] car with its studded tires is waiting for us." Last sentences of this first draft: "I am thinking also of what we didn't talk about, this anguish that France brandishes in the face of the world . . . that these years of wanting and chancing and fragile greatness may only be the drifting of clouds, similar to those riding with us over the snow. And this time it may possibly be over."

In this first draft, the head-to-head meeting with the General is very short. Some elements of the notes are used later, others reworked: "When I left," de Gaulle says, "age perhaps played a part, that is possible." Later, Malraux writes, "The tiredness of the last period of power has been dispelled."

His thoughts on France are still bound up in the marriage of de Gaulle to the nation: "He married her before Yvonne Vendroux." For Malraux, the General is "a thousand miles from thinking that France betrayed him for his successors: he has no successor. She cheated on him with destiny." Malraux asked (or says he asked) de Gaulle why he had to go.

"Because of the absurdity?" prompts Malraux.

De Gaulle: "Because of the absurdity."

In Malraux's subsequent drafts, de Gaulle says several times that he wants nothing to do with the current (George Pompidou's) government: "That doesn't concern me. It's not what I wanted. It is quite another thing."

Or again, when de Gaulle and Malraux are saying good-bye, the General insists, "Remember what I told you: that there is nothing in common between me and what is currently happening."

The General accepts—he knows how these things work—that so many Gaullist politicians are continuing to serve under Pompidou. But he did appreciate Malraux's decision to leave. The former ministre d'état sticks to a hard line: no Gaullism without the General. Malraux partially escapes his sorrows by writing. Politics was his aphrodisiac; literature remains his best therapy. One expression throws light on his approach when describing an important event in which he has taken part: "The link between two men, alone in this small, enclosed space . . . does it give rise to a muddled telepathy?" The telepathy with de Gaulle is easier than with Mao. Out of these thirty-one pages, thirteen are given over to the meeting of History with itself, the head-to-head. Afterward, de Gaulle called in Geoffroy de Courcel.[6] Malraux "chatted with Madame de Gaulle" somewhere else. "The meal finishes," writes Malraux; "I talked almost the whole time, as at the private dinners at the Élysée. The General doesn't talk much and hardly expounds at all except when one to one." The Malrucian monologue has not dried up. "Will I ever come back to this room?" wonders the writer.

Shortly afterward, Valéry Giscard d'Estaing asks for an interview with Malraux. Malraux refuses to see him. Then he at last grants an audience, in the presence of Corinne Godfernaux one evening, in calculated, murky light. Giscard wants to know what Charles de Gaulle said about him. Malraux replies that they talked of important things. Giscard's name was not mentioned.

On December 26, 1969, at Verrières, Louise de Vilmorin feels unwell after a siesta and dies of a heart attack.

Malraux starts to drink heavily again. Corinne Godfernaux discovers two revolvers. On the advice of Dr. Bertagna, she hides them, along with extra medicines that are knocking around. Later on, she returns the weapons to their place.

The former secretary general to the president's office, Bernard Tricot, still sees Charles de Gaulle regularly, and Malraux gets news of the General from him. Tricot dines with Malraux on July 7, 1970, chez Lasserre, of course,[7] and later notes:

> [Malraux] looks pale and tired: he broke a rib a few days ago. No tics this time. Long silences. He expresses himself briefly, in dense phrases. Lots of consideration for what the other person is thinking, not because he is particularly keen on being complimented but because he listens to what you say to him, thinks about it, and comes back to it. . . . As I am reminding him that the General is afraid not of apocalypse but subsidence and detours, he wonders, Won't we have drama at the reopening [of Parliament]? . . . I quote the General to André Malraux: "France will be fallow." . . . I tell him how complex the General's attitude was toward the question of succession and toward Pompidou himself. Of course, he says, that's not unusual, great statesmen always have ambiguous feelings about their successor. They want the good of the state, certainly, but it doesn't displease them that there should be a palpable difference. . . . Malraux is happy that the General is writing to him.[8]

The same day, Malraux says to Tricot, "The General is still alive, and we do not know what the future will bring." With others, he jokes about the Gaullists lapping up Pompidou's soup.

The writer thanks the General for sending him the first volume of *Memoirs of Hope*:

"For the content, you have known for years what I think. For the form (I don't mean form in the sense of style in literature but of styles in architecture), the criticism is the one we know. . . . You have no childhood, and fundamentally there is no Charles: if one were to translate the text into the third person, nothing essential would be changed. Where are the precedents? In Rome? The history (with and without a capital) of you and France is more like Greek tragedy than the accounts of Roman campaigns."[9]

The following month, on November 9, 1970, Charles de Gaulle dies. Malraux has been struck by two bereavements, with less than a year between them.[10] At the General's funeral the writer appears pained, distraught, and old.

In March 1971, he publishes *Les Chênes qu'on abat*.[11] Some find it Malraux's best work, not from a historical but from a literary point of view. The felled oak that Malraux raises in the book is, of course, the General. Several subtitles could have been appropriate: *De Gaulle as in Myself* or *De Gaulle and Me*. The plural oaks in the title come from an elegy by Victor Hugo, but if de Gaulle is the first, who is the second? The writer uses his last visit to Charles de Gaulle as an excuse to paint a portrait, full length, close up, full face, and in profile. He transforms thirty-five minutes of real dialogue (and with what art) into a head-to-head of at least two hours. Gide published delightful imaginary interviews in his lifetime; this book is Malraux's finest contribution to the genre. He comes across as grave, solemn, grandiose, but also jovial and lively, sarcastic, and fierce. On all sides of the book's central element, the author continues to mold historical variations on his own life, no more convincingly than in *Antimémoires* but just as poignantly.

The structural plan for *Les Chênes qu'on abat*, drawn up by Malraux's hand, shows us what is most important in his eyes, especially the phrases underlined in red. For the first chapter: "The dialogue between his will and the ageless snow . . . The contract with France . . . The greatness . . . America abandons Europe . . . Victor Hugo and Tintin . . . A character is not an individual. Why write and why live? Death . . . Religion . . ."

Malraux drives in the nail in his last draft. The chronic ailment of all politicians, especially French ones, is to be convinced that as soon as they have lost power, their country no longer has a future. A mournful General makes pompous predictions in front of his "genius" friend. He has always been "in the minority," he groans. This, from a man who polled 79.2 percent "yes" votes in 1958, 75.2 percent in 1961, and 90.6 percent in 1962! The former minister makes no reply to the General's morose historicism.

For the meetings with Mao and Nehru, Malraux embellished with relative impunity. For this interview with de Gaulle, he never pretends to be literally faithful; indeed, that would be pointless, in his view. He crosses out and adds onto the proofs, adds again. As in his youth, he finds space for repentant corrections. In the definitive version of *Les Chênes qu'on abat*, the criticized "Pompidou" is replaced by *"les anciens."* The *"pauvres types"* (poor bastards) of the Île de Sein in the first version who joined the General's Free France in 1940 become *"braves types"* (good guys) in the second version. Details count; every adjective speaks in this exceptional meeting. For the last version, the curtains at La Boisserie turn from "ugly" to "green." Malraux made fun in private of the General's bad taste. What place could ugly curtains have in History, or in the General's home?

Malraux is obsessed by de Gaulle. His text combines affection, respect, admiration, and tenderness. He asks himself why de Gaulle is a legendary character when he was neither a great war leader nor a saint. He looks for rational and irrational elements in the personality of the uncompromising liberator and discovers a partial answer, which enhances his own status indirectly: "The hero of History is the brother of the hero of the novel." For Malraux, the historical and the novelistic are twin brothers. The text dominates the raw events and complements them, like novelized journalism. Malraux makes mirrors of himself and the General, propped against each other, keeping each other up, genius against genius, face-to-face. They are so alike that de Gaulle, here, speaks like Malraux. They wonder in unison: Why write, why live, why is the world absurd? Banal questions, shared in a close volley.

It could be a meeting between two writers, building themselves up by writing, perhaps reassuring each other. According to Malraux, the General's life, when he saw him at Colombey, was "ordered by his memoirs." The writer saw lined up in Charles de Gaulle's study the "complete works of Bergson, a friend of his family, and mine, which he shows me with a wink." Malraux says, "Writing is also a powerful drug . . . there are suitcases full of blank pages wanting to be written." De Gaulle says, "Writing allows one to forget about the pack. It is important." And how much more important for a writer who needs to be around men of action. His narrative carries the reader along and the writer away so much that we do not, at moments, know who is the more present: the historic, living-dead General or his ex-minister, now full-time writer. It feels like two recumbent statues getting up, endowed with speech and movement.

In an additional tribute, Malraux converses with de Gaulle almost as if he were chatting with Gide. They talk literary technique, like actors discussing contracts or farmers the price of lamb. Malraux refers to the General's type of writing. De Gaulle has problems with adjectives, verbs, and a ternary rhythm that obsesses and irritates him. For once Malraux can place himself an inch above the General: "So far, he [de Gaulle] has not succeeded in overcoming it at all." An author can spot a colleague's literary habits more easily than his own.

Malraux writes, "To portray is to fix."[12] De Gaulle continues to evade Malraux ("There is no Charles," he repeats in half-simulated despair). Coquettish, but flat: "I do not know General de Gaulle. Who knows anybody?" He says of the General, "Intimacy, with him, is not talking about him (a taboo subject) but about France . . . or about death." In short, de Gaulle has never shown himself to Malraux in any degree of intimacy. To portray himself, Malraux retouches his own history again, adding interesting and completely new details on his military life during the Battle of Alsace: "A piece of shrapnel cuts my belt in two."

The writer also manages to attribute one of his own fantasies to de Gaulle: "Do you remember our conversation when you came back from the funeral of the president [Kennedy]? . . . You were talking to me about Mrs. Kennedy. I told you, 'She has played a very intelligent game: without getting involved in politics, she brought her husband prestige as a patron of the arts that he would not have had without her. Think of the dinner with the fifty Nobel Prize winners.' "

De Gaulle duly responds, "And what about yours [the dinner in your honor]!"

Malraux, skillfully, or getting carried away by his own game: "But you added, 'She is a plucky lady, very well brought up. As for her destiny, you are wrong: she is a star, and she will end up on some oil magnate's yacht.' "

"I said that to you? Well! . . . Actually, I'd rather have thought that she would marry Sartre or you!"

Malraux also claims that in 1958, more than ten years earlier, he took over "for some time" responsibility for "the security of the General." Another retrospective wish? For de Gaulle as a writer, Malraux was literary insurance, just as the General remains guarantor for Malraux as a politician. With *Les Chênes qu'on abat*, the writer protects de Gaulle like a son, or as a grandson would look after the antimemory of his grandfather.

Malraux, with his revived literary talent, is keen to "portray" the important passengers in his life. De Gaulle seems to be his masterstroke. He is less successful in portraying Picasso in *La Tête d'obsidienne*,[13] which grows out of *Le Musée imaginaire*. He admires the artist, not the man. He hints that Pablo and he were close—in genius—without being friends. The pretext for the work is thin: the artist's widow, Jacqueline Picasso, wanted to leave a collection of works amassed by the painter to the state. She called Malraux; he went down to Nice, and she showed him around the studio and the house. "With Pablito, this is where we used to have lunch." Malraux says honestly, "I never knew Pablo, a private person . . . I knew only Picasso." They bumped into each other, really talked twice, once in front of *Guernica*, before the war, once after. "Before the departure of *Guernica* for the Spanish Pavilion,[14] I said to Picasso, 'We do not really believe in subjects, but you have to admit it, this time the subject will have been useful to you!' He answered that indeed, he hardly believed in subjects but that he believed in themes—as long as they are expressed symbolically: 'We can express death with [Goya's painting] *Tres de Mayo* or with a skull, we have been doing that for a long time . . . but not with a car crash.' Then about the Goya: 'The black sky isn't a sky, it's just black. There are two sources of light. One of which we do not understand; it lights up everything, like moonlight. . . . And then there is the enormous lantern in the middle: it lights only him. The lantern is Death. Why? We don't know. Nor does Goya.' " Malraux also writes, "When he put on his naive expression (his comedy miller look, Braque called it), which was a favorite way to mystify whomever he was talking to, he would often express himself in questions: 'How do you expect a woman to do a good still life of a packet of tobacco if she doesn't smoke?' " Malraux answers:

"You know better than I do. Your works express what nobody else could. They shout it in unison. . . . They also say, 'Written on prison walls.' "[15]

The book offers the reader a museum tour with Malraux as a guide, which is not to be sneezed at, as he would say himself. He mistakes a Chardin for a Goya. How careless. . . . Ah, here are a Corot, a van Dongen, two Braques, two Mirós, a Modigliani; over here, a Courbet. . . . This one is weak, thinks Jacqueline Picasso. One tires of this artistic Who's Who through the centuries: Cézanne, Derain, Baudelaire, Dürer. . . . As I once said to Yehudi Menuhin, to Kahnweiler . . . Malraux here falls prey to unexpected cultural snobbishness. He shows surprise that Picasso should have existed and more still that André Malraux should have lived: "I feel the same as Picasso: all that is about some guy who has the same name as me."[16]

Around this time Malraux also publishes *Le Triangle noir*, devoted to Laclos, Saint-Just, and Goya, a reworking of known texts. The *NRF* at Gallimard prepares a review slip for the book bearing a ten-line biography. Malraux leaves in the entry: "Studied at the [École des] Langues Orientales." He has been showered with decorations and honors, but still he won't let go of this child's rattle of supposed attendance at university. But he deletes other elements: "1923: Archaeological missions in Indochina. 1926: Takes part in the civil war in China." 1936 and 1940 don't pose a problem for him. At first he wrote for one of the entries: "1942: Commands the maquis of Lot-et-Garonne and Corrèze." Then he clearly crossed out "Lot-et-Garonne and Corrèze" and replaced it vaguely with "Center." Not happy with that either, he crosses out the whole thing. He doesn't want to freeze his biography. Let them refer to his works! Could he be on the verge of admitting errors or exaggerations? He seems to be balanced on the line—a line that, for him, is often invisible—separating true from false.

Malraux is drinking again. Alcohol does not seem to affect his mental faculties too badly. He does not mind drinking until he is drunk. Great authors like Faulkner and Hemingway drink, he thinks. But Malraux doesn't talk about it; he respects a conventional moral and social position whereby one is not allowed to be an alcoholic. He is not depressed because he drinks, he drinks because he is depressive. Doctor Bertagna (the "best specialist in brain chemistry," according to Malraux) wants to wean him off it, but then there is the classic problem: If he stops drinking, how to stop getting depressed? He suffers an attack of polyneuritis.

At the beginning of November 1972, he is urgently admitted for alcoholism and nervous breakdown to the Salpêtrière Hospital. While he is in, he catches a pleuropulmonary infection. He suffers withdrawal from alcohol and becomes very fragile. On the first of November, All Saints' Day, he is not well at all. They ask him if he would like Bertagna to be called.

"No need," he says. "There must be an intern here."

Some of his nerve centers have been paralyzed. His sensory and motor functions appear to have been affected. It is not known if the primary functions of the cerebellum have been damaged irreversibly. Malraux spends twenty-nine days in hospital; he shows tremendous courage. They start him on Anafranil, an antidepressant that does not dull the mind. He bounces back in a way that is quite unexpected, not calculated: he writes a new book. In *Lazare*,[17] the author rediscovers a tone of authenticity. Starting from a clinical observation of his body, a source that cannot lie, he notes, "Sclerosis of the peripheral nerves and threat to the cerebellum, therefore threat of paralysis." An awareness of his body and its betrayals, which, perhaps, comes to all with age. While at the Salpêtrière, his legs "gave way several times"; he almost blacked out twice in one week. Never had he come so close to death, outside of war. He does not give the impression that he is playing a role: "Suffering, intravenous drips, injections, Green Pastures [nickname for one of the nurses] coming in, preceded by her laugh, other nurses who stop to chat, waiting for the time when I will be able to answer them, the next day, the day after that . . ." Then a turn of modesty about his pain: "Although I am not suffering much, I am a refugee in fever: the mind abandons itself to the groping of death as to sleep." In *Lazare*, the Grim Reaper keeps Malraux company at his bedside.

Malraux had the feeling of being without being himself; he has seen André Malraux from the outside. He denounces what is to him a "miserable little pile of secrets"; yet he does not give up those secrets. There is a silence about the alcoholism throughout the whole work.[18] The first sentence, "I was struck down by a sleeping sickness," sounds a lot better than "There I was in detox."

Whether or not the return of his appetite for life is due to the new woman in it, Sophie de Vilmorin, Louise's niece, the author does not say.

When he is on the verge of an intimate "secret," he tails off into silence. "For at the bedside of my dead father . . ." This prudery also prompts him to lay aside "I" and "me" in favor of an impersonal pronoun: "One can also kill oneself at the earliest opportunity." The same detached effect is achieved with some pleasing chiaroscuro aphorisms: "Capital decisions are rabbits we shoot as they pass; it is just as well to be a good shot."

In this context, his allusions to former books are less literary than psychological: " 'The self, that incomparable and fleeting monster that each of us cherishes in his heart,' I wrote in *La Condition humaine* forty years ago . . ." His "I" peers into his self. "I have read what concerns my books, not what concerns me," he says with affectation. "Inexplicably, this character, which haunts me at times, does not interest me here." So he admits that elsewhere it does, even to a point of obsession. "At times," he says— come on, André Malraux can do better than that!

At seventy-one, he knows that statistically his future is limited. At the time, the life expectancy of the average Frenchman of his social class is seventy-three. This leads the writer to zoom in on his present. He makes a discovery that is hardly surprising: "My past is a hindrance to me." He looks into his memory and dissects its various strata. A statement of fact and at the same time a confession: "My memory can never be applied to myself without an effort." A constant melody from one book to another: "I do not remember my childhood." The phenomenon is not unknown, but it is not, according to some psychiatrists, a happy one. Another confession of forgetfulness: "Nor even, without a deliberate effort, the women I have loved or thought I loved or my dead friends." "Few memories of feelings, even of love." This bitter—or just grandiose—acknowledgment turns him in his own eyes into an exceptional tragic figure: "Almost all those I have loved have been killed in accidents." In this morbid vein, he invents an exchange at the deathbed of Bernard Groethuysen (whom Malraux did not see when he was dying). Groet: "I would never have thought that this is what it was like to die."

Malraux attempts "to subject his images to an unsteady chronology." The author mixes everything up: his summer of 1939 in Montpellier, the (supposed) firing squad at Gramat, Hindu psalmodies, Saint Paul and Saint Francis, and his battle against illness. For some, Malraux makes a mistake by reusing passages from *Les Noyers de l'Altenburg*. When the book comes out, some of these copied or paraphrased pages are admired by readers and critics who do not know the writer well enough to know better.[19] One image returns insistently in *Lazare*: that of the author's father. "My father a little before his suicide: 'If I am to have another life, I don't want any other than my own.' " Can we be so sure? Malraux identifies himself with this father figure, more so than in *Les Noyers de l'Altenburg*.

In his action-packed exploits of the past, weathering the storm that almost broke his plane apart in the Algerian sky, coming under German fire during the Alsace campaign, Malraux showed himself to be a pretty sturdy little Lazarus. He not only survives his stay at the Salpêtrière but is resurrected. In the process, succinctly and without nostalgia, he assembles and condenses his life. "Writing," he wrote to his nephew, Alain, and to Grosjean, "is a permanent fistfight with oneself." He refuses to let himself be beaten by the illness or sink into a feeble convalescence and fights back with his best weapon: the sentence. The text is a confessional for the agnostic Malraux—he deforms the truth less here than elsewhere—or a consulting room for free association and (were such a thing possible) autopsychoanalysis. He hated "psychology" when he was younger.

Malraux is the object, not the source, of numerous rumors. He accepts few dinners and does not go out of his way to mix with the Paris set. He is above literary events, light-years ahead of them. Signing the odd manifesto with other greats, making a request with Sartre for a political pardon, why not? But meeting with him is out of the question. At these altitudes, the bets are already in. They are not going to invent any new rules. Pierre Viansson-Ponté, a journalist for *Le Monde*, wants (not for the first time) to reunite Malraux and Sartre. Malraux: "Do you see us playing Vadius and Trissotin?"[20]

Malraux does not know the price of a bus ticket or a pound of butter. When living with Madeleine, he asked about their washing machine, "Do you know how to make that work?" He still does not know how to put plates in a dishwasher. Yet as an occasional adviser at Gallimard, he has forgotten nothing of the qualities of different papers, formats, typefaces, justification. Each week he receives manuscripts and writes notes for those he recommends. The notes prove that, although little short of an emotional cripple in the attention he pays to others, he knows how to look at their works. To Claude Gallimard, on the work of a colleague: "You have perhaps seen Brigitte Friang's book *Regarde-toi qui meurs*, a best-seller with Laffont. She has just finished a novel. . . . She has a readership; but for memoirs, you'll have to judge."[21] He also recommends *Sexologie de l'Occident* (Western Sexology).[22] "Very big. (Publishable in several volumes? Don't know) . . . It is an 'Everything you always wanted to know on the subject' type of book to which one can refer for years, like the Larousse [encyclopedia]. The subject in question has a serious public. Just read the table of contents: it's analytical, it takes everything into account. With a clever bit of radio: 'Do you know when people started getting engaged and why?' It could sell well and for a long time. Or not . . ."

For Claude Gallimard, there is something sphinxlike about Malraux. If he signed a telephone directory, they would publish it; that's how successful he is. Despite his overdrawn account, he remains a prestigious figure and is treated with enormous consideration. Claude learns that a rival at Éditions Stock, Suarès, is going to publish an "iconographic album accompanied by the text of two interviews"—and that the interviews are with Malraux. Claude writes to his "Cher André": "My surprise is all the greater since when we had lunch together, hardly a fortnight ago, there was no mention of this. In my opinion it is regrettable that this publication, which the press and radio are already announcing as a book by you, should take place just as *La Tête d'obsidienne* is going on sale. It threatens to spoil the exceptional distribution efforts that I have undertaken to ensure substantial sales for your book." Claude is particularly unhappy that publication with a publisher other than Gallimard "could be interpreted as the sign of a disagreement that does not in any way correspond to the reality of our personal relationship." He adds, "If I am to judge from what you said into Jacques Chancel's microphone, this work constitutes a sort of complement to your *Antimémoires*, and that seems to me to be a contradiction that is incompatible with the spirit of our most recent agreements." If only Malraux had talked to him about the project. Immediate response from Malraux:[23]

My dear Claude,
    I prefer to think that some imbecile has been putting ideas in your head or that you have fallen on it (your head, not the imbecile). You write to me as if I were insidiously publishing books with Stock. You are joking, aren't you? . . .
    1. I do not believe in picture albums. If you had planned the publication of this one, I would have advised you against it. . . .
    2. I answered Guy Suarès's questions (as I did Jacques Chancel's) and gave him permission to use them—to help him out. . . .
    3. When Guy Suarès started his work, *Obsidienne* did not exist.
    I don't give a damn what anyone says about me; what counts is what I write about myself.
    4. I shall not ask Stock to defer its publication date. I have no rights over this book, it does not concern me. It is a book about me, not by me. And there is no question of using the transcripts, which are of no importance (except for an exhaustive volume, Pléiade style).
Malraux does not need to work on his PR, he just needs to watch it happen. He reassures Claude Gallimard by revealing to him that there will be a sequel to the very successful *Antimémoires*:
    5. It is not Guy Suarès' album that Chancel said belonged to *Antimémoires*, it's *Obsidienne*.
    6. Very best wishes, all the same.

Claude Gallimard is kind and understanding. Six months later, Malraux's account is in deficit to the tune of 199,203 francs.[24] It is a privilege to have Malraux in the catalog, even if he is costing them money. The writer is receiving a monthly payment of 20,000 francs ($4,160 in 1974). He regularly pays 3,500 francs of that to Clara—about the sum a fully qualified high school teacher would get. Major writers, with Gallimard and other publishers, negotiate from strength to strength with their editor. When the level of alarm about Malraux prompts the Accounts Department to barge in, Beuret intervenes and deals with them directly or preps them before bringing them to the writer.

Malraux sees himself above the Académie Française and far beyond the Nobel Prize: "I already have the Nobel."

It is the only prize worthy of him. He has often believed he would get it, but by now he has given up waiting. In 1967, a well-placed correspondent in Stockholm, Kjell Strömberg, tipped Gallimard off about the 1968 prize. Kösterling, the president of the Nobel Committee, had hinted that it would be "next year" for Malraux.[25]

The writer savors the letters of those he considers his equals, knights of the order of literature. *Lazare* has marked readers. Michel Leiris writes to him,[26] "I admire the way you deal with this subject among subjects, death, and the majority of Westerners treat it as something so tragic that they are incapable of talking about it without a thick screen of commonplaces." From the loyal and honest Jean Grosjean, one of the few to address him frankly:[27] "Thank you for this *Lazare* where, for the first time, you give up a part of your human adventure, which is not purely an adventure of the mind, with an ethereal liberty that mystics often bring to it. But for all that, you have not deserted the epic strength of a standard of human brotherhood, raised all the higher since the battle is more intimate." Grosjean was not embarrassed but dazzled by the remodeling of a scene from *Les Noyers de l'Altenburg*, the sapping before the release of poison gas: "You know that I take these pages to be one of the most fascinating jewels of this century." For many readers, the passage figures in their imaginary anthology of works by André Malraux.

Thanks to Bertagna's injunctions and Sophie de Vilmorin's presence, Malraux has not had a drink since 1972. Drugs ease his tics. From time to time, his Roman emperor's profile loses its puffiness. He seems to be staying on fairly good terms with himself and others. He mentions his only remaining child, his daughter, only twice in his books, but seems proud of her.[28] She has married the film director Alain Resnais, you know, not some Black Panther or some beatnik bum.

There's no way he would admit it, but Malraux seems serene. Radio and television are constantly approaching him, and he makes good use of them; although, without looking down on these media, he doesn't like the way he comes across. Malraux is part of the cultural landscape. His return to the literary scene has been astonishing, even to those who don't think much of his works or his personality. Rarely and oddly enough, even his silences make a noise. That man has visited the Kingdom of the Dead and brought back a book. He has traveled to the undiscover'd country and returned, in the role that suits him best. So he has a tendency to embroider the truth, they say, indulgently, tenderly. But Chateaubriand, but Byron, but . . . Perhaps that is just the price we pay for his verbal art?

CHAPTER THIRTY-SIX

Brilliant Pictures

SOME OF THE doodles Malraux puts on his letters and manuscripts are cats, some are *dyables* ("devyls"). His personal devyl is the demon of action, the historic gesture, preferably on the international stage. Since the General made his two exits in a row, from the Élysée and from this life, with no curtain call, the French stage has felt like a microscopic world of petty politicking.

Malraux is on the lookout for opportunities to infuse some History into his story and vice versa. He has a childish ambition just to get involved. In East Pakistan (out there in Asia, that's Malraux country), in March 1971, a majority of Bengali supporters of Sheikh Mujibur Rahman votes for a new regime; still Muslim, as in West Pakistan, but independent. Military leaders in Rawalpindi disregard the results of the election and send troops and tanks into East Pakistan to quell the "rebellion." India and her prime minister, Indira Gandhi, take sides with the independent insurgents. Millions of Bengalis flee East Pakistan (later to become Bangladesh) and take refuge in India. For Malraux, the situation is clear: it is another case of a popular nationalist movement standing up to a military regime. If the Bengali rebels are short of soldiers, especially officers, the resurrected Colonel Berger will provide them. He confides to the Indian ambassador, "I am extremely put out. Indira Gandhi invited me to participate in an intellectual roundtable she is organizing to try to resolve the Pakistan problem. I do not believe in that. Therefore I wrote to refuse, saying that words would be useless and that only action will be effective. My response has been interpreted to mean that I myself wanted to go and fight, and it has been published in the papers!"

"What are you going to do?"

"For the moment, I can't get out of it."[1]

He is alleged to have said, "The only intellectuals who have the right to defend the Bengalis with words are those who are ready to fight for them."[2] Over seventy, André Malraux is condemning himself to lead volunteers into Bengal and fight. The ideologue, adventurer, and warrior is reborn. "Soul of steel," remarks Brigitte Friang returning from Verrières. "The body appears more fragile." Brigitte Friang is a reporter and an excellent shot; she spent time in the fortified camp at the Battle of Dienbienphu. Malraux asks her to accompany him on this adventure.

Metamorphosis is also a historical concept for Malraux: "I feel History like an interrogation or a metamorphosis. . . . I think I stand in constant astonishment with regard to History, as Shakespeare did for what he chose." More telepathy? The colonel forms a sort of Foreign Legion. His correspondence at the end of this year shows not only that he cannot back out now but also how much he wants to return to Asia. To Canon Bockel, now archpriest at Strasbourg Cathedral, Malraux confides his intentions: "If you are in the Sahara and I am in Bengal, we will die together—and you should know that you will help me to die nobly."[3]

Malraux refuses an invitation to go to Hungary. He replies in writing, "As you may know, in a few weeks I will no longer be in Europe, for I shall have joined the Bengali troops."[4] A friend, Princess Elizabeth de Croÿ, offers to work in a refugee camp. On November 24, he suggests she organize an international collection of medicines: "I shall not be leaving for another three weeks because of the international regulations on vaccination. You will be in the same boat. If we should bump into each other in that world, that wouldn't be bad at all." For want of an available revolution in Europe, a national liberation war in Asia will do.

Indira Gandhi meets Malraux at the Indian Embassy in Paris. He must wait! The Indian Army will be quite sufficient. She, too, finds Malraux "tired," and persuades the writer Mulk Raj Anand to accompany him back. Colonel Berger does not get to be Colonel Lawrence, and this time Malraux plays neither one nor the other. He is a hindrance to the Indian government officials. Delhi is ready to accept Malraux's moral support but not his laughable physical presence.[5]

A privileged protector of Pakistan, Richard Nixon, sends an aircraft carrier and a few warships into the Bay of Bengal to dissuade Mrs. Gandhi from carrying out any ill-considered attacks. Malraux knows that he will not be fighting in Asia, but he has already convinced more than one hundred officers (or so he says) to go there with him. At the end of November, he sends a circular to his volunteers: "It is therefore probable that we will not go. I was awaiting our instructions on the first for a departure around the fifteenth. Why no word came, only History will teach us. We cannot have been unnecessary, at a time when we were offering the only help that

Bangladesh could obtain." Indian armored divisions are more effective than the Malrucian Foreign Legion would have been. Malraux continues to weave his legend: "The fact remains that when everything was at its worst, we were necessarily alone with the resistance forces; and in the name of the thousands of refugees, in the name of the government of a free Bengal of today and for tomorrow, I thank you."

He may not be in a tank, but Malraux can suddenly roll up on the front page of a newspaper, firing words. In *Le Figaro* on December 19, he publishes an open letter to Nixon. He berates the U.S. president for apparently supporting Pakistan. Malraux steps onto personal ground: "Do you remember our conversation with General de Gaulle? You had just come to power,[6] and you did me the honor of talking to me about American politics. I said to you, 'The United States is the first country to have become the most powerful in the world without having looked for it [Malraux had already said that to Kennedy, which would annoy Nixon if he knew]. Alexander wanted to be Alexander, Caesar wanted to be Caesar; you did not in the least want to be masters of the world. But you cannot afford the luxury of holding that position absentmindedly." Then, since a Mao-Nixon summit is planned, "You are going to try to establish with China a dialogue that the United States has been putting off for twenty years."

In February 1972, in preparation for this summit, Nixon invites Malraux to Washington. According to Malraux—something of an aficionado of retrospective prophecies—the General had said to the American president, "You cannot avoid confronting the problem of China. You have to get involved in this mad business."[7] Nixon had shown interest. The interview was reported to Chou En-lai by Étienne Manac'h, then French ambassador in Beijing.

Part of the reason for Nixon's invitation is his knowledge of Malraux's dealings with Kennedy. Nixon stresses that it will not be a "frilly" meeting. Artistic small talk may have suited the Camelot crowd, but he is planning a historic mission. Moreover, he wants to give himself a certain patina and escape the scorn of so many liberal intellectuals and other Americans. Nixon knows that Malraux was a minister under General de Gaulle; he is much less familiar with his stature as a writer. In one of his memos to a colleague, he writes the name of the illustrious Frenchman phonetically, referring to a "quotation by Andre Malrowe."[8]

Before leaving, Malraux asks Walter Langlois about Nixon's personality and talks with Senator Edward Kennedy in Paris. Malraux, with one eye on the geopolitical crystal ball, predicts that Mao will ask Nixon if "the richest nation in the world" is ready to help the poorest. The writer sets off for Washington with his aide, Corinne Godfernaux. At Orly Airport, a journalist from the ORTF (the French national broadcasting service) asks him, "Are you going to reveal things to him [Nixon] about the personality of President Mao that you know well?"

One of the fundamental truths about France at the time: steak-frites is the national dish, her wines are the best in the world, and Malraux knows Mao very well. He is irritated by the question: "He [Nixon] said in his press conference that he wanted to talk to somebody who knows Mao. There aren't that many to choose from." Translation: I am one of the few able to fathom this prodigious personality.

Malraux still benefits from a great advantage when it comes to reinforcing his legend: a double personality as both writer and politician. Again, literary columnists to whom advance copies of his works are sent are hardly interested in their historical veracity; or if they are aware of the question, they consider it of no importance. Specialists in foreign politics, in the papers, on radio and television channels either do not know about Malraux's maniac, mythomaniac, and megalomaniac escapades or do not judge it useful to allude to them. Faced with a body of work of such scope, who are they, surely, to issue judgment on a writer of this caliber? Heads, Malraux wins; tails, he doesn't lose.

When he arrives at Dulles International Airport, he is refused entry by immigration officers. There is no visa on his diplomatic passport. He is told to wait. Who is this Malrowe guy? He sits tight. The White House is informed and confirms that he is "the personal guest of the President of the United States." In Washington, Malraux stays at the French Embassy. The ambassador, Charles Lucet: "Dinner with Malraux . . . but is Malraux still well connected in People's China?" The writer makes the same remarks on "the richest nation . . ." "I replied," writes Lucet, "that this thought hardly corresponds to the image I have of Socialist China as a proud nation where beggars are chased off the streets."

Nixon is convinced that Malraux, the "great French writer and philosopher," "knew Mao Tse-tung and Chou En-lai in China in 1930" and that he "has maintained intermittent contact with them over the years."[9] The president of the United States seems about as well informed as a trainee journalist with the ORTF. He has done his homework, however: following recommendations from his advisers, he has read numerous extracts from articles and books by Western specialists on China. Among them are Edgar Snow, a favorite author of Malraux, Ross Terrill, Dennis Bloodworth, John Fairbank, Stuart Schram, C. P. Fitzgerald—and André Malraux. Nixon maintains that he has also read *Antimémoires*, "one of the most fascinating and precious pieces of reading I did in preparation for my trip." Which seems doubtful.

Malraux first sees Nixon on Monday, February 14, from 4 to 5.30 p.m., in the presence of the president's very special adviser Henry Kissinger and an interpreter from the State Department.[10] Malraux states there and then that his contacts with Mao have been "very close, a relationship of truths and untruths." Nixon points out in passing that Malraux is sitting in the same armchair de Gaulle sat in. Malraux insists on one point: "If Japan ceased to believe in American nuclear protection and were to find itself facing China with nuclear weapons," it would look for guarantees from the USSR. Malraux quickly points out that he is basing his remarks on a hypothesis, not on solid information. He does not always make a distinction between the two.

The same day, Nixon gives a dinner for twelve guests, including Ambassador Lucet, Secretary of State William Rogers, and another State Department interpreter who takes notes. Tried-and-tested remarks are recycled with Malrucian embellishments: "Mao's harbor is death." Malraux is asked for the details of the remarks he made in Paris to Edward Kennedy on the subject of Mao apparently looking for economic aid. He interrupts the question: "It was one of Senator Kennedy's jokes." Even if the subject is not frankly addressed, it still manages to dominate the meeting.

"Even with the war in Vietnam?" asks Nixon.

"Absolutely, even in that case. China's involvement in Vietnam is just a pretense [partly true]. There was a period of cloudless friendship between China and Russia, when the Chinese allowed Russian arms to pass over Vietnamese territory. But China has never helped anybody. Neither Pakistan nor Vietnam [false].[11] Chinese foreign policy is nothing but a brilliant lie. The Chinese don't believe it. They believe only in China, China alone."

Nixon asks him what his impression is of Mao.

"Five years ago," says Malraux, "Mao was afraid of one thing: that the Americans and the Russians, with ten atomic bombs, would destroy the industrial centers of China and set the country back fifty years to a time when Mao himself would be dead. He admitted to me, 'When I have six atomic bombs, nobody will be able to bomb my cities.' "

Neither in *Antimémoires* nor in his Cabinet report of the trip did Malraux allude to this substantial piece of information. That and other inventive remarks were heard, recorded, and presumably ignored by Nixon. The American president felt that Malraux was overflowing "with words and ideas." That's what the Kennedys had said, too, Jackie most of all. Malraux tells Nixon, "You will be dealing with a colossus, but a colossus who is facing death. The last time I saw him [the last time was the first time; Nixon does not know that, and perhaps, at this point, neither does Malraux] he said to me, 'We have no successor.' [A royal, Gaullian 'we': de

Gaulle also had no worthy successor.] Do you know what Mao will think when you see him for the first time? He will think: 'He is a lot younger than I am.' "

Malraux gives Nixon advice on the art of conducting a conversation with Mao: "Mr. President, you are going to meet a man who has had a fantastic destiny. . . . You will probably think that he is addressing himself to you, but in reality he will be addressing death."

This idea comes back again and again in the interviews about Mao. Malraux becomes Mao—or rather, the other way around. Over coffee, Malraux says, "You are going to try to do one of the most important things of our century. I am thinking of the explorers in the sixteenth century, who set sail with a very precise goal in mind but often on arriving made quite different discoveries."

Not, perhaps, very flattering or courteous to his host. At the end of the dinner, Nixon in turn pays his respects: "France has made many great gifts to America, but the greatest . . . has been that of its literary figures. Your name stands out among them for all those of us who were students and read the great French writers . . . Rousseau and others."

At the end of the evening, Nixon—more polite than Mao and in better health—sees Malraux to his car.

"I am not de Gaulle," says Malraux, "but I know what de Gaulle would have said if he were here. He would say, 'All those who comprise the venture on which you have embarked salute you.' "

A blessing for Nixon from de Gaulle, via his Malrucian intercessor.

John Scali, sometime journalist, sometime diplomat, was invited to the dinner as an adviser to the president. He had previously served as intermediary between the Soviets and Kennedy during the Cuba crisis, about ten years before.[12] Scali's report to Nixon contains a cruel commentary: "I was not impressed by André Malraux's assertions and musings. I found him muddled, contradictory, and too stubborn in his point of view. . . . Moreover, his remarks were littered with oversights and illogicalities." Malraux "takes on the characteristics he attributes to de Gaulle and Mao." He "does not address the person he is speaking to but an invisible audience that he aims to please and wants to disconcert, before leaving the stage, bathing in the applause of that invisible crowd." The conclusion is tough: "For my part . . . I felt I was listening to the insights of a pretentious old man weaving outdated ideas into a particular framework of the world as he would like it to be."[13] Scali's report is filed away by Nixon in an archive where the wily president knows it will remain for posterity.[14]

One of the twelve dinner guests was Leonard Garment, presidential adviser on internal and foreign affairs and one of the few to enjoy a part of

Nixon's trust (he would later be his special counsel during Watergate). Garment found Malraux "fascinating because he has a fascinating history." Malraux's observation that there was "something of the sorcerer in Mao" delighted Garment. He was convinced that his boss was treating the dinner as a rehearsal for his meeting with Mao, like an actor. In a brief note, Garment heaps praise upon the president for his "realism" and concludes by saying that Nixon prefers the pursuit of "larger meanings . . . more important than intellectual concerns."

Kissinger is very balanced in his judgment, simultaneously critical and admiring: "Unfortunately," he writes, "Malraux was grossly out of date on the Chinese issues and his predictions about China's immediate objectives were outrageously false." Kissinger, the éminence grise, has been secretly negotiating in Paris with the North Vietnamese, a fact of which Malraux seems curiously unaware. He agrees with the French ambassador, Lucet, about one thing: the possibility of Mao asking for economic aid. "The President [according to Malraux] would be judged on his capacity to come up with a new Marshall Plan for China. Given Mao's policy of independence, there was no danger of that happening; at best, Malraux was ahead by several years." Kissinger adds, however:[15] "Malraux's intuition proved that an artist's perception can often grasp the sense of problems better than experts or analysts from the intelligence service. Many of his judgments turned out to be remarkably incisive. The reconciliation between China and the United States was inevitable, inseparable from the Chinese-Soviet split. The Vietnam War would not be an obstacle because China's actions would depend on its economic requirements."

Kissinger later says about Malraux in Washington, "It was a stunning performance, not fully appreciated by an audience that was still prisoners of a decade of stereotyping. Words cascaded from Malraux's mouth while he fixed his visionary's stare on his listeners. He didn't so much give a coherent analysis as a series of brilliant pictures." After the customary applause comes Dr. Kissinger's final blow: "Malraux had not visited China for almost ten years; he had clearly not kept up to date with the latest developments; he had no documentation from the interior. All he had was his sensitivity, his brilliant perception, and his subtle intelligence." The men of the White House and the State Department were not playing the same games as Malraux, and Kissinger less than anybody: "Our task was to combine [Malraux's] intuition with the operational knowledge that we were accumulating little by little."

Back in Paris, Malraux declares, "Our conversations leave me with a rather strange impression; the president is a very warm person." Malraux must be one of the few great figures in the world to find Nixon warm. He continues, modestly, "I think I showed the president an area of reflection that he is not used to, for all his American colleagues have the same train-ing and the same view of China. So he was relatively surprised by what I had to say, and that seems to me very important. Everybody thinks that in Mao, they are going to find Lenin. Mao was a great revolutionary fifty years ago. Now, no longer."

Malraux seems happy with the attention Nixon paid to his writing and is convinced that the American president has read *Antimémoires* "closely."[16] Who manipulated whom with more success, the Frenchman or the American? In private and in public, Malraux does not rule out the possibility of Nixon's trip, at least on the face of it, coming to nothing. Much too much has been said about the Marshall Plan that Malraux fore-saw for China. He returns to the question in an interview—and suggests that a mistake was probably made in translation. And thanks to an uncanny talent for time travel that allows him to spend hours of 120, 240, or 360 minutes with Mao, Nehru, and de Gaulle, he now claims that he spoke with Nixon for five hours, not including meals, photo time, and translation. With a patronizing, professorial air, he points out that Nixon has consulted with some eminent specialists; but since the Americans have not set foot in China for twenty-five years, they have no specialists in Chi-nese life! Malraux, typically, without even having read Simon Leys,[17] broadcasts his edict: "The Americans have Sinologists, that's not the same thing." What is a China specialist, if not first and foremost a Sinologist? The only American really to master the subject of China, according to Malraux, is Edgar Snow; he knows the author well, but his writings are dropping in value. In international politics, as in history or art criticism, Malraux usually hates "specialists." Art is a standoff between culture and education; politics, a clash between intuition and facts. Edgar Snow dies on the day Nixon flies off to China. Malraux liked about the American president that he was apparently someone who was asking himself the question "What is someone who doesn't think like us thinking?"

As Malraux sees it, he has undertaken an exchange of vague general-izations with a minor counterpart, Nixon. Admittedly, the job and the title give the man a certain importance. But he is no equal.

Dyable politique des situations compliquées.

CHAPTER THIRTY-SEVEN

The Arts and Art

E VER SINCE HIS adolescence, without having been pushed into museums by his grandfather, his father, or the matriarchy in Bondy, Malraux had a passion for painting and sculpture. He loved them as much as literature. Architecture, apart from Le Corbusier and Alvar Aalto, attracted him less. He felt a physical need to examine and absorb drawings, prints, canvases, lithographs, busts, heads.[1] With the help of an astonishing memory—"abnormal" he would say—he put together an immense inner picture library. He would gallop through a gallery but still take in small details or works as a whole and reproduce them years later. Dictating advice for some friends who are going to Japan, René and Bronia Clair, two pages of details immediately spring into his mind about Tokyo, Kyoto, Nara, and Osaka: "Tokyo. Big museum, a mishmash. Two important areas: the Chinese bronzes (primitive vases) and the haniwas (pre-Buddhist statuettes). Washes by Gyokudo (or in Kyoto): it's the [style of] painting that broke with tradition (Manet for us). The Bridgestone collection (translation of the name of the Japanese owner) . . . Possible hotel . . ."

He talks about the arts from *La Tentation de l'Occident* onward and devotes remarks or cryptic dialogues to them in *La Voie royale, La Condition humaine, L'Espoir,* and *Les Noyers de l'Altenburg.* From 1947 to 1949, with Skira,[2] he published *Le Musée imaginaire, La Création artistique,* and *La Monnaie de l'absolu,* revising them for Gallimard in 1951 as *Les Voix du silence.* After that, as well as his essay on Goya, there follows *Le Musée imaginaire de la sculpture mondiale* (in three volumes), *L'Iréel,* and *L'Intemporel* (*The Timeless*), in the revised *La Métamorphose des dieux.* Art, with a menacing capital *A*, becomes a leitmotif with Malraux, like Revolution and Mankind. He sees the Essence of Art, beyond the appearance of specific types of art, as the supreme weapon against Death, an "antidestiny." Malraux writes as if every noun, especially when reinforced with a capital letter, referred to a substance. He finds the reticence shown toward these works distressing: "My books on art remain, by far, the least understood. I am grateful to you for contributing to the clarification of their meaning."[3] Some critics, such as André Brincourt, judge that Malraux's works on Art are as important as his novels.

Malraux has his own particular way of working. His library, after the war, includes at least 2,024 works, whether read or not.[4] Seventy-nine of them are annotated with comments on erroneous interpretations (in Malraux's opinion) and cutting remarks for some of the authors. The avid amateur scribbles on his twelve volumes (out of twenty-two) of *Summa Artis: Historia general del arte* by José Pijoán.[5] Bubbling over with excitement, Malraux will sometimes cut a passage he wants to use right out of a book with scissors.

For many of those who buy them, Malraux's art books are magnificent albums. The illustrations are as important as the text. In comparison, Élie Faure's works seem thin on images. Between the first volume of *Psychologie de l'art* (1947) and *L'Intemporel* (1976)—with its imperious device, "The artist is not transcriber of the world, he is its rival"—new reprographic techniques enrich the albums. In *Psychologie de l'art*, there were 19 color plates, 63 black and white; in *L'Intemporel*, 100 color and 84 black and white. The reader wavers and weaves between text and illustrations. Malraux plays with the editing, in the filmic sense, which at the time is quite new: instead of paraphrasing, he leaves the reader to fill in the gaps between words and illustrations. For Malraux, the works themselves are answers to his questions on the human condition, not just markers referring to the text.

In 1922, in his catalog preface for the painter Demetrios Galanis and his first essay on the plastic arts, Malraux sets the tone for his thinking about Art: he confronts. Art historians use vertical comparison—within a painter's works—and horizontal—comparing painters to other painters—to justify an attribution or establish chronology or affiliations. Malraux also compares, but in tremendous disorder, using intuition and instinct to establish links between one form and another. Art collectors did not wait for Malraux to reveal his enthusiasm, his inspiration, and his quirky erudition before hanging Greek and African works in the same drawing room. By juxtaposing works of different centuries and schools, Malraux draws the attention of the general public. If the masterpieces talk to one another, they have undergone a metamorphosis. The notion of metamorphosis—formulated in *La Voie royale* with regard to works of art—is at the heart of the writer's emotional and intellectual approach. The work is static, but the way we see it changes and its reception varies with the centuries. Sociologists talk of the reappropriation or resymbolization of a work and the observer being metamorphosed by it; Malraux talks of the metamorphosis of a work as a result of the passage of time. The passing centuries detach the piece from its original function and make it sacred. "Europe discovered African art when it looked at African sculptures between Cézanne and Picasso, not fetishes between coconuts and crocodiles. It discovered the great sculptures of China via Roman figures, not via chinoiserie ornaments." Each culture attains Universality and Truth.

"The work of art arises in its time and from its time, but it also becomes a work of art because of what escapes it," Malraux writes. He steps right over history, refusing to take its possible contributions into account, and supposes that the work of art contains all the keys to its own understanding. Culture is not about knowledge but about revelation. That is why Malraux steers clear of the specialists: in his view, art for them is a means of earning a living without exercising their sensibility. They are simply stationmasters who never board a train. They do not have a distinctive way of looking (and he does).

Malraux centers on "genius," a notion that is "not debatable." Genius accedes to Truth. Malraux's spontaneous, oral definition is this: "A genius, in art, is a man who creates things that had no expression before him."[6] In this way, genius is the equivalent of the historical hero. Heroes are "people who have a certain power that does not belong to them." This pivotal idea of genius comes from nineteenth-century Romanticism in Europe and from Hegel, especially from his *Introduction to Aesthetics*, probably his best contribution to the history of ideas. In contrast to Malraux, Hegel states that "it is a mistake to believe that the artist does not know what he is doing"; "the true originality of the work of art consists in the rationality of content that is true in itself, a rationality that must animate the artist as well as his work." Malraux goes beyond this meager philosophical fare to try to define irrationality in all the arts.

He wants to crack the mystery, the secret of creation, which he confesses has always "interested [him] more than perfection." He is not searching for Beauty. He does not believe in Beauty: it is, perhaps, reducible to a feeling of dazzling satisfaction within each of us. "The Greeks thought . . . that beauty was the sole reason for the work of art." For Malraux, that is "a vain abstraction." Art is the incarnation of immortality on Earth, of the infinite, of rebellion, revolt, the refusal of the everyday human condition.

His writings on art are like some strange poem or curious novel, where a Gothico-Buddhist head, a twelfth-century Christ figure, or a Rembrandt can converse with one man—an actor, André Malraux, turned

Shakespearian Prologue. He says himself in 1974 to Pierre Dumayet and Walter Langlois that there is no difference between his art books and his novels.[7] "The metaphysical" is, for him, not only possible, it is a driving force for some among us. It expresses the Truth—but he never gives a definition of that in his books. What if there were only truths? What if metaphysics, the last dead branch of philosophy, were an impossibility, an activity to be banished along with alchemy and astrology? For Malraux, it offers a way of pinning down certainty without having to formulate it, an incursion into the unattainable Absolute.[8]

Les Voix du silence provokes criticism as soon as it appears. Ernst Hans Gombrich, the Viennese-born British art historian, publishes a crucial article in the *Burlington Magazine*.[9] Gombrich finds that it is impossible to specify the nature of *La Psychologie de l'art*; as a whole, it seems to him a "romantic saga." Malraux's message appears inspired by the expressionist German criticism of the 1920s: "Malraux would prefer to have faith in an illusion, and that is why he makes a panegyric to Myth." The names and images Malraux reels off "function like the names of the divinities in ancient incantations to reassure the writer more than the reader." The author expresses anguish, authentic Angst, about the solitude "which would reign if art failed . . . if every man remained walled up in himself." Is Malraux escaping solitude and agnosticism by making Art into an "absolute" beyond the arts? In his novels, brotherhood was a way of escaping solitude. Art has replaced brotherhood.

In France in 1956, the critic Georges Duthuit publishes two volumes, with one volume of plates, called *Le Musée inimaginable*. Duthuit was a specialist in Byzantine art and as open to Van Gogh as to Nicolas de Staël. His aim: "to defend art against its most formidable defender," André Malraux. Duthuit picks out a number of errors with extreme polemical violence. He detects in these essays by the high priest and commissar of writings on art "ignorance," "negligence" or "counterfeiting," and "passionate ejaculation." He does not accept the "false eternity" that Malraux accords to works of art; Duthuit perceives the "dark drama that Malraux will one day be forced to confront, solitude. Which from now on will make his frenetic activity seem almost moving." For Duthuit, the "tall stories" peddled by Malraux—that "oracle of the imperfectly cultivated classes"—succeed only "because of an unparalleled style." Duthuit's three volumes never really make an impact.[10] Some critics are restrained by embarrassment; they do not want to express an opinion in opposition to the national institution that Malraux is.

Yet several points unite Malraux and Duthuit. In a letter to José Corti, his publisher, Duthuit says, "I hold to be particularly incompetent the scholars who have no contact with pieces, nor any intuition about art; that is, the vast majority if not all of them."[11] Duthuit suffers from not being accepted by museum curators; Malraux, apparently, not at all.

A full account of Malraux's ideas on aesthetics would require an analysis of a large number of phrases in G. E. Moore fashion. There is an accumulation of pithy formulae: "With Braque, it is not the peach that is velvety, it is the picture"; "It is not a matter of electing the unknowable but of circumscribing it"; "The representation of the world is succeeded by its annexation"; "For modern art to be born, the art of fiction has to come to an end and with it the myth of beauty"; "Art has evidently not become a religion, but it has become faith." The reader keeps stumbling over empty formulae forming concertina links: "Michelangelo is not possible in Egypt." One might as well say "Nefertiti is not possible in Florence." Malraux does not avoid truisms: "Nobody can speak of great painters without paintings, of great musicians without music." Well, no.

But if Malraux's formulae are not what logicians of the Vienna Circle would call propositions, they do often carry along suggestions of an imaginative and stimulating nature. The cut-and-dried phrases, the gratuitous (or inspired) parallels, with their factual errors, encourage readers to look at a painting differently. They coexist with sensible and enlightening remarks. This is the case when Malraux dwells at length on details that have been photographically enlarged. "The framing of a sculpture, the angle from which it is taken, above all, studied lighting give an imperious accent to what was hitherto only suggested." Photography is interpretation and metamorphosis; it gives another vision. Malraux perceives the dangers of modern techniques: "Reproduction has created fictitious arts by systematically falsifying the scale of objects, by presenting imprints of oriental seals as stamps on columns, amulets as statues; the unfinished work due to the small dimensions of an object becomes by enlargement an expansive style of modern expression. Roman silver and gold plate work joins with sculpture, at last finds its significance in the series of photos where reliquaries and statues have the same importance." Or again: "Rembrandt's shadow is not a use of light. If you want to make a live painting of a Rembrandt portrait or *The Night Watch*, shooting it on film, you can light it with all the extraordinary electric equipment of modern cinema; it is still absolutely impossible, because his light is false." Malraux's commentaries are occasionally user's manuals, instructions on how to look.

One senses that in the world of art historians, he sometimes benefits from an amused, even tender, critical sympathy (Well, he's a writer writing about art . . . he's bound to mix too many things together). But some experts today feel a clear gratitude toward him.[12] Yet if one digs deeper in the texts, the reading is somewhat spoiled. The very notion of an "imaginary museum," that every member of mankind could build up thanks to advances in reproduction, is odd. For Étienne Gilson, historian of philosophy, Malraux "spreads among the public the illusion that they are making themselves the owner of a sort of museum by buying a book and that in flipping through this book they have before their eyes works that are real enough to serve as the basis for an aesthetic appreciation . . . the only real means of access is the direct sight of the work of art."[13] Jean-François Revel, more scathing:

> But has Malraux by any chance heard of the existence of the book and of libraries? Does he know that for thousands of years, and even before the invention of printing, the book, curiously enough, has allowed a text to be transported into a different civilization from that of its author, with a fidelity to the original that is incredibly superior to that of the supposed "reproduction," often such a misnomer. From the fact that the Bibliothèque Nationale holds almost every work written by man, does he conclude that all these works, ever since libraries have existed, are instantaneously and simultaneously understood by each of us? For it is on this premise that the idea of the imaginary museum rests. . . . Malraux's museum is not in the least "unimaginable" (to recall Georges Duthuit's title)—or at least not because of any excessive abundance of material—but on the contrary, because of a shortage, an essential weakness: a lack of imagination. The imaginary museum, is, in short, the museum for people with no imagination.[14]

In radio and television interviews, Malraux does sometimes express himself clearly. If the text of the interview is to be published, it can be worked on later: the interviewee can add here and there and give the text the appearance of density. Malraux fans will prefer to see the process as a retrograde simplification of the final, written text for the benefit of the audiovisual medium. Most of those who interview Malraux align themselves with his system of thought or fall under his charm.

The print runs of the writer's works on art are not as long as those for his novels, either in the standard edition or in the Pléiade. To give an idea of the extent, the French sales of his novels in the Pléiade (first edition) up to 1999 were 160,142, and those of *Le Miroir des limbes*, which includes *Antimémoires*, had sold 226,242. On the art side, the Goya essay sold 14,750 and *Le Musée imaginaire* 61,169, impressive figures nonetheless considering the prices of these books.

From 1960, Malraux was also editor of the Gallimard collection *L'Univers des Formes*.[15] The title is reminiscent of Élie Faure's *L'Esprit des formes* and Henri Focillon's *La Vie des formes*. Malraux doesn't mind making use of specialists here. For his collection, he meets with Georges Salles in his office at the Louvre: "I'll look after the pictures, will you take care of the text?"

The two editors published forty-two volumes in the collection during Malraux's lifetime, making a wealth of documents available to academics and the general public. The series constitutes a sort of universal history of art, complete with superb illustrations and beautifully laid out. Multiple international contracts were required to cover the costs. A conflict of duty arose for some specialists, who detested Malraux's writings on art; but then again, a chance to collaborate on this collection with Gallimard . . . After painful mock debates, they generally succumbed. One exception was the exquisite Anthony Blunt, Poussin specialist and freelancer for Soviet espionage: he refused to touch the project. The first volumes sell well, at around 40,000 copies. After a while, the collection runs out of steam.

In 1974, Malraux takes one of the women in his life to Japan: *Mona Lisa*. Her "mysterious Glory . . . does not come only from genius. . . . The Italian genius bequeathed the most famous painting in the world to the last king of France to be armed as a knight. With his passing came the end of the great medieval soul that united mysticism and courage. Here, may she be welcomed by the only people to have united Zen and Bushido. And may the head of your government be commended for this in the name of the Japanese artists and heroes who, perchance, thank him from the depths of the grand funereal night."[16]

The *Mona Lisa* is hung behind a protective sheet of bulletproof glass in the Tokyo National Museum. This gives her a greenish tinge. Malraux sets about reinforcing the legend, trotting out like a veteran speaker: "*La Gioconda* is the only painting in the world to which mad people liken themselves; even madmen believe themselves to be *Mona Lisa*. Nobody thinks he or she is any other painting. *Mona Lisa* is the only painting that can be the target of an attack."

The former minister is received by the Japanese prime minister and by a war criminal the Americans spared, Emperor Hirohito.[17] The emperor gives the writer a Sengai picture. Malraux saw to it that he would not be in France for the presidential elections, a way of saying Giscard would not get his vote. He could have used a postal ballot, but didn't.[18] An interesting precedent for this occurred when Pompidou was elected president in June 1969 after de Gaulle's resignation: the General was in Ireland at the time.

His steps slowed by a growing portliness, his body weighed down with fatigue though his mind is still quick, Malraux indulges in his love of travel and goes with Sophie de Vilmorin to Haiti at the end of December 1975.

Haiti, the first black republic to win its independence, in 1803, at the cost of a massacre of settlers. The Creole, French-speaking slaves built a people against colonial exploitation, for the dignity of a nation. General Toussaint Louverture was practicing peasant guerrilla warfare long before Mao or Ho. Unfortunately, Napoleon, influenced by Josephine, re-established slavery there. In 1975, succeeding his father, François, Jean-Claude Duvalier, alias Baby Doc, petty tyrant of the Caribbean, is ruling Haiti, with the support of the Tontons Macoutes. But Malraux's trip is not of a political nature. He has for a long time been interested in Haitian painters. At the Festival of African Art in Dakar, the writer-minister met Jean-Claude Garoute, alias Tiga, who extended an invitation to him. Tiga, poet, hazy philosopher, and painter, and his friend Maud Robarts, "live" an artistic experience that Malraux wants to see firsthand.

At Port-au-Prince, visitors are dazzled by the cheerful violence of the colors on the shop signs and the gaudy tap-taps used as buses. André Malraux and his companion stay at the Hotel El Rancho and go around the art galleries. On December 29, they make their way up to Soissons-la-Montagne, a village of *spontanéiste* painters of the Saint Soleil School. The narrow road snakes across deep, verdant gorges. The profusion of flamboyants and plantain trees, the yellow, white, red, and mauve flowers suggest a Caribbean Tuscany as seen by Henri Rousseau. Huts and houses cling to the sides of the road amid smells of coffee, honey, grime, rice, and cocoa. In front of a famous cemetery, its tombs decorated with frescoes and concreted to protect the dead and keep in any bad spirits, there stands Baron Samedi, in the form of a cross.

"Sensational!" exclaims Malraux.

He discovers the immense Cul de Sac Plain running to the Étang Saumâtre. Budgerigars and coas—black birds that shriek like crows—fly off. A host of pictures descends toward Malraux, carried by their painters, led by Tiga. Small farmers, weavers, tradesmen, all pupils of Tiga, who gives them paints, paper, pencils, and clay. They do not sign their canvases like the naifs from "down below" (in Port-au-Prince). "Art for art's sake, and not for money," Tiga asserts, almost as volubly as Malraux, who in turn churns out his patent phrases, some crystal clear, some obscure: "There are naifs when there are firemen. . . . What is happening here with painting is what happened in the United States with jazz music. . . . It is a possessed painting. . . . The naif painter works by application, the Saint-Soleil painters by visitation. That is the point of starting to paint after the age of fifty: the psychological experience is completely different."

Malraux and Tiga each recognize the gifted actor in the other. Tiga speaks his line: "They [the painters present] know that they can create from dreams or naturally. . . . They do it effortlessly. There is no effort."

The two men talk with Maud and others until 4:30 in the afternoon. Back down in Port-au-Prince, Malraux writes, Sophie types. At seventy-four, the aging fighter knows just where he is. He is working on the definitive *Métamorphose des dieux* and inserts the pages written in Port-au-Prince after the unexpected ending of the third part, *L'Intemporel*, knocking out those on Goya.

Malraux and Sophie—she feels uneasy about it—attend a voodoo ceremony. Though tempted by the irrational and the *loas* (Haitian divinities), Malraux doesn't stay long. "Luckily," writes Sophie de Vilmorin, "he had understood enough about it." For those who love him, Malraux understands everything right away and in depth.

The part of Malraux that is interested in the irrational is attracted to possession, the spirit world, trance, language, magic, and these paintings of Christiano-voodoo inspiration. He skims over voodoo as he did Marxism: both are pretexts for touching stylistic exercises.

In Haiti he acquires eight paintings, including two on paper; two are bought, the others gifts, five from the Saint Soleil artists and one from Jean-Claude Duvalier. Malraux feels uncomfortable when invited to meet Baby Doc. After all, this is a private trip. The pocket dictator places a car at Malraux's disposal and a helicopter to get to Cap-Haitien. Malraux prefers a French Embassy car. What a headline it would have made: "André Malraux declines invitation from Haitian despot!"[19] The conversation between President Duvalier and Malraux centers on de Gaulle. Baby Doc—quite stupid, incidentally—asks, "What would the General do in my place?"[20] Malraux laughingly tells the ambassador that he had "no difficulty in answering."

In the conversations reported by Malraux in *L'Intemporel*, one often doesn't know who is talking, as is frequently the case with him. De Gaulle and a Haitian host are as one:

"What do they think will happen to the paintings they bring you [the painters of Saint Soleil]?"

"They will be with the others, find themselves among them. There is a community of paintings, like our community, our theater. Beyond that, it is vague. At least, I imagine so."

"What did they think of the exhibition at the museum [in Port-au-Prince]?" Tiga (probably) replies, "It disconcerted them. Like the museum. Funny idea. That's not what pictures are for."

"What did they think of their colleagues from down below?"

"The naifs? That they paint images in order to sell them. That doesn't interest them."

Malraux comes to life again: "Everything that makes reality float is important. Voodoo does not seem to me to be religious but supernatural.

It makes spirits and the dead as familiar as miracles were during the early Middle Ages." The last lines of *L'Intemporel*, written in 1976, seem to carry a feeling of helplessness: "Why should not art undergo a transformation as vast as that of beauty? Born together, the Imaginary Museum, the enigmatic value of art, the timeless, will doubtless all die together. And mankind will see that even timelessness is not eternal."

It's a long way from the confident opening pages of *Le Musée imaginaire*, written as the first volume of *Psychologie de l'art* in 1947. Malraux has brought some perspective to his search for Man, Art, and Truth. It is, he repeats, very "strange," "complicated," "important." As if he sensed the impossibility of his endeavor, he states, "To give an account of art is an insane enterprise."[21]

A derisory venture or a shattering adventure of backfiring, genius pretension? Or chimerical invention? The overheated Malraux, drugged up and supercharged on words, like Sartre, often writes on art faster than he thinks.[22] How are we to speak of art? Malraux, faced with an Art which escapes his words and passion, brings to mind T. S. Eliot:

> Words strain,
> Crack and sometimes break, under the burden,
> Under the tension, slip, slide, perish,
> Decay with imprecision, will not stay in place,
> Will not stay still.[23]

Returning to Verrières, Malraux hangs a Saint-Soleil painting of a *loa* next to a Rouault. He gives a dear friend, the Comtesse de Karolyi, a green-and-orange picture with two trees, a young plant, a straight man, and a hunched woman; in the background, a river flows from left to right—and out of the picture as Malraux escapes from the history of art. Can art be talked about the way Malraux saw it? His race against the inexpressible, the unreal, and the timeless might evoke, in a skeptical mind, the quip of the philosopher and mathematician F. P. Ramsey: "What we can't say we can't say, and we can't whistle it either."

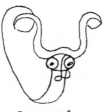

Dyable de la
dialectique

CHAPTER THIRTY-EIGHT

Pot-au-Feu and Caviar

I'LL SHOW THEM that I am the greatest writer of the century," said André Malraux to his nephew, Alain. He was no longer writing novels at the time. After the death of Montherlant, he sighed in front of Sophie, "Now there are only three of us: Sartre, Aragon, and me."

Malraux has depressive relapses, but much more rarely than before, and fewer tics. He lives embedded in public opinion, among his Caledonian masks and Greco-Buddhist sculptures, his Mexican cockerels and Thai bronzes, among his Braque, a *Head of a Hostage* by Fautrier, a head of Christ by Rouault, a Picasso lithograph, a small Poliakoff, a Chagall, a Dubuffet on the ground floor at Verrières or in his modest private apartment under the attic.

After Louise's death, he almost left and rented an apartment on the Quai Voltaire or in Rue Barbet-de-Jouy, or a house in Versailles, or a suite at the Crillon. He doesn't want to leave Verrières. He buys himself a rustic seventeenth-century Spanish table as a desk, declares himself to be on the point of moving out, and gets properly settled in. He has been dry since 1972 and has almost changed in nature: he now seems less vulnerable and aggressive.

When the subject of death crops up, he always insists—perhaps too much—on one point: his demise does not concern him. Who else has brushed with death as he has, who has related that state between life and death as well as he did in *Lazare*? Malraux talks little of his demise except in letters to friends, sometimes serious, sometimes playful. To Louis Martin-Chauffier:[1] "That such an old friendship, traversed by so many deaths, should remain has a mystery about it that is not so very far from the survival of works. For you, this is wrapped up in faith, but for me?" And then, as if regretting this confidence: "Anyway, you know that I have thought that there perhaps existed a heaven for me, where you would be welcoming me in Breton costume. I think I now know what it is, and I embrace you." Throughout his life, embracing and affection have not come easily to Malraux, even at the end of a letter.

He did at times contemplate suicide. Beuret conjured away a gun. Malraux grumbled to Grosjean, "They've taken away my revolver. I'm allowed to finish how I like."

If he were to succumb to a suicidal impulse, a gun is what he would use. Those closest to him are less aware of his bouts of depression. Bertagna, with his pharmacopoeia of tranquilizers, neuroleptics, anti-depressants, and soporifics, is never far away. He has gotten into the habit of dropping in at Verrières on Sundays. To his patient, a doctor is as fascinating as a priest or a lawyer. Bertagna is not obliged to keep the distance that a psychoanalyst would. Malraux is now treated mostly with Tofranil, an antidepressant.

Not many men or women can sound out Malraux. Jean Grosjean is permitted natural, unstaged visits; he has been seeing the writer regularly for more than thirty years, with pleasure and without fuss. With most people, including his companion, Sophie de Vilmorin, Malraux is in monologue mode. With Grosjean, he starts to dialogue. His whole life, the writer has had asymmetrical emotional relationships with others. With Grosjean, a balance has come about.

Since the day they met in 1940, each has been the gentle prisoner of the other, bound in a friendly dissimilarity. They talk about the Gospel according to Saint John, Aeschylus, Sophocles, Shakespeare. Their passions are similar: Hugo for one, Lamartine for the other. Their friendship is beyond propriety and everyday concerns, the tittle-tattle of Rue Sébastien-Bottin, where Grosjean works meticulously in the margins. They owe each other nothing if not their respect, consideration, and mutual criticism. Grosjean's passion for Malraux as a writer is discreet; his compassion for the man is clear. He knows what difficulties his friend has always had with writing. He senses that Malraux is afraid, above all, of "falling into the void." In this man, so assured in appearance, he detects anxiety, anguish. Grosjean is half poet, one fourth peasant; the rest is pure friend. Like Beuret, he is light-years away from the beggars, exploiters, and respectful profiteers who gravitate around Malraux. He knows the great man's permanent character traits: "Ambition, certainly. Or rather ambitions, and not always compatible ones: heroic and intellectual, financial and ethical, political and literary."[2]

Grosjean does not spend his time collecting comments from Malraux. But he throws a few impressions down on paper on returning from Verrières:[3]

At the bottom of a well
extreme kindness but this time from very far off
a sort of courtesy, both quite internal and almost
unreal.
It was a beautiful February in all its coldness and
all its grayness.
The shadow of his smile, the large fire through the
window
between the trembling of the bamboos and the great
dark cedar we saw the lawn rise up
a few birches of a great perfection through . . .
to which the Japanese screen behind A.M. seemed to be
responding.
"I have the tone of Bernanos and Claudel."
not quite true, but too modest since if his turn of
phrase is less sure his thinking goes further.
But not even a word to the cats anymore.
He inhabits his body and this world as a stranger.
One feels he is on a voyage.

Malraux is still flanked by Beuret, who is unconditional without being sanctimonious. He rejected Madeleine but accepted Louise and Sophie.[4] Albert and Sophie deal with practical problems. Malraux now has a more open relationship with his daughter, Florence. When Louise died, Florence was living in New York with her husband, Alain Resnais. The day of the burial, she kissed her father—a rare occurrence—and had the feeling that he was deeply moved. Malraux did not grieve for long. Louise, it would seem, was missed more by her family and Sophie than by her companion.

Sophie and André travel, a lot. Roaming the world is a way of finding one's youth and fleeing old age. You arrive, you leave. If death snatches you on the way, at least you don't see it coming as you do in hospital, where every dawn is a hope and every day's span a conquest. Sophie and André visit or revisit Japan, Nepal, and Bangladesh, where he is seen almost as a founding father of the new country. In India and Bangladesh, they combine tourism and political cruises. Malraux is awarded the Nehru Prize, in which his predecessors are Marshal Tito, Martin Luther King, Jr. (posthumously), Yehudi Menuhin, and Mother Teresa. Malraux gives the 100,000 rupees prize money to a foundation.

Having sorted Louise's archives after her death, Sophie starts on André's. They are lovers. The stewardess became partner one May 20, she records.[5] She watches over the writer, spares him the bothersome bits in the everyday life of an illustrious man, gives him injections of Gérovital, an "anti-aging" medicine that is no longer fashionable. Sophie is not a society woman. Malraux ventures, "Would you like us to entertain?"

"No."

Relief on the part of Malraux. He plans to marry Sophie, he says. He had thought about it for Louise. Slight snag, he was still married to Madeleine; he still is. A divorce would be complicated. Sophie considers herself, with justification, to be living with him, *en ménage*. Malraux, she discovers, is not even on record with the Social Security; the situation is sorted out with the help of the prime minister's office.

In his busy, ordered life, the writer rises at nine and works from ten until a quarter to one. Always the dandy, he likes Hermès ties, Lanvin suits, silk dressing gowns. With Sophie's care and attention, he stabilizes. He is, she knows, drugged with honor and respect. She is sometimes naive: she believes he read sacred Hindu texts "at seventeen." He suffers from polyneuritis in the legs. He doesn't complain. Sophie is there to keep him company. She knows when life is sweet: she has been through tough times herself. At the age of nine, she lost her mother. She worked as assistant in Christian Dior's boutique. Louise did not like to play second fiddle. Sophie is not looking to shine. She describes herself as "lateral."

Malraux pours down lemon tea and strong coffee. He sees visitors at the beginning of the afternoon, then returns to his "workbench." He remains courteous, even gallant when necessary. He talks abundantly about the Cathars with Jeanine Monnier, the governess-cum-cook from Toulouse, who takes care of various tasks around the house. But not the cleaning, which is the province of a Portuguese woman—and Malraux talks to her about sculptures too.

He has himself driven to dinners in Paris by Terzo Cricchi, his chauffeur and valet. The former minister doesn't seem to miss the Republican Guards, the pomp that surrounds a member of the government. Ludmilla Tcherina, a former star dancer at the Paris Opera, hangs around him. He finds that amusing: "She would like to make out that I am her lover. Whereas I have never done so much as kiss her, even on the cheek."

The Verrières dinners give way to sessions in front of the television set. Malraux listens to the news, follows a few debates, watches game shows and the odd film. But what Western can compare with his life? He doesn't think much of televised films. The screen seems too small for an Eisenstein or a Dreyer. If he starts to watch a film, he quickly tires of it.

"People think that television is cinema at home. But cinema is just a small part of what it will bring us," he says. They are talking about cable: cable television will transform our lives, and will drastically change the education system.

When Louise was asked what flaw she had the most indulgence for, she replied, "Mythomania." Sophie is happy, indulgent about everything. Quiet contentment can be contagious. Sophie never tires of marveling at Malraux, even if she can see his faults. He is her man, a great man, and she protects him. If he is depressed, she says he is "tired" or "bored." Sophie notices that Malraux still has his astonishing memory, and an imagination as dreamlike as it is realistic. She types his manuscripts, fields telephone calls, follows up correspondence, and, without keeping too close a watch over him, watches out for him.

Malraux knows that he has grown distant from many friends of many generations, particularly the younger ones. Two boys, Philippe and François de Saint-Chéron, motivated by boundless admiration, track him down. Knowing that Malraux often goes to Lasserre restaurant, they wait for him at the entrance. Sophie persuades him to see them. They arrive, swooning, at Verrières, and get to work sorting out photographs.[6] Sophie also introduces journalists, after filtering. Malraux works up some superb "numbers" like an excellent music hall artist, always on the same themes: Death, Stalin, Fate, Mao, the General. He adapts himself to the company, improvising with consummate skill and courtesy. With Claudine Vernier-Palliez:[7] "My cats have requested that I act as their spokesman with you. This is, for me, a great honor. Lustrée has come to listen and tell her friend Fourrure, who is out hunting, all about our conversation. What a nerve, chasing after field mice when she's stuffed already!"

"What relationship did de Gaulle have with cats?" asks Claudine Vernier-Palliez.

"When I asked him that question," says Malraux, "he answered, after a little thought, 'I do not scare them anymore.' Before, he was friends with a German shepherd. Then he had a Chartreux, a superb cat with a very distinguished name that Mme. de Gaulle preferred to call Grigri. Grigri won the General over by flattering him. The General was delighted to have a cat who was no longer afraid of him and even showed him an immense respect; he said to himself that here, at last, was a cat in his own image, an exceptional cat, a Cat-Lord."

Sophie puts up with Malraux's cats. Louise said, "I do not like cats, the cat is the pet of aristocrats and concierges."

Malraux moved into Verrières with two cats, Fourrure (black, gutter nobility) and Lustrée (beige). A male, Essuie-Plume, was entrusted to friends. It works as a good indicator: if he is being attentive to his animals, Malraux is doing well, if not . . .[8]

He has a pronounced weakness for pot-au-feu (beef stew), boeuf bourguignon, salt pork with lentils, Toulouse-style cassoulet, and caviar. He also likes cakes at every dessert, bought at Fauchon or chez Lenôtre.

Like many worriers, he consumes vast quantities of chocolate in little boxes, a little dish next to his bed, another on his desk. Chocolate is a good tranquilizer, a complement to Dr. Bertagna's pills.

Lasserre puts "Pigeon André Malraux" on the menu, which makes some, like Jean Lescure, smile. A serious-looking Malraux explains the dish to his guest, who is about to order: "Small, boned pigeon, stuffed, served with chanterelle mushrooms. Very good. Have it."

Lescure, laughing, but egged on by the tone of Malraux's remark: "There's one thing I don't understand. You are always saying to me, 'Writing is hard. Ah! Literature. Not easy. How can we do it. Precarious man, oh la la.' . . . And on the other hand you have said that Gutenberg is in the past, we are in the age of the image. So why carry on tiring yourself out? In fifty years, nobody will be reading; nobody will be reading you. In a food-loving country like France, your eternity is there [Lescure taps the menu], it's pigeon Malraux."

Malraux listens earnestly, angles a look up at the menu on the wall: "Chateaubriand. [A pause.] They've spelled it with a bloody *t*."

Lescure remembers the Egyptian Book of the Dead: "Nobody will achieve eternity if he has not been called by his name."[9]

Malraux is no longer active on the political scene. But he revives an epic and lyric tone for the celebrations at the fifth anniversary of the death of General de Gaulle: "The rival of Marx's *Manifesto* is not a Gaullist theory, it is the appeal of June 18 [1940]."

Of the General: "He spoke with the force of one who is saying what everybody knows, when everybody is keeping it quiet; he spoke to the land with simple words of love: You are necessary to me. . . . He takes on misfortune and hope together. . . . The goals it is most worth aimng for are those one never reaches."

As for his family, even now that he no longer leads the hectic life of a minister, it cannot be said that Malraux is very attached to them. He has no grandchildren, so the role of the good grandfather—which often offers itself to men who found themselves wanting as fathers—is not available. According to Sophie and others, he talks of his father but never of his mother. He has, at times, looked after his aunt, Marie Lamy. He writes to her, "My dear Aunt. The books have been sent to your address, and I suppose that you have now received them. The things we were talking about when you wrote to me signified, basically, that I shall probably take a command in Bengal. It is the best thing I can do. What you say is noble; some of us in the family will have had a gift for courage. I would have taken you to India, before, with confidence and joy. Now the evening is falling, perhaps it is just as well. What you say about your eyes does not concern the radio. Do you want me to send you a set? Yours affectionately." Again to his aunt: "I am happy to know that the set has arrived: I was on the other side of the Mediterranean. Finding a man in the business to set it up for you shouldn't be difficult: you only have to turn a knob and press on two buttons. Naturally, tell him to send me his bill. The Nobel Prize? No question. They will never give it to a Gaullist. So be it. . . . I will probably be in France until the end of the month: I am to meet Mrs. Gandhi on the 9th. I send lots of love to my dear aunt, affectionately yours."[10] His heart beats intermittently. He does not attend Marie Lamy's funeral.

Another woman is dear to him: "Gogo," very beautiful, of Hungarian origin, who works at Hermès as a draftswoman and designer. There is a furtive allusion to her in Malraux's embryonic novel *Non*, which he has picked up again and reread. "Gogo," Catherine Polya, Comtesse de Karolyi, is one of his "guardian demons," as he puts it. She has a long and deep loving friendship with Malraux. Eight years, interrupted by a quarrel.[11] Gogo had a childhood surrounded by painters and sculptors, and she talks a lot about art. She comes to dinner at Verrières every week, Wednesdays and Sundays. Sometimes, Terzo, driving the Citroën DS 21 Pallas, drops Malraux at her residence in Paris, then goes to buy a chocolate cake at Fauchon. The countess fascinates Malraux. He confides in her like an adolescent: "I am the last of the romantics."

To be translated as: And the first in my century. Which, for France, is perhaps not far off the mark. In a tête-à-tête with Gogo at Lasserre, he also says, "What do you think of death?"

"Nothing."

He looks at her. "Love is a myth, a poison of our time."

Catherine de Karolyi does not claim, like some others, to have been the writer's mistress, only his lover, in the sense of somebody who loves, and she finds herself tenderly liked in return. Malraux wonders in front of Gogo: "Why do we say '*fall* in love'?"

Gogo records in notebooks her memories of being with the writer:

Dinner chez Laurent: "I am so happy with you that I feel like kissing all men."

"Only the men?" says Malraux, laughing.[12]

A tiff that is difficult to decipher separates Malraux from Gogo. In her notebook:

Sunday . . . Sophie, this evening, says to me, "Isn't that right, Gogo, you still love your first husband?!!" Stunned, I say, "What's come over you, Sophie? It's as if I were to say the same thing to you!" André went white listening to "our dialogue" and said more or less, "It's not the same thing, Sophie has me"! . . .

Wednesday, one of the usual days for our dinners in the week, I was supposed to come. I didn't want to come, and I told Sophie so when she called me back . . . she insists: "But don't do that, Gogo, you can't not come, *you are his ray of sunshine!* etc. You know that it was only a mood thing, and so on, etc.!!! I didn't understand what was happening myself! I was as surprised as you . . . !!"

Is Sophie unhappy about this quarrel, which, for a while, separates André and Gogo? With a sense of the tragic, which was always there, Malraux announced to Gogo one evening in 1972, when dining alone with her at Verrières, "One day you will be able to say . . . I was in his arms, when he was in the arms of death."[13]

The two women observe each other. They love Malraux. Sophie is not jealous. She knows what she brings to her companion. She sees to his well-being. Gogo puts him in a good mood, but Sophie protects his steps: No, Gogo, no need to fetch that book, up there in Malraux's room, I'll go. Unsophisticated exchanges between women in love. Malraux is not innocent, without being completely guilty, of these feminine demands. After two cruises where the three of them traveled together, Sophie honorably explains to Gogo that Malraux does not want the countess to take part in another expedition to the Spitsbergen Islands. She and Malraux are to have each other to themselves. In fact, Monique de Vilmorin comes along on the trip. The writer fears solitude. He envelops himself in the admiration of women.

Terzo Cricchi leaves his job as Malraux's valet and chauffeur, having been offered a post with the Municipal Guard in Florence. He also wants to marry his fiancée, from the same village as he.[14] He has to think of his future.

Detached from French politics, Malraux re-emerges onto the forestage during the 1974 presidential election campaign, in support of the Gaullist candidate Jacques Chaban-Delmas, who is up against François Mitterrand and Valéry Giscard d'Estaing in the first round. Malraux's appearance is a disaster. During a broadcast, he appears to say that television will replace teachers in elementary and high schools. This aspect of his speech loses Chaban-Delmas the votes of Gaullist teachers, who are few enough to begin with. An astute remark made by Malraux on the importance of computers in the near future passes unnoticed. The film cuts to show Chaban, dumbfounded by the remarks of the man defending him.[15]

Malraux dispenses wishes and predictions: "Politically, the unity of Europe is a utopia. To achieve a common European unity would require a common enemy, but the only possible common enemy would be Islam."

On the mark.

"A rationalist culture can never be enough for the spirit. The West is looking everywhere for the irrationality it lacks. East and West have to elaborate, through a synthesis of their values, a new concept of Man to protect them against the attacks of industrialized society. Kipling was wrong: East and West are looking for each other, and their meeting, far from being impossible, will be one of the events of the end of the century."

Off the mark.

Malraux's speeches abroad and his tendency to put his foot in it are feared at the Quai d'Orsay, even if he is no longer a member of the government. What clanger is he going to drop next? When the Americans talked of providing arms to Pakistan, he added that Paris could supply seventeen planes to India. Then, to the astonishment of his audience, he explained in an aside to the French consul general that he had thought it a good idea to "take the initiative." Already recognized as one of the great French writers of his generation, what can he do to demonstrate that he is also (if only virtually, now) one of the great politicians of the century?

He invites writers to Verrières to inhale History. Seriously, not everybody can be Malraux. But men of letters will testify for posterity. Thus, Dominique de Roux, who counted on Malraux for Portugal after the fall of Salazar, notes, "Malraux invited me to Verrières. I had not seen him since a dinner with a prince of the empire where, out of breath and agitated, he put a stop to the Parisian prattling by warning the mistress of the house that he was going to throw himself on Dacca by parachute forthwith, all the while filling himself with profiteroles. The words bore no relation to reality."

I saw Malraux twice at Verrières, in October 1975. In a tweed suit, moccasins on his feet, his hair gray, he appeared in full possession of his faculties and his faults. His hands played with a pair of tortoiseshell glasses. The sentences simmered, bounced out, rose up in curls, filled the room. In the space of a few hours, Malraux went around the world, as if impatient to reach Mars. Despite the questions I had prepared to hold back this tsunami of a man, he found his way through to his totems, Mao and Trotsky; he ranged from psychoanalysis to pornography, from Vietnam to Portugal. He had signed an appeal with Sartre and Aragon in support of Spanish prisoners. Such an alliance was of the order of a "constellation," he said, without humility. Did he sometimes think about Sartre or Aragon? Never. Really? Even in a nasty way?

"Not at all in a nasty way. Here you can make yourself useful. Tell Sartre from me that when D'Annunzio was really blind, to allow him to write he had a thing that you must still be able to find today, when you use a machine like this one [Malraux indicated his stenotype machine]. It can't have been a unique device."

"The names Aragon, Malraux, and Sartre at the bottom of this anti-Francoist petition, does that mean anything?"

"Sartre took the initiative," Malraux replied. "He knew I would sign."

"Why?"

"That's just the way it is. If I had done it under the same conditions, I would have been sure that he would sign."

And what about Aragon? No, they no longer met. Malraux: "In twenty years, three half hours. Aragon, the last time was in 1966, at the Ministry of Culture: he wanted us to make the biggest possible fuss of a Russian naif artist. I had the exhibition done at the Marsan Pavilion [at the Louvre]. Aragon knows about painting."

And what about Spain, in the medium term?

"It is purely arbitrary," he said. "There is no 'yes' or 'no' answer. The French don't realize that the only realistic mass organization in Spain is the Anarchists. Will Franco's successor have a repressive streak? I do not see how it could be otherwise."

I pushed him on a few points about what is "true," what "false," and what "experienced":

"What is truth, to you?"

"My first response is banal: that which is verifiable."

"You are very much a positivist."

"That is old man Brunschvicg's theory. There is another answer: not to believe in a truth as the Bolsheviks did. It is an excessively precise thing. We're not really sure what dignity is, but we know very well what humiliation is. I'm not sure I know what truth is; I don't see it as the opposite of lying: I see it as the opposite of its absence. And the absence of truth, I know very well what that is."

We were on French interior politics: Pompidou and Pompidouism had succeeded Gaullism in 1969, and Giscardism had succeeded that in 1974.

"What is Giscardism?" I asked.

"Who was it that succeeded Napoleon again?"

"What do you think of Valéry Giscard d'Estaing?"

"Nothing, he is a courteous man."

And with the smile of a child stealing a pot of jam, Malraux put his hand over the microphone and said to me, "And that's about it!"

What of the Left, whence all three of them came, Aragon, Sartre, and himself?

"Did you see yourself, André Malraux, as the link between de Gaulle and the Left?"

"Yes, absolutely."

"Do you feel that was a success?"

"No. But we succeeded in other things."

"In twenty years, how will we present André Malraux to our grand-children? Will we say: writer, publisher, revolutionary, politician, art critic? Can you give me an epitaph for the moment when your life is 'transformed into destiny'?"

"It'd have to be 'writer.' One can imagine Gide: 'Writer, alas!' But I don't accept the 'alas' or the exclamation point."

In researching this biography, I at last understood, more than twenty years later, a remark Malraux made to me when seeing us (the photographer Françoise Viard, Alain Chouffan, and myself) out: "Ah, Ca-Mau, my youth, Ca-Mau . . . !"

I had sent him a novel, *Les Canards de Ca-Mao*, whose action takes place at the southern point of Vietnam.[16] He had written back to me. At Verrières, he recalled his effective defense of the peasants in his newspaper *L'Indochine* half a century earlier. At the time I didn't know about that.

IN 1975 AND 1976, Malraux remains present on several literary fronts—and how. At seventy-three and seventy-four, he puts the finishing touches to the portraits in *Hôtes de passage*. He corrects *Le Miroir des limbes*, comprising the revised *Antimémoires*. He finalizes his definitive work on art, *La Métamorphose des dieux*. He writes prefaces, including one for the correspondence between Jean Guéhenno and Romain Rolland. He revisits his distant youth with a homage to the painter and engraver Demetrios Galanis for an exhibition of work. He writes a flattering introduction to the book about Josette Clotis by her friend Suzanne Chantal—without, it would seem, having read it. He offers a text on the exhibition of Saint-John Perse's *Les Oiseaux* and the rest of his work for which, as a minister, he has presented a prize; in it he aims to make a characteristic link between painting and poetry: "The last pictures by Braque call on all his painting." At Verrières, he gazes at his Braque, a beach or bank of sand, a black sea, a blue mark, all surrounded by a big black frame.

Malraux chooses a selection of poems by Louise de Vilmorin. He wants to preserve his reserve and have them published as is. Claude Gallimard suggests "giving a text." "I think," says the publisher, "that it would be a shame if no writer were to pay her homage; can you think who we could ask?"[17] There is only one person: Malraux. He has already edited some of Louise's notebooks, containing the aphorisms at which she excelled: "I am not interested in what people who write think, I am interested in what they say." Was she talking about herself or André? In his preface to Louise's poems, Malraux is reserved but still describes himself: "A legend matters little when it does not disfigure the works." Conscious of Louise's legend, he takes the opportunity in his introduction to denounce the "episodic society gossip" that surrounded their life at Verrières and ricocheted onto him.

Malraux receives writers, commentators, and journalists he trusts at a staggering rate for a man of his age and prestige. He is not just hanging on to life; the living are hanging on to him. He likes the critic Frédéric Grover, a remarkable specialist on Drieu, which makes a difference to Malraux. When they meet in summer 1975,[18] Grover is struck by the attention Malraux openly pays to all things mysterious, irrational, and enigmatic. Before, the writer's alibis were more classical: Christianity, Hinduism. He confides to Grover, "What interests me, above all, is the question 'What can be transmitted to Man beyond what is intelligible?' "

Does this question mean anything? Malraux, without having read Wittgenstein, is getting close to what he called "mysticism," the ineffable beyond the bounds of the intelligible. The writer admits insistently, "In considering Man to be enigmatic, I am not at ease in the intelligible."

Briefly, Malraux thinks of another title for a work: the first volume of *La Métamorphose des dieux*, *Le Surnaturel*, could be called *L'Inaccessible*. He is still hunting for the Absolute, which, outside of mysticism, is inaccessible. Pilgrim visitors to Verrières are amazed at the way he talks about the Apocalypse and the Gospels, especially Saint John, Grosjean's favorite. Malraux's interest in Buddhism has almost disappeared. The same day as the conversation with Grover about the intelligible and the enigmatic, he talks to Sophie about his professional projects: "That's it, I've found a way to do what I have been wanting to for a long time: at last I can write *Les Métamorphoses de la littérature* as I wrote *La Métamorphose des dieux*."

With the encouragement of Claude Gallimard, he sets to work. For eleven years, from 1958 to 1969, the novelist and lover of literature was consumed by Art, through several books. Gallimard had asked him what he was going to write next. Malraux replied, "We're shutting up shop."

"You can get yourself forgiven," his editor parried. "Do the same thing on literature as you did on art."

André Malraux starts writing *L'Homme précaire et la littérature*, with frenetic application. It is an often impenetrable work, irritating and disconcerting yet admired.[19] Malraux wants, quite simply, to sum up literature. All of it. In his devotion to the plastic arts, he sought to uncover the secret of the gesture of genius. Now he wants to pin down the creative act in literature. He develops his ideas and shuffles them together. In his view the writer, like the painter or the sculptor, does not create to express himself but expresses himself in order to create. Man and literature are precarious, as Malraux is. The reader sometimes gets the feeling of whizzing through the literary centuries at supersonic speed in a surreal, *farfelu* film, espousing and exposing writers from Sophocles to Victor Hugo. And often Flaubert, who seems to hypnotize Malraux as much as he does Sartre.

He discusses the American detective novel and the Soviet novel, the latter in such a way as to consign it to the dustbin of history. He returns to his early love, the cinema, and compares it to Greek tragedy. Interspersing his work with abstruse elucidations, Malraux is not averse to making banal observations: "Fiction transmitted not only novelistic values but values in general." He prophesies with confidence, since it is also with hindsight: "One of the first ambitions of the novel, from that point on, would be to grasp the human experience through fiction; is that not how we would define *War and Peace*?"

In his search for the "unfathomable" (*l'insaisissable*) in literature, he acknowledges the impossibility of subjecting to reason "the problem of the meaning of life—less of a problem than an anxiety." Duly noted. A couple of years before,[20] he talked of this "moment in history where one becomes aware of metamorphosis as a law of the world." Isn't Malraux talking about himself here, from afar and from on high, with a dash of nostalgia? "The modern novel is a battle between the author and that part of the character which pursues him, always in vain, for this part is the mystery of Man." He repeats himself, his thought reaching further out but still forming a figure eight and coming back to the same point. He is still looking for a "vision of unfathomable forces" and the "metallic kingdoms of the absurd" that A.D., in *La Tentation de l'Occident*, perceived throughout the world. The quest might be considered vain, but it is his quest. Malraux was formerly interested in pataphysics, the "science" added on top of metaphysics. The attraction is still there.

On June 25, 1976, he receives a letter from Claude Gallimard: "I read *L'Homme précaire* attentively this week; I felt I was having one of the most troubling experiences of the mind and approaching the unfathomable in every powerful work. You have dizzyingly crossed the world of human creativity. I do not dare give you here an account of my thoughts, for I would only be paraphrasing you, which would be pointless [but useful]. I did, however, need to express to you my impressions after a first reading that gave me access to the world of the imaginary and to the secret of creation, but another reading will be necessary to get closer to the unfathomable."

The writer cannot accept the numerous projects offered him, especially films. He has written a will. When Grosjean sees Malraux, he finds his eyes black, shining, and dark but opaque. Malraux allows tenderness to show. His relations with his entourage are relaxed.

In August 1976, he is hospitalized at the Hartmann Clinic in Neuilly. They announce an ablation of the prostate. "Infectious tension," they say. "Treatment with antibiotics at home." France keeps quiet about the health of her *grands hommes*, ashamed or embarrassed about certain ill-nesses, especially cancer. Malraux is in fact suffering from "severely malig-nant cutaneous cancer, located in the pubic region and already having spread to the lymph nodes in the groin," writes Sophie de Vilmorin later. For a long time, neither André Malraux nor his companion utters the word "cancer." She thinks that Malraux has guessed the nature of his illness.

"You look a little tired this morning," she says.

"Don't say 'a little tired,' you know perfectly well that I am very ill."

He follows a course of chemotherapy by injection. Doctor Bertagna informs Florence. Only she and Sophie really know what is happening. Malraux tells his daughter, "You can't know how tired I am." In numerous letters, Sophie de Vilmorin explains that Malraux "is now happily cured but not yet convalescent."

After all the chemotherapy, it is congestion of the lungs that sends André Malraux to the Henri-Mondor Hospital in Créteil. Florence and Sophie, with her knitting machine, take turns at his bedside. Gogo de Karolyi rushes over. Words are found scrawled by Malraux on his bedside table: "It should have been otherwise." He dies of a pulmonary metastasis on November 23 at 9:36 a.m. He is buried at the cemetery at Verrières-le-Buisson. Two sprays of red flowers: one from the French Communist Party, the other from Lasserre restaurant. As much as a man, it is the dis-appearance of an institution, a myth. Tributes flood in from politicians and writers, old and new friends and enemies. Françoise Giroud, the junior minister for culture, has the flags in Rue de Valois flown at half-mast.

In February 1977, the unfinished book *L'Homme précaire et la littéra-ture* is released by Gallimard, having been printed without Malraux pass-ing it for press. A few pages, left in his desk, were inserted into the text by Beuret.[21]

In his will, André Malraux expresses a belated gratitude to Clara, bequeathing to her objects and items dating back to their original joint estate.

Legally, he is still the spouse of Madeleine Malraux. He made his daughter sole legatee and executrix for his work with Grosjean and Beuret. His two friends look after the essential part of his posterity. Trans-ferring his allegiance wholesale, Beuret puts himself at Florence's disposal for practical tasks. Malraux leaves debts to the tune of 3 million francs:[22] a third to Gallimard, a third to the tax office, a third miscellaneous. Galli-mard and the legatees absorb the debts by selling off pictures and the apartment on Rue Montpensier that Malraux bought before Louise's death. A revolver is found in a shoe box. Keeping a promise made to her father, "in case of death," Florence burns a thick envelope.

The fate, the chance, that Malraux so wanted to turn into necessity in some ways stole his death from him. Paul Nizan was killed by a German bullet, Jean Prévost died in the Resistance, Brasillach was shot by postwar justice, Drieu committed suicide. Malraux passed away quietly in his bed, like Gide. His work and his thrilling life seemed to invite a more heroic death. Then again, Rimbaud also died in a hospital bed.

L'Eternel
retour

Conclusion: Scars

To his contemporaries, fistfuls of gold coins were scattered by Malraux's hand. Counterfeit, often. For some who were twenty years old between 1930 and 1950, he reconciled action and literature, politics and ethics. Very early on, the writer wanted to score this world with "scars."

In the context of an ailing twentieth century, Malraux's tumultuous life sometimes looks like a prestigious comic strip. Apart from his wounds, real and imaginary, what does he pass on to us? A character and a body of work. Malraux's tone, the one that will be remembered, occurs first in *Les Conquérants*. The young man escaped from the insularity and the emotional agitation among the potted plants in Bondy and Dunkirk; he broke free of both provincialism and Parisianism. Not as a man of letters sequestered in his study but as a writer with a revolver on his belt—although he was a bad shot. He introduced striking left-wing militants into the novel, as Sartre would later place the café waiter into philosophy.

The pages of *Non* mark the dead end of this novelistic inspiration. In 1972, he spoke to Marc Chagall about his interest in this abortive work. He talked about *Non* in front of Admiral Philippe de Gaulle in Verrières in 1975 as if it were a book he was currently working on.[1] Did he know that he had already put the best of himself into the novels that posterity— "a stupid bet" according to Sartre—would retain? For Malraux, the classical novel was dead. He would doubtless have agreed with V. S. Naipaul: "The novel is not the fundamental intellectual form of our period. . . . It is no longer as important as when Balzac and Dickens started writing." Malraux genuinely believed in film as an alternative genre, but his readiness to think that the novel was moribund was also motivated by the fact that he had lost his touch for it. I no longer write novels, therefore the novel no longer exists. I shall therefore return to the novel that is me.

At sixty-six, Malraux the writer burst back onto the literary scene with a novelized account that was savored by the literary world at large and abhorred by historians: *Antimémoires*. Malraux clearly had a style, a tone of his own, but he did not invent a literary language as Proust, Joyce, or Céline did. Was Malraux a poet? One can read his texts on art as free verse; not as mode of explanation but as poetry, a means of expression; one lets one's mind wander. Will that style acquire the patina of age or just go rusty?

And then there are the words themselves, his preferred material; units of marvel and torture that he handled with intensity.

Malraux's rise in the 1930s coincided with the ascent of the two total-itarian systems invented by Europe. For years, he possessed his readers in the cafés on the Rive Gauche and the editors' offices on the Rive Droite. He was a genius at seduction, an authentic warrior, and a bogus combat-ant, in and out of service in Asia and Europe; a comrade and fellow trav-eler; an actor-director of himself; an unexpected cross between Oscar Wilde and Maurice Barrès. "My life does not interest me. That's clear, straight," he would say. In fact, his life interested him intensely. Malraux wanted to be, to do, and to seem more than he wanted to have and to hold. Yes, one can always be fascinated by his books and forget about the man, but one is depriving oneself of a character.

Before the age of eighteen, Malraux was a remarkable lower-middle-class youth with immense curiosity, intoxicated with words and his numerous talents. To his two sons and his nephew, he often quoted Hugo, a strong presence during his adolescence:

Mon père ce héros, au sourire si doux . . .[2]

Fernand Malraux, despite his handsome smile, was no hero. Did his son realize that? Emmanuel Berl said that Malraux regretted not having fought in the 1914–18 war; he would have liked to be decorated. And he was, eventually, more than his father. Was that a revenge on his childhood, a childhood without luxury but not without comforts? Did he want to erase his progenitor, the impenitent pretender? He replaced this untrust-worthy father with Literature, Adventure, Internationalism, Nation, Rev-olution, Art, and a range of totemic characters from his grandfather to Lenin and de Gaulle. His mother is a weighty absence. Do all mothers traumatize their sons? Some more than others. Berthe Lamy and the little brother who died made for a neurotic atmosphere. André Malraux tore himself away from it and escaped. Did that leave "scars"?

"That was his strength and his weakness," writes Jean Grosjean,[3] "to have triumphed over childhood without succumbing to the slightest maturity." During his entire life, Malraux was a rebellious teenager. "His death," Grosjean continues, "never contradicted his juvenile blend of ostentation and modesty . . . poverty dazzled him as much as splendor, but he had perhaps no less admiration for cynicism than for devotion."

Malraux saw himself as a politician and a statesman; he was Compagnon de la Libération and ministre d'état. From the largely Communist Left he turned away toward Gaullism, as did many French citizens, veterans of the ideological battle between the wars. Yet he was reproached for his desertion of communism, even by those outside the French Communist Party. Was his political evolution coherent, any more or less than theirs? Malraux avoided referring back to the Spanish period of his life in *Antimémoires*. In 1946, he passed on the idea of prefacing the French translation of Orwell's *Homage to Catalonia*. He could not, apparently, accept one of Orwell's fundamental ideas—that left-wing intellectuals had fought against the "brown" totalitarian regimes of Nazism, fascism, and Francoism—without also rejecting the "Red" totalitarianism of the Soviet Union and China. If the word "contradiction" means anything, the essential political contradiction of André Malraux is there. As an example of his century, he was, if not edifying, at least fairly typical. Yet he did not wait until the 1950s, as many others did, to turn his back on the Communist temptation. Still, we must also acknowledge that even afterward, he clung tight to Mao. André Wurmser, the Stalinist journalist, wrote in his obituary in *L'Humanité*, "Malraux made more Communists than he unmade."

Was Malraux really cut out to sink into the backseat of a ministerial Citroën DS and squeeze himself into a ministerial suit?

His decisions as minister in charge of cultural affairs can be approved of or disparaged on their own merits. The ministry itself is still part of the Fifth Republic, and it is often imitated abroad. Malraux helped to classify and save important parts of French heritage. He also contributed to the transformation of culture into an instrument of political power.

Malraux's influence on interior politics was limited by the fact that de Gaulle carefully avoided trusting his "genius friend" with a key ministry. Malraux was one of the first to claim that Gaullism ended with the departure of the General. As a ministre d'état he wanted to make his mark on international history. Unfortunately, he had the geopolitical weight of a butterfly.

He had a seventh sense for promotion, an aptitude for creating the propaganda to further a cause and advance his own character in one movement. Of all French writers of the twentieth century, he knew best how to use the press, the radio, and especially television. His imitators look foppish by comparison.

The lie, whether boastful, poetical, political, or risky, was a constant with Malraux. One thinks of Fernando Pessoa:[4]

> They say I pretend or lie
> All I write. No such thing.
> It simply is that I
> Feel by imagining.
> I don't use the heartstring.

Malraux the mythomaniac and his inventions are brilliantly justified, according to his loyal followers, from a literary point of view. Why shouldn't a writer elaborate a systematic vision of the world with lies (among other things) at its heart? It falls to the reader to accept or reject it. Jean Lescure was close to Malraux. He says today, "Is it my affection for Malraux that makes me claim that he never lied? We lied for him; he did not deny it. That didn't interest him."[5]

I asked Paul Nothomb if Malraux had always been a compulsive liar.

"Absolutely, as an artist, as a creator. For his sins he also mythicized History, which he took to be the modern form of destiny. And as such, he admired those who had played a role in it, such as Lenin and de Gaulle, the sort of role he dreamed of playing. But if you mean by that someone who ends up believing in the untrue things that he allows others to say about his life, even though he perhaps contributes to them to help cultivate his legend, then no. . . . He was playacting, but without ever, I am convinced, being fooled."[6]

I have my doubts about that. But the transpositions, myths, and metamorphoses that overlapped one another in his life were, on the whole, devoid of spite, malice, or pettiness.

Malraux forged an exceptional life for himself, not because of but despite and in opposition to his nervous tics. Like Mozart, Samuel Johnson, Émile Zola, and Franz Kafka, who also had to compromise with their Tourette's syndrome. Malraux overcompensated and dominated his physical difficulties. We still know almost nothing about the condition today. The disadvantages are talked about, but not the possible advantages for the exceptionally gifted. Might there be a creative connection between Malraux's Tourette's and his resolve, his lying, his apparent or real indifference? The dryness of his heart? What links also between his nervous tics, which he detested, and the spasms of his style? After 1972, Malraux stopped drinking and was less twitchy, physically, but his style often remained jerky. Without overemphasis, attention should be paid to this condition in the future. The syndrome does not explain Malraux, any more than Byron's clubfoot defines him, but it does perhaps allow us to understand him better.

Did he like himself? Did he like or love others? He enjoyed the brotherhood of soldiers, the friendship of priests, the company of women—not the same thing as loving women. The world according to Malraux is a masculine one. "It is true, women do not feature in my work. Not in Chateaubriand's either. The subject of my books did not lend itself to a feminine presence. . . . I cannot bring myself to imagine a female character." Several women dotted his life. Clara, for twelve years, and Madeleine, for twenty, were filled with wonder but not blinded. They lasted long and endured much. They knew too much. Josette Clotis did not understand the writer. Louise de Vilmorin entertained him. The devoted Sophie gave him a level old age. Gogo was a very pretty, brief, final, unrequited crush. "I think that M. has been very much loved by women," said Bergamin, "but I don't think he loved in return." "The father, the mother, the wife that Malraux loved the most was de Gaulle," says Florence Malraux with a laugh. Malraux admired himself but did not love himself. If it is true that one must love oneself a little in order to love others, Malraux carried a handicap, an invisible scar.

The writer had doubts about himself. After his death, a journalist interviewed Clara Malraux:

"And why did such a great man need to exaggerate?"

"I don't really know. . . . Probably because in the end he was not as sure of himself as one might think."

"And did he talk to you about his doubts?"

"No. But one felt them."[7]

Paul Morand, in the 1930s, saw in Malraux the only "living suicide victim." "He could not think about anxiety when he was very busy," emphasizes Grosjean. His whole life, Malraux battled against an internal panic and veiled it with panache. Humor was missing from his uneasy narcissism. Manès Sperber claimed that he had never known a man as unhappy as him. Was that an overstatement? Malraux's distance from women, his children, his friends concealed deep anxieties that Louis Bertagna helped him fight from 1966 onward.

Malraux asked himself questions about the Meaning of Life. He was a self-taught philosopher, and no doubt better off for it. His generation inherited the "death of God." "What is to be done with a soul if there is no God and no Christ?" asks Ch'en in *La Condition humaine*. Malraux wrote, "I am an agnostic, eager for transcendence, who has not had any 'revelations.' " What sort of transcendence? He managed to avoid that question: "We will talk more about this," he would mutter, when he hadn't talked about it yet. Malraux's giant albatross wings pinned him to the ground with his prophetic and apocalyptic tone: a huge issue . . . major point . . .

Doubtless Malraux benefited greatly from the capacities of the French language—the only one he knew—to pull off flashes of brilliance, rather than to make conceptual breakthroughs. Intuition, for Malraux, won hands down over reason. In his caves there glimmered flickering storm lanterns, the supernatural, fate, genius, and death. He believed no more in Reason and Progress than in the class struggle, scientific socialism, or other people's Gaullism. But he did believe, like many of his fellow citizens, that a higher knowledge exists; for him, it was metaphysics, encompassing all knowledge, revealing the essence of Man, touching the Absolute, piercing the secret of a masterpiece or of Art itself. Some believe in the possibility of "synthetic a priori propositions," to use the Kantian vocabulary. Such thoughts are matured in a study. Are not the real metaphysicians today those who work between the infinitely large and the infinitely small, astrophysicists and microbiologists, chemists, psychologists, psychiatrists, psychoanalysts, historians, sociologists, archaeologists, ethnologists, and demographers? In his last work, published after his death, Malraux came out with an odd question: "Why not accept God among the modern painters?"

While carrying out my investigations, I often thought of a quip of Jean Grosjean: "Malraux published more than he wrote." He also lived more than he wrote, but he lived in order to write. One must keep the man and the oeuvre together in one's mind. He invites us to do so: "I think I fought in Spain and in France for the same reasons that I wrote *Les Voix du silence*; it is absurd to think that I set art against the desire for justice. It is the same thing, in a different context." Very Malrucian logic.

Malraux was for a time a master of action for each new generation. He no longer is, but he has not ended up in the cruel scrap heap of politics, like Sartre, nor in a state of semisanctity, like Camus. All three survive primarily on the literary merits of their texts. Malraux, in addition, became a myth, as no other contemporary writer.[8]

In France, Malraux's "genius" is often acknowledged and discussed. Elsewhere his reputation remains disputed. The year after his death, the British historian Hugh Trevor-Roper declared that Malraux was a "charlatan" (then, shortly afterward, was unfortunately tripped up by a fake Hitler diary which he had guaranteed was authentic). Nabokov, who detested Malraux, stated that every great writer is an "illusionist." For me, the most endearing Malraux is the writer he was, and the loyal friend he could be, beneath the cracked masks of the militant, the prophet, and the minister. Was there a certain tenderness, an uncertain sentimentality even, behind his heart-handicapped selfishness?

"The uproar of trucks loaded with rifles covered a tense Madrid in the summer night . . . '¡Salud! . . .' " I pick up *L'Espoir* again with emotion. I reread the first part of *La Voie royale* with pleasure. The same goes for *Les Chênes qu'on abat* and *Antimémoires*, and fragments of *La Condition humaine.* I let myself be taken—had, if you like—by the funeral oration for Jean Moulin.

I accept the argument that the novelist has every right, that a piece of fiction is good or bad, not true or false, and that only a good novel "refutes" a bad one. The problem of truth arises elsewhere, in successive episodes of Malraux's life. Is the truth indispensable, salutary, worthless, or just impossible to establish? It would be unfair to say that this writer attached no importance to truth. From rare remarks on the subject ("I suppose that it is what is verifiable"), Malraux would seem to have opted for a coherence theory of truth—remarks that correspond among themselves—rather than a correspondence theory—the sum of the propositions that correspond to the facts. He built on what he experienced, and in a more assertoric mode than a demonstrative mode. Perhaps there is a link between his conception of the Truth, his yearning for power and his yearning to be seen as a thinker, his logorrhea and his graphorrhea, his refusal to say, "I don't know," his fear of an indifferent or absurd universe, and his Tourette's syndrome. Both the man and his work needed his mythomania to exist. It was an indispensable flaw, since his life was also, to him, an oeuvre, a creation, a statue. As he grew older, the split between his life and reality grew broader. A Jungian would perhaps say that his fantasies subjugated this reality by refusing it. He played with reality like an inventive child; he became his own favorite plaything.

In 1996, Malraux's ashes were transferred to the Panthéon in Paris. It was a ceremony on a national scale, without any blatant errors of taste.[9] Jacques Chirac, one year into his presidency, stood before the catafalque and gave a subdued speech. He used the vocative, most handy when speaking to the dead; you create an echo, but they don't answer you back. "André Malraux . . . You are the man of restlessness, of searching, he who opens his own path. . . . You will be one of those who take on the injustice of the world . . ." Chirac sang of Malraux's prescience, "Your exposure of Soviet totalitarianism, whose logic you understood very early on, earned you the ostracism of the Left while your past commitments seemed subversive to the Right." Very early? That evening, Malraux did not appear to be on the Left, the Right, or the Center. He was from elsewhere.

The ceremony, despite being initiated by intellectuals and academics, started with an error. The official program stated that Malraux had a "degree from the [School of] Oriental Studies." The first academic to propagate the myth of Malraux as student at the Langues Orientales was at the time a graduate from the École Normale Supérieure and a lecturer at the Institut d'Études Politiques de Paris: Georges Pompidou. By treating Malraux as a hero in his 1955 anthology *André Malraux: Pages choisies, romans,* Pompidou—who was not in the Resistance—was able to promote himself a little. Thus Malraux, after having gained access to the minipantheon of literature that is the Pléiade in 1947, was included in a scholastic pantheon at the age of fifty-four. Pompidou asserted that Malraux had been "wounded several times." He had fought "at Chiang Kai-shek's side." Malraux knew Pompidou; he let these slips of a panegyric go by uncorrected.

By a lucky coincidence, one year after Pompidou chose his "pieces," General de Gaulle gave his benediction to Malraux as a grand resistant with the publication of the second volume of his war memoirs (in June 1956). De Gaulle had been well informed, by Colonel André Passy, and knew that Malraux's involvement in the Resistance had been belated and symbolic. But he couldn't retract: Malraux had already been Compagnon de la Libération for more than ten years. Who, then, would have dared question these guarantors, Pompidou and de Gaulle? In the first volume of his *Mémoires d'espoir* in 1970, de Gaulle wrote, "On my right, I have and will always have André Malraux. The presence at my side of this genius friend, this devotee of higher destinies, makes me feel that I am shielded from the commonplace. The idea that this incomparable witness has of me helps to make me strong. I know that in debate, when the subject is serious, his lightning judgment will help me disperse shadows."

The same year as the Panthéon ceremony, the writer's Resistance reputation was still subject to inflation: "[Malraux] commands . . . the interior French forces, FFI of the Lot, the Dordogne, and Corrèze."[10] Yet ten years before, Guy Penaud had published *André Malraux et la Résistance*, a work that clearly undermined that reputation. The French press applied the law of silence to this book: it was an embarrassing document. Its author—neither a professional historian nor a member of the Parisian critical elite—was not consulted for the pantheonization. In Corrèze in 1996, the journalist Alain Galan attempted to sum up Malraux's life from 1942 to 1944. When it came to hearing witnesses' accounts and publishing them in their entirety, he ran into difficulties. His reports were unsettling. The legend of André Malraux, the immense Resistance fighter, suits Communists as well it does Gaullists, as much today as it did in 1996 or in 1946. Why the fakery? Everybody lied, everybody kept quiet, members and nonmembers of the Resistance protected one another with mutual secrecy: I'm going ahead, cover me. Not all the French were supporters of Pétain. Nor were they all members of the Resistance. Malraux, by joining the Resistance in the spring of 1944, is therefore an excellent average Frenchman. By predating his participation, he promotes the majority of his fellow citizens. The Alsace-

Lorraine Brigade was not enough. The national ego required an immaculate image.

On either side of the ceremony at the Panthéon, incense was wafted throughout France as an invitation to unite in ritual observance. Everywhere in the Métro, one read Malrucian quotes: "Death transforms Life into Destiny"; "I have learned that one life is worth nothing, but that nothing is worth one life." At the firm suggestion of the president's and prime minister's offices and the Ministry of Culture, the beast of bureaucracy was roused. The French State spent 22 million francs—$4.3 million—nothing at all, when you think that a summit for African heads of state cannot be organized for twice that amount.

The Comité National du Cinéma put on *Sierra de Teruel* in eight hundred cinemas. Suburbs and provinces were cajoled into action: Boulogne, where Malraux lived; Toulouse, where he was imprisoned; Strasbourg, which he liberated. A Malraux novel "at the teacher's discretion" was put onto the high school program for both the Literature and the Science Baccalaureate. How could France not have taken communion? Photographs of Malraux, in all his civilian and military costumes, were widely distributed, especially one of Malraux in 1945 in a beret, his colonel's stripes very apparent. *Elle* magazine launched a Malraux fashion with the advice "Copy the Malraux style . . . the literary look . . . cotton gabardine raincoat . . . in the Malraux look everything is irresistible . . . a style that will never go out of fashion." No writer had ever benefited from such official publicity. His sales doubled, for a time. Instant, homogenized biographies regurgitated all the simple, simplistic, distressing nonsense about him, the man. Everything and everyone was devoted to Malraux.

To see the writer beneath the man, to accommodate him, peeled clean of pretense, one has to screw up one's eyes; then one can detect his tragedies. He was an astounding character, unwilling to undergo a mediocre destiny. He believed himself obliged to correct reality, to metamorphose it with words. He let his militant self, the assiduous warrior within him, win over the writer. At the end of his life, he was as inebriated with himself as with words. His life fed his work—and very often fed on it.

But without this life where would the work be?

Camus recommended to Malraux some poems by Jean-Paul de Dadelsen. He wrote:

> *Nous somme nés pour porter le temps,*
> *Non pour nous y soustraire.*

> We were born to carry time,
> Not to elude it.

Malraux tried to carry his time. He was Barrès's literary son and
Chateaubriand's great-grandson. Did he make more of a success of his literary career than they? "My life is quite a novel," he often said, quoting
Napoleon. Who could deny that? For me, his two best novels will always
be the hybrid, powerful *L'Espoir* and his own staggering, rollicking life.

Dy able de la
Fidilils

ACKNOWLEDGMENTS

For their patience and assistance, for having entrusted me with their memories, letters, and unpublished documents, their critical commentaries and their savoir-faire, my sincere gratitude, among others, to the staff of the Bibliothèque Jacques-Doucet, the Archives Nationales de France in Paris, the Archives Militaires de l'Armée de Terre at Vincennes, the Ministry of Culture, the archives of the Musée de l'Ordre de la Libération, IMEC, the National Library of India in New Delhi, the Nehru Collection at the Indian National Archives, the Spanish Military Archives, the Archives of the Comintern, the Literary and General Archives in Moscow (which include documents taken from the French by the Germans, then from the Germans by the Soviets), the National Archives in Washington, the British SOE Archives in Kew, and so many members of the cultural relations departments ("*les cultureux*") of different countries. I am also indebted to the CIA, which showed me the file on Malraux, in part, but refused to show me mine; and to the holders of private archives, who sometimes wish to remain anonymous.

My thanks to Miguel Angel Aguilar, Victor Alba, Christine Albanel, Jean-Marc Alcalay, Henri Amouroux, Jacques Andrieu, René Andrieu, Agnès d'Angio, M.-A. Arold, Jean Astruc, François Avril, André Bach, Salim Bachi, Josette Barrera, Jacques Baumel, Paule-Renée Bazin, Jean-Jacques Bedu, Anthony Beever, Edward Behr, Yvon Bélaval, Nicolas Belorgey, Louis Bertagna, Nina Beskow, François Bizot, Peter Blake, Jacqueline Blanchard, Claude Blanchemaison, Délia Blanco, Carlos Blanco, Yves Bonnefoy, Claude Bourdet, Françoise Cachin, Madeleine Caglione, Agnès Callu, Jeanine Camp, Michèle Carteron, Curtis Cate, Alban Cerisier, Jacques Chaban-Delmas, Bertrand and Chantal Charpentier, Olga Chestakova, Jacques Chirac, Micheline Clavel, Hubert Colin de Verdières, Daniel Cordier, Olivier Corpet, José Courbil, Terzo Cricchi, Susheela Dayal, Catherine Delafosse, Jacques Delarue, Jean-Louis Desmeure, Hans-Georg Dillgard, Colette Dominique-Pia, Brigitte Drieu la Rochelle, Alain Dromson, Bernard Dumont, Jean-Jacques Dumont, Colette Durand-Pia, Élisabeth Dutartre, Bilge Ertugrul, Elvira Farrers, Isabelle Feldbrugge, Bertrand Fillaudeau, Michaâl Foot, Pierre Frechet, Diethard Freibig, Gisèle Freund, Elfriede Frischmuth, Robert Gallimard, Alain Galan, Augustin Girard, Françoise Giroud, Jean Gisclon, Henri Godard, Daniel Gotheil, José-Maria Grande-Urquijo, Sabine Gresens, Danielle Guéret, Yann and Olivier Guillaume, Philippe Guillemin, Claude Guy, André Haize, Jacqueline Hillaie, Georges Housset, Mireille Jean, Denis and Martine Jelen, Lionel Jospin, Catherine de Karolyi, Manfred Kehrig, Veena Kilam, Éva-Maria Koch, Alain Koniarz, M. Kushmar, Michel Laclote, Peter Lake, Jean-Claude Larrat, Hélène Lassalle, Jean Lassère, Marie-Ange Le Besnerais, Jacques Lecarme, Pierre Lefranc, Maggy Leroy, Marguerite Leroy, Jean Lescure, Jean Leymarie, Simon Leys, Karl-Heinz Loschke, Yves Mabin, Claude-Rolande Malraux de Wulf, Jean-Luc Marchand, Mariette Martin, Rachel and François Mazuy, Pierre Messmer, Pierre Moinot, Béatriz de Moura, Michaâl Niel, Valéri Nikitine, Patrick Nizan, Philippe Noble, J. Kevin O'Brian, Nikhil

Padgonkar, Jean-Louis Panné, Paolo Pasquale, Tomenec Pastor-Petit, Pierre Péan, Guy Penaud, Alain Peyrefitte, Lili Phan, Jean-Jacques Pimbert, Jacques Poirier, Jean Pouget, Lina Pournin, Clovis Prévost, Nicole Prévost, Rajesh Radha Sharma, Dom Hilari Raguer, Serge Ravanel, Michèle Renso, Jean-François Revel, Agnès Rich, Alain Richard, Maria-Fernanda Roa, Pierre Rosenberg, Michèle Roson, André Rossfelder, Pierre Salinger, François Samuelson, Sandrine Sanson, Claude Santelli, Walter Schäfer-Kehnert, Dominique Schnapper, Maurice Schumann, Dominique Seurin, Nadine Solé, Jenka Sperber, Bernard Spitz, Mathilde Sten, Duncan Stewart, Ezra Suleiman, Antoine Terrasse, Tiphaine Tesnière, Aurélia, Emmanuel and Samuel Todd, Catherine Trautmann, Bernard Tricot, Vladimir Trouplin, Ute Überschaer-Livonius, Hubert Védrine, Catherine Vellisaris, Marie Vidailhet, Corinne, Sophie and Sosthène de Vilmorin, and Arnim von Wieterscheim.

And a special mention to Florence Malraux, Georges Liébert, Claude Travi, Arnaud Jamin, Bénédicte Delorme-Montini, Sylvie Lanuci, Madeleine and Alain Malraux, Jean-Pierre Dauphin, Philippe Delpuech, and Jean Grosjean.

NOTES

I. HEROES AND CONFECTIONERS

1. 1868: Fernand-Jean; 1870: Georges; 1873: Georgina-Mathilde; 1875: Fernand-Jean (André's father); 1877: Édouard-Maurice; 1879: Marie-Mathilde; 1881: Mathias-Numa; 1883: Lucien-Alphonse. The two Fernand-Jeans explain the mistakes of biographers who attribute only five, six, or seven children to the prolific Alphonse.

2. Mathias-Numa was crushed by horses in the courtyard of his father's house.

3. The survivor must live up to his predecessor. Often, the dead child has a mysterious, threatening influence as an irreplaceable rival.

4. Current studies suggest that the cause of Gilles de la Tourette's syndrome is related to chemical imbalances affecting the neurological transmitters used by the brain to control movement and behavior. Research continues in biochemical, pharmacological, and genetic studies of Tourette's patients and their families. Today, as then, "Tourette's children" fare better in a school environment that is not too rigidly structured. The proceedings of the Salpêtrière Hospital in October 2000 established that the origin of the syndrome is unknown and that there is currently an absence of clinical consensus and uncertainty as to diagnostic criteria, a limited number of studied cases, and a multitude of theories. Malraux did not suffer from echolalia (the repetition of what other people have just said) or from coprolalia (recurrent obscene outbursts).

5. The official death certificate for Alphonse has him dying at sixty-seven years of age, not seventy-six. The document has misled the most careful editors and biographers, knowing the reinterpretation of Alphonse's death through legend: Malraux refers to it in *La Voie royale*, *Les Noyers de l'Altenburg*, and *Antimémoires*. In the first of these: "One day, intending to show a young, slow worker how they split the wood for the prow in his day, he was overcome by a giddy spell just as he was wielding the double-bladed ax and split his head open." André Malraux would often allow people to believe, and perhaps believed himself, that Alphonse had committed suicide.

6. Art lovers might compare this childhood work with a painting by Braque that Malraux later owned, now the property of Florence Malraux.

7. Both these works still exist. Madeleine Malraux collection.

8. Military files of Lieutenant Fernand Malraux. Army History Department, Vincennes archives.

9. Chevasson confirmed this in a television broadcast in 1981, "André Malraux, le destin d'un jeune homme," edited by Jean-Marie Rouart and Sylvie Genevoix. The story no longer exists—or is in the hands of a discreet collector.

10. To this day there is no convincing evidence one way or the other: no end-of-term reports, no notes from teachers. Biographers have taken their inspiration from Robert Payne's interview with Mlle. Thouvenin. Payne stated that Malraux was "first in history and drawing, second in spelling, third in French literature and English, fourth in geography and math, fifth in handwriting, sixth in chemistry and natural science." Malraux had no particular talent in physics, gymnastics, or singing. He did not do Greek or

Latin. He was taught clay modeling. In *seconde* (at sixteen) he was top of the class. Curtis Cate draws from Payne and adds that "he developed such a keen interest in clay modeling that he came first in this discipline. The following academic year (1917–18) he moved up to first place in handwriting, as in clay modeling, and to second place in French literature. He was placed third in diction and drawing and fifth in a course of 'civic instruction,' and sank to eighth place in the natural sciences. The most significant changes were the decline in his artistic skill with the pencil (from first to third place) and his ascension in French literature, where, according to one of his Turbigo schoolmates, Marcel Brandin, he was second only to the *lycée*'s star pupil." Who overtook him? A certain Perlman, "the son of a Jewish cloth-maker." This information is not improbable but cannot be verified and should be treated with caution.

11. Malraux talked of this later, with nostalgia, to Roger Stéphane.

12. Malraux is regularly quoted by biographers as saying that he "did not like his childhood," suggesting that it was a difficult one. The loyal Louis Chevasson denied this amiably.

2. ADOLESCENCE OF A LEADER

1. He later denied this repeatedly, declaring to his daughter Florence that he had never written any poems.

2. *Ô mon âme sensible et malade, ô mon âme, / Vois revenir le jour encore plus vide, vois / Près de la lampe éteinte et du foyer sans flammes / Revenir le jour pâle et triste comme toi. Hélas, amie, hélas! Tu te trahis toi-même! / Comme le sable au vent ton courage s'enfuit, / Fais de ton lourd dédain d'inutiles poèmes, / Tu vas vivre de force, ô mon âme, aujourd'hui.* Florence Malraux collection.

3. The owners of the manuscripts do not, for the present, wish them to be made public.

4. Curtis Cate, *André Malraux: A Biography* (Hutchinson, 1995).

5. Auguste Vaillant bombed the Chamber of Deputies on December 9, 1893. He was tried and executed within two months. Tailhade's comment: "*Qu'importe de vagues humanités, pourvu que le geste soit beau!*" (What do vague humanitarian considerations matter, as long as the deed is noble!) [Tr.]

6. October 1920, *Action*, no. 5.

7. In the preface to a catalog of first editions and pictorial works, 1929.

8. *The Books of Hell* by Pia, a classic, reprinted by Fayard, 1988.

9. Bernard Loliée collection.

10. Within the bound issues of the review *Littérature*. Bibliothèque Nationale.

11. See Madeleine Malraux and Inigo de Satrustegui, *André Malraux: Dessins* (Bordeaux: Ed. Mollat, 1998).

12. *Vers l'azur d'une autre rade / Loin de la terre malade / Du désir et de l'ennui / Et notre cœur s'est enfui / La rose de grenade / S'est ouverte enfin pour lui.*

13. Arrested in 1919 and accused of multiple murders, Henri Désiré Landru was a focus for the surrealists' fascination with "pulp" news stories. He was guillotined in 1922. [Tr.]

14. The grouped texts had appeared in *Tintamarre*, a literary journal. But who knew?

3. THE STRANGE FOREIGNER

1. In June 1921.

2. Picasso, at the time, used to keep a Browning on him. Again according to Clara, April 6, 1922.

3. Letter of October 2, 1921. Doucet collection.

4. See André Vandegans, *La Jeunesse littéraire d'André Malraux*. Vandegans, in his indispensable work, evokes Malraux's interest for *The Phantom Chariot*, the work of the filmmaker Victor Sjöström. Vandegans explains that Malraux, twenty years old in 1921, deserves credit for being interested in this avant-garde art. For Simone de Beauvoir, the cinema would primarily be an amusement for "skivvies."

5. The original titles: "Les hérissons apprivoisés," "Journal d'un pompier du jeu de massacre," "Écrit pour un ours en peluche," "Lapins pneumatiques dans un jardin français," and *Écrit pour une idole à trompe*, respectively.

6. These influences are also dissected by Vandegans in his book. His analyses are clear and subtle, if not always convincing.

7. The twelfth and final issue of *Action*, entitled *"Aspects d'André Gide."*

4 . FALSE THIEVES?

1. Élie Faure's *History of Art* in five volumes: *Ancient Art* (1909); *Medieval Art* (1911); *Renaissance Art* (1914); *Modern Art* (1921); *The Spirit of Forms* (1927).

2. See Pierre Assouline, *An Artful Life: A Biography of D. H. Kahnweiler, 1884–1979*, tr. Charles Ruas (Grove Weidenfeld, 1990).

3. French Overseas Archives, Aix-en-Provence. Most of the documents in this chapter come from this collection.

4. October 13, 1923.

5. December 16, 1923, on British India Steam Navigation Company paper. Miss Whitling is on her way, and she knows Angkor.

6. Telegram from the Office of Political Affairs, November 19, 1923.

7. The Groslier report says, "I notice after more detailed research that the *Banteay Srei*, the scene of Messrs. M. and C.'s exploits, is not the no. 575 of the inventory. It is another *Banteay Srei*, unnumbered, about ten miles to the north of 575. It does not appear in the inventory. Its mention should therefore be struck from my statement and replaced with 'Banteay Srei, near the Phnom Dei to the northwest of Angkor.'" The second "temple" was no more than a heap of stones.

8. This man knew how to be a lover "while remaining a friend," she says in her *Memoirs*.

9. Author's interview with Madeleine Giteau, 1998.

10. Judge Edmond Jodin's decision of July 21, 1924.

11. Today, pillaging in Cambodia is taking place on an industrial scale.

12. Roland Bonaparte (1858–1924): wealthy traveler, tireless photographer, would-be anthropologist, and Napoleon's great-nephew. [Tr.]

13. *L'Impartial*, November 15, 1924.

14. See Maurice Glaize, *Les Monuments du groupe d'Angkor*. In Angkor today, pirate copies of the book are sold.

15. See, among others, Daniel Wildenstein and Yves Stavidrès, *Marchands d'art* (Plon, 1999).

5 . TRUE REVOLUTIONARY?

1. This dialogue turns up in *La Condition humaine* (*Man's Fate*) nearly ten years later, between Kay and her husband.

2. French Indochina consisted of Cochin China, Annam, Tongking, Cambodia, Laos, and Kuangchou. [Tr.]

3. See letter from Malraux to Marcel Arland of March 19, 1925. Malraux talks

of "having Pia come almost immediately ... I am asking him to come first because he will have a practical role that you could not have or at any rate would not like. You will take mine; that will work better." Pia does not go to Saigon, and neither does Arland.

4. The council was composed of twenty-four members and had no real powers other than the ability to express opinion. The "French" had fourteen seats, eight of which were allocated at the discretion of the governor and the Chamber of Commerce. Ten "natives" were elected by 26,000 Cochin Chinese.

5. French Overseas Archives, Aix-en-Provence. Monguillot was acting governor-general.

6. A FAREWELL TO ARMS

1. In China, Malraux met nobody of any importance, and certainly not Borodine from *Les Conquérants*. So he did not go to Canton.

2. Still called *L'Indochine* on the cover.

3. Most come from the French trading posts in India.

4. Malraux (and Monin) are clear-sighted here. Up until the end of the Vietnam War (1975) the French authorities subsidized a French-language newspaper, *Le Journal d'Extrême-Orient*: cautious, conservative, and obedient. There is one significant difference between rats and politicians: the former draw certain conclusions when they get an electric shock at a particular point in a maze. After two or three tries, they avoid this point. Politicians don't.

5. *Section Française de l'Internationale Ouvrière*, the French Socialist Party. [Tr.]

6. Centrist coalition from 1924 to 1926. [Tr.]

7. This incident is *one* of the sources for the first scene of *La Condition humaine*. Monin, not Malraux, was the subject of an assassination attempt.

8. Walter Langlois collection. This letter on headed paper from the Continental Palace Hotel in Saigon is dated October 4, 1925. From Malraux's announcement that he has almost finished his book, we cannot deduce that it is true. He later gives information that is false: half of the work has *not* been translated into Chinese. There has been no prepublication in the Shanghai and Peking papers. In the definitive version there are hardly any annotations by one of "their Indian friends." Malraux, it would seem, wrote only a certain number of fragments during his newspaper's troubled period.

9. Malraux later published two texts about Indochina: an article in *Marianne* in 1933, and a preface to Andrée Viollis's book *Indochine S.O.S.*, in 1935. This silence surprises many commentators, as does the fact that he based no stories or novels on his Cochin Chinese sojourn, which is not the case for the Cambodian adventure. Monin remained a collaborator on the paper he founded with Malraux. He denounced Varenne's politics and actions more and more violently, especially when Varenne called for the dispatch of ten thousand reinforcement troops from Paris. He also had the new editor in chief, Le Thi Vinh, publish the entire text of the *Déclaration des Droits de l'Homme et du Citoyen* (Declaration of the Rights of Man and of the Citizen) even though the paper had only a few pages. Monin was no longer editor, but he remained the central pillar of the paper. He and his family left Indochina at the beginning of March 1926. The nine organizers of his leaving party, to which Annamese and "French friends from all classes of society" were invited, were Indochinese.

10. Gabriele D'Annunzio (1863–1938), Italian anarchist, First World War hero, and sometime French resident, who annexed the Yugoslavian port of Rijeka (Fiume in

Italian) in 1919 to Allied disapproval and subsequently declared Fiume an independent state. [Tr.]

11. Asked on television in 1967 by Roger Stéphane why he had gone to fool around in Indochina, Malraux answered, "It's the most intelligent thing I did!" Roger Stéphane, *Entretiens et précisions* (Gallimard, 1984).

7. EXOTIC PARISIAN

1. After the Perken from *La Voie royale*.

2. See the work of Philippe Noble, Du Perron specialist and translator of (among others) his *Un Néerlandais à Paris* (Méridon, 1997). The original edition of *Pays d'origine* dates from 1935, in Dutch. Héverlé figures in the *Pays d'origine* translated by Noble.

3. Translated as *The Temptation of the West* by Robert Hollander (New York: Vintage Books, 1961).

4. After the publication of *La Tentation de l'Occident* in *Les Nouvelles Littéraires* of July 31, 1926.

5. Some also see in Wang-Loh a sketch for Gisors from *La Condition humaine* because of his "great distinction" and his aristocratic allure.

6. *La Tentation de l'Occident* seems to present insurmountable difficulties to literary geneticists, with manuscripts and typescripts that are missing, incomplete, or composite. There is no final draft. One can suppose that Malraux took some *L'Indochine* headed paper away with him: some pages of *La Tentation de l'Occident* are written on this paper. In Saigon in the last months of his stay, Malraux had time to spare.

7. See Daniel du Rosay's notes in the first volume of the *Œuvres complètes* (Complete Works), published by Gallimard (Bibliothèque de la Pléiade) in 1989.

8. See Jean-Jacques Bedu, *Maurice Magre: Le Lotus perdu*, (Dire, 1999). Contrary to a persistent legend, Malraux was never an opium addict. He was not "on file" with the police, like some writers.

9. This article was in *Europe*, June 15, 1932. The other articles referred to here were for the *Nouvelle Revue Française* between 1926 and 1932.

10. Around 1927, undated letter. Gallimard Collection.

11. Letter of January 4, 1927. Gallimard Collection.

12. Letter of October 27, 1927. Gallimard Collection.

13. See *Europe*, November–December 1989, a presentation of André Malraux's letters to Jean Paulhan by Claire Paulhan and Christiane Moatti.

14. The text is apparently a fake written by a Viennese psychoanalyst. See Isabelle de Courtivron, *Clara Malraux: Une Femme dans le siècle* (Éditions de l'Olivier, 1992).

15. Letter of December 22, 1927.

16. A political work collectively written in 1594, worthy of inclusion in the canon for literary as well as historical reasons. [Tr.]

17. Group of poets from the end of the fifteenth to the beginning of the sixteenth century. [Tr.]

18. Malraux had the idea of this *Tableau de la littérature française* in 1928. The project later succeeded, with volume 2 (from Corneille to Chénier) appearing in 1939 and volume 1 (from Rutebeuf to Descartes) in 1962. A third volume (from Mme. de Staël to Rimbaud) was published in 1974.

19. See *Europe*, letter of 1928.

20. Ibid., 1928–1929.

21. Letter of April 15, 1929, published in no. 16 of *Cahiers François Mauriac*, Grasset, 1989 (from the Claude Mauriac collection).

22. In May 1927. For Malraux, this film is a masterpiece in the history of cinema and Eisenstein one of the great directors. "There is cinema before and after *Potemkin*, before and after *Mother*" (the film by Pudovkin, after the book by Gorky), he wrote in 1934 in one of his rare articles for *Marianne*.

23. From August 19 to 29, 1928.

8. ASIATIC PATHS

1. *The Conquerors*, trans. by Winifred Stephens Whale (New York: Harcourt, Brace, 1929).

2. *The Royal Way*, trans. Stuart Gilbert (Smith & Haas, Methuen, 1935).

3. Not with Clara but for others. Clara confided that she had never had to have an abortion, as did so many women at the time.

4. Mikhail Markovich Gruzenberg, aka Borodin (1884–1952). [Tr.]

5. With the benefit of hindsight, Malraux sees Garine like this more than twenty years afterward.

6. Letter from Malraux to Martin du Gard, October 23, 1928.

7. In *Mort de la pensée bourgeoise* in the spring of 1929.

8. "This book could immediately class its author among the greatest novelists of the time," proclaims Auguste Bailly in *L'Intransigeant*. Breathlessly, Robert Kemp murmurs for *La Liberté*, "Malraux is somebody." André Billy sighs in *L'Œuvre*, "We would not be turning away from novels if they were all like this one." In *Rond-Point des Champs-Élysées* (Grasset, 1935), Morand, detecting the obsession with death, writes, "His heroes all perish or disappear; isn't that because they all personify one of the questions to which our generation has not been able to find any answer? These ghosts that Malraux has fed with his anxiety obsess him, and he kills them off." In 1937, Morand publishes *Papiers d'iden-tité*, a more laudatory piece (dated 1929).

9. June 8, 1929.

10. See the preface by Jean Grosjean and the postscript by Philippe Delpuech in *La Vie de Napoléon par lui-même*.

11. Malraux makes copious corrections to these extracts for the forthcoming book.

12. My second "declaration of interest" (see introduction): I will admit to being (too much) influenced by Anglo-Saxon empiricists. Technically, the "meaning of mean-ing" presents similar difficulties to those of the principle of verification: How do we ver-ify the principle itself?

13. Some critics cannot cut the cords with the Banteay Srei affair. For them, Van-nec and Perken are crooks, "two rogues." Malraux makes some corrections in respect of these caustic remarks. See the text of *La Voie royale*, presented, established, and anno-tated by Walter Langlois in *Œuvres complètes*, vol. 1 of the Pléiade.

14. In *Candide*, November 13, 1930: "A Quarter of an Hour with André Malraux." Among the well-known critics in the running for the Lack of Insight Awards from 1925 onward, André Rousseaux would be a good candidate, for his work on Camus as well as Malraux.

9. COMMERCIAL TRAVELER

1. Letter of July 29, 1933.

2. Published in 1932, translated by Ralph Manheim as *Journey to the End of the Night*.

3. Irmgard Keun, 1932; new U.S. translation by Kathie von Ankum (Other Press, 2002).

4. Letter of September 8, 1933.

5. Thus, at Drouot, July 2 and 3, 1931, the collections of André Breton and Paul Éluard were sold at auction. "Sculptures from Africa, America, Oceania . . ." Africa: 30 pieces, statuettes, masks, bracelets . . . Oceania: 150 pieces, bird figure, decoration from boat, Kriss handle . . . America: 125 pieces, amulets, spoons, pipes . . .

6. Postcard to Chevasson in 1931.

7. The journalist was probably frightened off by this detail: the Hephthalite Huns, or White Huns, from Sogdiana and from the Bactrian reached Sassanid Persia, Gandhara, and, later on, the north of India.

8. From "L'écrivain archéologue" by Gaston Poulain in the January 2, 1931, issue of *Comœdia*. An indirect appeal in journalese: "Who sculpted the stones Mr. Malraux brought back from the Pamir?" Curtis Cate was the first to refer to this interview.

9. Most of the documents quoted here come from the gallery's archives. The other shareholders were Camille Ardant, Joseph Barnod, Philippe Clément, Frédéric Duché, Frédéric Delorme, Lorrain Maurice, Jean Parmentier, Joseph Simon, and Roland Tual.

10. Supplement to the report of the board of directors for 1933. A profit is foreseen, almost with sadness, for the year's activity in 1934. That's official accounting for you.

11. According to Curtis Cate, Strzygowski loses his way in proto-Nazism. He "detested the classic art of Greece, reserving his admiration for the art of nomads, particularly when it tended towards abstraction."

12. Letter of September 22, 1931.

13. The Sinologist Simon Leys: "This is a feeble and inappropriate characterization. The powerful originality and interest of the Ch'an come from the fact that it is the most *sinicized* form of Buddhism: Ch'an is basically Taoist philosophy dressed up in Buddhist clothes." Remarks made to the author, 2000.

14. Both knew Asia well. Segalen had cultural preoccupations, noting certain disastrous consequences of Western civilization. He aimed to banish any Eurocentric perspective. Claudel, an appointed diplomat, had come to the end of his third stay in the Far East in 1926. His outlook was large, and Malraux adored his poetry.

15. Maurice Martin du Gard, *Les Mémorables*, vol. 3 (Éditions Grasset; new edition by Gallimard, 1999). Preface by François Nourissier, annotations by Georges Liébert. In the course of my investigations, I have seen several very generous "gifts" from Malraux. Some beneficiaries or heirs prefer to remain anonymous.

16. The Prix Goncourt was to give him the means he needed. In 1935, he earned 6,000 francs ($400) from the gallery, and nothing at all after 1937. Numerous pieces were dispersed under the Occupation, between 1940 and 1944. Then Malraux claimed and received some pieces to sell or keep.

10. 1933

1. According to Nicole Racine, Malraux must have joined the AEAR in 1934. See *Le Mouvement Social*, no. 54, January–March 1966.

2. See, among others, Alan Sheridan's biography, *André Gide: A Life in the Present* (Harvard University Press, 1999).

3. These four works were translated as *The Fruits of the Earth* (Knopf, 1949), *Travels in the Congo* (Knopf, 1929), *Return to Chad* (Knopf, 1929), and *The Journals of André Gide, 1889–1949* (Knopf, 1947–1951).

4. Words reported by the publications of the AEAR and republished in *Mélange Malraux Miscellany*, 17 nos. 1–2 (1985).

5. *Ah Dieu! que la guerre est jolie / Avec ses chants ses longs loisirs* (from *L'adieu du cavalier*).

6. Alfred Dreyfus (1859–1935): Jewish French Army officer accused on flimsy evidence in 1894 of passing military secrets, stripped of his rank, and deported. Political forces on the Left (the *Ligue des Droits de l'Homme*) and the Right (the *Ligue de la Patrie Française*) were concentrated on either side of the question: it was the major political crisis of the period. Émile Zola's open letter "J'accuse" protested Dreyfus's innocence. Retried after five years, reconvicted, and pardoned, it was only in 1906 that his former rank was restored. Evidence exonerating Dreyfus conclusively was made public in 1930. [Tr.]

7. Archives of the *Académie Goncourt* in Nancy. The winner was not decided, or not unanimously, after the first round.

8. In 1934, Doctor Alexander Banyai corresponds with Robert Aron at Gallimard to negotiate with Malraux; he will, Aron says, be able to recover the movie rights. When Malraux and Eisenstein have worked seriously on a screenplay, Robert Aron continues to look for producers, thinking that Eisenstein's work will be "propaganda" and will not be able to be shown elsewhere. The rights would therefore be freed. Aron asks for an advance of 75,000 francs ($5,000) on a 3 percent cut of overall profits from the movie. Many movie and stage adaptations are made or planned, including a stage version of *La Condition humaine* by Anthony Broom in the United States in September 1937.

9. Letter from Malraux to Aron. Raymond Aron Institute. Sometime at the end of 1933. (Malraux has the bad habit of often failing to put a date on his letters. Those who have them have not always kept the envelopes. Why this absence of dates? Affectation or carelessness? A bid to outrun time or chased into haste? Or just to tease biographers?)

10. This is not Malraux's usual trick. He recognizes his debt toward Wieger in a letter to Suzanne Lain on June 7, 1958.

11. Séverine Charret, in her remarkable master's dissertation, "La 'Révolution chinoise' d'après *Les Conquérants* et *La Condition humaine* d'André Malraux" (University of Lyon–II, 1998), counts eighteen Chinese, "which is not many among the forty-two principal characters of *Les Conquérants* and *La Condition humaine*." In *As-tu vu Cremet?*, then *André Malraux, le roman d'un flambeur* (Hachette-Littératures, 2001), Roger Faligot and Rémi Kauffer have discovered a new documentary source for *La Condition humaine*, an ex-leader of the French Communist Party, Jean Cremet.

12. Before Mao, applying the original strategy of relying on the peasantry, took power in 1949.

13. Letter of August 24, 1933.

14. See Séverine Charret.

15. October 2, 1933.

16. Clara later confides, "At the time all men would withdraw." Reacting as a woman, a coquette, or a *bourgeoise*, Clara had decided that they would have a child—or rather, that she would get herself pregnant by Malraux. They "took precautions" but the Knaus Ogino method and *coitus interruptus* both carry risks.

17. She freely admits it only in 1945.

18. Alain Malraux, *Les Marronniers de Boulogne* (Bartillat, 1996).

19. Later, when her father is separated from Clara, Florence stops walking for a time.

20. It is risky to date the chronology of the meetings with Josette Clotis. Malraux shoveled sand over the tracks of his private life.

21. In French *un pingouin* is, strictly speaking, an auk; the exact word for penguin is *manchot*, although of course *pingouin* is commonly used for both. [Tr.]

22. Louis Chevasson's interview with Jean-Pierre Dauphin, February 21, 1977.

23. Most of the details given about the beginning of the affair and concerning its long continuation are drawn from Suzanne Chantal's book, to which Malraux wrote a preface—without, it would seem, having read it first. Suzanne Chantal makes Josette Clotis into a heroine. What she recounts, in abundant detail, may be true, or it may not. The overall effect is of a dialogue between two characters in a boulevard comedy. This is the sort of thing: "She is overcome by a distant self-absorption. . . . In her dreams, she lives with André in trouble-free harmony. . . . When he is there, her love for him destroys everything."

24. June 24, 1933.

I I. THE QUEEN OF SHEBA

1. Most of the sources for this chapter are from the files of the French Overseas Archives, Aix-en-Provence.

2. "Captain Chales" may be General Maurice Challe, later involved in the "Generals' putsch" in Algiers in 1961. It could also be the Captain Challe who, in December 1929, made the second direct flight between Europe and South America. Georges Guynemer (1894–1917) was a legendary hero of French aviation.

3. February 12, 1934; see Julien Caumier, *Leurs dossiers R.G.* (Flammarion, 2000). A report confirms that Malraux is a "pacifist and anti-Fascist," as well as a member of the Association des Artistes et Écrivains Révolutionnaires, president of the "Ligue de Défense contre l'Antisémitisme," president of the Comité de Libération de Dimitrov, president of the Comité de Libération de Thaelmann, honorary president of the Comité Directeur des Amis du Peuple chinois, and president of the "Comité Mondial Antifasciste."

4. He returns to it two years later, in a letter to Gaston Gallimard of June 12, 1936.

5. In *Antimémoires*, Malraux returns to the unfindable kingdom, the lost city, and this Arnaud, the ideal companion.

6. See Curtis Cate, *Malraux*.

7. Gabriel Dardaud, *Trente Ans au bord du Nil* (Lieu Commun, 1987).

8. Malraux's expedition leaves behind traces. Cf. the report of the French *chargé d'affaires* for the Kingdom of Saudi Arabia in Jedda, June 19, 1935. During these years, French diplomats undergo gentle reproach by the imam, who is convinced that Malraux is a spy. Two years later, the *chargé d'affaires* writes, "Judging by the observations made by those who saw Malraux's plane, it would seem that it got no farther than the plateau of Sanaa and the surrounding valleys. Our compatriot may unwittingly have mistaken for temples some relatively modern constructions made of large blocks of stone piled on top of each other. He did, I think, mention a very large water tank that I have myself seen, which in fact dates from the Himyarite era, but it is on the Sanaa plateau itself."

9. Gnome & Rhône flight logbook, April 1934.

10. To choose one of many masterpieces, *Scoop*.

11. Later, Malraux in *Antimémoires* recomposes the scene: "Here is the Negus . . . he is sitting on a sofa bought at Les Galeries Lafayette in front of his dignitaries in togas. . . . The interpreter calls M. Corniglion-Molinier *M. de la Molinière*, because the Negus received some German noblemen two days before." Malraux adds

that he hears "through the windows the roaring of the lions of Judah. Their cages have for centuries run along the great walkway of the Negus's Palace."

12. Malraux uses it, not long afterward, in *Le Temps du mépris*.

13. Letter to René Lalou, April 30, 1934. René Lalou, father of Étienne Lalou, was a literary critic and deliciously cranky English teacher at the Lycée Henri-IV.

14. The articles are interspersed in publication. Malraux publishes articles on May 3, 4, 6, 8, 9, 10, and 13; Corniglion-Molinier on May 5, 11, and 12.

15. See André Malraux, *La Reine de Saba*. A "geographical adventure." Text introduced and annotated by Philippe Delpuech, preface by Jean Grosjean (Gallimard, 1993).

16. To enjoy and understand Malraux's articles, see Philippe Delpuech's work: "The eternal traveler also knew that numerous expeditions had been attracted by the mysterious city of the queen of Sheba. That of Jean-Louis Burckhardt from Switzerland, who was the first European to get into Arabia and die there; that of the German Corsten Niebuhr, who had to flee before the hostile population near Mareb; that of Joseph Arnaud, a chemist from the French Lower Alps, who claimed to have found the capital of Balkis (the queen of Sheba) and copied inscriptions that no Westerner has ever seen since; that of Joseph Halévy, in 1870, who managed, disguised as a rabbi, to reach the city and take casts of the ruins; that of Glaser, an Austrian, who succeeded in entering the forbidden town four times and brought back eight hundred sketches; that of Germans Carl Rathjens and Hermann von Wissmann, who cleared the ruins of a temple devoted to Illumquh, god of the moon, and another devoted to Balkis, and indicated the ruins of a gigantic dam on the Adhanat river with two remaining towers."

17. Walter Langlois, one of the most eminent scholars of Malraux, is working on a book on the whole queen of Sheba episode.

12. TROTSKYIST TROPISM

1. France could have been better informed. Boris Kritchevski, the Moscow correspondent for *L'Humanité* (then a socialist paper), described the totalitarianism and use of terror from 1917 onward and understood the mechanism and effects of Leninist communism. See Christian Jelen, *L'Aveuglement* (Flammarion, 1984).

2. Plans for the project, if they ever existed, were apparently destroyed or removed from the Gallimard archives during the Second World War. The scheme was thought up in a somewhat boozy meeting with André Beucler.

3. April 1931.

4. A few years later, the Left's fascination with and admiration for terrorism gave way to a devotion to communism. Malraux, on this point, was a front-runner in the twentieth century.

5. August 1933. Two accounts of the meeting are combined: Malraux's own, published in April 1934 in *Marianne*, and Jean van Heijenoort's in Maurice Nadeau, *Sept Ans auprès de Léon Trotski* (*Les Lettres nouvelles*, 1978). The Malraux-Trotsky conversations took place on August 7 and 8.

6. In his account of the meeting, Malraux states that Trotsky "talked of the *Lenin* he was going to work on." According to Jean van Heijenoort, this book was not part of Trotsky's projects.

7. But he does send him *Le Temps du mépris* just before the International Writers' Congress of 1935.

8. See Jean-Louis Panné, *Boris Souvarine* (Laffont, 1993).

9. See Emmanuel Todd, *La Chute finale* and *Le Fou et le prolétaire* (Laffont, 1976 and 1979, respectively).

10. When Pierre de Boisdeffre expressed his amazement at finding no mention of Trotsky in *Antimémoires*, Malraux interrupted him: "That's because he's not in there yet!" However, he was never added. In a 1972 television program, "Légende du siècle," in front of Claude Santelli and Françoise Verny, Malraux did an imitation of Trotsky at their Saint-Palais meeting.

13. SOVIET COMRADES

1. *Lili Brik, Elsa Triolet: Correspondance, 1921–1970* (Gallimard, 2000).

2. The "journal," often in shorthand, comprises about sixty pages. Fonds Granville, a gift from Richard Anacréon.

3. Handwritten manuscript on *NRF* paper, July 29, 1934. Moscow Literary Archive.

4. The Soviet State Secret Service had several names. December 1917: Cheka. February 1922: Incorporated into the NKVD under the name GPU. July 1923: CGPU. July 1934: Reincorporated into the NKVD under the name GUGB. February 1941: NKGB. July 1941: Reincorporated into the NKVD under the name GUGB. April 1943: NKGB. March 1946: MGB. October 1947–November 1951: Foreign espionage transferred to KI. March 1953: Merged with the MVD to form a larger MVD. March 1954: KGB (today, FSB). I owe this information to Thierry Wolton. The KGB is not to be confused with the GRU, the Military Information Department, which also had outposts abroad. Competition between them obstructs the facts.

5. Koltsov was shot in 1942. Too many favors can be a bad thing. Ehrenburg, atypically, survived.

6. The rationing system was abolished for food items on October 1, 1935.

7. Interview in *Literaturnaya Gazeta* of June 16, 1934.

8. Author's conversations with Henriette Nizan, 1940–1975. Also by her, see *Libres mémoires*, collected by Marie-Josée Jaubert (Robert Laffont, 1989).

9. Letters pasted into a school exercise book, hidden during the war at La Merigote, their house near Poitiers. Some are signed "J. R. Bloch": these are shorter "notes." Now held at the Bibliothèque Nationale; brought to the author's attention by Rachel Mazuy.

10. Is there an allusion to Boleslava in *Lazare*? "Images of Spain start again to swirl in songs and in defeat. In Madrid I saw that girl again that I loved in Siberia when the light from the Soviet factories lit up at the foot of the steppes like the hope of the world."

11. Later English translation: *The Black Book and Schwambrania* (Moscow: Progress, 1978).

12. "André Malraux in Western Siberia," *Sibirskie Ogni*, no. 4, 1934.

13. See Sophie Cœuré, *La Grande Lueur à l'Est: Les Français et l'Union soviétique, 1917–1939* (Seuil, 1999).

14. Letter from Paul Nizan to his mother.

15. August 15, 1934: Congress begins. August 23, evening session: Malraux's speech. August 25, morning session: Unprogrammed speech by Malraux. September 1: Congress closes.

16. See Emmanuel Todd, *La Chute finale: Essai sur la décomposition de la sphère soviétique* (Laffont, 1976).

17. Some leave the stage altogether: of the seven hundred "writers," including translators and publishers' readers, participating in the 1934 conference, fewer than sixty survived to 1954 to take part in the second Writers' Congress. In 1934, 70 percent of them were younger than forty. Despite deaths due to the war, there should have been many more survivors. Socialist realism was unquestionably Stalinist and murderous.

18. In a daily paper called *New Life*, banned in July 1918. Gorky's article was entitled "Lenin and His Associates."

19. After the congress, Gorky's relationship with the government deteriorated. His son was allegedly liquidated by the NKVD. Before his death in 1936, Gorky was kept under surveillance in a luxury residence.

20. General Vitali Primakov, who was also eliminated.

21. Speech published in the *Moscow Journal*, September 1, 1934.

22. At Bukharin's request, Pasternak publishes a poem that, without naming him, celebrates Stalin as a "genius of action." He is considered an opponent after Bukharin's trial in 1938.

23. Malraux chatting to Muscovite journalists in August 1934, published in *Internatsionalnaya Literatura*.

24. This is where Malraux "saw" Stalin. On several occasions, before and after the Second World War, Malraux was asked if he had known Stalin and what he was like. Malraux replied, "The opposite of how they say. He looked like a kindly warrant officer. It is often said, memorably by Solzhenitsyn, that he was short. It is quite possible that he became shorter. General de Gaulle certainly lost between four and six inches. But the Stalin I knew was my height, five feet ten and a half, he wasn't short. Just as what they call his 'lost cat' mustache only came at the end. When I knew him, he was tall, he was sturdy. It was before the purges, although he had already done many things, but nobody considered him a tragic figure. He had this very benevolent air, a million miles from the tragic, Shakespearean ghost we have been told of." Stalin had started the purges *before* the Writers' Congress that Malraux attended and was not exactly considered a comic or benevolent character. Malraux *imagined* Stalin and also saw him through Charles de Gaulle's eyes.

25. See Robert Conquest, *The Great Terror* and *Harvest of Sorrow* (American Philological Association, 1986). The trials, which involved torture and false confessions, started in 1928. Andrei Bychinski, the most important piece in the mechanism, was deputy prosecutor from June 1933.

26. Malraux's friend Ilya Ehrenburg was allowed the rare favor of a large five-room apartment in Moscow. Specialists such as Alexis Berelovitch argue that a dacha is both a sign of enslavement and a place of discussion and freedom. An interesting point of view that deserves discussion.

27. August 28, 1934, under the headline "Foreign Avant-Garde Writers Attending Conference Give Us Their Opinion." The avant-garde is not very well thought of, formalism even less so. Jean-Richard Bloch is also interviewed.

28. Letter from Drieu to Nizan, September 5, 1935.

14. TIME TO CHOOSE

1. Translated as *Days of Wrath* by Haakon M. Chevalier (Random House, 1936).

2. Nos. 258, 259, and 260, from March to May 1935.

3. *Le Monde*, June 6, 1935.

4. Rirette Nizan told the author in the 1960s, "Paul-Yves [Nizan] laughed about this sort of article: '*Il faut ce qu'il faut*' [you have to do what you have to do]." The demands of history take precedence over literary quality.

5. *L'Humanité*, June 17, 1934.

6. File on Nizan. Comintern Archives, Moscow.

7. As they are in a striking way in *Antimémoires*, more than thirty years later.

8. These manuscripts are in the Malraux collection in the Bibliothèque Jacques-Doucet. They are referred to by Robert Jouanny in the Pléiade *Œuvres complètes*, vol. 1. Jouanny's work is also enlightening on the critical reception of *Le Temps du mépris*.

9. In front of Roger Stéphane, after the Second World War, Malraux called *Le Temps du mépris* "rubbish" (*un navet*). For a long time he refused to have it reprinted. This is one reason why so much fuss is made of the preface, which is less clear than it appears, and so little fuss is made of the story, which is less bad than people say.

10. See *L'Opium des intellectuels* by Raymond Aron, *La Tentation totalitaire* by Jean-François Revel, the work of François Furet and Ernst Nolte, and the work of George Orwell.

11. This subterfuge was revealed by Jean-Louis Panné.

12. In an interview with Jean Lacouture in January 1972, Malraux claims the merit of having invited Pasternak and Isaak Babel by force. But Babel was already in Paris on June 21.

13. See the retouched report in *Commune*, September 1935.

14. Comintern Archives.

15. In September 1935.

16. The young journalist Albert Camus later talks of "slavery" in Algeria.

15. FROM EISENSTEIN TO *L'HUMANITÉ*

1. Shorthand transcript of discussion about Malraux at the Soviet Writers' International Commission, February 19, 1935. Moscow Literary Archives.

2. His translation is deemed bad by the Writers' Union; a second translator is put on the job and helps himself freely to Romov's text.

3. September 2, 1934.

4. In 1954, Jean-Paul Sartre repeats similar nonsense.

5. For Malraux, Eisenstein, and political cinema, see John J. Michalczyk, *André Malraux, unité de l'œuvre* (La Documentation Française, 1989).

6. Annotation by Malraux: "Added to which, the works that strike us, the directors, as most significant, and that have made Russian cinema a success abroad, are not generally held in higher esteem here than many others; there is on this point an error of perspective."

7. Another annotation: "In the USSR, it is forbidden to enter the auditorium during a show."

8. See the Malraux-Eisenstein files in Moscow at the Special Archives and at the State Institute for Cinematography. Consulting the dossier, one has the feeling that Eisenstein and Malraux were thinking of different films.

9. This extensive synopsis is, with the text published by Gallimard, the only existing document concerning the Malraux-Eisenstein collaboration. In a letter to John J. Michalczyk, Malraux indicated (in 1971) that he had worked with Eisenstein "for a few days" but that Eisenstein "had prepared everything." Eisenstein apparently wrote and kept the shooting script. To the actor-director Jean Vilar, Malraux said that the text was

completely finished and that Eisenstein and he had written it together. The scenario in the Russian archives differs from that in the Pléiade *Œuvres complètes*: the latter is more like the novel.

10. From *Man's Fate*, trans. Haakon M. Chevalier (Smith & Haas, 1934).

11. Remarks and drawings by Eisenstein about *La Condition humaine* dated December 20 to January 6, 1935. Literary Archives, Moscow.

12. She disappeared or was shot between 1939 and 1944, partly because she knew the Malraux brothers. On her arrest, Babel asked his wife to warn Malraux immediately (see her account in Chris Marker's documentary film *The Last Bolshevik*).

13. For *Literaturnaya Gazeta*.

14. Confidential report by T. Rocotov to the Personnel Department of the Comintern, November 29, 1937.

15. He had not read Joyce's novel either. He liked only classic literature (and socialist realism). He did not understand formalist or symbolist poetry.

16. See the *Memoirs* of Ervin Chinko, who lived for a while in the same apartment as Babel and wrote down conversations with him.

17. Stalin had been present at the premiere of *Lady Macbeth*. He was seated too close to the orchestra and was bothered by the brass instruments. Hence the negative reviews across the board for Shostakovich, denounced as a formalist by some who loved the opera at the time. See Pierre Herbart, *La Ligne de force* (Gallimard, 1958).

18. See the memoirs of Antonina Pirozhkova, *Mémoires sur Babel*.

19. Unless the anecdote is an invention by Clara: wanting to destroy one myth, Clara sometimes constructs another.

20. The present author and his Russian colleague Olga Chestakova found nothing in the ritual "biog" prepared by every militant Communist invited by or sent to Moscow.

16. STALINIST TEMPTATION

1. The center obtained 526,615 votes, of which 125,714 were for the Basque Nationalists.

2. May 24, 1936.

3. For a historical perspective, see Renzo De Felice, *Interpretations of Fascism*, and Pierre Milza, *Mussolini*.

4. In *Avant-Poste* 3, October–November 1933.

5. "To become a Communist because one has read Marx," Malraux later said, "seems to me ill mannered. It is true that I don't like Marx. Without Groethuysen, I would not even have understood him." Interview with Dominique Desanti, published in *Le Nouvel Observateur*, November 29–December 5, 1976, under the title "Deux Fantômes Amis."

6. From June 19 to 23, 1936.

7. July 19, 1936.

8. See Andrée Bachoud, *Franco*.

9. In a telegram to Léon Blum, July 20, 1936.

10. See the journal *Icare* on the Spanish war, vol. 3, 1994, especially Ramón Salas Larrazabal, "Les Grandes Périodes de la guerre aérienne."

11. Many commentators claim that Malraux reached Spain on July 20. Others say that he was still in Paris on the twenty-second. One way or another, he got himself to the Spanish capital quickly.

12. *L'Humanité*, July 27, 1936.

13. See Daniel Cordier, who in *Jean Moulin: L'Inconnu du Panthéon* (Éditions JC Lattès, 1989), bases his comments on *documents*.

14. Henri Puget, the *directeur du cabinet*, Cordier notices, styles himself "the champion of nonintervention."

15. In 1937, Berl, for whom Stalin was a warmonger, explained his own position in a short essay, "*Le Fameux Rouleau compresseur.*" He opposed a Franco-Soviet alliance: he thought it would give Germany the impression that it was held in a vise and would provoke war.

16. From August 1 to 17.

17. Malraux often told this anecdote later. See, among others, his interview with Claude Santelli for *Les Cent Livres des hommes* published in *Télérama*, March 14, 1970.

18. At least that is what is claimed by the seemingly trustworthy historian Jesús Salas. The head of Republican aviation, the Communist aristocrat Hidalgo de Cisneros, later declared that 80 percent of planes were in the hands of the government.

19. They received $100 per week and 300 pesetas per month, with room and board paid for. At home, a mechanic would earn $80 a week or 230 pesetas per month. Others recruited by the American Communist Party in New York had monthly contracts: $1,500 for Bertram Acosta, for example. Another, Edwin Semons, bureaucracy only knows why, got only $750. See "La Question des contrats" by Angelo Emiliani, Italian historian of aeronautics, *Icare*, vol. 2, on the Spanish War.

20. Estimates vary. R. S. Thornberry sets the figure at 175. A member of the squadron who was present from the outset, Yann Stroobant, claims there were never more than 130.

21. Nothomb is anxious to point out that this was more of a title than a function.

22. Darry signed a contract in Madrid on October 12, 1936, for 50,000 francs, more than $3,000 a month.

23. There were two named Bourgeois in the España Squadron.

24. "L'aviation française et la guerre d'Espagne," by Victor Véniel, in *Icare*, *La guerre d'Espagne*, vol. 1. Véniel says of Bourgeois, "I know that in 1937, with no papers, he left for China with three other French pilots who had flown in Spain, Labussière, Boulingre, and Poivre. Like the others, he never came back."

25. These figures, corrected after a conversation with Paul Nothomb, were compiled by R. S. Thornberry in 1970. He obtained information from survivors himself. To this day, it seems, there exists no official list of members of the squadron, neither in France nor in Spain, nor in the Russian archives.

26. Yann Stroobant, corresponding with Claude Travi, furnished him with very useful information on the squadron's pilots and equipment.

27. There can be no doubt that he took part in some missions.

28. Letter from Yagüe to Franco, August 16. Pointed out to the author by Colonel Carlos Blanca Escolá and Miguel Angel Aguilar. The former has published a work on Franco's "military incompetence."

29. See Robert S. Thornberry, *André Malraux et l'Espagne* (Droz, 1977). It is not Malraux but his admirers that make it a decisive feat of arms. Even if *España* had been able to wipe out an entire column (around 525 men) throwing bombs by hand (with no bomb launcher), it would hardly have slowed the advance of Franco's several regiments—a minimum of 30,000 men in the area.

30. September 3, 1936.

31. See Jean Gisclon's books and interviews with the author, 2000.

32. It turns up in *L'Espoir* and at the heart of the film *Sierra de Teruel*.

33. From September 4 to 8.

34. This anecdote is aired again in 1945.

35. October 5, 1936.

36. Author's interview with Margot Devélere, 1997.

37. Patrick Lereau, "*Les Mercenaires et les volontaires*," in *Icare, la guerre d'Espagne*, vol. 2, 1989.

38. Interviews with the author, 1997 and 1998.

39. October 29, 1936.

40. See Julian Gorkin, *Les Communistes contre la révolution espagnole* (Belfond, 1978).

41. On August 27, 1936. See *The Black Book of Communism*, edited by S. Courtois, and the archives of the Comintern. The ambassador attends council sessions of the Republican government: our old friend Koltsov has an office at the War Ministry. Out of 3,000 Soviets in Spain, fewer than 100, mostly pilots, are in fighting units.

42. See Gustav Regler, *The Owl of Minerva*, 1960.

43. Report typed by Marty with alterations by hand, on the "overall situation of the international forces and brigades" as of February 19, 1937 (Comintern Archives, Moscow). Malraux is no longer in Spain at that point. The idea of liquidating Malraux and others buzzes away in Marty's head.

44. Reports by Marty, still extant in the Comintern archives, show a violent paranoia about intellectuals. The heaviest dates from the war. With Luc Durtain and Paul Nizan, André Malraux earns a paragraph: "[Malraux], at the beginning of the war [WWII], at the Chilean Embassy, in front of a Communist Embassy Councillor [*Conseiller d'ambassade* in G.D.), embarrassingly lost his cool. Aragon's wife was asking him for a signature for an appeal in favor of an intellectual. He went into a violent anger, declaring verbatim, 'Communists, you can just shut up / Keep quiet; for you there is only one solution: the wall.' " Quite the opposite of Malraux's position, as we shall see.

45. See Pierre Herbart, *La Ligne de force* (Gallimard, 1958).

46. Or so it is said. It is hard to see how, in a bomber cabin, he could have made himself heard. Max Aub's testimony on the radio. See also Denis Marion's work.

47. The Third Reich provides 600 aircraft, 100 tanks, about 1,000 heavy guns; il Duce throws in 660 aircraft, 150 tanks, and another 1,000 or so heavy guns.

48. Gide, *Journal*, September 4, 1936.

49. Dolores Ibarruri (1895–1989), known as "La Pasionaria," Communist member of the Cortes, militant Republican supporter, and orator. [Tr.]

50. Jan Ferak went on to pilot a Tupolev bomber. Jean Darry served the Republican Air Force until the end of 1938. He was shot down.

51. See David Diamant, *Combattants juifs dans l'armée républicaine espagnole* (Renonceau, 1974).

52. Julian Gorkin, *Les Communistes contre la Révolution espagnole*.

17. AGITPROP

1. R. S. Thornberry and Claude Travi have drawn up records that agree, except in a few details.

2. From a speech by Malraux, "Forging Man's Fate in Spain," *The Nation*, March 24, 1937.

3. March 7, 1937.

4. Some (rare) commentators claim that Malraux was a member of the Communist Party, with or without a membership card. The idea is inadmissible. His file in the Com-

intern archives does not contain the required "biog." Nor, apparently, does that of the KGB.

5. Translation published by Knopf as *Afterthoughts on the USSR*, 1938.

6. Isaac Deutscher is the first to notice this censorship, in his work devoted to the life of Trotsky.

7. March 1.

8. *The Nation* prints the complete text.

9. For a French example, see "André Malraux attaqué par Trotski," *Commune*, May 1937.

10. One of the most recent estimations. See Rémi Skoutelsky, *L'Espoir guidait leurs pas.*

11. April 20, 1937.

12. See Andrée Bachoud, *Franco.*

13. April 26.

14. April 2, 1937.

15. *Le Devoir,* April 5, 1937.

16. "Did you see any scars or wounds on his body?" I asked, in 1999, two women who were very close to Malraux. Loyally, one response, with a smile, was "I didn't look." The other: "No." Malraux's army medical records have disappeared from French military archives.

17. Interview with Edith Thomas, April 22, 1937.

18. *Commune*, September 1937.

19. Stephen Spender, *World Within World*, 1951, and conversation with the author at Cambridge, 1950.

20. July 3, 1937.

21. Impossible to say how much, given the current state of the archives.

22. See Jean-Sébastien Tourneur, *Bergamin*, "Cahiers pour un temps," Centre Georges-Pompidou, 1989.

23. Account in *Frente Rojo*, mouthpiece of the Communist Party of Valencia, July 5, 1937, taken up by Thornberry.

24. July 7.

25. Orwell published *Burmese Days* and *The Clergyman's Daughter* after his first book to be noticed: *Down and Out in Paris and London*, 1933.

26. Curtis Cate, *Malraux.*

18. WHAT HOPE?

1. A furnished apartment at 9 Rue Berlioz, in Josette's name, for 2,500 francs per month, then one in Royal Versailles, Rue de Marois, for 1,600 francs ($72 and $46, respectively).

2. Published in a translation by Stuart Gilbert and Alastair MacDonald as *Man's Hope* (Random House, 1938).

3. In his *Antimémoires*, the absence of his Spanish period is striking. He said to Roger Stéphane, "The weight of Spain is too great."

4. From October 11 to 22, 1938.

5. The manuscripts, writing paper, and notebooks referred to here are in the Malraux collection at the Bibliothèque Jacques-Doucet. For amateurs or specialists of literary accountancy in one form or another, the word "*fraternité*" occurs at least twenty-six times in the novel; the atmosphere, notion, and climate of brotherhood carry through the entire work. For an analysis of the different states of Malraux's novels, see Christiane

Moatti, *Le Prédicateur et ses masques: Les Personnages d'André Malraux* (Paris: Sorbonne, 1987).

6. Jean Carduner, in *La Création romanesque chez Malraux*, sees, in this music and the phonograph at the end of the book, "a discreet allusion to the symphonic composition of the book." Surely an exaggeration: the book's composition is rather filmic and journalistic (which is in no way a criticism).

7. Letter of October 26, 1937.

8. Letter from Malraux in the 1960s to John L. Brown, quoted by Brown in *Hemingway* (Gallimard, 1961). As usual, it would seem that Malraux imagines a meeting—neither true nor false but experienced—with all the force the imagination can bring to bear on the possible.

9. Among the last to have heard Malraux's unfavorable comments about Hemingway was Bruce Chatwin (see his *What Am I Doing Here?* [Cape, 1989]). Malraux succeeded in persuading Chatwin that he was a flying ace. Hemingway later punned cruelly that Malraux "pulled out of the war to write a materpisse."

10. Letter to Robert S. Haft, March 2, 1959. Doucet collection.

11. See *Homage to Catalonia*.

12. Colonel de Gaulle writes, almost at that time, in *Vers l'armée de métier*, that the leader "must keep in his possession a part that is secret."

13. Robert S. Thornberry has proposed definite, probable, or possible identifications of the characters of *L'Espoir*. Some critics face the following dilemma: Should we accuse Malraux of using mostly characters he had met or delight in the fact? Should he be criticized for not having given us completely convincing Anarchists, given that he hadn't spent much time with them?

14. Malraux later said, "When one introduces a love story into a revolutionary combat [*he must be thinking of Hemingway*], that really is the limit!" Radio broadcast on *Europe 1*, October 25, 1967.

15. In Spain, Malraux's admirers scratch their heads when faced with this character. Commenting on the novel with a smile, President Azaña apparently said that it had taken a French intellectual to make a colonel from the Guardia Civil talk in a such a metaphysical way.

16. The well-known historian and Republican Hilari Raguer, of the monastery of Montserrat near Barcelona, finds that Ximenez-Escobar "well deserves" Malraux's admiration. Meeting with the author, Montserrat, 1997, and letter of August 4, 1997. Raguer likes *L'Espoir*. He notes that the Nationalist soldiers are represented mostly by North Africans. "It seems that on the rebel side there are only Moors, with German and Italian planes, tanks and cannons."

17. Numerous critics take this, Clara's version of events, on board. It is plausible up to a point. Clara certainly made some suggestions, and more than Josette. From Malraux's manuscripts and documents alone, it is not possible to confirm or deny Clara's version.

18. Five pages (218 to 223) in the Pléiade *Œuvres complètes*.

19. See David Bevan, *André Malraux: Towards the Expression of Transcendence* (McGill-Queen's University Press, 1986).

20. See the rich pages of Pierre Daix's *Dictionnaire Picasso* ("La mauvaise réception de *Guernica*") and the pages on the world wars. Robert Laffont, 1995.

21. January 5, 1938.

22. January 1, 1938.

23. Henriette Nizan, conversations with the author, 1948–1975.

19. SIERRA DE TERUEL

1. Some critics, academic and otherwise, have suggested that *L'Espoir* was conceived for the screen or that Malraux had always had the adaptation of the novel for the cinema in mind. No oral or written evidence seems to support this hypothesis. On the other hand, that Malraux was taken by the process of editing film and that he used a quasi-filmic time frame in his novels are points beyond question. Josette Clotis's friend Suzanne Chantal claims that he was thinking of that film *before* having written a single page of the novel. That's another way of looking at it.

2. Later on, Malraux spoke of cinema as the "first world art" when, as minister of culture, he gave the closing speech at the Cannes Festival in 1959.

3. *Commune*, September 1936.

4. *Commune*, November 1934.

5. See Denis Marion, *André Malraux: Cinéma d'aujourd'hui* (Seghers, 1970).

6. Author's interview with Elvira Farreras, Barcelona, 1997.

7. Suzanne Chantal wrote that long afterward, Malraux remembered this contribution to the film: "A note from him, short and concise, three lines of his little writing, reminded me, while I was writing *Le Coeur battant*: 'You mustn't forget to say that the scene in the film where the women take the children away when the stretchers pass, on the way down the mountain, was Josette's and that she was very keen on it.' "

8. This is an allusion to an Alexandrine anecdote: during the performance of a play about the Median Wars in the theater at Antioch, the messenger announcing the arrival of the enemy fell, killed by a real arrow. Denis Marion *dixit*; see also Max Aub's account in the preface to the Mexican edition of *Sierra de Teruel* (Ediciones Era, 1968).

9. September 30 and December 6, 1938.

10. Clara dates it 1934–35.

11. August 18, 1939.

12. Jean Cocteau, *Journal, 1942–1945* (Gallimard, 1989).

13. Later, in 1975, he tells Georges Soria that he was short of money and that *Sierra de Teruel* could have been a very good film. See Georges Soria, *Guerre et révolution en Espagne 1936–1939* (Robert Laffont, 1975).

14. See André Vandegans, *La Jeunesse littéraire d'André Malraux*.

15. There are several versions of the film with variations in editing at the Library of Congress and the George Eastman House. Film buffs will find a screenplay, commentaries, and more in François Trécourt and Noël Burch, *Espoir Sierra de Teruel* (Gallimard, 1996), and Max Aub, *Sierra de Teruel* (Ediciones Era, 1968). The Malraux legend goes from strength to strength: on the videocassette of the film generally available in France, he is described as having "led for six months the first squadron in the Republican Air Force." The Republic did have *some* planes before the arrival of *el coronel*.

16. This "book" can be dated to this period, since Malraux very clearly says that his reflections are "born of experience" that he "acquired while filming parts of *L'Espoir*," from which he "tried to make a film." Modest for once, in the 1946 edition he says that the title, *Esquisse*, "is rather ambitious for some notes written seven years ago," which takes us back to the end of 1938 and the beginning of 1939.

17. It is in fact in "L'Œuvre d'art à l'ère de sa reproductivité technique," which appeared in the *Zeitschrift für Sozialforschung* in 1936.

18. Malraux, letter to his wife, October 1939.

19. Deposition of July 14, 1939.

20. THE PHONY WAR

1. *Sûreté* note, April 2, 1939.

2. See Paul Nothomb, *Malraux en Espagne;* also interviews with the author, 1999–2000.

3. $1,104, $276, and $125 respectively, at 1939's rates. Statement dated January 7, 1939.

4. This novel about David de Mayrena, the self-proclaimed king of the Sedang in Indochina, was apparently intended to be part of a huge ensemble called *Les Puissances du desert,* of which *La Voie royale* was to be the "tragic introduction." Malraux worked on the novel at the beginning of the 1930s but never finished it. It occurs as a scenario presented by Clappique in the first edition of *Antimémoires* in 1967. See Walter Langlois's notes to the Malraux Pléiade, vol. 1, pp. 1139–46.

5. Letter from Henriette Nizan to Malraux, undated.

6. "Intelligence, what a very small thing on the surface of ourselves. Deep down, we are emotional beings." Maurice Barrès, *Cahiers,* 1896.

7. Contrary to popular belief, the BBC never aired this fine and famous phrase.

8. Author's interviews with Jean Grosjean, 1997.

9. Translated by A. W. Fielding as *The Walnut Trees of Altenburg* (Lehmann, 1952).

10. Letter to the author from Jean Grosjean, September 2, 2000.

11. See *Europe,* November–December 1989, presentation of letters from André Malraux to Jean Paulhan by Claire Paulhan and Christiane Moatti and the IMEC archives.

12. Perhaps the only match for him in the twentieth century in this respect was Jacques Lacan during his lectures.

13. See *André Malraux, 1939–1942,* based on unpublished letters edited by Walter Langlois.

14. Letter of December 13, 1941.

15. May 29, 1941.

16. Letter to Louis Fischer, November 25, 1941.

17. Postcard dated September 22, 1941, communicated by Jacques Lecarme and Brigitte Drieu la Rochelle.

18. For more details on this correspondence, see the author's *Albert Camus: A Life* (Knopf, 1997).

19. Louis Veuillot (1813–1883), Catholic journalist and staunch defender of the infallibility of the pope. [Tr.]

20. A movement created—and blown up out of proportion—by François Mitterrand.

21. Author's conversation with Hans Schaul, East Berlin, 1962.

22. Published after his death in 1996 in *Œuvres complètes,* vol. 2.

23. See Jean Grenier, *Journal sous l'Occupation* (Éditions Claire Paulhan, 1999).

24. Postcard to Gaston Gallimard, January 21, 1942.

25. On July 16 and 17. After three days in the "*Vel d'hiv,*" they were transported to Auschwitz. The deportation is commemorated in Paris annually. [Tr.]

21. THE WAR OF THE PHONIES

1. Not all of Malraux's partners were as appreciative in this domain.

2. Letter dated 1941. See Alain Malraux, *Les Marronniers de Boulogne.*

3. The Special Operations Executive was created by Churchill over the summer of

1940 to organize operations in countries occupied by Germany. The SOE had one department per country.

4. Florence Malraux found the letter after the death of both her parents.

5. *Introduction to the Philosophy of History* (Beacon, 1961).

6. Letter of February 2, 1943.

7. Pataphysics, founded by Alfred Jarry, saw itself as "the science of what is added on top of metaphysics."

8. December 1942.

9. Letter from Josette Clotis to Drieu, September 24, 1943.

10. Author's interview with Maurice Schumann, 1996.

11. In November 1942, as the Americans and British landed in Morocco and Algeria, Pétain refused to do what many hoped he would: namely to leave France for North Africa with as much of the French fleet as possible, placing France alongside the Allies. [Tr.]

22. THE MALRAUXS OF THE RESISTANCE

1. The information in this chapter concerning the three Malraux brothers is drawn partly from the military files of the Bureau Résistance at Vincennes and the SOE archives in London, which have been accessible since 1999. Roland's dossier at the SOE no longer exists. André's is wafer-thin.

2. By Pierre Kaan, a teacher and friend of Sartre (author's interview with Daniel Cordier, Antibes, 2000); and by Bertrand de Jouvenel (see *Un voyageur dans le siècle, 1903–1945* [Robert Laffont, 1980]).

3. Which he puts to Louis Chevasson *in writing* on February 5, 1945. Doucet collection.

4. Other Malrauxs from around Dunkirk were active in the Resistance early on: an uncle, Lucien Malraux (member of the MLN), and a cousin, Pierre, who was arrested on June 4, 1941, and condemned to death. The sentence was commuted, and he was deported to Germany.

5. Author's conversations with Colonel André Passy in 1981 and Claude Bourdet in 1990.

6. Author's interviews with Peter Lake and M. R. D. Foot, London, 2000, and with Ralph Beauclerk, Wimbledon, 2000. Ralph Beauclerk told me, "Malraux imposed himself on us. He didn't give us orders. Personally, I wouldn't have accepted them. Charming man, Malraux!"

7. Malraux explained to General Jacquot that the day before the landings, he had taken part in the sabotage of railway lines. He talked about it several times. He was the only one to remember this operation.

8. See Max Hastings, *Das Reich* (Michael Joseph, 1981).

9. See Guy Penaud, *André Malraux et la Résistance*.

10. Guy Penaud, article in *L'Écho du centre*, November 23, 1976.

11. Guy Penaud's interviews with Marc Gerschel, used in his *André Malraux et la Résistance*.

12. Letter from Albert Uminski to Alain Galan, November 29, 1996.

13. Marcel Degliame (alias Fouché), military delegate of all the regional officials of the Resistance, assured me in Saint-Germain-en-Laye in 1958 that Malraux had had no military importance.

14. Remarks attributed to Malraux by Pierre Galante in *Malraux: Quel roman que sa vie*, translated by Haakon Chevalier as *Malraux* (Cowles, 1971). Galante is sometimes

more Malrucian than Malraux. Malraux saw the book but did not, as a rule, comment on biographical work about him.

15. The reader who knows *Antimémoires* will see that this account does not follow Malraux's own in its lyrical and inventive beauty. Nothing confirms the version of events described by Malraux: threat of execution, interrogation, misunderstanding. There is no trace of these events in the archives. The investigation of Guy Penaud and others, and my own, based on accessible evidence, largely invalidate André Malraux's beautiful account.

16. In *Antimémoires* and during an interview with Roger Stéphane. A lovely figment of his imagination.

17. Original: *L'Instant de ma mort* (Fata Morgana, 1994); translated by Lydia Davis (Barrytown, 1978).

18. Lieutenant Colonel Wilde's personal file in the German archives states that he was assistant commanding officer of the 11th Tank Division.

19. Claude Travi met the nun, Soeur Marguerite du Saint-Sacrement, or Marie Viguié in plainclothes. She showed him her copy of *Antimémoires* with a fine inscription by Malraux.

20. In *Antimémoires*, of course. General von Wieterscheim's son, Arnim von Wieterscheim, let me have details in 1999 that encourage skepticism, especially as far as the conversation of Colonel Berger and the general of the German division is concerned. There is no record of Malraux's arrest in the German archives (Auswärtige, AMT, Bundesarchiv) despite the *intensiven Recherchen* of Dr. Grotten and Herr Gresen. No trace of Malraux either in the works about the Das Reich Division.

21. According to his son, Arnim von Wieterscheim.

22. Even if, according to his son, Wieterscheim had a French-speaking Swiss nanny as a child, his military records specify that he needed an interpreter.

23. See André Culot's account in *La Dépêche du Midi* of November 23, 1976 (reported by Guy Penaud).

24. Letter from the paymaster of the Armées Départementales in Périgueux, December 29, 1944. Sums raised "for" are not necessarily sums actually paid. Guy Penaud in 2000 wrote, "Payment of a sum of 8,000,000F [$162,000 at the time] for the release of Colonel Berger (André Malraux) poses a problem, when we know that the writer was arrested by the Germans on July 22, 1944, in Gramat (Lot) and was not released (like all the other inmates) from Saint-Michel prison in Toulouse (Haute-Garonne), until the German troops had departed, August 19, 1944. The sum was apparently unfrozen by 'Léonie' . . . the treasurer of the AS in Corrèze . . . to have a clear conscience, but no more." Société Historique et Archéologique du Périgord.

25. Roland Trempé, history lecturer at the Université de Mirail, has investigated the "end" at Saint-Michel prison at length. See "À propos de la libération des résistants internés à la prison Saint-Michel à Toulouse," *Résistance R.* 4, 6, December 1978. See also the account of "Capitaine Georges" in *La Dépêche du Midi*, November 23, 1978. It is clear that Malraux let his imagination off the leash, not least from the fact that despite his prodigious memory, he had forgotten the circumstances of his liberation.

26. For Lake, Malraux was without a doubt an "asset" to the maquis. Interviews and correspondence between Peter Lake and the author.

27. Interviews with Henri Amouroux. See his *Grande Histoire des Français sous l'Occupation*. Amouroux states, "With 2 billion, 280 million francs, it was possible, in July 1944, to buy 43,000 calves weighing 100 kilos each, 12,000 pigs at 120 kilos, 10,000 tons of

potatoes at 4.50 francs a kilo, 25,000 kilos of Cantal cheese at 44 francs a kilo, and, to wash it all down, 20,000 barrels of wine at 2,200 francs a cask; or to feed, for ONE YEAR, *156,100 maquisards*, since the daily food ration of each maquisard cost 40 francs." The Banque de France freight car was attacked on July 26, four days after Malraux was arrested.

28. Thus a Mr. Hillaire, treasurer of the R5 section, paid back ten million francs allotted to the Mouvements Unis de Résistance (MUR). A few years later, the deposit and consignment office asked him what he wanted it to do with the interest. He stipulated that the money belonged to the state. Author's interview with Mme. Hillaire, Limoges, 1998.

29. So she boasted, at any rate. On this shady but fairly banal affair, see Guy Penaud, *Les Milliards du train de Neuvic* (Fanlac, 2001).

30. Hemingway's biographer Carlos Becker and others say that every time he told his version of the meeting with Malraux at the Ritz, Hemingway embellished the story.

23. THE ALSACE-LORRAINE CROSS

1. Documents quoted in this chapter come from the French Army Historical Department archives at Vincennes. See also Léon Mercadet, *La Brigade Alsace-Lorraine*.

2. To James Ellinger, September 30 issue, 1944.

3. The adolescents, of course, claim that they are older, but this is standard practice.

4. From Pierre Corneille, *Le Cid*: "The peril was impending, their brigade approaching."

5. We are the boys from Alsace / We've come a long way / We come from Haute-Savoie / To liberate the country / Roll the drums / To our loves . . .

6. Reported by Léon Mercadet.

7. *Combat*, the newspaper founded and distributed by the Resistance network of the same name. [Tr.]

8. Author's interview with B. Metz, 2000.

9. *Bulletin de l'Amicale des Anciens de la Brigade Alsace-Lorraine*, IV-76, no. 162.

10. This interview, one of Malraux's richest, was used by Stéphane in *Fin d'une jeunesse: Carnets, 1944–1947* (Table Ronde, 1954). I asked Roger Stéphane how he had gone about it: he had written part of the text the same evening. Afterward, he made alterations to the form.

11. On the night of March 30–31, 1945. See General de Lattre, *Histoire de la 1re Armée Française* (Plon, 1949). Curiously, in the first editions, de Lattre talks of *Boyer-Malraux*.

24. HISTORY, LEGEND, NOVEL

1. Until now, this file has never, to my knowledge, been consulted. It was pointed out to me by the Resistance office at Vincennes, with the authorization of Florence and Madeleine Malraux and the minister of defense at the time of writing, Alain Richard.

2. April 1945.

3. These officers admired his culture and his patter, as we have seen.

4. A notion communicated to me by M. R. D. Foot, who has had the opportunity to compare numerous exaggerated British dispatches with the *facts*.

5. Dated May 17, 1945. The document is in the archives of the Musée de l'Ordre de la Libération. Rebattet had no direct acquaintance with Malraux's activities in the Lot, Corrèze, and the Dordogne. Malraux's secretary, Madeleine Gaglione, takes up the same song on April 23, 1963: "Wounded three times, 1939–1945."

6. Respectively: November 17, 1945; August 17, 1945; April 24, 1946.

7. In July 1952.

8. The embryo of this novel, in several versions, is in the Malraux collection in the Bibliothèque Jacques-Doucet. No copy is longer than thirty pages. One is marked "1971." A reading of the first pages and Malraux's statements seem to indicate that they were written before then.

9. The Gestapo never searched Malraux's residence, according to the loyal Albert Beuret.

10. Conversations with and note from Jean Grosjean, 1998–2000. Grosjean says that for this "right to write," Malraux took a "massive" leap with *Antimémoires.*

25. CIVILIAN LIFE

1. See Frédéric J. Grover, *Six Entretiens avec André Malraux sur des écrivains de son temps* (Gallimard, 1978), and the *indirect* account of Drieu's brother via Brigitte Drieu la Rochelle. The issue of the pseudonym is still on hold.

2. One can choose to accept the version of the meeting written twenty-five years later by Malraux for *Antimémoires.* Or one can choose not to.

3. See Raymond Aron, *Mémoires.*

4. December 29, 1945.

5. The French subsequently did attempt to suppress resistance in Vietnam (formerly Tongking, Annam, and Cochin China), with the help of the British, but they signed an agreement with Ho Chi Minh in 1946. Then disagreement about whether Cochin China should be included led to the bloody French Indochina War, ending in French defeat at the Battle of Dienbienphu in May 1954. [Tr.]

6. In the first two weeks of October 1946. Letters by Falcoz communicated to the author by Jean Lescure. Malraux's interest in Indochina was revived in 1945. In *L'Indochine,* he foresaw the final result: the communization of "Viet-nam."

7. Letter of May 6, 1949.

8. Unpublished diary by Duff Cooper, communicated by Anthony Beever.

9. *Strategic Services Unit, War Department,* February 10–12, 1946. The same unit, one year before, had predicted that the relations "between the Communist members of his government and de Gaulle would be harmonious" and that de Gaulle would be too powerful to be "kicked out." The Americans' informer was Adrien Mouton, a member of the Central Committee of the PCF.

10. As an illustration, the print runs of Malraux's works on September 26, 1950, were *La Condition humaine,* 185,500 copies; *L'Espoir,* 64,900 copies; *Les Noyers de l'Altenburg,* 20,990 copies; *La Psychologie du cinéma,* 1,000 copies; *Saturne,* 15,000. These last two titles were not doing so well. Remaining in stock were 637 of the first and 9,714 of the second.

11. Letter from Gaston Gallimard, Paris, June 1, 1945. The amendment concerning the Pléiade is signed in March 1947.

12. The rights of *Les Conquérants* did belong to Grasset: he sold them to Gallimard. *L'Espoir* was included after the first edition.

13. A minister also has advantages: a car, chauffeur, and so on. A mystery remains about the "envelopes" from which his office (and therefore he) benefits. It was planned, in 1946, to increase the salary of a minister to 1,200,000 francs ($23,650).

14. Interview with Patrick Nizan, 1999. It was only from 1960 that the arrival of the densimeter allowed a scientific evaluation of colors. Then one could do without the

worker's eye, but one couldn't get rid of clients' exhausting remarks: "Bring up the red! Make it burn!"

15. They are in the Doucet collection.

16. See Pierre Hébey, *La NRF des Années sombres.*

17. Letter to Giono, September 11, 1944.

18. Sartre accused Céline of having been paid by the Germans to take an anti-Semitic stance. [Tr.]

19. Letter of May 26, 1951.

20. He turns up in the six volumes of Clara's memoirs. She writes well, even if, with Malraux as a model, she is sometimes too long and emphatic.

21. Clara kept the first drafts of some of her letters. The account of the reconciliation is by her.

22. Author's interviews with Madeleine Malraux, 1997–98.

23. Letter to Malraux, 1948 or 1949.

24. Letter of 1947.

25. Letter of March 8, 1951.

26. Letter of August 12, 1944.

26. THE MILITANT COMPANION

1. Claude Guy, *En écoutant le Général* (Grasset, 1996).

2. See Janine Mossuz-Lavau, *André Malraux et le gaullisme.*

3. Some Communists, including the author's mother, accompanied by her son and a unit secretary called M. Fourquien, distributed anti-Nazi leaflets in October 1940.

4. Author's interview with Jacques Baumel, Paris, 2000.

5. November 18, 1948.

6. April 14, 1948. Philippe Delpuech gave me many documents about Malraux's speeches.

7. Published in Geneva by Albert Skira in July 1948.

8. Letter dated June 27, 1947.

9. Interviews, March–April 1948, for *The Case for de Gaulle* (Random House, 1948).

10. The trilogy was translated by Stuart Gilbert as *The Psychology of Art* (Pantheon, 1949–1950).

11. December 13, 1949.

12. January 6, 1954.

13. Alain Malraux, *Les Marronniers de Boulogne.*

14. December 1948.

27. FAMILY LIFE

1. Alain Malraux, *Les Marronniers de Boulogne.*

2. *Éphémère*, June 1947.

3. Letter from André Malraux, 1953.

4. Undated letter from Malraux on headed Ministère des Affaires Culturelles paper, therefore after 1958.

5. Published in 1957, translated by Stuart Gilbert as *The Metamorphosis of the Gods* (Doubleday, 1960).

6. A French colony since 1830, Algeria saw increasing friction between French communities and Muslims after the war. The Algerian National Liberation Front

(FLN) was founded in 1954 and called for a general uprising. The Algerian war brought about the fall of the Fourth Republic in France and threatened the Fifth under de Gaulle. A referendum in France approved independence, and Algeria was proclaimed a republic in 1962.

28. POWER

1. He was invested as the head of government on June 1, 1958, and launched a raft of reforms within governmental institutions, including a huge increase in the power available to the president. The constitutional changes were approved by referendum on September 28, 1958, heralding the Fifth Republic, and de Gaulle began his presidency in December. [Tr.]

2. Doucet collection, undated.

3. Undated letter from de Bollardière to Malraux. Barberot and de Bollardière are, like Malraux, *Compagnons de la Libération.*

4. July 2, 1958.

5. Jacques Foccart, *Tous les soirs avec de Gaulle, 1965–1967* (Fayard/Jeune Afrique, 1997).

6. See Geneviève Poujol, "Aperçu sur la structuration politique et administrative du nouveau Ministère des Affaires Culturelles," in *André Malraux, ministre* (La Documentation française, 1996).

7. Interview with the author, 1988.

8. Diplomatic dispatches from the embassy, June 10 and 18, 1959.

9. Some Greeks in the French maquis groups did celebrate, without flags.

10. See Jean-François Revel, *Le Style du Général* (Julliard, 1959).

11. *Affaires Culturelles* budget presentation, November 17, 1959.

12. In March 1966.

13. See Jacques Foccart, *Tous les soirs avec de Gaulle.*

14. First published in 1961, translated by Bernard Frechtman as *The Screens* (Faber & Faber, 1963).

15. Garaudy's changing ideology took him from scouting to Stalinist communism to Islam. In comparison, Malraux's transition from companion of the Communist cause to companion of General de Gaulle seems logical and moderate.

16. A wordplay: "General de Gaulle never devaluates the currency/never loses in value."

29. JACKIE AND *LA GIOCONDA*

1. From May 31 to June 2, 1961.

2. Letter of thanks from Jacqueline Kennedy, June 21, 1961.

3. It is impossible to know if this question was "suggested" by the Kennedys or by Malraux himself, or if it was spontaneous.

4. May 12, from 4.30 p.m. Memorandum signed Mc.GB. Foreign Relations 1961–1963, vol. 13, National Archives, Washington, D.C.

5. See Alain Peyrefitte, *C'était de Gaulle*, vol. 1, and other sources.

6. Another political meeting takes place between André Malraux and John Kennedy on January 10, in the Oval Office.

7. From November 28 to December 5, 1962.

8. When the *Mona Lisa* was later sent to Japan, *all* the curators of the Louvre handed in their resignations (which were refused).

30. CRISES

1. It was not until November 2000 that an acknowledgment of the use of torture in Algeria was clearly and publicly made in France.

2. Parts of the French Army in Algeria, the Foreign Legion, the Organisation de l'Armée Secrète (OAS), and colonist vigilantes attempted to seize control in Algeria. The revolt was quashed after four days by the remaining French forces. This was the turning point in the Algerian War: thereafter the interests of the European settlers were no longer considered sacrosanct. Europeans were to be accorded equal rights for the first three years of independence (approved almost unanimously by referendum in France and Algeria in June and July 1962) but obliged to adopt Algerian citizenship or be declared aliens thereafter. [Tr.]

3. Napoleon's younger brother, the king of Westphalia. [Tr.]

4. Final and definitive separation in the spring of 1966.

31. MAO, MEMOIRS, *ANTIMÉMOIRES*

1. De Gaulle never went to China himself, but his successors visited Beijing: Pompidou in 1973, Giscard d'Estaing in 1980, Mitterrand in 1983.

2. See CIA report of July 30, 1965, "*French Government Position on Vietnam, no. 23,930.*"

3. Note no. 34,198, August 16, 1965.

4. Several versions of the interview between Malraux and Mao exist. 1. That of *Antimémoires*, the most literary and ample and the least trustworthy. 2. In "Vive la pensée de Mao Zedong," Beijing, 1969. 3. A transcription of the Chinese shorthand record in *Mondes asiatiques* in 1975, published with Malraux's consent. 4. The slightly censored shorthand account in the archives of the French Ministry of Foreign Affairs. 5. Malraux's notes for the Cabinet meeting of August 18, 1965, French National Archives. 6. Jean Lacouture's biography of Malraux and the typed interviews in the Malraux collection at the Bibliothèque Jacques-Doucet. The best analysis of the meeting to combine all the sources is Jacques Andrieu, "Mais que se sont donc dit Mao et Malraux?" *Perspectives chinoises*, no. 37, September–October 1996.

5. The timing can be calculated from the stenotype transcripts.

6. Translated by Terence Kilmartin as *Anti Memoirs* (Holt, Rinehart & Winston, 1968).

7. The keen literary geneticist and Malraux fan will read with pleasure the notes in the Pléiade *Œuvres complètes*, vol. 2, by Marius François Guyard, Jean-Claude Larrat, and François Trécourt.

8. Malraux never let go of this idea of Maoist China. In the 1970s, he said to Roger Stéphane, "The Chinese Communist masses that I have seen draw the best of their passion and their action from communism." He added unwisely that "at the current time, in China, they are not killing." He also said to Stéphane, "The major landowners have been fairly seriously cleared out"—not killed but *lessivé* (washed), and *fairly* seriously. There were millions of deaths. When militants come under criticism, their crimes are mistaken for *errors* made by communism.

9. July 19, 1967.

10. Author's interview with Arajeshwar Dayal, *La Nouvelle-Delhi*, 1997.

32. TEMPTATION OF THE EAST

1. The enlarged and revised version of *Le Musée imaginaire*, translated by Stuart Gilbert as *The Voices of Silence* (Doubleday, 1953).

2. *Saturne: Essai sur Goya* (Gallimard, 1950), translated by C. W. Chilton as *Saturn: An Essay on Goya* (Phaidon, 1957).

3. The Quai d'Orsay suggested that Malraux go to Pakistan after having seen an exhibition in Tokyo, thus avoiding a reaction by the military powers in Pakistan.

4. Alain Danielou, *Le Chemin du labyrinthe* (Robert Laffont, 1980).

5. Raja Rao, novelist and philosopher, was Malraux's principal intermediary in India. He readily Malrucized. In his forceful account of a Malraux-Nehru meeting in France in the 1930s, he proposes Malraux saying to Nehru, "Duality and death are the only two enemies of man. When you become prime minister of India, if you do, since Mahatma Gandhi will never be a member of any government—he is too much the leader of all men—then remember me." Raja Rao attributes to Malraux an unprecedented prescience about the constitution of India, more than a quarter of a century before its promulgation.

6. Today it houses the Nehru Museum and the Nehru archives (disappointing, as regards Malraux).

7. An almost complete reproduction of the dispatch is contained in a work published by the French Embassy in India, *Malraux et l'Inde: Itinéraire d'un émerveillement*.

8. See Raja Rao, *The Meaning of India* (Vision Books, 1996).

9. This detail and many others are to be found in a thesis by Yves Beigbeder, "André Malraux et l'Inde" (University of Paris–IV, 1983). Beigbeder is one of the few Malrucian scholars to admire Malraux without tipping over into hagiographic excess. He also points out the borrowed elements in Malraux's account of his conversations with Nehru in *Antimémoires*. Malraux "siphoned" considerably from works by Louis Fischer and Tibor Mende, in particular *Conversations with Mr. Nehru*. The same technique is used for the portrait of Mao in *Antimémoires*: Malraux borrowed from Edgar Snow.

10. Author's interview with Kushwant Singh, 1997.

11. In private, with Jean Grosjean, Malraux agrees that "the mental universe of India is unbreathable." Interview with the author, 2000.

12. Interview granted to Karthy Sishupal, 1974. In the same interview, Malraux says, "I had a great impression of poverty before in Delhi, but not now. For example, last year, I didn't see one untouchable in Delhi!" Malraux's physical blindness, here, is comparable to Sartre's political blindness when he stated that Soviet intellectuals were perfectly free.

13. An idea that stands out in the thesis of K. Madanagoblane, "André Malraux et l'Inde."

14. May 27, 1964.

15. Jean-Alphonse Bernard's expression.

16. Malraux's friends throw little light on his thoughts on Hindu philosophy. Dileep Padgonkar writes, "For the uninitiated, the abstract concepts of Self, being, and transcendence seem to be nothing but a string of words with no clear link between them. Whereas for Malraux, and the finest Indian minds, these Vedic axioms are manifested through the highest forms of Indian art, the most noble forms of Indian ethics, and—going one step further—in the weighty challenges the leaders of India have to take on. It took a thinker of Malraux's class, a thinker who was original, daring, and sympa-

thetic, to remind Indians trapped at this time by the chaos and anxiety of modernity that it is by a return to their sources that they will find, even in a limited way, grace and deliverance." "L'Inde de Malraux" in *Malraux et l'Inde*, French Embassy, Delhi.

17. De Gaulle is re-elected president on December 19.

18. December 15, 1965.

19. Malraux makes cuts in the second edition of his book.

20. For the second round of legislative elections, March 12, 1967.

21. December 15, 1965.

22. In brief letters of January 5, 1968, and January 3, 1969.

23. Letter of May 28, 1970. De Gaulle was no longer in power by then; he did have the time.

24. Letter of December 31, 1969.

25. Letter of June 3, 1970.

26. Translated by Terence Kilmartin as *Memoirs of Hope* (Weidenfeld and Nicolson, 1971). See the final chapter for a fuller extract.

33. THE ORATOR

1. Malraux treated de Gaulle as a father. Let us hazard an inevitable hypothesis: Would the General have liked to have the writer (or a calmer version of him) for a son?

2. Let us not forget that this was before starting on *Antimémoires*, at a time when he was severely depressed and breaking up with Madeleine after twenty years together.

3. Letters of April 5 and 13, 1971.

4. Letter dated October 15, 1968.

5. Although this comment by the General may, like so many others, have been invented by Jean Cau; see his *Croquis de mémoire*.

34. CLOUDS IN MAY

1. See José Bergamin, *Notes pour notre temps* (Paris: Centre Georges-Pompidou, 1989).

2. See, among others, Pierre Moinot, *Tous comptes faits*.

3. Letter to Georges Pompidou, September 24, 1957.

4. Claude Mauriac, *Le Temps immobile*, vol. 3, *Et comme l'espérance est violente*.

5. The remark may be an invention of Jean Cau, as many other "*mots du Général*" are known to be.

6. See interviews with Malraux broadcast on Yugoslav television on May 6, 1960, in particular the one conducted by Komnen Becirović on May 5.

7. Guy Mollet, secretary general of the SFIO, former prime minister and briefly a *ministre d'état* under de Gaulle before joining the opposition in 1959. [Tr.]

8. Jacques Foccart, *Le Général en mai* (Fayard/Jeune Afrique, 1998).

9. May 1971. Published by Claude Travi in the proceedings of the colloquium "André Malraux, l'homme des Univers," Verrières-le-Buisson, 1989.

35. LITERATURE STILL

1. It was to be his last public appearance before a large audience, in the flesh, in an electoral campaign.

2. And there he stays. Grosjean and Beuret in 1968 made fun of Malraux, thinking of Spain in 1939 and France in 1940, "You only need to espouse a cause." Malraux answered, "My friend Chiang Kai-shek isn't doing so badly."

3. Contemporary observation by the author as journalist with *Nouvel Observateur.*

4. A witness is also there in the form of Colonel d'Escrienne.

5. In a private collection, as are different "inventories" for and drafts of *Les Chênes qu'on abat*—a mine of information for the study of how the book came about. Malraux tore the manuscripts up, as he often did, before handing over the final version for typing.

6. It was only because d'Escrienne and de Courcel were present that Malraux didn't claim to have talked with de Gaulle for five hours. He lived half a century that day. Who's counting?

7. Having gotten this far, the reader deserves a restorative note: Lasserre's recipe for *Pigeon André Malraux*: For 4 persons, 4 pigeons of around 500 g (18 oz.) each. For the stuffing: 100 g (3½ oz.) fresh bacon fat, 100 g sliced cèpe mushrooms, 50 g (1¾ oz.) chopped scallions, 50 g cockscombs, 50 g fresh duck liver, 100 g salsify, cooked and chopped, 1 bouquet of thyme and bay, salt, and pepper. For the sauce: 100 ml (½ cup) dry white wine, 5 cl (3½ Tbsp.) Noilly Prat, 350 ml (¾ pt.) pigeon stock, 50 g butter (optional). Vegetables: 100 g cèpes, herbs. Bone and gut the pigeons from the backbone side, taking care only to cut them as far as the middle of the back. Leave as much skin on as possible around the pouch in order to seal in the stuffing. Only the drumsticks should remain. Keep the livers aside. Spread the pigeons out on the table, breast side down; season with salt and pepper; stuff them with about 60 g (2 oz.) of stuffing, prepared as follows. Melt and heat well 100 g cubed bacon fat in a high-sided pan; add the livers with the scallions, thyme, bay leaves, spices, salt, and pepper; firm up briskly on a high heat before they have time to give out their juices. Add 100 g cèpes, cut into cubes and quickly sautéed in a pan, 50 g of duck livers, diced and seared, 50 g cockscombs, previously cooked and well drained, and 100 g cooked salsify, cut into cubes. Mince the ingredients to obtain a fairly coarse stuffing. Fill the pigeons, reshape them, and tie them with string. Set them in a deep pan with a knob of butter and cook in the oven for thirty minutes at medium heat. The *sommelier* at Lasserre advises a bottle of Château Brondelles Graves 1985.

8. Told to the author by Bernard Tricot, 1998.

9. Letter of October 20, 1970.

10. The author begs to be excused for not lingering on the funerals.

11. Translated by Irene Clephane as *Fallen Oaks*, revised by Linda Asher as *Felled Oaks* (Holt, Rinehart & Winston, 1972).

12. With *Les Chênes qu'on abat*, Malraux was very aware of following *Antimémoires*. The works were published together in 1976 under the title *Le Miroir des limbes*: a revised version of *Antimémoires* as the first volume and *Hôtes de passage*, *Les Chênes qu'on abat*, *La Tête d'obsidienne*, and *Lazare* as the second volume, which also has its own title, *La Corde et les souris*.

13. Translated and annotated by June and Jacques Guicharnaud as *Picasso's Mask* (Holt, Rinehart & Winston, 1976).

14. At the Paris 1937 World's Fair.

15. See Pierre Daix, *Dictionnaire Picasso*.

16. When the Maeght Foundation, *not* at his behest, organized an exhibition called "André Malraux et le musée imaginaire."

17. Translated by Terence Kilmartin as *Lazarus* (Holt, Rinehart & Winston, 1977).

18. In interviews he said that he had tried alcohol and hashish "like everybody."

19. He told Françoise Giroud that she was the only one to have noticed.

20. Sparring poets in Molière's *Les Femmes Savantes*. [Tr.]

21. Letter of January 31, 1975.

22. Julien Cheverny, *Sexologie de l'Occident* (Hachette, 1976).

23. Claude Gallimard's letter, March 11, 1974; Malraux's answer, March 15.

24. $41,414 in 1974.

25. Letter to Gallimard's commercial manager, Louis-Daniel Hirsch, October 16, 1967.

26. December 19, 1974.

27. Letter of December 4, 1974.

28. One allusion in *Hôtes de passage*, used again in *Le Miroir des limbes*.

36. BRILLIANT PICTURES

1. Sophie de Vilmorin, *Aimer encore*. She writes affectionately, "He pretended . . . He loved fame, and the situation brought him a lot of it."

2. *France-Soir*, September 18, 1971. The source quoted is a French Press Agency dispatch from New Delhi. He is trapped in a similar way on September 18 on a television program.

3. Letter of October 4, 1971.

4. Letter to Gyula Illyes, November 8, 1971.

5. Author's interview with M. J. N. Dixit, former minister of foreign affairs, Haryana, 1996.

6. Nixon was in fact just a candidate at the time.

7. Widely distributed interview with Malraux by Jean Mauriac.

8. In a letter to Patrick Buchanan, March 4, 1971. Perhaps a typing error. Buchanan, in his reply accompanied by quotes requested by Nixon, does not make the same mistake.

9. Nixon, *Memoirs* (Grosset and Dunlop, 1978).

10. Memo from Henry Kissinger to Richard Nixon, dated February 14, 1972. National Archives, Washington, D.C.

11. Mao would later explain to Georges Pompidou that the artillery at the Battle of Dienbienphu was Chinese. In North Vietnam in 1965 and 1972, the author and countless other witnesses saw many Chinese products and light military equipment (individual weapons, trucks, etc.).

12. Branch chief of the KGB Aleksandr Komin and others remarked on Scali's involvement in the missile crisis in 1963. On his own initiative, Scali made "conditions" that pushed Khrushchev to give in.

13. Journalists such as Ken Freed, from the Associated Press, and Mel Elfin have the feeling that Malraux has lost his sense of reality.

14. The American Presidential Archives are filtered and skimmed, but less than the French ones.

15. Henry Kissinger, *White House Years* (Little, Brown, 1979).

16. Philippe Labro, interviewing Malraux in *Le Journal du dimanche*, February 20, 1972.

17. Simon Leys, whose *The Chairman's New Clothes: Mao and the Cultural Revolution* had appeared the previous year in France.

37. THE ARTS AND ART

1. Malraux never said he would have liked to become a painter. He didn't take seriously his doodles of seahorses, cats, and *dyables* on letters and manuscripts, collected by friends and colleagues. His indifference to music was that of his generation. From 1880 to 1900, in the wake of Wagner, literature and music were in symbiosis. There was a tendency for ignorance about or resistance toward music among writers from between the wars.

2. Skira was Swiss but worked in France from the 1930s onward, once photographic reproduction techniques improved. He published a small cultural paper called *Labyrinthe* for which Malraux gave a fragment of *Psychologie de l'art*.

3. Letter to Antoine Terrasse, December 26, 1973.

4. See the inventory of the publications on art in his library, published by the Musée National d'Art Moderne, Centre Georges-Pompidou, 1986.

5. Published in Madrid by Espasa-Calpe from 1945 to 1966.

6. To Santelli in *Le Légende du siècle*, 1972.

7. During the three ORTF films by Clovis Prévost, 1974.

8. From 1934–35 onward, French thought was often contaminated by *bits* of German philosophy. During his formative years, Malraux was closer to the concepts expressed by André Lalande in his 1926 *Vocabulaire technique et critique de la philosophie*, in which he rejoiced in the return to favor of metaphysics in France. From 1922, the early Wittgenstein marked out the limits due to language of possible metaphysical investigation. Clara and André Malraux went through Austria in the 1920s without knowing that the logical positivists of the Vienna Circle, Rudolf Carnap and Moritz Schlick, were working on these fundamental questions. As far as philosophy is concerned, Malraux remained an insular Frenchman, a pre-Kantian Parisian. He believed that metaphysics is a mode of consciousness, a supreme knowledge, and that the novel *and* artistic commentary—at *his* level—allow the Truth to be reached. Malraux wrote as if he believed that Art and Truth were *out there*, beyond their incantations in works, on the brink of the Absolute. He accepted the underlying idea that one can, by writing, unearth a rare substance that is reducible to words. A good writer may have a reverential but illogical approach to language, and even the most gifted may never be interested in where its limitations lie.

9. *Burlington Magazine*, "Andre Malraux and the Crisis of Expressionism," December 1954.

10. Only 3,000 copies of *Le Musée inimaginable* were ever printed; there were no translation and no second printing. By 1973, 1,147 copies had been sold. Compared with the 76,000 copies of *Le Musée imaginaire* and Malraux's reputation, Duthuit's book hardly carried much weight for the general public. In 1951, in the United States, *The Psychology of Art* sold better than any other art book.

11. Letter of April 26, 1955, communicated by Bertrand Fillaudeau. Corti Archives.

12. Such as Pierre Rosenberg, director of the Louvre, inspired by *Les Voix du silence* at the age of seventeen; and another art historian, François Avril, who describes the effect of Malraux's text on him as a young reader as "dazzling."

13. See Jean-François Sonnay, "La genèse du Musée Imaginaire de Malraux," *Études de lettres*, 1967. Sonnay seems to be one of those rare commentators who know how to talk about Malraux without either spitting blood or swooning in admiration.

14. Article of 1958, referred to in *Contrecensures* (J.-J. Pauvert, 1966).

15. See Alban Cerisier's exhaustive article in the special books issue by the École Nationale des Chartes, Paris, 2000. The collection ran from 1960 to 1997; Salles was codirector until 1966.

16. May 18, 1974. Amateurs will find variations on *La Gioconda* in *Les Voix du silence* (1951) and *L'Irréel* (1974).

17. Trip to Japan from May 13 to June 1, 1974.

18. Sophie de Vilmorin says, "André Malraux never voted." Author's interview, 2000.

19. In fact, he seems to have been perfectly willing or at least let himself be influenced by the ambassador, who was keen to butter up Duvalier Jr.

20. Ambassador Léon Deblé, interview with and letter to the author, 2000.

21. Oral comment made in Clovis Prévost's three films.

22. Malraux was quick to move from the real to the supernatural. As minister, he provided backing to the Louvre laboratory: he saw in the examination of paintings with microsampling, ultraviolet and infrared light "an introspection of the genius of artists such as da Vinci, Rembrandt, Corot." Jean-Pierre Mohen, "Note on Malraux," *Revue pour l'histoire du CNRS*, no. 2, Winter 2000.

23. *Burnt Norton*, 1935.

38. POT-AU-FEU AND CAVIAR

1. Letter of June 18, 1976.

2. Preface to vol. 1 of the Pléiade *Œuvres complètes*.

3. January 7, 1971. Shared with the author by Jean Grosjean, 1998.

4. He was, after the writer's death, totally devoted to Florence Malraux.

5. Sophie de Vilmorin, *Aimer encore* (Gallimard, 1999).

6. The Saint-Chéron brothers, one an academic, the other an essayist, have devoted their lives to Malraux.

7. Interview for *L'Express*, July 1976. Malraux *expected* to be asked to talk about cats.

8. Sartre, who didn't even have a hamster, claimed that people who love animals too much shouldn't be trusted. Malraux wouldn't have counted as one of them.

9. Notes communicated by Jean Lescure.

10. Letters to Marie Lamy, September and October 1971.

11. From 1968 to 1976; quarrel in 1972.

12. Notebook for 1971.

13. February 29, 1972. Gogo's letters to Malraux at Verrières have disappeared.

14. Interview with the author, Florence, 2000.

15. The author, who followed the candidate Chaban-Delmas for *Le Nouvel Observateur*, asked him, the day after the broadcast of this program, if he had known what Malraux was going to say. "More or less," he replied. He added, "We were both ahead of our time." That was true, for computers.

16. *Les Canards de Ca-Mao* (Laffont, 1975).

17. Letter of March 11, 1970.

18. Malraux-Grover interviews: about Drieu, June 1959; about Barrès, July 1, 1968; about Paulhan, August 20, 1971; about Céline, March 9, 1973. See also *Antimémoires*, June 20, 1975, and August 18, 1975.

19. For this last book, see a study by Henri Godard, very sympathetic to Malraux, *L'Autre Face de la littérature: Essais sur André Malraux et la littérature*.

20. *Le Monde*, March 15, 1974.

21. The manuscript included two possible endings. Beuret chose the more opti-

mistic, the one that went more in the direction of brotherhood. Pierre Brunel's account in the France-Culture radio program *Agora*, June 2, 1989.

22. More than $600,000 in 1976.

CONCLUSION: SCARS

1. Philippe de Gaulle, *Mémoires accessoires* (Plon, 2000).

2. "My father the hero, his smile so gentle . . ." (from Hugo's "Après la Bataille").

3. Introduction to the Pléiade *Œuvres complètes*.

4. *This*, 1933 (translated from the Portuguese by J. Griffin).

5. Manuscript communicated by Jean Lescure.

6. Letter to the author, May 28, 1999.

7. Television interview on *Antenne 2*, November 12, 1981.

8. Jean Lacouture played an eminent role in the mythogenesis of Malraux (as he did for Ho Chi Minh and François Mauriac). He was a member of the "pantheonization" committee. A few weeks before the ceremony, he wrote (in *Nouvel Observateur*, September 10–25, 1996) that: (1) Malraux had "not without informing the authorities pulled out a few statues and bas-reliefs from the practically abandoned temple of Banteay Srey"; (2) he had created "a squadron of about fifteen planes that constituted for one year the only forces of Republican aviation"; (3) "the bombing of the road from Medellín to Madrid . . . saved for several months the Republican capital." Errors from 1973, when Lacouture published his Malraux biography, needn't have been repeated and aggravated in 1996.

9. The worst was avoided by Bernard Spitz, a young member of the Council of State, who scrapped a plan to have Malraux's casket transported on an electric trolley steered by remote control. What if it had gone wrong?

10. Pascal Vacher, "*La Condition humaine*" (*1993*): *Malraux, résumé, personnages, thèmes* (Hatier, 1996).

SELECTED BIBLIOGRAPHY

BOOKS

Adams, Jad, and Phillip Whitehead. *The Dynasty: The Nehru-Gandhi Story.* Penguin, 1997.

Affaires culturelles au temps d'André Malraux, 1959–1969, Les. Documentation Française, 1996.

Ajchenbaum, Yves-Marc. *À la vie à la mort: Histoire du journal "Combat," 1941–1974.* Le Monde Éditions, 1994.

Alcalay, Jean-Marc. *André Malraux et Dunkerque: Une filiation.* Société Dunkerquoise d'Histoire et d'Archéologie, 1996.

Ali, Tariq. *The Nehrus and the Gandhis: An Indian Dynasty.* Picador, 1985.

Amouroux, Henri. *La Grande Histoire des Français sous l'Occupation: Un printemps de mort et d'espoir, joies et douleurs du peuple libéré, septembre 1943–août 1944.* Robert Laffont Bouquins, 1999.

Andreu, Pierre, and Frédéric Grover. *Drieu la Rochelle.* Hachette Littérature, 1979.

Aron, Raymond. *Mémoires.* Julliard, 1983.

Assouline, Pierre. *L'Épuration des intellectuels, 1944–1945: La mémoire du siècle.* Éditions Complexe, 1985.

———. *L'Homme de l'art: D.-H. Kahnweiler, 1884–1979.* Balland, Folio, 1988.

———. *Gaston Gallimard: Un demi-siècle d'édition française.* Balland, 1984.

Astruc, Alexandre. *Du stylo à la caméra . . . et de la caméra au stylo: Écrits (1942–1984).* L'Archipel, 1987.

Bachi, Salim. "La Mort dans la trilogie extrême-orientale d'André Malraux." Unpublished master's thesis, University of Paris–IV, 1996.

Bachoud, Andrée. *Franco.* Fayard, 1997.

Bartillat, Christian de. *Clara Malraux: Biographie-témoignage (le regard d'une femme sur son siècle).* Librairie Académique Perrin, 1985.

Baumel, Jacques. *Résister: Histoire secrète des années d'Occupation.* Albin Michel, 1999.

Bedu, Jean-Jacques. *Maurice Magre: Le Lotus perdu.* Dire Éditions, 1999.

Beigbeder, Yves. "André Malraux et l'Inde." Unpublished postgraduate thesis, University of Paris–IV, 1983.

Bergère, Marie-Claire, Lucien Bianco, and Jürgen Domes. *La Chine au XXᵉ siècle, de 1949 à aujourd'hui.* Fayard, 1990.

Beucler, André. *Plaisirs de mémoire,* vol. 2. Gallimard, 1982.

Biasini, Émile. *Sur Malraux, celui qui aimait les chats.* Éditions Odile Jacob, 1999.

Blanch, Lesley. *Romain, un regard particulier.* Actes Sud, 1998.

Bonhomme, Jacques (alias Jean-Jacques Pauvert). *André Malraux.* Éditions Régine Desforges, 1986.

Bothorel, Jean. *Louise, ou la vie de Louise de Vilmorin.* Grasset & Fasquelle, 1993.

Bourdet, Claude. *L'Aventure incertaine: De la Résistance à la Restauration.* Stock, 1975.

Brasillach, Robert, and Maurice Bardèche. *Histoire de la guerre d'Espagne.* Godefroy de Bouillon, 1995.

Brincourt, André. *Malraux: Le malentendu.* Grasset, 1986.

Bruneau, Jean-Baptiste. "Drieu la Rochelle: Mémoire et mythes." Unpublished master's thesis, University of Tours, 1996.

Cate, Curtis. *André Malraux.* Flammarion, 1994.

———. *André Malraux: A Biography.* Hutchinson, 1995.

Cau, Jean. *Croquis de mémoire.* Julliard, 1985.

Caumer, Julien. *Leurs dossier R. G.* Flammarion, 2000.

Chaban-Delmas, Jacques. *Mémoires pour demain.* Flammarion, 1997.

Chantal, Suzanne. *Le Cœur battant (Josette Clotis–André Malraux).* Bernard Grasset, 1976.

Charret, Séverine. "La 'Révolution chinoise' d'après *Les Conquérants* et *La Condition humaine* d'André Malraux." Unpublished master's thesis, University of Lyon-II, 1998.

Chentalinski, Vitali. *La Parole ressuscitée: Dans les archives littéraires du K.G.B.* Robert Laffont, 1993.

Cœure, Sophie. *La Grande Lueur à l'Est: Les Français et l'Union soviétique, 1917–1939.* Éditions du Seuil, 1999.

Cohen-Solal, Annie. *Sartre 1905–1980.* Gallimard, 1985.

Colloque de Cerisy under the direction of Christiane Moatti and David Bevan. *André Malraux: Unité de l'œuvre, Unité de l'homme.* Documentation française, 1989.

Conquest, Robert. *La Grande Terreur,* preceded by *Sanglantes moissons.* Latest French edition by Robert Laffont, Paris, 1995.

Cordier, Daniel. *Jean Moulin: La République des catacombes.* Gallimard, 1999.

Courtivron, Isabelle de. *Clara Malraux: Une Femme dans le siècle.* Éditions de l'Olivier, 1992.

Courtois, Stéphane, Nicolas Werth, and Jean-Louis Panné. *Le Livre noir du communisme: Crimes, terreur, répression.* Robert Laffont, 1997.

Daix, Pierre. *Dictionnaire Picasso.* Robert Laffont, 1995.

Damodaran, A. K. *Jawaharlal Nehru: A Communicator and Democratic Leader.* Radiant Publishers, 1997.

De Felice, Renzo. *Les Interprétations du fascisme.* Éditions des Syrtes, 2000.

de Gaulle, Charles. *Mémoires.* Edited by Marius-François Guyard, with an introduction by Jean-Louis Crémieux-Brilhac. Gallimard, Pléiade, 2000.

Du Perron, Eddy. *Le Pays d'origine.* Gallimard, 1980.

Faligot, Roger, and Rémi Kauffer. *As-tu vu Cremet?* Fayard, 1991.

Foot, M. R. D. *S.O.E. in France: An Account of the Work of the British Special Operations Executive in France, 1940–1944.* Her Majesty's Stationery Office, 1966.

Friang, Brigitte. *Un autre Malraux.* Plon, 1977.

Furet, François, and Mona Ozouf. *Dictionnaire critique de la Révolution française.* Flammarion, 1988.

Gabory, Georges. *Apollinaire, Max Jacob, Gide, Malraux et Cie.* Éditions Jean-Michel Place, 1988.

Gide, André. *Journal, 1942–1949.* Gallimard, 1950.

Gisclon, Jean. *La Désillusion: Espagne, 1936.* France-Empire, 1986.

Glaize, Maurice. *Les Monuments du Groupe d'Angkor.* J. Maisonneuve, 1993.

Godard, Henri. *L'Autre Face de la littérature: Essais sur André Malraux et la littérature.* Gallimard, 1990.

Gombrich, E. H. *L'Art et l'illusion. Psychologie de la représentation picturale.* Gallimard, 1996.

Gourevitch, Ivan Gervaise. *The Phenomenological Anthropology of Literature.* Nuf Ekoj Press, 1968.

Grossmann, Robert. *Le Choix de Malraux: L'Alsace, une seconde patrie.* La Nuée Bleue, 1997.

Gueret, Danielle. *Le Cambodge, une introduction à la connaissance du pays khmer.* Éditions Kailash, 1998.

Guillermaz, Jacques. *Une vie pour la Chine: Mémoires, 1937–1989.* Robert Laffont, 1989.

Hastings, Max. *Das Reich: Resistance and the March of the 2nd SS Panzer Division Through France, June 1944.* Michael Joseph, 1981.

Hebey, Pierre. *La NRF des années sombres, juin 1940–juin 1941: Des intellectuels à la dérive.* Gallimard, 1992.

Huyghe, René. *Psychologie de l'art: Résumé des cours du Collège de France, 1951–1976.* Éditions du Rocher, 1991.

———. *Sens et destin de l'art.* Vol. 1, *De la préhistoire à l'art roman.* Flammarion, 1967.

Jasper, Willi. *Hôtel Lutétia: Un exil allemand à Paris.* Éditions Michalon, 1994.

Jelen, Christian. *Hitler ou Staline: Le prix de la paix.* Flammarion, 1988.

Kissinger, Henry. *White House Years.* Little, Brown and Co., 1979.

———. *Years of Upheaval.* Little, Brown and Co, 1982.

Lacouture, Jean. *André Malraux: Une vie dans le siècle.* Éditions du Seuil, 1973.

Langlois, Walter G. *André Malraux.* Vol. 5, *Malraux et l'Histoire.* Revue des Lettres Modernes, Minard, 1982.

———. *André Malraux: L'Aventure indochinoise.* Mercure de France, 1967.

———. *Via Malraux.* Malraux Society, 1986.

Larrat, Jean-Claude. "André Malraux, théoricien de la littérature, des 'origines de la poésie cubiste' aux voix du silence, 1920–1951." Unpublished doctoral thesis, University of Paris–IV, vols. 1 and 2, 1991.

———. *Malraux, théoricien de la littérature, 1920–1951.* PUF Écrivain, 1996.

Lebovics, Herman. *Mona Lisa's Escort: André Malraux and the Reinvention of French Culture.* Cornell University Press, 1999.

Lescure, Jean. *Poésie et liberté: Histoire de messages, 1939–1946.* Éditions de l'IMEC, 1998.

Leys, Simon. *Essais sur la Chine.* Robert Laffont, 1998.

Lottman, Herbert R. *La Rive gauche: Du Front populaire à la guerre froide.* Éditions du Seuil, 1981.

Madanagobalane, K. "André Malraux et l'Inde." Unpublished postgraduate thesis, Karnataka University, Dharwad, 1973.

Malraux, Alain. *Les Marronniers de Boulogne: Malraux "père introuvable."* latest edition by Bartillat, 1996.

Malraux, Clara. *Le Bruit de nos pas.* 6 vols. Bernard Grasset, 1992.

Malraux, Madeleine, and Inigo Satrustegui. *André Malraux: Dessins.* Mollat Éditeur, 1998.

Martin du Gard, Maurice. *Les Mémorables 1918–1945.* Gallimard, 1993.

Mauriac, Claude. *Le temps immobile.* Vol. 3, *Et comme l'espérance est violente.* Bernard Grasset, 1976.

Mauriac, François. *Bloc-notes, 1965–1967*. Éditions du Seuil, 1993.

Mazuy, Rachel. *Croire plutôt que voir: Voyages en Russie soviétique, 1919–1939*. Odile Jacob, 2002.

Mercadet, Léon. *La Brigade Alsace-Lorraine*. Bernard Grasset, 1984.

Milza, Pierre. *Mussolini*. Fayard, 1999.

Moinot, Pierre. *Tous comptes faits*. Gallimard, 1997.

Moll, Geneviève. *Yvonne de Gaulle, l'inattendue*. Éditions Ramsay, 1999.

Morlino, Bernard. *Emmanuel Berl: Les tribulations d'un pacifiste*. La Manufacture, 1990.

Mossuz-Lavau, Janine. *André Malraux et le gaullisme*. Presses de la Fondation Nationale des Sciences Politiques, 1982.

Nadeau, Maurice. *Grâces leur soient rendues: Mémoires littéraires*. Albin Michel, 1990.

Naipaul, V. S. *India: A Million Mutinies Now*. Minerva, 1990.

———. *India: A Wounded Civilization*. Penguin Books, 1979.

Nizan, Henriette, and Marie-José Jaubert. *Libres Mémoires*. Éditions Robert Laffont, 1989.

Noble, Philippe. "Du Perron et la France." Unpublished master's thesis, University of Paris–III, 1973.

———. *Een Nederlander in Parijs: Eddy du Perron*. Cahiers du Méridon, 1994.

Noguères, Henri. *La Vie quotidienne des résistants de l'Armistice à la Libération*. Hachette Littérature, 1984.

Nothomb, Paul. *Malraux en Espagne*. Éditions Phébus, 1999.

Panné, Jean-Louis. *Boris Souvarine: Le premier désenchanté du communisme*. Robert Laffont, 1993.

Pastor-Petit, D. *La Guerra psicológica en las dictaduras*. Tangram, 1994.

Payne, Robert. *André Malraux*. Éditions Buchet/Chastel, 1996 (new edition).

Péan, Pierre. *Vies et morts de Jean Moulin*. Fayard, 1998.

Penaud, Guy. *André Malraux et la Résistance*. Éditions Fanlac, 1986.

———. *Les Milliards du train de Neuvic*. Éditions Fanlac, 2001.

Peyrefitte, Alain. *C'était de Gaulle*. Vol. 3, *Tout le monde a besoin d'une France qui marche*. Éditions de Fallois, Fayard, 2000.

Poirier, Jacques R. E. *La Girafe au long cou*. Éditions Fanlac, 1992.

Ragache, Gilles and Jean-Robert. *La Vie quotidienne des écrivains et des artistes sous l'Occupation, 1940–1944*. Hachette, 1988.

Rao, Raja. *The Meaning of India*. Vision Books, 1996.

Ravanel, Serge. *L'Esprit de résistance*. Éditions du Seuil, 1995.

Raymond, Gino. *André Malraux: Politics and the Temptation of Myth*. Avebury, 1995.

Saint-Pulgent, Maryvonne de. *Le Gouvernement de la culture*. Gallimard, Le Débat, 1999.

Sartre, Jean-Paul. *La Transcendance de l'ego: Esquisse d'une description phénoménologique*. Librairie Philosophique J. Vrin, 1996.

Schlumberger, Jean. *Notes sur la vie littéraire, 1902–1968*. Gallimard, "Les cahiers de la N.R.F.," 1999.

Singh, Khushwant. *Not a Nice Man to Know: The Best of Khushwant Singh*. Penguin Books, 1993.

———. *We Indians*. Orient Paperbacks, 1982.

Skoutelsky, Rémi. *L'Espoir guidait leurs pas: Les volontaires français dans les Brigades Internationales, 1936–1939*. Bernard Grasset, 1998.

Sondhi, Madhuri Santanam. *Modernity, Morality and the Mahatma*. Haranand Publications, 1997.

Sorensen, Theodore C. *The Kennedy Legacy.* Weidenfeld and Nicolson, 1969.

Stéphane, Roger. *Malraux: Premier dans le siècle.* Gallimard, 1996.

Suleiman, Susan Rubin. *Le Roman à thèse ou l'autorité fictive.* PUF Écriture, 1983.

Thomas, Hugh. *The Spanish Civil War.* Simon & Schuster, 1994.

Thompson, Brian, and Carl A. Viggiani. *Witnessing André Malraux.* Wesleyan University Press, 1984.

Thornberry, Robert S. *André Malraux et l'Espagne.* Librairie Droz, 1977.

Tully, Mark. *Jawaharlal Nehru: An Autobiography.* Mackays of Chatham, 1989.

Travi, Claude. *Dits et écrits d'André Malraux.* University of Burgundy, 2004.

Valenti, Elvira Farreras, and Joan Gaspar. *Memòries: Art i vida a Barcelona, 1911–1996.* La Campana, 1997.

Valynseck, Joseph, and Denis Grando. *À la découverte de leurs racines.* Intermédiaires des Chercheurs et Curieux, 1994.

van Rysselberghe, Maria. *André Gide: Les Cahiers de la Petite Dame, 1918–1929,* vols. 1 and 3. Gallimard, 1973–1975.

Villemot, Dominique. *André Malraux et la politique.* L'Harmattan, 1996.

Vilmorin, Sophie de. *Aimer encore.* Gallimard, 1999.

Viollis, Andrée. *Indochine S.O.S.* Gallimard, 1935.

Viswanathan, Ed. *Am I a Hindu? The Hinduism Primer.* Rupa & Co., 1993.

Vitoux, Frédéric. *La Vie de Céline.* Éditions Grasset & Fasquelle, 1988.

Wildenstein, Daniel, and Yves Stavrides. *Marchands d'art.* Plon, 1999.

Wilhelm, Bernard. "Hemingway et Malraux devant la guerre d'Espagne." Unpublished doctoral thesis, University of Berne, 1966.

Zarader, Jean-Pierre. *Malraux ou la pensée de l'art.* Éditions Vinci, 1996.

REVIEWS

1953 *Botteghe Oscure,* 12.

1972 *Les Calepins de Bibliographie,* 2 (*Revue des Lettres Modernes,* 304–309) (contains bibliography of English-language studies of Malraux's work).

1973 *Revue des Lettres Modernes,* 355–359. "André Malraux 2: Visages du romancier," ed. by Walter G. Langlois.

1975 *Revue des Lettres Modernes,* 425–431. "André Malraux 3: Influences et affinities," ed. by Walter G. Langlois.

1976 *Situation,* 36. Philippe Carrard, "Malraux ou le récit hybride: Essai sur les techniques narratives dans *L'Espoir.*"

1976 *Études Germaniques,* October–December.

1977 *La Nouvelle Revue Française,* 295. "Hommage à André Malraux (1901–1976)," July.

1978 *En Aulnove Jadis,* 6 (published by the Société Historique du Raincy et du Pays d'Aulnoye).

1978 *Revue des Lettres Modernes,* 537–542. "André Malraux 4: Malraux et l'art," P. Carrard, T. Conley, R. Riese Hubert, B. Knapp.

1979 *Twentieth Century Literature,* 24, 3 (Hofstra University Press).

1980 *Juffrouw Idastraat* 11. November 1980–February 1981.

1981 *Revue des Lettres Modernes,* 643–647. "André Malraux 5: Malraux et l'Histoire," ed. by Walter G. Langlois.

1986 *Revue André Malraux/André Malraux Review,* 18, 2 (bilingual).

1986 *Icare,* 118. "La guerre d'Espagne, 1936–1939: 1."

1987 *Revue des lettres modernes,* 739–744. "André Malraux 7: 'Les Conquérants': Mythe, politique et histoire," ed. by Christiane Moatti.

1989 *Icare*, 130. "La guerre d'Espagne, 1936–1939: 2."

1989 *L'Avant-scène Cinéma*, 385. "Sierra de Teruel, *Espoir*, André Malraux," October (bilingual dialogue).

1993 *L'Œil de bœuf*, 1. "Rencontre Jean Grosjean," June (quarterly).

1994 *Icare*, 149. "La guerre d'Espagne, 1936–1939: 3."

1995 *Nouveaux Cahiers François Mauriac*, 3.

1995 *Romans 20–50*, 19. "André Malraux, *Les Noyers de l'Altenburg, La Condition humaine*."

1996 *Discours prononcés à l'Assemblée Nationale, 1945–1976*. "André Malraux," Assemblée Nationale, November.

1996 *La Nouvelle Revue Française*, 526. "Le retour de Malraux," November.

1996 *Revue des Deux Mondes*. "Les mille et un visages de Malraux: Témoignages inédits," November.

1996 *Itinéraire d'un Émerveillement*. "Malraux, l'Inde & India" (French Embassy in India).

1996 *Archives du Quai d'Orsay*. "André Malraux: Hommage solennel de la nation à André Malraux," Ministère des Affaires Étrangères, 23 November.

1997 *Les Cahiers de la N.R.F.* Bernard Groethuysen, "Mythes et Portraits."

1997 *Questions, Florilège des Témoignages*, "Pourquoi Malraux prend un x" (supplement).

1997 *Espoir*, 111. "De Gaulle et Malraux" (Fondation et l'Institut Charles de Gaulle).

1999 *Cahiers de l'Herne*. "Mao Tsé-toung" (L'Herne-Fayard).

COMICS

Morera, Alfred, and Gilles Neret. *La Vie d'André Malraux*. Daniel Briand, Robert Laffont, 1986.

INDEX

PERMISSIONS ACKNOWLEDGMENTS

Grateful acknowledgment is made to the following for permission to reprint previously published material:

Harcourt, Inc.: Excerpt from "Burnt Norton" from *Four Quartets* by T. S. Eliot. Copyright 1936 by Harcourt, Inc. and renewed 1964 by T. S. Eliot. Reprinted by permission of Harcourt, Inc.

Penguin Group (UK): Excerpt from "This" from *Fernando Pessoa: Selected Poems* translated by Jonathan Griffin, (Penguin Books 1974, Second edition 1982). Copyright © 1974 by L. M. Rosa. Introduction and translation copyright © 1974, 1982 by Jonathan Griffin. Reprinted by permission of the Penguin Group (UK).

Random House Inc.: Excerpt from "Spain 1937," copyright 1940 & renewed 1968 by W. H. Auden, from *Collected Poems* by W. H. Auden. Reprinted by permission of Random House, Inc.

ILLUSTRATION CREDITS

© ADAGP: cartoon of Malraux carrying statue

AFP: Malraux with Mao Zedong; with statue of Shiva

Chamberlin/private collection: Berthe Lamy

Collette Durand-Pia: drawing by Malraux on p. xiii

Gilles Caron/Contact Press Images: Malraux and others before the Arc de Triomphe in 1968

Robert Disraeli Films: Malraux with Hemingway and Robert Haas

Dorka: Malraux with de Gaulle

Harcourt/Ministère de la Culture–France: Josette Clotis

M. Roy-D.R.: Malraux with Nehru

Paris-Match/dePotier: Malraux with Raja Rao

Paris-Match/Wurtz: Malraux in car

Paul and Margot Nothomb: Potez aircraft; Malraux in the cockpit

PPCM/Life: Malraux with Madeleine at the piano

Clovis Prévost: Malraux with raised arms, during filming of television show

Private collections: Fernand Malraux with his son; young Malraux; Clara Malraux; with Louis Chevasson; with writers for the NRF; with Meyerhold and Pasternak; form on which Malraux describes his war career; with Eddy Du Perron; with Khrushchev; with Jackie Kennedy; Florence Malraux; television stills; at ministry desk

Viollet: Malraux with cigarette

X-D.R.: Cartoon of Malraux scrubbing the Arc de Triomphe

A NOTE ABOUT THE AUTHOR

Olivier Todd was born in Paris in 1929. Educated at Cambridge and the Sorbonne, he has been a reporter and a columnist at *Le Nouvel Observateur* and *L'Express*. He has also contributed to *The Times Literary Supplement*, the *London Review of Books*, and *Newsweek International* and worked for the BBC and the first French television channel. The author of numerous books, including novels, essay collections, and biographies, Todd lives in Paris.

A NOTE ON THE TYPE

This book was set in Janson, a typeface long thought to have been made by the Dutchman Anton Janson, who was a practicing typefounder in Leipzig during the years 1668–1687. However, it has been conclusively demonstrated that these types are actually the work of Nicholas Kis (1650–1702), a Hungarian, who most probably learned his trade from the master Dutch typefounder Dirk Voskens. The type is an excellent example of the influential and sturdy Dutch types that prevailed in England up to the time William Caslon (1692–1766) developed his own incomparable designs from them.

Composed by North Market Street Graphics,
Lancaster, Pennsylvania
Printed and bound by Berryville Graphics,
Berryville, Virginia
Designed by Virginia Tan